Image Processing Based on Convolution Neural Network: 2nd Edition

Image Processing Based on Convolution Neural Network: 2nd Edition

Guest Editors

Shaozhang Niu
Jiwei Zhang

MDPI

Basel • Beijing • Wuhan • Barcelona • Belgrade • Novi Sad • Cluj • Manchester

Guest Editors
Shaozhang Niu
School of Computer Science
(National Pilot Software
Engineering School)
Beijing University of Posts
and Telecommunications
Beijing
China

Jiwei Zhang
School of Computer Science
Beijing University of Posts
and Telecommunications
Beijing
China

Editorial Office
MDPI AG
Grosspeteranlage 5
4052 Basel, Switzerland

This is a reprint of the Special Issue, published open access by the journal *Electronics* (ISSN 2079-9292), freely accessible at: https://www.mdpi.com/journal/electronics/special_issues/FT6LADH0R9.

For citation purposes, cite each article independently as indicated on the article page online and as indicated below:

Lastname, A.A.; Lastname, B.B. Article Title. *Journal Name* **Year**, *Volume Number*, Page Range.

ISBN 978-3-7258-7975-5 (Hbk)
ISBN 978-3-7258-7976-2 (PDF)
https://doi.org/10.3390/books978-3-7258-7976-2

Contents

About the Editors

Shaozhang Niu

Shaozhang Niu is affiliated with the School of Computer Science (National Pilot Software Engineering School) at Beijing University of Posts and Telecommunications, Beijing, China. His research interests include multimedia security and image recognition. He received his bachelor's degree from Beijing Normal University in 1985, his master's degree from Beijing Normal University in 1988, and his doctorate degree from Beijing University of Posts and Telecommunications (BUPT) in 2004. Today, he is mainly engaged in teaching and research work in network information security, network attack and defense technology, information content security, information hiding technology, digital rights management technology, software security, and computer forensics technology. He is currently the deputy director of the Digital Image Identification Expert Committee of the China Press Photographers Association and the deputy director of the Beijing Computer Education Research Association.

Jiwei Zhang

Jiwei Zhang is affiliated with the School of Computer Science (National Pilot Software Engineering School) at Beijing University of Posts and Telecommunications, Beijing, China. His research interests include artificial intelligence, computer vision, and the Internet of Things. He received his bachelor's degree in information and computing science from Yantai University and his Ph.D. in computer science and technology from Beijing University of Posts and Telecommunications. He has authored or coauthored more than 17 articles published in multiple international journals and conferences. He has been awarded more than three patents and software copyrights. He is a reviewer for six international conferences and journals.

Preface

This Reprint, "Image Processing Based on Convolution Neural Network: 2nd Edition," provides a comprehensive overview of the current landscape and emerging trends in this field. Convolutional Neural Networks (CNNs) have brought about a paradigm shift in image analysis, establishing data-driven hierarchical feature learning as the mainstream methodology. This approach has demonstrated outstanding performance in numerous applications including medical diagnosis, autonomous driving, and industrial quality inspection. However, it still faces three core challenges: high computational costs, insufficient model interpretability, and heavy reliance on annotated data. The papers collected in this volume have all undergone rigorous peer review. While demonstrating the performance advantages of CNNs, they also provide innovative solutions to the challenges mentioned above. We hope that these findings will offer new research directions for the academic community and promote the development of more efficient and reliable image processing technologies.

Shaozhang Niu and Jiwei Zhang
Guest Editors

electronics

MDPI

Article

Explainable Deep Learning for Thoracic Radiographic Diagnosis: A COVID-19 Case Study Toward Clinically Meaningful Evaluation

Divine Nicholas-Omoregbe [1], Olamilekan Shobayo [1,*], Obinna Okoyeigbo [2], Mansi Khurana [1] and Reza Saatchi [3]

1 School of Computing and Digital Technologies, Sheffield Hallam University, 151 Arundel Street, Sheffield S1 2NU, UK
2 Department of Engineering, Edge Hill University, Ormskirk L39 4QP, UK; obinna.okoyeigbo@edgehill.ac.uk
3 School of Engineering and Built Environment, Sheffield Hallam University, Pond Street, Sheffield S1 1WB, UK
* Correspondence: o.shobayo@shu.ac.uk

Abstract

COVID-19 still poses a global public health challenge, exerting pressure on radiology services. Chest X-ray (CXR) imaging is widely used for respiratory assessment due to its accessibility and cost-effectiveness. However, its interpretation is often challenging because of subtle radiographic features and inter-observer variability. Although recent deep learning (DL) approaches have shown strong performance in automated CXR classification, their black-box nature limits interpretability. This study proposes an explainable deep learning framework for COVID-19 detection from chest X-ray images. The framework incorporates anatomically guided preprocessing, including lung-region isolation, contrast-limited adaptive histogram equalization (CLAHE), bone suppression, and feature enhancement. A novel four-channel input representation was constructed by combining lung-isolated soft-tissue images with frequency-domain opacity maps, vessel enhancement maps, and texture-based features. Classification was performed using a modified Xception-based convolutional neural network, while Gradient-weighted Class Activation Mapping (Grad-CAM) was employed to provide visual explanations and enhance interpretability. The framework was evaluated on the publicly available COVID-19 Radiography Database, achieving an accuracy of 95.3%, an AUC of 0.983, and a Matthews Correlation Coefficient of approximately 0.83. Threshold optimisation improved sensitivity, reducing missed COVID-19 cases while maintaining high overall performance. Explainability analysis showed that model attention was primarily focused on clinically relevant lung regions.

Keywords: COVID-19; chest X-ray; explainable artificial intelligence (XAI); deep learning; Grad-CAM; medical image analysis

1. Introduction

Modern medical imaging has become a crucial component of modern medicine for diagnosing, treating, and detecting various diseases. Medical imaging technologies continue to evolve with advances in artificial intelligence (AI) and deep learning technologies, which have dramatically changed the way we create and produce medical imaging technologies. The World Health Organisation reported that over 3.6 billion diagnostic imaging procedures are conducted annually in global healthcare facilities and highlighted the importance of diagnostic imaging in modern healthcare services, and the importance it has in assisting with the detection and management of conditions like cancer, cardiovascular disease, and neurological disorders. X-ray, MRI, CT and ultrasound are some of the technologies being used for this purpose. The high demand for diagnostic imaging, coupled with the shortage of consultant radiologists, is placing substantial strain on health care services around the world to meet the growing need for imaging [1–3].

With deep learning tools and systems currently being used to assist with this need, Deep Learning technologies are becoming a significant asset to the healthcare industry. Convolutional Neural Networks (CNNs) are proven to classify and segment images with exceptional accuracy [4–6]. These models can identify subtle patterns in images that would otherwise be undetectable by humans, providing clinicians with vast improvements in their ability to make treatment decisions. For example, dermatology is finding great promise in utilising Convolutional Neural Networks to aid in the classification of skin lesions with an equivalent level of accuracy to Board Certified Dermatologists [7]. AI systems can match or exceed the performance of human radiologists in detecting pneumonia in patients based on chest X-rays [8].

Despite this progress, the clinical adoption of deep learning technologies is lagging behind demands, primarily due to the 'opaque' nature of deep learning models. Due to the inability of healthcare professionals to easily understand the inner workings of these models, they are often referred to as 'black-box' systems. Their "black-box" nature is a barrier, since predictions are frequently not transparent or easily interpretable [8–10]. This lack of transparency undermines clinician confidence and gives rise to ethical and regulatory concerns. The inability to understand or explain the predictions observed with these systems creates a distrust of Artificial Intelligence models by healthcare professionals, which raises a host of ethical and legal questions, as well as creating barriers to regulatory approval of these systems [11]. A recent survey of healthcare leaders reported that more than 60% of respondents indicated that the absence of 'explainability' is the primary barrier to the use of AI in hospitals [12]. It is important to clarify that the goal of explainable artificial intelligence in this study is not to replace clinical expertise or assume that expert interpretation is unreliable. In many healthcare settings, experienced radiologists achieve high diagnostic accuracy when interpreting medical images [5]. Instead, explainable AI is intended to function as a decision-support mechanism within a human-in-the-loop framework, where AI systems assist clinicians by providing complementary analysis and interpretable evidence supporting model predictions. Studies have also shown that the integration of interpretable AI tools can improve clinician trust and facilitate collaborative human–AI decision-making in medical imaging environments [13].

To address these issues, Explainable Artificial Intelligence (XAI) has emerged, attempting to provide techniques such as saliency maps, feature detection, and concept-based models to produce interpretable outputs [13,14]. XAI aims to overcome the lack of interpretability by providing methods that make AI model predictions transparent, understandable, and clinically meaningful [15]. Techniques, including SHAP (Shapley Additive Explanations) values and Concept Bottleneck Models, are attempting to make the connection between an insight from an algorithm and interpretation of how the AI reached its conclusions, but many of these techniques are still untested and have not yet made it into the clinical workflow [15,16].

Many of these techniques still need to be evaluated in the clinical workflow, creating a need for the current study on explainable deep learning models as applied to medical imaging. This study aims to develop and evaluate explainable deep learning models that enhance transparency, usability, and trust in Medical Imaging Analysis. This research aims to develop and evaluate an explainable deep learning framework for thoracic medical image analysis, integrating multi-channel feature preprocessing extraction to improve

https://doi.org/10.3390/electronics15071443

diagnostic accuracy and interpretability, guided by preprocessing and explainable artificial intelligence techniques.

Recent research has sought to include explainable AI in medical image analysis and chest radiograph interpretation. Multi-channel chest radiograph pipelines have been explored previously, for example, by constructing channels such as LBP, CLAHE, and contrast/edge-enhanced maps and learning from them using deep neural networks [17]. Reviews of deep learning for chest X-ray analysis have highlighted the importance of preprocessing, enhancement, and segmentation or masking choices for model performance and reliability [18,19]. While related feature-fusion strategies exist, an identical combination of these anatomically and diagnostically motivated channels was not identified in the reviewed literature.

Beyond input representation, prior studies in explainable AI for medical imaging have highlighted that saliency maps alone are often insufficient for reliable interpretation, particularly for non-technical stakeholders [20,21]. Grad-CAM is an established explainability technique; however, it is typically presented solely as a visual artefact, leaving interpretation to expert users [22,23]. While prior studies have explored either quantitative evaluation of saliency maps or textual explanation of model outputs, a structured rule-based translation of spatial attention metrics into clinician-oriented natural-language explanations has not been widely reported in the literature. The major contributions of this study are as follows:

- A novel four-channel input representation for thoracic chest X-ray analysis was proposed, integrating lung-region masking, frequency-domain enhancement, vesselness filtering, and texture-based features. While individual preprocessing and feature-enhancement techniques have been explored in prior chest radiograph studies, an identical combination of these anatomically and diagnostically motivated channels has not been identified in the reviewed literature. This novel four-channel combination provides complementary information beyond a single intensity channel, supporting improved sensitivity and anatomically aligned model attention when combined with explainable AI techniques.
- A structured, explainable deep learning framework was developed for thoracic medical image analysis, integrating the proposed multi-channel input representation with a modified deep convolutional neural network architecture. The framework is designed to balance diagnostic performance and interpretability, addressing the limitations of conventional single-channel pipelines and black-box deep learning models commonly reported in medical imaging literature.
- A novel approach to interpreting and communicating model attention was introduced by combining quantitative spatial attention analysis with rule-based natural-language explanations. Rather than presenting saliency maps solely as visual artefacts, this study quantified the distribution of model attention inside and outside lung regions and translated these measurements into concise, human-readable explanations. This structured explanation strategy improves the accessibility and interpretability of explainable AI outputs for non-technical users, including clinicians.
- The proposed framework enhances the clinical relevance and trustworthiness of AI-assisted diagnosis by ensuring that model attention is anatomically meaningful and aligned with lung regions of interest. This design supports transparent decision-making and addresses key ethical, regulatory, and usability concerns associated with the deployment of deep learning models in real-world clinical settings.
- The study provided practical insights into the integration of explainable AI within medical imaging workflows, demonstrating how anatomically guided preprocess-

https://doi.org/10.3390/electronics15071443

ing, multi-channel learning, and explainability mechanisms can be combined into a cohesive and computationally feasible diagnostic system.

2. Literature Review

In recent years, deep learning has transformed the way medical images can be interpreted by allowing for an expert level of performance in the areas of segmentation and classification. Deep learning provides healthcare systems with the ability to automate and extract important diagnostic features from imaging datasets that improve both the efficiency and quality of care [4,5]. Notably, deep learning has demonstrated diagnostic accuracy equivalent to that of human physicians working in radiology, ophthalmology, cardiology, and pathology [24,25].

Recent advances have further strengthened the role of deep learning in medical image interpretation by integrating explainability and multimodal feature learning techniques that improve model transparency and robustness [26–28]. These developments reflect a growing emphasis within the research community on designing systems that not only achieve high predictive accuracy but also provide interpretable and clinically meaningful insights.

2.1. Deep Learning for Chest X-Ray Classification

Classification of X-ray chest imaging is critical in diagnosing patients who may be experiencing respiratory failure at an early stage [18]. Several studies have found that convolutional neural networks (CNNs) have been particularly effective at analysing chest X-ray images because they can automatically learn feature representations directly from pixel data [4]. As the use of deep learning becomes increasingly accepted, knowledge and understanding of how deep learning produces results have become an issue [8,9,14].

In a study, researchers introduced CheXNet, a deep neural network with 121 layers that was trained on the NIH ChestX-ray14 dataset to predict pneumonia [29]. However, CheXNet focused primarily on classification accuracy and did not provide mechanisms for uncertainty handling or localisation of pathological regions. The strength of the CheXNet approach lies in its ability to leverage a large-scale dataset and deep convolutional architecture to achieve radiologist-level performance in pneumonia detection. This demonstrated the potential of deep learning models to assist clinicians in large-scale diagnostic screening tasks. However, the method also presents limitations. The model operates primarily as a classification system without explicitly identifying the anatomical regions responsible for its predictions. As a result, it provides limited interpretability and may reduce clinician trust when used in real-world clinical environments.

Similarly, the CheXpert dataset and associated models introduced uncertainty-aware learning but did not explicitly address whether model attention aligned with clinically meaningful lung regions [30]. A key advantage of the CheXpert dataset is its incorporation of uncertainty-aware labels, which improved the robustness of training when dealing with ambiguous radiological findings. This approach helped address the challenge of uncertain annotations commonly present in medical imaging datasets. However, despite this improvement in label handling, the associated models still did not fully address interpretability or whether predictions were based on clinically meaningful pulmonary features. Consequently, the diagnostic reasoning of these models remained largely opaque.

Other studies have explored alternative architecture and transfer learning strategies, demonstrating improved sensitivity and specificity in thoracic disease classification [31]. While these approaches improved performance, most did not assess whether increased accuracy translated into clinically interpretable model behaviour. These studies demonstrated that architectural design choices and transfer learning techniques can significantly improve classification performance, particularly when training data are limited. However,

https://doi.org/10.3390/electronics15071443

their primary focus remained on predictive accuracy, often without evaluating how models reached their decisions or whether the extracted features corresponded to medically relevant structures.

Research focused on COVID-19 diagnosis also demonstrated high reported accuracy using deep learning models such as COVID-Net and pre-trained CNNs, including ResNet50 and InceptionV3 [32,33]. COVID-Net introduced a tailored architecture specifically designed for COVID-19 detection and contributed an openly accessible dataset that supported rapid research development during the pandemic. The open-source nature of the framework enabled reproducibility and encouraged collaboration across the research community. However, concerns regarding dataset heterogeneity, overfitting, and shortcut learning limited confidence in clinical reliability [34,35]. Studies incorporating lung segmentation before classification demonstrated that constraining model input to anatomically meaningful regions improved diagnostic performance and reliability of visual explanations [36]. The use of lung segmentation represents an important methodological improvement because it restricts model attention to the pulmonary region, reducing the influence of irrelevant structures such as ribs, labels, or external artefacts. This approach helps ensure that the model focuses on clinically meaningful anatomical areas during prediction. However, segmentation-based pipelines may introduce additional sources of error if the segmentation algorithm fails to accurately isolate lung boundaries, potentially affecting downstream classification performance. Conversely, Grad-CAM-based explanations often reveal attention outside pathological regions, highlighting the limitations of explainability when applied without appropriate preprocessing [13,20,21].

Recent studies have introduced more advanced medical image processing and deep learning strategies to improve robustness, generalisation, and interpretability in chest X-ray analysis. For example, hybrid deep learning frameworks that integrate preprocessing pipelines with explainable AI mechanisms have been proposed to improve both diagnostic accuracy and transparency in clinical decision-support systems [26,37]. Other studies have explored multimodal feature learning and interpretable deep networks for medical imaging tasks, demonstrating improved model reliability when feature extraction, preprocessing, and explainability are jointly considered [27,38]. These developments highlight a growing research trend toward designing diagnostic models that combine high predictive performance with clinically interpretable reasoning, which motivates the design of the explainable multi-channel framework proposed in this study.

Overall, despite deep learning models providing good diagnostic performance in chest X-ray classification, some challenges remain. Many of the published accuracy results for these deep learning models are from either small or unbalanced datasets, which present an increased likelihood of overfitting and poor clinical generalisability. Additionally, most deep learning models utilise unaltered, raw images for diagnosing patients without removing or addressing the influence of other anatomical structures in the same imaging area, which therefore limits the reliability of their predictions. Although explainability methods such as Grad-CAM are applied, highlighted regions frequently lack alignment with radiological findings. Taken together, these observations indicate that existing approaches have made significant progress in improving diagnostic accuracy but still face important limitations related to interpretability, dataset bias, and clinical reliability. These limitations emphasise the need for research combining region-focused preprocessing, such as lung segmentation and bone suppression, with explainable deep learning methods to ensure predictions are accurate and clinically interpretable.

https://doi.org/10.3390/electronics15071443

2.2. Explainable Artificial Intelligence in Medical Imaging

Despite strong diagnostic performance, the black-box nature of deep learning systems remains a major barrier to clinical adoption [8,10]. XAI aims to address this limitation by offering explanations about how models generate predictions. It is therefore an essential element for both clinical decision support and regulatory approval for use within a healthcare environment [39]. Saliency-based methods such as Grad-CAM, Grad-CAM++, LIME, and SHAP are widely used to create visualisations of the areas of an image with the greatest impact on model prediction [13,34–36]. However, studies have revealed that areas that receive attention through these techniques do not consistently correspond to observable signs of disease in diagnostic imaging and may differ depending on the architecture and preprocessing strategy applied [20,21].

Concept- and prototype-based textual explanation approaches aim to link model predictions to clinical reasoning by matching the output of the model to rational explanations for decisions made [37,38,40]. These methods often require extensive human annotation, large multimodal datasets or creation of explanations that may not always be clinically valid [41]. Hybrid approaches that integrate several different methods of explainability have been presented to enhance robustness and enhance clinician trust. However, many of the same challenges associated with evaluating the consistency of these multiple methods, integrating them into the workflow, and establishing clinician trust persist [23,41].

The literature demonstrates progress in interpretability methods but highlights weaknesses limiting clinical applicability. Saliency-based methods may produce unstable heatmaps that do not reflect diagnostic reasoning [21]. Concept- and prototype-based methods require large, annotated datasets or fail to generalise. Textual explanation systems align with clinical language but are constrained by limited multimodal datasets and risk producing clinically irrelevant text [41].

Most XAI research remains retrospective, with limited validation in real clinical workflows. As noted in prior work, interpretability must be evaluated in collaboration with human experts to ensure that explanations are clinically meaningful and trustworthy [19]. The lack of standardised evaluation frameworks limits comparison and adoption. Overall, despite progress, existing approaches remain fragmented and inconsistently evaluated. These gaps motivate research that develops and evaluates explainability methods in terms of usability, reliability, and clinician trust. This article, therefore, positions explainable deep learning as a roadmap for transparent AI systems suitable for integration into health care practice.

2.3. Addressing Gaps and Advancing Knowledge

This research project addresses gaps in the current literature on deep learning applied to medical imaging. While convolutional neural networks (CNNs) have demonstrated strong performance across diagnostic problems, studies often note difficulties arising from limited dataset diversity, class imbalance, and lack of interpretability for clinical decision-making [33,42]. These problems become evident particularly in the classification of chest X-ray, where overlapping anatomical structures mask disease-relevant features, leading to a lack of visual clarity. This has had an impact on performance on thoracic diagnoses, leading to a lack of confidence in deployment in real-world healthcare situations [43].

The present research aims to address these shortcomings by incorporating a feature-focused preprocessing pipeline, including lung segmentation, bone suppression, and contrast enhancement, to improve the clarity of diagnostically relevant regions. This is in line with recent work, which emphasises the importance of CNN attention being steered towards meaningful anatomical features instead of background patterns [33,44]. In addition, the project utilises explainable AI methods such as Grad-CAM, which provide insight

https://doi.org/10.3390/electronics15071443

regarding areas that contribute to classification outcomes, thus improving transparency and clinical trust [13,45].

3. Proposed Methodology

This study introduces an explainable deep learning framework that integrates lung-focused preprocessing, multi-channel feature construction, and visual explanation techniques to address interpretability and reliability challenges in automated chest X-ray classification. The proposed method comprises systematic pulmonary region isolation, feature-specific image enhancement, and robust feature extraction using a modified Xception-based convolutional neural network, followed by interpretable predictions generated with Grad-CAM. Each component is designed to improve diagnostic performance while simultaneously ensuring anatomical relevance, clinical interpretability, and transparency. The proposed methodology is illustrated in Figure 1, with each phase of the solution formulation described in the following sections.

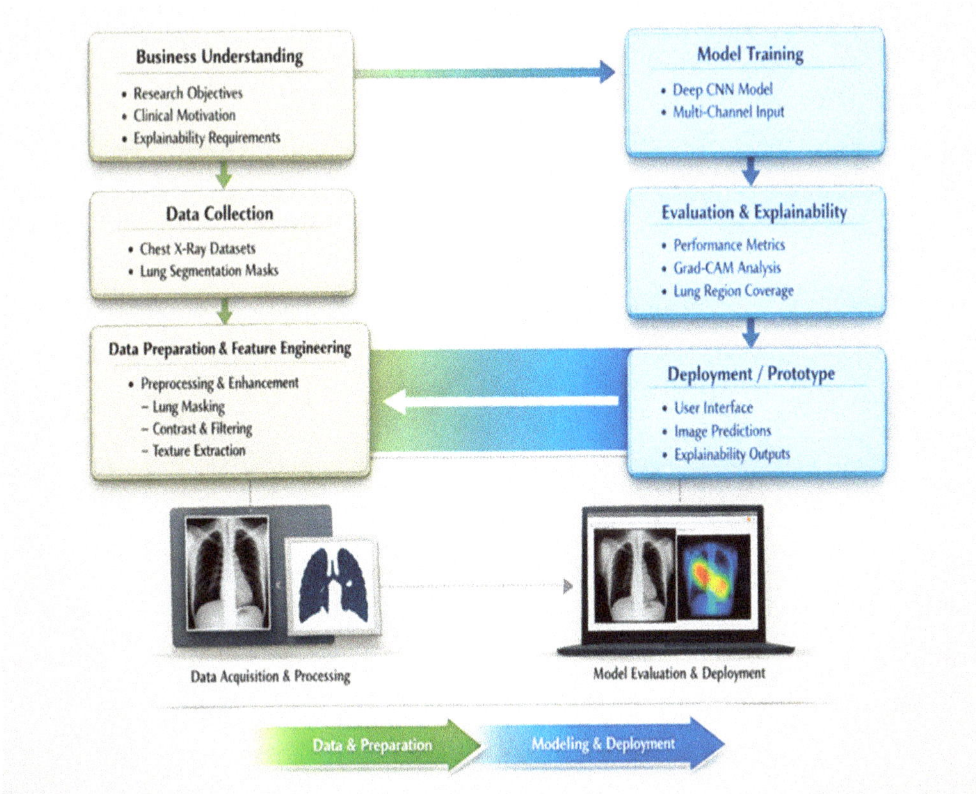

Figure 1. Workflow diagram of the proposed explainable DL framework.

This research is based on secondary data and utilises publicly available radiographic datasets. The data set provided annotated images suitable for this study [4]. The primary dataset selected for this study is the COVID-19 Radiography Database, a publicly available benchmark dataset compiled from publicly available clinical repositories [46]. The dataset contains 21,165 chest X-ray images taken from a posterior–anterior (PA) projection classified into four diagnostic categories: COVID-19, Normal, Lung Opacity, and Viral

https://doi.org/10.3390/electronics15071443

Pneumonia [46]. An important element in determining dataset appropriateness is the presence of segmented lung masks, made for each image, so that lung areas can be isolated and samples pre-processed consistently. This aspect of lung segmentation masks is crucial to explainable deep learning, whereby a model is limited to areas of anatomic significance that provide clinical insights. The details of these operations are included in the methodology section. A summary of COVID-19 radiography database dataset composition used in this study is provided in Table 1 and illustrated in Figure 2.

Table 1. Summary of COVID-19 radiography database dataset composition used in this study.

Diagnostic Class	Number of Images	Description
COVID-19	3616	Confirmed COVID-19 radiographs sourced from curated public repositories.
Normal	10,192	Chest radiographs with clear lung fields and no radiographic abnormalities.
Lung Opacity	6012	Images showing non-COVID-19 pulmonary opacities caused by various conditions.
Viral Pneumonia	1345	Radiographs depicting viral pneumonia distinct from COVID-19.

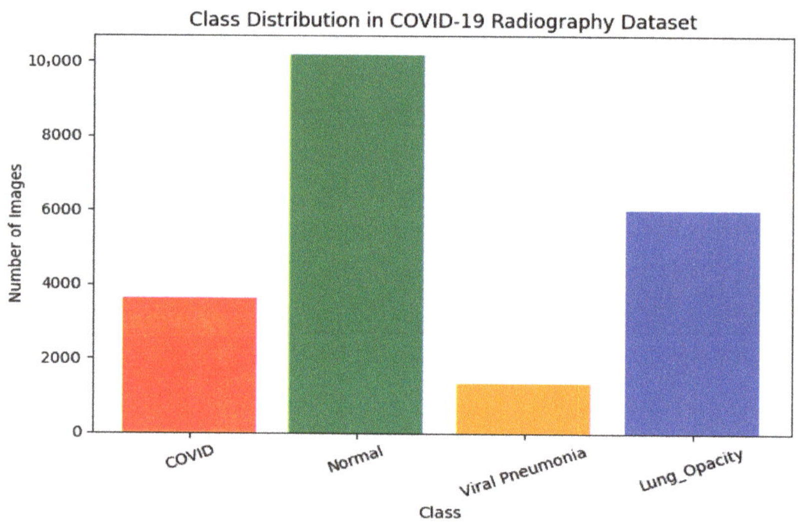

Figure 2. Distribution of the COVID-19 Radiography Database.

Rahman et al. established the COVID-19 Radiography Database to create an accessible database of COVID-related images for classification research [45]. Initial versions combined images from open-access datasets to reduce background noise, standardise metadata, and simplify analysis. A distinguishing feature is the inclusion of lung masks for every image, which enables the isolation of the lung region during preprocessing. This capability improves the reliability of preprocessing steps such as lung cropping, contrast enhancement, and XAI-based localisation. Studies suggest that a more tightly curated dataset with standardised PA-view images and corresponding lung masks supports more reliable preprocessing and region-of-interest extraction [45]. The dataset does not contain patient metadata, such as age, sex, or clinical history, but it includes consistent diagnostic labels and image quality, which supports reproducibility for deep learning research. Examples

https://doi.org/10.3390/electronics15071443

of chest x-ray class with corresponding lung mask in the dataset and their corresponding masks are shown in Figure 3.

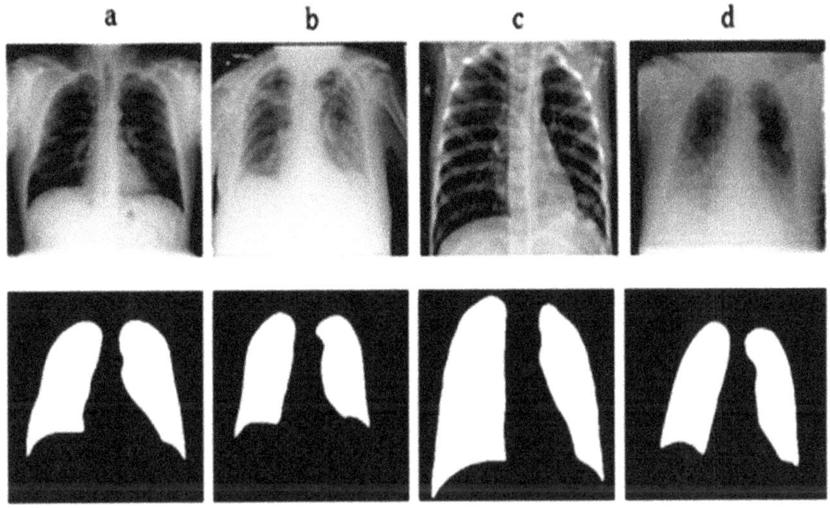

Figure 3. Examples of chest X-ray images (**top row**) and their corresponding masked lung shapes (**bottom row**) for different clinical categories: (**a**) Normal, (**b**) Lung Opacity, (**c**) Pneumonia, and (**d**) COVID-19.

Normal chest radiographs show clear lung fields with normal vascular markings. Lung Opacity and Viral Pneumonia cases display abnormal density patterns, including localised or diffuse opacification. Bilateral ground-glass opacities and haziness are often present in most cases of COVID-19; however, early-stage infection may not present with clearly visible radiographic abnormalities [47]. Therefore, the preprocessing of images and the use of XAI techniques will be necessary for the developed methods to yield clinically useful results. Lung-region masks obtained directly from the COVID-19 Radiography Database were used to isolate pulmonary regions during preprocessing. These masks were generated by the dataset authors using deep learning-based lung segmentation models trained on curated chest X-ray data and are provided as paired annotations for each image [45]. Although not manually delineated by medical practitioners, the masks exhibit consistent and anatomically plausible lung localisation and have been widely used in prior chest X-ray analysis studies [33,44]. To ensure the reliability and suitability of the secondary dataset used in this study, several validation considerations were applied. The chest radiograph images were obtained from publicly available repositories widely used in medical imaging research and benchmarking studies [46]. Such datasets are commonly adopted in medical AI research due to the challenges associated with acquiring large volumes of clinically annotated imaging data while maintaining patient privacy.

The dataset labels are based on expert radiological assessment, which serves as the ground truth for supervised model training. Expert annotation is widely recognised as the reference standard in medical imaging studies and ensures clinically meaningful diagnostic labels.

To further improve dataset suitability and reduce the influence of heterogeneity arising from multiple imaging sources and acquisition equipment, preprocessing procedures including lung-region isolation, image normalisation, contrast enhancement using CLAHE, and controlled data augmentation were implemented. These steps help reduce imaging artefacts, background variations, and scanner-related differences while preserving diag-

https://doi.org/10.3390/electronics15071443

nostically relevant pulmonary structures. Similar heterogeneity challenges in multi-source medical imaging datasets have been discussed in recent studies on heterogeneous medical image analysis tasks [48]. In addition, dataset distribution was examined to ensure balanced representation of diagnostic classes. Model performance was evaluated using multiple statistical metrics, including accuracy, sensitivity, specificity, and Matthews Correlation Coefficient (MCC), which provides a balanced assessment of classification performance in the presence of class imbalance [49]. These measures collectively support the reliability of the dataset for deep learning-based diagnostic modelling.

3.1. Image Preprocessing and Normalisation

Image processing is a crucial stage in medical imaging analysis, where data quality significantly impacts the performance and reliability of deep learning models. The preprocessing pipeline in this study was directed towards enhancing the visibility of clinically useful lung structures by reducing noise and undesirable features within the image. This process consisted of lung segmentation and suppression of surrounding bony structures, enhancement of contrast, normalisation of the data, and data augmentation. Figure 4 shows a visual representation of the preprocessing workflow implemented in this research.

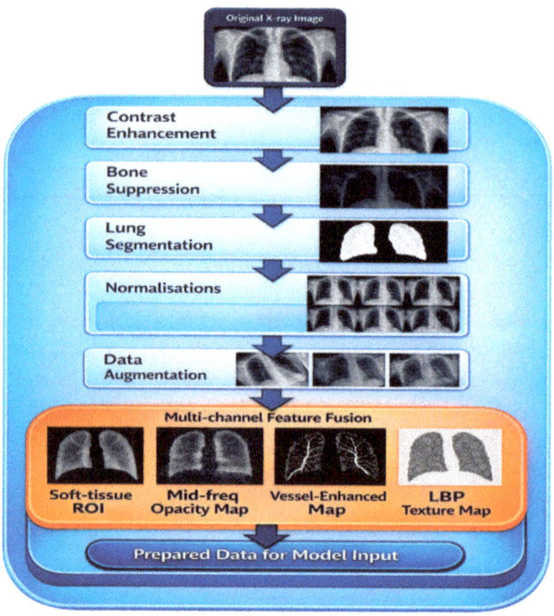

Figure 4. A visual representation of the preprocessing workflow implemented in this research.

3.1.1. Pulmonary Region of Interest (ROI) Extraction

Pulmonary region of interest (ROI) extraction was applied to isolate lung fields and enhance clinically relevant soft-tissue information while suppressing non-diagnostic structures. Lung segmentation was first used to restrict analysis to pulmonary regions, reducing the influence of surrounding anatomy and imaging artefacts [33,44]. Bone suppression was then applied to minimise the visual dominance of ribs and the spine, improving visibility of underlying lung pathology [43]. Finally, Contrast Limited Adaptive Histogram Equalisation (CLAHE) was used to increase local contrast, highlighting small patterns that can be seen in chest radiographs, such as ground-glass opacities or Consolidation [45,46].

https://doi.org/10.3390/electronics15071443

I. Lung Region Isolation

In this study, two types of lung masks were considered: dataset-provided lung masks and algorithmically generated masks. A key limitation observed in previous deep-learning studies for chest X-ray classification is the model's over-reliance on non-lung artefacts. Several studies have shown that classifiers used irrelevant cues like laterality markers, collars, and scanner-specific background noise, leading to inflated accuracy and limited clinical value [31,32]. To mitigate this issue, some researchers have employed automatic lung segmentation networks to constrain model attention to pulmonary regions [33,44]. However, such approaches may introduce additional uncertainty and segmentation-induced errors. In contrast, the availability of ground-truth lung masks within the COVID-19 Radiography Database enables precise pulmonary isolation without reliance on automated segmentation methods [43]. Consequently, this study adopted anatomically guided masking to explicitly remove non-pulmonary structures, following prior findings that lung-field extraction improves robustness and supports the reliability of explainable techniques such as Grad-CAM [13,28,33]. By reducing shortcut learning and constraining model attention to clinically meaningful regions, this approach enhanced interpretability and strengthened the validity of explanation-based performance assessment. A comparison between dataset-provided lung segmentation masks and algorithmically generated lung segmentation, visualised as overlays on the original chest X-ray image, is provided in Figure 5.

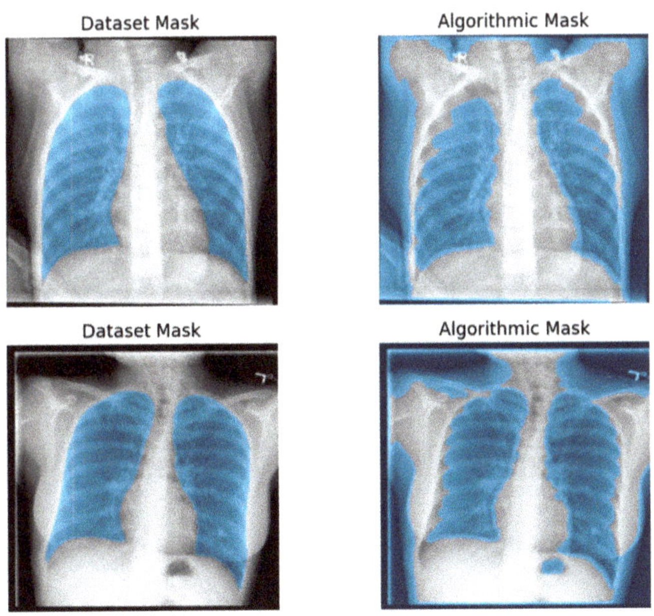

Figure 5. Comparison between dataset-provided lung segmentation masks and algorithmically generated lung segmentation, visualised as overlays on the original chest X-ray image.

As shown in Figure 5, the algorithmically generated lung masks occasionally over-segment into non-lung regions, particularly around the chest wall and shoulder areas. This variability can lead to inconsistent region-of-interest extraction, which can affect the model's performance. In contrast, the dataset-provided paired lung masks offer more stable and reliable lung localisation across samples with smoother edges, making them more suitable for ROI preprocessing and model training in this study.

https://doi.org/10.3390/electronics15071443

The dataset-provided masks were used during preprocessing and model training to ensure consistent and anatomically accurate pulmonary region extraction across all samples. These masks act as stable ROI constraints that remove non-pulmonary structures before feature construction and classification. In contrast, the algorithmically generated masks were not used during training. Instead, they were introduced only during the explainability evaluation stage to support quantitative Grad-CAM analysis. Specifically, the generated masks were used to measure the proportion of model attention located inside the lung region during explainability assessment. This separation ensures that potential segmentation noise from automatically generated masks does not influence model training while still enabling objective evaluation of whether the model focuses on clinically meaningful pulmonary regions.

The safe_lung_mask function follows a structured three-stage process consisting of (i) intensity-based segmentation, (ii) geometric filtering, and (iii) anatomical validation. which is a classical histogram-based segmentation technique widely used in medical image analysis. The mathematical formulation below follows the original method proposed by Otsu in 1979 [50]. This method is widely used in medical image segmentation due to its robustness, simplicity, and computational efficiency in separating foreground and background regions in grayscale images [50–52].

i. Segmentation Phase: Otsu's Thresholding

The otsu_lung_mask_simple step determines an optimal threshold t that separates darker lung regions from brighter surrounding anatomy by maximising the between-class variance. The optimal threshold is obtained by solving:

Let $I(x, y)$ denote a grayscale chest X-ray image defined on pixel domain Ω.

Let the image contain L possible intensity levels $\{0, 1, \ldots, L-1\}$.

Let:

- n_i = number of pixels with intensity level i;
- N = total number of pixels in the image.

The normalized histogram probability distribution is defined as

$$p_i = \frac{n_i}{N} \tag{1}$$

such that

$$\sum_{i=0}^{L-1} p_i = 1 \tag{2}$$

For a candidate threshold t, Otsu's method partitions the image into two classes:

- background class $C_0 = \{0, \ldots, t\}$;
- foreground class $C_1 = \{t+1, \ldots, L-1\}$.

Therefore,

$$t^* = arg\max_t \sigma_b^2(t) \tag{3}$$

where $\sigma_b^2(t)$ denotes the between-class variance associated with a candidate threshold t.

ii. Formula for Between-Class Variance:

$$\sigma_b^2(t) = \omega_0(t)\omega_1(t)[\mu_0(t) - \mu_1(t)]^2 \tag{4}$$

where

- $\omega_0(t), \omega_1(t)$ are the probabilities of the two classes;
- $\mu_0(t), \mu_1(t)$ are the corresponding mean intensities.

https://doi.org/10.3390/electronics15071443

The class probabilities are derived from the image histogram as

$$\omega_0(t) = \sum_{i=0}^{t} p_i, \omega_1(t) = \sum_{i=t+1}^{L-1} p_i \tag{5}$$

The class mean intensities are computed as

$$\mu_0(t) = \frac{1}{\omega_0(t)} \sum_{i=0}^{t} i\ p_i, \mu_1(t) = \frac{1}{\omega_1(t)} \sum_{i=t+1}^{L-1} i\ p_i \tag{6}$$

This formulation maximizes the separability between background and foreground classes and forms the basis of the classical Otsu thresholding algorithm.

iii. Binary Mask Result:

Once the optimal threshold t^* is determined, the binary segmentation mask is computed as

$$M\ (x,\ y) = \begin{cases} 1, & \text{if } I(x,\ y) < t \\ 0, & \text{otherwise} \end{cases} \tag{7}$$

where $I(x, y)$ denotes the intensity value at pixel location (x, y).

This mask identifies darker lung regions while suppressing brighter surrounding anatomical structures.

iv. Geometric Phase: Connected Components

The binary mask was treated as a set of connected components C_i. Each component's area is computed as

$$A_i = \sum_{(x,y)\in C_i} M(x, y) \tag{8}$$

where

$$M(x, y) = \begin{cases} 1 & \text{for foreground pixels} \\ 0 & \text{otherwise} \end{cases}$$

v. Assuming the lungs correspond to the two largest contiguous dark regions, the mask was filtered by retaining the two largest components:

$$M_{\text{filtered}} = \bigcup \{C_i \mid \text{rank}(A_i) \in \{1, 2\}\} \tag{9}$$

vi. Formula for Component Area:

$$A_i = \Sigma(x,\ y) \in C_i\ 1 \tag{10}$$

vii. Validation Phase: Area Fraction Heuristic

To ensure anatomical plausibility, the fraction of the image occupied by the detected lung region was computed:

$$\text{Area Fraction} = \frac{\sum_{x=1}^{W} \sum_{y=1}^{H} M_{\text{filtered}}(x, y)}{H \times W} \tag{11}$$

where H and W denote the image height and width.

https://doi.org/10.3390/electronics15071443

viii. Decision Rule

$$M_{\text{final}} = \begin{cases} M_{\text{filtered}}, & \text{if } 0.05 < \text{Area Fraction} < 0.80 \\ 1_{H\times W}, & \text{otherwise (fallback)} \end{cases} \quad (12)$$

This constraint ensures that only anatomically reasonable lung masks are accepted. Although algorithmically generated lung masks were not adopted for ROI preprocessing, they were still used during Grad-CAM analysis to constrain percentage activation measurements to the pulmonary region, ensuring that saliency measurements reflected model attention within the lung fields while avoiding the introduction of segmentation-related noise into the training pipeline.

II. Soft-Tissue Enhancement: CLAHE and Bone Suppression

Soft-tissue visibility is fundamental for detecting diffuse opacities associated with COVID-19 pneumonia. Contrast Limited Adaptive Histogram Equalisation (CLAHE) is widely used in radiographic image enhancement, and multiple COVID-19 studies have demonstrated that moderate local contrast enhancement improves convolutional neural network sensitivity without distorting anatomical structures or excessively amplifying noise [53,54].

Bones such as the ribs and clavicles can obscure subtle parenchymal changes; bone suppression techniques have therefore been explored to reduce this effect. Early work showed that suppressing rib shadows improves diagnostic accuracy, while more recent studies have confirmed that soft-tissue emphasis benefits the detection of COVID-19-related lesions [43].

Theory: CLAHE applies Histogram Equalisation to small image tiles, and limits contrast amplification using a clipping threshold (clipLimit = 3.0).

Formula (General Histogram Equalisation): The transformation function $T(r)$ maps the input intensity r to the output intensity s. The general histogram equalisation transformation is defined as

$$s = T(r) = (L-1)\sum_{j=0}^{r} p_r(j) \quad (13)$$

where

- $p_r(j)$ is the normalised histogram;
- $L = 256$ is the number of grayscale levels.

CLAHE applies this transformation locally to image tiles with contrast clipping (clipLimit = 3.0).

Where $p_r(j)$ is the normalised histogram of the image (or tile), and L is the number of intensity levels (256).

Bone suppression uses lightweight approximation to enhance fine details and reduce high-contrast bony structures.

Theory: The image was decomposed into a base (low-frequency structures) and a detailed component (high-frequency texture). Reducing the detailed component suppresses bone structures. A bilateral filter was used as it preserves edges better than Gaussian filtering.

Filter Used (Bilateral Filter): The output intensity I_F at pixel x is: Bilateral Filter

$$I_F(x) = \frac{1}{W_x}\sum_{\xi\in\Omega} I(\xi)\, f(\| x-\xi \|)\, g(| I(x)-I(\xi) |) \quad (14)$$

where

https://doi.org/10.3390/electronics15071443

W_x is a normalisation factor;
$f(\cdot)$ is the spatial Gaussian kernel (controlled by σ_{space});
$g(\cdot)$ is the range Gaussian kernel (controlled by σ_{color}).
Approximation Formula in Code:

$$\text{Base} = \text{BilateralFilter}(\text{Img}) \tag{15}$$

$$\text{Detail} = \text{Img} - \text{Base} \tag{16}$$

$$\text{Output} = \text{Base} + (0.18\ \text{Detail}) \tag{17}$$

The coefficient controlling the contribution of the detailed component was determined empirically through preliminary parameter exploration. Several candidate values in the range of 0.05–0.30 were evaluated to balance rib suppression and preservation of diagnostically relevant lung textures. Lower values (<0.10) excessively suppressed fine pulmonary structures, while higher values (>0.25) retained strong rib artefacts that reduced soft-tissue visibility. A value of 0.18 was therefore selected, as it provided a stable compromise between rib attenuation and preservation of parenchymal patterns, producing clearer lung structures while maintaining the radiographic detail that is relevant for deep learning feature extraction. Similar empirical parameter-tuning strategies are commonly adopted in lightweight bone-suppression and image-enhancement pipelines used in chest radiograph analysis, where parameters are selected based on visual quality and downstream model performance rather than fixed theoretical constants.

This study, therefore, combined CLAHE with bilateral-filter-based bone suppression to enhance soft-tissue visibility while reducing structural noise, improving interpretability and discriminative ability with lower computational cost than learning-based suppression models. Figure 6 represents raw chest X-ray images compared with pulmonary region of interest (ROI) representations following lung segmentation, bone suppression, and contrast enhancement. Typical raw chest X-ray images vs. pulmonary region of interest (ROI) representations are shown in Figure 6.

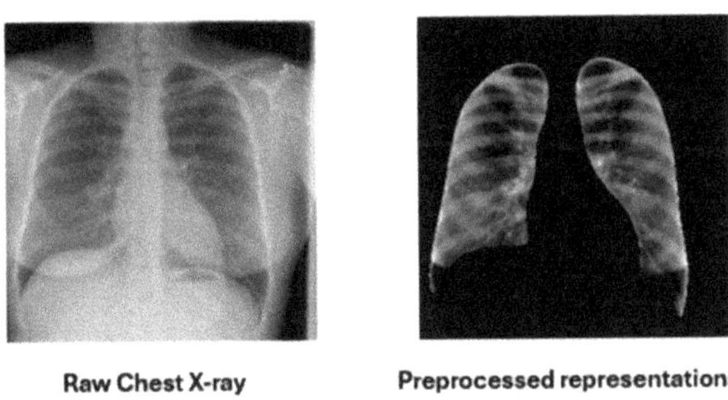

Figure 6. Raw chest X-ray images vs. pulmonary region of interest (ROI) representations.

3.1.2. Multi-Channel Feature Construction

Following core preprocessing, a multi-channel representation is constructed to provide complementary views of the same lung region. Rather than relying on a single greyscale image, this approach encodes multiple radiologically meaningful characteristics into separate channels, supporting richer and more anatomically aligned feature learning [17,18]. The lung-masked region of interest (ROI) forms the base channel, ensuring that all derived representations focus exclusively on clinically relevant pulmonary tissue. Frequency-based representations are included to emphasise diffuse opacity patterns commonly associated with infectious lung disease [55]. A vessel-enhanced channel highlights pulmonary vas-

https://doi.org/10.3390/electronics15071443

cular and airway-related structures linked to inflammatory changes [56–58]. Finally, a texture-based channel captures local lung texture variations that support differentiation between normal and pathological radiographic patterns [59].

Although frequency-domain opacity maps, vessel enhancement, and texture descriptors have each been used individually, they behave like three different "lenses" that highlight different visual clues in the same lung image. A single greyscale chest X-ray image may obscure subtle disease patterns because ribs, imaging noise, and illumination variations compete with weak pulmonary features, making early pathological signs difficult to distinguish [43,55]. Multi-channel representations address this limitation by providing complementary feature views of the same lung region, allowing deep learning models to capture opacity patterns, vascular structures, and fine texture variations simultaneously, thereby improving sensitivity to subtle radiographic abnormalities [17,18]. Similar multi-representation strategies have been shown to improve robustness and feature learning in medical imaging tasks [59].

Specifically, the frequency channel makes "cloudy" regions (diffuse opacities and haze) stand out by reducing lighting variation and fine noise, which supports the detection of subtle infectious patterns [55]. The vessel-enhanced channel makes thin tube-like structures clearer, helping the model observe vascular-related changes linked to pulmonary disease [56,58]. The texture channel (LBP) converts small local intensity changes into a consistent pattern code, which helps separate normal lungs from abnormal lungs when visual differences are small [59].

This combination is important for addressing inter-observer variability: different clinicians may focus on different visual cues such as opacity distribution, vascular changes, or local texture patterns, particularly in early or borderline cases where radiographic findings are subtle or ambiguous [18,42]. Previous studies have reported that multi-channel or multi-representation inputs can improve model robustness and classification performance compared with single-image representations, as the model can learn complementary diagnostic features from multiple visual perspectives [17,18]. For example, Nneji et al. [17] demonstrated that multi-channel deep learning inputs can enhance chest X-ray classification by allowing the model to learn complementary feature representations. Using multiple channels reduces dependence on one cue and makes the model more robust because it can agree across several complementary feature views rather than relying on a single appearance pattern [17,18]. Similarly, recent studies have explored multi-representation learning strategies that combine structural, texture, and frequency-based features to improve diagnostic performance and model robustness in medical image analysis [2,3,24]. However, these studies generally focus on generic feature fusion and do not explicitly integrate lung-region masking, frequency-based opacity mapping, vessel enhancement, and texture encoding within a single unified framework. Based on the reviewed literature and available studies in chest X-ray analysis, the joint combination of these four lung-focused representations has not been systematically explored for explainable chest X-ray classification. The proposed framework, therefore, integrates these complementary feature channels within anatomically constrained lung regions to capture subtle pulmonary patterns while supporting clinically interpretable predictions. Therefore, the multi-channel design is a formulated strategy to improve sensitivity to subtle radiographic findings and stability across variable interpretations.

I. Mid-frequency opacity mapping (Fourier band-pass filtering)

Mid-frequency textures associated with ground-glass opacities have been identified using radiomics-based texture analysis techniques [55]. Band-pass filtering improves visualisation by suppressing low-frequency illumination variations and high-frequency noise, thereby enhancing diagnostically relevant structural patterns. Prior medical imaging

https://doi.org/10.3390/electronics15071443

studies supported the diagnostic value of frequency-based feature decomposition for disease characterisation.

Theory: The 2D Discrete Fourier Transform (DFT) converts images to the frequency domain. A band-pass filter preserves frequencies within a radial range (r_1, r_2).

Formulas:

(a) 2D DFT:

$$F(u,v) = \sum_{x=0}^{M-1}\sum_{y=0}^{N-1} f(x,y)exp\left[-j2\pi\left(\frac{ux}{M} + \frac{vy}{N}\right)\right] \tag{18}$$

(b) Distance to Centre:

$$d(i,j) = \sqrt{(i - c_{row})^2 + (i - c_{col})^2} \tag{19}$$

(c) Filter Mask (Ideal Band-Pass):

$$Mask(i,j) = \begin{cases} 1, & r_1 < d(i,j) < r_2 \\ 0, & otherwise \end{cases} \tag{20}$$

(d) Filtered Transform:

$$F_{filtered}(i,j) = F_{shifted}(i,j) \cdot Mask(i,j) \tag{21}$$

(e) Inverse DFT:

$$Output(x,y) = \left|\mathcal{F}^{-1}\left\{F_{unshifted}(i,j)\right\}\right| \tag{22}$$

II. Vessel enhancement using the Frangi filter

The Frangi Vesselness filter enhances tubular structures by emphasising vascular morphology and suppressing background noise [56]. COVID-19 chest imaging studies have reported vascular thickening and dilation associated with inflammatory and thrombotic processes [57]. Prior pulmonary imaging research has demonstrated that vessel-enhanced representations can improve diagnostic sensitivity for pulmonary disease patterns [58].

Theory: The Frangi filter analyses the Hessian matrix and its eigenvalues to identify line-like structures across multiple scales. The eigenvalues (λ_1, λ_2) of the Hessian indicate the directions and magnitudes of maximum and minimum curvature.

Hessian Matrix:

$$H_I(x,y)\begin{bmatrix} \frac{\partial^2 I(x,y)}{\partial x^2} & \frac{\partial^2 I(x,y)}{\partial x \partial y} \\ \frac{\partial^2 I(x,y)}{\partial y \partial x} & \frac{\partial^2 I(x,y)}{\partial y^2} \end{bmatrix} \tag{23}$$

The maximum vesselness response across scales (1–8) is retained.

III. Texture encoding using Local Binary Patterns (LBP)

LBP are established texture descriptor for capturing local intensity variations and micro-texture information in images [59]. Prior chest X-ray studies have demonstrated that LBP features complement convolutional neural network representations by capturing fine-grained texture variations present in COVID-19 radiographs [17].

Theory: LBP compares a centre pixel with neighbouring pixels to generate a binary code.

LBP Formula (General):

$$LBP_{P,R}(x_c,\ y_c) = \sum_{p=0}^{P-1} s(i_p\ \ i_c)2^p \tag{24}$$

https://doi.org/10.3390/electronics15071443

where:

i_c is the grey value of the centre pixel (x_c, y_c).

i_p is the grey value of the p-th neighbour.

P is the number of neighbours ($P = 8$).

R is the radius of the circle ($R = 1$).

s(x) is the step function: $s(x) = \begin{cases} 1\ if\ x \geq 0 \\ 0\ if\ x < 0 \end{cases}$.

Collectively, these channels augment the soft-tissue ROI to form a four-channel tensor (ROI, Frequency, Vessel, LBP). This approach advances beyond single-channel studies and aligns with hybrid feature-learning strategies [17]. Figure 7 represents four-channel lung-focused feature representations.

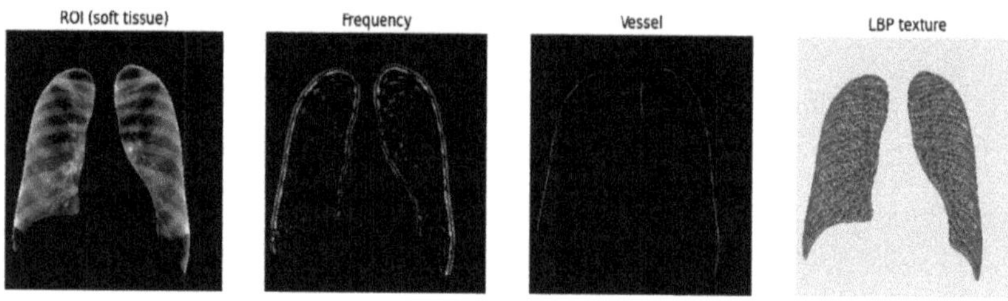

Figure 7. Four-channel lung-focused feature representations prepared for model input.

3.2. Normalisation, Class Balancing, and Augmentation

Minimum–maximum scaling was applied to preserve relative tissue intensity while ensuring numerical stability during training. Class imbalance was addressed using a controlled over-sampling strategy to balance COVID-19-positive and non-COVID-19 samples. Conservative data augmentation techniques, including horizontal flipping and small rotations, were applied to simulate acquisition variability while preserving radiological realism.

3.3. Model Architecture

The modelling phase involved constructing a deep convolutional neural network based on the Xception architecture. Xception was selected due to its effectiveness in medical imaging tasks requiring fine-grained feature extraction and its use of depth-wise separable convolutions. Xception was chosen because it replaces Inception's multi-branch modules with depthwise separable convolutions (depthwise spatial filtering followed by 1×1 channel mixing). In its original evaluation, Xception was shown to slightly outperform InceptionV3 at a comparable parameter scale, supporting it as a parameter-efficient backbone [60]. In transfer learning for small and imbalanced clinical datasets, this efficiency helps control overfitting, while stacked 3×3 convolutional blocks still provide a broad effective receptive field suitable for capturing diffuse thoracic patterns. Relative to ResNet50, it remains a robust and comparable architecture, while compared to EfficientNet, it is less parameter-efficient but often less sensitive to compound scaling strategies [61,62]. Limitations include reduced throughput of depthwise operations on certain hardware and the need for region-of-interest constraints and augmentation to mitigate shortcut learning. Recent studies in medical imaging have further confirmed the effectiveness of lightweight and depthwise-separable architectures for improving generalisation in clinical datasets [24]. The architecture was modified to accept four-channel input tensors corresponding to the proposed multi-channel representation. The first convolutional layer was adapted accordingly, and the classification head was replaced with a fully connected layer producing a single output logit for binary classification. Transfer learning was employed, and optimisation strategies were selected to ensure stable convergence and

https://doi.org/10.3390/electronics15071443

robustness to class imbalance. Conceptual architecture of the proposed 4-channel Xception-based model for this study is provided in Figure 8.

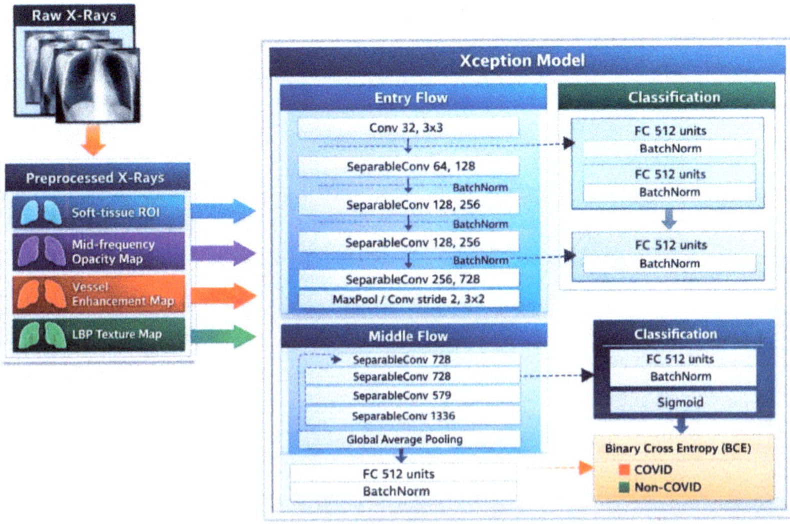

Figure 8. Conceptual architecture of the proposed four-channel Xception-based model for this study.

3.4. Explainability Integration

Explainability was incorporated as a core component of the proposed framework rather than as a post hoc addition. Gradient-weighted Class Activation Mapping (Grad-CAM) was used to generate localisation heatmaps highlighting image regions contributing to model predictions.

The explainability framework is strengthened through lung-field masking, ensuring that activation patterns reflect clinically meaningful pulmonary regions using lung-region coverage analysis. Both qualitative inspection and quantitative lung-region coverage analysis were used to assess the anatomical relevance of model attention, supporting transparent and clinically grounded interpretation.

3.5. Quantitative Explainability Assessment

Explainability is a critical requirement in medical AI systems, particularly in radiology, where model predictions must be grounded in clinically meaningful image regions.

In this study, explainability was implemented using Gradient-weighted Class Activation Mapping (Grad-CAM), which produced spatial heatmaps indicating image regions that contribute most strongly to the model's prediction by backpropagating gradients from the final convolutional layer. While visual inspection of Grad-CAM heatmaps provides intuitive insight, visual explanations alone are subjective and insufficient for rigorous evaluation. Global average pooling combined with attention and multi-scale feature representations can be interpreted clinically, as these mechanisms aggregate distributed evidence across lung fields while preserving spatial salience for focal abnormalities. This improves robustness to imaging artefacts when used alongside lung region constraints. Grad-CAM provides class-discriminative visual explanations that clinicians can inspect for anatomical plausibility [13]. However, interpretability claims should be supported by quantitative evaluation, including (i) lung-region CAM energy or coverage analysis, (ii) overlap metrics

https://doi.org/10.3390/electronics15071443

such as Dice or IoU where ground truth is available, and (iii) repeatability assessments across random seeds and augmentations, as recommended in saliency evaluation studies [22]. More recent studies have further emphasised the importance of combining visual explanations with quantitative validation to ensure clinical reliability and trustworthiness in medical AI systems [3]. To address this limitation, this study incorporated a quantitative explainability assessment based on lung-region coverage and CAM energy distribution, enabling objective measurement of anatomical relevance. The effectiveness of the proposed explainability framework is closely linked to the feature extraction strategy adopted in this study. Specifically, the multi-channel representation, comprising frequency-based opacity mapping, vessel enhancement, and texture-based descriptors, is designed to capture clinically relevant characteristics such as diffuse opacities, vascular alterations, and fine-grained texture variations associated with pulmonary disease. By combining these complementary feature representations with lung-region constraints, the model is encouraged to focus on diagnostically relevant patterns, thereby improving both predictive performance and the clinical interpretability of Grad-CAM visualisations.

Two complementary quantitative measurements are used.

(a) CAM Energy

CAM energy represents the total activation strength of the Grad-CAM heatmap and is computed as the sum of all pixel intensities in the heatmap:

$$E_{\mathrm{CAM}} = \sum_{x,y} H(x,y) \tag{25}$$

where $H(x,y)$ is the Grad-CAM activation value at pixel location (x,y).

This value reflects how strongly the model attends to image regions overall for a given prediction.

(b) Lung-Region CAM Energy Coverage

To assess anatomical relevance, CAM energy is separated into contributions inside and outside the lung region using a binary lung mask $M(x,y)$:

$$E_{\mathrm{lung}} = \sum_{x,y} H(x,y) \cdot M(x,y) \tag{26}$$

$$E_{\mathrm{total}} = \textstyle\sum_{x,y} H(x,y) \tag{27}$$

The lung-region coverage ratio is then defined as

$$\text{Lung Coverage } (\%) = \frac{E_{\mathrm{lung}}}{E_{\mathrm{total}}} \times 100 \tag{28}$$

This metric quantifies the proportion of model attention focused within anatomically valid pulmonary regions.

4. Experimental Results and Analysis

4.1. Implementation Setup

This section presents the experimental evaluation results for the proposed explainable deep learning framework for COVID-19 binary classification. The dataset was divided into training, validation, and test sets using stratified sampling to preserve class proportions. A stratified 70%–15%–15% split was adopted, which is widely used in medical AI to provide a reliable assessment of model generalisation when evaluating heterogeneous clinical data. The stratification also ensures that each split contains an equal proportion of COVID-19 cases. Model performance is assessed using standard classification metrics and threshold analysis, including accuracy, precision, recall (sensitivity), F1 score, Matthews Correlation Coefficient (MCC), and area under the receiver operating characteristic curve (AUC), while explainability was evaluated through qualitative visualisation and quantitative lung-region attention analysis. The objective was to demonstrate diagnostic performance, robustness, and clinically meaningful interpretability.

4.2. Model Training Configuration

The proposed model was trained using four-channel chest X-ray inputs with a spatial resolution of 512 × 512 pixels, where each sample consisted of the lung-isolated ROI, frequency-based opacity map, vessel-enhanced image, and texture-based LBP representation. Training was performed using a batch size of eight and the AdamW optimiser with an initial learning rate of 3×10^{-3} and weight decay of 1×10^{-4}. The Focal Loss function ($\alpha = 0.35$, $\gamma = 2.0$) was used instead of binary cross-entropy to improve robustness to class imbalance and reduce the influence of easily classified samples.

AdamW was used in this study because decoupled weight decay improves generalisation and provides more stable regularisation compared to standard Adam optimisation [63]. For fine-tuning, a practical weight decay range is approximately 10^{-5} to 10^{-3}, with common starting values between 1×10^{-4} and 5×10^{-4}. Focal Loss addresses class imbalance by down-weighting easy examples; $\gamma \approx 2$ is widely used, while α can be tuned based on class prevalence [64]. For learning rate scheduling, cosine annealing with a short warm-up phase (approximately 5–10% of training steps) provides stable convergence, while ReduceLROnPlateau offers a conservative alternative when validation performance stagnates. OneCycle scheduling can also accelerate convergence if an appropriate maximum learning rate is identified [65]. Recent work in medical deep learning optimisation has also highlighted the importance of adaptive optimisation and loss re-weighting strategies for handling class imbalance and improving convergence stability [2].

The model was trained for 20 epochs using a balanced training dataset, with performance monitored on the validation set. Training incorporated Automatic Mixed Precision (AMP) to improve computational efficiency, gradient clipping (threshold = 0.5) to stabilise optimisation, and cosine annealing learning rate scheduling with warm-up. Early stopping was applied based on the validation Matthews Correlation Coefficient (MCC) rather than the F1 score, as MCC provides a more reliable performance indicator under class imbalance conditions [49].

Prior to training, input tensors were normalised by scaling pixel intensities to the range [0,1] and subsequently standardised to [−1,1]. Conservative data augmentation was applied during training, including random horizontal flipping with probability 0.5 and random rotations between −7° and +7°, to simulate acquisition variability while preserving radiological realism.

Training metrics included loss, accuracy, precision, recall, and F1 score. The training history demonstrated stable convergence, with training and validation losses decreasing in parallel, indicating appropriate model capacity and optimisation strategy.

4.3. Quantitative Classification Performance

The results are summarised in Table 2 and the confusion matrix is shown in Figure 9. Initial evaluation was conducted using a default probability threshold of 0.50. At this threshold, the model achieved an accuracy of 95.3%, precision of 88.2%, recall of 83.8%, F1 score of 85.9%, MCC of 0.83, and an AUC of 0.983. The confusion matrix indicated that 2572 non-COVID-19 images were correctly classified, while 454 COVID-19-positive cases were correctly identified, with 88 false negatives and 61 false positives observed at this operating point.

https://doi.org/10.3390/electronics15071443

Table 2. Model evaluation metrics at different thresholds.

Threshold	Accuracy	Precision	Recall	F1	MCC
0.05	0.70	0.37	0.99	0.53	0.48
0.10	0.82	0.49	0.99	0.65	0.61
0.15	0.88	0.58	0.98	0.73	0.69
0.20	0.91	0.67	0.97	0.80	0.76
0.25	0.93	0.71	0.95	0.81	0.78
0.30	0.94	0.76	0.93	0.84	0.81
0.35	0.95	0.81	0.91	0.86	0.83
0.40	0.95	0.83	0.89	0.86	0.83
0.45	0.95	0.85	0.87	0.86	0.83
0.50	0.95	0.88	0.84	0.86	0.83
0.55	0.95	0.90	0.82	0.86	0.83
0.60	0.95	0.93	0.78	0.85	0.82
0.65	0.95	0.94	0.74	0.83	0.80
0.70	0.94	0.96	0.69	0.80	0.78
0.75	0.94	0.98	0.65	0.78	0.77
0.80	0.92	0.98	0.57	0.72	0.71
0.85	0.91	0.99	0.48	0.65	0.66
0.90	0.89	1.00	0.37	0.54	0.57
0.95	0.86	0.99	0.20	0.34	0.41

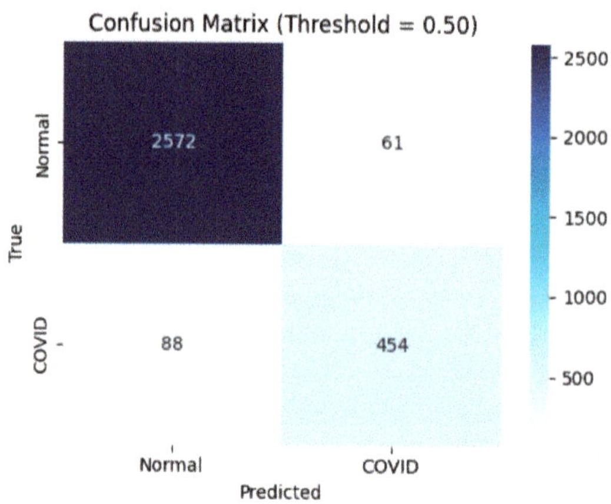

Figure 9. Confusion matrix at default threshold (0.50).

While the default threshold yielded strong overall performance, medical diagnosis often requires prioritising sensitivity. False negative predictions, corresponding to missed COVID-19 cases, pose a greater clinical risk than false positive classifications, particularly in screening-oriented applications. The model was therefore evaluated across probability thresholds ranging from 0.05 to 0.95 to identify an operating point that better balances sensitivity and specificity.

At a threshold of 0.40, the model achieved an accuracy of 95.1%, a precision of 83.4%, a recall of 89.1%, an F1 score of 86.2%, and the highest MCC (approximately 0.83). Lowering the threshold from 0.50 to 0.40 reduced the number of missed COVID-19 cases from 88 to 59, while increasing false positives from 61 to 96. This trade-off is clinically acceptable in screening contexts, as it substantially improves sensitivity at the cost of a moderate increase in false alarms. The confusion matrix at selected operating threshold 0.40 is shown in Figure 10.

https://doi.org/10.3390/electronics15071443

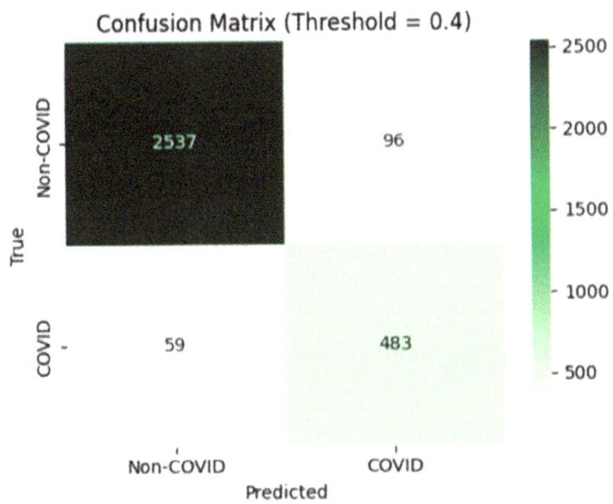

Figure 10. Confusion matrix at selected operating threshold (0.40).

The ROC curve (Figure 11) demonstrates strong class separability, with an AUC of approximately 0.98.

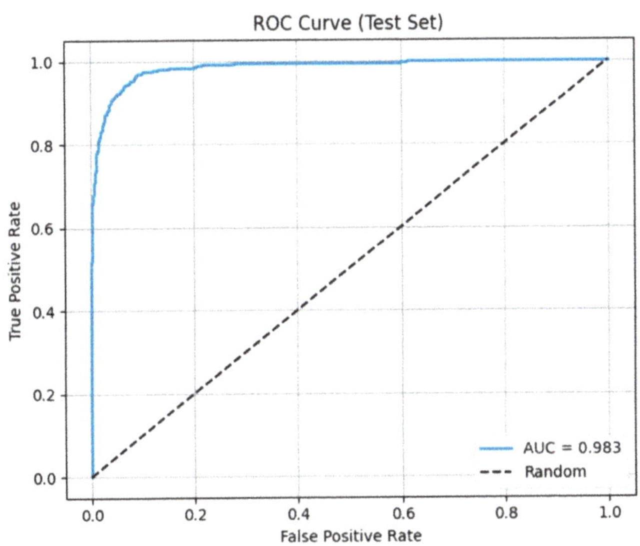

Figure 11. Receiver Operating Characteristic (ROC) curve on the test set.

Further analysis of MCC across thresholds (shown in Figure 12) revealed a broad optimal operating region between approximately 0.35 and 0.45, indicating robustness to minor threshold variations.

https://doi.org/10.3390/electronics15071443

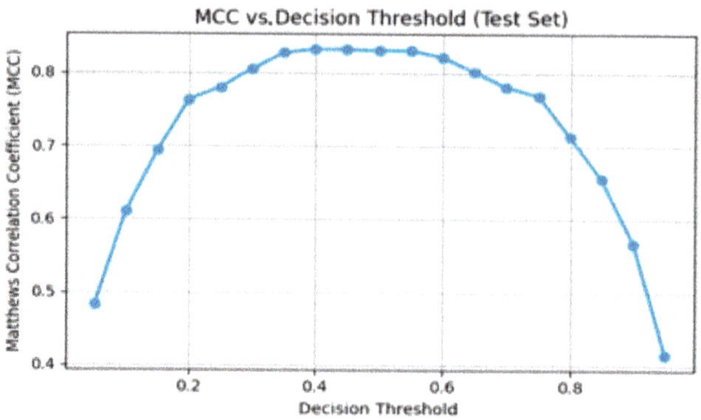

Figure 12. Matthews Correlation Coefficient (MCC) as a function of decision threshold.

5. Discussion

The modified Xception-based model demonstrated strong and reliable performance, particularly when evaluated using ROC-AUC, which is robust to class imbalance. The model achieved an AUC of 0.983, indicating excellent discrimination between COVID-19 and non-COVID-19 cases across varying decision thresholds. Unlike accuracy, which can be biassed toward majority classes, ROC-AUC reflects the model's ability to correctly rank positive and negative cases irrespective of class distribution. This highlights the effectiveness of the architecture and training strategy, including focal loss and threshold optimisation. The consistently high AUC confirms that the model maintains strong generalisation and sensitivity, making it suitable for imbalanced medical diagnostic tasks. For the explainability, which is the focus of this study, examples of the Grad-CAM explainability analysis for chest X-ray classification are included in Figure 13. Higher lung-region CAM energy indicates that the model relies predominantly on clinically relevant lung structures, such as parenchymal textures and opacity patterns, when making predictions. Conversely, lower coverage suggests reliance on non-diagnostic cues such as image borders, background artefacts, or acquisition markers. Increased concentrations of CAM energy within lung fields, therefore, provide objective evidence that the model's decision-making process is anatomically aligned and clinically meaningful, rather than driven by spurious correlations. This quantitative evaluation strengthens confidence in the interpretability and reliability of the model beyond qualitative heatmap inspection alone.

Quantitative evaluation was based on CAM energy distribution and lung-region coverage, measuring the proportion of model attention located within anatomically valid pulmonary regions. This explainability stage ensures that the developed COVID-19 classification model demonstrates behaviour that is interpretable, clinically grounded, and suitable for integration into diagnostic support workflows.

Explainability was incorporated as a core component of the framework through the integration of Grad-CAM and lung-region coverage analysis. Visual explanations and quantitative attention measurements confirmed that model predictions were predominantly driven by anatomically meaningful pulmonary regions rather than background artefacts. This combination of qualitative and quantitative explainability supports transparent and clinically grounded interpretation of model outputs and increases diagnostic confidence. Unlike purely visual XAI approaches, our method also introduces quantitative validation of interpretability, ensuring that predictions are grounded in anatomical regions. While parametric models offer transparency, they often lack the representational power required for complex imaging tasks. Our approach bridges this gap by combining high-performing deep learning with measurable explainability.

https://doi.org/10.3390/electronics15071443

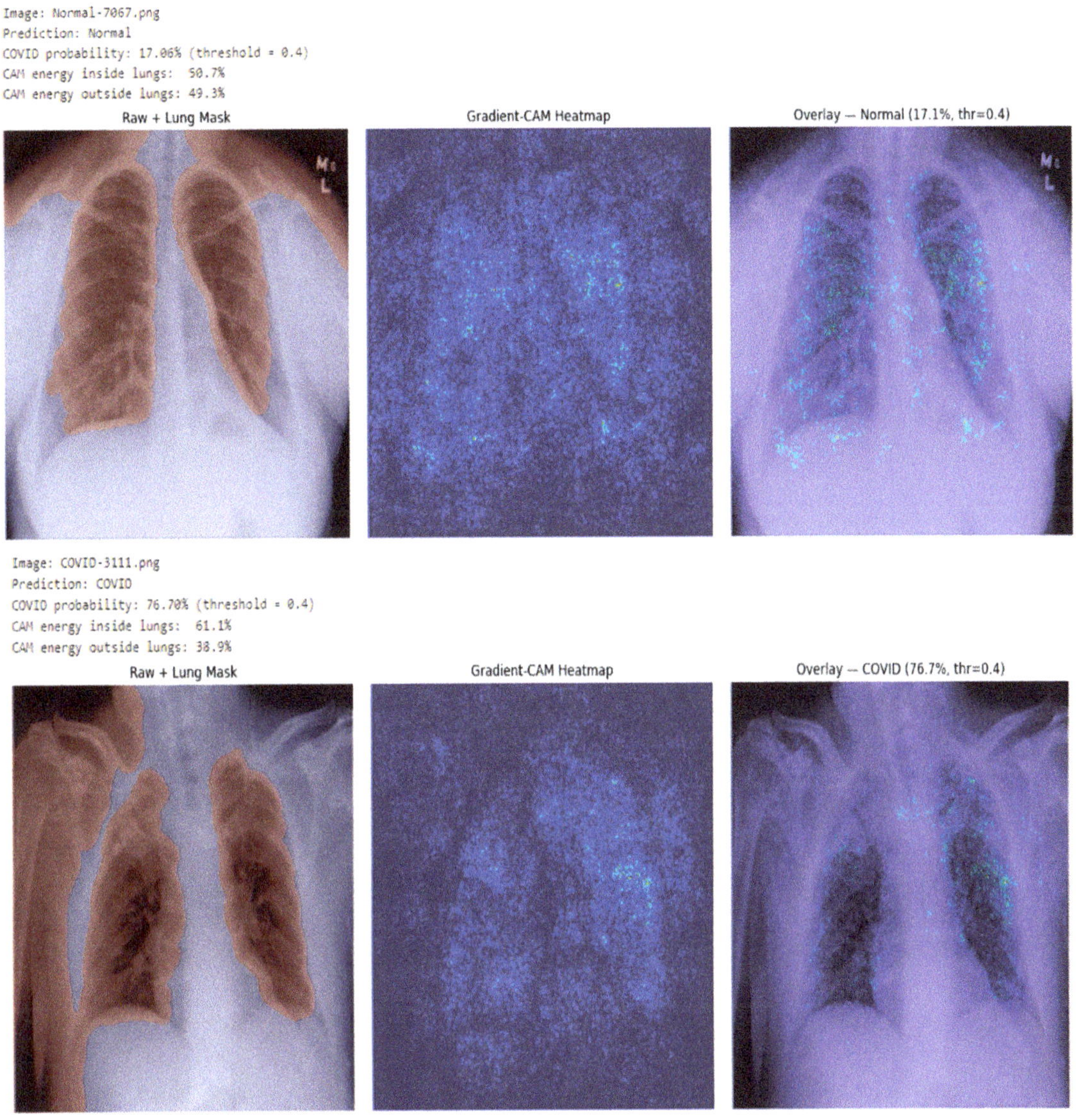

Figure 13. Grad-CAM explainability analysis for chest X-ray classification. Shown are (**left**) lung-masked chest X-ray, (**centre**) Grad-CAM heatmap, and (**right**) heatmap overlaid on the original image.

Beyond classification accuracy, an important contribution of this work is demonstrating how explainability can be incorporated as a measurable component of the diagnostic modelling process. Rather than treating explainability as a purely visual post hoc tool, the proposed framework introduces quantitative evaluation of model attention using lung-region coverage and CAM energy distribution. This approach enables objective assessment of whether deep learning predictions are grounded in clinically meaningful pulmonary structures. By combining anatomically guided preprocessing with quantitative explainability analysis, the framework helps bridge the gap between high-performing deep learning models and scientifically interpretable diagnostic systems suitable for clinical decision support.

https://doi.org/10.3390/electronics15071443

Overall, the findings indicate that combining anatomical guidance, a novel four-channel feature representation, and explainable artificial intelligence techniques can yield robust predictive performance while maintaining high interpretability. Although the proposed four-channel representation was designed to provide complementary anatomical, opacity, vascular, and texture information, the present study did not include a formal ablation analysis isolating the independent contribution of each individual channel. Therefore, while the overall framework demonstrated strong performance, the relative importance of each component cannot be quantified directly from the current experiments. This should be interpreted as a methodological limitation rather than evidence that all channels contribute equally. The proposed framework provides a foundation for explainable chest X-ray classification systems and supports the safe and trustworthy adoption of deep learning methods in medical imaging.

Future research should focus on extending the framework to multi-class respiratory disease classification, performing external and multi-centre validation to assess generalisability, conducting ablation experiments to quantify the independent contribution of each channel in the four-channel representation, incorporating clinical metadata to enhance contextual relevance, and evaluating performance through prospective clinical studies. Continued development of human-centred explainability methods will further strengthen the role of explainable deep learning systems in real-world healthcare applications.

The proposed explainable DL framework offered a robust and interpretable solution for COVID-19 detection from chest X-rays, supporting its potential integration into clinical decision-support workflows.

6. Conclusions

This paper presented an explainable deep learning framework for COVID-19 detection from chest X-ray images, addressing the need for accurate, interpretable, and clinically relevant diagnostic support systems. The proposed approach integrates anatomically guided preprocessing, a novel four-channel input representation, and explainable artificial intelligence techniques to enhance both predictive performance and transparency.

A modified Xception-based convolutional neural network was developed to process a four-channel representation comprising lung-isolated soft-tissue images, mid-frequency opacity maps, vessel enhancement maps, and texture-based features. This multi-channel formulation extends beyond conventional single-channel chest X-ray analysis and provides complementary anatomical, frequency-domain, vascular, and texture information. Experimental evaluation demonstrated strong classification performance, achieving high accuracy, recall, F1 score, Matthews Correlation Coefficient, and AUC. Threshold analysis further identified an operating point that prioritised sensitivity, reducing missed COVID-19 cases and aligning model behaviour with screening-oriented clinical requirements.

Author Contributions: Conceptualization, D.N.-O. and O.S.; methodology, D.N.-O. and O.S.; software, D.N.-O. and O.S.; validation, O.S., M.K., R.S. and O.O.; formal analysis, D.N.-O. and O.S.; investigation, D.N.-O. and O.S.; resources, O.S.; data curation, D.N.-O.; writing—original draft preparation, D.N.-O. and O.S.; writing—review and editing, O.S., M.K., R.S. and O.O.; supervision, O.S.; project administration, O.O., M.K., R.S. and O.S. All authors have read and agreed to the published version of the manuscript.

Funding: This research received no external funding.

Institutional Review Board Statement: Not applicable.

Informed Consent Statement: Not applicable.

https://doi.org/10.3390/electronics15071443

Data Availability Statement: The dataset is available at https://www.kaggle.com/datasets/tawsifurrahman/covid19-radiography-database (accessed on 25 September 2025).

Conflicts of Interest: The authors declare no conflicts of interest.

References

1. Mercaldo, F.; Belfiore, M.P.; Reginelli, A.; Brunese, L.; Santone, A. Coronavirus COVID-19 detection by means of explainable deep learning. *Sci. Rep.* **2023**, *13*, 462. [CrossRef]
2. Chadaga, K.; Prabhu, S.; Sampathila, N.; Chadaga, R.; Umakanth, S.; Bhat, D.; Shashi Kumar, G.S. Explainable artificial intelligence approaches for COVID-19 prognosis prediction using clinical markers. *Sci. Rep.* **2024**, *14*, 1783. [CrossRef]
3. Pham, N.T.; Ko, J.; Shah, M.; Rakkiyappan, R.; Woo, H.G.; Manavalan, B. Leveraging deep transfer learning and explainable AI for accurate COVID-19 diagnosis: Insights from a multi-national chest CT scan study. *Comput. Biol. Med.* **2025**, *185*, 109461. [CrossRef]
4. Litjens, G.; Kooi, T.; Bejnordi, B.E.; Setio, A.A.A.; Ciompi, F.; Ghafoorian, M.; Van Der Laak, J.A.; Van Ginneken, B.; Sánchez, C.I. A survey on deep learning in medical image analysis. *Med. Image Anal.* **2017**, *42*, 60–88. [CrossRef]
5. Esteva, A.; Robicquet, A.; Ramsundar, B.; Kuleshov, V.; DePristo, M.; Chou, K.; Cui, C.; Corrado, G.; Thrun, S.; Dean, J. A guide to deep learning in healthcare. *Nat. Med.* **2019**, *25*, 24–29. [CrossRef] [PubMed]
6. Shobayo, O.; Saatchi, R. Developments in Deep Learning Artificial Neural Network Techniques for Medical Image Analysis and Interpretation. *Diagnostics* **2025**, *15*, 1072. [CrossRef]
7. Esteva, A.; Kuprel, B.; Novoa, R.A.; Ko, J.; Swetter, S.M.; Blau, H.M.; Thrun, S. Dermatologist-level classification of skin cancer with deep neural networks. *Nature* **2017**, *542*, 115–118. [CrossRef] [PubMed]
8. El-Magd, L.M.A.; Dahy, G.; Farrag, T.A.; Darwish, A.; Hassnien, A.E. An interpretable deep learning based approach for chronic obstructive pulmonary disease using explainable artificial intelligence. *Int. J. Inf. Technol.* **2025**, *17*, 4077–4092. [CrossRef]
9. Adadi, A.; Berrada, M. Peeking inside the black box: A survey on explainable artificial intelligence (XAI). *IEEE Access* **2018**, *6*, 52138–52160. [CrossRef]
10. Solayman, S.; Aumi, S.A.; Mery, C.S.; Mubassir, M.; Khan, R. Automatic COVID-19 prediction using explainable machine learning techniques. *Int. J. Cogn. Comput. Eng.* **2023**, *4*, 36–46. [CrossRef]
11. Wachter, S.; Mittelstadt, B.; Floridi, L. Why a right to explanation of automated decision-making does not exist in the GDPR. *Int. Data Priv. Law* **2017**, *7*, 76–99. [CrossRef]
12. Singh, J.; Sillerud, B.; Yednock, J.; Larson, C.; Steffen, A.; Singh, A. Healthcare leaders' attitudes and perceptions on the use of artificial intelligence and artificial intelligence enabled tools in healthcare settings. *J. Med. Artif. Intell.* **2025**, *8*, 41. [CrossRef]
13. Selvaraju, R.R.; Cogswell, M.; Das, A.; Vedantam, R.; Parikh, D.; Batra, D. Grad-CAM: Visual explanations from deep networks via gradient-based localization. In Proceedings of the IEEE International Conference on Computer Vision (ICCV), Venice, Italy, 22–29 October 2017; pp. 618–626.
14. Gulum, M.A.; Trombley, C.M.; Kantardzic, M. A review of explainable deep learning cancer detection models in medical imaging. *Appl. Sci.* **2021**, *11*, 4573. [CrossRef]
15. Slack, D.; Hilgard, A.; Jia, E.; Singh, S.; Lakkaraju, H. Fooling LIME and SHAP: Adversarial attacks on post hoc explanation methods. In Proceedings of the AAAI Conference on Artificial Intelligence (AAAI), New York, NY, USA, 7–12 February 2020; pp. 180–187.
16. Holzinger, A.; Langs, G.; Denk, H.; Zatloukal, K.; Müller, H. Causability and explainability of artificial intelligence in medicine. *Wiley Interdiscip. Rev. Data Min. Knowl. Discov.* **2019**, *9*, e1312. [CrossRef]
17. Nneji, G.U.; Cai, J.; Deng, J.; Monday, H.N.; James, E.C.; Ukwuoma, C.C. Multi-channel based image processing scheme for pneumonia identification. *Diagnostics* **2022**, *12*, 325. [CrossRef]
18. Çallı, E.; Sogancioglu, E.; van Ginneken, B.; van Leeuwen, K.G.; Murphy, K. Deep learning for chest X-ray analysis: A survey. *Med. Image Anal.* **2021**, *72*, 102125. [CrossRef]
19. Ait Nasser, A.; Akhloufi, M.A. A review of recent advances in deep learning models for chest disease detection using radiography. *Diagnostics* **2023**, *13*, 159. [CrossRef]
20. Arun, N.; Gaw, N.; Singh, P.; Chang, K.; Aggarwal, M.; Chen, B.; Hoebel, K.; Gupta, S.; Patel, J.; Gidwani, M.; et al. Assessing the trustworthiness of saliency maps for localizing abnormalities in medical imaging. *Radiol. Artif. Intell.* **2021**, *3*, e200267. [CrossRef]
21. Liang, Z.; Zhao, K.; Liang, G.; Li, S.; Wu, Y.; Zhou, Y. MAXFormer: Enhanced transformer for medical image segmentation with multi-attention and multi-scale features fusion. *Knowl.-Based Syst.* **2023**, *280*, 110987. [CrossRef]
22. Adebayo, J.; Gilmer, J.; Muelly, M.; Goodfellow, I.; Hardt, M.; Kim, B. Sanity checks for saliency maps. In Proceedings of the 32nd Conference on Neural Information Processing Systems (NeurIPS), Montréal, QC, Canada, 3–8 December 2018; p. 31.
23. Tjoa, E.; Guan, C. A survey on explainable artificial intelligence (XAI): Toward medical XAI. *IEEE Trans. Neural Netw. Learn. Syst.* **2020**, *32*, 4793–4813. [CrossRef] [PubMed]

https://doi.org/10.3390/electronics15071443

24. Wani, N.A.; Kumar, R.; Bedi, J. DeepXplainer: An interpretable deep learning based approach for lung cancer detection using explainable artificial intelligence. *Comput. Methods Programs Biomed.* **2024**, *243*, 107879. [CrossRef] [PubMed]
25. Wang, X.; Peng, Y.; Lu, L.; Lu, Z.; Bagheri, M.; Summers, R.M. ChestX-ray8: Hospital-scale chest X-ray database and benchmarks on weakly supervised classification and localization of common thorax diseases. In Proceedings of the IEEE Conference on Computer Vision and Pattern Recognition (CVPR), Honolulu, HI, USA, 21–26 July 2017; pp. 2097–2106.
26. Irvin, J.; Rajpurkar, P.; Ko, M.; Yu, Y.; Ciurea-Ilcus, S.; Chute, C.; Marklund, H.; Haghgoo, B.; Ball, R.; Shpanskaya, K.; et al. CheXpert: A large chest radiograph dataset with uncertainty labels and expert comparison. In Proceedings of the AAAI Conference on Artificial Intelligence (AAAI), Honolulu, HI, USA, 27 January–1 February 2019; pp. 590–597.
27. Tang, Y.; Tang, Y.; Peng, Y.; Yan, K.; Bagheri, M.; Redd, B.A.; Brandon, C.J.; Lu, Z.; Han, M.; Xiao, J. Automated abnormality classification of chest radiographs using deep convolutional neural networks. *npj Digit. Med.* **2020**, *3*, 70. [CrossRef]
28. Wang, L.; Lin, Z.Q.; Wong, A. COVID-Net: A tailored deep convolutional neural network design for detection of COVID-19 cases from chest X-ray images. *Sci. Rep.* **2020**, *10*, 19549. [CrossRef]
29. Rajpurkar, P.; Irvin, J.; Zhu, K.; Yang, B.; Mehta, H.; Duan, T.; Ding, D.; Bagul, A.; Ball, R.L.; Langlotz, C.; et al. CheXNet: Radiologist-level pneumonia detection on chest X-rays with deep learning. *arXiv* **2017**, arXiv:1711.05225.
30. Narin, A.; Kaya, C.; Pamuk, Z. Automatic detection of coronavirus disease (COVID-19) using X-ray images and deep convolutional neural networks. *Pattern Anal. Appl.* **2021**, *24*, 1207–1220. [CrossRef]
31. Cohen, J.P.; Hashir, M.; Brooks, R.; Bertrand, H. On the limits of cross-domain generalization in automated X-ray prediction. In Proceedings of the International Conference on Medical Imaging with Deep Learning (MIDL), Montréal, QC, Canada, 6–8 July 2020; pp. 136–155.
32. Maguolo, G.; Nanni, L. A critical evaluation of methods for COVID-19 automatic detection from X-ray images. *Inf. Fusion* **2021**, *76*, 1–7. [CrossRef]
33. Sadre, R.; Sundaram, B.; Majumdar, S.; Ushizima, D. Validating deep learning inference during chest X-ray classification for COVID-19 screening. *Sci. Rep.* **2021**, *11*, 16075. [CrossRef]
34. Lundberg, S.M.; Lee, S.-I. A unified approach to interpreting model predictions. In Proceedings of the Advances in Neural Information Processing Systems (NeurIPS), Long Beach, CA, USA, 4–9 December 2017; pp. 4765–4774.
35. Aasem, M.; Javed Iqbal, M. Toward explainable AI in radiology: Ensemble-CAM for effective thoracic disease localization in chest X-ray images using weak supervised learning. *Front. Big Data* **2024**, *7*, 1366415. [CrossRef]
36. Chen, C.; Li, O.; Tao, D.; Barnett, A.; Rudin, C.; Su, J.K. This looks like that: Deep learning for interpretable image recognition. In Proceedings of the Advances in Neural Information Processing Systems (NeurIPS), Vancouver, BC, Canada, 8–14 December 2019.
37. Koh, P.W.; Nguyen, T.; Tang, Y.S.; Mussmann, S.; Pierson, E.; Kim, B.; Liang, P. Concept bottleneck models. In *Proceedings of the International Conference on Machine Learning; PMLR*; JMLR.org: Brookline, MA, USA, 2020; pp. 5338–5348.
38. Sultana, S.; Hossain, A.A.; Alam, J. COVID-19 detection from optimized features of breathing audio signals using explainable ensemble machine learning. *Results Control Optim.* **2025**, *18*, 100538. [CrossRef]
39. Samek, W.; Montavon, G.; Vedaldi, A.; Hansen, L.K.; Müller, K. *Explainable AI: Interpreting, Explaining and Visualizing Deep Learning*; Springer Nature: Berlin/Heidelberg, Germany, 2019; Volume 11700.
40. Kyrimi, E.; Dube, K.; Fenton, N.; Fahmi, A.; Neves, M.R.; Marsh, W.; McLachlan, S. Bayesian networks in healthcare: What is preventing their adoption? *Artif. Intell. Med.* **2021**, *116*, 102079. [CrossRef] [PubMed]
41. Mohammed, M.A.; Abdulkareem, K.H.; Garcia-Zapirain, B.; Mostafa, S.A.; Maashi, M.S.; Al-Waisy, A.S.; Subhi, M.A.; Mutlag, A.A.; Le, D.-N. A comprehensive investigation of machine learning feature extraction and classification methods for automated diagnosis of COVID-19 based on X-ray images. *Comput. Mater. Contin.* **2021**, *66*, 3289–3310. [CrossRef]
42. Suzuki, K.; Abe, H.; MacMahon, H.; Doi, K. Image-processing technique for suppressing ribs in chest radiographs by means of massive training artificial neural network. *IEEE Trans. Med. Imaging* **2006**, *25*, 406–416. [CrossRef]
43. Harrison, A.P.; Xu, Z.; Lu, L.; Summers, R.M.; Mollura, D.J.; US Department of Health. Progressive and Multi-Path Holistically Nested Networks for Segmentation. U.S. Patent 11,195,280, 7 December 2021.
44. Pisano, E.D.; Zong, S.; Hemminger, B.M.; DeLuca, M.; Johnston, R.E.; Muller, K.; Braeuning, M.P.; Pizer, S.M. Contrast limited adaptive histogram equalization image processing to improve the detection of simulated spiculations in dense mammograms. *J. Digit. Imaging* **1998**, *11*, 193–200. [CrossRef]
45. Rahman, T.; Khandakar, A.; Qiblawey, Y.; Tahir, A.M.; Kiranyaz, S.; Kashem, S.B.A.; Islam, M.T.; Al Maadeed, S.; Zughaier, S.M.; Khan, M.S.; et al. Exploring the effect of image enhancement techniques on COVID-19 detection using chest X-ray images. *Comput. Biol. Med.* **2021**, *132*, 104319. [CrossRef]
46. Rahman, T.; Chowdhury, M.E.H.; Khandakar, A. COVID-19 radiography database. *arXiv* **2020**, arXiv:2005.06794.
47. Jacobi, A.; Chung, M.; Bernheim, A.; Eber, C. Portable chest X-ray in coronavirus disease-19 (COVID-19): A pictorial review. *Clin. Imaging* **2020**, *64*, 35–42. [CrossRef]
48. Yue, L.; Tian, D.; Chen, W.; Han, X.; Yin, M. Deep learning for heterogeneous medical data analysis. *World Wide Web* **2020**, *23*, 2715–2737. [CrossRef]

https://doi.org/10.3390/electronics15071443

49. Chicco, D.; Jurman, G. The advantages of the Matthews correlation coefficient over F1 score and accuracy in binary classification evaluation. *BMC Genom.* **2020**, *21*, 6. [CrossRef] [PubMed]
50. Otsu, N. A threshold selection method from gray-level histograms. *IEEE Trans. Syst. Man Cybern.* **1979**, *9*, 62–66. [CrossRef]
51. Roslan, M.A.M.; Nasir, A.S.A.; Markom, M.A.; Andrew, A.M.; Haryanto, E.V. COVID-19 Chest X-Ray Lung Segmentation by Locally Adaptive Thresholding. *J. Adv. Res. Appl. Sci. Eng. Technol.* **2026**, *64*, 69–83. [CrossRef]
52. Malik, Y.S.; Tamoor, M.; Naseer, A.; Wali, A.; Khan, A. Applying an adaptive Otsu-based initialization algorithm to optimize active contour models for skin lesion segmentation. *J. X-Ray Sci. Technol.* **2022**, *30*, 1169–1184. [CrossRef]
53. Pizer, S.M.; Amburn, E.P.; Austin, J.D.; Cromartie, R.; Geselowitz, A.; Greer, T.; ter Haar Romeny, B.; Zimmerman, J.B.; Zuiderveld, K. Adaptive histogram equalization and its variations. *Comput. Vis. Graph. Image Process.* **1990**, *39*, 355–368. [CrossRef]
54. Salman, A.M.; Ahmed, I.; Mohd, M.H.; Jamiluddin, M.S.; Dheyab, M.A. Scenario analysis of COVID-19 transmission dynamics in Malaysia with the possibility of reinfection and limited medical resources scenarios. *Comput. Biol. Med.* **2021**, *133*, 104372. [CrossRef] [PubMed]
55. Frangi, A.F.; Niessen, W.J.; Vincken, K.L.; Viergever, M.A. Multiscale vessel enhancement filtering. In Proceedings of the International Conference on Medical Image Computing and Computer-Assisted Intervention (MICCAI), Cambridge, MA, USA, 11–13 October 1998; pp. 130–137.
56. Carotti, M.; Salaffi, F.; Sarzi-Puttini, P.; Agostini, A.; Borgheresi, A.; Minorati, D.; Galli, M.; Giovagnoni, A. Chest CT features of coronavirus disease 2019 (COVID-19) pneumonia: Key points for radiologists. *Radiol. Med.* **2020**, *125*, 636–646. [CrossRef]
57. Tajbakhsh, N.; Shin, J.Y.; Gotway, M.B.; Liang, J. Computer-aided detection and visualization of pulmonary embolism using a novel, compact, and discriminative image representation. *Med. Image Anal.* **2019**, *58*, 101541. [CrossRef]
58. Ojala, T.; Pietikäinen, M.; Mäenpää, T. Multiresolution gray-scale and rotation invariant texture classification with local binary patterns. *IEEE Trans. Pattern Anal. Mach. Intell.* **2002**, *24*, 971–987. [CrossRef]
59. Zhou, S.K.; Greenspan, H.; Davatzikos, C.; Duncan, J.S.; van Ginneken, B.; Madabhushi, A.; Prince, J.L.; Rueckert, D.; Summers, R.M. A review of deep learning in medical imaging: Imaging traits, technology trends, case studies with progress highlights, and future promises. *Proc. IEEE* **2021**, *109*, 820–838. [CrossRef]
60. Chollet, F. Xception: Deep learning with depthwise separable convolutions. In Proceedings of the IEEE Conference on Computer Vision and Pattern Recognition, Honolulu, HI, USA, 21–26 July 2017; pp. 1251–1258.
61. He, K.; Zhang, X.; Ren, S.; Sun, J. Deep residual learning for image recognition. In Proceedings of the IEEE Conference on Computer Vision and Pattern Recognition, Las Vegas, NV, USA, 27–30 June 2016; pp. 770–778.
62. Tan, M.; Le, Q. Efficientnet: Rethinking model scaling for convolutional neural networks. In Proceedings of the International Conference on Machine Learning; PMLR, Long Beach, CA, USA, 9–15 June 2019; pp. 6105–6114.
63. Loshchilov, I.; Hutter, F. Decoupled weight decay regularization. *arXiv* **2017**, arXiv:1711.05101.
64. Lin, T.; Goyal, P.; Girshick, R.; He, K.; Dollár, P. Focal loss for dense object detection. In Proceedings of the IEEE International Conference on Computer Vision, Venice, Italy, 22–29 October 2017; pp. 2980–2988.
65. Smith, L.N. A disciplined approach to neural network hyper-parameters: Part 1—Learning rate, batch size, momentum, and weight decay. *arXiv* **2018**, arXiv:1803.09820.

https://doi.org/10.3390/electronics15071443

electronics

MDPI

Article

Robust BEV Perception via Dual 4D Radar–Camera Fusion Under Adverse Conditions with Fog-Aware Enhancement

Zhengqing Li [1,2,3] and Baljit Singh [2,4,*]

1 School of New Energy and Intelligent Networked Automobile, University of Sanya, Sanya 572022, China; zhengqingli@sanyau.edu.cn
2 Faculty of Mechanical Engineering, Universiti Teknologi MARA, Shah Alam 40450, Selangor, Malaysia
3 New Energy and Intelligent Vehicle Engineering Research Center of Hainan Province, Sanya 572022, China
4 Solar Research Institute, Universiti Teknologi MARA, Shah Alam 40450, Selangor, Malaysia
* Correspondence: baljit@uitm.edu.my

Abstract

Bird's-eye-view (BEV) perception has emerged as a key representation for unified scene understanding in autonomous driving. However, current BEV methods relying solely on monocular cameras suffer from severe degradation under adverse weather and dynamic scenes due to limited depth cues and illumination dependency. To address these challenges, we propose a robust multi-modal BEV perception framework that integrates dual-source 4D millimeter-wave radar and multi-view camera images. The proposed architecture systematically exploits Doppler velocity and temporal information from 4D radar to model dynamic object motion, while introducing a deformable fusion strategy in the BEV space for accurate semantic alignment across modalities. Our design includes four key modules: a Doppler-Aware Radar Encoder (DARE) that enhances motion-sensitive features via velocity-guided attention; a Fog-Aware Feature Denoising Module (FADM) that suppresses modality inconsistency in low-visibility conditions through cross-modal attention and residual enhancement; a Multi-Modal Temporal Fusion Module (TFM) that encodes radar temporal sequences using a Transformer encoder for motion continuity modeling; and a confidence-aware multi-task loss that jointly supervises semantic segmentation, motion estimation, and object detection. Extensive experiments on the DualRadar dataset and adverse-weather simulations demonstrate that our method achieves significant gains over state-of-the-art baselines in BEV segmentation accuracy, detection robustness, and motion stability. The proposed framework offers a scalable and resilient solution for real-world autonomous perception, especially under challenging environmental conditions.

Keywords: BEV perception; 4D millimeter-wave radar; multi-modal fusion; Doppler velocity; adverse weather

1. Introduction

With the rapid development of autonomous driving and advanced driver assistance systems (ADAS), vehicles are required to perceive their surroundings with high accuracy and strong robustness. Among various perception paradigms, bird's-eye-view (BEV) perception has emerged as a key intermediate representation that bridges perception and downstream tasks such as planning and decision-making. By transforming multi-sensor observations into a unified top-down coordinate frame, BEV perception effectively eliminates perspective ambiguities and provides a geometrically consistent and structured scene representation, which is particularly beneficial for urban driving scenarios [1,2].

In recent years, camera-based BEV perception methods have achieved remarkable progress. By leveraging explicit or implicit view-lifting mechanisms, these approaches project 2D image features into 3D space or directly into the BEV domain, enabling fine-grained scene understanding and semantic mapping [3–6]. However, as passive sensors, cameras heavily rely on external illumination conditions. Their performance degrades significantly under adverse environments such as fog, rain, nighttime, or strong glare, leading to blurred object boundaries, missed detections of distant targets, and unstable perception of dynamic objects. This inherent limitation poses a critical challenge to the safety and reliability of vision-centric BEV perception systems in real-world autonomous driving [7,8].

To mitigate the vulnerability of vision-based perception, multi-sensor BEV fusion frameworks have gained increasing attention [9,10]. Among them, BEVCar [11] is a notable effort toward camera–radar BEV semantic segmentation. By introducing a learning-based radar point encoding and a radar-guided image feature lifting strategy, BEVCar demonstrates improved robustness under nighttime and rainy conditions compared with camera-only baselines. Despite these advances, several limitations remain. First, existing radar modeling in BEVCar primarily relies on sparse spatial point representations and does not fully exploit the rich dynamic information inherent in radar measurements [12]. Second, the employed radar configurations are mainly based on conventional automotive radars, leaving the potential of emerging 4D millimeter-wave radars underexplored. Third, under extreme adverse conditions such as dense fog, the noise mismatch between radar and visual features may still hinder effective fusion, limiting further performance gains [13,14].

Recently, 4D millimeter-wave radar has attracted considerable interest due to its ability to provide not only spatial location but also Doppler velocity and temporal information [15–17]. Compared with LiDAR, 4D radar offers lower cost and superior all-weather capability; compared with traditional automotive radar, it provides enhanced resolution and richer dynamic cues, making it particularly suitable for perceiving moving objects under low-visibility conditions [18–21]. Nevertheless, how to systematically and efficiently integrate 4D radar information with vision in the BEV domain remains an open research problem.

From a data perspective, the DualRadar dataset [22] offers a valuable opportunity to investigate this challenge. It provides multi-source millimeter-wave radar data (e.g., Arbe and ARS548), together with LiDAR and camera observations, enabling the study of multi-radar collaboration and cross-modal fusion in realistic driving scenarios. However, the dataset also introduces new difficulties, including sensor heterogeneity, data incompleteness, and increased noise under adverse conditions, which make it non-trivial to directly apply existing single-radar or simplified fusion approaches.

Motivated by these observations, this paper builds upon BEVCar and related works to investigate a robust BEV perception framework that jointly leverages Dual 4D millimeter-wave radar and vision under challenging environmental conditions. The core idea is to fully exploit the dynamic information provided by 4D radar, including Doppler velocity and temporal cues, and to incorporate environment-aware feature modeling within the BEV fusion process. By doing so, the proposed method aims to significantly enhance perception robustness and generalization in real-world adverse scenarios.

The main contributions of this paper can be summarized as follows:

- **Novel Motion-Aware BEV Architecture:** Unlike existing camera–radar frameworks such as BEVCar that primarily rely on static, sparse point representations for query initialization, we propose a fundamentally new fusion paradigm. We introduce a Motion-Aware Fusion Module (MAFM) that explicitly leverages 4D radar's Doppler

https://doi.org/10.3390/electronics15061284

velocity to modulate deformable attention in the BEV space, achieving superior spatiotemporal semantic alignment for dynamic objects.

- **Doppler-Aware Radar Encoding (DARE) for Heterogeneous Sensors:** We design a unified multi-radar modeling strategy that goes beyond simple point concatenation. By introducing a velocity-guided gating mechanism, DARE effectively standardizes and prioritizes dynamic features from heterogeneous 4D sensors (e.g., Arbe and ARS548), systematically filtering static clutter and addressing inherent discrepancies in resolution and noise distribution.
- **Dynamic Cross-Modal Denoising and Temporal Consistency:** To tackle modality inconsistency in extreme weather, we transition from assuming equal sensor reliability to a dynamic restoration approach. We propose the Fog-Aware Feature Denoising Module (FADM), which utilizes radar-guided cross-modal attention to restore degraded visual semantics, seamlessly integrated with a Multi-Modal Temporal Fusion Module (TFM) that encodes radar history to ensure trajectory continuity across frames.
- **Comprehensive Validation and Robustness Benchmark:** Extensive experiments on the DualRadar dataset and systematic adverse-weather simulations (fog and rain) demonstrate that our framework achieves significant gains over current state-of-the-art methods in BEV segmentation accuracy, detection robustness, and motion stability, establishing a highly resilient solution for low-visibility environments.

2. Related Work

In this section, we review prior works related to BEV perception, radar-based perception and sensor fusion, robustness under adverse weather conditions, as well as commonly used datasets for multi-modal autonomous driving research.

2.1. *BEV Perception from Multi-View Cameras*

Bird's-eye-view (BEV) perception has become a central research topic in autonomous driving due to its ability to provide a unified and geometrically consistent scene representation. Early camera-based BEV approaches focused on learning implicit mappings between image space and top-down representations using convolutional or variational architectures [23,24]. With the advent of transformer-based models, recent works have significantly improved BEV perception performance by explicitly modeling geometric relationships.

BEVFormer [25] introduces a spatiotemporal transformer that leverages camera calibration parameters and deformable attention to project multi-view image features into the BEV space, achieving state-of-the-art performance in vision-only 3D perception. BEVDet [26] and its variants further enhance efficiency and accuracy by adopting explicit depth estimation and voxel-based aggregation strategies. These methods demonstrate strong performance under favorable illumination but remain vulnerable to adverse environmental conditions due to their reliance on passive visual sensing.

To address robustness issues, BEVCar extends camera-based BEV perception by incorporating automotive radar. BEVCar proposes a learning-based radar point encoding and utilizes radar measurements to initialize BEV queries during image feature lifting. This design enables improved performance under rain and nighttime conditions compared with camera-only baselines. Nevertheless, BEVCar primarily exploits sparse spatial radar points and does not fully utilize the rich temporal and Doppler information available in modern 4D millimeter-wave radar systems.

2.2. *Radar Perception and Multi-Modal Fusion*

Radar sensors have long been recognized for their robustness to illumination and weather variations. Traditional radar perception research focused on standalone radar

https://doi.org/10.3390/electronics15061284

object detection or clustering [27], while recent studies increasingly explore radar–camera or radar–LiDAR fusion for autonomous driving.

M2-Fusion [28] demonstrates that fusing radar with LiDAR can improve 3D object detection robustness, particularly for distant and partially occluded targets. L4DR [29] further investigates multi-radar fusion under adverse weather conditions, proposing radar-aware feature modeling and fog simulation strategies to enhance robustness. These approaches highlight the importance of leveraging radar's physical sensing advantages, especially in degraded visibility scenarios.

Compared with conventional automotive radar, 4D millimeter-wave radar provides additional Doppler velocity and temporal information, offering richer cues for dynamic object perception. However, effectively integrating such high-dimensional radar information into BEV representations remains challenging. Existing fusion methods often treat radar points as static spatial inputs, limiting their ability to model motion patterns and temporal consistency in complex driving environments [30,31].

2.3. Robust Perception Under Adverse Weather Conditions

Robust perception under adverse weather, such as fog, rain, and snow, is critical for real-world autonomous driving. Several works have investigated sensor degradation modeling and data augmentation strategies to improve robustness. Fog simulation techniques for LiDAR [32] and camera sensors have been widely adopted to synthesize adverse conditions during training.

Recent studies emphasize that radar sensors maintain reliable measurements under low visibility, making them particularly suitable for adverse weather perception [33]. L4DR [29] explicitly incorporates fog simulation into radar-based learning, demonstrating improved performance under degraded conditions. However, most existing methods focus on detection tasks and do not systematically address BEV semantic understanding or joint map and object segmentation in adverse environments.

2.4. Autonomous Driving Datasets

Large-scale multi-modal datasets play a crucial role in advancing BEV perception research. The nuScenes dataset [34] provides synchronized multi-camera, LiDAR, and automotive radar data with comprehensive annotations and has become a standard benchmark for BEV-based perception. The View-of-Delft (VoD) dataset [35] further enriches radar research by offering high-resolution radar measurements suited for object detection.

More recently, the DualRadar dataset introduces multiple millimeter-wave radar sensors alongside LiDAR and camera data, enabling the study of multi-radar collaboration and heterogeneous sensor fusion in real-world driving scenarios. While these datasets provide valuable resources, effectively exploiting multi-radar and multi-modal information under challenging environmental conditions remains an open research problem.

2.5. Summary

To systematically clarify the architectural distinctions between our proposed framework and existing state-of-the-art methods, we provide a comprehensive comparison in Table 1. While early monocular BEV methods (e.g., BEVFormer, BEVDet) lack robustness in low-visibility environments, recent multi-modal approaches have introduced radar or LiDAR to compensate for visual degradation. Notably, BEVCar pioneers camera–radar BEV fusion but relies on sparse 3D point representations without exploiting radar dynamics. L4DR introduces weather-robust modeling but focuses on LiDAR–radar fusion rather than vision. In contrast, our approach is uniquely structured to fully harness Dual 4D radar by explicitly incorporating Doppler-guided attention, multi-modal temporal encoding, and dynamic cross-modal denoising.

https://doi.org/10.3390/electronics15061284

Table 1. Architectural comparison of the proposed framework with existing BEV and multi-modal fusion approaches.

Method	Primary Modalities	Fusion Space	4D Radar Integration	Doppler Utilization	Temporal Modeling	Adverse Weather Denoising
BEVFormer [25]	Camera	BEV	×	×	✓(Camera only)	×
BEVDet [26]	Camera	BEV	×	×	×	×
M2-Fusion [28]	LiDAR + 3D Radar	3D	×	×	×	×
BEVCar [11]	Camera + 3D Radar	BEV	×	×	×	✓(Implicit via Radar)
L4DR [29]	LiDAR + 4D Radar	3D	✓	✓	×	✓(Fog Simulation)
Ours	Camera + Dual 4D Radar	BEV	✓	✓(DARE & MAFM)	✓(Radar TFM)	✓(FADM)

In summary, while existing radar-assisted BEV methods have improved robustness, they still primarily underexploit the temporal and Doppler characteristics of 4D radar, leaving robust perception under extreme weather conditions insufficiently explored. These specific gaps motivate the proposed work, which aims to leverage Dual 4D millimeter-wave radar and vision to achieve resilient and reliable BEV perception in challenging real-world environments.

3. Method

To enhance the robustness of autonomous perception in complex dynamic environments and under adverse weather conditions, we propose a multi-modal BEV-based perception framework. This architecture integrates multi-view RGB images and dual-source 4D millimeter-wave radar data, and performs system-level optimization for dynamic object modeling and semantic understanding in the BEV domain. Built upon the BEVCar backbone, the proposed method introduces explicit motion-aware encoding, temporal sequence modeling, and sensor-level denoising strategies, which improve perceptual accuracy and stability under low illumination, occlusion, fog, and long-range sensing scenarios.

The overall system adopts an encoder–fusion–decoder architecture and consists of five core functional modules, as outlined below:

- Enhanced BEV backbone: Based on the BEVCar structure, we introduce a 4D radar-specific processing branch and a motion-aware guidance mechanism to jointly model and fuse multi-view camera and radar point cloud features, generating robust BEV representations under varying conditions.
- Doppler-aware radar encoder: A Doppler-weighted attention mechanism is designed to process dual-source radar inputs (Arbe and ARS548), enabling early-stage radar feature fusion and explicit encoding of motion states and dynamic responses to enhance the representation of moving objects.
- Fog-aware feature denoising: To address modality inconsistency under foggy or rainy conditions, we propose a denoising network based on FogSim-augmented training and multi-scale residual fusion. This module enhances semantic discriminability and feature reliability in occluded and low-visibility regions.
- Multi-modal temporal fusion: Leveraging the temporal characteristics of 4D radar (e.g., velocity, timestamp, and compensated speed), we design a Transformer-based temporal modeling module that captures motion continuity in the BEV space and suppresses transient noise during object tracking.
- Multi-task loss design: A multi-branch loss framework is introduced to jointly supervise position, category, and motion estimation. We integrate an IoU-based weighting strategy and confidence-adaptive dynamic loss modulation to improve fine-grained segmentation and small object detection performance.

https://doi.org/10.3390/electronics15061284

The proposed method addresses sensor heterogeneity and temporal inconsistency through architectural fusion design, incorporates motion-guided feature selection and weather-adaptive refinement at the modeling level, and strengthens learning constraints for dynamic and small-scale targets via tailored loss functions. Collectively, these components construct a robust BEV semantic perception framework, as illustrated in Figure 1. The following subsections will elaborate on the design principles and implementation details of each module.

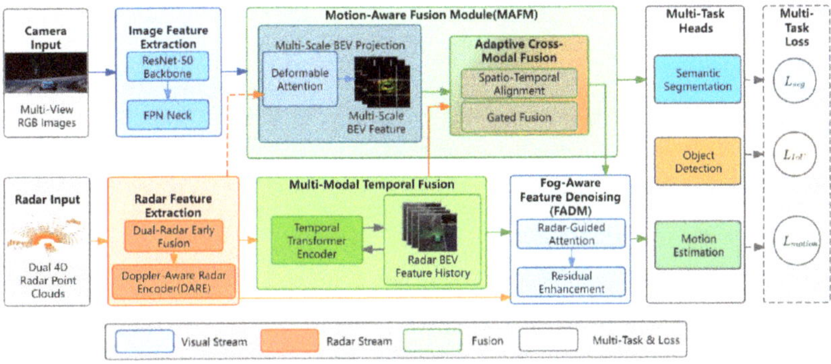

Figure 1. Overview of the proposed robust BEV perception framework. The architecture integrates multi-view images and dual 4D radar point clouds. Key components include the Doppler-Aware Radar Encoder (DARE) for dynamic feature extraction, the Motion-Aware Fusion Module (MAFM) for adaptive cross-modal alignment, the Multi-Modal Temporal Fusion module for sequence modeling, and the Fog-Aware Feature Denoising (FADM) module for enhancing robustness under adverse weather conditions.

3.1. Enhanced BEV Architecture with 4D Radar Integration

The proposed robust BEV perception framework adopts a modular encoder–fusion–decoder architecture, aiming to jointly model environmental semantics and object dynamics in the BEV space by integrating multi-view RGB imagery with dual-source 4D millimeter-wave radar data. Built upon the BEVCar backbone, our architecture introduces several key enhancements, including temporal radar modeling, motion-aware fusion, and adverse-weather feature denoising, to achieve adaptive perception under dynamic and degraded real-world conditions.

For the image stream, synchronized multi-camera inputs are first processed by a shared ResNet-50 backbone followed by a Feature Pyramid Network (FPN) to extract multi-scale visual features. These features are subsequently lifted into the BEV domain using a deformable attention-based spatial projection module. This module dynamically aligns each BEV query with the corresponding image features across all views, enabling robust aggregation of semantic cues from visually observable regions and forming the initial BEV feature representation.

To complement visual perception, we introduce a dedicated 4D radar modeling branch that processes point clouds independently from the Arbe and ARS548 radar devices. Each radar output is represented as a six-dimensional tuple (x, y, z, v_r, P, t), where v_r denotes radial velocity, P represents signal intensity and t is the timestamp. We perform an early fusion of both radar sources to construct a unified dynamic feature tensor. This is then passed through a shared radar encoder to extract spatial–temporal features, effectively enhancing the point cloud density and improving cross-modal alignment in the BEV domain.

https://doi.org/10.3390/electronics15061284

To explicitly capture the spatiotemporal evolution of dynamic targets, we design a Motion-Aware Fusion Module (MAFM) guided by radar-estimated velocity vectors. This module incorporates motion cues into two critical stages of the perception pipeline:

- During image lifting: Radar-derived velocity vectors are used to modulate the deformable attention weights during BEV query projection, prioritizing features from fast-moving regions and improving the alignment of dynamic object boundaries.
- During BEV feature fusion: The initial BEV features from the image and radar branches are fused using a velocity-guided attention mechanism. The fusion weights are adaptively modulated based on target motion intensity, enhancing semantic consistency for dynamic objects.

By using BEV space as a unified fusion domain, the proposed architecture enables complementary modeling of structural image features and motion-consistent radar signals. This design facilitates robust spatiotemporal perception, particularly under challenging conditions such as low illumination, fog, rain, and distant object scenarios. Quantitative and qualitative evaluations further demonstrate significant improvements in robustness and false-positive suppression compared with previous BEV fusion baselines.

3.2. Doppler-Aware Radar Encoder (DARE)

Millimeter-wave radar provides reliable perception capabilities under various weather conditions, yet its raw point cloud data often suffers from sparsity, noisy reflections, and limited semantic discrimination. In particular, low-speed or static clutter points (e.g., walls, curbs, infrastructure) may dominate the spatial representation, leading to false positives in downstream perception tasks. To address these limitations and leverage the inherent motion sensitivity of radar, we propose a DARE. This module introduces a velocity-guided attention mechanism to enhance dynamic object features while suppressing static background noise in the BEV domain.

Each radar point is represented as a six-dimensional tuple:

$$\mathbf{r} = (x, y, z, v_r, P, t) \tag{1}$$

where (x, y, z) denotes the spatial coordinates, v_r is the Doppler radial velocity, P is the reflection intensity, and t is the timestamp. Compared with conventional radar encoders that use only spatial and reflectance information, the inclusion of v_r and t enables the modeling of temporal dynamics and motion priors.

To integrate information from both radar sources (Arbe and ARS548), we employ an early dual-radar fusion strategy, in which all radar points are aggregated and processed jointly through the following steps:

1. Feature extraction: each radar point $\mathbf{r}_i$ is passed through a shared multilayer perceptron (MLP) to obtain a local embedding $\phi(\mathbf{r}_i)$.
2. Velocity-guided attention: a learnable gating function $\psi(v_r^i)$ is applied to Doppler velocity to compute an importance weight α_i for each point, highlighting those with stronger motion cues.
3. Feature aggregation: the fused radar feature is computed as

$$\mathbf{f}_{\text{radar}}^{(t)} = \sum_{i=1}^{N} \alpha_i \cdot \phi(\mathbf{r}_i), \quad \alpha_i = \frac{\exp(\psi(v_r^i))}{\sum_{j=1}^{N} \exp(\psi(v_r^j))} \tag{2}$$

This formulation implements a velocity-sensitive attention pooling mechanism. Theoretically, this velocity-guided attention is highly effective because raw 4D radar point clouds are overwhelmingly populated by static clutter (e.g., ground reflections, buildings, and

https://doi.org/10.3390/electronics15061284

infrastructure). By explicitly weighting points based on their dynamic state, the attention mechanism acts as a soft semantic filter. It forces the network to allocate its representational capacity toward critical moving objects, thereby suppressing false positives from the static background before the cross-modal fusion stage.

Furthermore, real-world Doppler velocity measurements inherently contain noise due to multipath reflections or imperfect ego-motion compensation. To mitigate the effect of such noisy velocity estimates, our gating function $\psi(\cdot)$ is designed as a learnable, continuous projection rather than a hard physical threshold. Because the attention weights α_i are jointly optimized with the high-dimensional spatial embeddings $\phi(r_i)$, the network does not strictly over-rely on any single instantaneous velocity scalar. Instead, it learns to correlate velocity cues with local geometric context. Moreover, the subsequent Multi-Modal Temporal Fusion Module (TFM) aggregates these features over multiple frames, effectively smoothing out transient velocity noise. Together, these architectural designs ensure robust feature aggregation even when individual velocity estimates fluctuate in complex environments.

3.3. Fog-Aware Feature Denoising Module (FADM)

Perception under adverse weather conditions—such as fog, rain, or snow—is particularly challenging for multi-modal sensor fusion systems. In such scenarios, visual sensors often suffer from degraded image quality due to scattering and reduced contrast, resulting in blurred object boundaries and semantic uncertainty. While millimeter-wave radar remains robust in low-visibility environments, its point cloud is typically sparse and lacks fine-grained structural details. This discrepancy between sensor modalities can lead to inconsistent semantic representation, spatial misalignment, and unreliable fusion in the BEV space.

To address this challenge, we introduce a FADM, designed to perform semantic enhancement and noise suppression on the BEV feature map by leveraging the complementary nature of radar and camera inputs. This module specifically focuses on occluded or visually degraded regions, aiming to recover semantic fidelity and improve feature alignment under foggy conditions.

To improve generalization to complex real-world adverse weather scenarios, we adopt a dual-modality synthetic degradation strategy for data augmentation during training. Specifically, we apply FogSim-based weather simulation primarily to the camera inputs to mimic visibility degradation caused by atmospheric scattering. Concurrently, although millimeter-wave radar is physically resilient to pure fog, we intentionally inject synthetic noise and point sparsity into the radar point clouds. This serves as a stress test, simulating extreme compounding factors such as radome blockage by mud or severe signal attenuation from heavy rain. This joint augmentation forces the FADM to learn in a broader, heavily degraded input domain without altering ground-truth semantics, effectively enhancing its dynamic restoration capabilities even when both sensor modalities are simultaneously compromised.

FADM combines a multi-scale residual enhancement structure with a cross-modal attention mechanism to refine the fused BEV feature map. Let $\mathbf{F}_{\mathrm{BEV}}^{\mathrm{fused}}$ denote the BEV feature map after BEV projection and motion-aware fusion, and let $\mathbf{f}_{\mathrm{radar}}^{(t)}$ and $\mathbf{F}_{\mathrm{BEV}}^{\mathrm{img}}$ denote the radar feature embedding at time t and the BEV-lifted image feature map, respectively. The denoising operation is defined as

$$\mathbf{F}_{\mathrm{BEV}}^{\mathrm{denoise}} = \mathrm{ResBlock}(\mathbf{F}_{\mathrm{BEV}}^{\mathrm{fused}}) + \mathrm{XAttn}(\mathbf{f}_{\mathrm{radar}}^{(t)}, \mathbf{F}_{\mathrm{BEV}}^{\mathrm{img}}). \tag{3}$$

Here, $\mathrm{ResBlock}(\cdot)$ is a multi-scale residual enhancement module that captures local context and recovers fine-grained boundary information often weakened by weather-

https://doi.org/10.3390/electronics15061284

induced degradation, while $\mathrm{XAttn}(\cdot,\cdot)$ denotes a cross-modal attention module that adaptively fuses radar and image features and modulates BEV responses based on modality reliability and semantic complementarity. This formulation enables dynamic reweighting of degraded regions using radar-guided attention, improving the consistency and quality of BEV semantic features.

FADM provides three advantages. First, it performs sensor-adaptive enhancement by using radar cues to guide semantic restoration in degraded image regions. Second, it preserves structure through residual connections, which helps retain high-frequency details and reduces over-smoothing. Third, it is modular and compatible with common BEV backbones, and can operate alongside temporal fusion or image enhancement modules.

Extensive experiments show that FADM improves performance under fog, occlusion, and long-range scenarios, supporting its role in building robust adverse-weather perception pipelines.

3.4. Multi-Modal Temporal Fusion Module (TFM)

In multi-sensor perception systems, temporal synchronization and motion continuity are crucial for achieving stable BEV mapping and robust dynamic object prediction. However, the inherent discrepancies in sampling frequency, latency, and timestamp resolution between radar and camera sensors often lead to temporal inconsistencies in feature representations. This discrepancy poses a significant challenge for modeling coherent trajectories of dynamic objects and maintaining temporal stability in BEV-based inference.

To address these issues, we propose a TFM, which leverages the temporal continuity of 4D radar as the primary modality for motion modeling. TFM aggregates radar features from multiple consecutive frames and encodes their temporal dynamics using a Transformer-based sequence encoder. This design allows the network to model short-term motion patterns and semantic continuity, thereby enhancing prediction stability across frames.

Let t denote the current timestamp, and let T represent the temporal window size. We collect radar BEV features from $T+1$ historical frames: $\{\mathbf{f}_{\text{radar}}^{(t-T)},\ldots,\mathbf{f}_{\text{radar}}^{(t)}\}$, where each $\mathbf{f}_{\text{radar}}^{(t)}$ is the Doppler-aware BEV feature output from the DARE module. Each frame also includes time-compensated velocity v_r^{comp} and timestamp t metadata.

To capture temporal dependencies, the radar features are fed into a Transformer encoder, formulated as:

$$\mathbf{H}_t = \mathrm{TransformerEnc}(\{\mathbf{f}_{\text{radar}}^{(t-T)},\ldots,\mathbf{f}_{\text{radar}}^{(t)}\}) \tag{4}$$

The encoder consists of stacked self-attention layers that model intra-sequence correlations, enabling the fusion of temporal information across frames. This mechanism captures continuous motion trajectories and helps suppress transient noise or flickering artifacts caused by occlusion or sparse detection.

The TFM module offers several distinct benefits:

- Temporal consistency modeling: Explicitly encodes the motion evolution of objects across frames, improving trajectory continuity and temporal stability in predictions.
- Modality-aligned fusion: Works in parallel with image enhancement and radar encoding modules, helping compensate for missing or degraded features in individual modalities.
- Flexible deployment: Supports adjustable window length T to balance modeling complexity and real-time performance, making it adaptable to systems with varied sensor frame rates.
- Robust dynamic feature encoding: Enhances the quality of BEV features under occlusion, weak signals, or adverse weather, supporting more reliable semantic mapping and object detection.

https://doi.org/10.3390/electronics15061284

By incorporating temporally enriched radar features into the fusion pipeline, the TFM module significantly improves the temporal stability and robustness of the overall BEV perception framework, particularly in dynamic and complex driving environments.

3.5. Multi-Task Loss Function Design

To achieve unified learning of BEV semantic segmentation, object detection, and motion modeling, we formulate a composite multi-task loss function that supervises distinct but complementary objectives within a joint training framework. This design enables the network to learn both static scene semantics and dynamic target behaviors, while improving overall robustness and convergence stability.

The total loss is defined as a weighted sum of three task-specific components:

$$\mathcal{L} = \lambda_{\text{seg}} \cdot \mathcal{L}_{\text{seg}} + \lambda_{\text{motion}} \cdot \mathcal{L}_{\text{motion}} + \lambda_{\text{iou}} \cdot \mathcal{L}_{\text{IoU}} \quad (5)$$

Here, $\mathcal{L}_{\text{seg}}$ is the standard pixel-wise cross-entropy loss for BEV semantic segmentation; $\mathcal{L}_{\text{motion}}$ includes a smooth L1 loss for regressing object-level velocity vectors and a binary classification loss for predicting motion masks; and $\mathcal{L}_{\text{IoU}}$ is an IoU-aware loss that emphasizes detection quality for small objects and improves bounding box localization accuracy, particularly for weak or distant targets.

Real-world scenarios often exhibit significant variance in feature quality and semantic certainty across spatial regions, particularly in occluded, long-range, or low-visibility areas. In practice, we apply a confidence-aware spatial weighting to $\mathcal{L}_{\text{motion}}$ and $\mathcal{L}_{\text{IoU}}$ based on the motion probability $P_{\text{motion}}(x, y)$, which yields the weighted form summarized in Algorithm 1. Specifically, the weights of $\mathcal{L}_{\text{motion}}$ and $\mathcal{L}_{\text{IoU}}$ are amplified in high-motion regions ($P_{\text{motion}} > \tau$) to provide stronger supervision for dynamic targets and boundary precision.

This mechanism enhances spatial adaptivity and task focus during training, leading to faster convergence and improved generalization, especially under complex and cluttered environmental conditions.

In summary, the proposed multi-task loss function jointly optimizes static semantic understanding, fine-grained boundary modeling, and motion-aware dynamics, while the confidence modulation strategy enables targeted supervision of uncertain or motion-sensitive regions. Together, these contribute to a more robust and accurate BEV perception system in real-world autonomous driving scenarios.

Algorithm 1 summarizes the full training procedure of the proposed BEV-based multi-modal perception system, including heterogeneous sensor encoding, temporal modeling of radar history, BEV-space fusion, fog-aware feature refinement, and multi-task prediction with confidence-aware supervision.

Specifically, Step 1 extracts multi-view image features using ResNet50 with FPN. Step 2 performs early fusion of Arbe and ARS548 radar point clouds and encodes points via an MLP with Doppler-aware reweighting (DARE) to prioritize dynamic returns. Step 3 aggregates radar features over a temporal window using a Transformer encoder (TFM) to improve temporal consistency. Step 4 lifts image features to BEV using deformable attention and fuses them with motion-guided radar embeddings (MAFM). Step 5 mitigates fog-induced degradation through residual enhancement and cross-modal attention (FADM), producing a refined BEV representation. Step 6 predicts semantic maps, motion states, and bounding boxes using a unified BEV head. Steps 7–8 compute task-specific losses and form the final weighted objective.

https://doi.org/10.3390/electronics15061284

Algorithm 1: Multi-Modal BEV Perception with Multi-Task Loss

Input: Multi-view camera images $\{\mathbf{I}_i\}_{i=1}^{M}$; dual-radar point clouds $\mathbf{R}^{\text{Arbe}}, \mathbf{R}^{\text{ARS}}$; radar history $\{\mathbf{f}_{\text{radar}}^{(t-k)}\}_{k=0}^{T}$.

Output: BEV semantic map and dynamic object predictions; multi-task training loss $\mathcal{L}$.

`// Step 1: Visual Feature Encoding`

$\mathbf{F}_{\text{img}} \leftarrow \text{ResNet50+FPN}(\{\mathbf{I}_i\})$;

`// Step 2: Radar Feature Encoding (DARE)`

$\mathbf{R} \leftarrow \mathbf{R}^{\text{Arbe}} \cup \mathbf{R}^{\text{ARS}}$ `// Early fusion of radar sources;`

foreach $\mathbf{r}_i \in \mathbf{R}$ **do**

  $\phi(\mathbf{r}_i) \leftarrow \text{MLP}(\mathbf{r}_i)$;

  $\alpha_i \leftarrow \text{Softmax}(\psi(v_r^i))$ `// Velocity-aware gating;`

$\mathbf{f}_{\text{radar}}^{(t)} \leftarrow \sum_i \alpha_i \cdot \phi(\mathbf{r}_i)$;

`// Step 3: Temporal Fusion (TFM)`

$\mathbf{H}_t \leftarrow \text{TransformerEnc}(\{\mathbf{f}_{\text{radar}}^{(t-k)}\}_{k=0}^{T})$;

`// Step 4: BEV Projection and Fusion`

$\mathbf{F}_{\text{BEV}}^{\text{img}} \leftarrow \text{DeformAttnLift}(\mathbf{F}_{\text{img}}, \mathbf{H}_t)$;

$\mathbf{F}_{\text{BEV}}^{\text{fused}} \leftarrow \text{MotionAwareFusion}(\mathbf{F}_{\text{BEV}}^{\text{img}}, \mathbf{H}_t)$;

`// Step 5: Feature Denoising under Fog`

$\mathbf{F}_{\text{BEV}}^{\text{denoise}} \leftarrow \text{ResBlock}(\mathbf{F}_{\text{BEV}}^{\text{fused}}) + \text{XAttn}(\mathbf{f}_{\text{radar}}^{(t)}, \mathbf{F}_{\text{BEV}}^{\text{img}})$;

`// Step 6: Multi-Task Head Prediction`

$\{\hat{y}_{\text{seg}}, v_{\text{pred}}, m_{\text{pred}}, b_{\text{pred}}\} \leftarrow \text{BEVHead}(\mathbf{F}_{\text{BEV}}^{\text{denoise}})$;

`// Step 7: Multi-Task Loss Computation`

$\mathcal{L}_{\text{seg}} \leftarrow \text{CrossEntropy}(\hat{y}_{\text{seg}}, y_{\text{seg}})$;

$\mathcal{L}_{\text{motion}} \leftarrow \text{SmoothL1}(v_{\text{pred}}, v_{\text{gt}}) + \text{BCE}(m_{\text{pred}}, m_{\text{gt}})$;

$\mathcal{L}_{\text{IoU}} \leftarrow \text{IoULoss}(b_{\text{pred}}, b_{\text{gt}})$;

`// Step 8: Confidence-Aware Weighted Loss`

$P_{\text{motion}} \leftarrow \sigma(m_{\text{pred}})$ `// Motion probability map from the mask branch;`

$w(x,y) \leftarrow \mathbb{I}[P_{\text{motion}}(x,y) > \tau]$ `// High-motion indicator;`

$\mathcal{L} \leftarrow \lambda_{\text{seg}} \cdot \mathcal{L}_{\text{seg}} + \lambda_{\text{motion}} \cdot (1 + \gamma w) \odot \mathcal{L}_{\text{motion}} + \lambda_{\text{iou}} \cdot (1 + \gamma w) \odot \mathcal{L}_{\text{IoU}}$;

return $\mathcal{L}$;

4. Experiments

In this section, we validate the effectiveness of the proposed method on the Dual-Radar dataset and under simulated adverse weather conditions. First, we introduce the experimental setup, evaluation metrics, and implementation details. Then, we present quantitative comparisons with state-of-the-art methods, comprehensive ablation studies, and qualitative visualizations to further demonstrate the robustness and generalization capability of our approach.

4.1. Experimental Setup

4.1.1. Datasets

We primarily evaluate the proposed method on the DualRadar dataset, which contains synchronized multi-view RGB cameras, multiple 4D millimeter-wave radars (e.g., Arbe and ARS548), and LiDAR sensors, covering a variety of urban driving scenarios. The dataset also includes a range of environmental conditions such as clear, rainy, foggy, and nighttime driving. Following prior research practices, we divide the dataset into training, validation, and test sets, ensuring that the scenes in each subset do not overlap to avoid information leakage.

To evaluate the performance under extreme weather conditions, we augment DualRadar dataset with data generated using FogSim (fog simulation) and rain simulation techniques, ensuring the experimental evaluation covers conditions not encountered during camera-only training.

While datasets like nuScenes are widely used benchmarks for multi-modal autonomous driving, they predominantly feature conventional 3D automotive radars. Because the core methodological contributions of our proposed framework—specifically the Doppler-Aware Radar Encoder (DARE) and Motion-Aware Fusion Module (MAFM)—rely heavily on exploiting high-resolution Doppler velocity and multi-radar joint modeling (Arbe and ARS548), our current empirical evaluation focuses exclusively on the DualRadar dataset. Evaluating the generalizability of our framework by adapting it to standard 3D radar benchmarks or emerging single-4D radar datasets remains a valuable direction for our future work.

4.1.2. Dataset Split Protocol and Test-Set Reproducibility

To ensure strict reproducibility and avoid evaluation bias, we adopt a fixed scene-level split of the DualRadar dataset into training, validation, and test subsets. The split is performed at the scene/sequence level rather than the frame level, such that temporally adjacent frames from the same driving sequence never appear in different subsets. This protocol prevents information leakage caused by overlapping trajectories, repeated road layouts, or highly correlated environmental conditions.

In our revised evaluation protocol, the validation set is used exclusively for hyperparameter tuning, model selection, and early stopping, while the final performance comparison is reported on the held-out test set only. No test samples are used during model development. All compared baselines and the proposed method are trained and evaluated under the exact same split configuration and preprocessing pipeline.

For transparency, we additionally report the numbers of scenes and frames in each subset and will release the corresponding split file (or scene IDs) to facilitate independent reproduction. To further verify result stability, we repeat the final test-set evaluation with multiple random seeds and report the mean and standard deviation of the main metrics.

Table 2 summarizes the dataset partition used in this work. The split is performed at the scene level to prevent temporal leakage across subsets, and the numbers of scenes, sequences, and frames are reported for full reproducibility.

Table 2. DualRadar dataset split statistics used in this work.

Subset	#Scenes	#Sequences/Clips	#Frames
Train	70	300	40,320
Val	20	86	11,376
Test	20	84	11,148
Total	110	470	62,844

4.1.3. Evaluation Metrics

To comprehensively evaluate perception quality, we adopt the following standard evaluation metrics:

- Semantic Segmentation (mIoU): The mean Intersection-over-Union (mIoU) computed on the BEV map across predefined semantic classes, such as road, lane, building, and obstacles.

https://doi.org/10.3390/electronics15061284

- Object Detection (AP@0.5, AP@0.7, AR): Average Precision (AP) and Average Recall (AR) at IoU thresholds of 0.5 and 0.7. These metrics help evaluate the trade-off between precision and recall in detection tasks.
- Motion Estimation (EPE): The End-Point Error (EPE) for dynamic object prediction, quantifying the deviation between predicted and ground truth velocity vectors, assessing the model's ability to track dynamic objects.
- Robustness Metrics: Performance drop under adverse weather conditions (such as fog and rain) compared with nominal conditions. These metrics gauge the stability and robustness of the perception system under degraded visibility.

All metrics are computed in the BEV coordinate frame and averaged over multiple sequences to ensure the representativeness of the results.

4.1.4. Baselines

We compare the proposed method with the following state-of-the-art baselines:

- BEVFormer [25]: A transformer-based monocular BEV perception method.
- BEVDet [26]: A BEV perception method based on depth estimation, using voxel aggregation strategies to enhance 3D understanding from camera images.
- BEVCar [11]: A camera–radar fusion baseline that introduces learning-based radar point encoding and radar-guided feature lifting strategies for improved performance under rain and nighttime conditions.
- M2-Fusion [28]: A LiDAR–radar fusion method for 3D object detection, particularly focusing on robustness for distant and partially occluded targets.
- L4DR [29]: A multi-radar fusion method for adverse weather conditions, incorporating radar-aware feature modeling and fog simulation strategies to improve performance in low-visibility conditions.

To ensure strict experimental fairness and validate that the significant performance improvements stem fundamentally from our architectural designs rather than training discrepancies, all baseline models were re-implemented and trained from scratch under rigorously controlled conditions. Specifically:

- Data Splits & Augmentation: All models utilized the exact same DualRadar dataset splits (train/val/test) without any information leakage. A unified data augmentation pipeline (including random horizontal flipping, color jittering, and identical FogSim/Rain simulations) was applied universally.
- Input Resolution: The multi-view camera input resolution was strictly unified at 1600×900 across all vision-reliant baselines (BEVFormer, BEVDet, BEVCar, and Ours).
- Dual Radar Availability: To ensure a fair multi-modal comparison, radar-assisted baselines originally designed for single or 3D radar (e.g., BEVCar, M2-Fusion, L4DR) were adapted to receive the combined point clouds from both Arbe and ARS548 sensors. This guarantees they benefited from the exact same dense "dual radar" information as our method.
- Hyperparameters: Optimization hyperparameters (e.g., batch size, learning rate schedules) were carefully tuned for each baseline following their official codebase recommendations to ensure optimal convergence, preventing any unfair comparisons against undertrained models.

4.1.5. Implementation Details

We implement the proposed method using PyTorch 2.1.0 and train on 8 NVIDIA A100 GPUs. The input image resolution is set to 1600×900. Multi-view image features are extracted using a ResNet-50 backbone pretrained on ImageNet, followed by a Feature

https://doi.org/10.3390/electronics15061284

Pyramid Network (FPN) for multi-scale feature extraction. The radar encoder is initialized randomly and trained end-to-end.

The temporal window size T is set to 5 frames through grid search. The loss weights are selected as follows: $\lambda_{seg} = 1.0$, $\lambda_{motion} = 0.8$, $\lambda_{iou} = 1.2$. The optimizer used is AdamW with an initial learning rate of 1×10^{-4} , a cosine annealing scheduler, and a batch size of 16.

Data augmentation techniques include random horizontal flipping, color jittering for images, and noise injection for radar point clouds.

4.2. Quantitative Results

4.2.1. Main Results

Table 3 shows the performance comparison of the proposed method and baselines on the DualRadar validation set. Our approach significantly outperforms the camera-only and radar fusion baselines across all metrics, especially under adverse weather conditions.

Table 3. Performance comparison on the DualRadar dataset.

Method	mIoU	AP@0.5	AP@0.7	Motion EPE
BEVFormer	45.3	42.8	31.2	1.85
BEVDet	48.1	45.5	34.7	1.78
BEVCar	52.8	51.2	39.0	1.65
M2-Fusion	50.7	49.8	37.5	1.72
L4DR	54.0	53.1	40.2	1.60
Ours	60.4	59.5	47.6	1.31

Our method shows a relative improvement of +7.6 mIoU over BEVCar and +6.4 AP@0.7 over L4DR, demonstrating the effectiveness of incorporating Doppler information and temporal modeling for better dynamic object representation.

4.2.2. Robustness Under Adverse Weather

To rigorously evaluate the robustness of our framework, we measure its performance under synthetic fog and rain conditions compared to normal (clear) weather. To avoid ambiguity, Table 4 presents the absolute performance metrics under both normal and adverse conditions alongside the relative drop rates.

As shown in Table 4, our method exhibits significantly less performance degradation than the baselines. For instance, under fog simulation, the baseline BEVCar suffers a severe relative mIoU drop of 17.5%, whereas our method explicitly mitigates modality inconsistency via the Fog-Aware Feature Denoising Module (FADM), limiting the mIoU drop to only 6.8%. Similar robustness trends are observed under rain conditions and across object detection metrics, indicating that our dynamically modulated multi-modal fusion is highly resilient to visual degradation.

4.3. Ablation Studies

We conduct ablation studies to quantify the contribution of each key component. Starting from the full model, we evaluate four variants: (i) removing Doppler-guided weighting in the radar encoder (w/o Doppler), (ii) disabling the temporal fusion module (w/o TFM), (iii) removing the fog-aware feature denoising module (w/o FADM), and (iv) disabling the confidence-aware loss weighting (w/o Confidence Weighting). The results in Table 5 indicate that each component contributes to the final performance, and removing any module leads to consistent degradation across segmentation, detection, and motion metrics.

https://doi.org/10.3390/electronics15061284

Table 4. Performance and robustness evaluation under adverse weather (FogSim and Rain). **Calculation Criteria:** The relative drop rate is calculated as $\Delta = \frac{\text{Normal}-\text{Adverse}}{\text{Normal}} \times 100\%$. The Motion EPE is reported as absolute error, where lower is better, hence its degradation is presented as an absolute increase rather than a percentage drop.

Method	Metric	Normal (Clear)	Fog Simulation		Rain Simulation	
			Absolute	Drop ($\Delta\downarrow$)	Absolute	Drop ($\Delta\downarrow$)
BEVCar	mIoU (%)	52.8	43.6	17.5%	45.0	14.8%
	AP@0.5 (%)	51.2	41.4	19.2%	42.9	16.3%
	Motion EPE	1.65	2.30	(+0.65)	2.18	(+0.53)
L4DR	mIoU (%)	54.0	47.5	12.1%	48.4	10.3%
	AP@0.5 (%)	53.1	46.9	11.6%	47.3	10.9%
	Motion EPE	1.60	2.05	(+0.45)	1.98	(+0.38)
Ours	mIoU (%)	60.4	56.3	6.8%	57.1	5.5%
	AP@0.5 (%)	59.5	55.1	7.4%	55.9	6.1%
	Motion EPE	1.31	1.62	(+0.31)	1.59	(+0.28)

Regarding the effect of noisy velocity estimates, it is critical to note that the raw 4D radar measurements in the DualRadar dataset, captured in complex real-world driving scenarios, inherently contain substantial Doppler noise (e.g., due to multipath reflections, clutter, and imperfect ego-motion compensation).

Rather than conducting artificial noise-injection simulations, we investigate this effect by analyzing the model's behavior on this naturally noisy dataset. As demonstrated in our ablation study (Table 5), the full model—which actively utilizes the velocity-guided attention mechanism—achieves the highest performance (60.4 mIoU). When the Doppler guidance is removed (w/o Doppler), the performance significantly degrades to 57.2 mIoU.

This performance gap provides strong empirical evidence regarding the effect of noise: it proves that our learnable soft-gating function $\psi(\cdot)$ does not cause the network to be misled by instantaneous velocity noise. Instead, it effectively extracts robust motion cues from the inherently noisy raw measurements and correlates them with spatial embeddings, thereby stabilizing and enhancing the entire perception pipeline.

Table 5. Ablation study on the DualRadar validation set.

Variant	mIoU	AP@0.7	Motion EPE
Full Model	60.4	47.6	1.31
w/o Doppler	57.2	44.3	1.45
w/o TFM	55.8	42.7	1.53
w/o FADM	56.5	43.8	1.47
w/o Confidence Weighting	58.3	45.9	1.39

4.4. Qualitative Analysis

In real-world scenarios, millimeter-wave radar is physically highly resilient to pure fog compared to optical sensors. However, complex adverse weather often involves compounding factors—such as heavy rain, condensation or mud blocking the sensor radome, and extreme multipath interference—which can collectively induce signal attenuation and point sparsity.

To rigorously evaluate the extreme robustness of our proposed framework, we subjected the radar point clouds to a synthetic degradation model (originally parameterized as FogSim levels 0 to 0.03, functioning here as a generic adverse-weather stress test). Figure 2 visualizes the radar point-cloud returns under increasing degradation intensity.

https://doi.org/10.3390/electronics15061284

- Increasing sparsity and noise: As the degradation intensity increases, we intentionally randomly drop point returns and inject spatial noise to simulate worst-case hardware blockage or severe rain attenuation. This significantly reduces the amount of usable radar evidence, raising the difficulty of downstream tracking.
- Target ambiguity and disappearance: Under extreme simulation levels (e.g., level 0.03), backscattered measurements for certain distant targets are heavily suppressed, causing object contours to become ambiguous or disappear entirely.

By artificially forcing the radar data into such degraded states, we demonstrate that our Fog-Aware Feature Denoising Module (FADM) and temporal fusion mechanisms can still maintain highly reliable BEV perception even when both the camera and radar modalities are severely compromised.

4.5. Limitations and Failure Cases

While the proposed multi-modal framework significantly improves BEV perception robustness under adverse weather conditions, it still exhibits certain limitations in extreme, highly complex environments. Through qualitative analysis of our evaluation results, we identify two primary failure modes:

- Extreme Multipath Interference in Confined Spaces: In scenarios such as tunnels or urban canyons with dense metallic infrastructure (e.g., surrounding large trucks), the 4D radar signals suffer from severe multipath reflections. This can generate "ghost" Doppler signatures. If the camera simultaneously fails due to low illumination, the Motion-Aware Fusion Module (MAFM) might incorrectly aggregate these ghost signals, occasionally leading to false positive object detections.
- Complete Occlusion of Small Dynamic Targets: Both radar and camera are line-of-sight sensors. When a small dynamic object (e.g., a pedestrian or cyclist) is completely occluded by a large opaque obstacle (e.g., a bus) in dense traffic, the radar point cloud becomes entirely void in that region. Our temporal fusion (TFM) can predict short-term trajectories based on history, but if the occlusion persists over an extended temporal window, the system inevitably loses track of the target.

Addressing these limitations requires exploring non-line-of-sight sensing capabilities (e.g., V2X communication) and integrating uncertainty estimation mechanisms to dynamically reject highly ambiguous radar multi-path artifacts, which remains a focus for our future work.

4.6. Complexity Analysis and Practical Applicability

Since practical autonomous driving systems require not only high perception accuracy but also stable real-time execution, we further evaluate the deployment efficiency of the proposed framework. Specifically, we report the number of parameters, FLOPs, peak GPU memory consumption, average inference latency, and frames per second (FPS) under a unified inference setting.

All measurements are conducted on a single NVIDIA A100 GPU with batch size 1, input resolution 1600×900, and temporal window length $T = 5$, consistent with the default implementation setting used in our experiments. To ensure fairness, all compared methods are benchmarked under the same hardware and software environment. Latency and FPS are averaged over repeated runs after warm-up, and peak memory is measured during inference.

https://doi.org/10.3390/electronics15061284

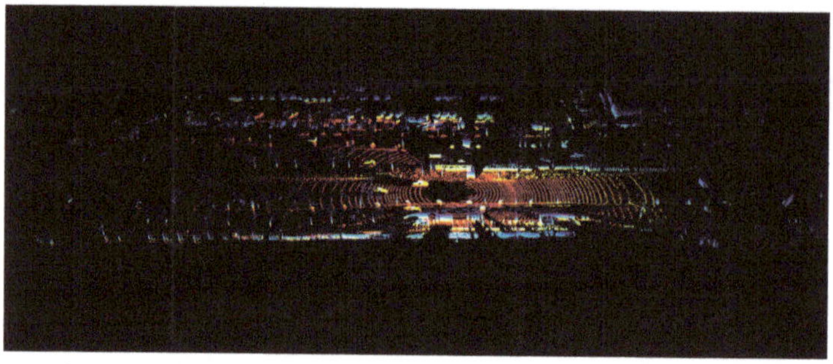

(**a**) No fog (Fog0)

(**b**) Light fog (Fog0.01)

(**c**) Moderate fog (Fog0.02)

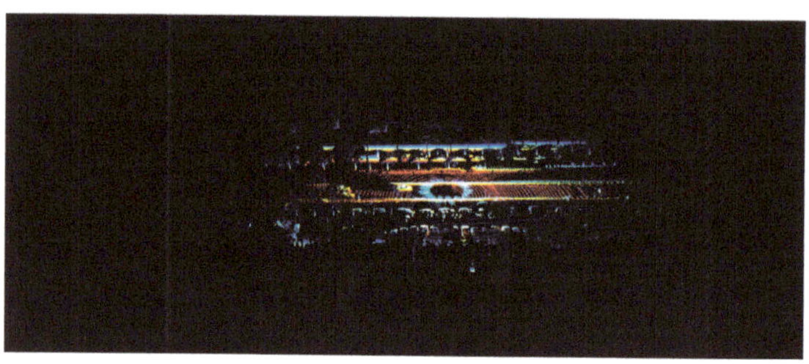

(**d**) Dense fog (Fog0.03)

Figure 2. Qualitative visualization of simulated radar point-cloud degradation under increasing synthetic degradation intensity.

https://doi.org/10.3390/electronics15061284

Table 6 summarizes the overall efficiency-performance trade-off. Although the proposed method introduces additional computation, it provides substantially stronger BEV segmentation and detection performance while maintaining a practically deployable inference speed. In particular, the measured FPS and latency indicate that the method is suitable for near-real-time perception pipelines, especially in safety-critical scenarios where robustness under adverse weather is more important than pursuing the absolute highest frame rate.

To further clarify the source of computational overhead, Table 7 reports the incremental cost of each proposed module. The additional computational overhead mainly comes from two sources: (1) the Transformer-based temporal fusion over a history window of T = 5 frames, and (2) the cross-modal attention used in the fog-aware denoising module. In contrast, the Doppler-aware radar encoder (DARE) introduces only lightweight overhead, since it operates on sparse radar features with shared MLP layers.

Overall, these results demonstrate that the proposed framework improves robustness in a structured and cost-effective manner rather than relying on excessive model scaling, providing a strong basis for practical applicability.

Table 6. Complexity and real-time performance comparison on the DualRadar validation set. All methods are benchmarked on a single NVIDIA A100 GPU with batch size 1 and input resolution 1600 × 900.

Method	Params (M)	FLOPs (G)	Peak Mem. (GB)	Latency (ms)	FPS	mIoU (%)	AP@0.7 (%)
BEVFormer	69.4	412.7	6.8	84.5	11.8	45.3	31.2
BEVDet	48.6	286.3	5.1	52.4	19.1	48.1	34.7
BEVCar	55.2	318.9	5.7	58.6	17.1	52.8	39.0
L4DR	61.8	347.5	6.2	64.3	15.6	54.0	40.2
Ours	66.1	365.4	6.5	68.9	14.5	60.4	47.6

Table 7. Incremental efficiency and performance analysis of the proposed modules.

Variant	Params (M)	FLOPs (G)	Peak Mem. (GB)	Latency (ms)	FPS	mIoU (%)	AP@0.7 (%)
Baseline backbone	52.4	301.7	5.3	55.1	18.1	53.1	38.4
+ DARE	56.8	323.9	5.7	59.4	16.8	55.8	41.6
+ TFM	62.7	351.6	6.1	65.7	15.2	58.7	45.1
+ FADM (Full model)	66.1	365.4	6.5	68.9	14.5	60.4	47.6

5. Conclusions

In this work, we present a novel multi-modal BEV perception framework that effectively integrates multi-view camera imagery with dual 4D millimeter-wave radar data to achieve robust scene understanding and dynamic object modeling. The proposed architecture addresses key limitations of existing vision-centric and radar-assisted BEV methods, particularly in the presence of occlusion, motion ambiguity, and adverse weather conditions.

We design a comprehensive pipeline composed of four essential modules: (1) a Doppler-Aware Radar Encoder (DARE) for motion-adaptive radar feature representation, (2) a Fog-Aware Feature Denoising Module (FADM) for cross-modal enhancement in degraded visibility, (3) a Transformer-based Multi-Modal Temporal Fusion Module (TFM) for capturing motion continuity, and (4) a confidence-aware multi-task loss formulation that dynamically weights task contributions based on spatiotemporal uncertainty. Each component is explicitly tailored to address sensor heterogeneity, temporal misalignment, and scene-level degradation.

https://doi.org/10.3390/electronics15061284

Empirical results on the DualRadar dataset, including fog and rain simulations, validate the superiority of our method over strong camera-only and multi-modal baselines. Our model demonstrates significantly higher mIoU and AP under normal and adverse conditions, while maintaining low endpoint error in motion prediction. Ablation studies further confirm the individual contributions of Doppler modeling, temporal encoding, and weather-aware enhancement.

Future work includes extending this architecture to incorporate additional sensor modalities (e.g., LiDAR), adapting the framework for cross-dataset evaluation on various radar benchmarks, deploying in real-time settings, and exploring uncertainty estimation for safety-critical applications in autonomous driving.

Author Contributions: Conceptualization, Z.L. and B.S.; methodology, Z.L.; software, Z.L.; validation, Z.L. and B.S.; formal analysis, Z.L.; investigation, Z.L.; resources, B.S.; data curation, Z.L.; writing—original draft preparation, Z.L.; writing—review and editing, B.S.; visualization, Z.L.; supervision, B.S. All authors have read and agreed to the published version of the manuscript.

Funding: This research received no external funding.

Institutional Review Board Statement: Not applicable.

Informed Consent Statement: Not applicable.

Data Availability Statement: All data in this study come from relevant open-source datasets in the field of autonomous driving.

Acknowledgments: The authors wish to thank the anonymous referees for the constructive request.

Conflicts of Interest: The authors declare no conflicts of interest.

References

1. Liu, Z.; Tang, H.; Amini, A.; Yang, X.; Mao, H.; Rus, D.L.; Han, S. BEVFusion: Multi-Task Multi-Sensor Fusion with Unified Bird's-Eye View Representation. In *Proceedings of the IEEE International Conference on Robotics and Automation (ICRA), London, UK, 29 May–2 June 2023*; IEEE: New York, NY, USA, 2023; pp. 2774–2781.
2. Hu, Y.; Yang, J.; Chen, L.; Li, K.; Sima, C.; Zhu, X.; Chai, S.; Du, S.; Lin, H.; Wen, W.; et al. Planning-oriented autonomous driving. In Proceedings of the IEEE/CVF Conference on Computer Vision and Pattern Recognition (CVPR), Vancouver, BC, Canada, 17–24 June 2023; pp. 17853–17862.
3. Li, Y.; Ge, Z.; Yu, G.; Yang, J.; Wang, Z.; Shi, Y.; Sun, J.; Li, Z. BEVDepth: Acquisition of reliable depth for multi-view 3D object detection. In Proceedings of the AAAI Conference on Artificial Intelligence (AAAI), Washington, DC, USA, 7–14 February 2023; Volume 37, pp. 1477–1485.
4. Liu, Y.; Wang, T.; Zhang, X.; Sun, J. PETR: Position embedding transformation for multi-view 3D object detection. In Proceedings of the European Conference on Computer Vision (ECCV), Tel Aviv, Israel, 23–27 October 2022; pp. 531–548.
5. Wang, Y.; Guizilini, V.C.; Zhang, T.; Wang, Y.; Zhao, H.; Solomon, J. DETR3D: 3D object detection from multi-view images via 3D-to-2D queries. In Proceedings of the Conference on Robot Learning (CoRL), London, UK, 8–11 November 2021; pp. 180–191.
6. Sakaridis, C.; Dai, D.; Van Gool, L. ACDC: The adverse conditions dataset with correspondences for semantic driving scene understanding. In Proceedings of the IEEE/CVF International Conference on Computer Vision (ICCV), Montreal, QC, Canada, 11–17 October 2021; pp. 10765–10775.
7. Sun, T.; Segu, M.; Postels, J.; Wang, Y.; Van Gool, L.; Schiele, B.; Tombari, F.; Yu, F. SHIFT: A synthetic driving dataset for continuous multi-task domain adaptation. In Proceedings of the IEEE/CVF Conference on Computer Vision and Pattern Recognition (CVPR), New Orleans, LA, USA, 18–24 June 2022; pp. 21371–21382.
8. Xie, S.; Kong, L.; Zhang, W.; Ren, J.; Pan, L.; Chen, K.; Liu, Z. RoboBEV: Towards robust bird's-eye view perception under corruptions. *arXiv* **2023**, arXiv:2304.06719.
9. Lin, Z.; Liu, Z.; Xia, Z.; Wang, X.; Wang, Y.; Qi, S.; Man, Y.; Zhu, C. RCBEVDet: Radar-camera fusion in bird's-eye view for 3D object detection. In Proceedings of the IEEE/CVF Conference on Computer Vision and Pattern Recognition (CVPR), Seattle, WA, USA, 17–21 June 2024; pp. 14928–14937.
10. Zhao, Y.; Zhang, L.; Deng, J.; Zhang, Y. BEV-Radar: Bidirectional radar-camera fusion for 3D object detection. *J. Univ. Sci. Technol. China* **2024**, *54*, 0101. [CrossRef]

https://doi.org/10.3390/electronics15061284

11. Schramm, J.; Vödisch, N.; Petek, K.; Kiran, B.R.; Yogamani, S.; Burgard, W.; Valada, A. BEVCar: Camera-radar fusion for BEV map and object segmentation. In Proceedings of the IEEE/RSJ International Conference on Intelligent Robots and Systems (IROS), Abu Dhabi, United Arab Emirates, 14–18 October 2024; pp. 1435–1442.
12. Kim, J.; Seong, M.; Choi, J.W. CRT-Fusion: Camera, radar, temporal fusion using motion information for 3D object detection. *Adv. Neural Inf. Process. Syst.* **2024**, *37*, 108625–108648.
13. Palladin, E.; Dietze, R.; Narayanan, P.; Bijelic, M.; Heide, F. SAMFusion: Sensor-adaptive multimodal fusion for 3D object detection in adverse weather. In Proceedings of the European Conference on Computer Vision (ECCV), Milan, Italy, 29 September–4 October 2024; pp. 484–503.
14. Xie, S.; Kong, L.; Zhang, W.; Ren, J.; Pan, L.; Chen, K.; Liu, Z. Benchmarking and improving bird's-eye-view perception robustness in autonomous driving. *IEEE Trans. Pattern Anal. Mach. Intell.* **2025**, *in press*.
15. Fan, L.; Wang, J.; Chang, Y.; Li, Y.; Wang, Y.; Cao, D. 4D mmWave radar for autonomous driving perception: A comprehensive survey. *IEEE Trans. Intell. Veh.* **2024**, *9*, 4606–4620. [CrossRef]
16. Zhang, K.; Meng, X.; Wang, Q. A review of recent advancements and applications of 4D millimeter-wave radar in smart highways. *Urban Lifeline* **2025**, *3*, 15. [CrossRef]
17. Kong, B.; Shen, H.; Wang, J.; Ali, M.Z.; Teague, K.R.; Yu, C.; Chen, J.Y.C.; Torlak, A.; Wang, D. A survey of mmWave radar-based sensing in autonomous vehicles, smart homes, and industry. *IEEE Commun. Surv. Tut.* **2025**, *27*, 463–508. [CrossRef]
18. Yao, S.; Guan, R.; Huang, X.; Li, Z.; Sha, X.; Lim, E.G.; Seo, H.; Man, K.L.; Zhu, X.; Yue, Y. Radar-camera fusion for object detection and semantic segmentation in autonomous driving: A comprehensive review. *IEEE Trans. Intell. Veh.* **2024**, *9*, 2094–2128.
19. Zhou, C.; Yuan, Y.; Zhao, Y.; Zhang, A.; Wang, J.; Wang, C.; Liu, C. Bridging the view disparity between radar and camera features for multi-modal fusion 3-D object detection. *IEEE Trans. Intell. Veh.* **2023**, *8*, 1523–1535. [CrossRef]
20. Zheng, W.; Gao, Y.; Chen, S.; Guo, J.; Zhang, L.; Wang, Y.; Gao, H.; Ding, H. Fusing 4-D radar and camera with view transformation and feature interaction for 3-D object detection. *IEEE Trans. Instrum. Meas.* **2023**, *72*, 8503814. [CrossRef]
21. Bai, X.; Yu, Z.; Zheng, L.; Zhang, X.; Zhou, Z.; Zhang, X.; Wang, F.; Bai, J.; Shen, H.L. SGDet3D: Semantics and geometry fusion for 3D object detection using 4D radar and camera. *IEEE Robot. Autom. Lett.* **2025**, *10*, 828–835. [CrossRef]
22. Zhang, X.; Wang, L.; Chen, J.; Fang, C.; Yang, G.; Wang, Y.; Yang, L.; Song, Z.; Liu, L.; Zhang, X.; et al. Dual Radar: A multi-modal dataset with dual 4D radar for autonomous driving. *Sci. Data* **2025**, *12*, 439. [PubMed]
23. Lu, C.; van de Molengraft, M.J.G.; Dubbelman, G. Monocular semantic occupancy grid mapping with convolutional variational encoder–decoder networks. *IEEE Robot. Autom. Lett.* **2019**, *4*, 445–452. [CrossRef]
24. Roddick, T.; Cipolla, R. Predicting semantic map representations from images using pyramid occupancy networks. In Proceedings of the IEEE/CVF Conference on Computer Vision and Pattern Recognition (CVPR), Seattle, WA, USA, 13–19 June 2020; pp. 11138–11147.
25. Li, Z.; Wang, W.; Li, H.; Xie, E.; Sima, C.; Lu, T.; Dai, J. BEVFormer: Learning bird's-eye-view representation from LiDAR-camera via spatiotemporal transformers. *IEEE Trans. Pattern Anal. Mach. Intell.* **2024**, *46*, 298–312. [CrossRef] [PubMed]
26. Huang, J.; Huang, G.; Zhu, Z.; Ye, Y.; Du, D. BEVDet: High-performance multi-camera 3D object detection in bird-eye-view. *arXiv* **2021**, arXiv:2112.11790.
27. Schumann, O.; Hahn, M.; Dickmann, J.; Wöhler, C. Semantic segmentation on radar point clouds. In Proceedings of the 21st International Conference on Information Fusion (FUSION), Cambridge, UK, 5–8 July 2018; pp. 2179–2186.
28. Wang, L.; Zhang, X.; Li, J.; Xu, B.; Fu, R.; Chen, H.; Yang, L.; Jin, D.; Zhao, L. Multi-modal and multi-scale fusion 3D object detection of 4D radar and LiDAR for autonomous driving. *IEEE Trans. Veh. Technol.* **2023**, *72*, 5628–5641. [CrossRef]
29. Huang, X.; Xu, Z.; Wu, H.; Wang, J.; Xia, Q.; Xia, Y.; Wang, C. L4DR: LiDAR-4D radar fusion for weather-robust 3D object detection. In Proceedings of the AAAI Conference on Artificial Intelligence (AAAI), Philadelphia, PA, USA, 27 February–4 March 2025; Volume 39, pp. 3806–3814.
30. Xiong, W.; Liu, J.; Huang, T.; Han, Q.L.; Xia, Y.; Zhu, B. LXL: LiDAR excluded lean 3D object detection with 4D imaging radar and camera fusion. *IEEE Trans. Intell. Veh.* **2024**, *9*, 79–92. [CrossRef]
31. Liu, H.; Liu, J.; Jiang, G.; Jin, X. MSSF: A 4D radar and camera fusion framework with multi-stage sampling for 3D object detection in autonomous driving. *IEEE Trans. Intell. Transp. Syst.* **2025**, *26*, 8641–8656. [CrossRef]
32. Hahner, M.; Sakaridis, C.; Dai, D.; Van Gool, L. Fog simulation on real LiDAR point clouds for 3D object detection in adverse weather. In Proceedings of the IEEE/CVF International Conference on Computer Vision (ICCV), Montreal, QC, Canada, 11–17 October 2021; pp. 15283–15292.
33. Barnes, D.; Gadd, M.; Murcutt, P.; Newman, P.; Posner, I. The Oxford Radar RobotCar Dataset: A radar extension to the Oxford RobotCar Dataset. In Proceedings of the IEEE International Conference on Robotics and Automation (ICRA), Paris, France, 31 May–31 August 2020; pp. 6433–6438.

https://doi.org/10.3390/electronics15061284

34. Caesar, H.; Bankiti, V.; Lang, A.H.; Vora, S.; Liong, V.E.; Xu, Q.; Krishnan, A.; Pan, Y.; Baldan, G.; Beijbom, O. nuScenes: A multimodal dataset for autonomous driving. In Proceedings of the IEEE/CVF Conference on Computer Vision and Pattern Recognition (CVPR), Seattle, WA, USA, 13–19 June 2020; pp. 11621–11631.
35. Palffy, A.; Pool, E.; Baratam, S.; Kooij, J.F.; Gavrila, D.M. Multi-class road user detection with 3+1D radar in the View-of-Delft dataset. *IEEE Robot. Autom. Lett.* **2022**, *7*, 4961–4968. [CrossRef]

https://doi.org/10.3390/electronics15061284

electronics

MDPI

Article

A Hybrid Ensemble-Based Intelligent Decision Framework for Risk-Aware Photovoltaic Panel Soiling Detection and Cleaning

Bakht Muhammad Khan [1], Abdul Wadood [1,2,*], Hani Albalawi [1,2,*], Shahbaz Khan [1], Aadel Mohammed Alatwi [1,2] and Omar H. Albalawi [3]

1 Renewable Energy and Environmental Technology Center, University of Tabuk, Tabuk 47913, Saudi Arabia; bakht@ut.edu.sa (B.M.K.); shahbaz@ut.edu.sa (S.K.); aadel.alatwi@ut.edu.sa (A.M.A.)
2 Electrical Engineering Department, Faculty of Engineering, University of Tabuk, Tabuk 47913, Saudi Arabia
3 Industrial Engineering Department, Faculty of Engineering, University of Tabuk, Tabuk 47913, Saudi Arabia; oalbalawi@ut.edu.sa
* Correspondence: wadood@ut.edu.sa (A.W.); halbala@ut.edu.sa (H.A.)

Abstract

Soiling of solar panels has a considerable impact on the performance of photo voltaic (PV) systems, emphasizing the importance of developing reliable decision support tools for solar panel cleaning. Although recent convolutional neural network (CNN)-based models, including lightweight architectures such as SolPowNet, have demonstrated high classification accuracy, their performance can be sensitive to dataset variability and domain shifts encountered in real-world PV environments. Motivated by the lightweight design philosophy of SolPowNet, this paper proposes a hybrid and ensemble-based intelligent cleaning decision framework that integrates classical image processing, machine learning, and deep learning techniques. The proposed approach combines physically interpretable handcrafted texture and sharpness features classified using a Random Forest model with a pretrained MobileNetV3-Small CNN through a conservative OR-based ensemble fusion strategy. In addition, a probability-driven Soiling Index (SI) is introduced to translate classification confidence into actionable cleaning decisions, including no cleaning, light cleaning, and full cleaning. Experimental results on multiple PV image datasets demonstrate that, under domain-shift conditions where individual models may experience performance degradation, the proposed ensemble framework achieves an accuracy of up to 85.93% and attains a dusty-panel detection rate of 0.90 on the unseen dataset. On the in-distribution evaluation, the proposed OR-ensemble achieves an average accuracy of 0.9663 ± 0.0177 with dusty recall of 0.9896 ± 0.0104 over repeated stratified runs. Importantly, the conservative fusion strategy minimizes high-risk false negative cases while avoiding excessive misclassification of clean panels. Overall, the proposed framework offers a robust, scalable, and deployment-ready solution for intelligent PV cleaning decision support, advancing CNN-based soiling detection toward practical and risk-aware operation and maintenance systems.

Keywords: photovoltaic panel soiling; intelligent cleaning decision; ensemble learning; MobileNetV3-Small; Random Forest; risk-aware classification; computer vision for PV systems; condition-based maintenance

1. Introduction

The depletion of fossil fuel resources and their adverse environmental impacts have accelerated the global transition toward renewable energy sources. Among the available alternatives, solar energy has emerged as one of the most promising solutions due to its sustainability, widespread availability, and critical role in ensuring long-term energy security. PV technology, which directly converts solar radiation into electrical energy, has consequently experienced rapid growth, shown in Figure 1, with the global installed capacity projected to exceed 8000 GW by 2050 [1].

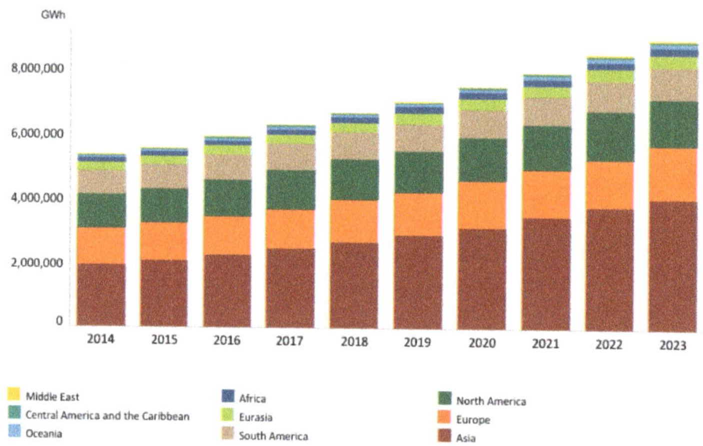

Figure 1. Global rise in electricity power installation using renewable energy sources. The statistics are taken from https://www.irena.org (accessed on 7 January 2026).

Despite all these advantages, the operational efficiency of PV systems is highly sensitive to environmental factors. Prolonged exposure to dust, sand, air pollution, rainfall residues, and changes in meteorological conditions causes soiling of the PV panels. Soiling causes the loss of incident solar radiation and hence affects the efficiency of the PV system [2]. It has been observed in various studies that the efficiency loss of PV systems due to soiling varies between 10 and 60% [3]. Such extreme losses have been observed in different geographical locations. In Saudi Arabia, 50% efficiency loss has been observed in six months [4]. In Nepal, 76% efficiency loss has been observed in 29 months [5]. In India, 30% efficiency loss has been observed in two months [6]. In Kuwait, 65% efficiency loss has been observed in two months [7]. In addition to efficiency loss, soiling of PV panels causes the trapping of moisture, leading to corrosion and structural degradation of the panels [8]. Figure 2 shows various types of dirt accumulated on solar panels.

Figure 2. Various types of dirt and birds waste found on solar panels.

https://doi.org/10.3390/electronics15061192

All these effects, collectively, underscore the need to ensure effective monitoring, timely cleaning, and effective maintenance strategies for large-scale solar power plant installations. However, it is not practical to use conventional methods such as image processing and cleaning strategies for solar power plant installations due to their high costs, labour requirements, and scalability. Hence, image processing and AI-based monitoring systems have drawn considerable attention as a cost-effective solution to monitor solar power plant conditions [9]. This is to ensure intelligent scheduling strategies to reduce energy production costs. Recent advances in image processing and AI have made significant contributions to various applications, including surveillance, disease detection, and medical image analysis [6]. Similarly, image processing and AI have made significant contributions to solar power plant monitoring. Specifically, CNN models have shown promising potential to learn discriminative features from images to detect soiling on solar panel surfaces. However, most state-of-the-art models have a large number of parameters to be trained, which may require significant computational resources, such as GPUs. Moreover, the model architecture and classification-oriented outputs may not be suitable for risk-based decision-making [10,11].

In order to overcome these challenges, lightweight CNN architectures have been proposed to reduce the computational cost while achieving reasonable classification performance. Among these, SolPowNet proposed an efficient CNN architecture specifically designed for solar panel dust detection, which showed promising results under controlled experimental conditions. However, it is observed that most CNN-based methods proposed so far use a single CNN model to perform classification on the given dataset, with limited focus on predicting the cleanliness level of the solar panels. Moreover, these methods do not use prediction confidence to make decisions. These limitations restrict the applicability of CNN-based methods to real-world PV operation and maintenance scenarios. With these observations in mind, this paper proposes an intelligent cleaning decision framework that is inspired by the SolPowNet architecture. The proposed framework utilizes the benefits of classical image processing techniques, machine learning methods, and lightweight deep learning architectures. The proposed system uses physically interpretable handcrafted features to represent the intuitive soiling features, while the high-level semantic features are represented using a lightweight CNN architecture. Unlike existing CNN-based methods, the proposed system uses an ensemble approach to make decisions, thereby reducing high-risk classification.

1.1. Paper Contributions

The main contributions of this research work are briefly summarized as follows:

- A hybrid ensemble method that combines a handcrafted feature-based Random Forest classifier and a lightweight CNN architecture, namely MobileNetV3-Small, to enhance the robustness of soiling detection results.
- A conservative OR-based ensemble fusion method that ensures minimal false negatives in dusty-panel detection, which is critical in PV maintenance decision-making.
- A probability-based SI that utilizes confidence probability to inform decision-making in PV panel maintenance, including no cleaning, light cleaning, and heavy cleaning, which redefines soiling detection as decision-making rather than classification.
- Experimental evaluation of the proposed method on various PV panel image datasets to demonstrate improved reliability in dusty panel detection and decision-making under different environmental conditions.

Novelty and innovation: While several existing methods report high classification accuracy, their primary focus is typically on classifier performance under a fixed dataset setting. The novelty of this work is the introduction of a risk-aware maintenance deci-

https://doi.org/10.3390/electronics15061192

sion framework that (i) integrates physically interpretable handcrafted features with a lightweight CNN to exploit complementary cues, (ii) employs a conservative OR-based fusion rule specifically designed to reduce maintenance-critical missed soiling events (false negatives), and (iii) converts probabilistic confidence into an actionable Soiling Index (SI) with explicit cleaning thresholds. Together, these design choices emphasize maintenance outcomes and deployment-oriented decision support, rather than only maximizing headline accuracy.

Risk-aware problem statement: In PV operation and maintenance, the cost of a false negative (dusty panel predicted as clean) is typically higher than that of a false positive, because missed soiling can delay cleaning and cause cumulative energy loss. Therefore, the objective of this work is to design a soiling detection system that explicitly prioritizes reducing dusty false negatives (i.e., improving dusty recall) while maintaining acceptable overall classification performance.

Hypothesis (risk-aware fusion): Because handcrafted texture–sharpness features (RF branch) and CNN features respond differently to environmental and imaging variations, fusing the two branches using a conservative OR-based ensemble rule (flagging *dusty* if either model predicts soiling) will reduce missed soiling events (false negatives) and improve dusty-panel recall, thereby providing more reliable maintenance-oriented cleaning decisions when combined with the probability-driven Soiling Index (SI).

1.2. Paper Roadmap

The rest of this paper is organized as follows. Section 2 discusses the relevant literature on solar panel soiling detection and intelligent monitoring systems. Section 3 introduces the proposed hybrid ensemble approach along with its architectural components. Section 4 introduces the experiment design along with the evaluation approach. Section 5 contains a detailed discussion of the results. Section 6 concludes the paper and presents directions for future research.

2. Related Work

In recent years, various image processing and deep learning-based techniques have been extensively researched and explored for the purpose of automatic evaluation of PV panel cleanliness. CNN architectures have been found to possess excellent potential in learning discriminative features from images of PV panels and classifying them into clean and dusty panels quickly and accurately. Such developments in this field have greatly aided in the automation of monitoring and maintenance activities in solar power plants, and this has resulted in an increased interest in this field of research. Various studies were conducted on developing a deep learning framework for the purpose of detecting and classifying dust on solar panels. Sun et al. used a YOLO-based architecture for improving the detection of dust pollution on PV panels, and it was found to perform better in terms of accuracy and speed compared to conventional deep learning models. The precision and recall of this model were 89.71% and 90.23%, respectively, making it highly suitable for practical applications [12]. In addition to this, some studies were conducted to explore the physical effects of dust on solar panels using experimental measurements. Maghami et al. conducted comparative experiments using two identical PV panels, one of which was cleaned and the other left uncleaned, and it was found that an energy loss of 11.61 kWh occurred in the uncleaned panel, thereby validating the direct proportionality between dust and power loss [13].

In addition to this, various studies have focused on combining deep learning with traditional machine learning paradigms to create a hybrid model that leverages CNN features and traditional machine learning classification algorithms. Mehta and Singh

https://doi.org/10.3390/electronics15061192

created a CNN–SVM model that utilized a CNN to obtain deep features and then employed a support vector machine classifier to classify those features. This model was able to achieve 95% accuracy even when subjected to adverse environmental conditions while keeping the implementation costs low [14]. Ghosh et al. employed a CNN model inspired by AlexNet to detect dust on solar panels and was able to achieve 85% accuracy, thus proving that CNN can be employed to automate PV cleaning processes [15]. Other more complex architectures combine residual learning and attention mechanisms with physics-informed approaches to achieve higher robustness and accuracy. Fan et al. created a residual network model that was enhanced with image preprocessing capabilities and was thus able to achieve an R^2 accuracy of 78.7% and a mean absolute error of 3.67%, thus proving to be more accurate than other such models [16]. Bashirr et al. created a model that combined CNN with a Random Forest classifier and was thus able to achieve 98% accuracy by first converting characteristics of an electric I–V curve into an RGB image and then extracting features using a CNN model [17].

Apart from fixed camera image analysis techniques, various drone-assisted and sensor-based vision techniques have been proposed in the recent literature for large-scale PV system monitoring. In this context, various techniques have been proposed that use unmanned aerial vehicles (UAVs), cameras, and computer vision techniques for the automation of data acquisition and analysis for large-scale solar farms. Some specific techniques proposed in the literature include cell-level soiling analysis techniques, hybrid CNN-tree-based techniques, attention-based CNN-Transformer techniques, and physics-informed deep learning techniques. A comparative summary of various techniques proposed in the recent literature is given in Table 1.

Table 1. Summary of representative studies on PV panel soiling detection and analysis.

Study	Methodology	Key Contributions	Reported Performance
Dust Accumulation Analysis on Desert Solar Panels: A CNN–Transformer Approach [18]	CNN with attention mechanisms and Transformer layers using transfer learning and data augmentation	Lightweight fusion architecture robust to illumination variability and suitable for embedded systems	Accuracy: 98%
Deep Learning-Based Detection of Solar Panel Condition in Power Plants [19]	Histogram equalization preprocessing combined with deep learning classification	Real-time dust detection implemented using an AI-enabled drone platform	F1-score: 97%
Efficient Combination of Deep Learning and Tree-Based Models for Solar Panel Dust Detection [20]	Hybrid framework combining CNN/ViT-based feature extraction with Random Forest and XGBoost classifiers	Enhances dust detection performance through feature fine-tuning and ensemble-based tree classification	Accuracy: 97%
Solar Panel Dust Detection Using Deep Learning Models [21]	CNN-based feature extraction followed by SVM classification	Comparative evaluation of VGG, ResNet, DenseNet, MobileNet, Xception, and NASNet architectures	Accuracy: 96.5%, Loss: 0.083
A Novel Vision-Based Technique for Dust and Soil Detection on PV Panels [22]	RGB image analysis using HSV colour space and GLCM texture features with linear classification	Cost-effective dust detection using standard camera sensors and handcrafted features	Accuracy: 82%

https://doi.org/10.3390/electronics15061192

Table 1. *Cont.*

Study	Methodology	Key Contributions	Reported Performance
Dust Accumulation and Aggregation on PV Panels [23]	Mathematical modelling of dust impact on PV output and cleaning efficiency	Integrates soiling loss indices, power derating factors, and bilinear power models for cleaning assessment	Cleaning efficiency up to 90%
Experimental Study of Dust Deposition and Cleaning Effects on PV Panels [24]	Physics-informed deep neural network integrating irradiation, temperature, and pollution parameters with visual features	Combines physical constraints with data-driven learning for accurate energy efficiency prediction	Energy prediction error < 3%
CNN-Based Dust Detection with Economic Benefit Analysis [25]	Adam-optimized CNN models including ResNet-18, VGG-16, and MobileNetV2	Unified optimization framework incorporating warm-up and cosine annealing strategies	Performance reported across multiple CNN architectures
Cell-Resolved PV Soiling Measurement Using Drone Images [26]	Drone-based RGB image acquisition combined with optical–electrical correlation analysis	Enables visualization and quantification of cell-level soiling losses validated through electrical measurements	RMSE $\approx$ 1%

Despite these advances, most existing methods emphasize classification accuracy without explicitly addressing decision confidence or the operational risks associated with false negative soiling detections.

3. Proposed Hybrid Ensemble Framework

In this section, a SolPowNet-inspired hybrid and ensemble-based intelligent cleaning decision framework is presented for the automatic detection of dust on PV panels, with the overall workflow illustrated in Figure 3.

The section first describes the datasets used in this study, highlighting their main characteristics, class distributions, and variability in environmental and imaging conditions, which form the basis for training, validation, and independent testing. It then introduces the core components of the proposed framework, including a classical image processing branch that extracts handcrafted texture, sharpness, and statistical features and classifies them using a Random Forest model, alongside a lightweight deep learning branch based on transfer learning that employs a convolutional neural network for high-level feature extraction from RGB images. The "complementary" nature of these two branches is exploited through the implementation of a conservative ensemble fusion strategy with the aim of increasing robustness while minimizing the likelihood of risky misclassification, especially with regard to the misclassification of soiled panels as clean. Additionally, the formulation of a probability-driven SI is presented with the aim of mapping model outputs to actionable cleaning decisions, namely no cleaning, light cleaning, and full cleaning, thereby effectively transforming the soiling detection problem from a binary classification one to a more applicable one. Lastly, the criteria employed in the performance evaluation are presented, namely accuracy, precision, recall, F1-score, confusion matrix analysis, with special emphasis being given to the reliable detection of dusty panels.

https://doi.org/10.3390/electronics15061192

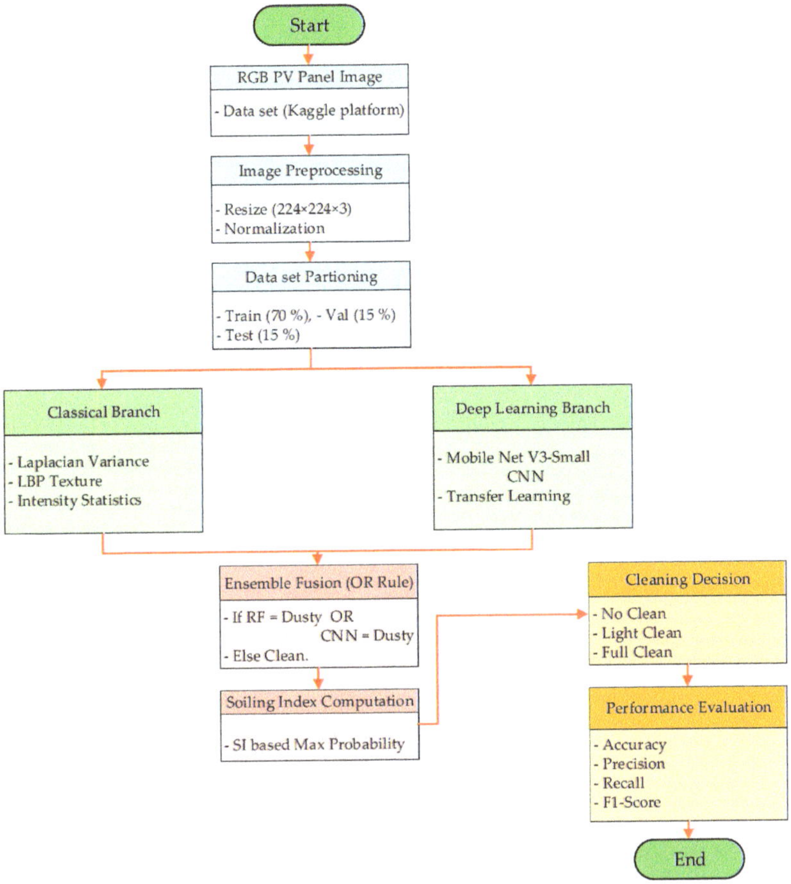

Figure 3. Proposed hybrid ensemble framework work flow.

3.1. Effect of Dust on Light Attenuation in PV Panels

The electrical performance of PV panels is directly influenced by the amount of solar irradiance reaching the cell surface. Under standard operating conditions, the output power of a PV module can be expressed as [27]:

$$P_{out} = P_{\mathrm{STC}} \times \frac{G}{G_{\mathrm{STC}}} \times [1 + \gamma \times (T - T_{\mathrm{STC}})] \quad (1)$$

where P_{out} denotes the output power, G is the incident solar irradiance on a clean panel surface, γ is the temperature coefficient, and T represents the ambient temperature. P_{STC}, G_{STC}, and T_{STC} correspond to values under Standard Test Conditions.

In real outdoor environments, PV panels are exposed to dust and airborne contaminants that attenuate incoming solar radiation through absorption and scattering effects [28–30]. The effective irradiance received by a dust-covered panel can be modelled as:

$$G_d = G \times e^{-\tau d} \quad (2)$$

where G_d denotes the irradiance under dusty conditions and τd represents the dust-induced optical attenuation coefficient.

https://doi.org/10.3390/electronics15061192

To quantify soiling-induced degradation, the Soiling Loss Index (SLI) is defined as:

$$SLI = \frac{G_d - G}{G} \times 100 \tag{3}$$

The SLI provides a normalized indicator of irradiance loss due to surface contamination and directly reflects the severity of dust accumulation. Incorporating the soiling effect into the power model yields:

$$P_{out} = P_{STC} \times \frac{G \times (1 + SLI)}{G_{STC}} \times [1 + \gamma \times (T - T_{STC})] \tag{4}$$

This formulation highlights the combined influence of irradiance attenuation, temperature variation, and surface soiling on PV output power, thereby motivating the need for accurate soiling detection and intelligent cleaning decision mechanisms.

3.2. Dataset Description

The data used by the research is collected from an openly accessible photovoltaic panel soiling dataset provided by Afroz and shared on the Kaggle platform [31]. The dataset consists of RGB images of photovoltaic panels collected under different environmental conditions, with different lighting, surface contamination levels, viewing angles, and background environments. The images are classified as clean or dusty photovoltaic panels.

In total, the dataset comprises 383 images, with 193 images classified as clean and 190 images classified as dusty photovoltaic panels, which can be considered almost equally distributed. Because the dataset is modest in size for CNN training, it applies lightweight data augmentation during MobileNetV3-Small training to improve generalization while preserving physically meaningful soiling cues. Specifically, the training images are augmented using random horizontal flipping, small-angle rotations (±5°), and mild colour jittering; augmentation is applied only to the training subset (see Section 4.2 for details). The images were originally collected at different spatial resolutions; however, all of these images are resized to a uniform size of 224 × 224 × 3 pixels. This uniform size is appropriate for the input data for the MobileNetV3-Small CNN and meets the criteria for the conventional and deep learning components of the CNN. Figure 4 shows some examples of clean and dusty photovoltaic panels.

Figure 4. Sample images illustrating clean and dirty PV panels.

https://doi.org/10.3390/electronics15061192

To assess model robustness beyond controlled experimental conditions, additional evaluation was performed using an independent unseen dataset, enabling the investigation of cross-dataset generalization under domain-shift scenarios. Details regarding dataset partitioning, training–validation–testing splits, and evaluation protocols are provided in Section 4.1.

Independent Unseen Dataset (Domain-Shift Evaluation Dataset)

To assess model robustness beyond the development dataset, additional evaluation has been performed using an independent unseen dataset to examine cross-dataset generalization under domain shift. In this study, domain shift refers to a change in the image distribution between the development dataset and the external dataset due to differences in acquisition and environmental conditions (e.g., illumination, camera viewpoint/orientation, background content, and soiling appearance). The unseen dataset was obtained from a separate Kaggle PV soiling dataset and was not used during training, validation, or model selection. It contains 2562 images, comprising 1493 clean and 1069 dusty samples (clean: dusty ratio $\approx$ 1.40:1).

Labelling procedure: Images were labelled into clean and dusty classes according to the Kaggle dataset annotations (class folders/labels). These provided labels used directly for evaluation to ensure consistency with the dataset ground truth.

Details regarding dataset partitioning, training–validation–testing splits, and evaluation protocols are provided in Section 4.1, while cross-dataset performance under domain shift is reported in Section 5.8.

3.3. *Image Preprocessing*

Before the feature extraction or classification, each image of the PV panel undergoes an image preprocessing step, which is unique to the needs of the two branches in the suggested framework, namely, the classical machine learning branch and deep learning approaches. In the classical machine learning, the images are converted from RGB to grayscale. The rationale for this is to optimize the calculation of texture and sharpness-related features, as well as those associated with dust buildup. The image is converted to grayscale to reduce redundancy in the colour data, but the essential intensity and spatial irregularities are preserved, reflecting the impact of the dust on the PV panel surface. The dust primarily affects the image in terms of contrast, brightness, and high-frequency texture, and these are the dimensions in the image data in the case of the grayscale image, which are the most relevant to the calculation of the Laplacian variance, Local Binary Pattern (LBP), and other statistical intensity-related features.

An illustrative example of this conversion is presented in Figure 5, where a dusty PV panel in RGB format (Figure 5a) and its corresponding grayscale representation (Figure 5b) are shown. As observed, the grayscale image retains dust-related texture non-uniformities and shading variations, which are critical for classical feature modelling, while simplifying the data representation.

In the deep learning branch, the images are used in RGB to ensure the presence of colour and semantic information in the image data, as explained in the following paragraphs. All the images are resized to $224 \times 224 \times 3$ pixels and are normalized using the ImageNet dataset's mean and variance values to ensure the stability of the learning process and the convergence of the deep learning model. This dual preprocessing strategy ensures that each branch operates on an input representation optimized for its respective modelling paradigm, thereby enhancing complementary feature learning within the hybrid ensemble framework.

https://doi.org/10.3390/electronics15061192

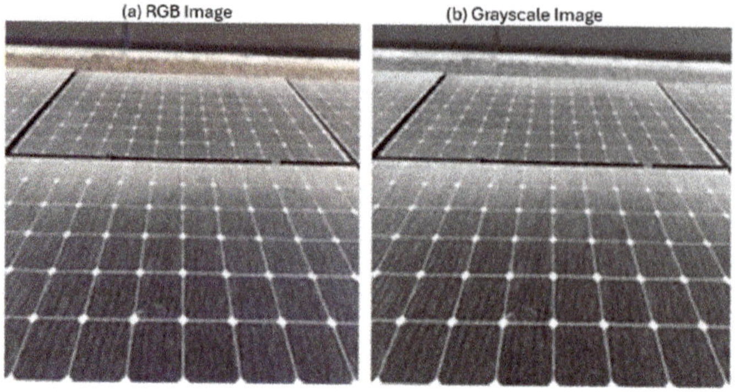

Figure 5. (**a**) Example RGB image of a dusty PV panel; (**b**) Corresponding grayscale representation used for handcrafted texture and sharpness feature extraction.

3.4. Handcrafted Feature Extraction and Random Forest Classification

Inspired by classical image processing techniques, a set of handcrafted features is extracted to capture physically interpretable soiling characteristics from PV panel images. Image sharpness and surface clarity are quantified using the Laplacian variance, which measures the amount of high-frequency content in the image. The Laplacian operator applied to a grayscale image $I(x,y)$ is defined as

$$\nabla^2 I(x,y) = \frac{\partial^2 I}{\partial x^2} + \frac{\partial^2 I}{\partial y^2}, \quad (5)$$

and the corresponding Laplacian variance is computed as

$$\sigma^2{}_{Lap} = Var\left(\nabla^2 I(x,y)\right) \quad (6)$$

Moreover, the histograms of Local Binary Pattern (LBP) are utilized to extract the local texture variations introduced by dust accumulation. For a central pixel with intensity I_c, the LBP code is expressed as

$$LBP_{P,R} = \sum_{p=0}^{P-1} s(I_p - I_c)2^P, \\ s(x) = \begin{cases} 1, & x \geq 0, \\ 0, & x < 0, \end{cases} \quad (7)$$

Here, I_p represents the intensity of neighbouring pixels within a circular neighbourhood of radius R. The resulting LBP codes are accumulated into histograms that describe local texture distributions.

Furthermore, statistical intensity measures are computed to capture global brightness and contrast variations caused by surface contamination. These include the mean intensity

$$\mu_I = \frac{1}{MN}\sum_{x=1}^{M}\sum_{y=1}^{N} I(x,y) \quad (8)$$

While the standard deviation is computed as

$$\sigma_I = \sqrt{\frac{1}{MN}\sum_{x=1}^{M}\sum_{y=1}^{N}(I(x,y) - \mu_I)^2} \quad (9)$$

https://doi.org/10.3390/electronics15061192

The root mean square (RMS) contrast, which reflects overall intensity contrast, is defined as

$$RMS = \sqrt{\frac{1}{MN}\sum_{x=1}^{M}\sum_{y=1}^{N}(I(x,y) - \mu_I)^2}, \quad (10)$$

and the local intensity variation is computed as the average of local standard deviations over K neighbourhoods,

$$\sigma_{local} = \frac{1}{K}\sum_{k=1}^{K}\sigma_k \quad (11)$$

All extracted descriptors are concatenated to form a compact feature vector representing each image. These feature vectors are classified using a Random Forest classifier, selected for its robustness to overfitting, ability to model nonlinear feature interactions, and reliable performance on medium-sized datasets. In addition to predicted class labels, the RF model provides class probability estimates, which are later incorporated into the ensemble fusion strategy and the cleaning decision formulation.

The Random Forest classifier was configured as follows: number of trees n_estimators = 400, maximum depth max_depth = None (i.e., nodes are expanded until pure or until the minimum split constraint is reached), and feature selection at each split max_features = "sqrt", meaning that a random subset of $\sqrt{d}$ candidate features is considered at each split (where d is the number of handcrafted input features). The split criterion was Gini impurity, and class imbalance was handled using class_weight = "balanced". The full handcrafted feature vector is provided to the RF; the max_features setting controls the random subset of candidate features evaluated at each node split.

3.5. *Lightweight CNN Architecture (MobileNetV3-Small)*

To complement the physically interpretable handcrafted features, a lightweight CNN based on MobileNetV3-Small is employed to automatically learn high-level visual representations directly from RGB PV panel images. MobileNetV3-Small is specifically designed for efficiency-critical applications and offers an optimal trade-off between classification accuracy and computational complexity, making it particularly suitable for deployment in resource-constrained environments such as edge devices, embedded systems, and drone-based inspection platforms. This claim is supported by the CPU inference-time and model-size benchmarks reported in Section 5.9. The choice of MobileNetV3-Small is motivated not only by deployment efficiency but also by its reduced parameter count (~2.5M), which helps mitigate overfitting risks in limited-data scenarios.

In this work, transfer learning is applied by initializing the network with ImageNet-pretrained weights and replacing the final classification layer with a two-node output corresponding to the clean and dusty classes. Fine-tuning enables the network to adapt to PV-panel-specific soiling patterns while retaining the compact structure and fast inference capability of the original architecture.

MobileNetV3-Small is composed of stacked convolutional blocks that integrate depth wise separable convolutions, inverted residual bottleneck structures, and squeeze-and-excitation (SE) attention mechanisms. Compared with conventional CNN architectures, this design significantly reduces the number of trainable parameters and floating-point operations while preserving strong representational capacity.

3.5.1. Convolutional and Depth Wise Separable Convolution Layers

Instead of standard convolutions, MobileNetV3-Small predominantly employs depth wise separable convolutions, which decompose a conventional convolution into two sequential operations: a depth wise convolution and a pointwise convolution. For an input

https://doi.org/10.3390/electronics15061192

feature map X and convolution kernel K, a standard two-dimensional convolution is expressed as

$$T(i,j) = (X \times K)(i,j) = \sum_{m=1}^{n} \sum_{n=1}^{n} K(m,n) \times X(i+m, j+n) \tag{12}$$

In depth wise separable convolution, the operation is factorized as

$$T_d = X \times K_d, T_p = T_d \times K_p \tag{13}$$

where K_d represents the depth wise kernel applied independently to each input channel, and the term K_p represents a pointwise convolution operation of size 1×1, which combines the responses of each channel. This factorization reduces the computation significantly and enables the model to learn discriminative texture and intensity features related to dust accumulation on the surface of PV panels. The model enables fast inference and retains sufficient representation capacity to model surface soiling.

3.5.2. SE Attention Mechanism

To enhance the discriminability of features, MobileNetV3-Small introduces SE modules that dynamically weight channel-wise feature responses. Given a feature map $U \in \mathbb{R}^{H \times W \times C}$, the squeeze operation collects global spatial features through global average pooling along the height and width:

$$z_c = \frac{1}{HW} \sum_{i=1}^{H} \sum_{j=1}^{W} U_c(i,j) \tag{14}$$

The excitation operation computes channel-wise weights using a gating mechanism:

$$s = \sigma(W_2 \times \delta(W_1 \times z)) \tag{15}$$

In this equation, δ (·) denotes the ReLU activation function, and σ (·) denotes the sigmoid activation function, with learnable parameters W_1, and W_2. This configuration enables the network to focus on more informative feature channels about dust information and suppress less informative ones.

3.5.3. Pooling and Fully Connected Layers

The pooling operations gradually decrease the spatial resolution of the feature maps while retaining the significant structural details. After the feature extraction process, fully connected layers are used for classification. The last layer is adjusted to produce two outputs for clean PV panels and dusty PV panels. The SoftMax activation function is used for class probability estimation, and the results are used for ensemble fusion and Soiling Index calculation.

The detailed layer-wise configuration of the fine-tuned MobileNetV3-Small model employed in this study is summarized in Table 2.

Table 2. Fine-tuned MobileNetV3-Small architecture used in this study (input size: 224 × 224 × 3).

Layer Block	Input Size	Parameters (From MobileNetV3-Small Spec)	Output Size
Conv1	224 × 224 × 3	3 × 3 Conv, out = 16, stride = 2, NL = HS	112 × 112 × 16
BNeck1	112 × 112 × 16	k = 3, exp = 16, out = 16, SE = ✓, NL = RE, stride = 2	56 × 56 × 16
BNeck2	56 × 56 × 16	k = 3, exp = 72, out = 24, SE =–, NL = RE, stride = 2	28 × 28 × 24
BNeck3	28 × 28 × 24	k = 3, exp = 88, out = 24, SE =–, NL = RE, stride = 1	28 × 28 × 24

https://doi.org/10.3390/electronics15061192

Table 2. *Cont.*

Layer Block	Input Size	Parameters (From MobileNetV3-Small Spec)	Output Size
BNeck4	28 × 28 × 24	k = 5, exp = 96, out = 40, SE = ✓, NL = HS, stride = 2	14 × 14 × 40
BNeck5	14 × 14 × 40	k = 5, exp = 240, out = 40, SE = ✓, NL = HS, stride = 1	14 × 14 × 40
BNeck6	14 × 14 × 40	k = 5, exp = 240, out = 40, SE = ✓, NL = HS, stride = 1	14 × 14 × 40
BNeck7	14 × 14 × 40	k = 5, exp = 120, out = 48, SE = ✓, NL = HS, stride = 1	14 × 14 × 48
BNeck8	14 × 14 × 48	k = 5, exp = 144, out = 48, SE = ✓, NL = HS, stride = 1	14 × 14 × 48
BNeck9	14 × 14 × 48	k = 5, exp = 288, out = 96, SE = ✓, NL = HS, stride = 2	7 × 7 × 96
BNeck10	7 × 7 × 96	k = 5, exp = 576, out = 96, SE = ✓, NL = HS, stride = 1	7 × 7 × 96
BNeck11	7 × 7 × 96	k = 5, exp = 576, out = 96, SE = ✓, NL = HS, stride =1	7 × 7 × 96
Conv2 (1 × 1)	7 × 7 × 96	1 × 1 Conv, out = 576, stride = 1, NL = HS	7 × 7 × 576
Global AvgPool	7 × 7 × 576	7 × 7 pooling → global feature	1 × 1 × 576
Conv3 (1 × 1)	1 × 1 × 576	1 × 1 Conv, out = 1024, NBN, NL = HS	1 × 1 × 1024
Classifier (1 × 1/FC)	1 × 1 × 1024	1 × 1 Conv (or FC), out = k = 2, NBN	1 × 1 × 2

Note: BNeck = inverted residual bottleneck block (1 × 1 expand → depth wise k × k → SE (optional) → 1 × 1 project), exp = expansion channels inside the block, SE: ✓ = Squeeze-and-Excitation used, NL: RE = ReLU, HS = h-swish, k = 2 (our two classes).

3.6. Ensemble Fusion Strategy

Risk-aware fusion objective: The ensemble fusion strategy is designed to reflect maintenance risk, where missing a dusty panel (false negative) is more costly than incorrectly flagging a clean panel (false positive). Accordingly, a conservative OR-based rule has been adopted that marks a panel as dusty if either the RF branch or the MobileNetV3-Small branch detects soiling, and marks it clean only when both agree it is clean. This design directly supports maintenance outcomes by reducing missed cleaning events that can lead to avoidable energy losses.

To leverage the best of traditional machine learning and deep learning without overcomplicating things, a cautious ensemble of a Random Forest classifier and a MobileNetV3-Small CNN has been used. Both models work on the same input image of a PV panel independently and produce a label and a confidence score for it.

Instead of relying on a single source of truth, an OR-based fusion rule has been used to make a final decision, which is more focused on not missing dusty panels. In this approach, a panel is marked dusty if either model marks it dusty, and it is marked clean only if both models agree on a clean state.

In addition to providing the final classification result, the ensemble system also retains the probabilistic results from each of the models, which are then used as input to a probability-driven SI. With the interpretability of the handcrafted features and the high-level semantic information provided by the CNN, the ensemble system moves beyond the simple classification task and into the realm of decision support, providing risk-based cleaning decisions that are critical for large-scale monitoring systems.

3.7. Soiling Index and Cleaning Decision Formulation

A Soiling Index (SI) is introduced as a continuous measure of PV panel soiling severity, translating classification outputs into actionable maintenance advice. Rather than providing a binary "clean/dusty" decision, SI encodes the model's confidence and supports risk-adjusted cleaning actions aligned with PV operation and maintenance requirements.

Let $p_{\text{dusty}}^{\text{RF}}$ and $p_{\text{dusty}}^{\text{CNN}}$ denote the dusty-class probabilities predicted by the Random Forest classifier and the MobileNetV3-Small CNN, respectively. In accordance with the conservative OR-based ensemble strategy adopted in this study, the ensemble dusty confidence is computed as

$$p_{\text{dusty}}^{\text{ens}} = \max\left(p_{\text{dusty}}^{\text{RF}}, p_{\text{dusty}}^{\text{CNN}}\right) \tag{16}$$

https://doi.org/10.3390/electronics15061192

The Soiling Index is then defined on a normalized scale from 0 to 100 as

$$SI = 100 \times p_{dusty}^{ens} \tag{17}$$

This strategy focuses on the reliable detection of panels that might be dusty by always choosing the highest confidence score from one of the classifiers. This strategy aims to reduce high-risk false negatives while remaining responsive to various levels of surface contamination.

With the SI value calculated, three cleaning levels are established:

- No Cleaning (SI < 30): little to no soiling is detectable;
- Light Cleaning ($30 \leq$ SI < 60): some soiling is present, with minimal impact on energy output;
- Full Cleaning (SI $\geq$ 60): heavy soiling is expected, with noticeable energy losses.

The probabilistic confidence incorporated in the decision process converts the soiling detection problem from a simple yes/no question into a useful decision support system. This helps in the scheduling of condition-based maintenance, minimizes unnecessary cleaning, and keeps automated vision-based detection in tune with cost-effective PV cleaning strategies.

3.8. Performance Evaluation Metrics

In the study "Assessing the proposed hybrid ensemble framework and its individual classifiers," classification metrics such as accuracy, precision, recall, F1-score and Area Under the ROC Curve (AUC) were utilized, which are commonly applied when classifying images. These metrics provide a comprehensive overview, such as overall correctness, reliability of classifiers when classifying dusty panels, as well as sensitivity to surface contamination.

The evaluation criteria are derived from the confusion matrix, where the predicted results are categorized into True Positives (TPs), False Negatives (FNs), True Negatives (TNs), and False Positives (FPs). In the context of PV panel maintenance, the interest is particularly in the recall value of the dusty class because a false negative result, which is a dusty panel missed, may cause a delay in cleaning and result in energy losses.

The definitions of these metrics are provided in Table 3. These metrics are computed uniformly over all models and evaluation settings, as described in this section, to provide a fair comparison. The numerical results and side-by-side analysis are provided in Section 5.

Table 3. Mathematical formulas and explanations for the evaluation metrics.

Metric and Formula	Description
$\text{Accuracy} = \frac{TP+TN}{TP+TN+FP+FN}$	Represents the proportion of all cases the model gets right, including both clean and dusty panels.
$\text{Precision} = \frac{TP}{TP+FP}$	This metric shows the proportion of panels classified as dusty that are actually dusty. The more precise the model is, the fewer false positives there are.
$\text{Recall} = \frac{TP}{TP+FN}$	Measures the model's ability to find all dusty panels, which is crucial to avoid false negatives regarding cleaning actions.
$\text{F1-score} = 2 \times \frac{\text{Precision} \times \text{Recall}}{\text{Precision} + \text{Recall}}$	Represents the harmonic mean of precision and recall, providing a balanced view of the classifier's performance, especially if one class is more frequent than the other.
$\text{AUC} = \int_0^1 TPR(FPR)d(FPR)$	This quantifies the overall discriminative ability of the classifier over all possible decision thresholds. If the AUC value is close to 1, it implies that the separability between clean and dusty classes is high, thus showing the robustness of the classifier at different thresholds.

https://doi.org/10.3390/electronics15061192

In addition to the metrics based on the confusion matrix, AUC is said to evaluate the threshold-independent separability of clean and dusty PV panels, as highlighted in the ROC curve in Section 5.

3.9. Implementation Environment

All experiments were performed using Python-based libraries for image processing, machine learning, and deep learning techniques. The classical feature extraction and classification using the Random Forest classifier were implemented using OpenCV, NumPy, and scikit-learn libraries, while the CNN was implemented using the PyTorch library. Due to the lightweight nature of the MobileNetV3-Small architecture used for the CNN, the experiments can be performed efficiently using a CPU-based workstation, with the option to use a GPU for the CNN training process. This implementation of the proposed framework is suitable for deployment in resource-constrained environments.

4. Experimental Setup

This section describes the process of testing the proposed hybrid and ensemble-based intelligent soiling detection framework. The division of data, training of models, steps of the algorithm, and performance metrics will be discussed in this section.

4.1. Dataset Partitioning and Evaluation Protocol

The dataset obtained in Section 3.2 was divided using a stratified method to maintain class balance. In particular, 70% of the images were used for training, 15% for validation, and the remaining 15% for testing. A fixed random seed was used to make the results reproducible.

Statistical reliability protocol: In addition to reporting single-split results, 10 independent repetitions of the stratified 70%/15%/15% train/validation/test partitioning were performed using different random seeds. For each repetition, the RF, MobileNetV3-Small, and OR-ensemble models were trained and evaluated using the same hyperparameters and preprocessing. The research work reports mean $\pm$ standard deviation across runs and 95% confidence intervals (CIs) for accuracy, dusty recall, dusty F1-score, and AUC using a t-based interval computed from the per-run metric distribution.

In addition to testing on the same dataset, it is also tested for the generalization performance across datasets by performing batch inference on a separate PV image dataset obtained under different conditions. This protocol enables assessment of model robustness under domain shift, including variations in illumination, camera viewpoint, and soiling characteristics, which are commonly encountered in real-world PV monitoring scenarios.

The distribution of images across the training, validation, and testing subsets is summarized in Table 4.

Table 4. Distribution of images in the training, validation, and test sets.

Image Split	Percentage (%)	Clean PV Panels	Dusty PV Panels
Training images	70%	135	133
Validation images	15%	29	29
Test images	15%	29	28
Total images	100%	193	190

4.2. Training Configuration

The CNN branch was fine-tuned using MobileNetV3-Small initialized with ImageNet-pretrained weights. The final classification layer was replaced to output two classes (clean vs. dusty), and the network was fine-tuned end-to-end (no layers were frozen during

https://doi.org/10.3390/electronics15061192

training). Training used a learning rate of 1×10^{-4}, batch size of 32, the AdamW optimizer with weight decay of 1×10^{-4}, and the cross-entropy loss function. The maximum number of epochs was set to 50, with early stopping applied based on validation accuracy to prevent overfitting (the best-performing checkpoint on the validation set was retained). Data augmentation was applied only to the training split and included random horizontal flipping, small-angle rotations (±5°), and mild colour jittering.

The Random Forest (RF) classifier was implemented using scikit-learn with 400 decision trees (n_estimators = 400). The split criterion was Gini impurity (criterion = "gini"), the maximum depth was set to max_depth = None (unrestricted depth), and the feature selection strategy at each split was max_features = "sqrt" (i.e., a random subset of $\sqrt{d}$ features is considered at each node, where d is the number of handcrafted features). Class imbalance was handled using class_weight = "balanced". Class probability estimates were obtained via predict_proba for integration into the ensemble fusion strategy.

All hyperparameters were kept fixed across experiments to ensure consistency and reproducibility. The final configuration used in this study is reported in Table 5.

Table 5. Final hyperparameters used in the experimental setup.

Parameter	Value
Image size	224 × 224 × 3
Batch size	32
Learning rate	1×10^{-4}
Epochs (max)	50
Optimizer	AdamW
Weight decay	1×10^{-4}
Loss function	Cross-Entropy
Data augmentation	Flip + rotation (±5°) + mild colour jitter (train only)
CNN backbone	MobileNetV3-Small (ImageNet pretrained)
Frozen layers	None (end-to-end fine-tuning)
RF implementation	scikit-learn
RF number of trees	400
RF max depth	None
RF max features	"sqrt"
RF class weight	"balanced"
Ensemble strategy	OR-based fusion

Given the relatively small dataset size (383 images), several measures were implemented to mitigate potential overfitting risks. First, a lightweight backbone architecture (MobileNetV3-Small) was selected to limit model capacity and reduce the number of trainable parameters. Second, transfer learning was employed by initializing the network with ImageNet-pretrained weights, allowing the model to leverage generalized visual representations. Third, data augmentation techniques—including random horizontal flipping, small-angle rotations, and colour jittering—were applied to increase effective data variability. Additionally, weight decay regularization and early stopping based on validation accuracy were incorporated to prevent excessive fitting to the training data. The number of training epochs was selected conservatively to balance convergence and generalization.

4.3. Algorithmic Implementation

To clearly formalize the experimental procedure, the proposed framework is described through two complementary algorithms. Algorithm 1 describes the training procedure for MobileNetV3-Small CNN while the Algorithm 2 describes the Hybrid Ensemble-Based Soiling detection and cleaning decision frame work.

https://doi.org/10.3390/electronics15061192

Algorithm 1. Training Procedure for MobileNetV3-Small CNN

Input: Labelled PV panel image dataset
Output: Trained MobileNetV3-Small CNN model

1. Resize all RGB images to 224 × 224 × 3224\times 224\times 3224 × 224 × 3.
2. Split the dataset into training and validation subsets using stratified sampling.
3. Initialize MobileNetV3-Small with ImageNet-pretrained weights.
4. Replace the final classification layer with a two-class output layer.
5. Set training hyperparameters (learning rate, batch size, number of epochs).
6. For each epoch:
    a. Perform forward propagation on training images.
    b. Compute cross-entropy loss.
    c. Update network parameters using the Adam optimizer.
7. Save the trained CNN model with the best validation performance.

Algorithm 2. Hybrid Ensemble-Based Soiling Detection and Cleaning Decision Framework

Input: RGB PV panel image
Output: Final panel condition and cleaning decision

1. Acquire RGB image of a PV panel.
2. Resize the image to 224 × 224 × 3224\times 224\times 3224 × 224 × 3.
3. Classical branch:
    a. Extract handcrafted features (Laplacian variance, LBP histograms, statistical intensity measures).
    b. Classify the feature vector using the trained RF model.
    c. Obtain RF predicted label and class probability.
4. Deep learning branch:
    a. Feed the resized RGB image into the trained MobileNetV3-Small CNN.
    b. Obtain CNN predicted label and class probability via SoftMax.
5. Ensemble fusion:
   If (RF predicts dusty) OR (CNN predicts dusty):
   → Final decision = dusty
   Else:
   → Final decision = clean
6. Compute the probability-based Soiling Index (SI).
7. Map the SI value to a cleaning action (no cleaning, light cleaning, or full cleaning).

4.4. Evaluation Metrics and Testing Protocol

The performance of the model was evaluated based on the metrics discussed in Section 3.8, including accuracy, precision, recall, and F1-score, all of which are extracted from the confusion matrix. The performance of the model was evaluated based on the validation data, test data, and unseen data, giving us a comprehensive view of the performance of the model, including its generalization. The precision of the dusty class was of major concern, considering that false negatives could be very detrimental, resulting in unnecessary delays in cleaning, which could cause loss of energy in photovoltaic systems. The metrics were all derived based on the same evaluation process, giving us a fair basis for comparing the performance of the models. For the

https://doi.org/10.3390/electronics15061192

repeated-run analysis (Table 6), the research work used 10 seeds (100–109). For visualization and representative examples, a fixed seed (42) is used.

Table 6. Performance across 10 repeated stratified runs (mean ± std; 95% CI).

Model	Accuracy	Dusty Recall	Dusty F1-Score	AUC
Random Forest (handcrafted)	0.8534 ± 0.0338 (95% CI: 0.8293–0.8776)	0.8966 ± 0.0488 (95% CI: 0.8617–0.9314)	0.8594 ± 0.0321 (95% CI: 0.8365–0.8824)	0.9380 ± 0.0272 (95% CI: 0.9185–0.9574)
MobileNetV3-Small (CNN)	0.8897 ± 0.0260 (95% CI: 0.8711–0.9082)	0.8172 ± 0.0631 (95% CI: 0.7721–0.8624)	0.8801 ± 0.0320 (95% CI: 0.8571–0.9030)	0.9623 ± 0.0106 (95% CI: 0.9547–0.9699)
Proposed OR-Ensemble	0.9663 ± 0.0177 (95% CI: 0.9537–0.9790)	0.9896 ± 0.0104 (95% CI: 0.9822–0.9970)	0.9592 ± 0.0295 (95% CI: 0.9381–0.9803)	0.9920 ± 0.0102 (95% CI: 0.9847–0.9993)

5. Results and Discussion

This segment provides an in-depth evaluation of the proposed hybrid ensemble-based intelligent PV panel soiling detection framework. It commences with an evaluation of the MobileNetV3-Small CNN's learning mechanism and continues through quantitative performance evaluation, error evaluation, assembling effects, and statistical evaluation. In this context, it is important to consider the implications for PV panel maintenance, especially in terms of detecting dusty panels.

5.1. Learning Behaviour and Convergence Analysis

The training process of the MobileNetV3-Small CNN was evaluated by observing the training and validation accuracy and loss at each epoch, as presented in Figures 6 and 7. Generally, the CNN model has a stable training process with continuous improvement in validation performance as training progresses.

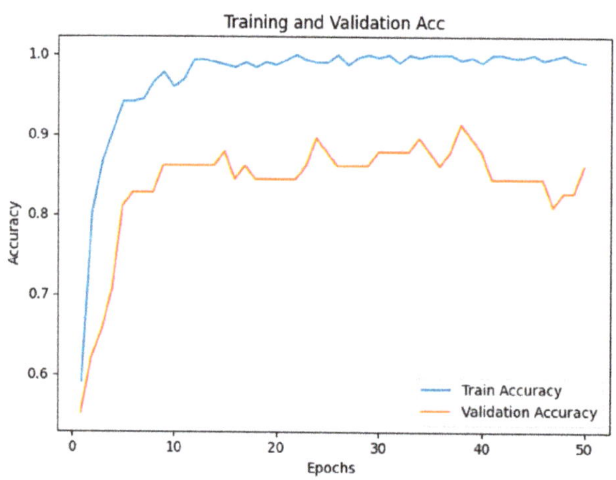

Figure 6. Training and validation accuracy of the proposed MobileNetV3-Small CNN.

During training, the validation accuracy increases rapidly, indicating effective adaptation of the pretrained backbone to PV soiling characteristics. Moving forward, it can be seen that the training and validation accuracy curves stabilize at a range, with minor fluctuations in the validation curve. The fluctuations are due to the messy nature of the limited data, the varying lighting, angles, and textures of the PV panels.

https://doi.org/10.3390/electronics15061192

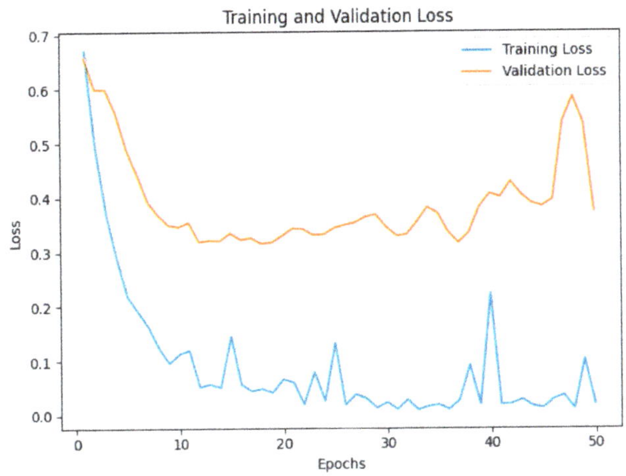

Figure 7. Training and validation loss curves of the proposed MobileNetV3-Small CNN.

Meanwhile, the training loss decreases rapidly while the validation loss gradually plateaus without any extreme behaviour. The minor gap between the two curves does not indicate any extreme overfitting. The overall observations suggest that the model's performance with the MobileNetV3-Small backbone is favourable for effective feature learning, optimization, and generalization, which is beneficial for the model fusion process. Although the dataset size is moderate for deep learning applications, the observed training–validation curves demonstrate stable convergence without severe divergence between training and validation accuracy. The relatively small gap between training and validation metrics indicates that overfitting is effectively controlled. Furthermore, the ensemble framework improves robustness by combining complementary representations, thereby reducing sensitivity to limited sample variability. These findings suggest that the lightweight transfer-learning approach is suitable for practical PV monitoring scenarios with moderate dataset sizes.

5.2. Core Performance Metrics Obtained

To provide a quantitative assessment of the proposed framework, the research work reports standard performance metrics derived from the confusion matrix and predicted probabilities (accuracy, dusty-class recall, dusty-class F1-score, and AUC). To address variability and strengthen comparative conclusions, metrics are reported over 10 repeated stratified 70%/15%/15% runs as mean ± standard deviation with 95% confidence intervals. The results for the Random Forest (handcrafted features), MobileNetV3-Small CNN, and the proposed OR-based ensemble fusion framework are summarized in Table 6.

Table 6 shows that the proposed OR-ensemble achieves the highest dusty-panel recall (0.9896 ± 0.0104, 95% CI: 0.9822–0.9970), which aligns with the PV maintenance objective of minimizing missed soiling events (false negatives). In addition, the OR-ensemble attains the highest mean accuracy (0.9663 ± 0.0177) and highest AUC (0.9920 ± 0.0102) among the compared methods. These results indicate that combining the complementary RF and CNN detectors using the conservative OR fusion rule improves the reliability of dusty-panel identification, while maintaining strong overall discriminative performance. This behaviour is consistent with risk-aware operation and maintenance, where reducing false negatives is typically prioritized due to the energy-loss cost of undetected soiling. These findings directly support the risk-aware hypothesis stated in the Introduction: the OR-based fusion improves maintenance-relevant performance by reducing missed soiling

https://doi.org/10.3390/electronics15061192

events through higher dusty-panel recall. Table 6 reports performance on the seen (in-distribution) dataset using repeated stratified runs; cross-dataset results under domain shift on an independent unseen dataset are reported separately in Table 7.

Table 7. Cross-dataset performance on the unseen dataset (domain-shift evaluation).

Model	Accuracy (%)	Dusty Recall	Dusty F1-Score
Random Forest (handcrafted)	67.10	0.69	0.64
MobileNetV3-Small (CNN)	74.55	0.76	0.71
Proposed OR-Ensemble	85.93	0.90	0.87

5.3. Confusion Matrix of the Proposed OR-Based Ensemble Model

The confusion matrix for the proposed OR-based ensemble model is shown in Figure 8 as an illustrative evaluation on the full seen dataset (N = 383). The primary quantitative results are reported in Table 6, which summarizes performance over 10 repeated stratified splits.

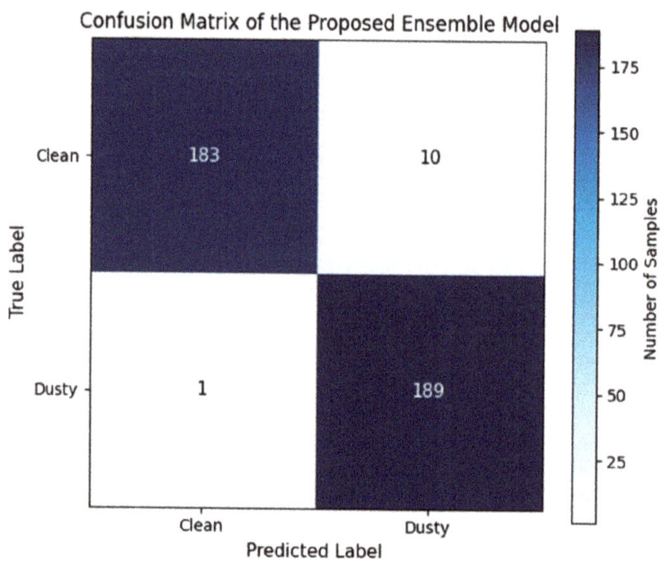

Figure 8. Confusion matrix of the proposed OR-based ensemble model on the full seen dataset (N = 383) (illustrative visualization). Primary performance statistics over repeated splits are reported in Table 6.

In this illustrative evaluation, only a small number of misclassifications occur. False negatives (dusty predicted as clean) are more critical in PV maintenance because they may delay cleaning and lead to cumulative energy losses, whereas false positives primarily trigger earlier inspection or cleaning. The conservative OR decision rule labels a panel as dusty if either the Random Forest or the MobileNetV3-Small CNN predicts soiling, thereby reducing the risk of false negatives and supporting deployment-oriented PV cleaning decision support.

5.4. Ensemble Impact on Decision Reliability

To illustrate the impact of the proposed ensemble method on the reliability of soiling detection, Figure 9 provides a visual representation of the dusty-panel recall of the models under consideration. Recall has been emphasized in this figure because this parameter has a

https://doi.org/10.3390/electronics15061192

direct relationship with the capability of the model to correctly identify soiled photovoltaic panels, thus avoiding unnecessary cleaning operations and the associated energy losses.

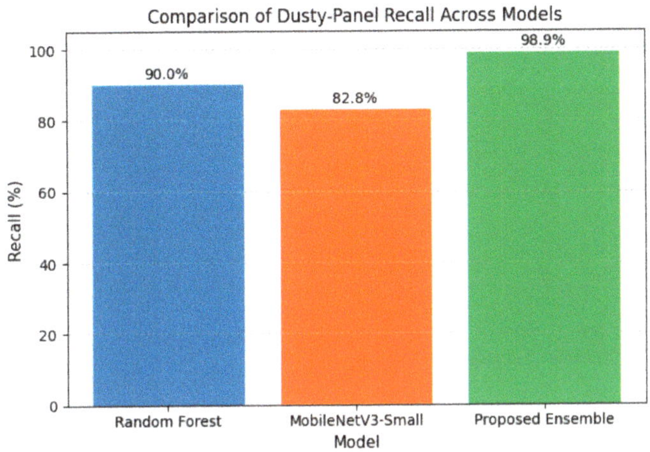

Figure 9. Comparison of dusty-panel recall across the Random Forest classifier, MobileNetV3-Small CNN, and the proposed OR-based ensemble framework.

As illustrated in Figure 9, the standalone Random Forest classifier peaks at a recall of 90%. This is because it uses physically interpretable handcrafted features that are quite sensitive to texture and sharpness changes. The MobileNetV3-Small CNN classifier follows with a slightly lower recall of 82.8%, likely because it uses learned features that are quite sensitive to lighting changes and contamination patterns. The OR-based ensemble framework, however, aims to achieve a much higher dusty-panel recall of 98.9%, demonstrating its effectiveness in preventing false negatives. By conservatively classifying a panel as dusty if either the CNN or the Random Forest classifier detects soiling, the ensemble framework effectively leverages the complementary strengths of both classifiers. This side-by-side comparison demonstrates the benefits of the ensemble approach to improving the reliability of soiling detection over a single classifier.

Overall, the results demonstrate that the proposed ensemble framework provides a more robust and risk-conscious solution to PV panel soiling detection, particularly in real-world use cases where false negatives can significantly impair performance.

5.5. Receiver Operating Characteristic (ROC) Analysis

To further evaluate the discriminative capability of the proposed framework under varying decision thresholds, ROC analysis was conducted for the standalone Random Forest classifier, the MobileNetV3-Small CNN, and the proposed OR-based ensemble model. The ROC curve illustrates the trade-off between the true positive rate (recall/sensitivity) and the false positive rate (1 − specificity) across different classification thresholds, providing a threshold-independent assessment of model performance. In this study, AUC is computed on the held-out evaluation set using the dusty-class probability score (dusty treated as the positive class) to ensure consistent and reproducible reporting.

Figure 10 shows ROC curves for a representative split of the seen dataset (seed = 42) to visualize the operating characteristics of the RF, MobileNetV3-Small CNN, and the proposed OR-ensemble. Because ROC/AUC values can vary across data partitions—particularly for modest dataset sizes—the research work reports the statistical reliability of AUC in Table 6, which summarizes the mean ± standard deviation and 95% confidence intervals over 10 repeated stratified runs. Accordingly, Figure 10 serves as a qualitative visualization of classifier behaviour, while Table 6 provides the primary aggregated quantitative AUC results.

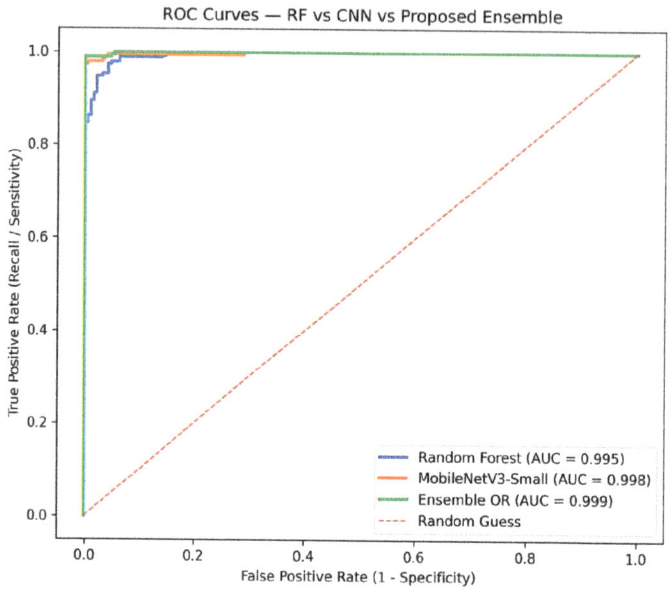

Figure 10. ROC curves for a representative split (seed = 42) comparing RF, MobileNetV3-Small CNN, and the proposed OR-ensemble. Aggregated AUC statistics across 10 repeated runs are reported in Table 6.

Overall, the ROC analysis indicates that the models maintain meaningful discriminative capability across thresholds, consistent with the AUC values reported in Table 6. While the CNN and the OR-ensemble show comparable threshold-independent discrimination, the OR-ensemble is specifically designed to prioritize dusty-panel recall and reduce missed soiling events, which is critical for PV maintenance decision support.

5.6. PV-Oriented Operational Implications

Accurate detection of dusty panels is vital to PV system operation and maintenance. Among the reported metrics, dusty-class recall most directly reflects the system's ability to identify panels that require cleaning. As shown in Table 6, the proposed OR-ensemble achieves the highest dusty recall on average across repeated runs, indicating improved sensitivity to soiling under variations in illumination, partial soiling, and reflections.

5.7. Statistical Significance Analysis

To address variability and strengthen comparative conclusions, the research work evaluated all models over 10 repeated stratified runs (70%/15%/15%) using different random seeds. For each run, the Random Forest, MobileNetV3-Small CNN, and the proposed OR-ensemble were trained and evaluated under the same protocol. Accordingly, Table 6 reports the performance distribution as mean ± standard deviation together with 95% confidence intervals computed from the per-run metric values. The results show that the proposed OR-ensemble consistently improves dusty-panel recall across repeated runs, supporting the reliability of the risk-aware fusion strategy.

https://doi.org/10.3390/electronics15061192

5.8. Domain-Shift Evaluation on an Unseen Dataset (Cross-Dataset Testing)

To examine robustness under domain shift, the research work performed cross-dataset testing using an independent unseen PV soiling dataset that was not used during training. This dataset contains 1493 clean and 1069 dusty images (total 2562) and exhibits different acquisition conditions (e.g., illumination, camera viewpoint/orientation, background, and soiling appearance), which alter the data distribution relative to the training dataset. The research work evaluated the RF baseline, the MobileNetV3-Small CNN baseline, and the proposed OR-ensemble on this unseen dataset using the same inference pipeline.

As shown in Table 7, the proposed OR-ensemble achieves the strongest performance under domain shift, reaching 85.93% accuracy, 0.90 dusty recall, and a 0.87 dusty-class F1-score on the unseen dataset. This directly supports the conservative OR-based design decision: compared with the standalone CNN (dusty recall = 0.76) and RF (dusty recall = 0.69), OR fusion substantially reduces missed soiling events; for example, at dusty recall $\approx$ 0.90 on 1069 dusty samples, the expected number of false negatives is approximately 107. This indicates improved cross-dataset generalization compared with either standalone model and demonstrates enhanced capability to detect dusty panels—an essential requirement for PV operation and maintenance, where missed soiling events (false negatives) can lead to cumulative energy losses. Overall, these results clarify that "robustness under domain shift" in this study refers to maintaining reliable dusty-panel detection when acquisition conditions differ from those observed during training.

5.9. Computational Complexity and Edge Inference Benchmarking

To validate suitability for resource-constrained deployment, the research works benchmarked inference latency per image and model size on a standard CPU environment (PyTorch 2.9.1 + cpu, Python 3.13.7). The research work reports median and 95th-percentile (p95) latency over repeated runs (with warm-up) for the Random Forest (RF) pipeline (preprocessing + feature extraction + RF inference), the MobileNetV3-Small CNN, and the complete OR-ensemble (RF + CNN + fusion). Results are summarized in Table 8. The OR-ensemble latency reflects the cumulative cost of both branches and the fusion step, while remaining within practical limits for near real-time PV monitoring and decision support.

Table 8. CPU inference-time and model-size benchmarking (single-image inference).

Component	Device	Median Latency (ms)	p95 Latency (ms)	Throughput (Images/s)	Model Size (MB)
RF (preprocess + features + RF)	CPU	67.00	96.94	14.92	2.32
CNN (MobileNetV3-Small)	CPU	18.73	76.45	53.39	5.93
OR-Ensemble (RF + CNN + fusion)	CPU	116.06	210.56	8.62	8.24

Note: median and p95 are computed over repeated runs after warm-up; throughput is computed as 1000 median latency.

6. Conclusions

In this study, a hybrid intelligent decision framework for risk-aware photovoltaic (PV) panel soiling detection and cleaning support using an ensemble approach has been proposed. The framework combines physically meaningful handcrafted features classified by a Random Forest (RF) model with high-level representations learned by a lightweight MobileNetV3-Small CNN. A conservative OR-based fusion rule is employed to improve the reliability of dusty-panel detection and to reduce high-risk false negative cases. To strengthen the reliability

https://doi.org/10.3390/electronics15061192

of the reported results, performance was evaluated over 10 repeated stratified 70%/15%/15% runs, and metrics were reported as mean ± standard deviation with 95% confidence intervals. Across these repeated runs, the proposed OR-ensemble achieved 0.9663 ± 0.0177 accuracy (95% CI: 0.9537–0.9790), 0.9896 ± 0.0104 dusty-panel recall (95% CI: 0.9822–0.9970), 0.9592 ± 0.0295 dusty-class F1-score (95% CI: 0.9381–0.9803), and 0.9920 ± 0.0102 AUC (95% CI: 0.9847–0.9993). These results demonstrate that the proposed fusion strategy consistently prioritizes the detection of dusty panels—an essential requirement for PV operation and maintenance—while maintaining strong overall discriminative performance.

Furthermore, the probability-driven Soiling Index (SI) transforms the detection outputs into actionable cleaning recommendations, making the framework suitable for deployment-oriented PV cleaning management. Overall, this work enhances image-based PV soiling detection by integrating risk awareness and decision support, providing a practical and scalable approach for intelligent PV panel cleaning management.

Author Contributions: Conceptualization and methodology were performed by A.W., B.M.K., H.A., S.K. and A.M.A. Investigation was performed by A.W., B.M.K. and H.A. Formal analysis, data curation, resources, and software development were performed by A.W., B.M.K. and H.A. Validation was performed by A.W., B.M.K., H.A., S.K., O.H.A. and A.M.A. Visualization was performed by A.W. and H.A. Funding acquisition and project administration were performed by H.A. and A.M.A. Writing—original draft was performed by A.W., B.M.K. and H.A. Writing—review and editing was performed by all authors (A.W., B.M.K., H.A., S.K., A.M.A. and O.H.A.). All authors have read and agreed to the published version of the manuscript.

Funding: This article is derived from a research grant funded by the Research, Development, and Innovation Authority (RDIA)—Kingdom of Saudi Arabia—with grant number (13385-Tabuk-2023-UT-R-3-1-SE).

Data Availability Statement: The original contributions presented in this study are included in the article. Further inquiries can be directed to the corresponding author.

Acknowledgments: The authors extend their appreciation to the Research, Development, and Innovation Authority (RDIA), Saudi Arabia, for funding this work through grant number (13385-Tabuk-2023-UT-R-3-1-SE).

Conflicts of Interest: The authors declare no conflicts of interest.

Abbreviations

The following abbreviations are used in this manuscript:

PV	Photo Voltaic
CNN	Convolution neural network
SI	Soiling Index
UAVs	Unmanned Air vehicles
SLI	Soiling Loss Index
LBP	Local Binary Pattern
RMS	Root Mean Square
SE	Squeeze-and-Excitation
TP	True Positive
FN	False Negative
TN	True Negative
FP	False Positive
ROC	Receiver Operating Characteristic
AUC	Area Under the ROC Curve

https://doi.org/10.3390/electronics15061192

References

1. Qi, J.; Dong, Q.; Song, Y.; Zhao, X.; Shi, L. Combining Dust Scaling Behaviors of PV Panels and Water Cleaning Methods. *Renew. Sustain. Energy Rev.* **2025**, *212*, 115394. [CrossRef]
2. Onim, M.S.H.; Sakif, Z.M.M.; Ahnaf, A.; Kabir, A.; Azad, A.K.; Oo, A.M.T.; Afreen, R.; Hridy, S.T.; Hossain, M.; Jabid, T.; et al. SolNet: A Convolutional Neural Network for Detecting Dust on Solar Panels. *Energies* **2023**, *16*, 155. [CrossRef]
3. Hussain, A.; Batra, A.; Pachauri, R. An Experimental Study on Effect of Dust on Power Loss in Solar Photovoltaic Module. *Renew. Wind Water Sol.* **2017**, *4*, 9. [CrossRef]
4. Adinoyi, M.J.; Said, S.A.M. Effect of Dust Accumulation on the Power Outputs of Solar Photovoltaic Modules. *Renew. Energy* **2013**, *60*, 633–636. [CrossRef]
5. Paudyal, B.R.; Shakya, S.R. Dust Accumulation Effects on Efficiency of Solar PV Modules for off Grid Purpose: A Case Study of Kathmandu. *Sol. Energy* **2016**, *135*, 103–110. [CrossRef]
6. Vaishak, S.; Bhale, P.V. Effect of Dust Deposition on Performance Characteristics of a Refrigerant Based Photovoltaic/Thermal System. *Sustain. Energy Technol. Assess.* **2019**, *36*, 100548. [CrossRef]
7. Mekhilef, S.; Saidur, R.; Kamalisarvestani, M. Effect of Dust, Humidity and Air Velocity on Efficiency of Photovoltaic Cells. *Renew. Sustain. Energy Rev.* **2012**, *16*, 2920–2925. [CrossRef]
8. Noura, H.N.; Chahine, K.; Bassil, J.; Abou Chaaya, J.; Salman, O. Efficient Combination of Deep Learning Models for Solar Panel Damage and Soiling Detection. *Measurement* **2025**, *251*, 117185. [CrossRef]
9. Abdelsattar, M.; Rasslan, A.A.A.; Emad-Eldeen, A. Detecting Dusty and Clean Photovoltaic Surfaces Using MobileNet Variants for Image Classification. *SVU-Int. J. Eng. Sci. Appl.* **2025**, *6*, 9–18. [CrossRef]
10. Sladojevic, S.; Arsenovic, M.; Anderla, A.; Culibrk, D.; Stefanovic, D. Deep Neural Networks Based Recognition of Plant Diseases by Leaf Image Classification. *Comput. Intell. Neurosci.* **2016**, *2016*, 3289801. [CrossRef]
11. Yilmaz, A. Brain Tumor Detection from MRI Images with Using Proposed Deep Learning Model: The Partial Correlation-Based Channel Selection. *Turk. J. Electr. Eng. Comput. Sci.* **2021**, *29*, 2615–2633. [CrossRef]
12. Sun, T.; Gao, H.; Fan, S.; Hu, X. Enhancing Dust Detection on Photovoltaic Panels with PP-YOLO: A Deep Learning Approach. In *Proceedings of the 2024 4th International Conference on Machine Learning and Intelligent Systems Engineering (MLISE), Zhuhai, China, 28–30 June 2024*; IEEE: Piscataway, NJ, USA, 2024; pp. 24–28.
13. Maghami, M.; Hizam, H.; Gomes, C. Impact of Dust on Solar Energy Generation Based on Actual Performance. In *Proceedings of the 2014 IEEE International Conference on Power and Energy (PECon), Kuching, Malaysia, 1–3 December 2014*; IEEE: Piscataway, NJ, USA, 2014; pp. 388–393.
14. Mehta, S.; Singh, M. Optimizing Solar Energy Output Through Automated Dust Detection Using CNN-SVM. In *Proceedings of the 2024 5th International Conference on Smart Electronics and Communication (ICOSEC), Trichy, India, 18–20 September 2024*; IEEE: Piscataway, NJ, USA, 2024; pp. 920–924.
15. Ghosh, A.; Afrin, S.; Tithy, R.S.; Nahid, F.; Alam, F.; Reza, A.W. Improving Solar Panel Efficiency: A CNN-Based System for Dust Detection and Maintenance. In Proceedings of the 2nd International Conference on Big Data, IoT and Machine Learning, Dhaka, Bangladesh, 6–8 September 2023; Volume 867, pp. 673–684.
16. Fan, S.; Wang, Y.; Cao, S.; Zhao, B.; Sun, T.; Liu, P. A Deep Residual Neural Network Identification Method for Uneven Dust Accumulation on Photovoltaic (PV) Panels. *Energy* **2022**, *239*, 122302. [CrossRef]
17. Bashir, S.B.; Farag, M.M.; Hamid, A.-K.; Adam, A.A.; Bansal, R.C.; Mbungu, N.T.; Elnady, A.; Abo-Khalil, A.G.; Hussein, M. Innovative Dust Detection and Efficient Cleaning of PV Panels: A CNN-RF Approach Using I–V Curve Data Transformed into RGB Mosaics. *Energy Convers. Manag. X* **2025**, *27*, 101079. [CrossRef]
18. Li, M.; Wang, Y. Deep Learning for Dust Accumulation Analysis on Desert Solar Panels: A CNN-Transformer Approach. *IEEE Access* **2025**, *13*, 69857–69872. [CrossRef]
19. Ozer, T.; Turkmen, O. An Approach Based on Deep Learning Methods to Detect the Condition of Solar Panels in Solar Power Plants. *Comput. Electr. Eng.* **2024**, *116*, 109143. [CrossRef]
20. Bassil, J.; Noura, H.N.; Salman, O.; Chahine, K.; Guizani, M. Efficient Combination of Deep Learning and Tree-Based Classification Models for Solar Panel Dust Detection. *Intell. Syst. Appl.* **2025**, *26*, 200509. [CrossRef]
21. Alatwi, A.M.; Albalawi, H.; Wadood, A.; Anwar, H.; El-Hageen, H.M. Deep Learning-Based Dust Detection on Solar Panels: A Low-Cost Sustainable Solution for Increased Solar Power Generation. *Sustainability* **2024**, *16*, 8664. [CrossRef]
22. Abuqaaud, K.A.; Ferrah, A. A Novel Technique for Detecting and Monitoring Dust and Soil on Solar Photovoltaic Panel. In *Proceedings of the 2020 Advances in Science and Engineering Technology International Conferences (ASET), Dubai, United Arab Emirates, 4 February–9 April 2020*; IEEE: Piscataway, NJ, USA, 2020; pp. 1–6.
23. Khalid, H.M.; Rafique, Z.; Muyeen, S.M.; Raqeeb, A.; Said, Z.; Saidur, R.; Sopian, K. Dust Accumulation and Aggregation on PV Panels: An Integrated Survey on Impacts, Mathematical Models, Cleaning Mechanisms, and Possible Sustainable Solution. *Sol. Energy* **2023**, *251*, 261–285. [CrossRef]

https://doi.org/10.3390/electronics15061192

24. Abd, H.S.; Judran, H.K.; Aun, S.H.A.; Jaddoa, A.A.; Hammoodi, K.A.; Kadhim, S.A.; Daif, J.M. Dust Deposition and Cleaning Effect on PV Panel: Experimental Approach. *Results Eng.* **2025**, *27*, 106041. [CrossRef]
25. Shao, Y.; Zhang, C.; Xing, L.; Sun, H.; Zhao, Q.; Zhang, L. A New Dust Detection Method for Photovoltaic Panel Surface Based on Pytorch and Its Economic Benefit Analysis. *Energy AI* **2024**, *16*, 100349. [CrossRef]
26. Winkel, P.; Wilbert, S.; Roger, M.; Krauth, J.J.; Algner, N.; Nouri, B.; Wolfertstetter, F.; Carballo, J.A.; Alonso-Garcia, M.C.; Polo, J.; et al. Cell-Resolved PV Soiling Measurement Using Drone Images. *Remote Sens.* **2024**, *16*, 2617. [CrossRef]
27. Al-Addous, M.; Dalala, Z.; Alawneh, F.; Class, C.B. Modeling and Quantifying Dust Accumulation Impact on PV Module Performance. *Sol. Energy* **2019**, *194*, 86–102. [CrossRef]
28. Fatima, K.; Faiz Minai, A.; Malik, H.; Garcia Marquez, F.P. Experimental Analysis of Dust Composition Impact on Photovoltaic Panel Performance: A Case Study. *Sol. Energy* **2024**, *267*, 112206. [CrossRef]
29. Yakubu, S.; Samikannu, R.; Gawusu, S.; Wetajega, S.D.; Okai, V.; Shaibu, A.K.S.; Workneh, G.A. A Holistic Review of the Effects of Dust Buildup on Solar Photovoltaic Panel Efficiency. *Sol. Compass* **2025**, *13*, 100101. [CrossRef]
30. Chen, L.; Fan, S.; Sun, S.; Cao, S.; Sun, T.; Liu, P.; Gao, H.; Zhang, Y.; Ding, W. A Detection Model for Dust Deposition on Photovoltaic (PV) Panels Based on Light Transmittance Estimation. *Energy* **2025**, *322*, 135284. [CrossRef]
31. Afroz. Solar Panel Images Clean and Faulty Images. Available online: https://www.kaggle.com/datasets/pythonafroz/solar-panel-images (accessed on 31 December 2025).

https://doi.org/10.3390/electronics15061192

electronics

MDPI

Article

Physics-Informed Neural Network for Denoising Images Using Nonlinear PDE

Carlos Osorio Quero [1,*,†] and Maria Liz Crespo [2,*,†]

1 Instituto Nacional de Astrofísica, Óptica y Electrónica (INAOE), Puebla 72840, Mexico
2 Multidisciplinary Laboratory (MLab), Science, Technology and Innovation Unit, Abdus Salam International Centre for Theoretical Physics (ICTP), 34151 Trieste, Italy
* Correspondence: caoq@inaoep.mx (C.O.O.); mcrespo@ictp.it (M.L.C.)
† These authors contributed equally to this work.

Abstract

Noise remains a persistent limitation in coherent imaging systems, degrading image quality and hindering accurate interpretation in critical applications such as remote sensing, medical imaging, and non-destructive testing. This paper presents a physics-informed deep learning framework for effective image denoising under complex noise conditions. The proposed approach integrates nonlinear partial differential equations (PDEs), including the heat equation, diffusion models, MPMC, and the Zhichang Guo (ZG) method, into advanced neural network architectures such as ResUNet, UNet, U2Net, and Res2UNet. By embedding physical constraints directly into the training process, the framework couples data-driven learning with physics-based priors to enhance noise suppression and preserve structural details. Experimental evaluations across multiple datasets demonstrate that the proposed method consistently outperforms conventional denoising techniques, achieving higher PSNR, SSIM, ENL, and CNR values. These results confirm the effectiveness of combining physics-informed neural networks with deep architectures and highlight their potential for advanced image restoration in real-world, high-noise imaging scenarios.

Keywords: physics-informed neural networks (PINNs); image denoise; deep learning; PDE; encoder–decoder; image processing

1. Introduction

Image denoising is a crucial task in image processing aimed at removing noise while preserving the underlying structures [1,2]. As high-resolution digital imagery becomes increasingly accessible, especially with novel modalities such as single-pixel imaging (SPI) [3,4], UAV or SAR Images [5,6], and other computer image applications, there is a growing demand for denoising algorithms that deliver high effectiveness and computational efficiency. In recent years, deep learning-based approaches have shown superior performance in image denoising, surpassing traditional hand-made methods [7]. These approaches employ convolutional neural networks (CNNs) to learn the mapping between noisy and clear from noisy to clean images, training on large datasets of paired noisy–clean difference between the network output and the corresponding clean image [8].

One of the key advantages of deep learning-based denoising methods is their ability to learn complex [9], nonlinear relationships between noisy and clean image patches [10,11]. This enables networks to capture both local and global image structures and patterns, resulting in more accurate and visually pleasing denoising results (see Table 1). Image

https://doi.org/10.3390/electronics15030560

priors [12], including nonlocal self-similarity (NSS) models [13], median filters [14], sparse models [15], gradient models [16], Markov models [17], BM3D [18], LSSC [19], NCSR [20], and WNNM [21], address the challenge of noise removal. More recently, deep learning-based denoising models, such as standard CNNs [22], residual networks (ResNets) [23], and generative adversarial networks (GANs) [24], have emerged as effective solutions. The standard CNN model learns a direct mapping from noisy to clean images, while the ResNet model uses skip connections to learn residual mappings, resulting in more efficient training and improved denoising performance. GAN-based models further enhance denoising by incorporating a generator that produces denoised images and a discriminator that differentiates between real and generated images, leading to more realistic and visually consistent results [24,25].

Physics-informed neural networks (PINNs) have emerged as a novel approach in artificial intelligence [26], particularly by using partial differential equations (PDEs) for efficient image denoising [27]. PDE-based models such as heat diffusion [28], Perona–Malik (PM) [29], MPMC [30], and the Black-Zhichang Guo model [31] are effective in addressing noise reduction in images. In the PINN framework, a neural network is utilized to approximate the solution of a PDE by minimizing a loss function that includes terms representing the mismatch of the residual PDE and its boundary conditions. The nonlinearity of PDEs and the varying boundary conditions do not pose significant challenges when employing neural networks, offering a distinct advantage over traditional numerical methods. However, integrating PDEs into deep learning frameworks also introduces challenges, including balancing accuracy and stability, managing computational complexity, and ensuring interpretability [32]. Many existing approaches address these issues only partially, leaving room for improvement in terms of generalization, computational efficiency, and preservation of fine-scale structures.

This work presents a physics-informed deep learning framework that couples nonlinear PDE priors—heat, diffusion-based regularization, Mean Curvature Motion (MPMC), and the Zhichang Guo (ZG) model—with modern denoising backbones including ResUNet, UNet, U2Net, and Res2UNet. We focus on these four PDEs because they offer complementary denoising behavior while remaining computationally predictable and suitable for future FPGA/embedded-GPU deployment [33,34]. Specifically, heat provides a stable isotropic baseline, diffusion introduces edge-aware anisotropy, MPMC enforces curvature-driven geometric smoothing, and ZG improves robustness under speckle and other multiplicative degradations.

By embedding physical constraints directly into the network training process, the proposed method improves denoising performance, preserves fine structural details, and reduces dependence on large-scale labeled datasets. This hybrid approach combines the interpretability and stability of PDE-based modeling with the representational power of deep learning, offering a robust and scalable solution for image denoising in challenging noise environments. To rigorously assess the performance of the framework, a comprehensive set of evaluation metrics is used, including the peak signal-to-noise ratio (PSNR), the structural similarity index measure (SSIM), the equivalent number of looks (ENL), and the contrast-to-noise ratio (CNR). Our experiments consistently achieve PSNR values greater than 20 dB and SSIM values greater than 0.5, demonstrating the effectiveness of the model in enhancing image quality while maintaining computational efficiency.

The main contributions of this work are summarized as follows:

- The integration of physics-informed neural networks (PINNs) with PDE-based models for effective image denoising leverages physical priors to enhance noise suppression and structural preservation.

https://doi.org/10.3390/electronics15030560

- This study introduces a rigorous and diverse set of evaluation metrics for denoising in remote sensing imagery, spanning pixel-level fidelity and perceptual quality.
- The proposed framework demonstrates superior performance compared to classical denoising algorithms and existing deep learning-based methods, achieving higher image quality and robustness across multiple datasets.

Table 1. Overview of the main advantages and drawbacks of the implemented denoising approaches.

Method	Advantages	Drawbacks
Supervised CNN [35]	High reconstruction quality with sufficiently large labeled training sets.	Requires extensive paired datasets; weaker generalization outside the training domain.
Self-supervised CNN [36]	Training does not require paired clean labels; it can learn directly from noisy data.	May exhibit residual bias and relies on masking/noise assumptions that can be violated.
Wavelet/Sparse [37]	Often excellent PSNR/SSIM for additive Gaussian noise; interpretable transform-domain representation.	Can leave granular residue for speckle-like noise; requires careful parameter tuning.
Score-based diffusion [38]	Naturally integrates explicit forward noise models; very strong perceptual quality.	Computationally demanding due to long sampling chains with many denoising steps.
Variance-stabilized PDE [39]	Simple pipeline combining variance-stabilizing transform and PDE evolution; fast and lightweight.	Inverse-VST can introduce bias; performance degrades for strongly spatially varying noise.
Nonlocal PDE/NL-TV [40]	Preserves fine textures and details by exploiting nonlocal similarities; texture-aware regularization.	Sensitive to patch and hyper-parameter choices; typically higher runtime.
Classical PDE [41]	Conceptually simple, interpretable, and numerically stable with low computational cost.	Parameter sensitive and prone to over-smoothing fine structures and textures.
PINN–PDE [42]	Physics-informed formulation enables adaptation across sensors with limited retuning.	More complex training procedure and higher computational cost than analytical PDE solvers.
Transformer-based denoisers [43]	Easy to add noise-level maps, prompts, or multi-scale features.	Can overfit to training noise statistics; may generalize poorly to unseen sensors/artifacts.
Diffusion-model denoisers [44]	Robust when noise/artifacts are heavy or complex (with good conditioning).	Expensive to train. Strong generative prior may introduce plausible but incorrect details—bad.
DIP-TV [45]	Can work reasonably even when the noise model is not well specified.	DIP can start fitting noise; results depend on stopping criterion/hyperparameters.
SwinIR [46]	Strong on PSNR/SSIM, preserves edges and textures well with long-range context.	Needs supervised (or well-designed self-supervised) training; may generalize poorly to unseen sensors/noise statistics.
DDPMs [47]	Can handle complex noise/artifacts when properly conditioned.	Many denoising steps; even accelerated samplers can be heavy.
DDRM [48]	Designed for restoration/inverse problems; can incorporate the measurement/degradation model more directly than plain DDPM denoising.	Inference remains multi-step, often similar order to diffusion sampling.

https://doi.org/10.3390/electronics15030560

The outline of this article is as follows. Section 2 reviews previous work on image denoising, with an emphasis on PDE-based approaches. In Section 3, we introduce the specific nonlinear PDE formulations used in our framework. Section 4 describes the architecture of the general physics-informed denoising, while Section 5 details the neural network backbones used, and Section 6 discusses refinement through PINN denoising. The numerical benchmark results appear in Section 7 and conclude with key lessons and directions for future work in Section 8.

2. Related Work

2.1. *Deep Learning Methods for Image Denoising*

Deep learning methods can be classified into supervised [1], semi-supervised [49], and unsupervised learning approaches [50].

2.1.1. Supervised Learning

It relies on labeled data to guide the model in learning parameters for tasks such as image denoising [51]. For example, consider a denoising model defined as $y = x + \epsilon$ where x, y, and ϵ represent the clean image, noisy image, and additive Gaussian noise (AWGN) with a standard deviation of σ, respectively. Based on this model and Bayesian inference, learning the model parameters depends on a dataset of paired examples $\{(x_k, y_k)\}_{k=1}^N$, where x_k and y_k denote clean and noisy images k-th, and N is the total number of samples. The relationship can be expressed as $x_k = f(y_k, \theta, m)$, where θ denotes the model parameters and m is the known noise level.

2.1.2. Unsupervised Learning

Does not require labeled data [52]. Instead, it identifies the underlying patterns within the input data to perform tasks such as domain transfer or image enhancement. For example, the Cycle-in-Cycle GAN (CinCGAN) [53] architecture performs super-resolution by first estimating a high-resolution label and then refining this estimate using loss functions and unlabeled data.

2.1.3. Semi-Supervised Learning

Combines labeled and unlabeled data [54]. It is particularly useful in scenarios with limited labeled samples, such as in medical diagnostics [55]. For example, the Semi-Supervised Learned Sinogram Restoration Network (SLSR-Net) [56] initially learns feature distributions from paired sinograms through a supervised component and then applies this knowledge in an unsupervised manner to reconstruct high-quality sinograms from unlabeled low-dose data [57].

2.2. *CNNs for Image Denoising*

Convolutional neural networks (CNNs) have demonstrated remarkable success in image processing tasks due to their flexible plug-and-play architectures [58]. LeNet [59], one of the first CNN models, used convolutional kernels of various sizes to effectively extract features for image classification. However, its reliance on the sigmoid activation function led to slow convergence, limiting its applicability in real-world scenarios [60]. The introduction of AlexNet marked a significant milestone in the field of deep learning. Its success stemmed from several key innovations: leveraging the computational power of GPUs, employing dropout to mitigate overfitting [61], using the ReLU activation function to accelerate stochastic gradient descent (SGD) [62], and incorporating data augmentation techniques. Despite its strong performance, the large convolutional kernels of AlexNet

https://doi.org/10.3390/electronics15030560

required significant memory [63], which restricted its use in resource-limited applications, such as smart cameras.

2.3. Recent Image Denoising Methods

Transformer-based denoisers, such as Swin Transformer/SwinIR-style models [64], use windowed self-attention to capture long-range dependencies and typically deliver strong PSNR/SSIM with fast, single-pass inference. In contrast, DIP-TV [45] (Deep Image Prior with Total Variation) is a training-free, per-image optimization approach that can work without clean datasets, but is slower and can over-smooth fine textures. Diffusion models (DDPMs) [65] provide powerful generative priors and often achieve excellent perceptual denoising, yet require iterative sampling with higher computational cost and potential hallucination if not constrained. DDRM [44] adapts diffusion priors to restoration by enforcing data consistency with an explicit degradation model, often improving fidelity over unconstrained diffusion, but still inherits multi-step inference and sensitivity to forward-model mismatch.

2.4. Recent Progress in PDE-Based Image Denoising

Recent work has progressed along three converging research directions (Table 2), with several studies emphasizing the implementation of PDE-based image denoising techniques.

i New and generalized PDE formulations for denoising (including multiplicative/speckle noise): Variable- and fractional-order PDEs have been proposed to better adapt the smoothing strength to local structure and speckle statistics, improving detail preservation over classical anisotropic diffusion. Examples include a variable spatially exponent PDE for multiplicative noise [66] and fractional-order PDEs that enhance edge/texture fidelity while suppressing ultrasound noise [67]. Anisotropy-stabilized formulations continue to evolve, e.g., tunable despeckling guided by anisotropic diffusion within a degradation framework [68]. These works collectively report gains in PSNR/SSIM and texture retention compared to standard PM/TV baselines.

ii Hybrid PINN/PDE–DL schemes that enforce physics during learning: PINN-style training that embeds PDE residuals and boundary conditions into loss has been shown to improve robustness and interpretability in imaging tasks. For image denoising and edge preservation, physics-informed blending of PDE priors has demonstrated improved artifact control over CNNs driven purely by data [69]. Beyond natural images, PINN denoisers have been specialized for modality-specific physics (e.g., high b-value diffusion MRI), showing superior fidelity under limited data [70]. Physics-informed microscopy reconstruction similarly integrates forward optics into a diffusion-conditioned architecture to suppress hallucinations [71].

iii Generative diffusion models tailored to SAR despeckling with explicit noise physics have emerged as the state of the art. Regional DDPMs and diffusion posterior sampling strategies explicitly consider block-wise structure and speckle statistics to reduce texture loss and over-smoothing [72,73]. Conditional/efficient DDPMs further incorporate the SAR noise model and achieve strong quantitative and visual performance in synthetic and real scenes [74,75]. These methods consistently report gains in ENL/CNR while maintaining edges.

https://doi.org/10.3390/electronics15030560

Table 2. Implementation case studies of PDE-based image denoising.

Method (PDE)	Noise Model	Dataset/Application	Ref.
Heat diffusion	Additive Gaussian	USC–SIPI, Kodak24; baseline smoothing	[76]
SRAD	Multiplicative speckle (Gamma)	Ultrasound, SAR	[77]
Nonlocal PDE/NL-TV	Multiplicative speckle	Gaussian test images; texture preservation	[78]
Complex diffusion	Additive Gaussian	Various natural images	[79]
Variance-stabilized PDE	Poisson	Microscopy images	[39]
Fourth-order PDE	Additive Gaussian	Various natural images	[80]
TV-Poisson (TV-KL)	Poisson	Various natural images	[81]
CED	Additive Gaussian	Fingerprint images	[82]

3. Denoising PDE Models

Partial differential equations (PDEs) are widely applied in various image processing tasks [42]. One powerful approach to solving PDEs using neural networks, particularly (FNNs) [83], is the physics-informed neural network framework (PINN) [69]. In a PINN, a neural network is designed to serve as a surrogate model for the PDE solution. Consider an FNN that takes inputs x and t, with hidden layers composed of n_l neurons. The objective is to train the neural network to approximate the solution $u(x,t)$ using a function $f(x,t,\theta)$, where θ denotes the parameters of the network, including weight matrices and bias vectors. The output of the FNN is generated through an activation function, typically the hyperbolic tangent function tanh.

To enforce the PDE constraints, the PINN calculates the required k-th order derivatives of $f(x,t,\theta)$ regarding its inputs using automatic differentiation (AD) [84]. The backpropagation algorithm, an AD technique, is employed to calculate these derivatives within the neural network. AD consists of two main phases: a forward pass to compute variable values and a backward pass to compute their derivatives. The neural network is then restricted to satisfy the given PDE and its associated boundary and initial conditions. The training dataset τ includes two subsets of points: those sampled from the interior domain and those on the boundary. These points are collectively referred to as residual points. A loss function $L(\theta,\tau)$ is defined as a weighted sum of $L_2 - norms$ of the residuals of the PDE and the boundary conditions. This loss quantifies the deviation of the neural network from satisfying the problem constraints. The goal is to minimize $L(\theta,\tau)$ to identify an optimal set of parameters θ. Gradient-based optimization algorithms are used for this minimization. To achieve a high level of accuracy, it is essential to carefully tune various hyperparameters, including the network size, the number of residual points, and other model-specific settings.

These models form the mathematical backbone for traditional and modern image denoising techniques, including physics-informed neural networks (PINNs) that integrate such equations into their training process:

- **Modified Perona–Malik Curvature Model (MPMC) Model:** The MPMC model enhances classic Perona–Malik anisotropic diffusion by incorporating curvature in-

https://doi.org/10.3390/electronics15030560

formation to better preserve edges during denoising. The Equation (1) [30] is as follows:

$$\frac{\partial u}{\partial t} = \nabla \cdot (g(|k|)\nabla u) \tag{1}$$

where $u(x, y, t)$ is the image intensity, k is the curvature of the level lines, and $g(\cdot)$ is an edge-stopping function that controls diffusion strength.

- **Zhichang Guo (ZG) Model:** A PDE model combining second- and fourth-order anisotropic diffusion was proposed to simultaneously smooth flat regions and preserve fine details. The Equation (2) [31] is as follows:

$$\frac{\partial u}{\partial t} = \lambda_1 \nabla \cdot (g_1(|\nabla u|)\nabla u) - \lambda_2 \triangle^2 u \tag{2}$$

where λ_1, λ_2 are regularization weights, $g_1(\cdot)$ is an edge-preserving function, and $\triangle^2 u$ is the biharmonic operator for fourth-order diffusion.

- **Heat Equation Residual Model:** The heat equation is the simplest form of isotropic diffusion used for image smoothing. The Equation (3) [85] is as follows:

$$\frac{\partial u}{\partial t} = \triangle u \tag{3}$$

This model blurs both noise and edges uniformly. The residual form is often used in deep learning to guide the network's output $f(x, t, \theta)$ through a physics-informed loss Equation (4):

$$R(x, t) = \frac{\partial f}{\partial t} - \triangle f \tag{4}$$

- **General Diffusion Model:** This model is a general formulation for anisotropic diffusion. The Equation (5) [44] is as follows:

$$\frac{\partial u}{\partial t} = \nabla \cdot (D(x, y, t)\nabla u) \tag{5}$$

where $D(x, y, t)$ is a diffusion tensor that controls the direction and strength of the smoothing, adaptable based on the characteristics of the image.

Speckle Model for Data Generation

Speckle noise in coherent imaging systems, such as SA,R is commonly modeled using a *multiplicative noise model* [86]:

$$Y = NX, \tag{6}$$

where $Y \in \mathbb{R}^{W \times H}$ is the noisy image observed (intensity domain), $X \in \mathbb{R}^{W \times H}$ is the underlying speckle-free image, and $N \in \mathbb{R}^{W \times H}$ is a positive random variable representing the speckle. For a multi-look SAR image with L independent looks, N follows a Gamma distribution with unit mean and variance $1/L$, whose probability density function (PDF) is

$$p(N) = \frac{L^L N^{L-1} e^{-LN}}{\Gamma(L)}, \quad N \geq 0,\ L \geq 1, \tag{7}$$

where $\Gamma(\cdot)$ is the Gamma function.

- **Amplitude image:** Many SAR processors work on the *amplitude* image, defined as the square root of the intensity: $x = \sqrt{X}$ for the clean image and $y = \sqrt{Y}$ for the observed one. The same multiplicative model applies:

$$y = n\,x, \tag{8}$$

https://doi.org/10.3390/electronics15030560

where n is the multiplicative speckle affecting the amplitude domain. In this case, n follows a Nakagami distribution with PDF:

$$p(n) = \frac{2L^L n^{2L-1} e^{-Ln^2}}{\Gamma(L)}, \quad n \geq 0, \ L \geq 1. \tag{9}$$

- **Single-look image:** A *single-look* ($L = 1$) SAR image is obtained from one coherent measurement without multi-look averaging; it contains the strongest speckle fluctuations. For $L = 1$, the Nakagami distribution in Equation (9) reduces to the Rayleigh distribution, which characterizes the amplitude speckle in single-look data (see Figure 1). This formulation allows us to synthesize speckle-corrupted images in either the intensity or the amplitude domain by drawing samples from the corresponding PDFs for any chosen number of looks L.

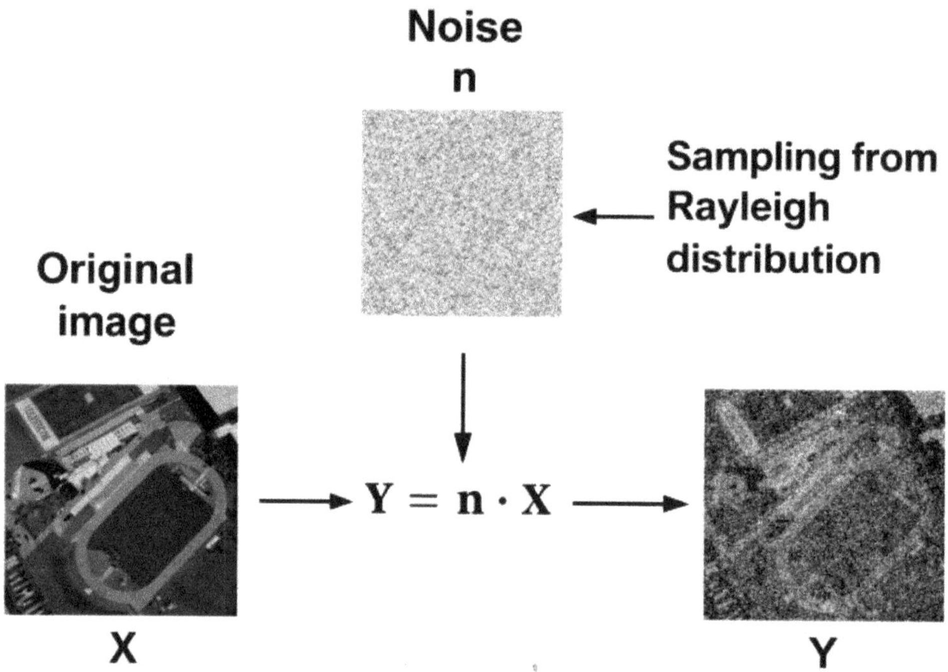

Figure 1. Dataset generation process for speckle-corrupted images. The original clean image X is multiplied by a noise sample n drawn from a Rayleigh distribution to produce the speckle-corrupted observation $Y = n \cdot X$. This simulates the multiplicative noise model commonly used in image degradation.

Image denoising is evaluated across additive levels of Gaussian white noise (AWGN) $\sigma \in \{15, 25, 50\}$, Poisson–Gaussian $\lambda \in \{1, 4, 8\}$, and speckle $\Gamma \in \{1, 4, 8\}$ in 8-bit images (range 0–255), following common practice. When images are normalized to $[0, 1]$, the corresponding standard deviation, for example, by AWGN is $\hat{\sigma} = \sigma/255$ and the variance is $\hat{\sigma}^2 = (\sigma/255)^2$, which yields $\hat{\sigma^2} \simeq \{1.2010^{-5}, 9.6010^{-5}, 3.8410^{-4}\}$.

4. Proposed Framework

The present study proposes the framework illustrated in Figure 2, which integrates classical PDE priors into a deep neural network through a composite loss function. The

https://doi.org/10.3390/electronics15030560

network processes a noisy image, denoted as $\hat{X}_N$, to produce a denoised output. Training is driven by Equation (10):

$$L_{\text{total}} = L_{\text{PDE}} + \lambda_1 L_{\text{perceptual}} + \lambda_2 L_{\text{data}} + \lambda_3 L_{\text{IC}} + \lambda_4 L_{\text{BC}} \quad (10)$$

The total loss $\mathcal{L}_{\text{total}}$ used to train the physics-informed neural network (PINN) comprises multiple components, each designed to enforce the fidelity, physical consistency, and perceptual quality of the data. The weighting coefficients λ are carefully tuned based on the validation performance to achieve an optimal balance between accurate data reconstruction and adherence to the underlying physical laws. Here, individual terms are defined as follows:

- **PDE Loss:** This term enforces that the prediction of the network $\hat{X}_r$ satisfies the underlying residual of the PDE $\mathcal{N}\theta(\cdot)$ by Equation (11). For each model, the derivatives in Equations (1)–(5) are obtained by automatic differentiation, ensuring exact gradients in terms of network parameters:

$$L_{\text{PDE}} = |\mathcal{N}\theta(\hat{X}_r)|_2^2 \quad (11)$$

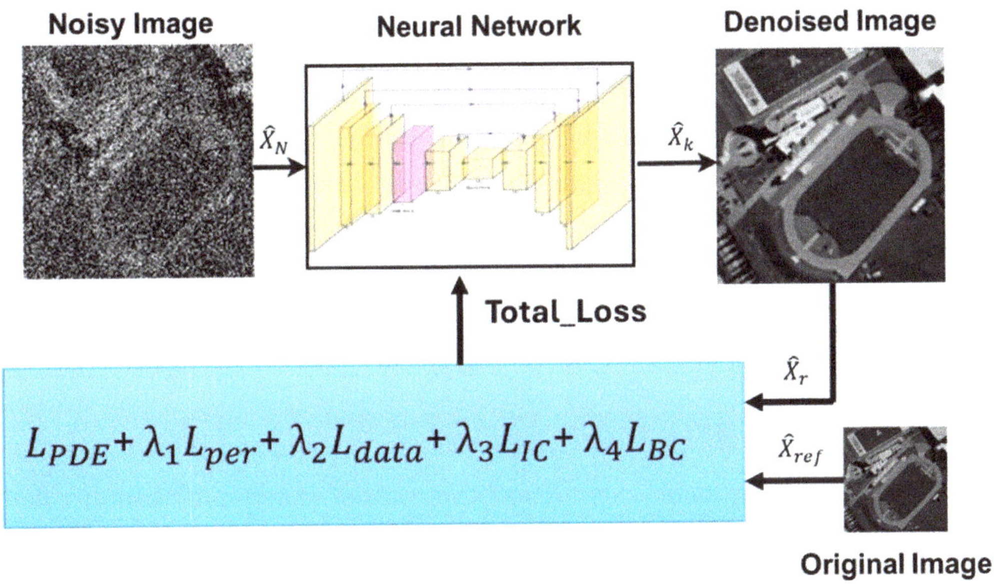

Figure 2. Denoising framework PINNs. A neural network processes the noisy input image $\hat{X}_N$ to produce a denoised output. The training is guided by a total loss function composed of a PDE-based loss (L_{PDE}), perceptual loss ($L_{perceptual}$), MSE loss data (L_{data}), initial condition loss (L_{IC}), and a boundary condition loss (L_{BC}), which enforces physical constraints derived from a partial differential equation (PDE). The network aims to minimize the discrepancy between the denoised image $\hat{X}_r$ and the original clean reference $\hat{X}_{ref}$.

- **Perceptual Loss:** The term "feature-space" ensures that the predicted image $\hat{X}_r$ remains perceptually close to the original clean image X_{ref} using the ℓ_1 norm by Equation (12). Let $\phi_l(\cdot)$ denote the activation in the layer l and w_l its weight:

$$L_{\text{perc}} = \sum_{l \in \mathcal{S}} w_l \left\| \phi_l(\hat{X}_r) - \phi_l(X_{\text{ref}}) \right\|_1. \quad (12)$$

https://doi.org/10.3390/electronics15030560

- **Data Loss:** This is a standard mean squared error term that compares the predicted and original images by Equation (13):

$$L_{\text{data}} = \left|\hat{X}_r - X_{ref}\right|_2^2 \tag{13}$$

- **Initial Condition Loss:** This term penalizes the deviation of the predicted field at $t = 0$ from the known initial image X_0:

$$L_{\text{IC}} = \frac{1}{|\Omega|} \sum_{p\in\Omega} w_{\text{IC}}(p) \left\|\widehat{X}_r(p,0) - X_0(p)\right\|_2^2, \tag{14}$$

  where $w_{\text{IC}}(p) \geq 0$ is an optional spatial weight or mask (e.g., to ignore unknown pixels). When the ground truth at $t = 0$ is not available, we set X_0 to the observed input (or a priori).

- **Boundary Condition Loss:** We support standard BC types on $\partial\Omega$; n denotes the normal outward unit. *Dirichlet BC* ($\widehat{X}_r = g$ on $\partial\Omega$):

$$L_{\text{BC}} = \frac{1}{|\partial\Omega|} \sum_{q\in\partial\Omega} w_{\text{BC}}(q) \left\|\widehat{X}_r(q,t) - g(q,t)\right\|_2^2. \tag{15}$$

5. Integrating PDE with Network DL Denoising

Four neural network architectures—UNet, ResUNet, U2Net, and ResU2Net—each integrated with the PDE formulation described in Section 3. All models were implemented in PyTorch and trained with the Adam optimizer using an early stopping criterion of loss $< 10^{-4}$ or a maximum of 500 epochs.

- **Case 1:** A UNet-based architecture was used for PDE-guided image denoising (see Figure 3). The network was specifically adapted to accommodate multi-scale feature extraction, incorporating a symmetric structure composed of downsampling and upsampling paths. The architecture consisted of two main stages:
  1. **Downsampling Path:** The encoder utilized a sequence of convolutional layers followed by max-pooling operations to progressively reduce the spatial dimensions of the input noisy image $\hat{X}_N$. The resolution of the feature map was sequentially downscaled through levels of 32, 64, 128, and 256 channels, allowing the abstraction of hierarchical features at multiple scales.
  2. **Upsampling Path:** The decoder used upsampling operations and convolutional layers to gradually restore the spatial resolution of the encoded features. Skip connections were integrated between the corresponding encoder and decoder layers to preserve fine-grained spatial details that are critical for accurate reconstruction.

  During training, the UNet was optimized not only to minimize the reconstruction error between the denoised output $\hat{X}_R$ and the ground truth image $\hat{X}_{ref}$, but also to satisfy a governing partial differential equation (PDE) model embedded within a composite loss function. Specifically, the total loss function combined three components: (i) a residual PDE loss enforcing physical consistency, (ii) an initial condition (IC) loss ensuring correct initialization behavior, and (iii) a boundary condition (BC) loss enforcing consistency along image borders. This physics-informed loss formulation guided the UNet to denoise in a manner aligned with the underlying diffusion dynamics, thereby improving generalization and preserving important structural features.

https://doi.org/10.3390/electronics15030560

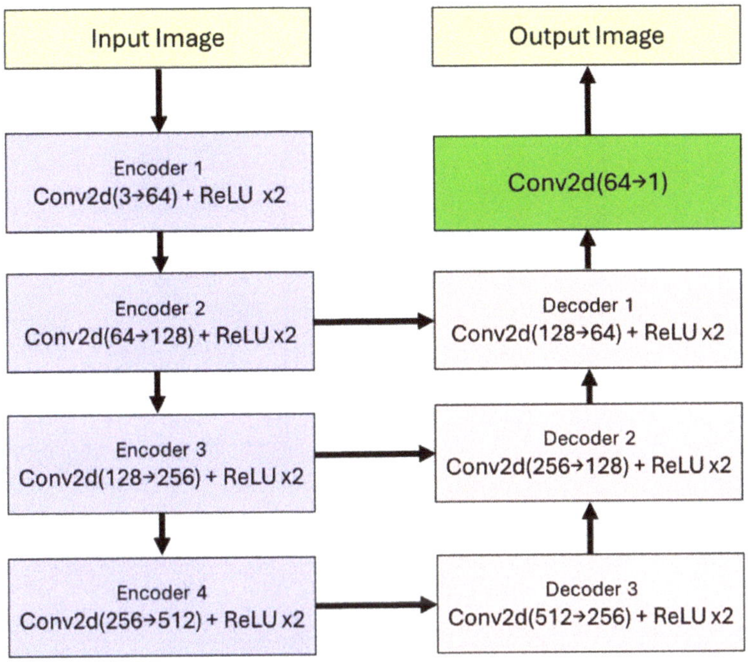

Figure 3. Denoise neural network model architecture UNet model.

- **Case 2:** Residual U-Net (ResUNet) architecture was used to perform image denoising under partial differential equation (PDE) constraints (see Figure 4). The model takes as input a noisy image $\hat{X}_N$ and outputs a denoised image $\hat{X}_R$. The ResUNet structure incorporates deep residual learning into the classical encoder–decoder U-Net design to facilitate better gradient flow and capture complex features critical for PDE-driven restoration tasks. The architecture consists of the following main components:

    1. **Encoder:** The encoder progressively extracts hierarchical characteristics through a sequence of downsampling stages. Each stage consists of a ResidualBlock, which applies two convolutional layers (with Batch Normalization and ReLU activation) and a skip connection that directly adds the input to the output. The encoder maps the noisy input $\hat{X}_N$ into a compact feature representation through the following encoder layer: enc1$\rightarrow$ enc2 $\rightarrow$ enc3 $\rightarrow$ enc4.
    2. **Decoder:** The decoder reconstructs spatial resolution by successive upsampling operations (using transposed convolutions), followed by residual blocks. Skip connections are used between encoder and decoder layers to preserve spatial information lost during downsampling. Before concatenation, a cropping operation ensures that the dimensions of feature maps align with the decoder layer: dec3 $\longleftarrow$ dec2 $\longleftarrow$ dec1.
    3. **Output Layer:** A final 1×1 convolution maps the feature space to a single-channel image $\hat{X}_R$, corresponding to the denoised reconstruction.

https://doi.org/10.3390/electronics15030560

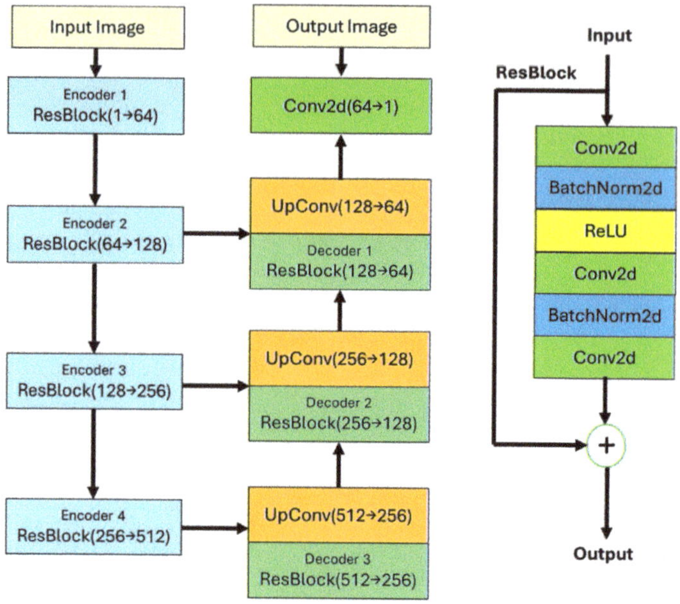

Figure 4. Denoise neural network model architecture: ResUNet model.

- **Case 3:** This case presents the U2Net architecture to perform image denoising under a physics-informed learning framework (see Figure 5a). The U2Net model, illustrated by the above class definition, processes a noisy image input $\hat{X}_N$ and outputs a denoised prediction $\hat{X}_R$, while leveraging a composite loss that includes PDE constraints. The U2Net is a deeply nested U-structure network composed of residual U-blocks (RSUs) at each stage. The model architecture can be summarized as follows:

  1. **Encoder:** The input noisy image $\hat{X}_N$ is first passed through multiple encoding stages: stage1 $\longrightarrow$ pool12 $\longrightarrow$ stage2 $\longrightarrow$ pool23 $\longrightarrow$ stage3 $\longrightarrow$ stage6.
  2. **Decoder:** After reaching the deepest feature representation ($hx6$), the network performs upsampling and decoding operations: stage5d $\longrightarrow$ to $\longrightarrow$ stage1d. Skip connections are implemented by concatenating encoder features with corresponding decoder layers, ensuring fine-grained spatial information is preserved.
  3. **Side Outputs:** Intermediate outputs (d1, d2, d3, d4, d5, d6) are generated at different resolutions through 1 × 1 convolutional layers, which are later fused to form the final denoised prediction d0.
  4. **Final Prediction:** The final denoised image $\hat{X}_R$ is obtained by applying a sigmoid activation function to the fused side outputs: $\hat{X}_R = \sigma(d0)$.

- **Case 4:** ResU2Net model, a lightweight variant of the U2Net architecture, was adapted to incorporate PDE priors for physics-informed noise removal (see Figure 5b). The network takes as input a noisy image $\hat{X}_N$ and produces a denoised output $\hat{X}_R$. The architecture is composed of multiple residual U-shaped (RSU) blocks, each designed to effectively capture multi-scale spatial features while maintaining computational efficiency:

  1. **Encoder:** The noisy image $\hat{X}_N$ is successively processed through six RSU stages (Stage 1 to Stage 6), where each stage refines the spatial representations using residual encoding. As shown in the schematic, each RSU block comprises a

https://doi.org/10.3390/electronics15030560

Conv2D+BatchNorm+ReLU stack, which applies downsampling to enlarge the receptive field while reducing spatial resolution.

2. **Decoder:** After the final encoder stage (Stage 6), the model reconstructs high-resolution features via a mirrored decoder structure. Each decoder stage (from Stage 5 to Stage 1) receives upsampled features concatenated with skip connections from its corresponding encoder stage, followed by residual RSU decoding blocks to recover spatial details. This design enables efficient feature reuse and context fusion.
3. **Residual Connections:** As highlighted in the image, skip connections and element-wise summation between encoder and decoder outputs enhance feature propagation and support robust gradient flow during training.
4. **Side Outputs and Deep Supervision:** The architecture includes six intermediate side outputs (denoted as d1 through d6), each extracted from a corresponding decoder stage. These outputs undergo upsampling and contribute to deep supervision, encouraging multi-scale feature learning.
5. **Final Reconstruction:** All side outputs are fused through a final convolutional layer (outconv) to generate the denoised output image $\hat{X}_R$.

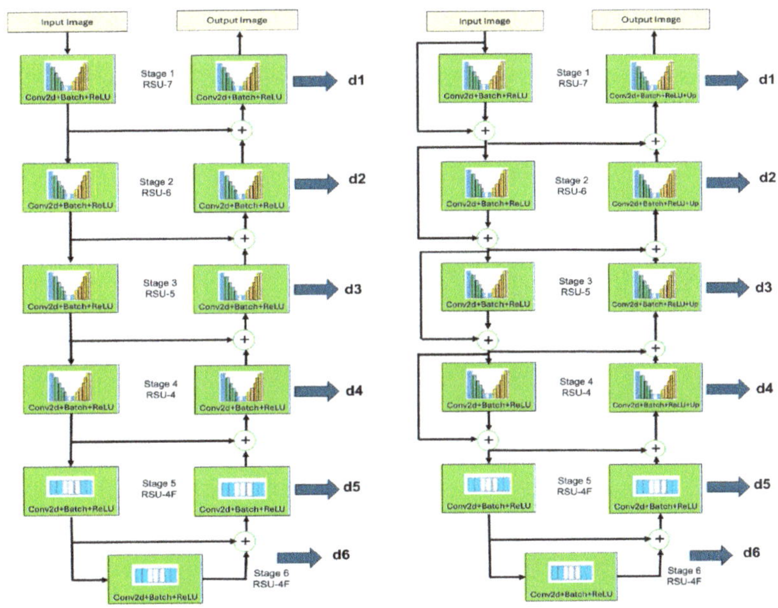

(a) (b)

Figure 5. Denoise neural network model architecture: (**a**) U2Net model. (**b**) Res-U2Net model.

6. Progressive Refinement via Physics-Informed Neural Network Denoising

Figure 6 illustrates the progressive improvement in image quality over iterations of the PINN-based denoising process [26]. Starting from the original and noisy inputs (top row), the bottom sequence shows how the model gradually reconstructs structural details while suppressing speckle noise. Early iterations retain high levels of noise and artifacts, whereas later stages achieve clearer and sharper restorations that closely resemble the ground truth. This highlights the capacity of the physics-informed approach to balance noise reduction with feature preservation throughout the training process.

https://doi.org/10.3390/electronics15030560

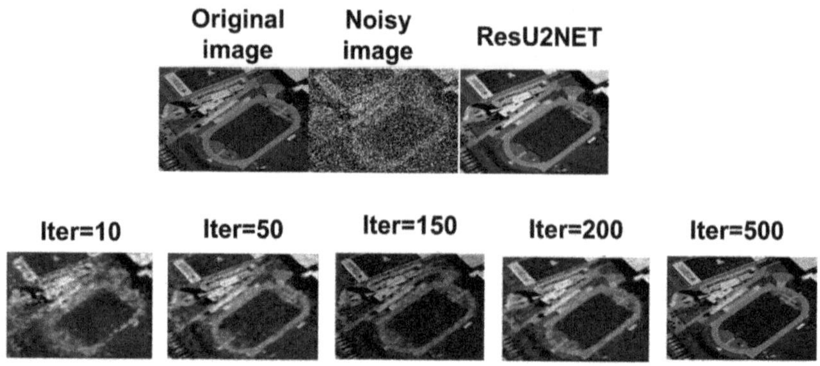

Figure 6. Evolution of the image denoising process using the proposed physics-informed neural network (PINN) framework. The top row shows the clean image, the speckle-corrupted noisy input, and the final denoised output. The bottom row illustrates the iterative refinement over multiple training steps, where the PINN progressively suppresses noise and restores structural details, converging toward the clean reference image.

PINN-Based Image Denoising: Pseudocode

The proposed algorithm (see Algorithm 1) performs image denoising (see Figure 7) based on PINN by integrating a neural network backbone, such as UNet or ResUNet, with a residual based on diffusion-based partial differential equations (PDE), following principles similar to those described in [44]. First, the chosen model is constructed with symmetric encoder–decoder stages (with skip connections or residual blocks). During training, each noisy input Y is passed through the network to produce a prediction $\widehat{u}$:

1. Data fidelity loss L_{data} (mean squared error between $\widehat{u}$ and the clean image X).
2. PDE loss L_{PDE} enforcement $\kappa\,\Delta\widehat{u} - \text{model}(\widehat{u}) \approx 0$.
3. Perceptual loss L_{perc} (L_1 distance).
4. Boundary Condition Loss$L_{\text{BC}} \rightarrow \text{MSE}(\hat{u}, 0)$.
5. Loss of initial condition $L_{\text{IC}} \rightarrow \text{MSE}(\hat{X}_{r0}, X_0)$.

The total loss is a weighted sum of these terms and is minimized via the Adam optimizer over a fixed number of epochs. Periodic logging of individual loss components ensures stable convergence. The final output is the denoised image $\widehat{X} = \text{model}(Y)$, which effectively suppresses the speckle while preserving structural details.

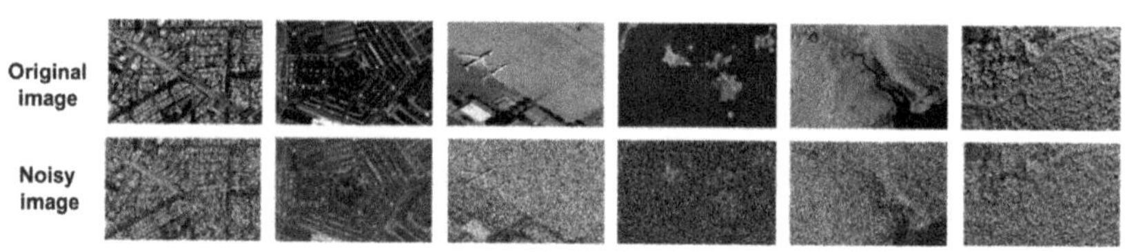

Figure 7. Visual comparison of original and speckle-corrupted images from the RESISC and AID datasets used in the PINN-based denoising simulation.

https://doi.org/10.3390/electronics15030560

Algorithm 1 Physics-informed PINN–PDE image denoising scheme

Require: Clean image X, noisy image Y, number of epochs E, architecture *arch*
Ensure: Denoised image $\widehat{X}$

Model construction

function BUILDMODEL(*arch*)
  if *arch* = "UNet" **then**
    Define encoder–decoder with standard UNet blocks
  else if *arch* = "ResUNet" **then**
    Define encoder–decoder with residual UNet blocks
  else if *arch* = "U2Net" **then**
    Define encoder–decoder with nested U^2 blocks
  else if *arch* = "ResU2Net" **then**
    Define encoder–decoder with residual U^2 blocks (ResU2Net–ZG backbone)
  end if
  return model_θ
end function

PDE residual

function DIFFUSIONRESIDUAL(u, model_θ, κ)
  Compute discrete Laplacian Δu using a fixed convolution kernel
  $\widehat{f}_\theta(u) \leftarrow \text{model}_\theta(u)$
  return $r(u) = \kappa\, \Delta u - \widehat{f}_\theta(u)$
end function

Loss function

function COMPUTELOSS($\widehat{u}$, X, model_θ)
  $L_{\text{data}} \leftarrow \text{MSE}(\widehat{u}, X)$
  $L_{\text{IC}} \leftarrow \text{MSE}(X_r, X_0)$ ▷ Initial-condition consistency
  $L_{\text{BC}} \leftarrow \text{MSE}(\widehat{u}_{|\partial\Omega}, 0)$ ▷ Boundary condition
  $L_{\text{PDE}} \leftarrow \text{MSE}(\text{DiffusionResidual}(\widehat{u}, \text{model}_\theta, \kappa), 0)$
  $L_{\text{perc}} \leftarrow L_1(\widehat{u}, X)$
  $L_{\text{total}} \leftarrow L_{\text{data}} + L_{\text{PDE}} + 0.1\, L_{\text{perc}} + 0.03\, L_{\text{IC}} + 0.02\, L_{\text{BC}}$
  return L_{total}
end function

Training loop

function TRAINPINN($X, Y, E, arch$)
  $\text{model}_\theta \leftarrow$ BUILDMODEL(*arch*)
  Initialize the Adam optimizer for parameters θ
  for $e = 1$ to E **do**
    $\widehat{u} \leftarrow \text{model}_\theta(Y)$
    Resize/crop $\widehat{u}$ to match the spatial size of X
    $L \leftarrow$ COMPUTELOSS($\widehat{u}, X, \text{model}_\theta$)
    Update θ with one Adam step using $\nabla_\theta L$
    if $e \bmod 100 = 0$ **then**
      Log e, L, L_{PDE} and L_{perc}
    end if
  end for
  return $\text{model}_\theta(Y)$
end function

Main procedure

Load X and generate Y (e.g., $Y \leftarrow \text{add\_speckle}(X)$)
$\widehat{X} \leftarrow$ TRAINPINN(X, Y, 500, "ResU2Net")
Display and/or save $\widehat{X}$

7. Experimental Results

The performance of the proposed PINN–PDE denoising framework was evaluated using a dedicated protocol (see Table 3). Specifically, we applied the system to aerial scene images from the RESISC and AID datasets [87,88]. To simulate noise (see Figures 8 and 9) and testing in the laboratory (see Figure 10), we used the widely accepted multiplicative noise model defined as $Y = N \cdot X$, where $Y \in \mathbb{R}^{W\times H}$ denotes the observed noisy image, $X \in \mathbb{R}^{W\times H}$ is the underlying clean image, and $N \in \mathbb{R}^{W\times H}$ represents the speckle component modeled using a Nakagami–Rayleigh distribution [86]. The enhanced (denoised) images were subsequently assessed using the neural network architecture described in Section 5. Methods were evaluated and compared using PSNR, SSIM, ENL, and CNR to validate the PINN approach across multiple neural network configurations (see Tables 4 and 5). PSNR quantifies the fidelity of the reconstruction in decibels (higher values are better; values >20 dB typically indicate acceptable quality). SSIM measures the perceptual similarity of luminance, contrast, and structure (higher is better; values >0.5 denote moderate to strong similarity). For speckle, the equivalent number of looks (ENL) gauges residual multiplicative noise within homogeneous regions (higher ENL indicates stronger speckle suppression). Finally, CNR assesses edge/target visibility relative to background noise (higher CNR is better suited for contrast and boundary preservation). Reporting all four metrics—PSNR/SSIM for fidelity, and ENL/CNR for speckle-specific behavior—provides a balanced basis for comparison with previous work [89,90].

Table 3. PDE-based deep learning denoising on 256 × 256 image inputs using different backbone architectures and GPU platforms.

Model	GeForce RTX 3060	Jetson Nano	Jetson Xavier
UNet	Real-time (20–30 FPS)	Slow (1–3 FPS)	Moderate (8–12 FPS)
ResUNet	Fast (15–20 FPS)	Slow (0.5–2 FPS)	Moderate (6–10 FPS)
U^2Net	Moderate (10–15 FPS)	Very slow (< 1 FPS)	Slow (4–7 FPS)
ResU^2Net	Moderate (8–12 FPS)	Not feasible without quantization	Slow (3–6 FPS)

Table 4. PSNR (dB) ↑ and SSIM ↑ scores for denoised images obtained with the heat, diffusion, MPMC, and ZG PDE models.

Method	Heat (PSNR/SSIM)	Diffusion (PSNR/SSIM)	MPMC (PSNR/SSIM)	ZG (PSNR/SSIM)
UNet	15.01/0.75	16.63/0.78	17.25/0.75	20.95/0.77
ResUNet	27.13/0.78	20.03/0.88	15.72/0.89	29.90/0.87
U2Net	26.70/0.79	25.69/0.90	16.44/0.93	30.82/0.89
ResU2Net	32.24/0.89	34.72/0.91	37.24/0.97	42.24/0.98

Table 5. ENL ↑ and CNR ↑ scores for denoised images obtained with the heat, diffusion, MPMC, and ZG PDE models. Higher values indicate better speckle suppression and contrast preservation.

Method	Heat (ENL/CNR)	Diffusion (ENL/CNR)	MPMC (ENL/CNR)	ZG (ENL/CNR)
UNet	8.01/2.55	10.00/2.12	8.30/2.25	9.69/4.36
ResUNet	9.10/6.06	9.58/3.41	10.24/6.46	11.21/4.53
U2Net	9.11/5.55	10.47/4.31	16.76/6.96	11.72/7.36
ResU2Net	9.61/6.43	11.60/4.46	18.58/8.30	22.24/9.61

https://doi.org/10.3390/electronics15030560

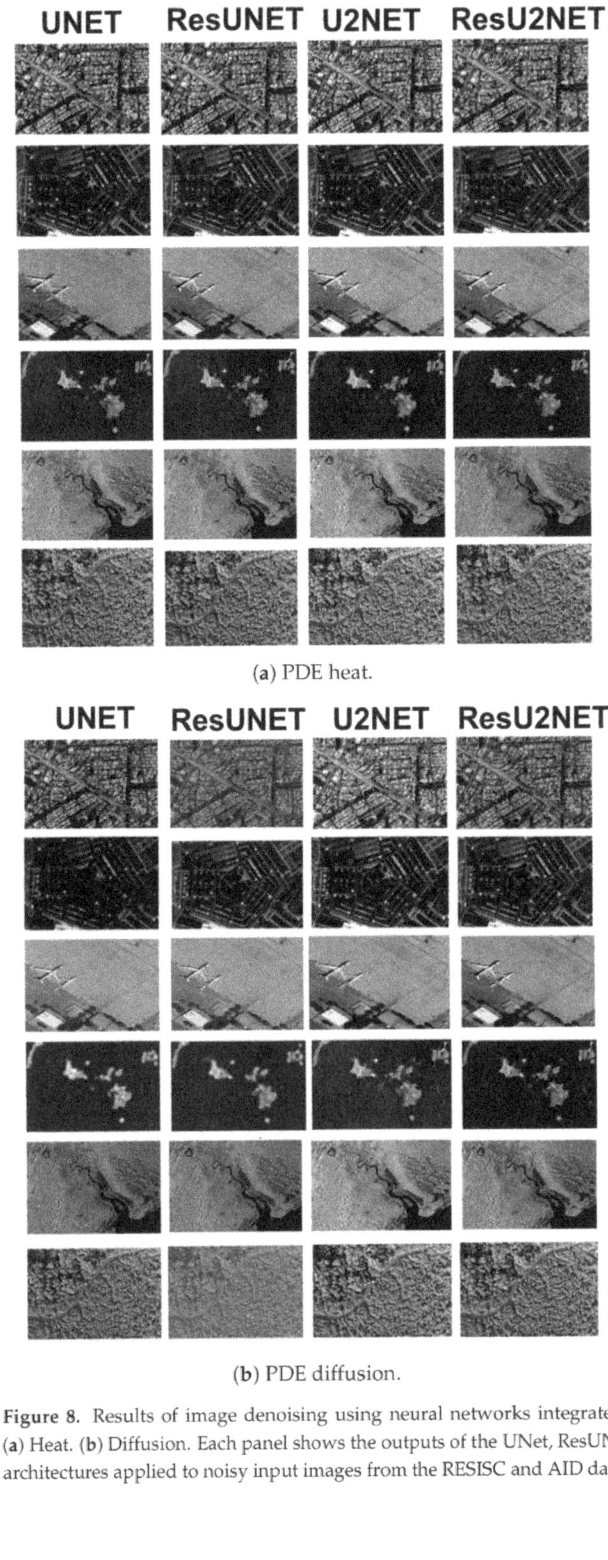

Figure 8. Results of image denoising using neural networks integrated with two PDE models: (**a**) Heat. (**b**) Diffusion. Each panel shows the outputs of the UNet, ResUNet, U2Net, and ResU2Net architectures applied to noisy input images from the RESISC and AID datasets.

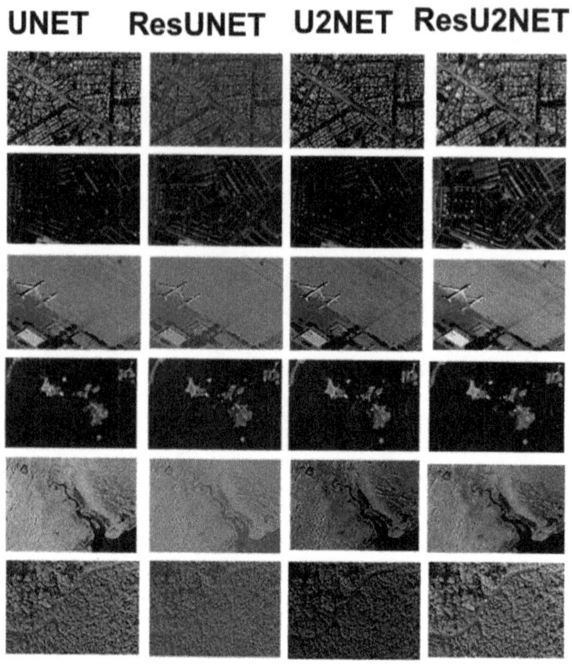

(a) PDE MPMC.

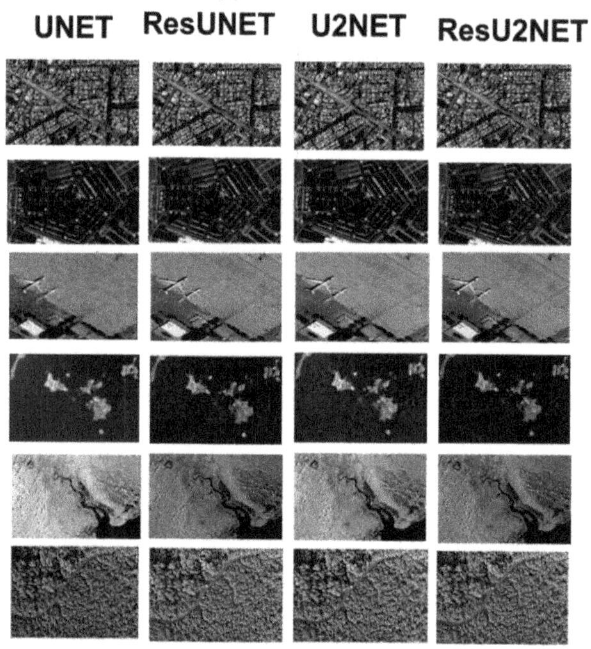

(b) PDE ZG.

Figure 9. Results of image denoising using neural networks integrated with four PDE models: (**a**) MPMC. (**b**) ZG. Each panel shows the outputs of the UNet, ResUNet, U2Net, and ResU2Net architectures applied to noisy input images from the RESISC and AID datasets.

https://doi.org/10.3390/electronics15030560

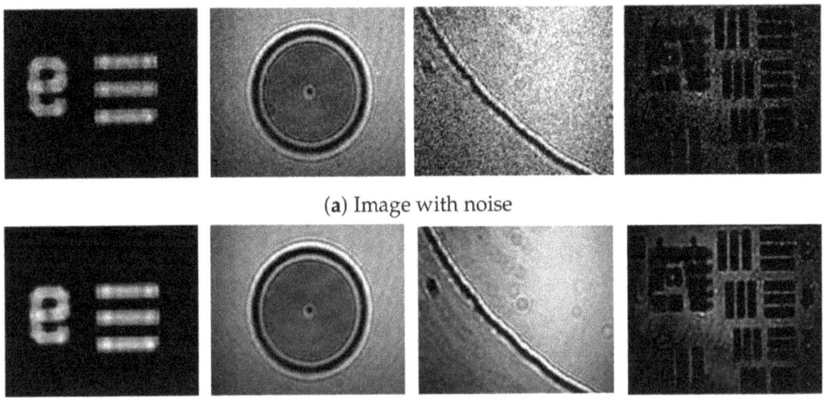

(**a**) Image with noise

(**b**) Denoised image

Figure 10. Experimental laboratory evaluation of image denoising performance using a ResU2Net architecture regularized by the ZG PDE model.

7.1. Correctness and Reliability Analysis

Given a noisy input image y, our network produces a reconstruction $\hat{x} = f_\theta(y)$ by minimizing a composite training objective:

$$\mathcal{L}_{\text{total}}(\theta) = \lambda_{\text{PDE}}\mathcal{L}_{\text{PDE}}(\hat{x}) + \lambda_1\mathcal{L}_{\text{per}}(\hat{x}) + \lambda_2\mathcal{L}_{\text{data}}(\hat{x}, x_{\text{ref}}) + \lambda_3\mathcal{L}_{\text{IC}}(\hat{x}) + \lambda_4\mathcal{L}_{\text{BC}}(\hat{x}), \quad (16)$$

where the PDE loss enforces numerical consistency with the selected prior through a discrete residual operator $\mathcal{R}(\cdot)$:

$$\mathcal{L}_{\text{PDE}}(\hat{x}) = \frac{1}{|\Omega|}\sum_{p\in\Omega}\|\mathcal{R}(\hat{x})(p)\|_2^2. \quad (17)$$

For the linear priors (heat/diffusion), $\mathcal{R}$ is a local, bounded finite-difference operator; hence $\mathcal{L}_{\text{PDE}}$ acts as a structured Tikhonov-like regularizer that stabilizes the mapping $y \mapsto \hat{x}$ by discouraging high-frequency components inconsistent with the PDE prior. For nonlinear priors (MPMC/ZG), $\mathcal{R}$ remains local and curvature-/edge-aware, providing a physically meaningful constraint that suppresses noise while preserving geometry. Although the overall optimization is non-convex due to f_θ, the PDE residual term improves reliability by shrinking the feasible set toward PDE-consistent reconstructions, reducing sensitivity to spurious solutions.

7.2. Repeatability Across Images and Noise Levels

Table 6 reports the PSNR standard test images under three Gaussian noise levels ($\sigma \in \{15, 25, 50\}$). A key reliability property is *consistent dominance*: our method attains the highest PSNR for *every image* and *every noise level*, indicating that performance is not driven by a small subset of favorable cases.

To quantify the effect size, we compare against the strongest deep baseline in Table 6 on a per-image basis and report the mean improvement with a 95% confidence interval (CI) over the 10 images:

$$\sigma = 15: \quad \Delta\text{PSNR} = 8.48\text{ dB } [7.21,\ 9.74]; \quad (18)$$

$$\sigma = 25: \quad \Delta\text{PSNR} = 9.33\text{ dB } [7.89,\ 10.78]; \quad (19)$$

$$\sigma = 50: \quad \Delta\text{PSNR} = 7.50\text{ dB } [5.09,\ 9.90]. \quad (20)$$

https://doi.org/10.3390/electronics15030560

Moreover, the improvement holds for images at each noise level, yielding a sign-test probability of $p = 2^{-10} \approx 9.77 \times 10^{-4}$ per noise level, which supports the notion that the gain is systematic rather than incidental. At the aggregate level (Average column in Table 6), our PSNR is also substantially higher: 41.19 vs. 32.87 dB ($\sigma = 15$), 39.58 vs. 30.43 dB ($\sigma = 25$), and 34.64 vs. 27.14 dB ($\sigma = 50$), confirming a large accuracy margin under increasingly severe corruption.

Table 6. PSNR (dB) achieved by competing image denoising methods on standard test images based on the ResU2Net–ZG method.

Method	C.Man	House	Peppers	Starfish	Monar	Airpl	Parrot	Boat	Man	Couple	Average
					$\sigma = 15$						
BM3D [18]	31.92	34.94	32.70	31.15	31.86	31.08	31.38	32.14	31.93	32.11	32.38
WNNM [91]	32.18	35.15	32.97	31.83	32.72	31.40	31.61	32.28	32.12	32.18	32.70
EPLL [92]	31.82	34.14	32.58	31.08	32.03	31.16	31.40	31.91	31.97	31.90	32.10
TNRD [93]	32.19	34.55	33.03	31.76	32.57	31.47	31.63	32.15	32.24	32.11	32.51
DnCNN-S [94]	32.62	35.00	33.29	32.23	33.10	31.70	31.84	32.42	32.47	32.47	32.87
MemNet [95]	32.51	35.10	33.31	32.12	33.04	31.53	31.73	32.43	32.45	32.49	32.83
Ours	**38.27**	**43.53**	**38.33**	**41.40**	**42.22**	**42.50**	**41.39**	**41.06**	**41.53**	**41.68**	**41.19**
					$\sigma = 25$						
BM3D	29.45	32.86	30.16	28.56	29.25	28.43	28.93	29.91	29.62	29.72	29.98
WNNM	29.64	33.23	30.40	29.03	29.85	29.69	29.12	30.03	29.77	29.82	30.26
EPLL	29.24	32.04	30.07	28.43	29.30	28.56	28.91	29.29	29.63	29.48	29.63
TNRD	29.71	32.54	30.55	29.02	29.86	28.98	29.18	29.92	29.88	29.71	30.66
DnCNN-S	30.19	33.09	30.85	29.40	30.23	29.13	29.42	30.22	30.11	30.12	30.43
MemNet	30.02	33.25	30.87	29.35	30.24	29.03	29.30	30.21	30.08	30.14	30.41
Ours	**37.90**	**42.99**	**35.57**	**39.80**	**41.84**	**40.40**	**37.47**	**38.72**	**41.02**	**40.13**	**39.58**
					$\sigma = 50$						
BM3D	26.13	29.69	26.68	25.04	25.82	25.10	25.90	26.78	26.81	26.46	26.73
WNNM	26.42	30.33	26.91	25.43	26.32	25.42	26.09	26.97	26.94	26.64	27.04
EPLL	26.02	28.76	26.63	25.04	25.78	25.24	25.84	26.65	26.72	26.24	26.35
TNRD	26.62	29.48	27.10	25.42	26.31	25.59	26.16	26.94	26.98	26.50	26.81
DnCNN-S	27.00	30.02	27.29	25.70	26.77	26.46	26.88	27.19	27.24	26.90	27.14
MemNet	27.24	30.70	27.51	25.76	27.19	26.96	26.50	27.06	27.24	27.14	27.40
Ours	**35.88**	**41.19**	**28.53**	**35.57**	**37.86**	**35.73**	**33.93**	**35.60**	**30.97**	**31.16**	**34.64**

7.3. Discussions

The simulation Figure 9 of the results demonstrates the effectiveness of the proposed PINN–PDE-based denoising framework in improving image quality and suppressing speckle noise across a variety of neural network backbones and PDE models. In Table 4, the PSNR and SSIM metrics consistently improve when any of the heat, diffusion, MPMC, or ZG PDE models are applied. Among these, the ZG model yields the highest overall gains in both metrics across all architectures. For example, ResU2Net achieves the best performance, reaching a PSNR of 42.24 dB and an SSIM of 0.98, indicating highly effective noise removal while preserving structural image details. The observed performance trend, heat < diffusion < MPMC < ZG, suggests that progressively more sophisticated PDE formulations provide stronger regularization and structural fidelity in the denoising process.

Similarly, Table 5 shows clear improvements in ENL and CNR, which are critical for evaluating speckle suppression and contrast preservation. Again, the ZG model stands out, with ResU2Net achieving the highest scores. ENL = 22.24 and CNR = 9.61 dB, indicating excellent homogeneity in flat regions and strong contrast between regions of interest. Notably, the MPMC and diffusion models also show competitive results, outperforming simpler models like heat, particularly in terms of CNR.

https://doi.org/10.3390/electronics15030560

Compared with traditional methods (see Tables 6 and 7) such as models based on BM3D, EPLL, TNRD, MEmNet, SAR-DRN, WNNM, and PDE, our proposed methods show moderate performance, with PSNR values below 32 dB and SSIM scores ranging from 0.81 to 0.89. Deep learning-based models such as DnCNN, ECNDNet, and RSIDNet achieve better results, with PSNR around 31.6–31.9 dB and SSIM up to 0.94. In particular, ADNet, an attention-guided CNN, achieves the best among these with 34.14 dB PSNR and 0.96 SSIM. However, the proposed PINN-ResU2Net model significantly outperforms all others, achieving a PSNR of 42.24 dB and an SSIM of 0.98, demonstrating the effectiveness of combining physics-informed neural networks with the ResU2Net architecture for high-quality image denoising.

Although the proposed PINN–PDE-based denoising framework demonstrates state-of-the-art performance in PSNR, SSIM, ENL, and CNR, several limitations remain. The current evaluation relies mainly on simulated and benchmark datasets, which may not fully reflect the variability and complexity of real-world noise patterns. Joint optimization of PDE residuals and network parameters also introduces additional computational cost, particularly for large-scale or high-resolution images. Moreover, the framework currently employs a fixed set of PDE models (heat, diffusion, MPMC, and ZG), which may limit its adaptability to different noise characteristics. Future work will focus on extending the framework to real-world and multimodal datasets, enhancing computational efficiency through model compression and hardware acceleration, and incorporating adaptive PDE selection strategies. Integration of uncertainty estimation into the PINN formulation is also planned to improve the interpretability and reliability of the model.

The proposed model achieves strong accuracy in speckle-degraded images (see Table 8), outperforming classical and several modern baselines in our setting while remaining interpretable through its PDE priors. Compared with transformer denoisers and diffusion models, it is lighter and more data-efficient; although those methods can reach higher peaks on natural images at a greater memory/compute cost. Unlike self-supervised/SAR-specific approaches, our supervised, physics-guided design preserves structures more reliably when clean supervision is available and generalizes well across backbones; however, it introduces extra loss terms and training overhead. Deep-unrolling and plug-and-play frameworks offer strong generalization but incur iterative inference; GAN variants enhance perceptual sharpness, yet risk hallucinations; wavelet-domain nets are efficient but less flexible. In general, our method strikes a practical balance of quality, robustness, and interpretability for speckle denoising, with the main trade-off being the additional computation of physics-informed losses.

The results in Tables 9 and 10 demonstrate the scalability and versatility of the proposed denoising framework across a wide range of datasets with different image characteristics and under varying noise conditions. Consistently high PSNR and SSIM values across all noise levels indicate robust generalization, particularly for challenging scenarios such as high variability AWGN ($\sigma = 50$) and strong multiplicative noise ($\Gamma = 8$). Performance remains stable across both natural and remote sensing datasets, highlighting the adaptability of the method to varying image domains and noise distributions.

https://doi.org/10.3390/electronics15030560

Table 7. Numerical evaluations on image denoising and speckle suppression. The proposed ResU2Net–ZG method consistently outperforms competing approaches.

Method	PSNR (dB) ↑	SSIM ↑	Model
SAR-DRN [96]	27.93	0.81	UNet with TV regularization.
RSIDNet [97]	31.84	0.94	CNN-based encoder–attention–decoder architecture.
DnCNN [94]	31.90	0.93	Feed-forward denoising convolutional neural network.
ECNDNet [98]	31.60	0.93	Convolutional neural denoising network.
ADNet [99]	34.14	0.96	Attention-guided denoising convolutional neural network.
WNNM [91]	31.90	0.85	Weighted nuclear norm minimization.
$TV\text{-}L^2$ [100]	30.28	0.89	Nonlinear PDE-based total variation model (L^2 fidelity).
$TV\text{-}H^{-1}$ [100]	31.53	0.89	Nonlinear PDE-based total variation model (H^{-1} fidelity).
Pureformer [43]	29.64	0.86	Transformer-based Image Denoising.
Diffusion Models [101]	31.64	—	Denoising Diffusion Models with Iteratively Preconditioned Guidance.
Self-argumented(ViT) [102]	25.53	0.75	Noise2Noise Image Denoising.
Deep Image Prior [103]	33.10	0.961	Deep Image Prior for image denoising.
Ours	**42.24**	**0.98**	**PINN–ResU2Net (physics-informed ResU2Net with ZG prior).**

Table 8. Overview comparison between modern image denoising techniques and the proposed ResU2Net–ZG model.

Method	PSNR/SSIM	Pros	Cons
Transformer denoisers [104]	51.16/0.99	High reconstruction quality on natural images.	Increased memory footprint and computational cost.
Diffusion models [101]	32.40/—	Flexible modeling of complex noise distributions.	High training and sampling complexity.
Self-supervised/unsupervised [105]	32.46/0.81	Do not require clean target images for training.	Typically trail supervised state-of-the-art performance.
Deep unrolling [106]	30.19/0.80	Strong generalization linked to iterative optimization priors.	Requires careful tuning and model-specific design.
GAN-based denoisers [107]	32.87/—	Good perceptual quality and sharper textures.	Training and stabilization are more difficult.
Wavelet-domain deep learning [108]	28.55/—	Good detail recovery in the transform domain.	May be less flexible across diverse noise types.
Speckle-specific self-supervised [109]	30.61/0.88	Preserves structural information in speckle-dominated images.	Performance can be sensitive to acquisition conditions.
Ours (ResU2Net–ZG)	**42.24/0.98**	**Robust denoising when labeled data are scarce; physics-informed prior.**	**More complex loss design and higher computational cost.**

Table 9. Quantitative comparison of denoising performance of ResU2Net–ZG across multiple datasets and noise models (AWGM and Poisson–Gaussian).

Dataset	AWGM			Poisson–Gaussian		
	$\sigma = 15$	$\sigma = 25$	$\sigma = 50$	$\lambda = 1$	$\lambda = 4$	$\lambda = 8$
AID [88]	33.00/0.90	38.20/0.96	39.49/0.98	38.26/0.96	40.23/0.98	40.60/0.98
BSD68 [110]	36.81/0.97	29.54/0.88	28.45/0.84	38.77/0.98	37.70/0.97	37.47/0.97
Urban100 [111]	40.69/0.97	39.23/0.96	28.04/0.87	39.43/0.97	39.26/0.96	38.64/0.96
DIV2K [112]	40.37/0.97	39.17/0.97	38.72/0.97	41.68/0.98	40.00/0.97	39.20/0.96
Kodak24 [113]	39.41/0.96	39.15/0.96	33.69/0.87	38.61/0.96	39.69/0.97	40.93/0.97
Set12 [1]	33.48/0.92	33.50/0.91	36.88/0.95	36.96/0.96	37.11/0.95	38.02/0.96
RESISC [87]	40.65/0.97	36.58/0.92	33.24/0.86	41.27/0.98	40.16/0.97	40.48/0.97

https://doi.org/10.3390/electronics15030560

Table 10. Quantitative comparison of denoising performance of ResU2Net–ZG across multiple datasets for speckle noise.

Dataset	Speckle		
	$\Gamma = 1$	$\Gamma = 4$	$\Gamma = 8$
AID [88]	40.18/0.97	38.94/0.97	38.64/0.96
BSD68 [110]	39.86/0.98	38.53/0.97	36.12/0.97
Urban100 [111]	39.57/0.98	38.79/0.95	38.03/0.95
DIV2K [112]	41.90/0.97	40.19/0.97	39.79/0.96
Kodak24 [113]	38.65/0.95	39.07/0.96	39.29/0.96
Set12 [1]	37.37/0.96	38.33/0.96	38.49/0.96
RESISC [87]	40.79/0.98	40.16/0.96	37.37/0.95

8. Conclusions and Future Work

This study presented a physics-informed denoising framework that integrates four partial differential equation (PDE) priors: heat, diffusion, MPMC, and ZG—into deep neural network architectures to address image denoising and speckle suppression. Theoretically, the work establishes a bridge between classical PDE-based modeling and modern deep learning, enhancing interpretability and improving noise suppression by embedding physical priors into the learning process. Practically, the proposed framework demonstrates strong reconstruction performance, achieving high PSNR, SSIM, ENL, and CNR values on the RESISC and AID aerial datasets, with the ZG prior in combination with ResU2Net providing the most consistent results. This confirms the effectiveness of the PINN–PDE approach in restoring speckle-degraded imagery across different backbones of the network.

The main contributions of this research are threefold. First, it introduces a unified PINN–PDE denoising strategy that is generalizable across architectures. Second, it provides a systematic comparison of the PDE priors, identifying the ZG model as particularly effective. Third, it validates the framework for challenging aerial imagery, achieving state-of-the-art results in multiple quality metrics. These contributions highlight the value of incorporating physics-based constraints into deep learning for robust image restoration. In practical terms, the framework offers several advantages. By leveraging PDE priors, it reduces dependence on large labeled datasets, making it suitable for real-world applications where ground truth is limited. Its modular structure enables easy integration with existing neural models, and the enhanced preservation of structural details makes it well-suited for downstream tasks such as classification, object detection, and change analysis. Moreover, the use of interpretable PDE dynamics increases trust and traceability, which are critical in sensitive domains such as environmental monitoring and medical imaging.

The experiments rely mainly on simulated and benchmark datasets, which may not fully capture the complexity of real-world noise. Joint optimization of PDE residuals and network parameters increases computational costs, particularly for high-resolution images. Furthermore, the use of fixed PDE priors constrains the adaptability of the framework to complex or mixed noise types. Future research will address these challenges by developing adaptive PDE learning strategies that dynamically tune the priors during training and incorporate attention mechanisms and multi-scale representations to better preserve edges and fine structures. We will also extend the framework to realistic noise and acquisition conditions through systematic stress tests, including saturation/clipping augmentation with censored-loss training, EMI-like artifact modeling (stripe/impulse/burst corruption), and misregistration robustness via controlled shifts/warps and joint alignment–denoising. Finally, we will optimize the method for efficient, low-power deployment (FPGA/embedded-GPU), enabling integration into operational imaging pipelines and edge devices, thereby increasing its practical impact.

https://doi.org/10.3390/electronics15030560

Author Contributions: Conceptualization, C.O.Q.; Methodology, C.O.Q.; Software, C.O.Q.; Validation, C.O.Q.; Investigation, C.O.Q.; Writing—original draft, C.O.Q. and M.L.C.; Writing—review & editing, C.O.Q. and M.L.C.; Supervision, M.L.C. All authors have read and agreed to the published version of the manuscript.

Funding: This research received no external funding.

Data Availability Statement: The data presented in this study are available on request from the corresponding author.

Acknowledgments: The first author is thankful to Consejo Nacional de Ciencia y Tecnología (CONACYT) for his scholarship with No. CVU: 661331. I would like to acknowledge support from the ICTP through the Associates Program (2024-2029).

Conflicts of Interest: The authors declare no conflicts of interest.

Abbreviations

The following abbreviations are used in this manuscript:

AWGN	Additive White Gaussian Noise
CNN	Convolutional Neural Networks
CNR	Contrast-to-Noise Ratio
ENL	Equivalent Number of Looks
GPU	Graphics Processing Unit
MPMC	Modified Perona–Malik Curvature
PDE	Partial Differential Equation
PINNs	Physics-Informed Neural Networks
PSNR	Peak Signal-to-Noise Ratio
SAR	Synthetic Aperture Radar
SSIM	Structural Similarity Index
VIS	Visible Wavelengths
ZG	Zhichang Guo

References

1. Fan, L.; Zhang, F.; Fan, H.; Zhang, C. Brief review of image denoising techniques. *Vis. Comput. Ind. Biomed. Art* **2019**, *2*, 7. [CrossRef]
2. Osorio Quero, C.A.; Durini, D.; Rangel-Magdaleno, J.; Martinez-Carranza, J. Single-pixel imaging: An overview of different methods to be used for 3D space reconstruction in harsh environments. *Rev. Sci. Instruments* **2021**, *92*, 111501. [CrossRef] [PubMed]
3. Osorio Quero, C.; Durini, D.; Martinez-Carranza, J. ViT-Based Classification and Self-Supervised 3D Human Mesh Generation from NIR Single-Pixel Imaging. *Appl. Sci.* **2025**, *15*, 6138. [CrossRef]
4. Osorio Quero, C.; Durini, D.; Rangel-Magdaleno, J.; Martinez-Carranza, J.; Ramos-Garcia, R. Single-Pixel Near-Infrared 3D Image Reconstruction in Outdoor Conditions. *Micromachines* **2022**, *13*, 795. [CrossRef]
5. Chan, D.; Gambini, J.; Frery, A. Speckle Noise Reduction In Sar Images Using Information Theory. In *2020 IEEE Latin American GRSS & ISPRS Remote Sensing Conference (LAGIRS)*; IEEE: New York, NY, USA, 2020; pp. 456–461. [CrossRef]
6. Quero, C.O.; Martinez-Carranza, J. Unmanned aerial systems in search and rescue: A global perspective on current challenges and future applications. *Int. J. Disaster Risk Reduct.* **2025**, *118*, 105199. [CrossRef]
7. Yapici, A.; Akcayol, M.A. A Review of Image Denoising with Deep Learning. In *2021 2nd International Informatics and Software Engineering Conference (IISEC)*; IEEE: New York, NY, USA, 2021; pp. 1–6. [CrossRef]
8. Ghose, S.; Singh, N.; Singh, P. Image Denoising using Deep Learning: Convolutional Neural Network. In *2020 10th International Conference on Cloud Computing, Data Science & Engineering (Confluence)*; IEEE: New York, NY, USA, 2020; pp. 511–517. [CrossRef]
9. Ahamed, B.; Yuvaraj, D.; Priya, S.S. Image Denoising with Linear and Non-linear Filters. In *2019 International Conference on Computational Intelligence and Knowledge Economy (ICCIKE)*; IEEE: New York, NY, USA, 2019; pp. 806–810. [CrossRef]
10. Pushpavalli, R.; Srinivasan, E.; Himavathi, S. A New Nonlinear Filtering Technique for Image Denoising. In *2010 International Conference on Advances in Recent Technologies in Communication and Computing*; IEEE: New York, NY, USA, 2010; pp. 1–4. [CrossRef]

https://doi.org/10.3390/electronics15030560

11. Thakur, R.S.; Chatterjee, S.; Yadav, R.N.; Gupta, L. Image De-Noising with Machine Learning: A Review. *IEEE Access* **2021**, *9*, 93338–93363. [CrossRef]
12. Hou, X.; Luo, H.; Liu, J.; Xu, B.; Sun, K.; Gong, Y.; Liu, B.; Qiu, G. Learning Deep Image Priors for Blind Image Denoising. In *2019 IEEE/CVF Conference on Computer Vision and Pattern Recognition Workshops (CVPRW)*; IEEE: New York, NY, USA, 2019; pp. 1738–1747. [CrossRef]
13. Zha, Z.; Yuan, X.; Wen, B.; Zhang, J.; Zhou, J.; Zhu, C. Simultaneous Nonlocal Self-Similarity Prior for Image Denoising. In *2019 IEEE International Conference on Image Processing (ICIP)*; IEEE: New York, NY, USA, 2019; pp. 1119–1123. [CrossRef]
14. Rees, W.G.; Satchell, M.J.F. The effect of median filtering on synthetic aperture radar images. *Int. J. Remote Sens.* **1997**, *18*, 2887–2893. [CrossRef]
15. Liu, H.; Zhang, J.; Xiong, R. CAS: Correlation Adaptive Sparse Modeling for Image Denoising. *IEEE Trans. Comput. Imaging* **2021**, *7*, 638–647. [CrossRef]
16. Li, Z.; Liu, H.; Cheng, L.; Jia, X. Image Denoising Algorithm Based on Gradient Domain Guided Filtering and NSST. *IEEE Access* **2023**, *11*, 11923–11933. [CrossRef]
17. Chen, T.L. A Markov Random Field Model for Medical Image Denoising. In *2009 2nd International Conference on Biomedical Engineering and Informatics*; IEEE: New York, NY, USA, 2009; pp. 1–6. [CrossRef]
18. Alnuaimy, A.N.H.; Jawad, A.M.; Abdulkareem, S.A.; Mustafa, F.M.; Ivanchenko, S.; Toliupa, S. BM3D Denoising Algorithms for Medical Image. In *2024 35th Conference of Open Innovations Association (FRUCT)*; IEEE: New York, NY, USA, 2024; pp. 135–141. [CrossRef]
19. Zhao, B.; Sveinsson, J.R.; Ulfarsson, M.O.; Chanussot, J. Local Spatial-Spectral Correlation Based Mixtures of Factor Analyzers for Hyperspectral Denoising. In *IGARSS 2020—2020 IEEE International Geoscience and Remote Sensing Symposium*; IEEE: New York, NY, USA, 2020; pp. 1488–1491. [CrossRef]
20. Liu, Y.; Xu, S.; Lin, Z. An Improved Combination of Image Denoisers Using Spatial Local Fusion Strategy. *IEEE Access* **2020**, *8*, 150407–150421. [CrossRef]
21. Jia, L.; Zhang, Q.; Shang, Y.; Wang, Y.; Liu, Y.; Wang, N.; Gui, Z.; Yang, G. Denoising for Low-Dose CT Image by Discriminative Weighted Nuclear Norm Minimization. *IEEE Access* **2018**, *6*, 46179–46193. [CrossRef]
22. Liu, Z.; Yan, W.Q.; Yang, M.L. Image denoising based on a CNN model. In *2018 4th International Conference on Control, Automation and Robotics (ICCAR)*; IEEE: New York, NY, USA, 2018; pp. 389–393. [CrossRef]
23. Ren, H.; El-khamy, M.; Lee, J. DN-ResNet: Efficient Deep Residual Network for Image Denoising. In *Computer Vision—ACCV 2018*; Jawahar, C., Li, H., Mori, G., Schindler, K., Eds.; Springer International Publishing: Cham, Switzerland, 2019; pp. 215–230.
24. Tran, L.D.; Nguyen, S.M.; Arai, M. GAN-Based Noise Model for Denoising Real Images. In *Computer Vision—ACCV 2020*; Ishikawa, H., Liu, C.L., Pajdla, T., Shi, J., Eds.; Springer International Publishing: Cham, Switzerland, 2021; pp. 560–572.
25. Momen-Tayefeh, M.; Momen-Tayefeh, M.; Hasheminasab, F.Z.; Ghahramani, S.A.G. SNRGAN: The Semi Noise Reduction GAN for Image Denoising. In *2024 20th CSI International Symposium on Artificial Intelligence and Signal Processing (AISP)*; IEEE: New York, NY, USA, 2024; pp. 1–5. [CrossRef]
26. Farea, A.; Yli-Harja, O.; Emmert-Streib, F. Understanding Physics-Informed Neural Networks: Techniques, Applications, Trends, and Challenges. *AI* **2024**, *5*, 1534–1557. [CrossRef]
27. Zhang, X.; Wang, R.; Jiao, L.C. Partial Differential Equation Model Method Based on Image Feature for Denoising. In *2011 International Workshop on Multi-Platform/Multi-Sensor Remote Sensing and Mapping*; IEEE: New York, NY, USA, 2011; pp. 1–4. [CrossRef]
28. Lakshmi, K.; Parvathy, R.; Soumya, S.; Soman, K.P. Image denoising solutions using heat diffusion equation. In *2012 International Conference on Power, Signals, Controls and Computation*; IEEE: New York, NY, USA, 2012; pp. 1–5. [CrossRef]
29. Yu, J.; Chen, L.; Zhou, S. A Fractional Differential Fidelity-based PDE Model for Image Denoising. In *2018 Chinese Automation Congress (CAC)*; IEEE: New York, NY, USA, 2018; pp. 3727–3731. [CrossRef]
30. Perona, P.; Malik, J. Scale-space and edge detection using anisotropic diffusion. *IEEE Trans. Pattern Anal. Mach. Intell.* **1990**, *12*, 629–639. [CrossRef]
31. Zaabouli, Z.; Hakoume, A.E.; Afraites, L.; Laghrib, A. A novel coupled p(x) and fractional PDE denoising model with theoretical results. *Int. J. Comput. Math.* **2024**, *101*, 1300–1325. [CrossRef]
32. Ashouri, F.; Eslahchi, M.R. A new PDE learning model for image denoising. *Neural Comput. Appl.* **2022**, *34*, 8551–8574. [CrossRef]
33. Shen, J.; Cheng, X.; Yang, X.; Zhang, L.; Cheng, W.; Lin, Y. Efficient CNN Accelerator Based on Low-End FPGA with Optimized Depthwise Separable Convolutions and Squeeze-and-Excite Modules. *AI* **2025**, *6*, 244. [CrossRef]
34. Kang, W.; Wu, X.; Zhang, M.; Zhang, X.; Huang, X.; Sun, B.; Zhou, Q. Improvement and Hardware Design of Image Denoising Algorithm Based on Deep Learning. In *2024 9th International Conference on Integrated Circuits and Microsystems (ICICM)*; IEEE: New York, NY, USA, 2024; pp. 671–676. [CrossRef]
35. Ilesanmi, A.E.; Ilesanmi, T.O. Methods for image denoising using convolutional neural network: A review. *Complex Intell. Syst.* **2021**, *7*, 2179–2198. [CrossRef]

https://doi.org/10.3390/electronics15030560

36. Fang, W.; Li, H. A self-supervised CNN for image denoising with self-similarity prior. In *2022 16th IEEE International Conference on Signal Processing (ICSP)*; IEEE: New York, NY, USA, 2022; Volume 1, pp. 66–69. [CrossRef]
37. Li, H.; Liu, F. Image Denoising Via Sparse and Redundant Representations Over Learned Dictionaries in Wavelet Domain. In *2009 Fifth International Conference on Image and Graphics*; IEEE: New York, NY, USA, 2009; pp. 754–758. [CrossRef]
38. Zaman, F.A.; Jacob, M.; Chang, A.; Liu, K.; Sonka, M.; Wu, X. Surf-CDM: Score-Based Surface Cold-Diffusion Model for Medical Image Segmentation. In *2024 IEEE International Symposium on Biomedical Imaging (ISBI)*; IEEE: New York, NY, USA, 2024; pp. 1–5. [CrossRef]
39. Azzari, L.; Foi, A. Variance stabilization in Poisson image deblurring. In *2017 IEEE 14th International Symposium on Biomedical Imaging (ISBI 2017)*; IEEE: New York, NY, USA, 2017; pp. 728–731. [CrossRef]
40. Jin, Y.; Jiang, X.; Jiang, W. An image denoising approach based on adaptive nonlocal total variation. *J. Vis. Commun. Image Represent.* **2019**, *65*, 102661. [CrossRef]
41. Liua, J.; Shi, C.; Gao, M. Image denoising based on BEMD and PDE. In *2011 3rd International Conference on Computer Research and Development*; IEEE: New York, NY, USA, 2011; Volume 3, pp. 110–112. [CrossRef]
42. Che, J.; Guan, Q.; Wang, X. Image denoising based on adaptive fractional partial differential equations. In *2013 6th International Congress on Image and Signal Processing (CISP)*; IEEE: New York, NY, USA, 2013; Volume 1; pp. 288–292. [CrossRef]
43. Gautam, A.; Pawar, A.; Joshi, A.; Tazi, S.N.; Chaudhary, S.; Hambadre, P.; Dudhane, A.; Vipparthi, S.K.; Murala, S. Pureformer: Transformer-Based Image Denoising. In *2025 IEEE/CVF Conference on Computer Vision and Pattern Recognition Workshops (CVPRW)*; IEEE: New York, NY, USA, 2025; pp. 1–9. [CrossRef]
44. Liu, J.; Wang, Q.; Fan, H.; Wang, Y.; Tang, Y.; Qu, L. Residual Denoising Diffusion Models. In *2024 IEEE/CVF Conference on Computer Vision and Pattern Recognition (CVPR)*; IEEE: New York, NY, USA, 2024; pp. 2773–2783. [CrossRef]
45. Zhang, C.; Yen, K.S. Exploration of explicit regularization terms in deep image prior. In *International Conference on Green Energy, Computing and Intelligent Technology 2024 (GEn-CITy 2024)*; IET: London, UK, 2024; Volume 2024; pp. 50–55. [CrossRef]
46. Liang, J.; Cao, J.; Sun, G.; Zhang, K.; Van Gool, L.; Timofte, R. SwinIR: Image Restoration Using Swin Transformer. In *2021 IEEE/CVF International Conference on Computer Vision Workshops (ICCVW)*; IEEE: New York, NY, USA, 2021; pp. 1833–1844. [CrossRef]
47. Jiang, H.; Imran, M.; Zhang, T.; Zhou, Y.; Liang, M.; Gong, K.; Shao, W. Fast-DDPM: Fast Denoising Diffusion Probabilistic Models for Medical Image-to-Image Generation. *IEEE J. Biomed. Health Inform.* **2025**, *29*, 7326–7335. [CrossRef]
48. Kaya, M.O.; Oktem, F.S. DDRM-PR: Fourier phase retrieval using denoising diffusion restoration models. *Appl. Opt.* **2025**, *64*, A95–A105. [CrossRef] [PubMed]
49. Chen, B.H.; Yin, J.L.; Li, Y. Image Noise Removing Using Semi-supervised Learning on Big Image Data. In *2017 IEEE Third International Conference on Multimedia Big Data (BigMM)*; IEEE: New York, NY, USA, 2017; pp. 338–345. [CrossRef]
50. Pang, T.; Zheng, H.; Quan, Y.; Ji, H. Recorrupted-to-Recorrupted: Unsupervised Deep Learning for Image Denoising. In *2021 IEEE/CVF Conference on Computer Vision and Pattern Recognition (CVPR)*; IEEE: New York, NY, USA, 2021; pp. 2043–2052. [CrossRef]
51. Young, S.I.; Dalca, A.V.; Ferrante, E.; Golland, P.; Metzler, C.A.; Fischl, B.; Iglesias, J.E. Supervision by Denoising. In *IEEE Transactions on Pattern Analysis and Machine Intelligence*; IEEE: New York, NY, USA, 2023; pp. 1–12. [CrossRef]
52. Lim, B.; Son, S.; Kim, H.; Nah, S.; Lee, K.M. Enhanced Deep Residual Networks for Single Image Super-Resolution. In *2017 IEEE Conference on Computer Vision and Pattern Recognition Workshops (CVPRW)*; IEEE: New York, NY, USA, 2017; pp. 1132–1140. [CrossRef]
53. Yuan, Y.; Liu, S.; Zhang, J.; Zhang, Y.; Dong, C.; Lin, L. Unsupervised Image Super-Resolution Using Cycle-in-Cycle Generative Adversarial Networks. In *2018 IEEE/CVF Conference on Computer Vision and Pattern Recognition Workshops (CVPRW)*; IEEE: New York, NY, USA, 2018; pp. 814–81409. [CrossRef]
54. Sajjadi, M.; Javanmardi, M.; Tasdizen, T. Regularization with stochastic transformations and perturbations for deep semi-supervised learning. In *Proceedings of the 30th International Conference on Neural Information Processing Systems*; NIPS'16; Curran Associates Inc.: Red Hook, NY, USA, 2016; pp. 1171–1179.
55. Pan, Y.; Gou, F.; Xiao, C.; Liu, J.; Zhou, J. Semi-supervised recognition for artificial intelligence assisted pathology image diagnosis. *Sci. Rep.* **2024**, *14*, 21984. [CrossRef]
56. Meng, M.; Li, S.; Yao, L.; Li, D.; Zhu, M.; Gao, Q.; Xie, Q.; Zhao, Q.; Bian, Z.; Huang, J.; et al. Semi-supervised learned sinogram restoration network for low-dose CT image reconstruction. In *Medical Imaging 2020: Physics of Medical Imaging*; Chen, G.H., Bosmans, H., Eds.; International Society for Optics and Photonics, SPIE: San Diego, CA, USA, 2020; Volume 11312, p. 113120B. [CrossRef]
57. Xie, E.; Ni, P.; Zhang, R.; Li, X. Limited-Angle CT Reconstruction with Generative Adversarial Network Sinogram Inpainting and Unsupervised Artifact Removal. *Appl. Sci.* **2022**, *12*, 6268. [CrossRef]

https://doi.org/10.3390/electronics15030560

58. Ranjan, A.; Azeemuddin, S.M. Image Denoising using Convolutional Neural Network. In *2022 4th International Conference on Advances in Computing, Communication Control and Networking (ICAC3N)*; IEEE: New York, NY, USA, 2022; pp. 2315–2319. [CrossRef]
59. Zhu, Y.; Zhu, D.; Liu, J. RA-LENet:R-Wave Attention and Local Enhancement for Noise Reduction in ECG Signals. In *2024 International Joint Conference on Neural Networks (IJCNN)*; IEEE: New York, NY, USA, 2024; pp. 1–9. [CrossRef]
60. Lin, X.; Ren, C.; Liu, X.; Huang, J.; Lei, Y. Unsupervised Image Denoising in Real-World Scenarios via Self-Collaboration Parallel Generative Adversarial Branches. In *2023 IEEE/CVF International Conference on Computer Vision (ICCV)*; IEEE: New York, NY, USA, 2023; pp. 12608–12618. [CrossRef]
61. Lin, C.H.; Liao, W.M.; Liang, J.W.; Chen, P.H.; Ko, C.E.; Yang, C.H.; Lu, C.K. Denoising Performance Evaluation of Automated Age-Related Macular Degeneration Detection on Optical Coherence Tomography Images. *IEEE Sensors J.* **2021**, *21*, 790–801. [CrossRef]
62. Chen, S.; Xu, S.; Chen, X.; Li, F. Image Denoising Using a Novel Deep Generative Network with Multiple Target Images and Adaptive Termination Condition. *Appl. Sci.* **2021**, *11*, 4803. [CrossRef]
63. Gurrola-Ramos, J.; Dalmau, O.; Alarcón, T.E. A Residual Dense U-Net Neural Network for Image Denoising. *IEEE Access* **2021**, *9*, 31742–31754. [CrossRef]
64. Li, M.; Liu, W.; Chen, W. An Image Denoising Method Based on Swin Transformer V2 and U-Net Architecture. In *2024 IEEE 16th International Conference on Advanced Infocomm Technology (ICAIT)*; IEEE: New York, NY, USA, 2024; pp. 204–209. [CrossRef]
65. Deshpande, R.; Özbey, M.; Li, H.; Anastasio, M.A.; Brooks, F.J. Assessing the Capacity of a Denoising Diffusion Probabilistic Model to Reproduce Spatial Context. *IEEE Trans. Med Imaging* **2024**, *43*, 3608–3620. [CrossRef]
66. Laghrib, A.; Afraites, L. Image denoising based on a variable spatially exponent PDE. *Appl. Comput. Harmon. Anal.* **2024**, *68*, 101608. [CrossRef]
67. Zhang, Y.; Liu, T.; Chen, Y.; Wang, J.; Shi, M. An efficient fractional-order PDE based image denoising algorithm with optimal adaptive strategy for ultrasound medical image-based diagnostics. *J. Comput. Appl. Math.* **2025**, *460*, 116400. [CrossRef]
68. Ran, Y.; Guo, Z.; Li, J.; Li, Y.; Burger, M.; Wu, B. A tunable despeckling neural network stabilized via diffusion equation. *Signal Process.* **2026**, *239*, 110324. [CrossRef]
69. Namaki, N.; Eslahchi, M.; Salehi, R. The use of physics-informed neural network approach to image restoration via nonlinear PDE tools. *Comput. Math. Appl.* **2023**, *152*, 355–363. [CrossRef]
70. Lin, Q.; Yang, F.; Yan, Y.; Zhang, H.; Xie, Q.; Zheng, J.; Yang, W.; Qian, L.; Liu, S.; Yao, W.; et al. Physics-informed neural networks for denoising high b-value diffusion-weighted images. *Comput. Med Imaging Graph.* **2025**, *124*, 102579. [CrossRef]
71. Li, R.; della Maggiora, G.; Andriasyan, V.; Petkidis, A.; Yushkevich, A.; Deshpande, N.; Kudryashev, M.; Yakimovich, A. Microscopy image reconstruction with physics-informed denoising diffusion probabilistic model. *Commun. Eng.* **2024**, *3*, 186. [CrossRef]
72. Wang, Z.; Han, J.; Zhang, C. Diffusion Posterior Sampling for SAR Despeckling. *IEEE Trans. Geosci. Remote Sens.* **2025**, *63*, 5204619. [CrossRef]
73. Paul, A.; Savakis, A. On Denoising Diffusion Probabilistic Models for Synthetic Aperture Radar Despeckling. *Sensors* **2025**, *25*, 2149. [CrossRef]
74. Pan, Y.; Zhong, L.; Chen, J.; Li, H.; Zhang, X.; Pan, B. SAR Image Despeckling Based on Denoising Diffusion Probabilistic Model and Swin Transformer. *Remote Sens.* **2024**, *16*, 3222. [CrossRef]
75. Guo, Z.; Hu, W.; Zheng, S.; Zhang, B.; Zhou, M.; Peng, J.; Yao, Z.; Feng, M. Efficient Conditional Diffusion Model for SAR Despeckling. *Remote Sens.* **2025**, *17*, 2970. [CrossRef]
76. Wei, G. Generalized Perona-Malik equation for image restoration. *IEEE Signal Process. Lett.* **1999**, *6*, 165–167. [CrossRef]
77. Yu, Y.; Acton, S. Speckle reducing anisotropic diffusion. *IEEE Trans. Image Process.* **2002**, *11*, 1260–1270. [CrossRef]
78. Gilboa, G.; Osher, S. Nonlocal Operators with Applications to Image Processing. *Multiscale Model. Simul.* **2009**, *7*, 1005–1028. [CrossRef]
79. Gilboa, G.; Sochen, N.; Zeevi, Y. Image enhancement and denoising by complex diffusion processes. *IEEE Trans. Pattern Anal. Mach. Intell.* **2004**, *26*, 1020–1036. [CrossRef]
80. You, Y.L.; Kaveh, M. Fourth-order partial differential equations for noise removal. *IEEE Trans. Image Process.* **2000**, *9*, 1723–1730. [CrossRef]
81. Zhang, J.; Wu, C. Fast optimization for multichannel total variation minimization with non-quadratic fidelity. *Signal Process.* **2011**, *91*, 1933–1940. [CrossRef]
82. Dong, G.; Guo, Z.; Zhou, Z.; Zhang, D.; Wo, B. Coherence-enhancing diffusion with the source term. *Appl. Math. Model.* **2015**, *39*, 6060–6072. [CrossRef]
83. Lim, J.; Sung, K. FNN (Feedforward Neural Network) Training Method Based on Robust Recursive Least Square Method. In *Advances in Neural Networks—ISNN 2007*; Liu, D., Fei, S., Hou, Z., Zhang, H., Sun, C., Eds.; Springer: Berlin/Heidelberg, Germany, 2007; pp. 398–405.

84. Chiu, P.H.; Wong, J.C.; Ooi, C.; Dao, M.H.; Ong, Y.S. CAN-PINN: A fast physics-informed neural network based on coupled-automatic–numerical differentiation method. *Comput. Methods Appl. Mech. Eng.* **2022**, *395*, 114909. [CrossRef]
85. Shi, K. Coupling local and nonlocal diffusion equations for image denoising. *Nonlinear Anal. Real World Appl.* **2021**, *62*, 103362. [CrossRef]
86. Goodman, J.W. Some fundamental properties of speckle∗. *J. Opt. Soc. Am.* **1976**, *66*, 1145–1150. [CrossRef]
87. Cheng, G.; Han, J.; Lu, X. Remote Sensing Image Scene Classification: Benchmark and State of the Art. *Proc. IEEE* **2017**, *105*, 1865–1883. [CrossRef]
88. Xia, G.S.; Hu, J.; Hu, F.; Shi, B.; Bai, X.; Zhong, Y.; Zhang, L.; Lu, X. AID: A Benchmark Data Set for Performance Evaluation of Aerial Scene Classification. *IEEE Trans. Geosci. Remote Sens.* **2017**, *55*, 3965–3981. [CrossRef]
89. Heusel, M.; Ramsauer, H.; Unterthiner, T.; Nessler, B.; Hochreiter, S. GANs Trained by a Two Time-Scale Update Rule Converge to a Local Nash Equilibrium. In *Proceedings of the 31st International Conference on Neural Information Processing Systems*; Curran Associates Inc.: Red Hook, NY, USA, 2017; pp. 6629–6640.
90. Argenti, F.; Lapini, A.; Bianchi, T.; Alparone, L. A Tutorial on Speckle Reduction in Synthetic Aperture Radar Images. *IEEE Geosci. Remote Sens. Mag.* **2013**, *1*, 6–35. [CrossRef]
91. Gu, S.; Zhang, L.; Zuo, W.; Feng, X. Weighted Nuclear Norm Minimization with Application to Image Denoising. In Proceedings of the IEEE Conference on Computer Vision and Pattern Recognition (CVPR), Columbus, OH, USA, 23–28 June 2014 .
92. Zoran, D.; Weiss, Y. From learning models of natural image patches to whole image restoration. In *2011 International Conference on Computer Vision*; IEEE: New York, NY, USA, 2011; pp. 479–486. [CrossRef]
93. Chen, Y.; Pock, T. Trainable Nonlinear Reaction Diffusion: A Flexible Framework for Fast and Effective Image Restoration. *IEEE Trans. Pattern Anal. Mach. Intell.* **2017**, *39*, 1256–1272. [CrossRef]
94. Zhang, K.; Zuo, W.; Chen, Y.; Meng, D.; Zhang, L. Beyond a Gaussian Denoiser: Residual Learning of Deep CNN for Image Denoising. *IEEE Trans. Image Process.* **2017**, *26*, 3142–3155. [CrossRef]
95. Tai, Y.; Yang, J.; Liu, X.; Xu, C. MemNet: A Persistent Memory Network for Image Restoration. In *2017 IEEE International Conference on Computer Vision (ICCV)*; IEEE: New York, NY, USA, 2017; pp. 4549–4557. [CrossRef]
96. Lattari, F.; Gonzalez Leon, B.; Asaro, F.; Rucci, A.; Prati, C.; Matteucci, M. Deep Learning for SAR Image Despeckling. *Remote Sens.* **2019**, *11*, 1532. [CrossRef]
97. Han, L.; Zhao, Y.; Lv, H.; Zhang, Y.; Liu, H.; Bi, G. Remote Sensing Image Denoising Based on Deep and Shallow Feature Fusion and Attention Mechanism. *Remote Sens.* **2022**, *14*, 1243. [CrossRef]
98. Tian, C.; Xu, Y.; Fei, L.; Wang, J.; Wen, J.; Luo, N. Enhanced CNN for image denoising. *CAAI Trans. Intell. Technol.* **2019**, *4*, 17–23. [CrossRef]
99. Tian, C.; Xu, Y.; Li, Z.; Zuo, W.; Fei, L.; Liu, H. Attention-guided CNN for image denoising. *Neural Netw.* **2020**, *124*, 117–129. [CrossRef]
100. Halim, A.; Kumar, B.R. A TV-L2-H-1 PDE model for effective denoising. *Comput. Math. Appl.* **2020**, *80*, 2176–2193. [CrossRef]
101. Garber, T.; Tirer, T. Image Restoration by Denoising Diffusion Models with Iteratively Preconditioned Guidance. In *2024 IEEE/CVF Conference on Computer Vision and Pattern Recognition (CVPR)*; IEEE: New York, NY, USA, 2024; pp. 25245–25254. [CrossRef]
102. Limsuebchuea, A.; Duangsoithong, R.; Phukpattaranont, P. Self-Augmented Noisy Image for Noise2Noise Image Denoising. *IEEE Access* **2024**, *12*, 71076–71087. [CrossRef]
103. Zhang, C.; Yen, K.S. A survey on Deep Image Prior for image denoising. *Digit. Signal Process.* **2025**, *163*, 105235. [CrossRef]
104. Zhang, D.; Zhou, F. Self-Supervised Image Denoising for Real-World Images with Context-Aware Transformer. *IEEE Access* **2023**, *11*, 14340–14349. [CrossRef]
105. Wang, X.; Fan, S.; Zhao, C.; Liu, D.; Chen, W. A Self-Supervised Method Using Noise2Noise Strategy for Denoising CRP Gathers. *IEEE Geosci. Remote Sens. Lett.* **2023**, *20*, 7503505. [CrossRef]
106. Vu, H.; Cheung, G.; Eldar, Y.C. Unrolling of Deep Graph Total Variation for Image Denoising. In *ICASSP 2021—2021 IEEE International Conference on Acoustics, Speech and Signal Processing (ICASSP)*; IEEE: New York, NY, USA, 2021; pp. 2050–2054. [CrossRef]
107. Singh, V.; Deepthi, T.; Ginnare, J.; Pavani, K.; Rathour, M.; Sonu, I.; Tiwary, U.S. Performance Analysis of GANs for De-Noising Images. In *2023 International Conference on Information Technologies (InfoTech)*; IEEE: New York, NY, USA, 2023; pp. 1–7. [CrossRef]
108. Zhao, Q.; Wu, S.; Zhang, Z.; Sun, Y.; Fu, Y.; Wang, H. SAR Image Noise Reduction Based on Wavelet Transform and DnCNN. In *2021 2nd China International SAR Symposium (CISS)*; IEEE: New York, NY, USA, 2021; pp. 1–4. [CrossRef]
109. Shan, H.; Fu, X.; Lv, Z.; Xu, X.; Wang, X.; Zhang, Y. Synthetic aperture radar images denoising based on multi-scale attention cascade convolutional neural network. *Meas. Sci. Technol.* **2023**, *34*, 085403. [CrossRef]
110. Martin, D.; Fowlkes, C.; Tal, D.; Malik, J. A Database of Human Segmented Natural Images and its Application to Evaluating Segmentation Algorithms and Measuring Ecological Statistics. In *Proceedings of the Eighth IEEE International Conference on Computer Vision. ICCV 2001*; IEEE: New York, NY, USA, 2001; Volume 2, pp. 416–423.

https://doi.org/10.3390/electronics15030560

111. Huang, J.B.; Singh, A.; Ahuja, N. Single Image Super-Resolution From Transformed Self-Exemplars. In *Proceedings of the IEEE Conference on Computer Vision and Pattern Recognition (CVPR)*; IEEE: New York, NY, USA, 2015.
112. Agustsson, E.; Timofte, R. NTIRE 2017 Challenge on Single Image Super-Resolution: Dataset and Study. In Proceedings of the IEEE Conference on Computer Vision and Pattern Recognition (CVPR) Workshops, Honolulu, HI, USA, 21–26 July 2017.
113. Soniya, S.; Sriharipriya, K.C. Datasets for Testing Denoised Image. 2024. Available online: https://figshare.com/articles/dataset/Datasets_for_Testing_Denoised_Image/26827765/1 (accessed on 22 January 2026).

https://doi.org/10.3390/electronics15030560

electronics

MDPI

Article

Lightweight Neural Network Ensemble Models for Medical Image Classification with MedMNIST Dataset

Marina Prvan *, Josip Musić, Duje Čoko and Ante Kristić

Faculty of Electrical Engineering, Mechanical Engineering and Naval Architecture, University of Split, R. Boškovića 32, 21000 Split, Croatia; jmusic@fesb.hr (J.M.); dcoko@fesb.hr (D.Č.); akristic@fesb.hr (A.K.)
* Correspondence: mprvan@fesb.hr

Abstract

Over the last decade, convolutional neural networks (CNNs) have demonstrated significant potential in assisting medical diagnosis. Research has focused on implementing such networks, particularly in the context of embedded medical systems. This can be challenging due to CNNs' large memory footprint, high computational requirements, and need for retained performance. One of the common approaches for high model accuracy is to use an ensemble of several deep neural networks (DNNs). Recently, the authors have discussed the high computational demands of DNN ensembles. Therefore, in this paper, lightweight ensemble solutions are investigated. Three separate types of ensembles are classified: DNN-only (consisting of deep-of-the-shelf networks), CNN-only (consisting of customized CNNs), and a hybrid ensemble (combining the former two architectures). Experiments were conducted on each class using three public datasets from the MedMNIST database, and classes were compared and contrasted. The results show that a higher sensitivity and a smaller memory footprint can be achieved with CNN-only compared to with DNN-only. Moreover, a hybrid ensemble approach is proposed as the best compromise between the two, being the most lightweight, as it reduces the number of FLOPs, with the performance result comparable to previous work. The performance drop is ~0.3%, ~0.4%, and ~2% for PathMNIST, OrganAMNIST, and OCTMNIST, but the memory footprint is reduced by ~65%, ~77%, and ~82% compared to the recent state of the art. Thus, the proposed hybrid ensemble approach is compliant with the requirements of a resource-constrained device and suitable for implementation in a smart medical system.

Keywords: MedMNIST; neural network; classification; ensemble learning

1. Introduction

The early diagnosis of a disease is one of the key steps in the patient treatment process [1–4]. Typically, medical experts make diagnoses using appropriate biomedical images and manual classification of histological tissue samples. However, in the last decade, the development of reliable machine learning (ML)-based approaches such as neural networks (NNs) and their application in automatic computer-aided diagnosis of many diseases has emerged [1,2,4]. Convolutional neural networks (CNNs) are extremely popular, outperforming the other ML-based methods and reducing the time and effort for the pathologist to analyze histological images [5]. The CNN is often associated with "deep learning" in medical applications and is the de facto standard in the ML community. The deeper the deep neural network (DNN) architecture, the better the accuracy, but at the cost of an increased number of calculations and a prolonged learning time [6,7].

Nowadays, in the era of the Internet of Medical Things (IoMT) and the constant development of embedded medical systems with various resource-constrained end-devices [8–10], research has been directed towards simplification of DNNs. Scientists tend to compress DNNs as much as possible, while retaining a satisfactory performance. These models can be referred to as "lightweight" because they are small in memory footprint and easy to implement on an edge device for real-time application [7,11,12]. Floating-point (FP) operations of the full-precision networks are especially expensive, so they are often replaced by fixed-point or integer calculations with a reduced number of bits [8,13–15]. Compressed DNNs have smaller memory footprints and lower computational requirements. Furthermore, they are more suitable for a real-time application due to their increased timing efficiency and faster inference time [7,15].

Many different solutions exist for smart medical edge applications, such as ARM Central Processing Unit (CPU) processors, Graphics Processing Unit (GPU)-embedded systems, or Field Programmable Gate Arrays (FPGAs). In this study, an FPGA is considered over other edge technologies, as it exhibits better performance in domain-specific tasks that require real-time monitoring, low-latency data throughput, high-accuracy decision making, and improved energy efficiency critical for battery-constrained environments. FPGAs offer the highest potential for ML algorithms and especially image processing tasks to be run at the edge device, minimizing the need for data transmission and storage requirements [16]. A more detailed comparison of the advantages of FPGAs versus other solutions for NN inference in medical edge computing can be found in [17].

The authors have shown that only sufficiently small NN models can fit into the available memory of a resource-constrained device, such as an FPGA. For example, in the case of the Xilinx Virtex 7 FPGA, model size should be compressed to a maximum of 8.5 MB for it to be stored directly in the on-chip memory [18]. This fact from the literature is considered in this paper, and it is calculated that the threshold for the acceptable FP size of the model is $\leq$34 MB, with the assumption that it will be further compressed to an 8-bit integer (int8). Naturally, weights and activations could be quantized into even lower-bit formats, and the authors are already moving towards this in the recent literature [19].

There is another important factor besides model complexity that should be taken into account when designing NNs, and that is the performance of the model. While the complexity is measured in the total number of parameters and in total model size, the performance is usually the accuracy or the sensitivity of the implemented model. This is especially crucial in medical applications, so authors constantly seek solutions that would enhance the capability of the classification prediction scores. One of these approaches is called ensemble learning [20,21], where models with statistically different predictions in multi-class problems are combined to improve performance. This is still a hot topic in medical diagnostics, where up to five base learners are combined into an ensemble scheme [22]. Usually, the state-of-the-art DNN models are selected in studies, and they are carefully fine-tuned and adjusted for a new task. A pre-trained model is normally obtained via a transfer learning (TL) approach, and final predictions are combined to improve classification prediction [23–26]. There are also studies combining deep state-of-the-art DNNs with a custom-designed CNN network [27].

However, the authors in [6,11] recently discussed the ensemble-based combination of deep networks as highly computationally demanding, and propose to concentrate more on exploring ensemble techniques on simpler and smaller models, as is achieved in this paper. Furthermore, the authors in [28] demonstrated that rather simple CNNs may achieve results comparable to deeper networks when applied to medical image classification problems. Using the fact that the ensemble has high complexity, and that the entire network must be implemented within a device with limited resources, this paper aims to identify the best approach: to use only existing DNNs (like, for example, the ones from the ResNet, MobileNet, or VGG family), to use a combination of DNNs and custom CNNs, or to make an ensemble only from the smallest and most efficient custom CNNs. Three different classes of ensemble types are defined:

- DNN-only ensemble—consisting only of the common deep state-of-the-art NN models such as the ones from MobileNet, ResNet, VGG family, etc.;
- CNN-only ensemble—consisting only of the customized NN models, i.e., the classical ones consisting of convolutional, pooling, and fully connected layers;
- Hybrid ensemble—combining the two former types of architectures.

This study investigates and compares the most lightweight models that can be designed with the three types of ensembles above. The classification approach for the definition of these ensemble types is based on taxonomy, where each category is a predefined and well-known type of neural network model. The purpose of this study is to help researchers decide which type of model or ensemble model design strategy to use in medical image classification tasks. To the best of our knowledge, this is the first time that such classes are compared and contrasted, at the same time minimizing complexity and maximizing performance, with the goal of finding the best trade-off ensemble type. Moreover, this study proposes a novel "best"-candidate-selection methodology that combines Pareto analysis with weighted radar-area scoring to compare the performance of various ensemble combinations. Classical radar plots [29–31] are upgraded with a weighting function inspired by [32], used to adjust the complexity axes for a fairer comparison. In total, three complexity and four performance metrics were included in the evaluation, and the areas of the obtained polygons are used as final evaluation scores. This study is general, and the presented methodology could be applied for any dataset. Furthermore, the findings of this study are confirmed using three publicly available datasets from the MedMNIST database introduced in [33].

This paper is organized as follows. In Section 2, an overview of the literature is provided using common state-of-the-art networks for medical image classification. Section 3 ensures the repeatability of the study, describing the experimental setup and the methodology used. The performance evaluation of the proposed models towards the baseline is provided in Section 4, and Section 5 derives the limitations of the work. A conclusion is given in Section 6, followed by the references used.

2. Brief Literature Review

There is an extensive amount of previous work on the automated classification of medical images. Various datasets are used in these studies, but the number of publicly available datasets is rather low. Recently, Yang et al. [33,34] developed MedMNIST, a public dataset that consists of many different preprocessed medical datasets. Among them is PathMNIST, a lightweight collection of colorectal cancer histopathological images, standardized for research and educational purposes. Many authors have utilized the benefits of this dataset [7,12,33–37]. Yang et al. [33] tested the performance of PathMNIST classification using two DNN models, Resnet50 and Resnet18, and obtained performance scores of 91.1% and 90.7%, respectively. Salehin et al. [12] surpassed previous work and developed a model called MedvCNN, which yields 84.1% mean accuracy but has twice as few parameters as compared to ResNet18 (5.56 M).

As improving the performance of classification models is a key factor for medical applications, recent works have begun to demonstrate new ideas for increasing efficiency, one of which is the development of an ensemble that combines multiple classifiers. For example, Yang et al. [38] developed a combination of three fine-tuned DNN classifiers. Similarly, the authors in [39] merged five DNNs for fine-tuning and optimized the computations in each

https://doi.org/10.3390/electronics15071470

classifier. In their work, various ensemble methods are compared, like majority voting, simple averaging, and weighted averaging, to enhance the performance of COVID-19 infection identification.

The works of Kundu et al. [21,40] propose novel approaches to enhancing methods for combining the base model outputs and assigning weights to the base classifiers. They also use pre-trained deep models to enhance the classification performance using chest X-ray images. Ghosh et al. [20] went a step further and proposed an ensemble of deep networks, but combined it with the merged input datasets. These authors showed that by increasing the diversity of the input data, the overall classification score improves. Recently, the authors in [6] considered an ensemble-based combination of deep networks such as the one from [20] as highly computationally demanding and suggested a hybrid deep learning method that outperforms existing models in efficiency and computational complexity. An additional ensemble of lightweight NNs is proposed in [11], and it is shown that it is more accurate than state-of-the-art methods and deployable in practice. A different idea to enhance the performance of classification models is to include other information besides medical images in the data training procedure [35,41]. However, the inclusion of additional learnable characteristics causes additional costs in parameters and memory.

Recently, the authors in [6] discussed the computational complexity vs. accuracy trade-off for various DNNs. They also suggest hybrid deep learning models that outperform existing methods in efficiency and time, such as ResNet, used via transfer learning (TL) [42], or the ensemble-based structure [20]. The work of [43] presents a TL-based approach for organ classification and emphasizes the need for using lightweight pre-trained DNN architectures in the ensemble. They suggest utilizing the ones with a minimal parameter count and targeted for mobile edge devices, i.e., VGG19, EfficientNetB0 (EffB0), and MobileNetV2 (MobV2). Hsia et al. [7] proposed the reduction in size, the number of FLOPs, and trainable parameters of the existing DenseNet. They modified it to be more suitable for real-time purposes, with an accuracy of 95%. The work in [3] compared a larger ResNet18 model to a lightweight SqueezeNet variant, and found that the latter is less effective for predicting colon cancer and requires a larger training dataset to improve classification performance.

The work in [9] presents a lightweight fast NN for tumor patch classification that has fewer trainable parameters (0.22 M) and a smaller operation count (210 M) compared to the well-known lightweight DNNs. Similarly, Kumar et al. [14] proposed a small and efficient CNN model for histopathology image classification based on MobileNet. The model was implemented on several resource-constrained edge devices, after being compressed using a lower-bit representation for the weights instead of the typical 32-bit floating point. Moreover, other works [15,44] have also reported their efforts in applying the usual compression techniques such as model pruning and quantization. For example, the work in [15] demonstrated a variant of DenseNet, which exhibited superior performance over the lightweight MobileNetV2 or ShuffleNet. The authors in [44] also gradually reduced pre-trained DNNs in size and obtained a hardware-friendly integer model representation. They analyzed the impact of different quantization techniques on the accuracy, model size, and inference time for each of the selected models and improved their memory, power, and computational requirements without affecting the classification performance.

Recently, lightweight CNNs were replaced by vision transformer models for mobile vision tasks [37,45,46]. In their method, the image is divided into patches and transformer layers are applied due to their relation to benefiting the classification score. The performance is measured as a trade-off between accuracy and complexity, expressed as the total number of trainable parameters. The study in [47] employs a hybrid model combining

https://doi.org/10.3390/electronics15071470

transformer and CNN models, and shows comparable performance to the existing work in image classification tasks on the MedMNIST database.

Since most authors often combine deep off-the-shelf models when designing an ensemble, and sometimes include a custom CNN architecture, the main contribution of this study is providing answers to the following several posed research questions (RQ) that arise:

- RQ1: The first answer provided in this study addresses the question of whether it is worthwhile to design a custom CNN ensemble at all, or if we can rely on a combination of existing deep networks adapted to the new application.
- RQ2: Next, an answer is found to the question of whether it is possible to use only custom-designed CNN models, which could have more FP operations than existing deep networks like MobileNet or ResNet (but again, as many as the FPGA device supports), but will be smaller and/or more efficient than a combination of existing deep networks.
- RQ3: Finally, the findings in this study answer the question of whether a combination of both model types, i.e., a hybrid ensemble approach, is the best compromise.

3. Materials and Methods

3.1. Dataset

The MedMNISTv2 [33] is a publicly available MNIST-like dataset with 12 types of biomedical images widely used in medical image analysis. Original images of size 224 × 224 were preprocessed into a lightweight size of 28 × 28. The images contain the corresponding classification labels such that no background knowledge is needed from the medical domain. The current experiment is conducted on three selected MedMNIST datasets. PathMNIST is a subset of the MedMNIST containing histopathology color scans of colorectal cancer tissues. The dataset has nine classes, and these are adipose, background, debris, lymphocytes, mucus, smooth muscle, normal colon mucosa, cancer-associated stroma, and colorectal adenocarcinoma epithelial. The OrganAMNIST dataset is an axial grayscale view of the eleven 3D computed tomography (CT) organ scans: bladder, left femur, right femur, heart, left kidney, right kidney, liver, left lung, right lung, pancreas, and spleen. The OCTMNIST grayscale image dataset comprises four diagnosis classes: choroidal neovascularization, diabetic macular edema, drusen, and a normal retina. For simplicity, classes from the former three datasets are referred to as numbers 0–8, 0–10, and 0–3 throughout the paper. Details of the datasets are given in Table 1. The visualization of random images from the datasets is given in Figure 1a–c.

Table 1. Details of the datasets used in this paper.

Dataset	Image Size [Width × Height × Color]	Num. of Classes	Num. of Samples	Train/Validation/Testing
PathMNIST	28 × 28 × 3	9	107,180	84%/9.3%/6.7%
OrganAMNIST	28 × 28 × 1	11	58,850	58.8%/11%/30.2%
OCTMNIST	28 × 28 × 1	4	109,309	89.2%/9.9%/0.9%

3.2. Baseline Models

3.2.1. DNN Classification Architectures

The selection of the baseline architectures is made depending on whether the architectures are reported in the literature as high-performing or suitable for implementation on edge devices. Hence, it is decided to use five DNNs: ResNet50, MobileNetV2, MobileNetV3Large (MobV3), EfficientNetB0, and DenseNet121. Overall, the parameter size of the selected models is such that they utilize up to 100 MB, so it is possible to fit them in the

https://doi.org/10.3390/electronics15071470

limited memory of the edge device. The smallest models are especially interesting, as they could fit even into the most limited hardware on-chip memory [18].

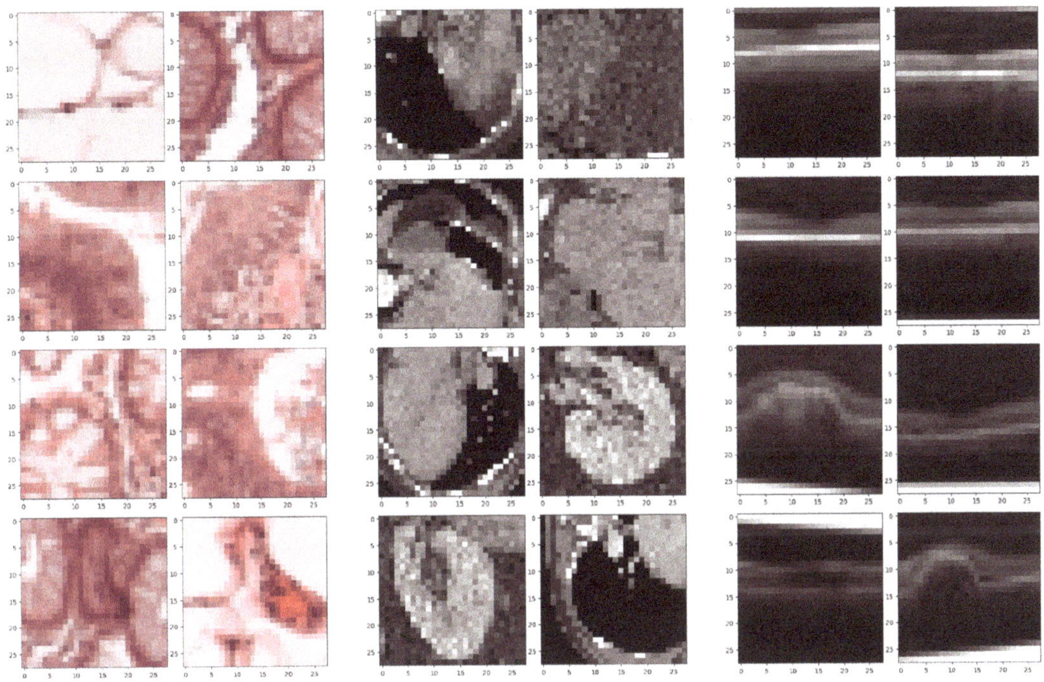

(a) PathMNIST (b) OrganAMNIST (c) OCTMNIST

Figure 1. Visualization of random images from the used MedMNIST datasets [33].

ResNet architectures are rather popular in biomedical image classification, although they have a large number of trainable parameters. On the other hand, the MobileNet family of architectures is described in the literature as lightweight and memory-efficient, with a low computational cost, and thus is able to run on limited edge devices such as mobile phones [48,49]. There are two common generations of lightweight variants with increased classification efficiency and modest latency, MobileNetV2 and MobileNetV3, and it was considered useful to include both in this research. EfficientNet follows the same strategy as MobileNet to compress the network and reduce computational cost [9]. There are eight variants of EfficientNet available in the Tensorflow framework, labeled from B0 to B7 [13]. It is stated in [50] that EfficientNetB0 is the most efficient and uses fewer parameters, so it is included in this study. Furthermore, DenseNet121 [51] is selected to be tested for the implementation on the edge device due to its high accuracy and a comparable number of parameters to EfficientNetB0. There are some other DNN architectures marked in the literature as lightweight, like Squeezenet [49] or ShuffleNet [9]. However, several researchers have highlighted a number of issues with them [1,3,52,53], so it was decided not to use them in this study.

3.2.2. The Customized State-of-the-Art CNN Architectures

Recently, the authors in [36] designed a customized CNN for the classification of low-level medical images. They used the PathMNIST dataset and showed that using a CNN is a preferable choice for this type of classification problem. Hence, this model is adopted from the literature and used as a baseline architecture. The details of the implementation are

https://doi.org/10.3390/electronics15071470

shown in Figure 2a. The model contains five blocks of 2D convolution layers, with batch normalization and ReLU activations for the output features on each block. Finally, the output of the last block is fed to a Max pooling layer to reduce computational complexity. The most prominent image features are processed by three fully connected or dense layers, where the first two utilize a ReLU function, and the last layer uses Softmax to calculate the final probabilities [36]. This architecture is referred to as CNN5 throughout the paper because it has five convolutional layers. It is also referred to as Model A.

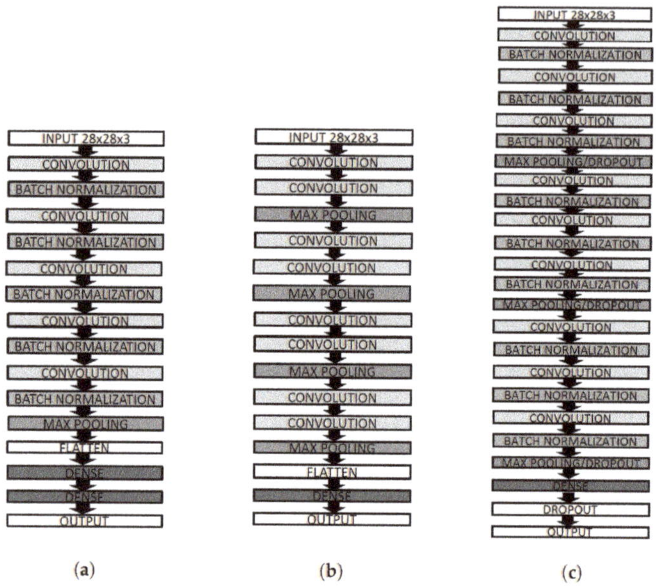

Figure 2. The classification models A, B, and D used in this paper (all datasets). (**a**) Adjei_CNN5 (A) from [36]; (**b**) Diniz_CNN8 (B4) from [54]; (**c**) DaSilva_CNN9 (D3) from [55].

Other customized state-of-the-art solutions are taken from [54–56]. The authors use principles of genetic programming, and develop a methodology that resulted in the development of novel optimized CNN architectures. First, Diniz et al. [54] proposed an architecture from Figure 2b. This architecture has eight convolutional layers, so it is referred to as CNN8. In fact, it has four blocks of double convolutional layer + pooling layer, so the architecture is also referred to as Model B4. In addition, variants smaller than CNN8 are derived, consisting of three blocks (six convolutional layers), two blocks (four convolutional layers), and a single block (two convolutional layers). Similarily, these models are referred to as CNN6 (B3), CNN4 (B2), and CNN2 (B1), respectively.

Next, da Silva et al. [56] designed architectures specifically generated for each dataset, i.e., for PathMNIST, OrganAMNIST, and OCTMNIST. They are visualized in Figure 3, and they have six or nine convolutional layers arranged in two or three blocks depending on the dataset. Smaller and larger variants of each architecture are developed here. For example, a smaller model (CNN3 or C1) and a larger model (CNN9 or C3) were designed for PathMNIST. Two smaller variants (CNN2 or C1 and CNN4 or C2) and a larger variant (CNN8 or C4) were developed for OrganAMNIST. Two smaller variants (CNN3 or C1 and CNN6 or C2) were developed for the OCTMNIST dataset.

Finally, the authors in [55] proposed the architecture visualized in Figure 2c, with alternating layers of convolutional and batch normalization blocks. It has three blocks of three convolution + batch normalization layers, and each block ends with a pooling layer.

https://doi.org/10.3390/electronics15071470

The total number of convolutional layers is nine, so the architecture is called CNN9, or D3 (if the total number of blocks is counted). Furthermore, smaller variants are developed here, i.e., CNN6 (D2) and CNN3 (D1).

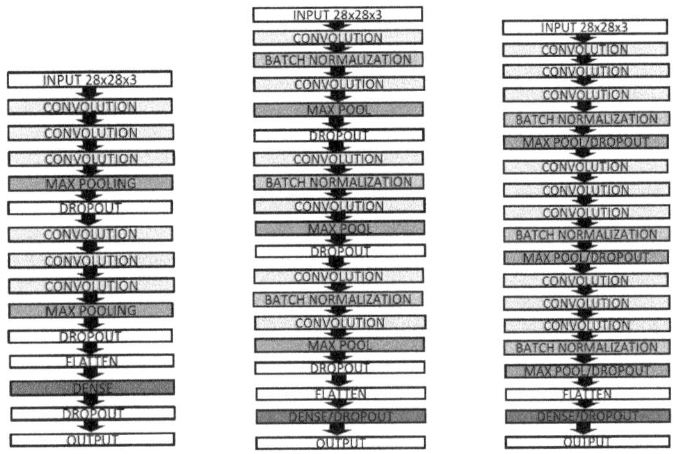

(**a**) DaSilva_CNN6 (C2) (**b**) DaSilva_CNN6 (C3) (**c**) DaSilva_CNN9 (C3)

Figure 3. Classification models from [56] used for (**a**) PathMNIST, (**b**) OrganAMNIST, and (**c**) OCTMNIST.

3.3. Experimental Setup

Using a TL-based approach with a model pre-trained on ImageNet data is popular in medical image classification [5,43,57]. In this work, the strategy could have been to use randomly initialized weights or to set the initial weights to the previously trained ImageNet model. A test was performed with the deepest ResNet50 (PathMNIST), and the pre-trained model achieved higher accuracy (87.4%) than when trained with random weights (78.3%), while the training parameters remained the same. Additional tests were performed with MobileNetV2 and EfficientNetB0 (OrganAMNIST), where the efficiency dropped to 67.43% and 84.66%, compared to the initial ImageNet pre-trained scores of 91.9% and 92.9%, respectively. Hence, all baseline-selected DNN models were imported with weights initialized on ImageNet data but without the final classification layer. Then, two additional layers of Max pooling (2 $\times$ 2) and flattening were added on top of the base model. Finally, a new fully connected output layer was added. All layers of the base model were kept trainable, as well as the additional layers.

The basic approach in the experiment involved reconstructing state-of-the-art DNN and CNN models from the literature and then using them to develop ensemble combinations. As the CNNs and DNNs trained on the MedMNIST dataset were not publicly available, they were reconstructed based on the information available in the literature. To obtain the DNN benchmarks, the ImageNet-pre-trained DNNs were imported from the Keras Application module and fine-tuned for a new application. The inputs were adjusted to the form of the data the network was trained on to accomplish a successful adaptation of the architecture to a new domain [58,59]. Therefore, as suggested in TensorFlow Keras documentation (https://www.tensorflow.org/api_docs/python/tf/keras/applications (accessed on 25 March 2026)), a preprocessing function to scale the pixels to [−1,1] was applied for MobileNetV2. This preprocessing step was included since the literature confirms it as a common part of a medical pipeline with machine learning classifiers [59]. A small ablation-type study confirmed that the MobileNetV2 performance result is independent of

https://doi.org/10.3390/electronics15071470

the preprocessing applied in the current application (for different MedMNIST datasets). Furthermore, due to the architectures being pre-trained on RGB ImageNet data, grayscale inputs were replicated to three single-channel images. The input size was 28 × 28 × 3 for all DNNs except MobileNetV3 and DenseNet, where the input was zero-padded to 32 × 32 × 3 to be adjusted for the pre-trained networks in the TensorFlow framework.

The CNN benchmarks were reconstructed based on the description provided in the literature. The authors in [54–56] provided enough details for the reconstruction of CNN models B, C, and D. The specific hyperparameters for each convolutional block are given in Table 2. On the other hand, for the reconstruction of CNN Model A, some details were missing [36], so a Keras Tuner tool (https://github.com/keras-team/keras-tuner (accessed on 25 March 2026)) was applied to find a number of filters in each convolutional layer so that results from the literature could be replicated as closely as possible. A Bayesian optimization algorithm was used with the objective to minimize validation loss. In total, 15 trials on a maximum of five epochs were examined, with the number of filters per layer selected from {32, 64, 128}. The configuration of 32, 64, 128, 128, and 64 filters on each convolutional layer provided the best result and was selected for the CNN5 model's implementation. Each dense layer had 64 filters, except the final one, where the number of filters was set to the number of classes.

Table 2. Details of the hyperparameters for each convolutional block.

Convolutional Block	Model B	Model C (PathMNIST)	Model C (OrganAMNIST)	Model C (OCTMNIST)	Model D
1	{32, 32}	{32, 32, 64} *{64, 64, 64}	{32, 32}	{32, 32, 64}	{32, 32, 64}
2	{64, 64}	{64, 128, 128}	{64, 64}	{64, 128, 128}	{64, 128, 128}
3	{128, 128}	{256, 256, 512}	{128, 128}	{256, 256, 512}	{256, 256, 512}
4	{256, 256}	-	{256, 256}	-	-

* The hyperparameters for the C2 version of the model.

To ensure a fair comparison across model families (CNN and DNN), the input preprocessing pipeline was standardized to minimize variations between them. Fairness was ensured wherever possible, and the schematic is shown in Figure 4. The raw and unscaled inputs were used for all architectures except for MobileNetV2, and input resizing was carried out only when specifically required (MobileNetV3 and DenseNet). The grayscale-to-RGB replication was applied for all architectures when dealing with grayscale datasets. The formation of hybrid ensemble combinations was carried out using CNN and DNN benchmarks, so the comparison of CNNs and DNNs with the hybrid ensembles was fair and did not require any further adjustments.

The training protocol was uniform for all architectures. The hyperparameters were not optimized for the learning process because the training configuration setup was taken from the literature [36]. Hence, a variant of the Adam optimizer called AdamW was used, with the advantage of being computationally efficient, easy to implement, and low in its memory requirement [36,48]. It was employed with a fixed learning rate of 0.0001. Training was performed with a batch size of 64. Sparse categorical cross-entropy was used as a loss function, and an early stopping mechanism was employed to prevent over-fitting if the validation loss did not decrease after five epochs. The learning curves obtained during training of the selected models on PathMNIST dataset are given in Figure 5a–c.

All architectures were trained and tested in the Google Colab environment with the Python 3 Google Compute Engine backend and 12.7 GB of RAM. The TensorFlow 2.18.0 Keras framework was used with the latest version v3.0.2 of the MedMNIST image database. Due to the memory and processing constraints, models were trained for a maximum of 20 epochs.

https://doi.org/10.3390/electronics15071470

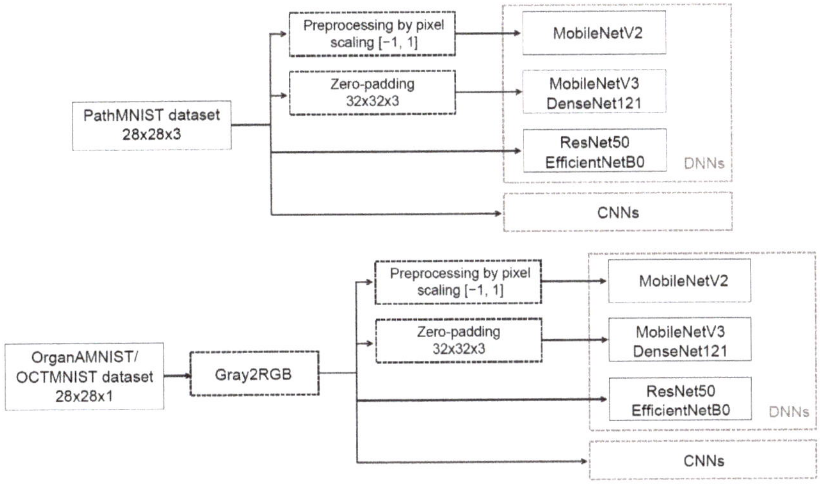

Figure 4. Preprocessing pipeline for all architectures.

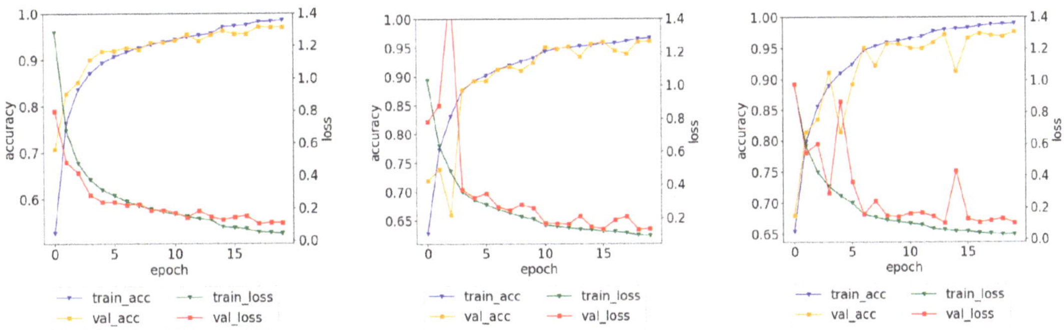

(**a**) DaSilva_CNN9 (C3) (**b**) DaSilva_CNN6 (D2) (**c**) DaSilva_CNN9 (D3)

Figure 5. Learning curves for training and validation accuracy/loss (PathMNIST).

3.4. Evaluation Metrics

In the current multi-class problem, weighted recall (wR), weighted precision (wP) as in Equation (1), F1 score (Equation (2)), and AUC are used to evaluate the model's performance, and they are calculated using the number of true positive (TP), true negative (TN), false positive (FP), and false negative (FN) samples. Weighted recall is also called weighted sensitivity (wS) throughout this paper, as it represents the models' ability to predict truly positive samples as positive, which is crucial in medical applications.

$$wP = \sum_{i=1}^{n} w_i \frac{TP_i}{TP_i + FP_i}, \quad wR = wS = \sum_{i=1}^{n} w_i \frac{TP_i}{TP_i + FN_i}, \quad w_i = \frac{TP_i + FN_i}{TP + FP + FN + TN}. \quad (1)$$

$$F1 = \sum_{i=1}^{n} w_i (2 \times \frac{\frac{TP_i}{TP_i+FP_i} \times \frac{TP_i}{TP_i+FN_i}}{\frac{TP_i}{TP_i+FP_i} + \frac{TP_i}{TP_i+FN_i}}) \quad (2)$$

$$BA = \frac{\sum_{i=1}^{n} \frac{TP_i}{TP_i+FN_i}}{n} \quad (3)$$

The parameter w_i in Equations (1) and (2) is the weight applied for a class i in the total of n classes, and it represents the support for class i in the dataset. This is the most commonly used method for this type of classification task, as PathMNIST and OrganAMNIST datasets are not fairly balanced. A weighted score is the mean of all class scores, calculated by summing the individual scores per class, each multiplied by the number of true samples of the class in the dataset. It is to note that although weighted metrics are used to handle class imbalance, incorporating a weighted loss function during the actual training could potentially yield even better results for minority classes. The AUC is the area under the Receiver Operating Characteristics (ROC) curve, which is important for unbalanced datasets and measures the ability of the model to distinguish between classes. It is computed as an unweighted macro AUC, with a one-vs-rest (OvR) strategy. Unlike the weighted metrics, it treats each class equally, regardless of its prevalence in the dataset, and is useful when a minority class's performance is critical.

Furthermore, the overall accuracy of the models is measured as the ratio of correctly predicted images over the total number of images in the dataset, and this is needed for the comparison of the obtained results with the literature. All metrics are retrieved from Scikit-learn (https://scikit-learn.org/stable/api/sklearn.metrics.html (accessed on 25 March 2026)). However, two out of the three used datasets are imbalanced enough that macro-averaged metrics or balanced accuracy (BA) should also be reported in addition to the overall accuracy. This one is calculated by using the metrics from the same library, i.e., the average of the recall obtained on each class (Equation (3)). For a balanced OCTMNIST dataset, both types of accuracy yield the same value.

The parameters used to evaluate the model complexity include model size, inference time, and the number of parameters and floating-point arithmetic operations (FLOPs). Since the targeted models are the ones that might fit the memory of an edge medical device, their size is evaluated here, being proportional to the total number of trainable parameters. Model parameter count, as well as the number of FLOPs, enables one to estimate the speed of a model when implemented on an edge device [14]. The FLOPs are estimated by the number of memory accumulation (MAC) instructions since each instruction takes a single floating-point computation for the CPU and GPU. The model analyzer package from Tensorflow Profiler (https://pypi.org/project/keras-flops (accessed on 25 March 2026)) is used to calculate these computations in hardware. Furthermore, the inference time is an important metric, revealing the time needed on the edge device to predict the classes in the input image [9]. In this experiment, the inference time is measured on the batch of images consisting of the full test portion of the dataset, i.e., on 7180 (PathMNIST), 17,780 (OrganAMNIST), and 1000 (OCTMNIST) test images.

3.5. The Proposed Methodology for Best Candidate Selection

Before the candidate-selection procedure, a corresponding search space was constructed. The ensemble combinations were formed by the conventional approach [57], with predictions derived from baseline models and combined through averaging to yield the final prediction scores of an ensemble. This is a form of a late ensemble, as it deals with the predictions of the individual learners. The description of the search space formed and tested for each ensemble type (CNN-only, DNN-only, and hybrid) is the following:

- The DNNs with the lowest footprint are combined such that the total size of the ensemble is $\leq$34 MB, and the combinations are formed consisting of the top three DNNs with the maximal wS scores (from Table 3).
- There were 39, 28, and 25 CNN ensemble combinations tested with the PathMNIST, OrganAMNIST, and OCTMNIST datasets, respectively: 23, 16, and 15 by combining CNNs of similar size ($\pm$1 convolutional layer); 8, 7, and 3 by combining CNNs with the maximal wS (from Table 4); and 8, 5, and 7 formed ensembles of up to five CNN

https://doi.org/10.3390/electronics15071470

combinations having the highest wS value (>88%, 91%, and 76% threshold) that are combined with the other CNNs such that the total size is ≤34 MB.

- There were 54, 40, and 33 combinations tested with hybrid models for PathMNIST, OrganAMNIST, and OCTMNIST, respectively: 9 combining the top two CNNs and top two DNNs with the highest wS (from Tables 3 and 4); 9 combining the top two CNNs and top two DNNs with the lowest footprint; 15, 7, and 2 trade-off hybrid combinations; and 21, 15, and 13 ensembles of up to five CNN combinations with the highest wS (>88%/91%/76%) combined with DNNs such that the total size is ≤34 MB.

Table 3. The efficiency of existing DNNs. Models are sorted by wS for each dataset.

MNIST Dataset	Model	★wS	wP	F1	BA	AUC	Size [MB]	FLOPs (M)	Params	Inference Time [s]
Path	DenseNet121	**0.886**	**0.891**	**0.887**	**0.854**	0.976	26.88	115.712	7,046,729	46
	ResNet50	0.873	0.883	0.876	0.845	0.975	89.90	158.495	23,564,498	44
	MobileNetV2	0.871	0.877	0.872	0.846	0.980	**8.66**	**11.428**	**2,269,513**	**11**
	EfficientNetB0	0.860	0.875	0.865	0.826	**0.981**	22.62	29.326	5,930,841	21
	MobileNetV3	0.833	0.843	0.836	0.801	0.958	11.46	11.857	3,005,001	13
OrganA	DenseNet121	**0.942**	**0.943**	**0.942**	**0.937**	**0.996**	26.89	116.607	6,965,131	77
	EfficientNetB0	0.929	0.929	0.928	0.923	0.994	22.63	29.694	5,872,795	34
	ResNet50	0.927	0.927	0.926	0.919	0.995	90.07	150.781	23,557,131	83
	MobileNetV2	0.919	0.919	0.918	0.916	0.994	**8.67**	**11.769**	**2,237,963**	**21**
	MobileNetV3	0.907	0.907	0.906	0.897	0.991	11.47	12.113	2,982,523	28
OCT	MobileNetV2	**0.734**	0.766	**0.702**	**0.734**	**0.943**	**8.63**	**11.751**	**2,228,996**	**4**
	ResNet50	0.727	0.763	0.696	0.727	0.939	90.01	150.753	23,542,788	10
	DenseNet121	0.724	**0.784**	0.695	0.724	0.939	26.89	116.592	6,957,956	14
	MobileNetV3	0.706	0.749	0.673	0.706	0.902	11.44	12.100	2,975,796	9
	EfficientNetB0	0.703	0.745	0.668	0.703	0.916	22.60	29.676	5,863,828	11

Bold values indicate the best scores. Inference time is measured on the full test portion of the dataset. ★ Primary performance metric.

Next, the set of best ensemble combinations was selected for comparison between CNN-only, DNN-only, and hybrid ensembles. The proposed best-candidate-selection procedure is shown in Figure 6. It is a two-stage mechanism combining Pareto analysis with weighted radar-area scoring. The Pareto analysis is a standard when dealing with the design of resource-constrained smart devices, as it combines performance and device-aware constraints, and results in the best models for multiple optimization objectives [60–62]. Therefore, the first stage of the selection procedure consists of two steps, and performs a multi-objective Pareto algorithm (in step 1), extracting the trade-off models (temporary best candidates) that are on the Pareto frontier. These models are considered equally good, and they are better than the Pareto-dominated models in terms of all the optimization objectives [62]. The Pareto analysis used here is performed as a classical multiple 2D analysis in parallel, but in a simplified form. Namely, the authors in [60] demonstrated that when the number of objectives is more than two, the Pareto front becomes more complicated, so in the proposed setup, a single performance metric is fixed (wS) and tested versus each of the three complemented complexity metrics ($Size^C$, $FLOPs^C$, and $Time^C$) separately. The former values $Size^C$, $FLOPs^C$, and $Time^C$ are calculated by normalizing the complexity parameters (size [MB], FLOPs (M), and inference time [s]) w.r.t. the maximal value and calculating their complement (Equation (4)), such that the final goal in each analysis is to maximize both objectives.

$$Size^C = 1 - Size_{norm}, FLOPs^C = 1 - FLOPs_{norm}, Time^C = 1 - Time_{norm}. \quad (4)$$

Table 4. The classification efficiency of existing CNNs using the MedMNIST dataset.

MNIST Dataset	Model	★wS	wP	F1	BA	AUC	Size [MB]	FLOPs (M)	Params	Inference Time [s]
Path	Adjei_CNN5 (A)	0.851	0.853	0.846	0.806	0.979	4.280	495.324	1,123,081	45
	Diniz_CNN2 (B1)	0.796	0.813	0.799	0.759	0.966	6.17	**19.097**	1,618,345	**8**
	Diniz_CNN4 (B2)	0.845	0.853	0.846	0.803	0.981	3.32	39.205	870,953	11
	Diniz_CNN6 (B3)	0.841	0.850	0.842	0.800	0.979	**3.10**	60.345	**813,865**	14
	Diniz_CNN8 (B4)	**0.852**	**0.859**	**0.851**	**0.814**	**0.983**	5.48	88.144	1,436,969	16
	small_CNN3 (C1)	0.859	0.869	0.860	0.816	0.980	6.24	**48.071**	1,635,561	**11**
	DaSilva_CNN6 (C2)	**0.894**	**0.900**	**0.894**	**0.869**	**0.988**	**4.16**	147.708	**1,091,113**	28
	large_CNN9 (C3)	0.875	0.879	0.875	0.845	0.979	12.98	350.592	3,402,281	54
	small_CNN3 (D1)	0.798	0.824	0.804	0.768	0.959	12.37	**51.486**	3,242,729	**13**
	small_CNN6 (D2)	0.824	0.859	0.831	0.804	0.978	**7.24**	149.645	**1,896,105**	29
	DaSilva_CNN9 (D3)	**0.852**	**0.872**	**0.855**	**0.823**	**0.976**	17.01	353.127	4,455,081	59
OrganA	Diniz_CNN2 (B1)	0.837	0.843	0.839	0.821	0.979	6.18	**19.097**	1,618,859	**12**
	Diniz_CNN4 (B2)	0.861	0.866	0.862	0.843	0.983	3.32	39.206	871,467	18
	Diniz_CNN6 (B3)	0.872	0.874	0.873	**0.865**	0.988	**3.11**	60.346	**814,379**	24
	Diniz_CNN8 (B4)	**0.879**	**0.880**	**0.879**	**0.865**	**0.990**	5.48	88.145	1,437,483	34
	small_CNN2 (C1)	0.886	0.886	0.885	0.872	0.991	1.57	**16.735**	412,395	**10**
	small_CNN4 (C2)	0.908	0.911	0.908	0.899	0.994	**1.02**	38.073	**267,243**	26
	DaSilva_CNN6 (C3)	0.915	0.917	0.915	0.906	**0.995**	1.60	59.644	419,307	28
	large_CNN8 (C4)	**0.918**	**0.921**	**0.919**	**0.909**	**0.995**	4.73	87.846	1,239,531	37
	small_CNN3 (D1)	0.896	0.897	0.896	0.888	0.993	12.37	**51.487**	3,243,243	**27**
	small_CNN6 (D2)	0.915	0.917	0.915	0.906	0.996	**7.24**	149.646	**1,896,619**	59
	DaSilva_CNN9 (D3)	**0.931**	**0.933**	**0.931**	**0.922**	**0.997**	17.01	353.128	4,455,595	121
OCT	Diniz_CNN2 (B1)	0.691	0.742	0.646	0.691	0.918	6.17	**19.094**	1,617,060	**1**
	Diniz_CNN4 (B2)	0.699	0.745	0.660	0.699	0.925	3.32	39.202	869,668	2
	Diniz_CNN6 (B3)	0.721	0.774	0.693	0.721	**0.941**	**3.10**	60.342	**812,580**	3
	Diniz_CNN8 (B4)	**0.735**	**0.775**	**0.712**	**0.735**	0.940	5.48	88.142	1,435,684	3
	small_CNN3 (C1)	0.737	0.800	0.703	0.737	0.949	3.17	**46.564**	831,908	**1**
	small_CNN6 (C2)	0.762	**0.826**	0.735	0.762	**0.965**	**2.63**	147.055	**689,124**	4
	DaSilva_CNN9 (C3)	**0.777**	0.824	**0.758**	**0.777**	0.964	10.99	349.747	2,878,436	11
	small_CNN3 (D1)	0.717	0.787	0.679	0.717	0.942	12.37	**51.484**	3,241,444	**2**
	small_CNN6 (D2)	**0.793**	0.831	0.774	**0.793**	**0.966**	**7.23**	149.642	**1,894,820**	5
	DaSilva_CNN9 (D3)	0.790	**0.833**	**0.776**	0.790	0.953	17.00	353.125	4,453,796	7

Bold values indicate the best scores. Inference time is measured on the full test portion of the dataset. ★ Primary performance metric.

The output of each Pareto analysis (wS vs. $Size^C$, wS vs. $FLOPs^C$, and wS vs. $Time^C$) is a set P_i, $i = 1,2,3$ that contains the temporary "best" candidates from each Pareto frontier. Due to the different nature of the analysis, set P_i values do not necessarily contain the same candidates, so an intersection is performed to find the set of candidates $Q = P1 \cap P2 \cap P3$) containing the "best" ensembles in all three Pareto contexts. The ensemble combinations that are found in at least one of the Pareto frontiers are calculated as the union $U = P1 \cup P2 \cup P3$. The former stage 1 is repeated for each class separately, i.e., for CNN-only, DNN-only, and hybrid ensembles. Hence, the sets Q_{CNN}, Q_{DNN}, and Q_{HYBRID} are extracted and forwarded to the filtering process in the next stage, where, once again, there are two separate steps. First, the union $F = Q_{CNN} \cup Q_{DNN} \cup Q_{HYBRID}$ is calculated, containing the "best" ensembles from each class. Then, the resulting set F with the filtered candidates is re-evaluated using a weighted radar-area scoring in step 2. Finally, the best architectures from each class, F_{CNN}, F_{DNN}, F_{HYBRID}, are extracted, as well as a single best architecture, F_{best}.

https://doi.org/10.3390/electronics15071470

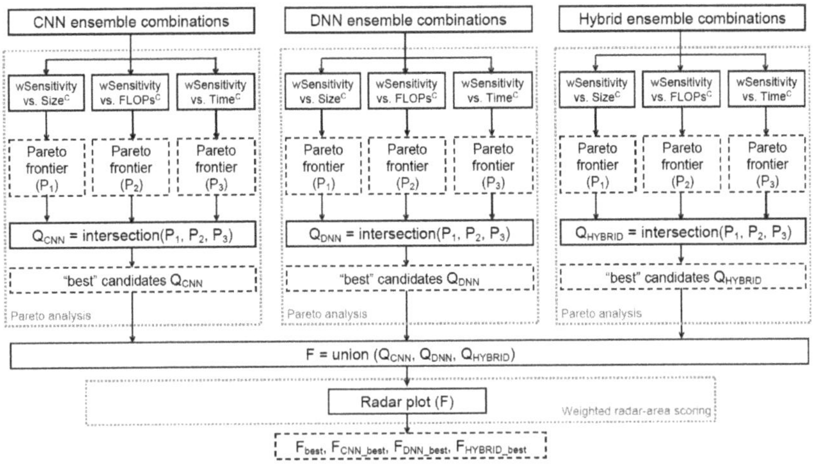

Figure 6. The proposed methodology combining the Pareto analysis and weighted radar-area scoring.

Radar plots are a standardized way to visually compare the data by means of multiple parameters displayed along their axis [30]. The authors in the literature either use only performance-related or complexity-related metrics on the radar plot, where a model (polygon) having a larger or smaller area is better than the other [31,63], or they combine both metrics [29]. In the proposed framework, the latter approach is adopted, but with the complemented complexity axis, such that the maximal polygon area is required. The area of the polygon is calculated by a simple mathematical formula using the polygon vertices' coordinates [64]. Seven metrics in total, i.e., three complexity and four performance metrics, are included in the evaluation. Parameter $F1$ is excluded from the plot as it is considered redundant, since other metrics like wS, wP, and BA are used. The performance metrics are already in the range [0–1], and the simplest solution for the complexity metrics (size [MB], FLOPs (M), and inference time [s]) would be to normalize them with respect to the maximal value and complement them. However, this could create a bias towards low-complexity models, and to accomplish a fairer comparison, a weighted radar plot is constructed, assigning weights equal to 1 for the performance metrics, while the complexity metrics are scaled with weights w_{size}, w_{FLOPs}, and w_{time}. This idea was inspired by [32], who used an inverse-variance weighting approach to reduce the impact of high-variance features during training.

The complexity parameters (size [MB], FLOPs (M), and inference time [s]) are first normalized with respect to the maximal value, and the normalized values $Size_{norm}$, $FLOPs_{norm}$, and $Time_{norm}$, are scaled by weights $w_s = 1/m_s, w_f = 1/m_f$, and $w_t = 1/m_t$, where m_s, m_f, and m_t are the mean values of each metric (before normalization). The final complemented values for the complexity axes in the radar plot are calculated by Equation (5).

$$Size^C = 1 - w_s * Size_{norm}, FLOPs^C = 1 - w_f * FLOPs_{norm}, Time^C = 1 - w_t * Time_{norm}. \quad (5)$$

The weighted radar-area scoring mechanism extracts the selected ensemble candidates from each category, i.e., $F_{CNN_{best}}$, $F_{DNN_{best}}$, and $F_{HYBRID_{best}}$, and F_{best} is the final best ensemble. However, if the final goal is to select the "implementable" architecture that can fit the posed FPGA memory requirement of ≤34 MB, the set of ensembles in the Pareto frontier (F) could be refined by the mentioned constraint before the radar-area scoring procedure. To differentiate between these two sets throughout this paper, the filtered set F containing the "implementable" architectures only is denoted with F'. Furthermore, the

https://doi.org/10.3390/electronics15071470

candidates extracted by the radar plot ranking the filtered set F' are denoted as $F'_{CNN_{best}}$, $F'_{DNN_{best}}$, $F'_{HYBRID_{best}}$, and $F'best$.

4. Results and Discussion

4.1. The Efficiency of the Existing Single CNNs and DNNs

Considering the complexity of DNNs in Table 3, the results show that MobileNetV2 offers lower complexity than MobileNetV3 (it is 2.8 MB smaller in size and requires ~0.4 M fewer FLOPs), followed by a higher performance score, which is in concordance with [10]. The exact increase in the obtained wS score is ~3.8%, ~1.2%, and ~2.8%, for PathMNIST, OrganAMNIST, and OCTMNIST, respectively. The inference time for both MobileNet variants is lower than with other architectures because their total number of parameters is smaller. However, MobileNetV2 stands out in terms of time and memory requirements, providing the best compromise and being the most lightweight among the selected DNN baseline architectures [39].

The results in Table 4 confirm that customized CNNs from the literature provide higher performance and reduced memory requirements than state-of-the-art DNNs [55,56]. Moreover, results are in concordance with Da Silva et al. [56], whose custom CNN solution is better than the one from Diniz et al. [54]. To summarize, the results show that the best CNN is always better in wS performance than MobileNetV2 (~2.3%, ~1.2%, and ~5.9%) for all three datasets, while the size is ±5 MB depending on the dataset used. Nevertheless, the best CNN is on average up to five times slower than MobileNetV2 (and even slower than DenseNet in terms of inference). Furthermore, considering FLOPs as a measurement of how easy it is to implement a model in hardware, DNNs win over custom CNNs, as the latter requires ~350 M operations to be executed, whereas for MobileNetV2, it is ~11 M (and ~100 M for DenseNet). One could explain this as MobileNetV2 being a highly optimized architecture, specifically designed for computational efficiency. For example, FLOPs are reduced using depthwise convolutions and residual blocks. In contrast, a custom CNN often uses standard convolution layers with a larger number of filters that involve more MAC operations, or the architectural design with convolutional, pooling, and fully connected layers is less efficient, increasing FLOPs.

4.2. The Efficiency of the Average Ensemble Models

4.2.1. The Ensemble of CNNs

The example of the Pareto analysis procedure selecting the best CNN-only ensembles and a visualization of the search space for the OrganAMNIST dataset are presented in Figure 7. For convenience, the other two datasets (PathMNIST and OCTMNIST) are included in Appendix A (Figures A1 and A2). The result of the top-N CNN ensembles that were found in at least one of the Pareto frontiers during the analysis is given in Table 5. As explained, the candidates constitute the union set U_{CNN}, and are shown for each dataset, i.e., the U_{CNN} for PathMNIST, OrganAMNIST, and OCTMNIST, respectively. Gray shade indicates the best-trade-off CNN-only ensembles selected by the Pareto algorithm. As explained in the methodology, these candidates constitute the set Q_{CNN}, and are found in the resulting Pareto frontier of all three Pareto contexts.

It can be seen that in this first stage of the proposed best model selection procedure, A_B4_C2_C3 and A_C2 are selected as the best-performing models for the PathMNIST dataset. For OrganAMNIST, models C3_D3 and B1_C1 are extracted, while for OCTMNIST, C3_D3, C2_D2, and B3_C2 are highlighted. As each model corresponds to the Pareto frontier set of points, they are optimal at least in one of the objectives, allowing any of them to be designated as the top performer in this stage.

https://doi.org/10.3390/electronics15071470

Table 5. The performance evaluation metrics for the top-N CNN ensembles that were found in at least one of the Pareto frontiers during the Pareto analysis (U_{CNN}). Gray shade indicates the selected best-trade-off CNN-only ensembles in all three Pareto contexts (Q_{CNN}).

MNIST Dataset	Model	*wS	wP	F1	BA	AUC	Size [MB]	FLOPs (M)	Inference Time [s]
Path	A_B4_C2_C3	**0.899**	**0.903**	**0.899**	**0.867**	0.988	21.160	1081.768	54
	B4_C2_C3_D2	0.897	0.902	0.897	**0.867**	0.988	29.860	736.089	54
	A_C2	0.896	0.901	0.896	0.865	0.986	8.440	643.032	45
	B4_C2_D3	0.891	0.896	0.891	0.859	**0.989**	26.650	588.979	59
	B4_C2	0.888	0.892	0.888	0.857	0.988	9.640	235.852	28
	B3_C2	0.879	0.884	0.879	0.844	0.987	**7.260**	208.053	28
	B2_C1	0.871	0.880	0.873	0.830	0.983	9.560	87.276	**11**
	B1_C1	0.840	0.850	0.840	0.797	0.981	12.410	**67.168**	**11**
OrganA	C3_D3	**0.932**	**0.933**	**0.932**	**0.922**	**0.996**	18.610	412.772	121
	B4_C3_C4_D2	0.925	0.927	0.926	0.917	**0.996**	19.050	385.281	59
	B3_B4_C3_C4_D2	0.924	0.926	0.925	0.917	**0.996**	22.160	445.627	37
	B3_C3_D2	0.924	0.925	0.924	0.918	0.995	11.950	269.636	59
	C3_D2	0.922	0.924	0.922	0.913	0.996	8.840	209.290	59
	B3_C4	0.913	0.914	0.914	0.910	0.995	7.840	148.192	37
	B2_C2_D1	0.908	0.910	0.908	0.900	0.994	16.710	128.766	27
	C2_D1	0.907	0.909	0.907	0.900	0.995	13.390	89.560	27
	B3_C3	0.903	0.904	0.903	0.898	0.994	4.710	119.990	28
	C1_D1	0.903	0.903	0.902	0.894	0.993	13.940	68.222	27
	B2_C2	0.891	0.894	0.892	0.878	0.994	4.340	77.279	26
	B1_C1	0.866	0.869	0.866	0.852	0.990	**1.750**	**35.832**	**12**
OCT	C3_D3	**0.796**	**0.836**	**0.781**	**0.796**	0.966	27.990	702.872	11
	C3_D2	0.794	**0.836**	0.773	0.794	**0.972**	18.220	499.389	11
	C2_D2	0.785	**0.836**	0.762	0.785	0.970	9.860	296.697	5
	B4_D2	0.772	0.812	0.750	0.772	0.964	12.710	237.784	5
	B3_D2	0.760	0.815	0.735	0.760	0.965	10.330	209.984	5
	B3_C2	0.744	0.803	0.714	0.744	0.964	5.730	207.397	4
	C1_D1	0.735	0.803	0.698	0.735	0.952	15.540	98.048	2
	B2_C1	0.726	0.782	0.692	0.726	0.947	**6.490**	85.766	2
	B1_C1	0.716	0.778	0.670	0.716	0.948	9.340	**65.658**	**1**

Bold values indicate the best scores. The values are sorted by the wS score. * Primary performance metric. Inference time is estimated based on the slowest model in the ensemble.

The mean difference in sensitivity between selected models (when compared to the best result marked in bold) is $\Delta wS \sim 0.3\%$, $\Delta wS \sim 6.6\%$, and $\Delta wS \sim 3.2\%$ for PathMNIST, OrganAMNIST, and OCTMNIST, while the complexity in terms of individual metrics (size, FLOPs, and time) differs for more than ~50%.

As expected, the maximal performance that can be obtained by the ensembled CNN models is enhanced compared to using single CNN networks, i.e., 89.4% to 89.9%, 93.1% to 93.2%, and 79.3% to 79.6%, for PathMNIST, OrganAMNIST, and OCTMNIST, respectively. Furthermore, the size of the ensemble increases (4.16 MB to 21.16 MB, 17.01 MB to 18.61 MB, and 7.23 MB to 27.99 MB).

4.2.2. The Ensemble of DNNs

The result of selecting top-N DNN ensemble combinations with the Pareto analysis is given in Table 6. The search process for OrganAMNIST is visualized in Figure 8, while, again, for convenience, other datasets are included in Appendix A (Figures A3 and A4). The results show that the efficiency of a DNN ensemble is higher than using single DNNs.

https://doi.org/10.3390/electronics15071470

The maximal sensitivity increases from 88.6% to 89.9% (PathMNIST), 94.2% to 94.9% (OrganAMNIST), and 73.4% to 76.6% (OCTMNIST), and the size of the ensemble increases from 26.88 MB to 35.54 MB, 26.89 MB to 49.52 MB, and 8.63 MB to 125.53 MB for PathMNIST, OrganAMNIST, and OCTMNIST, respectively. Following a premise with the posed memory requirement for the FPGA (≤34 MB size), only two combinations from the listed U_{DNN} architectures are useful and fit the device's on-chip memory for all datasets (MobNetV2_EffB0 and MobNetV2_MobV3).

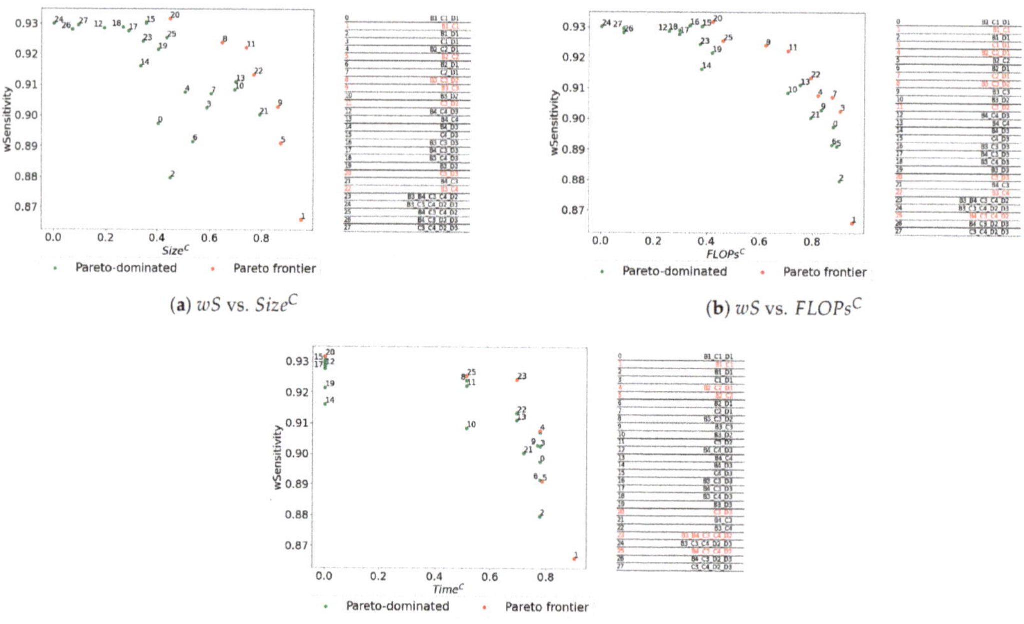

(**a**) wS vs. $Size^C$ (**b**) wS vs. $FLOPs^C$ (**c**) wS vs. $Time^C$

Figure 7. Pareto analysis results extracting the CNN-only ensembles that constitute the Pareto frontier (OrganAMNIST). These points (denoted in red) constitute the sets P_1, P_2, and P_3. The search space is visible in the tables next to the plots. To ensure figure clarity, some point labels in high-density regions are omitted to prevent overlap.

Table 6. The performance evaluation metrics for the top-N DNN ensembles that were found in at least one of the Pareto frontiers during the Pareto analysis (U_{DNN}). Gray shade indicates the selected best trade-off DNN-only ensembles in all three Pareto contexts (Q_{DNN}).

MNIST Dataset	Model	★wS	wP	F1	BA	AUC	Size [MB]	FLOPs (M)	Inference Time [s]
Path	Dense121_MobNetV2	**0.899**	0.902	0.899	0.872	0.988	35.54	127.14	46
	MobNetV2_MobV3_EffB0	**0.899**	**0.904**	**0.900**	**0.875**	**0.989**	42.74	52.611	21
	MobNetV2_EffB0	0.895	0.899	0.895	0.869	0.988	31.28	40.754	21
	MobNetV2_MobV3	0.882	0.887	0.882	0.856	0.984	**20.12**	**23.285**	**13**
OrganA	Dense121_Res50_EffB0	**0.949**	**0.950**	**0.949**	**0.946**	**0.997**	139.59	297.082	83
	Dense121_EffB0	**0.949**	0.949	0.948	**0.946**	**0.997**	49.52	146.301	77
	MobNetV2_MobV3_EffB0	0.941	0.941	0.940	0.937	**0.997**	42.77	53.576	34
	MobNetV2_EffB0	0.938	0.938	0.937	0.933	0.996	31.30	41.463	34
	MobNetV2_MobV3	0.934	0.934	0.933	0.930	0.996	**20.14**	**23.882**	**28**

https://doi.org/10.3390/electronics15071470

Table 6. *Cont.*

MNIST Dataset	Model	★wS	wP	F1	BA	AUC	Size [MB]	FLOPs (M)	Inference Time [s]
OCT	MobNetV2_Dense121_Res50	**0.766**	**0.818**	**0.735**	**0.766**	**0.957**	125.53	279.096	14
	MobNetV2_Res50	0.749	0.780	0.717	0.749	0.953	90.01	162.504	10
	MobNetV2_Dense121	0.740	0.790	0.708	0.740	0.951	35.52	128.343	14
	MobNetV2_MobV3_EffB0	0.733	0.779	0.698	0.733	0.948	42.67	53.527	11
	MobNetV2_MobV3	0.726	0.767	0.689	0.726	0.945	**20.07**	**23.851**	**9**

Bold values indicate the best scores. The values are sorted by the wS score. ★ Primary performance metric. Inference time is estimated based on the slowest model in the ensemble.

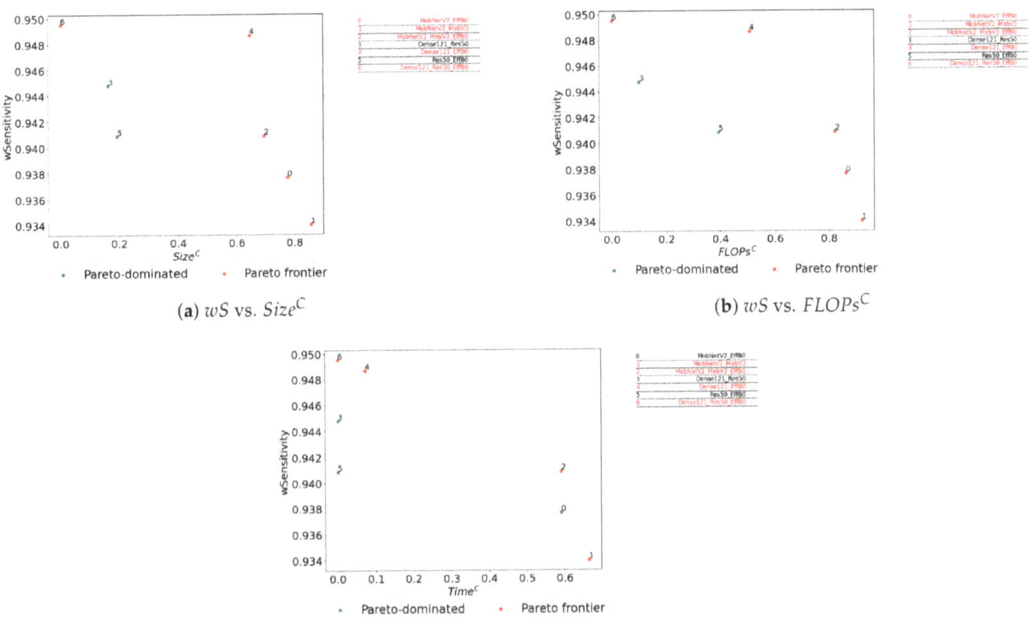

(**a**) wS vs. $Size^C$ (**b**) wS vs. $FLOPs^C$ (**c**) wS vs. $Time^C$

Figure 8. Pareto analysis results extracting the DNN-only ensembles that constitute the Pareto frontier (OrganAMNIST). These points (denoted in red) constitute the sets P_1, P_2, and P_3. The search space is visible in the tables next to the plots.

It can be seen in Table 6 that the MobNetV2_MobV3 combination is always among the best trade-off models from the set Q_{DNN} for all three datasets (highlighted in gray). It has ∼1.7%, ∼1.5%, and ∼4% lower wS scores than the best-performing model for the PathMNIST, OrganAMNIST, and OCTMNIST datasets, while the complexity in terms of size, FLOPs, and time is decreased for more than ∼50%. In the case of the OCTMNIST dataset, the biggest savings are accomplished, as this DNN-only ensemble provides a ∼84% and ∼90% decrease in size and FLOPs compared to the best-performing MobNetV2_Dense121_Res50 combination (marked in bold).

4.2.3. Hybrid Ensemble Models Combining CNNs and DNNs

The Pareto analysis compares the hybrid ensemble combinations results with the U_{HYBRID} set of models listed in Table 7. The top-N selected Pareto optimal ones are indicated in gray and constitute the set Q_{HYBRID}. This process is visualized in Figure 9 (OrganAMNIST), as well as in Appendix A Figures A5 (PathMNIST) and A6 (OCTMNIST).

https://doi.org/10.3390/electronics15071470

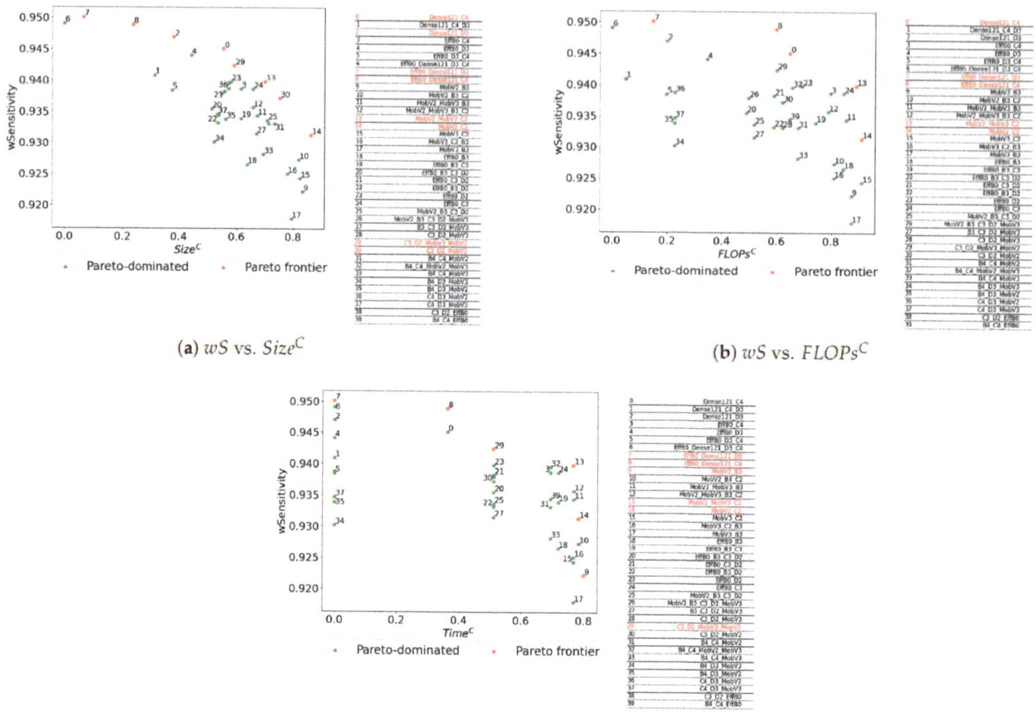

(**a**) wS vs. $Size^C$ (**b**) wS vs. $FLOPs^C$ (**c**) wS vs. $Time^C$

Figure 9. Pareto analysis results extracting the hybrid ensembles that constitute the Pareto frontier (OrganAMNIST). These points (denoted in red) constitute the sets P_1, P_2, and P_3. The search space is visible in the tables next to the plots. To ensure figure clarity, some point labels in high-density regions are omitted to prevent overlap.

It can be seen that the Dense121_Res50_C2_C3, MobNetV2_MobV3_C2_D2, and MobNetV2_B2 combinations are the best for PathMNIST. The hybrid classification models EffB0_Dense121_D3, EffB0_Dense121_C4, MobNetV2_MobV3_C2, and MobNetV2_C2 are extracted for OrganAMNIST. The OCTMNIST dataset has three top architectures, i.e., MobNetV2_C3_D2, MobNetV2_D2, and MobNetV2_C2. The mean difference in sensitivity between the selected models (when compared to the best result marked in bold) is $\Delta wS \sim 1.3\%$, $\Delta wS \sim 1\%$, and $\Delta wS \sim 1.9\%$ for PathMNIST, OrganAMNIST, and OCTMNIST, while the complexity in terms of size, FLOPs, and time differs for more than ~50%.

Table 7. The performance evaluation metrics for the top-N hybrid ensembles that were found in at least one of the Pareto frontiers during the Pareto analysis (U_{HYBRID}). Gray shade indicates the selected best trade-off hybrid ensembles in all three Pareto contexts (Q_{HYBRID}).

MNIST Dataset	Model	★wS	wP	F1	BA	AUC	Size [MB]	FLOPs (M)	Inference Time [s]
Path	Dense121_Res50_C2_C3	**0.911**	**0.913**	**0.911**	**0.883**	**0.991**	133.920	772.507	54
	MobNetV2_MobV3_C2_D2	0.908	**0.913**	0.908	0.882	0.990	31.520	320.638	29
	Dense121_C2	0.906	0.908	0.905	0.877	0.991	31.040	263.420	46
	MobNetV2_MobV3_A_C2	0.905	0.908	0.905	0.877	0.990	28.560	666.317	45
	MobNetV2_A_C2	0.902	0.907	0.902	0.873	0.990	17.100	654.460	45
	MobNetV2_B4_C2	0.902	0.906	0.902	0.876	0.991	18.300	247.280	28
	MobNetV2_C2	0.898	0.901	0.897	0.873	0.991	12.820	159.136	28

https://doi.org/10.3390/electronics15071470

Table 7. *Cont.*

MNIST Dataset	Model	★wS	wP	F1	BA	AUC	Size [MB]	FLOPs (M)	Inference Time [s]
Path	MobNetV2_MobV3_B2	0.893	0.896	0.893	0.864	0.988	23.440	62.490	14
	MobNetV2_B2	0.888	0.891	0.888	0.859	0.988	11.980	**50.633**	**11**
	MobNetV2_B3	0.887	0.892	0.887	0.858	0.987	**11.760**	71.773	14
OrganA	EffB0_Dense121_D3	**0.950**	**0.951**	**0.950**	**0.946**	**0.998**	66.530	499.429	121
	EffB0_Dense121_C4	0.949	0.950	0.949	0.945	**0.998**	54.250	234.147	77
	Dense121_D3	0.947	0.948	0.947	0.941	**0.998**	43.900	469.735	121
	Dense121_C4	0.945	0.946	0.945	0.940	0.997	31.620	204.453	77
	C3_D2_MobV3_MobV2	0.942	0.943	0.942	0.938	0.997	28.980	233.172	59
	MobV2_MobV3_C2	0.940	0.940	0.939	0.936	0.997	21.160	61.955	28
	C3_D2_MobV2	0.937	0.938	0.937	0.932	0.997	17.510	221.059	59
	MobV2_C2	0.931	0.932	0.931	0.928	0.996	**9.690**	**49.842**	26
	MobV2_B3	0.922	0.922	0.922	0.920	0.995	11.780	72.115	**24**
OCT	MobNetV2_C3_D2	**0.791**	**0.837**	**0.769**	**0.791**	**0.968**	26.850	511.140	11
	MobNetV2_C3	0.788	0.832	0.767	0.788	0.963	19.620	361.498	11
	MobNetV2_D2	0.781	0.823	0.758	0.781	0.963	15.860	161.393	5
	MobNetV2_C2_D2	0.781	0.828	0.757	0.781	0.967	18.490	308.448	5
	MobNetV2_C2	0.763	0.818	0.731	0.763	0.963	**11.260**	158.806	4
	MobNetV2_B3	0.748	0.799	0.718	0.748	0.952	11.730	**72.093**	4

Bold values indicate the best scores. The values are sorted by the wS score. ★ Primary performance metric. Inference time is estimated based on the slowest model in the ensemble.

4.3. The Comparison Between CNN-Only, DNN-Only, and Hybrid Ensembles

In the second stage of the proposed best-candidate-selection procedure, the selected Pareto-optimal combinations (7, 10, and 9 in total from PathMNIST, OrganAMNIST, and OCTMNIST, respectively) are compared using a weighted radar-area scoring. In Figure 10, all models from the set F are evaluated. In Figure 11, the "non-implementable" architectures are first filtered out, such that the resulting set F' of 5 (PathMNIST), 5 (OrganAMNIST), and 7 (OCTMNIST) remaining models is constructed before radar-plot evaluation. When considering the rank of the individual ensemble types (CNN-only, DNN-only, and hybrid), evaluated by comparing the maximal area scores for each, it can be seen that hybrid ensembles are always better than DNN-only (for all three datasets). Moreover, a hybrid approach outperforms CNN-only ensembles in two out of three datasets, as for OCTMNIST, the CNN-only architecture is selected as the best one. All the resulting radar-evaluated rankings are reasonable, and can be confirmed by comparing the best results (marked in bold) from Tables 5–7.

Overall, the extracted best models in each ensemble category ($F_{CNN_{best}}$, $F_{DNN_{best}}$, and $F_{HYBRID_{best}}$) from Figure 10 are the following:

- A_C2, A_B4_C2_C3, Dense121_MobNetV2, MobNetV2_MobV3_C2_D2 (PathMNIST);
- C3_D3, Dense121_EffNetB0, and EffB0_Dense121_C4 (OrganAMNIST);
- C2_D2, MobNetV2_Dense121_Res50, and MobNetV2_D2 (OCTMNIST).

The single best architectures selected by the candidate-selection procedure is MobileNetV2_MobV3_C2_D2 (PathMNIST), EffB0_Dense121_C4 (OrganAMNIST), and C2_D2 (OCTMNIST). Hence, a hybrid model is selected in two out of these three cases.

To better understand why the CNN-only ensemble outperformed the hybrid ensemble with OCTMNIST, and why the above-mentioned exceptions exist in the class-based rankings of the ensembles for OCTMNIST and OrganAMNIST, the Pareto analysis is performed between all models from set F. For OrganAMNIST, models C3_D3 ($F_{CNN_{best}}$) and Dense121_EffNetB0 ($F_{DNN_{best}}$) are both equally good concerning wS vs. $Size^C$ analysis, but regarding the trade-off between sensitivity and $FLOPs^C$ and $Time^C$, the DNN-only representative will dominate. Similarly, with the OCTMNIST dataset, its best hybrid representative (MobileNetV2_D2) is dominated by the best one from CNN-only (C2_D2) in both wS vs. $Size^C$ and wS vs. $Time^C$ analysis, while they are equally good or Pareto-optimal when evaluating wS vs. $FLOPs^C$. However, when $FLOPs^C$ are considered, a hybrid solution could be even better, offering a negligible drop in performance (a wS score of 78.1% compared to 78.5%), but having a much better complexity of ∼45% less FLOPs (∼161 M compared to ∼297 M). In addition, calculating the distance from the best point (C2_D2) to all other points, it can be seen that although dominated, the hybrid model (MobileNetV2_D2) is the closest point in the Pareto plane. For reference, the visualization of the Pareto analysis is given in Appendix A Figure A7.

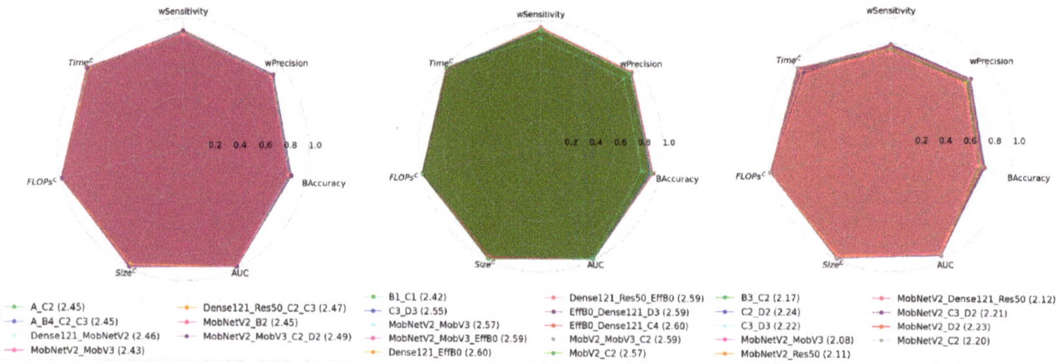

(a) PathMNIST (b) OrganAMNIST (c) OCTMNIST

Figure 10. A radar chart with seven metrics and N polygons for comparing all Pareto-optimal best ensembles (from set F) with weighted radar-area scoring and extracting $F_{CNN_{best}}$, $F_{DNN_{best}}$, and $F_{HYBRID_{best}}$. Model with the largest area is the best of all (F_{best}).

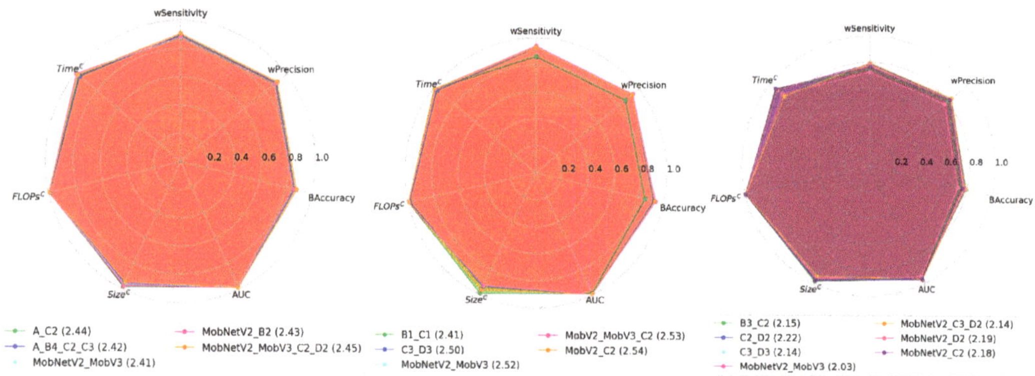

(a) PathMNIST (b) OrganAMNIST (c) OCTMNIST

Figure 11. A weighted radar chart comparing only the "implementable" trade-off ensembles extracted from Pareto analysis (from set F') and extracting $F'_{CNN_{best}}$, $F'_{DNN_{best}}$, and $F'_{HYBRID_{best}}$. Model with the largest area is the best of all (F'_{best}).

However, some selected models from Figure 10 (Dense121_MobNetV2, Dense121_EffB0, EffB0_Dense121_C4, and MobNetV2_Dense121_Res50) do not fit the FPGA memory requirement assumption, as their total sizes are 35.54 MB, 49.52 MB, 54.25 MB, and 125.53 MB, respectively (≥34 MB). When the filtered set F', containing only the "implementable" architectures, is imported into the radar plot evaluation (Figure 11), the extracted best models for each ensemble category that can fit within the theoretical FPGA resources are the following:

- A_C2, MobNetV2_MobV3, and MobNetV2_MobV3_C2_D2 (PathMNIST);
- C3_D3, MobNetV2_MobV3, and MobNetV2_C2 (OrganAMNIST);
- C2_D2, MobNetV2_MobV3, and MobNetV2_D2 (OCTMNIST).

The single best architecture selected by the candidate's selection procedure is MobNetV2_MobV3_C2_D2 (PathMNIST), MobNetV2_C2 (OrganAMNIST), and C2_D2 (OCTMNIST). Hence, a hybrid model is once again selected in two out of three cases, whereas the hybrid MobNetV2_D2 is closest to the selected C2_D2 with the OCTMNIST dataset.

The DNN-only ensembles that are selected from all three datasets (MobNetV2_MobV3) are "implementable". They improve accuracy compared to a single MobileNetV3 on all datasets, but outperform MobileNetV2 on two out of three datasets. The lower performance of the ensemble for OCTMNIST (72.6%) is due to the averaging method applied between the two models, as the difference between the MobileNetV2 and MobileNetV3 performances is too large (73.4% and 70.6%), causing a drop in the mean result when averaging their prediction scores. Still, the reduction in FLOPs and timing is significant for the MobV2_MobV3 architecture, causing it to be the more "lightweight" in that sense. When comparing DNN-only and CNN-only, the latter wins in two out of three datasets, as with OrganAMNIST, the CNN-only ensemble is the least efficient of all.

Overall, the hybrid ensemble is the winning architecture against all three datasets. It offers a good compromise between performance and complexity, as it incorporates the benefits of both ensemble types. The total number of FLOPs is decreased compared to CNN-only, and it uses up less memory than DNN-only. Its performance in terms of wS value is 90.8%, 93.1%, and 78.1%, for PathMNIST, OrganAMNIST, and OCTMNIST, respectively. The size [MB], FLOPs (M), and time [s] of the models are 31.52 MB, 320.638 M, and 29 s (PathMNIST); 9.69 MB, 49.842 M, and 26 s (OrganAMNIST); and 15.86 MB, 161.393 M, and 5 s (OCTMNIST). Therefore, the hybrid ensemble is proposed as the final solution for potential implementation on a resource-constrained device such as an FPGA.

4.4. *Performance with Other Ensemble Strategies*

4.4.1. Stacking Ensemble

To improve the performance of the ensembles, another version of the late fusion, instead of averaging, was tested. It is called stacking—an ensemble strategy where the predictions of several base models are input to a meta-model, which gives a final prediction. The two versions of the meta-model are examined, having a single or a double hidden dense layer. The optimization is carried out by varying the number of neurons on each dense layer; 8, 16, 32, 64 for a single and 8_16, 8_32, 8_64, 16_32, 16_64, 32_64 combinations for a double meta-layer. For simplicity, only CNN-based ensembles were tested, and a single dataset is shown here, i.e., the smallest one—OrganAMNIST. The results of the other two datasets (PathMNIST and OCTMNIST) are given in Appendix B, Tables A1 and A2. Furthermore, two metrics are kept as representatives of performance (wS, AUC) and complexity (size, FLOPs). Table 8 shows that the results are very similar to averaging. The Mann–Whitney U-test confirms that there are no significant statistical differences between the stacking and averaging results ($U = 40$, $p = 0.469$; $U = 48$, $p = 0.909$). Furthermore, there is no statistically significant difference in performance when using a single or double meta-layer ($U = 42.5$, $p = 0.594$). Hence, there is no point in stacking the individual learners and spending time on re-training the meta-learner, as a simpler algorithm with averaging offers similar results (and adding meta-learner layers to the network would slightly increase the total model size).

https://doi.org/10.3390/electronics15071470

Table 8. The efficiency for stacking with a meta-learner (OrganAMNIST).

Fusion Method	Num of Hidden Layers in Meta-Learner	Model	★wS	AUC	Size [MB]	FLOPs (M)
Average ensemble (no meta-learner)	-	C3_D3	**0.932**	0.996	18.61	412.772
		B3_C3_D3	0.930	0.996	21.72	473.118
		C4_D3	0.930	**0.997**	21.74	440.974
		B4_C3_C4_D2	0.925	0.996	19.05	385.281
		B3_C3_D2	0.924	0.995	11.95	269.636
		C3_D2	0.922	0.996	8.84	209.29
		B3_C4	0.913	0.995	7.84	148.192
		B4_C3	0.900	0.995	**7.08**	**147.789**
Stacking with meta-learner	single	C3_D3_64	0.920	**0.992**	18.64	412.776
		B3_C3_D3_64	0.929	0.990	21.74	473.124
		C4_D3_64	**0.931**	0.991	21.77	440.978
		B4_C3_C4_D2_8	0.924	0.989	19.08	385.282
		B3_C3_D2_8	0.921	0.990	11.99	269.637
		C3_D2_32	0.921	0.992	8.86	209.292
		B3_C4_8	0.901	0.989	7.86	148.193
		B4_C3_8	0.888	0.986	**7.10**	**147.790**
	double	C3_D3_16_64	**0.933**	0.989	18.64	412.774
		B3_C3_D3_32_64	0.927	**0.990**	21.74	473.126
		C4_D3_32_64	0.931	0.989	21.79	440.981
		B4_C3_C4_D2_8_32	0.925	0.986	19.08	385.283
		B3_C3_D2_16_64	0.921	0.989	12.01	269.638
		C3_D2_16_64	0.921	0.989	8.88	209.292
		B3_C4_8_64	0.900	0.988	7.87	148.195
		B4_C3_16_32	0.889	0.983	**7.13**	**147.792**

Bold values indicate the best scores. Values are sorted by the order of models in average ensemble. ★ Primary performance metric.

4.4.2. Early Fusion

To answer the question of whether or not the earlier fusion ensemble could increase the classification results, an early fusion of the features is implemented instead of the late one. Again, for simplicity and speed, only OrganAMNIST was used, being the smallest dataset. Two feature selection strategies were examined: first, a feature vector is outputted from the dense layer before the Softmax layer (usually the penultimate layer of the network), and second, features are extracted from the output of the layer before the aforementioned dense layer. The extracted features in both scenarios are inputted to the meta-learner with a single hidden dense layer or two hidden dense layers. Table 9 shows that the results in the first scenario are very similar to averaging. The Mann–Whitney U-test confirms that there are no significant statistical differences between the early fusion (first scenario) and averaging results regarding sensitivity (U = 17, p = 0.128; U = 27.5, p = 0.672). Furthermore, there is no statistically significant difference between having a single or double meta-layer in early fusion (U = 17, p = 0.127).

The results in the second scenario are also similar to averaging, and it is confirmed that there are no statistically significant differences in performance between the early fusion (second scenario) and averaging results (U = 22, p = 0.314; U = 24, p = 0.429). There is no statistically significant difference in having a single or double meta-layer (U = 30.5, p = 0.916). Just as for stacking, an early fusion ensemble requires additional training of the meta-learner. Based on these results, it is concluded that it is not worth spending time on re-training, as the model performance would not significantly increase compared to a simpler averaging strategy.

The fusion analysis with both ensemble strategies tested on the PathMNIST and OCTMNIST datasets confirms the previously derived conclusions (Tables A1 and A2).

Table 9. The efficiency for early fusion strategies with a meta-learner (OrganAMNIST).

Fusion Method	Num of Hidden Layers in Meta-Learner	Model	*wS	AUC	Size [MB]	FLOPs (M)
Early fusion (first scenario)	single	C3_D3_8	0.920	**0.996**	18.63	412.782
		B3_C3_D3_32	0.920	0.995	21.79	473.156
		C4_D3_16	**0.924**	**0.996**	21.76	440.985
		B4_C3_C4_D2_8	0.922	**0.996**	19.07	385.291
		B3_C3_D2_64	0.915	0.995	12.09	296.711
		C3_D2_32	0.913	0.995	8.88	209.311
		B3_C4_32	0.919	**0.996**	7.88	148.213
		B4_C3_32	0.911	0.995	**7.12**	**147.810**
	double	C3_D3_16_64	0.925	**0.996**	18.63	412.786
		B3_C3_D3_16_64	**0.927**	**0.996**	21.76	473.140
		C4_D3_8_64	0.923	**0.996**	21.75	440.982
		B4_C3_C4_D2_32_64	0.925	**0.996**	19.14	385.328
		B3_C3_D2_16_32	0.916	0.995	11.99	269.656
		C3_D2_16_64	0.917	0.995	8.87	209.304
		B3_C4_32_64	0.925	**0.996**	7.89	148.218
		B4_C3_32_64	0.914	0.995	**7.13**	**147.815**
Early fusion (second scenario)	single	C3_D3_64	**0.930**	**0.996**	19.30	413.072
		B3_C3_D3_32	0.921	0.995	23.22	473.905
		C4_D3_16	**0.930**	**0.996**	22.30	441.269
		B4_C3_C4_D2_32	0.915	0.995	20.32	385.945
		B3_C3_D2_16	0.915	0.995	12.58	269.968
		C3_D2_32	0.917	0.995	9.33	209.790
		B3_C4_64	0.918	0.994	8.59	148.587
		B4_C3_32	0.899	0.993	**7.46**	**147.986**
	double	C3_D3_32_64	0.929	**0.996**	19.20	413.372
		B3_C3_D3_16_32	0.925	**0.996**	22.47	473.513
		C4_D3_16_32	**0.930**	**0.996**	22.31	441.271
		B4_C3_C4_D2_32_64	0.918	0.995	20.33	385.950
		B3_C3_D2_16_64	0.917	0.995	12.59	269.971
		C3_D2_16_64	0.917	0.995	9.33	209.590
		B3_C4_16_64	0.915	0.994	8.03	148.294
		B4_C3_8_64	0.900	0.992	**7.18**	**147.841**

Bold values indicate the best scores. Values are sorted by the order of models in average ensemble. * Primary performance metric.

4.5. Ablation Study on Input Preprocessing with the Proposed Models

To examine the impact of input preprocessing on the proposed models, the three types of input data were defined: input scaling of [−1, 1], no preprocessing (raw input data), and input scaling of [0, 1]. The proposed ensemble model for PathMNIST has four components (MobNetV2_MobV3_C2_D2), while the proposed models for OrganAMNIST and OCTMNIST have two constituents each (MobNetV2_C2 and MobNetV2_D2). Therefore, there were in total 81, 9, and 9 combinations of different input preprocessings tested in the case of PathMNIST, OrganAMNIST, and OCTMNIST, respectively. Each combination was encoded by treating the input data variables as digits in a base-3 number system, where the input data variables were the following: 0 = [−1, 1]; 1 = raw; and 2 = [0, 1]. The results are shown in Table 10. For simplicity with PathMNIST, only the top four best results, the combination used in the proposed model, and the top four worst performance results are given.

The Mann–Whitney U-test confirms that there are no significant statistical differences between the best performance result and the worst performance result when compared to the proposed one regarding all metrics (PathMNIST: U = 3.0, $p = 0.2$; U = 12.0, $p = 0.343$. OrganAMNIST: U = 7.0, $p = 0.886$. U = 13.0, $p = 0.2$; OCTMNIST: U = 12.0, $p = 0.343$).

https://doi.org/10.3390/electronics15071470

Table 10. The proposed models' mixed preprocessing results. Gray shade indicates the preprocesing combination used in this paper. The meaning of the input data preprocessing combination is the following: 0 = preprocessing [−1, 1]; 1 = no preprocessing; 2 = preprocessing [0, 1].

MNIST Dataset	Model	Preprocessing Combination	★wS	wP	F1	AUC
Path	MobNetV2_MobV3_C2_D2	0212	**0.917**	**0.918**	**0.915**	0.990
		2112	0.916	0.917	**0.915**	0.991
		0110	0.916	**0.918**	**0.915**	0.991
		0110	0.914	0.917	0.914	**0.992**
		0111	0.908	0.913	0.908	0.990
		2011	0.898	0.907	0.897	0.989
		1001	0.898	0.905	0.897	0.990
		2001	0.898	0.904	0.897	0.990
		1021	0.897	0.905	0.896	0.990
OrganA	MobNetV2_C2	00	**0.932**	0.931	**0.931**	**0.996**
		01	0.931	**0.932**	**0.931**	**0.996**
		11	0.931	0.931	0.930	**0.996**
		02	0.930	0.930	0.930	**0.996**
		10	0.930	0.930	0.930	**0.996**
		12	0.928	0.928	0.928	0.995
		21	0.927	0.928	0.927	**0.996**
		20	0.927	0.927	0.926	0.995
		22	0.924	0.924	0.923	0.995
OCT	MobV2_D2	01	**0.781**	**0.823**	0.758	**0.963**
		02	0.780	0.820	**0.759**	0.959
		00	0.771	0.816	0.746	0.960
		20	0.744	0.782	0.715	0.953
		22	0.742	0.777	0.716	0.954
		21	0.740	0.769	0.713	0.960
		12	0.724	0.768	0.682	0.951
		11	0.719	0.758	0.676	0.959
		10	0.716	0.761	0.672	0.951

Bold values indicate the best scores. Values are sorted by the wS score. ★ Primary performance metric.

4.6. The 8-Bit Integer Compression of the Proposed Models

The simulation of the 8-bit quantization of both weights and activations in the proposed models is performed using dynamic integer post-quantization. The intention is to demonstrate the validity of the theoretical assumptions used in this paper and the chosen compressed model size threshold. The compression is simulated by using the Tensorflow optimization code (https://www.tensorflow.org/model_optimization/guide/quantization/post_training (accessed on 25 March 2026)). Table 11 shows that the proposed models are successfully compressed to an 8-bit integer format, with the total model size lowered by ∼4 times without compromising their performance. Hence, the simulated compression confirms that the used assumptions regarding integer quantization are logically sound, and that the chosen size threshold applied on model size during the experiment truly preserves the achieved accuracy.

It is to note that a simulated dynamic-range integer post-quantization as conducted here is a good approximation of an integer-based inference, with integer weights and activations of a compressed model, but keeping the inputs and outputs in an FP 32-bit format. This means that the 8-bit MAC result in the output of the model's inner computational block will be de-quantized back into a FP 32-bit format. For a model to be fully compliant with integer-only devices, it should have all-integer-based operations, and all input and output data inside the model should be converted to integers. Another limitation that should be considered here is that a representative dataset is required during the conversion of the model to estimate the range of values that the model had during training and validation.

https://doi.org/10.3390/electronics15071470

Table 11. The 8-bit compression of the proposed models.

MNIST Dataset	Model	wS	wP	F1	AUC	Size [MB]
Path	MobNetV2_MobV3_C2_D2_FP32	**0.908**	**0.913**	**0.908**	**0.990**	31.52
	MobNetV2_MobV3_C2_D2_8bits	0.906	0.912	0.906	**0.990**	**8.88**
OrganA	MobNetV2_C2_FP32	**0.931**	**0.932**	**0.931**	**0.996**	9.69
	MobNetV2_C2_8bits	0.930	0.931	0.930	0.995	**2.86**
OCT	MobNetV2_D2_FP32	**0.781**	0.823	**0.758**	**0.963**	15.86
	MobNetV2_D2_8bits	0.777	**0.824**	0.751	0.954	**4.44**

Bold values indicate the best scores.

4.7. Comparison of the Proposed Ensembles with the Existing Models from the Literature

The comparison of proposed hybrid models with the existing models from the literature is shown in Table 12. This table is constructed taking into account the recently reported results from [12,33,34,37]. There are similar papers in the literature such as the ones from [37,47,65] that deal with the same dataset, but their use of upscaled images (224 × 224 px or 92 × 92 px) excludes them from direct comparison. Furthermore, the architectures from [45,46] make it rather complex to estimate their number of parameters based on the number of depths, dimensions, and patches. A base ViT model could have been assumed for complexity estimation purposes of the model in [45], but this is only one of the three processing phases in the entire framework, making the estimation quite unreliable. A similar problem is present in [46], where relying on the PVT-Tiny model assumption for evaluation purposes was not sufficient, given that the architecture includes parameter extraction with parts of ResNet18 and several ViT blocks in multiple multi-scale output feature schemes.

Usually, accuracy and AUC are reported for the existing models, whereas the former is expressed in terms of the standard overall accuracy, i.e., the ratio of correctly classified samples over the total number of samples, without taking into account class balance. The complexity is normally expressed in the literature as the total number of parameters, and it is rarely expressed in size or FLOPs. To provide a more fair and more robust comparison regarding the complexity of the proposed models and the competitor architectures, the total parameter count is taken from [12,37]. Next, the size of the model in MB is calculated by using the total number of parameters and assuming their 32-bit floating-point representation. Finally, to make the table as informative as possible, the FLOPs complexity metric is evaluated objectively for all models by using the FLOPs estimation tool.

Overall, values in Table 12 that are not reported in the available literature or calculated are denoted with N/A. The metrics used throughout this paper are reported here for the best trade-off between the CNN-only, DNN-only, and hybrid ensemble representative (selected by the radar plots). For consistency with the related work, the reported performance for the proposed models is expressed as the "overall accuracy" when it refers to the obtained wS score. Moreover, it is to note that the reported recall and precision for the proposed models are wR and wP, respectively. As per-class recall scores were available for MedvCNN [12], its performance was estimated in terms of wS using Equation (1).

From this table, it is evident that the proposed hybrid ensembles are always better in terms of size and number of parameters compared to existing models, so smaller networks are obtained. In this sense, the models presented here are more lightweight. Furthermore, FLOPs are decreased in OrganAMNIST compared to the lowest value estimated for the competitors (68.925 M), and the value is 49.842 M, while an increase in FLOPs is present for PathMNIST (320.638 M) and for OCTMNIST (161.393 M). Overall, the proposed models outperform the ones presented in the literature for two out of three complexity metrics on all three datasets. Additionally, the proposed hybrid ensembles are comparable to the existing competitors [33]. The drop in performance is ∼0.3%, ∼0.4%, and ∼2% towards the best accuracy result reported from the literature (marked in bold in Table 12) for PathMNIST,

OrganAMNIST, and OCTMNIST, respectively. The memory footprint is reduced for ~65%, ~77%, and ~82% compared to the same architectures (ResNet50 and ResNet18).

Table 12. The comparison with MedMNIST classification efficiency reported in the literature. Gray shade indicates the proposed architectures.

MNIST Dataset	Ref.	Model	★Acc	Prec	Rec	F1	AUC	Size [MB]	FLOPs (M)	Params (M)
Path	[34]	Resnet18	0.844	N/A	N/A	N/A	0.972	*42.72	**68.925	11.2
		Resnet50	0.864	N/A	N/A	N/A	0.979	*89.65	**158.495	23.5
	[33]	Resnet18	0.907	N/A	N/A	N/A	0.983	*42.72	**68.925	11.2
		Resnet50	**0.911**	N/A	N/A	N/A	**0.990**	*89.65	**158.495	23.5
	[12]	MedvCNN	†0.871	**0.84**	**0.86**	**0.86**	0.985	*22.24	N/A	**5.56**
		A_C2	0.896	0.901	0.896	0.896	0.986	**8.44**	643.032	**2.21**
		MobNetV2_MobV3	0.882	0.887	0.882	0.882	0.984	20.12	**23.285**	5.28
		MobNetV2_MobV3_C2_D2	**0.908**	**0.913**	**0.908**	**0.908**	**0.990**	31.52	320.638	8.26
		Dense121_MobNetV2	0.899	0.902	0.899	0.899	0.988	35.54	127.14	9.32
OrganA	[34]	Resnet18	0.921	N/A	N/A	N/A	0.995	*42.72	**68.925	11.2
		Resnet50	0.916	N/A	N/A	N/A	0.995	*89.65	**150.781	23.5
	[33]	Resnet18	**0.935**	N/A	N/A	N/A	**0.997**	*42.72	**68.925	11.2
		Resnet50	**0.935**	N/A	N/A	N/A	**0.997**	*89.65	**150.781	23.5
	[12]	MedvCNN	†0.781	**0.79**	**0.77**	**0.78**	0.990	*22.24	N/A	**5.56**
		C3_D3	0.932	0.933	0.932	0.932	0.996	18.610	412.772	4.87
		MobNetV2_MobV3	0.934	0.934	0.934	0.933	0.996	20.14	23.882	5.220
		MobNetV2_C2	0.931	0.932	0.931	0.931	0.996	**9.69**	**49.842**	**2.51**
		Dense121_EffB0	**0.949**	0.949	**0.949**	0.948	0.997	49.52	146.301	12.84
		EffB0_Dense121_C4	**0.949**	**0.950**	**0.949**	**0.949**	**0.998**	54.25	234.147	14.08
OCT	[34]	Resnet18	0.758	N/A	N/A	N/A	0.951	*42.72	**68.925	11.2
		Resnet50	0.745	N/A	N/A	N/A	0.939	*89.65	**150.753	23.5
	[33]	Resnet18	0.743	N/A	N/A	N/A	0.943	*42.72	**68.925	11.2
		Resnet50	**0.762**	N/A	N/A	N/A	**0.952**	*89.65	**150.753	23.5
	[12]	MedvCNN	†0.685	**0.73**	**0.68**	**0.5**	0.947	*22.24	N/A	**5.56**
		C2_D2	**0.785**	**0.836**	**0.785**	**0.762**	**0.970**	**9.86**	296.679	**2.58**
		MobNetV2_D2	0.781	0.823	0.781	0.758	0.963	15.86	161.393	4.12
		MobNetV2_MobV3	0.726	0.767	0.726	0.689	0.945	20.07	**23.851**	5.205
		MobNetV2_Dense121_Res50	0.766	0.818	0.766	0.735	0.957	125.53	279.096	32.73

Bold values indicate the best scores. Values denoted with ** are estimated using the FLOPs estimation tool. ★ Primary performance metric. Values denoted with * are estimated assuming 32-bit floating-point parameters. Values denoted with † are calculated wS scores using Equation (1).

Figure 12 visualizes confusion matrices obtained with the proposed hybrid ensembles, and Figure 13 presents per-class scores. Classes 5 and 7 are always the most problematic on the PathMNIST dataset. This is in accordance with the literature, where these classes are referred to as the most similar ones that are usually misclassified, especially with CNN models [35]. It is interesting to note that the obtained recalls for classes 5 and 7 in Figure 12a are 81% and 53%, while the corresponding results from [35] are 55.5% and 44.1%. On the other hand, Salehin et al. [12] demonstrated better results for these two classes (90% and 80%), but exhibited the lowest recall on class 3 (72%), which is 99% in this paper. As far as the OrganAMNIST dataset is concerned, the recall of class 4 is the lowest of all the classes (76%). This is confirmed with the confusion matrix in [65], although a better score of 88% is accomplished. For OCTMNIST, class 2 remains the most problematic as in the literature, causing the lower overall performance on this dataset [45]. The recall for class 2 in Figure 12c is better than in [45], i.e., it is 35% compared to the reported 16%. Examples of random misclassifications across all three datasets are illustrated in Figure 14.

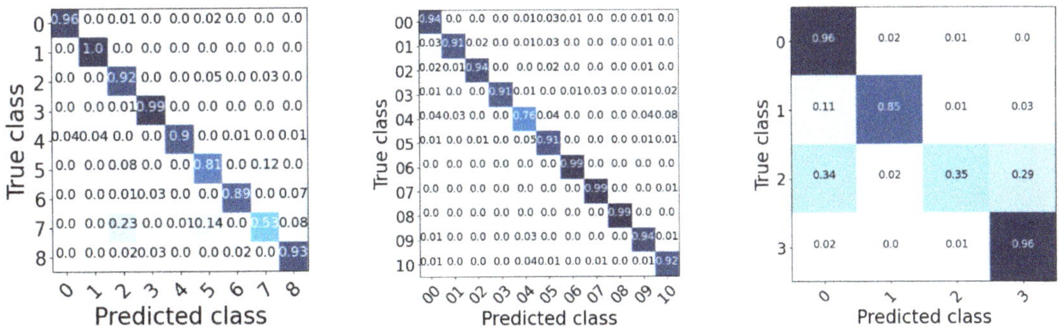

(a) MobNetV2_MobV3_C2_D2 (PathMNIST)

(b) MobNetV2_C2 (OrganAMNIST)

(c) MobNetV2_D2 (OCTMNIST)

Figure 12. Confusion matrices of the proposed lightweight hybrid ensembles.

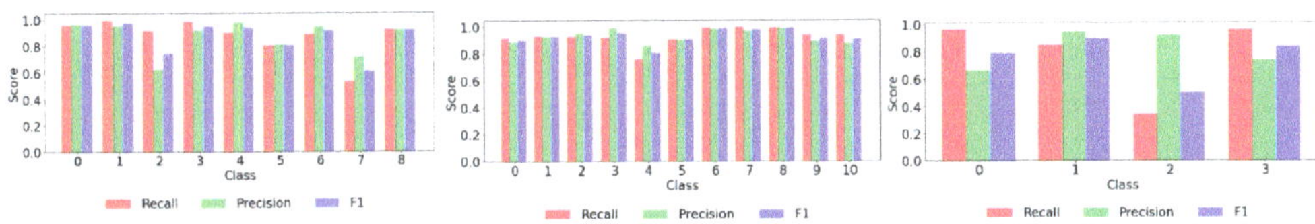

(a) MobNetV2_MobV3_C2_D2 (PathMNIST)

(b) MobNetV2_C2 (OrganAMNIST)

(c) MobNetV2_D2 (OCTMNIST)

Figure 13. Per-class recall/precision/F1 scores of the proposed lightweight hybrid ensembles.

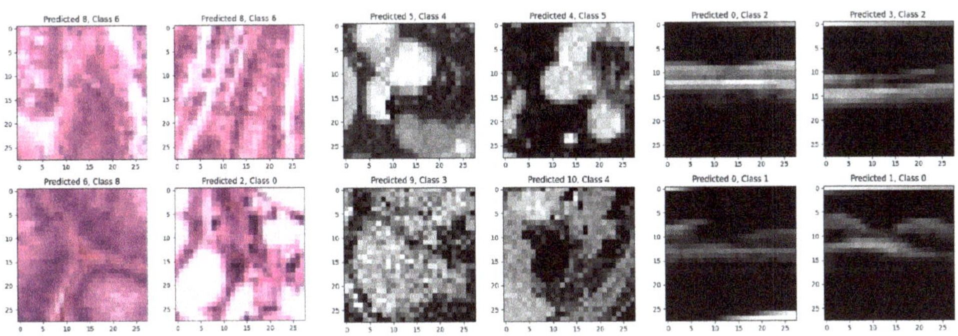

(a) PathMNIST

(b) OrganAMNIST

(c) OCTMNIST

Figure 14. Examples of misclassified images from each dataset.

It is to note that some hybrid models are not proposed as final solutions (as those are not the best trade-off architectures), even though they provide a higher performance than that in the existing work (when compared to the best result marked bold in Table 12). For example, for OrganAMNIST, DNN-only Dense121_EffB0 and hybrid EffB0_Dense121_C4 have higher performance than the related work (94.9%), and are comparable in size (49.52 MB and 54.25 MB) to the reported ResNet18 (42.69 MB). They have more FLOPs (146.301 M and 234.147 M). However, these models are declared as "non-implementable" as they do not fit the memory cap on assumed int8 effects.

Table 13 lists all models from the conducted research, classified as CNN-only, DNN-only, or hybrid, that are better than the existing work in terms of performance. Values given as accuracy are wS scores. As reported, no purely CNN-based model surpasses the established benchmarks in the literature for OrganAMNIST and PathMNIST, and it is the same for DNN-only models when PathMNIST and OCTMNIST are concerned. On the other hand, there are hybrid models that outperform the existing work for every dataset, which confirms once again that using a hybrid approach is the best option for forming the ensemble structure. Performance is exactly 91.1%, as is the maximal result reported in the literature, for PathMNIST (accomplished with Dense121_Res50_C2_C3). The sensitivity with the hybrid models spans from 0.2% to up to 1.5% higher for OrganAMNIST, and from 0.5% to up to 0.8% higher for OCTMNIST, whereas the size is lowered for up to 58.98% and for up to 54.58%, with a compromise of more FLOPs.

Radar plots are constructed in Figure 15, and they compare the proposed hybrid ensembles to the related work, but taking into account only the metrics that are fully reported in Table 12; these are accuracy, AUC, size, and the number of parameters. Radar plots show that polygon areas of the hybrid ensembles consistently exceed those of prior work, establishing them as the the best-performing architectures.

Table 13. All ensembles outperforming the existing work based on sensitivity. Gray shade indicates models that surpass established benchmarks in the literature in both wS and size.

MNIST Dataset	CNN-Only	DNN-Only	Hybrid Ensemble
Path	-	-	Dense121_Res50_C2_C3 (0.911, 133.92)
OrganA	-	MobV2_EffB0 (0.938, 31.3) Dense121_EffB0 (0.949, 49.59) Dense121_Res50_EffB0 (0.949, 139.59) MobNetV2_MobV3_EffB0 (0.941, 42.77)	C3_D2_MobV2 (0.937, 17.51) MobV2_MobV3_C2 (0.940, 21.16) C3_D2_MobV3_MobV2 (0.942, 28.98) Dense121_C4 (0.945, 31.62) Dense121_D3 (0.947, 43.9) EffB0_Dense121_C4 (0.949, 54.25) EffB0_Dense121_D3 (0.950, 66.53)
OCT	C2_D2 (0.785, 9.86) C3_D2 (0.794, 18.22) C3_D3 (0.796, 27.99)	-	MobV2_C3 (0.788, 19.62) MobV2_C3_D2 (0.791, 26.85)

Value in parenthesis is a wS score and total size is in MB.

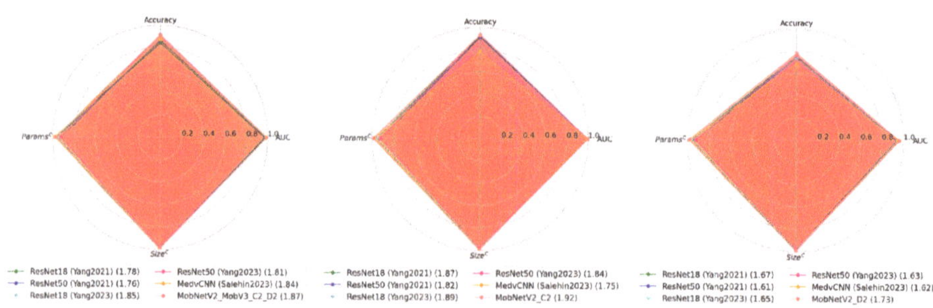

(**a**) PathMNIST (**b**) OrganAMNIST (**c**) OCTMNIST

Figure 15. A radar chart comparing the proposed hybrid ensembles to the reported results from the literature [12,33,34].

5. Limitations of the Work

The limitations of this study should be addressed, and the first one concerns the experimental setup. Due to the limited resources that are freely available in the Google Colab environment, the total number of training epochs is fixed to a maximum of 20 for all architectures. This fixed parameter ensures a fair training protocol and a fair comparison between models to avoid performance bias caused by different training strategies. Although this computational constraint, together with an early stopping criterion included in the experiment, justifies the used setting, it could be argued that it is always better to use a larger number of epochs to train these complex networks on a more powerful machine. To ensure that the proposed models have truly converged, they were retrained on a larger number of epochs using NVIDIA GeForce GTX 1060 6 GB by keeping the early stopping mechanism. The models' early convergence without overfitting was confirmed, proving that the 20-epoch setup was sufficient and that models were not under-trained. Furthermore, a single train–validation–test ratio, as prepared inside the MedMNIST dataset, is used in this study. Although the used strategy is sufficient for the current analysis, where the existing benchmarks were repeated and compared to the literature, it should be noted that in general, by averaging over results of multiple folds, the results become more stable, yielding a more reliable study than using a single data split. The mean performance across multiple folds in this study confirms a robust and stable result for the proposed models.

Next, concerning the input data, preprocessing was adjusted such that models were fairly comparable. Other preprocessing schemes should be examined, as they might result in even higher classification performances. Furthermore, a fusion of different preprocessing algorithms could be potentially useful for ensembles, especially when it comes to base learner stacking in the classification of medical images. Regarding the ensemble's limitations, it could be argued that using the simplest ensemble approach, such as averaging, could influence the obtained results. Possibly, the performance of the models could be enhanced by using a more sophisticated ensemble function, or one might further optimize the models by implementing a high-level ensemble concept with a hierarchical combining of features and predictions. This could require extensive computational power due to the complex operations involved, but it would be interesting to examine the performance of the resulting hierarchical ensemble schemes.

6. Conclusions

Increasing the classification model performance is normally carried out using the ensemble learning approach, and the need for a retained model performance is crucial for its implementation on a resource-constrained device, such as on an FPGA. However, the complexity of the overall structure is often too complex, and this study confirms how important it is to investigate lightweight combinations of ensemble models before defining the ensemble structure itself. The main target here is that the architecture of the overall model is as small as possible (with as few parameters), but with a retained performance value. In particular, this paper used the fact that the available memory size of an FPGA device is about 8.5 MB, and that a larger model cannot fit in the device memory. The average late fusion is employed for the ensemble, justified by comparing the effectiveness with an earlier feature extraction, which increases complexity but does not provide a significant performance gain.

The answers to the posed research questions were found through the conducted study, and this is precisely the contribution this study brings:

- RQ1: By looking separately at three ensemble types in particular (CNN-only, DNN-only, and a hybrid approach), it was shown that it is worth designing new customized CNN solutions because a comparable or even more efficient model can be achieved with the CNN-only compared to DNN-only ensemble for all datasets. The sensitivity increased for $\sim$1.4% and $\sim$5.9% depending on the dataset, while a smaller memory footprint was obtained.
- RQ2: Since the number of FLOPs is much higher for CNNs than DNNs ($\sim$10 times), as these are generally not highly optimized architectures and have no mechanisms for reducing their number of operations, it is most useful to combine them with existing DNNs.

https://doi.org/10.3390/electronics15071470

- RQ3: A hybrid ensemble approach combining CNNs and DNNs is the best compromise, as it incorporates the benefits of both architecture types; it reduces the number of FLOPs and retains performance, with a size that could fit the device memory.

The performances of the proposed hybrid models are 90.8%, 93.1%, and 78.1%, for PathMNIST, OrganMNISTA, and OCTMNIST, and these results are comparable to the work reported in the literature. For PathMNIST, the performance is ~0.3% lower than in previous work, and the model is ~65% smaller. The drop in performance is ~0.4% and ~2% for OrganAMNIST and OCTMNIST, but the memory footprint is reduced by ~77% and ~82% compared to the recent state-of-the-art solutions. This means that the proposed hybrid ensemble models could be successfully deployed on a resource-constrained device with a limited memory. With the compromise of a larger number of necessary FLOPs operations, even better-performing models can be achieved. The increased sensitivity that can be offered compared to the related work is ~1.4% with the hybrid ensemble (OrganAMNIST) and ~2.3% with CNN-only (OCTMNIST).

Future work will further refine the proposed selection mechanism by incorporating more advanced techniques. Namely, in the proposed best-candidate-selection procedure, the wS score is treated as the most important performance metric in the first-stage Pareto analysis since the goal was to find the ensemble combinations that exhibit the best overall performance across all classes. The current selection incorporates AUC in the second stage of extracting the best models, and future work will investigate how to include AUC and other performance metrics in the earlier stage of the multi-variable Pareto selection. The theoretical assumptions used in this paper for the edge deployment are logically sound, and rely on the standardly used complexity metrics for the model's deployment and implementation. As a next step in our research, the Pareto analysis will be repeated by using the complexity of the models implemented on real physical hardware. Another possible extension of our work could focus on exploring the strategies for addressing limited data availability in medical studies.

Moreover, in future research, we plan to expand the compression of the proposed models with efficient quantization and pruning strategies to confirm that the models could be successfully implemented in the resource-constrained device using integer-only arithmetic. A simulation of the 8-bit dynamic integer quantization of the proposed models confirms that the used assumptions regarding integer quantization are logically sound and that the compression of the proposed models' weights and activations to 8 bits can indeed preserve the achieved accuracy. The next focus will be towards the implementation of these models on a real edge device (for example, on an FPGA) and their testing in the more realistic environment of an embedded medical system.

Author Contributions: Conceptualization, M.P. and J.M.; methodology, M.P. and J.M.; software, M.P. and D.Č.; validation, M.P., D.Č., and J.M.; formal analysis, J.M. and A.K.; investigation, M.P. and D.Č.; resources, M.P., D.Č., and A.K.; data curation, J.M. and A.K.; writing—original draft preparation, M.P. and D.Č.; writing—review and editing, M.P., J.M., and D.Č.; visualization, M.P. and D.Č.; supervision, J.M. and A.K.; project administration, J.M. and A.K. All authors have read and agreed to the published version of the manuscript.

Funding: This research received no external funding.

Data Availability Statement: The input data used in this study are openly available from the official MedMNIST website (https://medmnist.com/, accessed on 25 March 2026) and the Zenodo repository (https://zenodo.org/records/10519652, accessed on 25 March 2026). The original contributions presented in this study are included in this article. Further inquiries can be directed to the corresponding author.

Conflicts of Interest: The authors declare no conflicts of interest.

Appendix A. Pareto Analysis Results (PathMNIST and OCTMNIST Dataset)

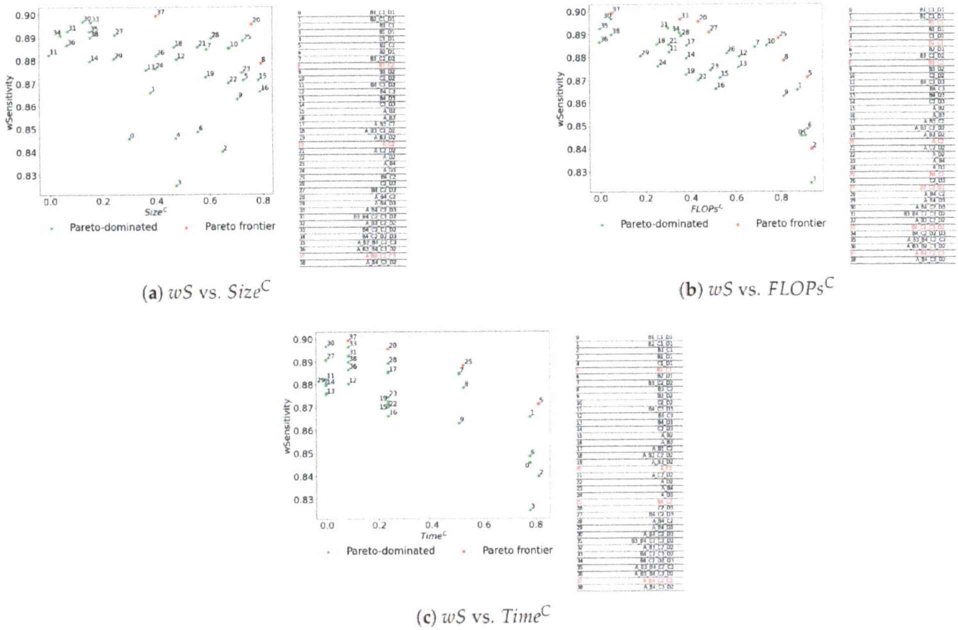

(**a**) wS vs. $Size^C$ (**b**) wS vs. $FLOPs^C$ (**c**) wS vs. $Time^C$

Figure A1. Pareto analysis results extracting the CNN-only ensembles that constitute the Pareto frontier (PathMNIST). These points (denoted in red) constitute the sets P_1, P_2, and P_3. The search space is visible in the tables next to the plots. To ensure figure clarity, some point labels in high-density regions are omitted to prevent overlap.

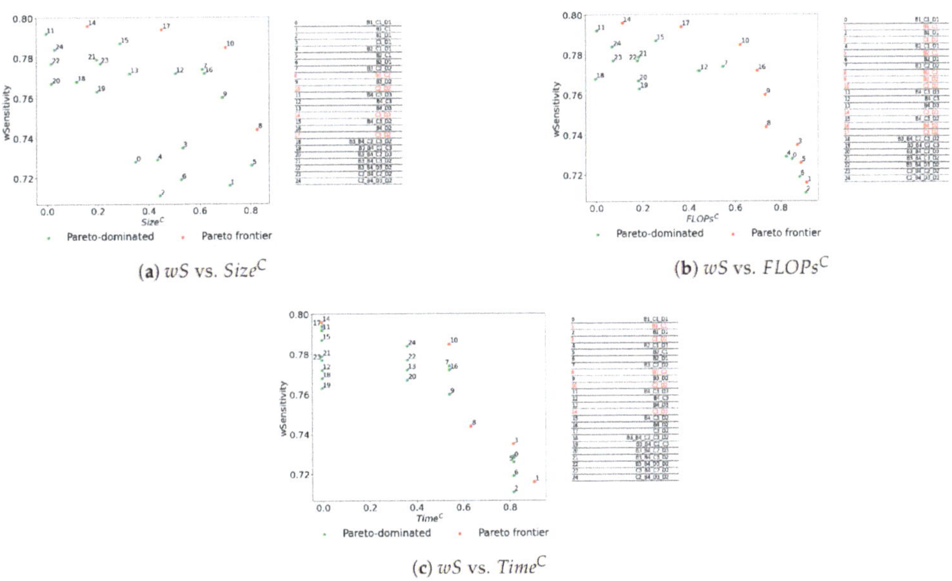

(**a**) wS vs. $Size^C$ (**b**) wS vs. $FLOPs^C$ (**c**) wS vs. $Time^C$

Figure A2. Pareto analysis results extracting the CNN-only ensembles that constitute the Pareto frontier (OCTMNIST). These points (denoted in red) constitute the sets P_1, P_2, and P_3. The search space is visible in the tables next to the plots. To ensure figure clarity, some point labels in high-density regions are omitted to prevent overlap.

https://doi.org/10.3390/electronics15071470

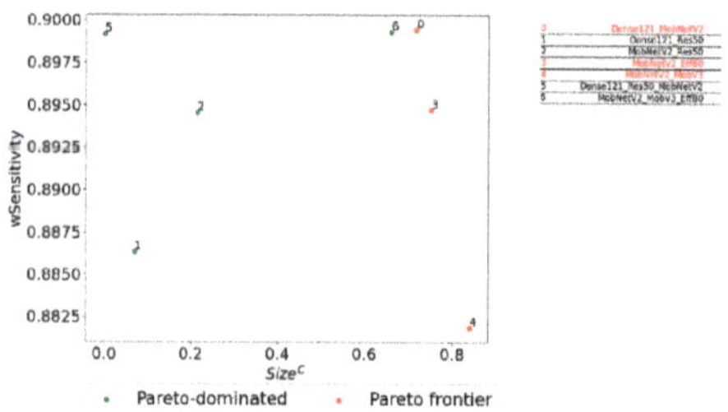

(**a**) wS vs. $Size^C$

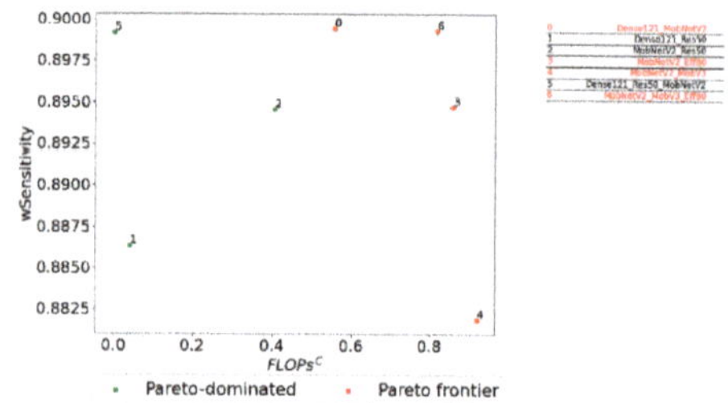

(**b**) wS vs. $FLOPs^C$

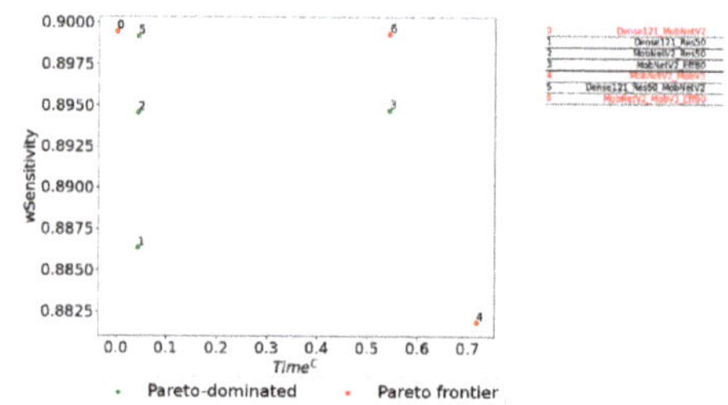

(**c**) wS vs. $Time^C$

Figure A3. Pareto analysis results extracting the DNN-only ensembles that constitute the Pareto frontier (PathMNIST). These points (denoted in red) constitute the sets P_1, P_2, and P_3. The search space is visible in the tables next to the plots.

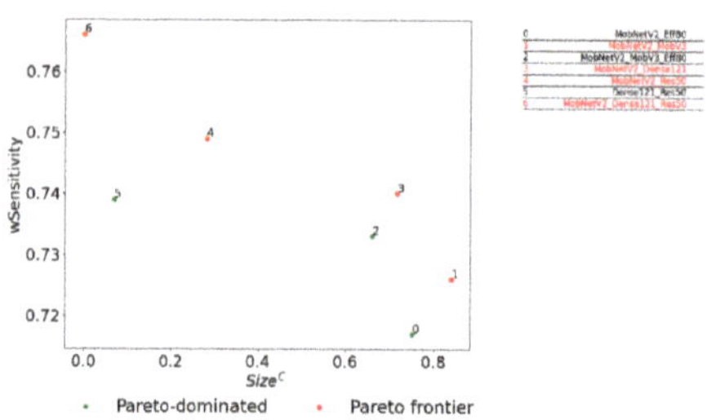

(**a**) wS vs. $Size^C$

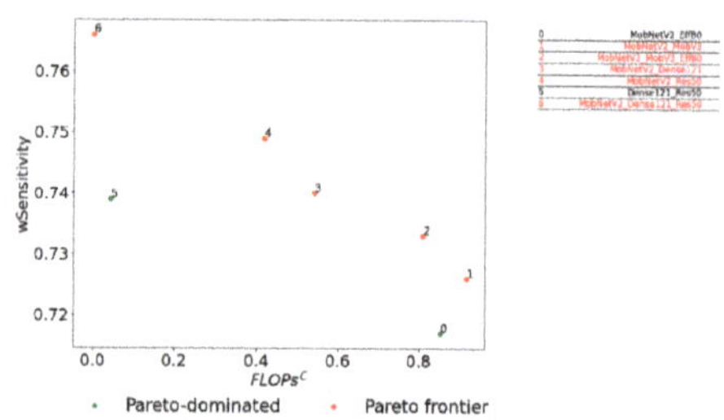

(**b**) wS vs. $FLOPs^C$

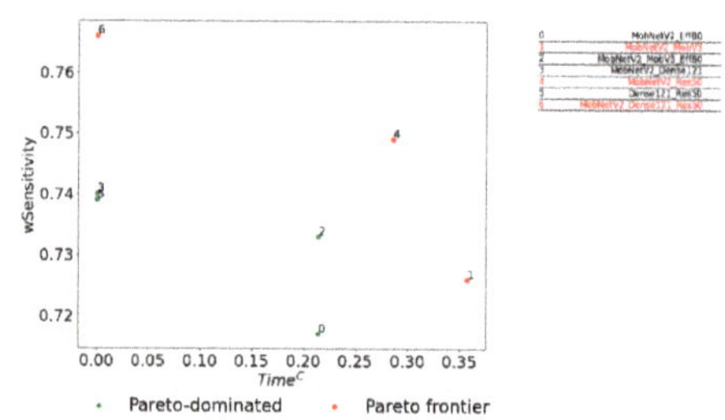

(**c**) wS vs. $Time^C$

Figure A4. Pareto analysis results extracting the DNN-only ensembles that constitute the Pareto frontier (OCTMNIST). These points (denoted in red) constitute the sets P_1, P_2, and P_3. The search space is visible in the tables next to the plots.

https://doi.org/10.3390/electronics15071470

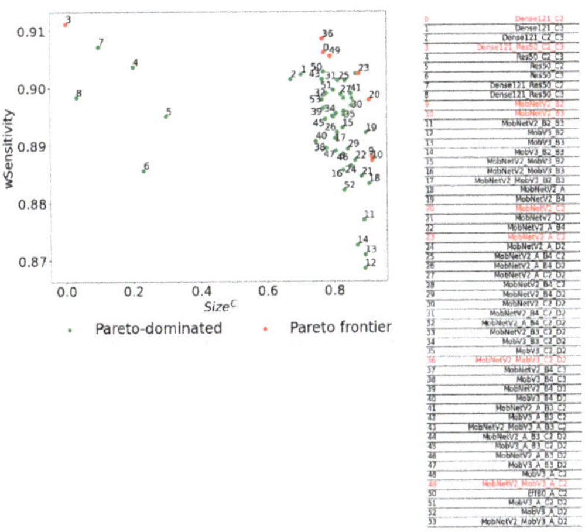

(**a**) wS vs. $Size^C$

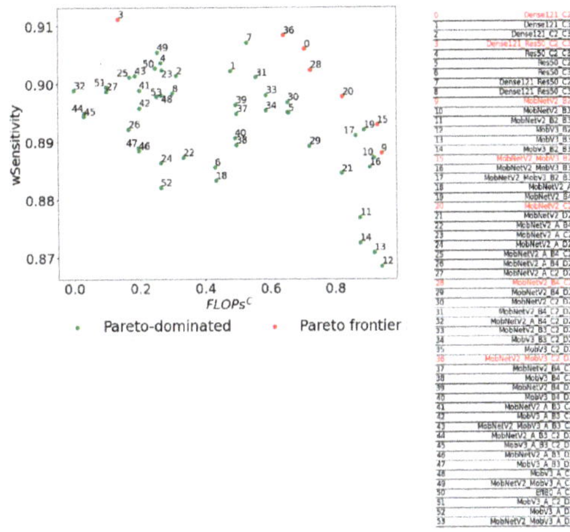

(**b**) wS vs. $FLOPs^C$

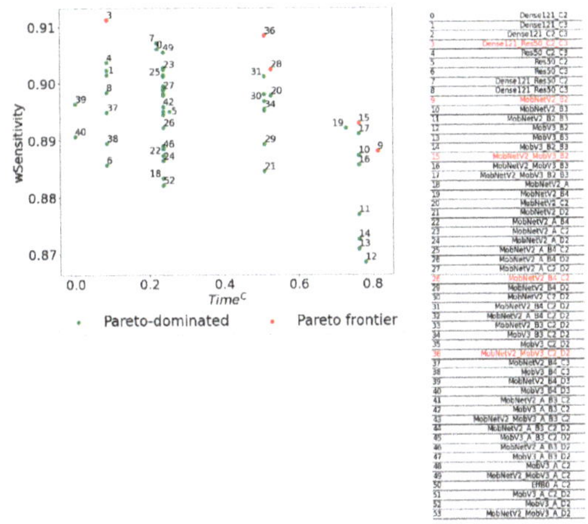

(**c**) wS vs. $Time^C$

Figure A5. Pareto analysis results extracting the hybrid ensembles that constitute the Pareto frontier (PathMNIST). These points (denoted in red) constitute the sets P_1, P_2, and P_3. The search space is visible in the tables next to the plots. To ensure figure clarity, some point labels in high-density regions are omitted to prevent overlap.

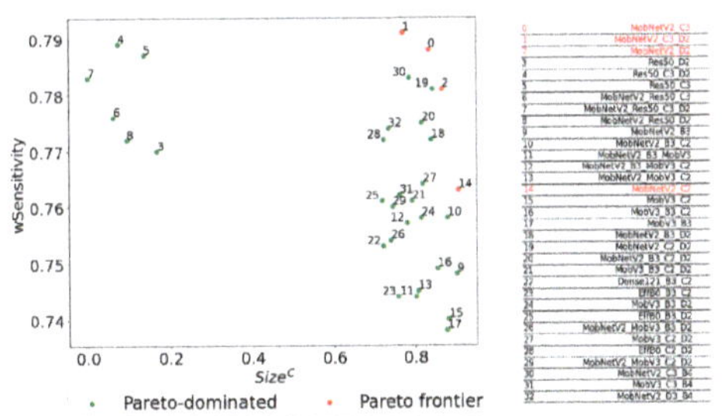

(**a**) wS vs. $Size^C$

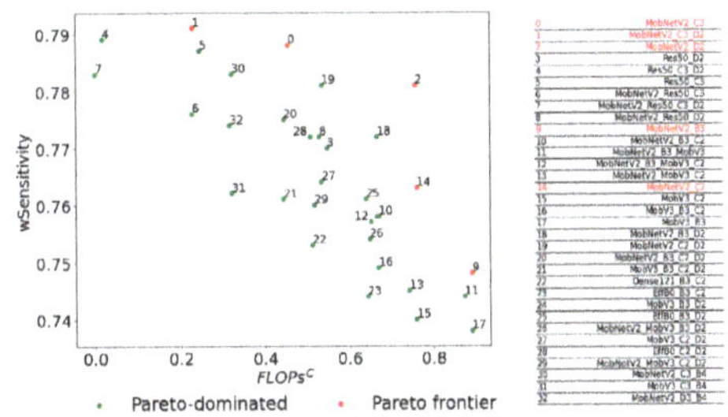

(**b**) wS vs. $FLOPs^C$

Figure A6. *Cont.*

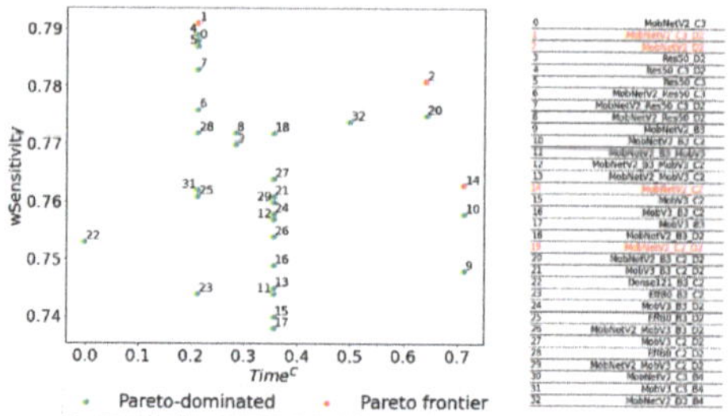

(**c**) wS vs. $Time^C$

Figure A6. Pareto analysis results extracting the hybrid ensembles that constitute the Pareto frontier (OCTMNIST). These points (denoted in red) constitute the sets P_1, P_2, and P_3. The search space is visible in the tables next to the plots. To ensure figure clarity, some point labels in high-density regions are omitted to prevent overlap.

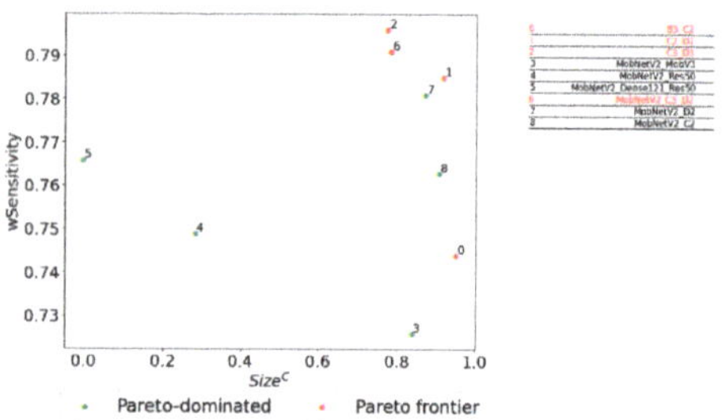

(**a**) wS vs. $Size^C$

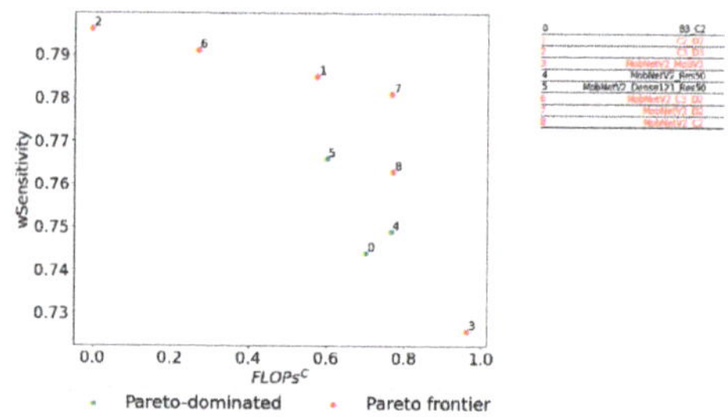

(**b**) wS vs. $FLOPs^C$

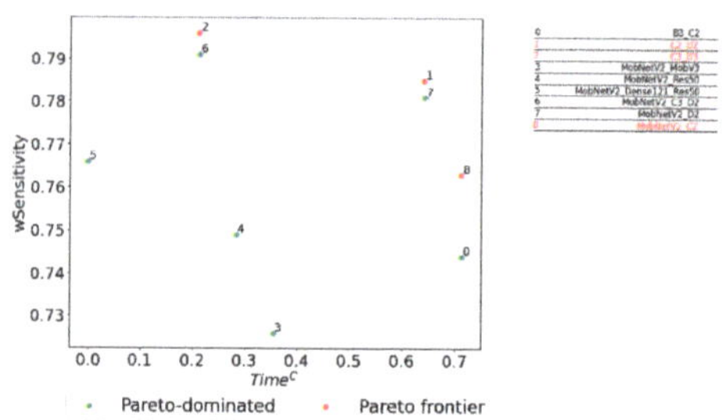

(**c**) wS vs. $Time^C$

Figure A7. Pareto analysis results comparing the selected architectures from the set F (OCTMNIST). These points (denoted in red) constitute the sets P_1, P_2, and P_3. The search space is visible in the tables next to the plots.

Appendix B. Performance with Other Ensemble Strategies (PathMNIST and OCTMNIST)

Table A1. The efficiency for stacking with a meta-learner (PathMNIST and OCTMNIST).

Fusion Method	Num of Hidden Layers in Meta-Learner	MNIST Dataset	Model	★wS	AUC	Size [MB]	FLOPs (M)
Average ensemble (no meta-learner)	-	Path	A_B4_C2_C3	**0.899**	**0.988**	21.160	1081.768
			B4_C2_C3_D2	0.897	**0.988**	29.860	736.089
			A_C2	0.896	0.986	**8.440**	**643.032**

Table A1. *Cont.*

Fusion Method	Num of Hidden Layers in Meta-Learner	MNIST Dataset	Model	*wS	AUC	Size [MB]	FLOPs (M)
Average ensemble (no meta-learner)	-	OCT	C3_D3	**0.796**	0.966	27.990	702.872
			C3_D2	0.794	**0.972**	18.220	499.389
			C2_D2	0.785	0.970	**9.860**	**296.697**
Stacking with meta-learner	single	Path	A_B4_C2_C3_8	0.888	0.972	21.161	1081.768
			B4_C2_C3_D2_8	0.888	**0.980**	29.861	736.089
			A_C2_64	**0.890**	0.977	**8.447**	**643.035**
		OCT	C3_D3_8	0.787	0.942	27.990	702.872
			C3_D2_16	**0.797**	**0.953**	18.221	499.389
			C2_D2_64	0.790	0.938	**9.863**	**296.698**
	double	Path	A_B4_C2_C3_8_16	**0.890**	0.976	21.162	1081.769
			B4_C2_C3_D2_8_16	0.886	**0.978**	29.862	736.090
			A_C2_8_64	**0.890**	0.977	**8.445**	**643.034**
		OCT	C3_D3_8_32	0.785	0.937	27.992	702.872
			C3_D2_8_32	**0.797**	**0.951**	18.222	499.389
			C2_D2_8_16	0.792	0.925	**9.861**	**296.697**

Bold values indicate the best scores. Values are sorted by the order of models in the average ensemble. * Primary performance metric.

Table A2. The efficiency for early fusion strategies with a meta-learner (PathMNIST and OCTMNIST).

Fusion Method	Num of Hidden Layers in Meta-Learner	MNIST Dataset	Model	*wS	AUC	Size [MB]	FLOPs (M)
Early fusion (first scenario)	single	Path	A_B4_C2_C3_16	0.888	0.984	21.196	1081.786
			B4_C2_C3_D2_32	**0.894**	**0.988**	29.955	736.138
			A_C2_8	0.883	0.977	**8.446**	**643.035**
		OCT	C3_D3_32	0.775	0.941	28.03	702.892
			C3_D2_64	**0.790**	**0.957**	18.299	499.430
			C2_D2_16	0.773	0.951	**9.88**	**296.707**
	double	Path	A_B4_C2_C3_16_32	0.888	0.979	21.198	1081.788
			B4_C2_C3_D2_32_64	**0.892**	**0.986**	29.964	736.143
			A_C2_8_16	0.888	0.984	**8.447**	**643.035**
		OCT	C3_D3_32_64	0.776	0.937	28.038	702.897
			C3_D2_8_32	**0.796**	**0.957**	18.231	499.394
			C2_D2_16_32	0.777	0.952	**9.882**	**296.708**
Early fusion (second scenario)	single	Path	A_B4_C2_C3_8	0.886	0.980	22.016	1082.216
			B4_C2_C3_D2_16	**0.896**	**0.982**	31.19	736.785
			A_C2_64	0.872	0.980	**13.04**	**645.441**
		OCT	C3_D3_16	**0.793**	0.949	28.99	703.396
			C3_D2_64	0.774	**0.951**	21.75	501.240
			C2_D2_16	0.768	0.950	**10.626**	**297.098**
	double	Path	A_B4_C2_C3_8_16	0.884	**0.985**	22.017	1082.217
			B4_C2_C3_D2_16_64	**0.891**	0.981	31.19	736.788
			A_C2_16_64	0.877	0.980	**9.59**	**643.637**
		OCT	C3_D3_32_64	**0.794**	0.950	30.0	703.925
			C3_D2_16_32	0.785	**0.962**	19.105	499.853
			C2_D2_16_32	0.774	0.960	**10.628**	**297.099**

Bold values indicate the best scores. Values are sorted by the order of models in the average ensemble. * Primary performance metric.

References

1. Tsai, M.J.; Tao, Y.H. Deep learning techniques for colorectal cancer tissue classification. In *Proceedings of the 2020 14th International Conference on Signal Processing and Communication Systems (ICSPCS)*; IEEE: New York, NY, USA, 2020; pp. 1–8.

https://doi.org/10.3390/electronics15071470

2. Paladini, E.; Vantaggiato, E.; Bougourzi, F.; Distante, C.; Hadid, A.; Taleb-Ahmed, A. Two ensemble-CNN approaches for colorectal cancer tissue type classification. *J. Imaging* **2021**, *7*, 51. [CrossRef]
3. Vasu, K.; Kumar, D.P. Effective Classification of Colon Cancer using Resnet-50 in Comparison with Squeezenet. *J. Pharm. Negat. Results* **2022**, *13*, 261913771.
4. Davri, A.; Birbas, E.; Kanavos, T.; Ntritsos, G.; Giannakeas, N.; Tzallas, A.T.; Batistatou, A. Deep learning on histopathological images for colorectal cancer diagnosis: A systematic review. *Diagnostics* **2022**, *12*, 837. [CrossRef]
5. Tsai, M.J.; Tao, Y.H. Deep learning techniques for the classification of colorectal cancer tissue. *Electronics* **2021**, *10*, 1662. [CrossRef]
6. Khazaee Fadafen, M.; Rezaee, K. Ensemble-based multi-tissue classification approach of colorectal cancer histology images using a novel hybrid deep learning framework. *Sci. Rep.* **2023**, *13*, 8823.
7. Hsia, S.C.; Wang, S.H.; Chang, C.Y. Convolution neural network with low operation FLOPS and high accuracy for image recognition. *J. Real-Time Image Process.* **2021**, *18*, 1309–1319. [CrossRef]
8. Ma, H.; Qiu, H.; Gao, Y.; Zhang, Z.; Abuadbba, A.; Xue, M.; Fu, A.; Zhang, J.; Al-Sarawi, S.F.; Abbott, D. Quantization backdoors to deep learning commercial frameworks. *IEEE Trans. Dependable Secur. Comput.* **2023**, *21*, 1155–1172. [CrossRef]
9. Xiao, P.; Qin, Z.; Chen, D.; Zhang, N.; Ding, Y.; Deng, F.; Qin, Z.; Pang, M. FastNet: A lightweight convolutional neural network for tumors fast identification in mobile-computer-assisted devices. *IEEE Internet Things J.* **2023**, *10*, 9878–9891.
10. Lee, H.; Lee, N.; Lee, S. A method of deep learning model optimization for image classification on edge device. *Sensors* **2022**, *22*, 7344. [CrossRef]
11. Bhatt, H.; Shah, M. A Convolutional Neural Network ensemble model for Pneumonia Detection using chest X-ray images. *Healthc. Anal.* **2023**, *3*, 100176. [CrossRef]
12. Salehin, I.; Islam, M.S.; Amin, N.; Baten, M.A.; Noman, S.; Saifuzzaman, M.; Yazmyradov, S. Real-Time Medical Image Classification with ML Framework and Dedicated CNN–LSTM Architecture. *J. Sens.* **2023**, *2023*, 3717035. [CrossRef]
13. Tobiasz, R.; Wilczyński, G.; Graszka, P.; Czechowski, N.; Łuczak, S. Edge devices inference performance comparison. *arXiv* **2023**, arXiv:2306.12093. [CrossRef]
14. Kumar, A.; Sharma, A.; Bharti, V.; Singh, A.K.; Singh, S.K.; Saxena, S. MobiHisNet: A lightweight CNN in mobile edge computing for histopathological image classification. *IEEE Internet Things J.* **2021**, *8*, 17778–17789. [CrossRef]
15. Wang, R.J.; Li, X.; Ling, C.X. Pelee: A Real-Time Object Detection System on Mobile Devices. In *Proceedings of the 32nd International Conference on Neural Information Processing Systems*; Curran Associates Inc.: Red Hook, NY, USA, 2018.
16. Alçalar, Y.U.; Cao, Y.; Akçakaya, M. Edge Computing for Physics-Driven AI in Computational MRI: A Feasibility Study. In *Proceedings of the 2025 12th International Conference on Future Internet of Things and Cloud (FiCloud)*; IEEE: New York, NY, USA, 2025; pp. 34–38. [CrossRef]
17. Aridhi, E.; Laabidi, K.; Mami, A. FPGA Technology in Healthcare: A Comprehensive Review of Hardware and Software Solutions for Diagnostics, Imaging, and Patient Care. *Array* **2025**, *28*, 100622. [CrossRef]
18. Iandola, F.N.; Han, S.; Moskewicz, M.W.; Ashraf, K.; Dally, W.J.; Keutzer, K. SqueezeNet: AlexNet-level accuracy with 50× fewer parameters and <0.5 MB model size. *arXiv* **2016**, arXiv:1602.07360.
19. Frantar, E.; Alistarh, D. Optimal brain compression: A framework for accurate post-training quantization and pruning. *Adv. Neural Inf. Process. Syst.* **2022**, *35*, 4475–4488.
20. Ghosh, S.; Bandyopadhyay, A.; Sahay, S.; Ghosh, R.; Kundu, I.; Santosh, K. Colorectal histology tumor detection using ensemble deep neural network. *Eng. Appl. Artif. Intell.* **2021**, *100*, 104202. [CrossRef]
21. Kundu, R.; Singh, P.K.; Mirjalili, S.; Sarkar, R. COVID-19 detection from lung CT-Scans using a fuzzy integral-based CNN ensemble. *Comput. Biol. Med.* **2021**, *138*, 104895. [CrossRef]
22. Mahajan, P.; Uddin, S.; Hajati, F.; Moni, M.A. Ensemble Learning for Disease Prediction: A Review. *Healthcare* **2023**, *11*, 1808. [CrossRef]
23. Albashish, D. Ensemble of adapted convolutional neural networks (CNN) methods for classifying colon histopathological images. *PeerJ Comput. Sci.* **2022**, *8*, e1031. [CrossRef]
24. Das, A.; Hazra, A. Classification of colorectal cancer tissues using stacking ensemble learning. In *Proceedings of the International Conference on Communication, Devices and Networking*; Springer: Berlin/Heidelberg, Germany, 2024; pp. 107–123.
25. Sundaravalli, N. An Enhanced Diagnostic and Classification Process of COVID-19 Chest X-Ray Images Using Ensemble Convolutional Neural Network (ECNN). *Eksplorium-Bul. Pus. Teknol. Bahan Galian Nukl.* **2025**, *46*, 1376–1398.
26. Prezja, F.; Annala, L.; Kiiskinen, S.; Lahtinen, S.; Ojala, T.; Ruusuvuori, P.; Kuopio, T. Improving performance in colorectal cancer histology decomposition using deep and ensemble machine learning. *Heliyon* **2024**, *10*, e37561. [CrossRef] [PubMed]
27. Santosh, K.; Ghosh, S. COVID-19 versus lung cancer: Analyzing chest CT images using deep ensemble neural network. *Int. J. Artif. Intell. Tools* **2022**, *31*, 2250049. [CrossRef]
28. Wilhelmi, M.; Rusiecki, A. Simple CNN as an alternative for large pretrained models for medical image classification-MedMNIST case study. *Procedia Comput. Sci.* **2024**, *239*, 1298–1303. [CrossRef]

https://doi.org/10.3390/electronics15071470

29. Succetti, F.; Rosato, A.; Araneo, R.; Panella, M. Deep neural networks for multivariate prediction of photovoltaic power time series. *IEEE Access* **2020**, *8*, 211490–211505. [CrossRef]
30. Oyelade, O.N.; Ezugwu, A.E. A bioinspired neural architecture search based convolutional neural network for breast cancer detection using histopathology images. *Sci. Rep.* **2021**, *11*, 19940. [CrossRef]
31. Xu, W.; Song, Y.; Gupta, S.; Jia, D.; Tang, J.; Lei, Z.; Gao, S. Dmixnet: A dendritic multi-layered perceptron architecture for image recognition. *Artif. Intell. Rev.* **2025**, *58*, 129. [CrossRef]
32. Mai, V.; Khamies, W.; Paull, L. Batch Inverse-Variance Weighting: Deep Heteroscedastic Regression. *arXiv* **2021**, arXiv:2107.04497. [CrossRef]
33. Yang, J.; Shi, R.; Wei, D.; Liu, Z.; Zhao, L.; Ke, B.; Pfister, H.; Ni, B. Medmnist v2-a large-scale lightweight benchmark for 2d and 3d biomedical image classification. *Sci. Data* **2023**, *10*, 41. [CrossRef]
34. Yang, J.; Shi, R.; Ni, B. Medmnist classification decathlon: A lightweight automl benchmark for medical image analysis. In *Proceedings of the 2021 IEEE 18th International Symposium on Biomedical Imaging (ISBI)*; IEEE: New York, NY, USA, 2021; pp. 191–195.
35. Dao, H.N.; Quang, T.N.; Paik, I. Transfer learning for medical image classification on multiple datasets using PubMedCLIP. In *Proceedings of the 2022 IEEE International Conference on Consumer Electronics-Asia (ICCE-Asia)*; IEEE: New York, NY, USA, 2022; pp. 1–4.
36. Adjei-Mensah, I.; Zhang, X.; Baffour, A.A.; Agyemang, I.O.; Yussif, S.B.; Agbley, B.L.Y.; Sey, C. Investigating vision transformer models for low-resolution medical image recognition. In *Proceedings of the 2021 18th International Computer Conference on Wavelet Active Media Technology and Information Processing (ICCWAMTIP)*; IEEE: New York, NY, USA, 2021; pp. 179–183.
37. Manzari, O.N.; Ahmadabadi, H.; Kashiani, H.; Shokouhi, S.B.; Ayatollahi, A. MedViT: A robust vision transformer for generalized medical image classification. *Comput. Biol. Med.* **2023**, *157*, 106791. [CrossRef]
38. Yang, Z.; Ran, L.; Zhang, S.; Xia, Y.; Zhang, Y. EMS-Net: Ensemble of multiscale convolutional neural networks for classification of breast cancer histology images. *Neurocomputing* **2019**, *366*, 46–53. [CrossRef]
39. Sakthivel, R.; Thaseen, I.S.; Vanitha, M.; Deepa, M.; Angulakshmi, M.; Mangayarkarasi, R.; Mahendran, A.; Alnumay, W.; Chatterjee, P. An efficient hardware architecture based on an ensemble of deep learning models for COVID-19 prediction. *Sustain. Cities Soc.* **2022**, *80*, 103713.
40. Kundu, R.; Das, R.; Geem, Z.W.; Han, G.T.; Sarkar, R. Pneumonia detection in chest X-ray images using an ensemble of deep learning models. *PLoS ONE* **2021**, *16*, e0256630. [CrossRef]
41. Mahmood, T.; Kim, S.G.; Koo, J.H.; Park, K.R. Artificial intelligence-based tissue phenotyping in colorectal cancer histopathology using visual and semantic features aggregation. *Mathematics* **2022**, *10*, 1909. [CrossRef]
42. Hamida, A.B.; Devanne, M.; Weber, J.; Truntzer, C.; Derangère, V.; Ghiringhelli, F.; Forestier, G.; Wemmert, C. Deep learning for colon cancer histopathological images analysis. *Comput. Biol. Med.* **2021**, *136*, 104730. [CrossRef]
43. Islam, S.; Tabassum, F.; Rizwan, S.; Chowdhury, T.M. Transfer Learning-based Ensemble Approach for Organ Classification: An Empirical Study. In *Proceedings of the 2022 12th International Conference on Electrical and Computer Engineering (ICECE)*; IEEE: New York, NY, USA, 2022; pp. 52–55.
44. Garifulla, M.; Shin, J.; Kim, C.; Kim, W.; Kim, H.; Kim, J.; Hong, S. A Case Study of Quantizing Convolutional Neural Networks for Fast Disease Diagnosis on Portable Medical Devices. *Sensors* **2021**, *22*, 219. [CrossRef] [PubMed]
45. Saraei, M.; Kozak, I.; Lee, E.J. ViT-2SPN: Vision Transformer-based Dual-Stream Self-Supervised Pretraining Networks for Retinal OCT Classification. *arXiv* **2025**, arXiv:2501.17260.
46. Liu, J.; Li, Y.; Cao, G.; Liu, Y.; Cao, W. Feature pyramid vision transformer for medmnist classification decathlon. In *Proceedings of the 2022 International Joint Conference on Neural Networks (IJCNN)*; IEEE: New York, NY, USA, 2022; pp. 1–8.
47. Liu, Y. Medical Image Classification Based on Transformer Model and Ordinal Loss. In *Proceedings of the 1st International Conference on Engineering Management, Information Technology and Intelligence—EMITI*; SciTePress: Setúbal, Portugal, 2024; pp. 708–713. [CrossRef]
48. Xu, W.; Chen, B.; Shi, H.; Tian, H.; Xu, X. Real-time COVID-19 detection over chest x-ray images in edge computing. *Comput. Intell.* **2023**, *39*, 36–57. [CrossRef]
49. Howard, A.; Sandler, M.; Chen, B.; Wang, W.; Chen, L.C.; Tan, M.; Chu, G.; Vasudevan, V.; Zhu, Y.; Pang, R.; et al. Searching for MobileNetV3. In *Proceedings of the 2019 IEEE/CVF International Conference on Computer Vision (ICCV)*; IEEE Computer Society: Los Alamitos, CA, USA, 2019; pp. 1314–1324. [CrossRef]
50. Tan, M.; Le, Q. EfficientNet: Rethinking Model Scaling for Convolutional Neural Networks. In *Proceedings of the 36th International Conference on Machine Learning*; Chaudhuri, K., Salakhutdinov, R., Eds.; ICML: San Diego, CA, USA, 2019; Volume 97, pp. 6105–6114.
51. Amin, H.; Darwish, A.; Hassanien, A.E.; Soliman, M. End-to-End Deep Learning Model for Corn Leaf Disease Classification. *IEEE Access* **2022**, *10*, 31103–31115. [CrossRef]

https://doi.org/10.3390/electronics15071470

52. Kather, J.; Krisam, J.; Charoentong, P.; Luedde, T.; Herpel, E.; Weis, C.A.; Gaiser, T.; Marx, A.; Valous, N.; Ferber, D.; et al. Predicting survival from colorectal cancer histology slides using deep learning: A retrospective multicenter study. *PLoS Med.* **2019**, *16*, e1002730. [CrossRef] [PubMed]
53. He, Y.; Pan, Z.; Li, L.; Shan, Y.; Cao, D.; Chen, L. Real-Time Vehicle Detection from Short-range Aerial Image with Compressed MobileNet. In *Proceedings of the 2019 International Conference on Robotics and Automation (ICRA)*; IEEE: New York, NY, USA, 2019; pp. 8339–8345. [CrossRef]
54. Diniz, J.B.; Cordeiro, F.R.; Miranda, P.B.; da Silva, L.A.T. A grammar-based genetic programming approach to optimize convolutional neural network architectures. In *Proceedings of the Encontro Nacional de Inteligência Artificial e Computacional (ENIAC)*; BRACIS & SBBD: Ceará, Brasil, 2018; pp. 82–93.
55. da Silva, C.A.; Rosa, D.C.; Miranda, P.B.; Cordeiro, F.R.; Si, T.; Nascimento, A.C.; Mello, R.F.; de Mattos Neto, P.S. A multi-objective grammatical evolution framework to generate convolutional neural network architectures. In *Proceedings of the 2021 IEEE Congress on Evolutionary Computation (CEC)*; IEEE: New York, NY, USA, 2021; pp. 2187–2194.
56. da Silva, C.A.; Miranda, P.B.; Cordeiro, F.R. A new grammar for creating convolutional neural networks applied to medical image classification. In *Proceedings of the 2021 34th SIBGRAPI Conference on Graphics, Patterns and Images (SIBGRAPI)*; IEEE: New York, NY, USA, 2021; pp. 97–104.
57. Hossain, M.M.; Hossain, M.M.; Arefin, M.B.; Akhtar, F.; Blake, J. Combining state-of-the-art pre-trained deep learning models: A noble approach for skin cancer detection using max voting ensemble. *Diagnostics* **2023**, *14*, 89. [CrossRef]
58. Ahamed, K.U.; Islam, M.; Uddin, A.; Akhter, A.; Paul, B.K.; Yousuf, M.A.; Uddin, S.; Quinn, J.M.; Moni, M.A. A deep learning approach using effective preprocessing techniques to detect COVID-19 from chest CT-scan and X-ray images. *Comput. Biol. Med.* **2021**, *139*, 105014. [CrossRef]
59. Demircioğlu, A. The effect of feature normalization methods in radiomics. *Insights Imaging* **2024**, *15*, 2. [CrossRef] [PubMed]
60. Dong, J.D.; Cheng, A.C.; Juan, D.C.; Wei, W.; Sun, M. Dpp-net: Device-aware progressive search for pareto-optimal neural architectures. In *Proceedings of the European Conference on Computer Vision (ECCV)*; ECCV: Zurich, Switzerland, 2018; pp. 517–531.
61. Mih, A.N.; Rahimi, A.; Kawnine, A.; Palma, F.; Wachowicz, M.; Dubay, R.; Cao, H. Achieving Pareto Optimality using Efficient Parameter Reduction for DNNs in Resource-Constrained Edge Environment. In *Proceedings of the Canadian Conference on Artificial Intelligence*; Canadian Artificial Intelligence Association: Waterloo, ON, Canada, 2024. Available online: https://caiac.pubpub.org/pub/2gh9r4xc (accessed on 25 March 2026).
62. Preuveneers, D.; Tsingenopoulos, I.; Joosen, W. Resource usage and performance trade-offs for machine learning models in smart environments. *Sensors* **2020**, *20*, 1176. [CrossRef]
63. Sathish, R.; Khare, S.; Sheet, D. Verifiable and energy efficient medical image analysis with quantised self-attentive deep neural networks. In *Proceedings of the International Workshop on Distributed, Collaborative, and Federated Learning*; Springer: Berlin/Heidelberg, Germany, 2022; pp. 178–189.
64. Ochilbek, R. A new approach (extra vertex) and generalization of Shoelace Algorithm usage in convex polygon (Point-in-Polygon). In *Proceedings of the 2018 14th International Conference on Electronics Computer and Computation (ICECCO)*; IEEE: New York, NY, USA, 2018; pp. 206–212.
65. Rajoria, R.; Kanodia, B.; Saha, D.; Kopets, E.; Voznesensky, A.; Kaplun, D.; Singh, P.K. Attention-Based Deep Neural Networks for Automatic Organ Classification from 2D CT Scan Images. In *AI and ML Techniques in Image Processing and Object Detection*; Springer: Berlin/Heidelberg, Germany, 2025; pp. 1–27.

https://doi.org/10.3390/electronics15071470

electronics

MDPI

Article

Prex-NetII: Attention-Based Back-Projection Network for Light Field Reconstruction

Dong-Myung Kim and Jae-Won Suh *

Department of Electronics Engineering, College of Electrical and Computer Engineering, Chungbuk National University, Cheongju 28644, Republic of Korea; dmkim@chungbuk.ac.kr
* Correspondence: sjwon@cbnu.ac.kr; Tel.: +82-43-261-3268

Abstract

We propose an attention-based back-projection network that enhances light field reconstruction quality by modeling inter-view dependencies. The network uses pixel shuffle to efficiently extract initial features. Spatial attention focuses on important regions while capturing inter-view dependencies. Skip connections in the refinement network improve stability and reconstruction performance. In addition, channel attention within the projection blocks enhances structural representation across views. The proposed method reconstructs high-quality light field images not only in general scenes but also in complex scenes containing occlusions and reflections. The experimental results show that the proposed method outperforms existing approaches.

Keywords: light field reconstruction; angular super-resolution; convolutional neural network

1. Introduction

Light field imaging enables the reconstruction of 3D information by capturing both spatial and angular information [1,2]. Due to this property, light field imaging has been applied in various fields [3–8]. However, to extend its applications further, the angular resolution of light field imaging needs to be improved. One of the primary challenges in this task is processing a large number of views. This requirement substantially increases the number of network parameters. In addition, parallax between views complicates the reconstruction process. Moreover, factors such as light reflections and occlusions make the restoration process more difficult. Consequently, enhancing light field resolution remains a highly challenging problem.

Conventional view synthesis methods [9–13] generate novel views using classical approaches. Geometry-based techniques [9,11] use estimated depth or disparity maps to guide pixel rearrangement. They perform well in simple scenes but have difficulty handling occlusions, complex lighting, or strong reflections. To address these limitations, Zhou et al. [14] proposed learning an appearance mapping from input images via appearance flow, thus avoiding explicit depth estimation. While this method can yield high-quality reconstructions under favorable conditions, it is still challenged by occlusions and regions not visible in the input views. Moreover, its reliance on flow-based warping limits flexibility in handling novel pixels and complex scenes.

Recently, deep learning-based methods [15–26] have been introduced for light field reconstruction. These approaches are categorized into depth-based and non-depth-based methods. Depth-based methods generate novel views by predicting a depth map from the input images. However, inaccurate depth estimation causes problems that reduce the quality of the novel view. Non-depth-based methods can avoid these issues since they do not rely on depth maps. However, due to the inherent complexity of light field, the quality of the reconstructed images remains limited. To overcome this limitation, non-depth-based approaches focus on efficiently utilizing the intrinsic information across light field views without relying on explicit depth estimation.

In our previous work, we proposed Prex-Net [27], which progressively fused feature maps across views using a modified back-projection structure [28]. We extend our previous approach and propose Prex-NetII, an improved algorithm for high-quality light field reconstruction. Unlike our previous network [27], Prex-NetII employs pixel shuffle and spatial attention for initial feature extraction. The pixel shuffle approach efficiently aggregates multi-view information with fewer parameters than 3D convolution.

In addition, the spatial attention module improves the network's capacity to capture spatial correlations across sub-aperture images. Furthermore, channel attention is incorporated into the up- and down-projection modules within the refinement network to better exploit inter-view dependencies and underlying 3D structural information. To further stabilize training and improve reconstruction performance, long skip connections are applied before and after the refinement network. The main contributions of this work are summarized as follows:

- Efficiently extracts the initial feature map using pixel shuffle, reducing the number of parameters compared to our previous work.
- Enhanced training stability achieved by adopting long skip connections around the refinement network.
- Improved cross-view representation through attention mechanisms that better capture structural dependencies across views.

2. Related Works

A common strategy for synthesizing novel views is to predict a depth map and warp the input images. The accuracy of the estimated depth map directly determines the quality of the resulting views. Traditional depth-based light field reconstruction methods have explored various approaches. Wanner and Goldluecke [9] introduced a variational framework for disparity estimation and angular super-resolution, deriving disparity maps from local slope estimations to generate warp maps. However, this approach is limited to local regions and shows reduced performance in areas with complex structures or strong specular reflections. Mitra and Veeraraghavan [10] proposed a patch-based method using Gaussian mixture model to model disparity patterns, integrating patches to reconstruct high-resolution light field images. This method struggles when the patch sizes are smaller than the maximum disparity in the light field.

With the introduction of deep learning, CNN-based methods have been applied to light field reconstruction. Flynn et al. [15] demonstrated a method for synthesizing novel views from wide-baseline stereo images, providing guidelines for disparity-based CNN synthesis. However, generating views using only two input images limits the total number of novel views. Kalantari et al. [16] proposed a framework that estimates depth from densely sampled light field images, warps the inputs accordingly, and refines intermediate synthesis images through color estimation. Although effective, this method requires cropping boundary regions due to missing data in warped inputs and is computationally expensive when producing multiple views. Jin et al. (LFASR-geometry) [17] addressed speed limitations by predicting multiple depth maps simultaneously, but remaining inaccuracies in depth estimation still cause distortions. Jin et al. (LFASR-FS-GAF) [18] further enhanced intermediate synthesis by incorporating attention maps and plane sweep volumes (PSVs), improving synthesis quality, but limitations remain in improving the accuracy of depth maps. Chen et al. [19] proposed a hybrid method that combines depth-based and non-depth-based synthesis through region-wise disparity guidance. However, it still suffers from detail loss and artifacts due to disparity estimation errors.

Several methods reconstruct light fields without estimating depth explicitly, relying on structural cues or frequency-domain information instead. Shi et al. [12] restored the sparsity of light field images in the Fourier domain via nonlinear gradient descent, although their approach required specific sampling along image borders and diagonals. Vagharshakyan et al. [13] applied adaptive discrete shearlet transforms and EPI-based inpainting, but sequential synthesis along axes slowed processing and limited occlusion handling.

As in depth-based methods, CNN-based models have been proposed to reconstruct light fields without explicit depth estimation. Yoon et al. [20] proposed a network to synthesize an intermediate view from two adjacent views, but it had a limitation in the location of synthesized views. Gul and Gunturk [21] fed lenslet stacks into a network to achieve angular super-resolution more efficiently, yet simple architectures caused quality degradation. Wu et al. [22] reconstructed light fields via EPIs using a blur-restoration-deblur framework, but the reconstruction failed for scenes with disparities beyond a certain range. To address this, Wu et al. [23] proposed a shear-aware light field reconstruction network that integrates learnable shearing, downscaling, and prefiltering into the rendering process. It reduces aliasing in epipolar-plane images by processing and fusing multiple sheared inputs. Wang et al. (DistgASR) [24] combined MacPI structures and multiple filters to extract spatial and angular features simultaneously, achieving high quality with minor inference delays. Fang et al. (GLGNet) [25] proposed an EPI-based framework that incorporates a bilateral upsampling module to perform angular super-resolution at arbitrary interpolation rates. However, the method tends to lose fine details in scenes with complex textures. Salem et al. (LFR-DFE) [26] integrated dual feature extraction and macro-pixel upsampling, producing high-quality reconstructions under sparse inputs, but the approach struggled with complex occlusion boundaries.

In summary, inaccurate depth estimation causes distortions in the reconstructed views of depth-based methods. Although non-depth-based approaches can avoid this issue, they still suffer from image artifacts and loss of fine details in regions with complex occlusions or reflections. This is because existing models have difficulty capturing the spatial–angular relationships required for accurate reconstruction. To solve these problems, we propose an attention-based back-projection network that enhances feature interaction across views and improves reconstruction quality.

3. Proposed Network

The proposed network consists of an initial feature extraction network and a refinement network. The initial feature extraction network integrates spatial and angular information from multiple input views. It generates a fused feature representation of the corner sub-aperture images through pixel shuffle. This allows the use of 2D convolutions to capture spatio-angular dependencies with a low computational cost. A spatial attention module is then applied to focus on informative regions. The initial feature map is then fed into the refinement network for reconstruction. The refinement network adopts a back-projection structure to refine the extracted features. The refinement network consists of multiple up- and down-projection blocks that reduce reconstruction errors and recover fine spatial details while maintaining consistency across views.

As shown in Figure 1, the initial feature extraction network concatenates corner images LF_{LT}, LF_{RT}, LF_{LB}, and $LF_{RB} \in \mathbb{R}^{H \times W \times 1}$ of the 7×7 light field image to create $LF_{concat} \in \mathbb{R}^{H \times W \times 4}$, where H and W are the height and width of light field images, respectively. Then, LF_{concat} is rearranged to $LF_{ps} \in \mathbb{R}^{rH \times rW \times 4/r^2}$ by pixel shuffle, where r is the upscaling factor and is set to 2. Consequently, the input images of the four corners are rearranged into a single-channel feature map with double the spatial resolution. This allows the network to efficiently extract spatio-angular features from multiple images using only 2D convolution.

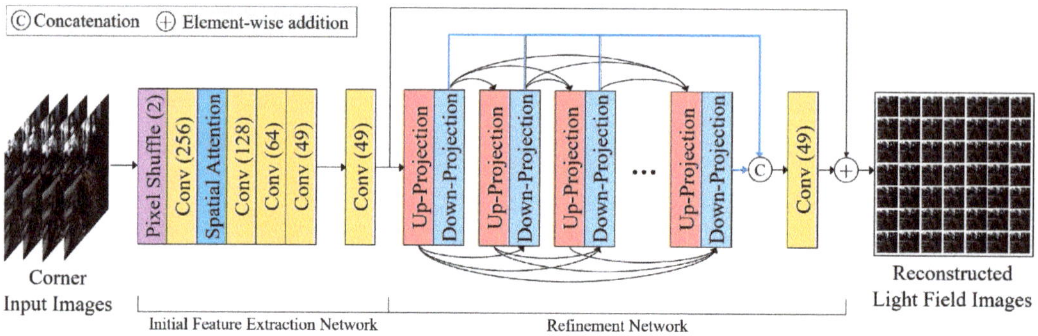

Figure 1. Overall architecture of the proposed Prex-Net. The network consists of two stages: (1) an initial feature extraction network that integrates spatial and angular information using pixel shuffle and spatial attention, and (2) a refinement network that refines features through multiple up- and down-projection blocks.

The pixel-shuffled image LF_{ps} passes through 2D convolution layers of 256, 128, 64, 49, and 49 with 3 × 3 kernels. The spatial attention module is inserted after the first convolution layer to improve spatial features. As a result, the initial feature map F_{init} is obtained. The stride and padding of all convolution layers are set to 1, except for the last layer. To match the spatial resolution of the initial feature map F_{init} and the input light field image, the stride of the last convolution layer is set to 2 and the padding is set to 1. Each convolution layer is followed by LeakyReLU with a negative slope of 0.01.

In the spatial attention module, the input feature map is processed through both average and max pooling to produce two spatial maps. These maps are concatenated and passed to a 2D convolution layer with a 7 × 7 kernel, stride 1, and padding 1. This layer generates the spatial attention map. The 7 × 7 kernel size is adopted to provide a wider receptive field for capturing long-range spatial correlations. The attention map is normalized using a sigmoid activation and multiplied with the original feature map to obtain spatially refined features. The structure of the spatial attention module is shown in Figure 2.

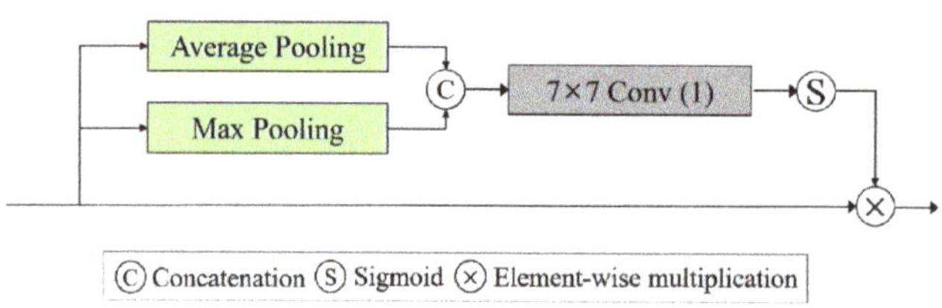

Figure 2. Structure of the spatial attention module. Average and max pooling are first applied to the input feature map to generate spatial features, which are then concatenated and passed through a 7 × 7 convolution, followed by a sigmoid activation to produce the spatial attention map.

To capture the inherent correlations in the initial feature map, we introduce a refinement network based on a back-projection structure [28]. As shown in Figure 1, the up- and down-projection blocks of the refinement network are densely connected to each other. The first up-projection block takes the initial feature map as input. The subsequent up-projection blocks concatenate the outputs of the down-projection blocks from the previous stage and use them as input. Similarly, the first down-projection block takes the output of the first up-projection block as input, and the following down-projection blocks concatenate the outputs of the up-projection blocks from the previous stage and use them as input.

The input of the last convolution layer is the concatenated outputs of the down-projection blocks. The last convolution layer has a filter size of 3 × 3 and is not followed by an ReLU. Finally, the output feature map $\boldsymbol{F}_{refine}$ of the refinement network is added to the initial feature map $\boldsymbol{F}_{init}$, via a long skip connection, to generate the final reconstructed light field images. This long skip connection helps to improve the quality of the reconstructed light field images and enables stable training of the proposed network.

3.1. Up-Projection Bock

The up-projection block is shown in Figure 3. The input feature map U^i_{in} of the up-projection block is the initial feature map or the concatenated outputs of the down-projection blocks. It can be expressed as

$$U^i_{in} = \begin{cases} \boldsymbol{F}_{init}, & i = 1 \\ concatenate(D^1_{out}, \cdots, D^{i-1}_{out}), & i = 2, \ldots, 12, \end{cases} \tag{1}$$

where i represents the i-th block. As i increases, the number of channels of the input feature map U^i_{in} increases by 49 × i. Therefore, a 1 × 1 convolution layer is employed to set the channel number of the input feature map U^i_{in} to 49. The following 3 × 3 convolution layer expands the 49-channel feature map to a 196-channel feature map. The expanded 196-channel feature map is passed through a channel attention module to assign weights to each channel. This expanded feature map enhances feature representation and captures more complex spatial relationships. Subsequently, the feature map is rearranged into a 49-channel feature map u^i_1 using pixel shuffle with an upscaling factor of 2. The pixel-shuffled 49-channel feature map u^i_1 is processed by a 6 × 6 convolution layer with a stride of 2 and padding of 2. This operation produces a 49-channel feature map u^i_2 with spatial resolution matching that of the input light field image. The feature map u^i_2 becomes a residual feature map by subtracting u^i_0. This 49-channel residual feature map passes through a 3 × 3 convolution layer for channel expansion and pixel shuffle with an upscaling factor of 2. Each convolution layer is followed by LeakyReLU with a negative slope of 0.2. The resulting u^i_3 is then added to u^i_1 to produce U^i_{out}. The final output of the up-projection block can be expressed as

$$U^i_{out} = \mathcal{F}(u^i_0) + \mathcal{F}\Big(\phi(g(u^i_1)) - u^i_0\Big), \tag{2}$$

where $\mathcal{F}(\cdot) = \phi(\mathcal{P}_2(\mathcal{A}_c(q(\cdot))))$. Here, $\phi(\cdot)$ represents the LeakyReLU activation function, $\mathcal{P}_2(\cdot)$ denotes the pixel shuffle operation, and $\mathcal{A}c(\cdot)$ denotes the channel attention module, while $q(\cdot)$ and $g(\cdot)$ refer to 3 × 3 and 6 × 6 convolution layers, respectively.

The channel attention module is shown in Figure 4. First, a feature map with 196 channels is input and compressed into a channel-wise descriptor by applying average pooling. Although max pooling can also be used in this step, we used only average pooling to reduce the computational cost. The average-pooled feature map with a shape of (196 × 1 × 1) is passed through two fully connected layers to generate the attention map, where the reduction ratio is set to 14. Here, the feature dimension is reduced from 196 to 14 and then expanded back to 196. This enables the network to learn channel-wise weights that represent the importance of each channel. An ReLU activation is applied between the layers. The resulting attention map is normalized using a sigmoid activation function and then multiplied element-wise with the input feature map. This produces the final channel-attended feature representation.

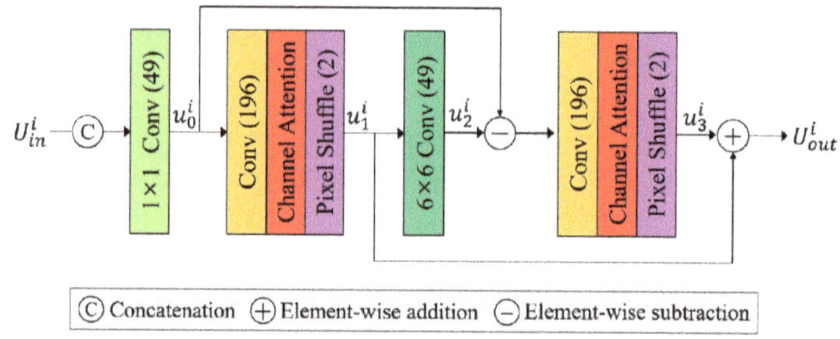

Figure 3. Structure of the up-projection block. Stacked inputs are compressed, enhanced with channel attention, and spatially aggregated using a 6 × 6 convolution.

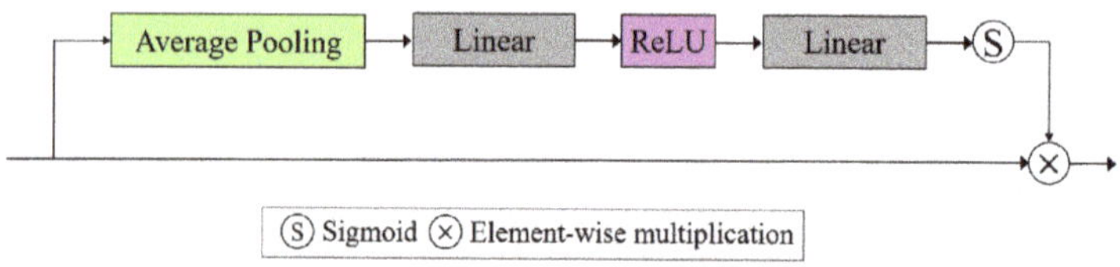

Figure 4. Structure of the channel attention module. Global average pooling and two fully connected layers generate attention weights, which scale channel features.

3.2. Down-Projection Bock

The down-projection block is shown in Figure 5. The input feature map D^i_{in} of the down-projection block is the concatenated outputs of the up-projection blocks. It can be expressed as

$$D^i_{in} = concatenate(U^1_{out}, \cdots, U^i_{out}), i = 1, 2, \ldots, 12. \tag{3}$$

Similar to the up-projection block, each increment in i increases the channels of the input feature map for the down-projection block by $49 \times i$. Therefore, a 1×1 convolution layer is employed to set the channel number of the input feature map D^i_{in} to 49. Unlike the up-projection block, the spatial resolution of the feature map D^i_{in} is double that of the input light field image. Therefore, we resize it using a 6×6 convolution layer with a stride of 2 and padding of 2. The 49-channel feature map d^i_1 is expanded to 196-channel feature map using a 3×3 convolution layer. The 196-channel feature map is then passed through the channel attention module and subsequently rearranged into a 49-channel feature map d^i_2 by pixel shuffle with an upscaling factor of 2. The 49-channel feature map d^i_2 becomes a residual feature map by subtracting the feature map d^i_0 previously generated by the 1×1 convolution layer. This 49-channel residual feature map passes through a 6×6 convolution layer to match the spatial resolution of the input light field image. It is then added to d^i_1 to produce the output of the down-projection block. It can be expressed as

$$D^i_{out} = d^i_1 + \phi\Big(g(\mathcal{F}(d^i_1) - d^i_0)\Big). \tag{4}$$

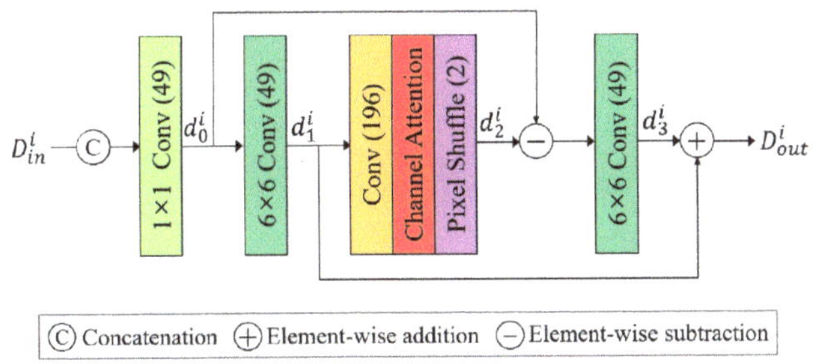

Figure 5. Structure of the down-projection block. The block compresses concatenated inputs, applies channel attention for feature enhancement, and employs convolution and pixel shuffle operations to restore residual information.

4. Simulation Results

For training, we used the Stanford Lytro light field archive [29] and the Kalantari dataset [16]. These datasets have an angular resolution of 14 × 14 and a spatial resolution of 376 × 541. We used only the 7 × 7 light field images from the center of the 14 × 14 light field images. We converted RGB color images to YCbCr color images and conducted experiments using only luminance. For testing, we used real-world light field images named 30Scenes [16], Occlusions [29], and Reflective [29] datasets. The 30Scenes dataset consists of general images, the Occlusions dataset contains images with overlapping objects, and the Reflective dataset includes images with reflective areas. In particular, light field images with occlusions or diffuse reflections make it difficult to predict the pixels of the reconstructed light field images. We evaluated the performance of the proposed method using datasets with various characteristics.

We used randomly cropped patches with a spatial resolution of 96 × 96 for training, and the cropped patch was augmented by flipping and rotation. To avoid memory limitation issues, the batch size was set to 1. For optimization, we used Adam optimizer with $\beta_1 = 0.9, \beta_2 = 0.999$. The learning rate was initialized as 10^{-4} and decreased to 10^{-6} by 10^{-1} every 5000 epochs. The proposed network was trained using the Charbonnier loss [30], which minimizes the error between the original high-resolution (HR) light field image and the reconstructed light field image. This loss function is adopted for its robustness to outliers and its smooth approximation of the L_1 norm. The loss is defined as

$$\mathcal{L} = \sqrt{||L^{HR} - \hat{L}^{HR}||^2 + \epsilon^2}, \tag{5}$$

where L^{HR} and $\hat{L}^{HR}$ denote the ground-truth and predicted HR light field images, respectively. The value of ϵ is set to 1×10^{-3}, which is commonly used in image reconstruction tasks.

To evaluate the performance of the proposed method, various metrics were compared with those of existing approaches. Table 1 presents the PSNR comparison results. Non-depth-based methods [24,26,27] achieve better performance than early depth-based approaches [16,18] as they reconstruct images directly without relying on depth estimation. On average, the PSNR of the proposed method was 2.33 dB, 1.44 dB, 0.61 dB, 0.38 dB, and 0.27 dB higher than that of Kalantari et al. [16], LFASR-FS-GAF [18], DistgASR [24], Prex-Net [27], and LFR-DFE [26], respectively. The proposed method consistently outperformed competing approaches across the entire dataset, regardless of its characteristics.

Table 1. Quantitative comparison of PSNR and SSIM between our proposed method and existing methods for $2 \times 2 \rightarrow 7 \times 7$ reconstruction.

Methods	30Scenes	Occlusions	Reflective	Average
Kalantari et al. [16]	41.42/0.984	37.46/0.974	38.07/0.953	38.98/0.970
LFASR-FS-GAF [18]	42.75/0.986	38.51/0.979	38.35/0.957	39.87/0.974
DistgASR [24]	43.61/0.995	39.44/0.991	39.05/0.977	40.70/0.988
Prex-Net [27]	43.49/0.987	40.00/0.983	39.30/0.961	40.93/0.977
LFR-DFE [26]	43.62/0.987	40.08/0.983	39.42/0.960	41.04/0.977
Prex-NetII	**43.79/0.988**	**40.35/0.984**	**39.80/0.962**	**41.31/0.978**

To analyze the influence of the number of projection blocks, we conducted experiments by varying the number of blocks in the refinement network. All models were trained under identical conditions, and their reconstruction performance was evaluated in terms of PSNR and SSIM. As shown in Table 2, the performance improved as the number of projection blocks increased. However, as the number of projection blocks increased, the performance gain gradually decreased. We determined the optimal number of up- and down-projection blocks to be 12 for each, considering the trade-off between performance and model parameters. In addition, the proposed model achieved better performance while reducing the number of parameters compared to our previous work [27].

Table 2. Quantitative comparison of PSNR and SSIM with varying numbers of projection blocks.

Number of Blocks	30Scenes	Occlusions	Reflective	Average	Param. (M)
Prex-Net [27]	43.49/0.987	40.00/0.983	39.30/0.961	40.93/0.977	8.10
Blocks 3	43.20/0.986	39.55/0.981	39.23/0.958	40.66/0.975	2.11
Blocks 6	43.51/0.987	39.95/0.983	39.48/0.956	40.98/0.975	3.85
Blocks 9	43.66/0.987	40.06/0.983	39.75/0.962	41.16/0.977	5.63
Blocks 12	**43.79/0.988**	**40.35/0.984**	**39.80/0.962**	**41.31/0.978**	7.46

We conducted a series of experiments to validate the effectiveness of the proposed method. This ablation study was conducted to evaluate the contribution of the applied attention blocks to performance improvement. We applied different attention modules to the initial feature extraction and projection blocks. As shown in Table 3, the results indicate that the best performance was achieved when spatial attention was applied at the initial feature extraction stage and channel attention was integrated within the projection block.

Spatial attention applied at an early stage helped the network to focus on relevant regions in the input image, improving spatial feature learning. Channel attention within the projection block refined the features by strengthening channel-wise correlations, which led to improved reconstruction performance.

Table 3. Ablation results on spatial and channel attention modules.

Variants	Initial Feature Extraction	Projection Block	PSNR(dB)/SSIM
w/o	✗	✗	41.20/0.977
1	channel attention	spatial attention	40.86/0.975
2	channel attention	channel attention	41.24/0.978
3	spatial attention	spatial attention	40.85/0.975
4	spatial attention	channel attention	**41.31/0.978**

Figure 6 presents a comparison between the proposed method and existing methods using both error maps and cropped image regions. The error maps show the pixel-wise differences between the reconstructed and ground-truth images. Smaller errors are shown in blue, while larger errors are shown in red. For clearer comparison, error values were clipped to the range of 0 to 0.1, with values above 0.1 truncated to 0.1. As shown in Figure 6, the proposed method more accurately reconstructs the ground-truth images than existing methods.

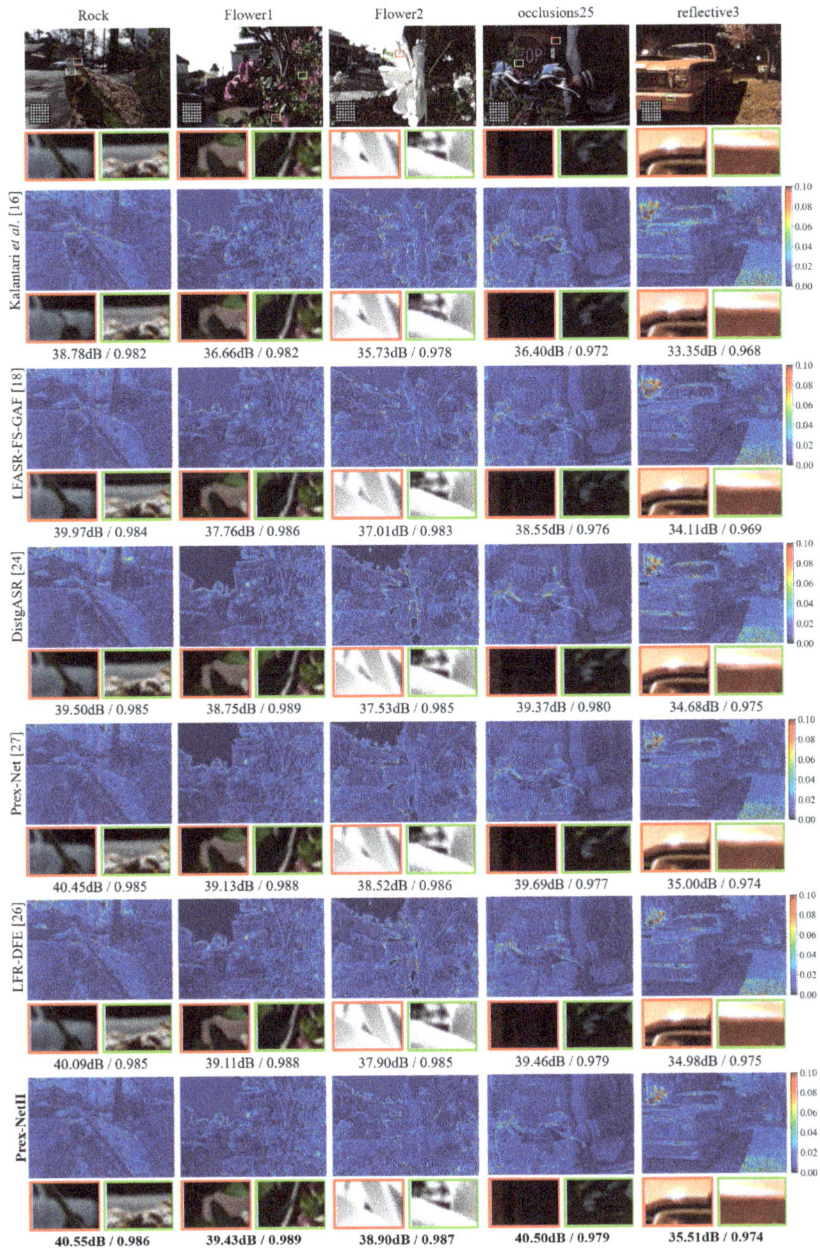

Figure 6. Visual comparison of central novel view result images.

Methods that rely on depth maps reconstruct light field images by warping input views based on estimated depth. As shown in Figure 6, blur or artifacts can be seen because the predicted depth map is inaccurate. In contrast, methods that do not rely on depth maps avoid such issues. However, the figure shows that they may not fully exploit angular correlations in the light field data, which leads to reduced texture quality.

For example, in the first cropped region of the *Flower2* scene, the proposed method recovers the background object between the petals more accurately than existing methods. In the second crop of the *Occlusion25* scene, the proposed method recovers leaf textures more clearly than existing methods. This indicates that the proposed method provides consistently higher-quality reconstructions across these examples. In the first crop of the *Reflective3* scene, the proposed method restores reflected light that closely matches the ground truth. Additionally, in the second crop of the same scene, existing methods tend to produce unwanted white lines in reflective regions due to interference from neighboring regions. The results show that the proposed method is more robust in handling reflections.

5. Conclusions

In this paper, we proposed Prex-NetII to increase the angular resolution of light fields using an attention-based back-projection network. Compared with our previous work, the proposed network included several improvements to enhance reconstruction performance. The proposed network adopted pixel shuffle for initial feature extraction, which efficiently extracted features while reducing the number of parameters. By employing attention mechanisms, the network effectively captured inter-view correlations and selectively enhanced important spatial features. In addition, long skip connections were applied around the refinement network to stabilize training and preserve structural details across views. The experimental results showed that our method achieved higher PSNR and SSIM compared with existing approaches, demonstrating the benefit of integrating projection-based refinement with attention-driven feature fusion. The proposed light field reconstruction method can be applied to various industrial domains, such as CCTV systems, visual recognition, and AR/VR applications. Future work will focus on reducing model complexity while maintaining reconstruction accuracy.

Author Contributions: Conceptualization, D.-M.K.; methodology, D.-M.K.; software, D.-M.K.; formal analysis, D.-M.K.; investigation, J.-W.S.; resources, J.-W.S.; data curation, D.-M.K.; writing—original draft preparation, D.-M.K.; writing—review and editing, D.-M.K. and J.-W.S.; validation, D.-M.K. and J.-W.S.; visualization, D.-M.K.; supervision, J.-W.S.; project administration, J.-W.S.; funding acquisition, J.-W.S. All authors have read and agreed to the published version of the manuscript.

Funding: This work was supported by the National Research Foundation of Korea grant funded by the Korea government (MSIT) (No. 2022R1A5A8026986).

Institutional Review Board Statement: Not applicable.

Informed Consent Statement: Not applicable.

Data Availability Statement: The datasets used in this paper are public datasets. The code used for evaluation of the proposed method can be accessed at https://github.com/dmkim17/Prex-Net2 (accessed on 22 August 2025).

Conflicts of Interest: The authors declare no conflicts of interest.

References

1. Adelson, E.H.; Bergen, J.R. The plenoptic function and the elements of early vision. In *Computer Models of Visual Processing*; MIT Press: Cambridge, MA, USA, 1991; pp. 3–20.
2. Levoy, M.; Hanrahan, P. Light field rendering. In Proceedings of the 23rd Annual Conference on Computer Graphics and Interactive Techniques (SIGGRAPH '96), New Orleans, LA, USA, 4–9 August 1996; pp. 31–42. [CrossRef]
3. Kim, C.; Zimmer, H.; Pritch, Y.; Sorkine-Hornung, A.; Gross, M. Scene reconstruction from high spatio-angular resolution light fields. *ACM Trans. Graph.* **2013**, *32*, 73. [CrossRef]

4. Yücer, K.; Sorkine-Hornung, A.; Wang, O.; Sorkine-Hornung, O. Efficient 3D object segmentation from densely sampled light fields with applications to 3D reconstruction. *ACM Trans. Graph.* **2016**, *35*, 22. [CrossRef]
5. Wang, Y.; Yang, J.; Guo, Y.; Xiao, C.; An, W. Selective light field refocusing for camera arrays using bokeh rendering and superresolution. *IEEE Signal Process. Lett.* **2019**, *26*, 204–208. [CrossRef]
6. Yan, T.; Zhang, F.; Mao, Y.; Yu, H.; Qian, X.; Lau, R.W.H. Depth estimation from a light field image pair with a generative model. *IEEE Access* **2019**, *7*, 12768–12778. [CrossRef]
7. Wang, Y.; Wu, T.; Yang, J.; Wang, L.; An, W.; Guo, Y. DeOccNet: Learning to see through foreground occlusions in light fields. In Proceedings of the IEEE Winter Conference on Applications of Computer Vision (WACV), Snowmass Village, CO, USA, 1–5 March 2020; pp. 118–127. [CrossRef]
8. Wang, T.-C.; Chandraker, M.; Efros, A.A.; Ramamoorthi, R. SVBRDF-invariant shape and reflectance estimation from light-field cameras. In Proceedings of the IEEE Conference on Computer Vision and Pattern Recognition (CVPR), Las Vegas, NV, USA, 27–30 June 2016; pp. 5451–5459. [CrossRef]
9. Wanner, S.; Goldluecke, B. Variational light field analysis for disparity estimation and super-resolution. *IEEE Trans. Pattern Anal. Mach. Intell.* **2013**, *36*, 606–619. [CrossRef] [PubMed]
10. Mitra, K.; Veeraraghavan, A. Light field denoising, light field superresolution and stereo camera based refocussing using a GMM light field patch prior. In Proceedings of the 2012 IEEE Computer Society Conference on Computer Vision and Pattern Recognition Workshops, Providence, RI, USA, 16–21 June 2012; pp. 22–28. [CrossRef]
11. Seitz, S.M.; Dyer, C.R. View Morphing. In Proceedings of the 23rd Annual Conference on Computer Graphics and Interactive Techniques (SIGGRAPH '96), New Orleans, LA, USA, 4–9 August 1996; pp. 21–30. [CrossRef]
12. Shi, L.; Hassanieh, H.; Davis, A.; Katabi, D.; Durand, F. Light field reconstruction using sparsity in the continuous Fourier domain. *ACM Trans. Graph.* **2014**, *34*, 12. [CrossRef]
13. Vagharshakyan, S.; Bregovic, R.; Gotchev, A. Light field reconstruction using shearlet transform. *IEEE Trans. Pattern Anal. Mach. Intell.* **2017**, *40*, 133–147. [CrossRef] [PubMed]
14. Zhou, T.; Tulsiani, S.; Sun, W.; Malik, J.; Efros, A.A. View synthesis by appearance flow. In Proceedings of the European Conference on Computer Vision (ECCV), Amsterdam, The Netherlands, 11–14 October 2016; pp. 286–301. [CrossRef]
15. Flynn, J.; Neulander, I.; Philbin, J.; Snavely, N. DeepStereo: Learning to predict new views from the world's imagery. In Proceedings of the IEEE Conference on Computer Vision and Pattern Recognition (CVPR), Las Vegas, NV, USA, 27–30 June 2016; pp. 5515–5524. [CrossRef]
16. Kalantari, N.K.; Wang, T.-C.; Ramamoorthi, R. Learning-based view synthesis for light field cameras. *ACM Trans. Graph.* **2016**, *35*, 193. [CrossRef]
17. Jin, J.; Hou, J.; Yuan, H.; Kwong, S. Learning light field angular super-resolution via a geometry-aware network. In Proceedings of the AAAI Conference on Artificial Intelligence, New York, NY, USA, 7–12 February 2020; pp. 11141–11148. [CrossRef]
18. Jin, J.; Hou, J.; Chen, J.; Zeng, H.; Kwong, S.; Yu, J. Deep coarse-to-fine dense light field reconstruction with flexible sampling and geometry-aware fusion. *IEEE Trans. Pattern Anal. Mach. Intell.* **2020**, *44*, 1819–1836. [CrossRef] [PubMed]
19. Chen, Y.; Zhang, X.; Li, J.; Wang, L.; Guo, Y. Enhanced light field reconstruction by combining disparity and texture information in PSVs via disparity-guided fusion. *IEEE Trans. Comput. Imaging* **2023**, *9*, 665–677. [CrossRef]
20. Yoon, Y.; Jeon, H.-G.; Yoo, D.; Park, J.; Kweon, I.S. Light-field image super-resolution using convolutional neural network. *IEEE Signal Process. Lett.* **2017**, *24*, 848–852. [CrossRef]
21. Gul, M.; Gunturk, B.K. Spatial and angular resolution enhancement of light fields using convolutional neural networks. *IEEE Trans. Comput. Imaging* **2018**, *27*, 2146–2159. [CrossRef] [PubMed]
22. Wu, G.; Wang, Y.; Wang, L.; Yu, J.; Guo, Y. Light field reconstruction using convolutional network on EPI and extended applications. *IEEE Trans. Pattern Anal. Mach. Intell.* **2018**, *41*, 1681–1694. [CrossRef] [PubMed]
23. Wu, G.; Wang, Y.; Wang, L.; Yu, J.; Guo, Y. Revisiting light field rendering with deep anti-aliasing neural network. *IEEE Trans. Pattern Anal. Mach. Intell.* **2021**, *44*, 5430–5444. [CrossRef] [PubMed]
24. Wang, Y.; Wang, L.; Wu, G.; Yang, J.; An, W.; Yu, J.; Guo, Y. Disentangling light fields for super-resolution and disparity estimation. *IEEE Trans. Pattern Anal. Mach. Intell.* **2022**, *45*, 425–443. [CrossRef] [PubMed]
25. Fang, L.; Wang, Q.; Ye, L. GLGNet: Light field angular superresolution with arbitrary interpolation rates. *Vis. Intell.* **2024**, *2*, 6. [CrossRef]
26. Salem, A.; Elkady, E.; Ibrahem, H.; Suh, J.-W.; Kang, H.-S. Light field reconstruction with dual features extraction and macro-pixel upsampling. *IEEE Access* **2024**, *12*, 121624–121634. [CrossRef]
27. Kim, D.-M.; Yoon, Y.-S.; Ban, Y.; Suh, J.-W. Prex-Net: Progressive exploration network using efficient channel fusion for light field reconstruction. *Electronics* **2023**, *12*, 4661. [CrossRef]
28. Haris, M.; Shakhnarovich, G.; Ukita, N. Deep back-projection networks for super-resolution. In Proceedings of the 2018 IEEE/CVF Conference on Computer Vision and Pattern Recognition (CVPR), Salt Lake City, UT, USA, 18–23 June 2018; pp. 1664–1673. [CrossRef]

29. Raj, A.S.; Lowney, M.; Shah, R.; Wetzstein, G. *Stanford Lytro Light Field Archive*; Stanford Computational Imaging Lab: Stanford, CA, USA, 2016.
30. Charbonnier, P.; Blanc-Féraud, L.; Aubert, G.; Barlaud, M. Two deterministic half-quadratic regularization algorithms for computed imaging. In Proceedings of the 1st International Conference on Image Processing (ICIP), Austin, TX, USA, 13–16 November 1994; pp. 168–172. [CrossRef]

electronics

MDPI

Article

The Effective Highlight-Detection Model for Video Clips Using Spatial—Perceptual

Sungshin Kwak [1], Jaedong Lee [2,*] and Sohyun Park [2,*]

1 Department of Artificial Intelligence Convergence, Graduate School, Dankook University, Yongin 16890, Republic of Korea; sungshin98@dankook.ac.kr

2 Department of Software Science, SW Convergence College, Dankook University, Yongin 16890, Republic of Korea

* Correspondence: letsdoit@dankook.ac.kr (J.L.); sohyunpark@dankook.ac.kr (S.P.); Tel.: +82-031-8005-3254 (J.L. & S.P.)

Abstract

With the rapid growth of video platforms such as YouTube, Bilibili, and Dailymotion, an enormous amount of video content is being shared worldwide. In this environment, content providers are increasingly adopting methods that restructure videos around highlight scenes and distribute them in short-form formats to encourage more efficient content consumption by viewers. As a result of this trend, the importance of highlight extraction technologies capable of automatically identifying key scenes from large-scale video datasets has been steadily increasing. To address this need, this study proposes SPOT (Spatial Perceptual Optimized TimeSformer), a highlight extraction model. The proposed model enhances spatial perceptual capability by integrating a CNN encoder into the internal structure of the existing Transformer-based TimeSformer, enabling simultaneous learning of both the local and global features of a video. The experiments were conducted using Google's YT-8M video dataset along with the MR.Hisum dataset, which provides organized highlight information. The SPOT model adopts a regression-based highlight prediction framework. Experimental results on video datasets of varying complexity showed that, in the high-complexity group, the SPOT model achieved a reduction in mean squared error (MSE) of approximately 0.01 (from 0.090 to 0.080) compared to the original TimeSformer. Furthermore, the model outperformed the baseline across all complexity groups in terms of mAP, Coverage, and F1-Score metrics. These results suggest that the proposed model holds strong potential for diverse multimodal applications such as video summarization, content recommendation, and automated video editing. Moreover, it is expected to serve as a foundational technology for advancing video-based artificial intelligence systems in the future.

Keywords: highlight extraction; video understanding; Transformer; CNN; short-form video

1. Introduction

With the rapid proliferation of video platforms such as YouTube, Bilibili, and Dailymotion, an enormous amount of video content is being shared online [1,2]. In this environment, content providers have actively adopted strategies that extract only the highlight scenes and reorganize them into short-form videos to enable viewers to consume content more quickly and easily [3,4].

This approach serves as an effective means of rapidly attracting viewer interest and delivering key information in a compressed format, thereby increasing viewer engagement and driving higher viewership [5,6]. Alongside this shift in content consumption patterns, the short-form video market has also experienced rapid growth, attracting significant attention. Platforms such as TikTok, YouTube Shorts, and Instagram Reels have gained explosive popularity among users worldwide [7,8], and the practice of delivering key information in a short time span is becoming increasingly common [9,10].

Recent studies have analyzed this trend, noting that "short-form videos have revolutionized digital consumption experiences due to fast consumption habits and mobile-friendly designs" [11]. In particular, the proliferation of short-form content is closely tied to strategies aimed at encouraging users to watch full-length videos by effectively exposing them to key scenes. As a result, the importance of highlight detection technologies capable of automatically extracting key moments from long videos has become increasingly emphasized [12].

However, the creation of such short-form content still largely depends on manual editing, which is both time-consuming and inefficient, given the exponential increase in video data. Consequently, there is a growing need for automated highlight detection methods that can efficiently and accurately identify the most engaging moments in long videos. Nevertheless, automatic highlight extraction remains a significant challenge, as it requires effectively selecting moments of interest from among the vast number of scenes within long videos [7,8].

Consequently, the growing demand for more sophisticated and efficient highlight extraction techniques has actively driven research efforts. Notable examples include MH-DETR [13], LD-DETR [14], SC-HVPPNet [15], and other recent approaches [16,17], which aim to improve highlight detection performance in complex video data. These highlight extraction techniques have evolved based on video understanding technologies, which are designed to comprehend both visual and contextual information within videos. Video understanding is a technology that goes beyond the analysis of individual frames to comprehensively interpret events, activities, object relationships, and contextual information across sequences [18,19].

In this process, the complementary learning of local and global information is crucial [20,21], as highlights are determined not only by subtle changes in objects but also by the overall contextual flow of the video [22]. Local information refers to fine-grained patterns and object-level changes occurring within limited regions of a frame, such as variations in facial expressions or hand gestures. In contrast, global information encompasses relationships and contextual flows across entire frames or sequences of frames, serving as key elements for understanding narrative development, scene transitions, and the overall atmosphere of the video.

To effectively leverage both local and global information, prior research on highlight extraction has largely evolved in two directions. The first approach is based on 2D/3D CNN models [23,24], which excel at detecting local patterns but face limitations in capturing relationships between segments and understanding broader video context [25]. The second approach employs Transformer-based models [26], which leverage self-attention to learn long-range spatiotemporal dependencies and global contextual information. However, because they process inputs by dividing them into patches, these models often struggle to capture subtle, fine-grained local variations within frames [27,28].

While both CNN- and Transformer-based approaches possess unique strengths, they exhibit structural limitations when applied independently—often failing to jointly model fine-grained local variations and long-range contextual dependencies. This structural gap, as discussed in prior studies [29,30], underscores the need for a unified model capable of integrating both aspects effectively. However, despite these advances, existing approaches remain limited in their ability to jointly capture both fine-grained local variations and long-range contextual dependencies. Most prior studies have focused on either local or global information in isolation, leaving a gap in effectively integrating the two for robust highlight detection.

To address these limitations, we propose SPOT, which combines a CNN with the Transformer-based TimeSformer [31]. The SPOT architecture extends TimeSformer by incorporating a CNN branch in parallel with its Spatial Encoder, enabling the model to simultaneously learn local and global features and effectively fuse them. This integrated design is particularly beneficial in videos with high visual complexity or frequent local variations, where TimeSformer alone often struggles. Under such conditions, SPOT demonstrates improved highlight prediction accuracy compared to the baseline TimeSformer.

In this study, video complexity was calculated by analyzing the degree of change between consecutive frames. Recent studies have emphasized the importance of video complexity analysis for adaptive encoding and streaming. For instance, the Video Complexity Analyzer (VCA) [32] estimates spatial and temporal complexity by leveraging block-based DCT energy and its temporal variations. Inspired by such approaches, we adopt a computationally simple calculation based on inter-frame variations to categorize videos into different complexity levels for model evaluation.

Using this metric, the dataset was categorized into different complexity levels to compare the performance of the proposed SPOT model with that of TimeSformer. Experimental results revealed that SPOT consistently outperformed TimeSformer across key evaluation metrics such as Coverage Ratio [33] and mean average precision (mAP) [34] as video complexity increased. Notably, in the high-complexity group, SPOT achieved up to a 0.01 reduction in mean squared error (MSE) [35] compared to TimeSformer. This demonstrates that SPOT is more sensitive to local visual variations within videos, thereby exhibiting superior highlight detection capabilities even in highly complex scenes.

Furthermore, to analyze in greater depth the impact of visual complexity on model performance, we included MH-DETR, a representative state-of-the-art (SOTA) model in the field of highlight detection, as an additional comparison baseline. Through this, we aimed to experimentally verify that SPOT demonstrates competitive performance not only compared to pure Transformer-based architectures but also against the latest designs that leverage cross-modal attention for integrating spatiotemporal features.

These results demonstrate that SPOT maintains high performance even in dynamic video content, supporting its applicability to real-world tasks such as automated editing and video summarization. While this study focuses on the visual modality for highlight extraction, the use of multimodal datasets [36] suggests the potential for future expansion to additional modalities such as audio and subtitles.

2. Related Research

Research on highlight extraction has evolved within the broader field of video understanding and can be broadly categorized into CNN-based, attention-based, Transformer-based, and multimodal methods. Each of these approaches has contributed to important advances: CNNs are effective for learning local spatial features, attention-based models improve the focus on salient regions, and Transformers provide strong global context modeling, and multimodal methods enrich visual information with complementary cues such as audio or text. Nevertheless, several limitations remain. CNNs often fail to capture long-range dependencies, attention mechanisms may struggle with fine-grained spatiotemporal patterns, and Transformers are computationally expensive and relatively insensitive to subtle local variations, and multimodal methods introduce challenges of modality alignment and increased complexity. To address these issues in a unified manner, this study proposes

SPOT, a model designed to integrate the complementary strengths of these approaches while mitigating their respective limitations.

2.1. Video Understanding

Video understanding is a technology that interprets visual data in videos to recognize objects, scenes, actions, and contextual information, and it has recently expanded into diverse applications such as highlight extraction, action recognition, and video summarization. Early studies in video understanding primarily leveraged convolutional neural networks (CNNs) [37], which had demonstrated strong performance in image recognition, to learn local patterns at the frame level or employed 3D CNNs [38] to capture spatiotemporal features. Subsequently, recurrent neural networks (RNNs) and long short-term memory (LSTM) networks [39] were introduced to model temporal dependencies. The integration of attention mechanisms further enhanced the ability to focus on important frames and regions. More recently, Transformer-based models [40] have activated research that emphasizes understanding global context, offering improved performance in various video understanding tasks. In parallel, matching-based methods have been proposed to address few-shot and fine-grained recognition challenges. For instance, M^3Net [41] introduces a multi-view encoding, matching, and fusion framework that leverages intra-frame, intra-video, and intra-episode relationships to improve recognition performance in low-data regimes. In addition, the incorporation of multimodal techniques [42] and large language models (LLMs) [43] has enabled more advanced forms of video understanding, such as video captioning, question answering, and streaming summarization.

2.2. CNN-Based Approaches

Early studies on highlight extraction were largely developed based on CNN [44] models, which had been successfully applied in image recognition. These models typically extracted spatial features from individual frames and then connected them along the temporal axis to detect or summarize highlight scenes within videos. While 3D CNNs demonstrated strong capabilities in capturing local visual information, they faced limitations in modeling sequential changes between scenes or detecting events likely to capture viewer interest. In particular, their architectures were often inadequate for handling patterns involving rapid visual changes or scene transitions within short time spans.

2.3. Attention-Based Approaches

Attention mechanisms enable models to focus on the most relevant parts of a video by dynamically attending to spatial and temporal features, thereby allowing them to effectively capture key scenes and fine-grained details. Attention-based models compute weights that represent the relevance of each element in an input sequence to all others, enabling the efficient extraction of important information even from long sequences. This approach addresses some of the limitations of CNNs by allowing models to respond more sensitively to event sequences and transitions between scenes.

2.4. Transformer-Based Approaches

Transformer architectures, built upon attention-based neural networks, extend the self-attention mechanism and have marked a turning point in video understanding. Notable examples include MH-DETR and LD-DETR, which utilize Transformer-based designs to improve highlight detection and video moment localization. However, while Transformer-based models excel at learning global context, prior studies have noted that they can be relatively less effective at capturing fine-grained local patterns. This tendency may affect tasks such as highlight detection, where sensitivity to subtle visual changes is important.

2.5. Multimodal-Based Approach

Recent studies have increasingly focused on integrating multimodal information to further enhance highlight extraction performance. These approaches utilize not only visual information from videos but also incorporate audio, subtitles, and metadata to more accurately identify key moments. For example, highlights may be detected by considering the co-occurrence of specific sound events and visual scenes or by analyzing dialog content alongside visual context to select highlight candidates.

3. SPOT Model

3.1. Structure of SPOT Models

Previous studies have primarily focused on effectively learning global context through Transformer-based architectures; however, viewers' actual interests are often based on subtle object changes or localized movements within videos. This study distinguishes itself by combining the global representation learning capabilities of Transformers with the local pattern extraction strengths of convolutional neural networks (CNNs), thereby enabling the capture of fine-grained spatial information that conventional models often overlook and achieving more precise highlight prediction. The overall architecture of the proposed model is illustrated in Figure 1.

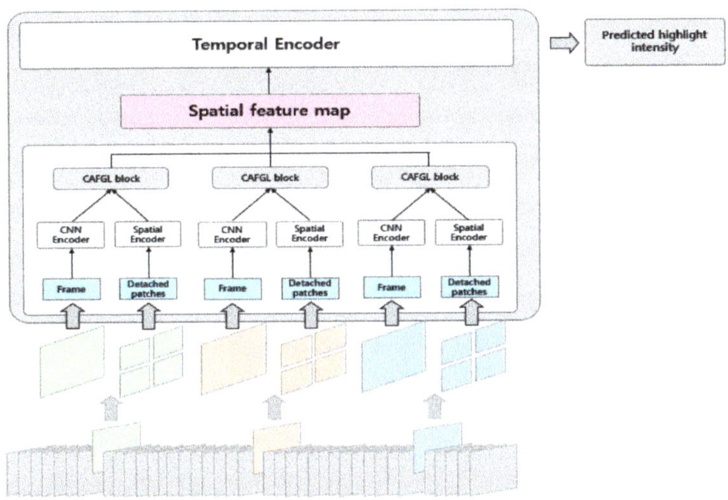

Figure 1. SPOT model architecture.

As illustrated in Figure 1, the proposed SPOT model follows a network architecture that combines a CNN-based encoder and the Transformer-based TimeSformer in parallel to simultaneously capture both local and global features in videos. Specifically, the architecture operates through the following five stages.

First, the input frame sequence is divided into patches, and each patch is transformed into an input token through a linear embedding process. The resulting tokens are then processed by the Spatial Encoder in the Frame's Global Feature Extraction Branch, which is responsible for learning the global visual information of each frame.

Second, each frame is fed into a pre-trained CNN encoder, such as ResNet-18, to extract local features. This CNN encoder constitutes the Frame's Local Feature Extraction Branch and effectively encodes fine-grained patterns within each frame, including localized objects, boundaries, and movements (e.g., the motion of a ball in sports videos) that are likely to attract viewer attention.

Third, the frames extracted from the two branches are fused through the CAFGL (Cross-Attention Fusion of Global and Local features) block, as illustrated in Figure 2, by using the local features as the Value (V) and the global features as the Query (Q) and Key (K). The CAFGL block performs two successive cross-attention operations to iteratively update the local and global features. In each stage, the softmax function converts the Q–K similarity into a probability distribution, which is then used to compute a weighted sum of V, thereby enabling the two feature types to exchange information and achieve effective fusion.

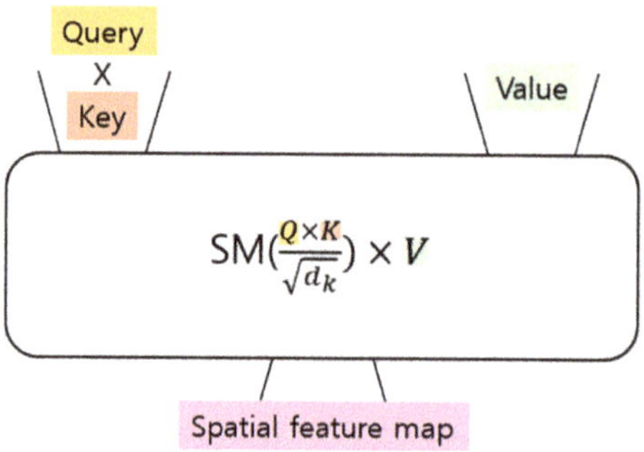

Figure 2. CAFGL Block.

Fourth, the Spatial feature map is processed by the Temporal Encoder to learn temporal relationships and sequential dynamics along the time axis. This stage plays a critical role in capturing the temporal context of the video.

Finally, a fully connected regression head predicts an intensity score for each video segment, representing the level of viewer engagement. This prediction is formulated as a regression problem and is trained to minimize the mean squared error (MSE). The model's performance is further evaluated using metrics such as mean average precision (mAP).

The baseline model used for comparison in this study follows the TimeSformer-based processing pipeline, as outlined in Algorithm 1.

Algorithm 1 TimeSformer

```
Input     video
Output    Tf_prediction
1         def timesformer(video):
2           split video to video_frames
3           For frame in video_frames:
4               split frame to frame_patch
5               Flatten and embed frame_patch to patch_tokens
6               Spatial_token ← Spatial_encoder(patch_tokens)
7               Add Spatial_token into Spatial_tokens
8           Temporal_tokens ← Temporal_encoder(Spatial_tokens)
9           Tf_prediction ← Prediction_head(Temporal_tokens)
10          Return Tf_prediction
```

In Algorithm 1, the TimeSformer receives a video as its input. From lines 2 to 5, the input video is divided into fixed-size patches for each frame, which are then flattened and embedded to generate *Patch_tokens*. In line 6, the generated *Patch_tokens* are processed by the Spatial Encoder to extract spatial features. Subsequently, in line 7, the extracted

Spatial_token from each frame is aggregated sequentially to form *Spatial_tokens*. In line 8, the Temporal Encoder learns the visual relationships among the *Spatial_tokens*, thereby capturing contextual information across the temporal dimension. Finally, in line 9, the Prediction Head produces the output *Tf_prediction*, representing the final prediction. The parameters used in Algorithm 1 are presented in Table 1.

Table 1. Parameters of Algorithm 1.

Variable Name	Description
Video	Input video sequence
Tf_prediction	The output of Prediction_head, i.e., the final predicted value of the TimeSformer model
video_frames	List/arrangement of frames divided by video (T frames)
frame	Single frame in video_frames
frame_patch	As a result of dividing the frame into smaller patches (for example, 16×16)
patch_tokens	Token vector embedded with frame_patch unfolded (linear projection)
Spatial_token	Output of spatial encoder (set of tokens in one frame)
Spatial_tokens	Sequence that gathers the spatial_token of all frames (stacked by the time axis)
Temporal_tokens	Temporary encoder results (final token sequence with added time context)

In addition, the proposed SPOT model is presented in Algorithm 2. This model adopts the TimeSformer framework illustrated in Algorithm 1 as its backbone. However, unlike the original architecture, a CNN encoder is integrated during the frame feature extraction stage to enhance the features extracted from each frame. Specifically, the local features (*LC_feature*) obtained from the CNN encoder and the global features (*GL_feature*) extracted by the Spatial Encoder are fused through the CAFGL block before being fed into the Temporal Encoder.

Algorithm 2 SPOT

```
Input     video
Output    SPOT_prediction
def SPOT(video):
    split video to video_frames
    For frame in video_frames:
        split frame to frame_patch
        Flatten and embed frame_patch to patch_tokens
        GL_feature ← Spatial_encoder(patch_tokens)
        LC_feature ← CNN_encoder(frame)
        Fusion_feature ← CAFGL(GL_feature, LC_feature)
        Add Fusion_feature into Fusion_features
    Temporal_tokens ← Temporal_encoder(Fusion_features)
    SPOT_prediction ← Prediction_head(Temporal_tokens)
    Return SPOT_prediction
```

The parameters used in Algorithm 2 are summarized in Table 2.

Table 2. Parameters of Algorithm 2.

Variable Name	Description
Video	Input video sequence
SPOT_prediction	Final prediction value (e.g., highlight score)
Video_frame	List/array of frames obtained from video segmentation
frame	A single frame within video_frames
frame_patch	Result of dividing a frame into small patches
patch_tokens	Token vector obtained by embedding a frame patch
GL_feature	Global feature extracted from the Spatial Encoder
LC_feature	Local feature extracted from the CNN Encoder
CAFGL	Module for dynamically fusing local and global features based on cross-attention
Fusion_feature	Fused feature obtained by integrating GL_feature and LC_feature through the CAFGL block
Fusion_features	Sequence of fusion features from all frames arranged in temporal order
Temporal_tokens	Temporal Encoder output (tokens with temporal context incorporated)

The baseline SPOT model in Algorithm 2 employs ResNet-18 as the CNN encoder. By introducing this architectural modification, the structural differences between the processing flow of the original TimeSformer (Algorithm 1) and that of the proposed SPOT model (Algorithm 2) enable performance improvements to be achieved.

3.2. *Mathematical Definition of SPOT*

3.2.1. Input Clip

The SPOT model takes video clips as input, represented as a tensor $X \in \mathbb{R}^{H \times W \times C \times F}$. Here, C denotes the number of channels in each frame ($C = 3$ for RGB), and F represents the number of RGB frames sampled from the original video. Each frame has a spatial resolution of $H \times W$.

3.2.2. Decomposition into Patches

Since the proposed SPOT model is based on TimeSformer, it decomposes the input video clips into patches in the same manner as the original model within the Spatial block. Each frame is divided into N non-overlapping patches of size $P \times P$. This process ensures that all N patches completely cover the entire frame, where $N = HW/P^2$. Here, $p = 1, \ldots,$ N denotes the spatial locations.

In addition, the CNN block (e.g., ResNet-18), which operates in parallel with the Spatial block, decomposes each frame into overlapping regions (overlapping patches). The CNN applies a kernel of size $K \times K$, stride S, and padding P to the input image $X \in \mathbb{R}^{H \times W \times C}$ to extract patches. Each location (i, j) in the resulting feature map corresponds to a region of the input image $X[i \cdot S : i \cdot S + K, j \cdot S : j \cdot S + K]$. When $S < K$, the patches overlap, resulting in overlapping regions across the feature map.

3.2.3. Local Feature Extraction (CNN Encoder)

In the CNN encoder is designed to capture local features, each convolutional layer performs the operation described in Equation (1) on the input feature map $F^{(\ell-1)}$.

$$F_{i,j,c}^{(\ell)} = \sum_{u=1}^{K}\sum_{v=1}^{K}\sum_{d=1}^{C} W_{u,v,d,c}^{(\ell)} \cdot F_{i+u,j+v,d}^{(\ell-1)} + b_c^{(\ell)} \tag{1}$$

In Equation (1), H_ℓ, W_ℓ, and C_ℓ represent the height, width, and number of channels of the output feature map, respectively. After the convolution operation defined in Equation (1), a nonlinear activation function $\sigma(\cdot)$, such as ReLU, is applied to introduce nonlinearity, as expressed in Equation (2).

$$F_{i,j,c}^{(\ell)} = \sigma\left(F_{i,j,c}^{(\ell)}\right) \tag{2}$$

After repeating the operation in Equation (2) across multiple layers, the final feature map $F_{CNN}^{(t)} \in \mathbb{R}^{H\prime \times W\prime \times C\prime}$ is obtained from the last layer. This feature map has a downsampled spatial resolution (H′, W′) and a final channel size C′. Here, t = 1, . . . , F denotes the frame index in the video sequence.

3.2.4. Global Feature Extraction (Spatial Attention Encoder)

Each patch is then linearly mapped into a D-dimensional embedding vector $z_{(p,t)}^{(0)}$ using a learnable projection matrix $E \in \mathbb{R}^{D \times 3P^2}$, as follows.

$$z_{(p,t)}^{(0)} = Ex_{(p,t)} + e_{(p,t)}^{pos} \tag{3}$$

In Equation (3), $e_{(p,t)}^{pos}$ represents the positional embedding that encodes the spatiotemporal locations of each patch. The resulting embedding sequence $z_{(p,t)}^{(0)}$ is then used as the input to the Transformer.

The Transformer consists of L encoding blocks, where each block ℓ computes the Query, Key, and Value vectors from the output of the previous block $z_{(p,t)}^{(\ell-1)}$, as defined in Equation (4).

$$\begin{aligned} q_{(p,t)}^{(\ell,a)} &= W_Q^{(\ell,a)} \cdot LN(z_{(p,t)}^{(\ell-1)}) \\ k_{(p,t)}^{(\ell,a)} &= W_K^{(\ell,a)} \cdot LN(z_{(p,t)}^{(\ell-1)}) \\ v_{(p,t)}^{(\ell,a)} &= W_V^{(\ell,a)} \cdot LN(z_{(p,t)}^{(\ell-1)}) \end{aligned} \tag{4}$$

In Equation (4), LN $(\cdot)$ denotes the LayerNorm operation, a = 1, . . . , A represents the attention head index, and $D_h = D/A$ indicates the dimensionality of the latent representation for each head. TimeSformer adopts a Pre-LN architecture, in which LayerNorm is applied prior to the computation of Query, Key, and Value (Q/K/V) vectors. This design helps to stabilize the self-attention distribution when modeling the spatiotemporal characteristics of videos.

The self-attention weights are computed using the dot-product and the SoftMax (SM) function, as defined in Equation (5).

$$a_{(p,t)}^{(\ell,a)} = SM\left(\frac{q \cdot k^T}{\sqrt{D_h}}\right) \tag{5}$$

Using the weights computed in Equation (5), a weighted sum of the Value vectors is calculated to obtain the final encoded representation for each patch. This process is defined in Equation (6).

$$s^{(\ell,a)}_{(p,t)} = a^{(\ell,a)}_{(p,t).(0,0)} v^{(\ell,a)}_{(0,0)} + \sum_{p\prime=1}^{N} \sum_{t\prime=1}^{F} a^{(\ell,a)}_{(p,t).(p',t')} v^{(\ell,a)}_{(p\prime,t\prime)} \tag{6}$$

The outputs $s^{(\ell,a)}_{(p,t)}$ from all attention heads are concatenated and then passed through a linear projection and a multi-layer perceptron (MLP). The resulting representation is updated via residual connections, as defined in Equations (7) and (8).

$$z^{(\ell)\prime}_{(p,t)} = W_0 \left[s^{(\ell,1)}_{(p,t)}, \ldots, s^{(\ell,A)}_{(p,t)} \right] + z^{(\ell-1)}_{(p,t)} \tag{7}$$

$$z^{(\ell)}_{(p,t)} = MLP(LN(z^{(\ell)\prime}_{(p,t)})) + z^{(\ell)\prime}_{(p,t)} \tag{8}$$

3.2.5. Feature Fusion Block (CAFGL)

To learn richer representations by fusing the local features from the CNN encoder and the global features from the Spatial encoder, the CAFGL (Cross-Attention Fusion for Global and Local) module was employed. In this process, the output of the CNN encoder $F^{(\ell)}_{i,j,c}$ is used as the Query, while the final output of the Spatial encoder $z^{(\ell)}_{(p,t)}$ serves as the Key and Value. These are mapped to the Q/K/V representations, and the cross-attention is computed as defined in Equation (9).

$$\begin{aligned} Q_{(i,j)} &= W_Q \cdot F^{(i,j)}_{(p,t)} \\ K_{(p,t)} &= W_K \cdot z^{(\ell)}_{(p,t)} \\ V_{(p,t)} &= W_V \cdot z^{(\ell)}_{(p,t)} \end{aligned} \tag{9}$$

In Equation (9), W_Q, W_K, and W_V denote learnable weight matrices. The CAFGL module computes the scaled dot-product between the Query and Key, followed by the application of a SM function to obtain the attention weights $a_{(i,j)(p,t)}$, as defined in Equation (10).

$$a_{(i,j)(p,t)} = SM\left(\frac{Q \cdot K^T}{\sqrt{D_h}}\right) \tag{10}$$

The attention weights computed in Equation (10) are then used to calculate the final fused features by performing a weighted sum of the Value vectors, as defined in Equation (11).

$$S_{(i,j)} = \sum_{p=1}^{N} \sum_{t=1}^{F} a_{(i,j)(p,t)} V_{(p,t)} \tag{11}$$

Finally, the local and global features are combined, as defined in Equation (12).

$$H^{(i,j)}_{fusion} = MLP\left(\left[S_{(i,j)}; F^{(i,j)}_{CNN}\right]\right) \tag{12}$$

3.2.6. Temporal Encoder

The output of the CAFGL module, $H^{(i,j)}_{fusion}$, is passed to the Temporal Encoder to learn temporal continuity. Since $H^{(i,j)}_{fusion}$ is a spatial feature map, it is partitioned into non-overlapping patches, following the same procedure used in the Spatial Encoder, and subsequently transformed into $z_{time(p,t)}$, as defined in Equation (13).

$$z_{time(p,t)} = P\left(H_{fusion}\right) \tag{13}$$

In Equation (13), P( ) denotes the operation of partitioning $H_{fusion}^{(i,j)}$ into $P \times P$ patches. Using the resulting sequence $z_{time(p,t)}$, each block ℓ of the Temporal Encoder computes the Query, Key, and Value vectors as defined in Equation (14).

$$\begin{aligned} q_{time(p,t)}^{(\ell,a)} &= W_{Qtime}^{(\ell,a)} \cdot LN(H_{fusion}^{(i,j)}) \\ k_{time(p,t)}^{(\ell,a)} &= W_{Ktime}^{(\ell,a)} \cdot LN(H_{fusion}^{(i,j)}) \\ v_{time(p,t)}^{(\ell,a)} &= W_{Vtime}^{(\ell,a)} \cdot LN(H_{fusion}^{(i,j)}) \end{aligned} \tag{14}$$

Temporal attention learns the relationships between the Query and all Key vectors across different time frames at the same spatial location p. The attention score $a_{time(p,t)}^{(\ell,a)}$ is computed as defined in Equation (15).

$$a_{time(p,t)}^{(\ell,a)} = SM\left(\frac{q_{time} \cdot k_{time}^{T}}{\sqrt{D_h}}\right) \tag{15}$$

Subsequently, the attention scores $a_{time(p,t)}^{(\ell,a)}$ from Equation (15) are used to compute the weighted sum of the Value vectors, as defined in Equation (16).

$$s_{time(p,t)}^{(\ell,a)} = \sum_{t\prime=1}^{F} a_{time(p,t).t\prime}^{(\ell,a)} \cdot v_{(p,t\prime)}^{(\ell,a)} \tag{16}$$

The outputs from all attention heads are concatenated and then passed through a linear projection and a multi-layer perceptron (MLP), as defined in Equation (17), to obtain the final representation.

$$z_{(p,t)}^{(\ell)} = MLP\left(LN\left(W_0\left[s_{time(p,t)}^{(\ell,1)}, \cdots, s_{time(p,t)}^{(\ell,A)}\right]\right)\right) + W_0\left[s_{time(p,t)}^{(\ell,1)}, \cdots, s_{time(p,t)}^{(\ell,A)}\right] \tag{17}$$

The final representation is processed through a downstream regression head to generate an intensity score for each segment of the video, representing the level of viewer interest. Subsequently, the scipy.signal.find_peaks algorithm is applied to the resulting intensity score sequence to automatically detect highlight segments based on local maxima. In this context, highlight detection is defined as the set of points that satisfy the condition expressed in Equation (18).

$$P(y) = \left\{t_p \middle| y(t_p) > y(t_p - 1), y(t_p) > y(t_p - 1), y(t_p) > T_{height}, \Delta T_{distance}\right\} \tag{18}$$

This process effectively identifies sections of successive frames with soaring interest and is used to determine the start and end points of each highlight.

4. Experimental Results

4.1. *Dataset for SPOT Models*

In this study, we collected video data from the YouTube-8M (YT8M) dataset using the metadata employed in MR.Hisum [45], a previous study on highlight dataset creation. This metadata contains the information summarized in Table 3.

Table 3. Columns in the metadata.

Column Name	Description
video_id	A unique identifier assigned to distinguish each video within the dataset
yt8m_file	The file name of the corresponding video in the YouTube-8M dataset

Table 3. *Cont.*

Column Name	Description
random_id	A randomly generated ID created during the data randomization process
youtube_id	The actual YouTube video ID (https://www.youtube.com/watch?v=%E2%80%98youtube_id%E2%80%99 (accessed on 8 September 2025))
duration	The total playback duration of the video
views	The number of views for the video
entry 2	The set of topics or categories associated with the video

Using the youtube_id from the metadata, the YouTube-8M (YT-8M) dataset provided by the YouTube platform is collected, following the sequence illustrated in Figure 3.

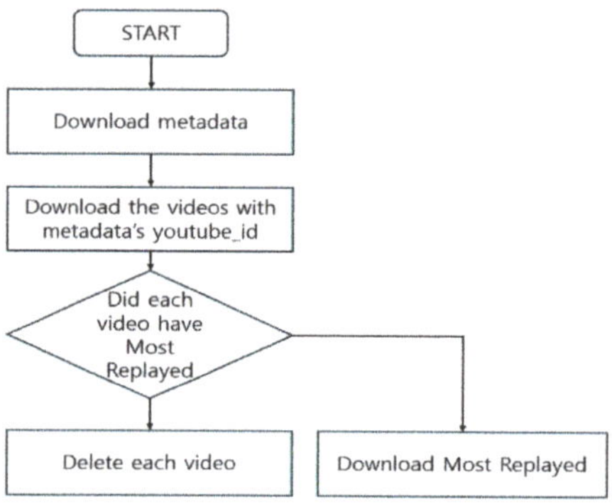

Figure 3. Download flowchart of dataset.

Specifically, it includes video (visual), audio, and subtitle information, providing a rich dataset that allows the analysis of not only visual elements but also auditory and linguistic contexts.

In this study, we focused primarily on the visual modality for highlight extraction. We selectively utilized videos for which highlight information was provided by YouTube's "Most Replayed" feature. "Most Replayed" appears as a graph on the playback bar, indicating sections of the video that users have frequently rewatched.

The "Most Replayed" feature, as shown in Figure 4, is displayed above the YouTube playback bar and visualizes the frequency with which specific segments are repeatedly viewed by users. This information can be collected from the HTML source of the video page, and the replay frequency data for the entire video is stored in the macroMarkersListEntity field in the format shown in Table 4.

Figure 4. YouTube's "Most Replayed".

Table 4. macroMarkersListEntity's data.

Name	Description	Type
startMillis	Start time in milliseconds	String
durationMillis	Duration in milliseconds	String
intensityScoreNormalized	Normalized intensity score	Float

The segment with the highest replay frequency among these is labeled as the "Most Replayed." This process leverages automatically generated segment replay information from YouTube, which is based on user viewing patterns, enabling reliable highlight labeling that reflects the actual audience response for each video. In this study, to utilize this feature, we collected the HTML data of each video and extracted the highlight segments using the macroMarkersListEntity field, storing the results in JSON format.

In addition, video complexity was calculated by analyzing inter-frame pixel differences, after a light, standardized preprocessing (all frames resized to 224 × 224, sampled at 24 FPS, converted to the luminance channel with pixel values normalized to [0, 1]). Let $\{I_t\}_{t=1}^{T}$ denote the resulting frame sequence.

$$D_t = \frac{1}{HW}\sum_{x=1}^{H}\sum_{y=1}^{W}|I_t(x,y) - I_{t-1}(x,y)| \quad (19)$$

As shown in Equation (19), we first computed the mean absolute pixel-wise difference D_t between consecutive frames, normalized by image size (H,W). This simple calculation captures overall changes in intensity and texture between frames.

To aggregate over time, we computed the mean variation score:

$$C = \frac{1}{T-1}\sum_{t=2}^{T} D_t \quad (20)$$

Finally, I min–max normalizes C across the dataset to obtain $\hat{C} \in [0, 1]$, which enables stratification into three complexity regimes using empirical quantiles: Low ($\hat{C} \leq$ q0.33), Medium (q0.33 < $\hat{C} \leq$ q0.66), and High ($\hat{C}$ > q0.66). For each regime, the dataset was further divided into training, validation, and test sets in a ratio of 7:1.5:1.5 to ensure balanced evaluation across complexity levels.

4.2. Comparison with Baselines

In this study, to compare the highlight prediction performance of the proposed SPOT model with that of the conventional TimeSformer model, experiments were conducted based on the mean squared error (MSE) across different levels of video complexity. The performance metrics used in the evaluation are shown in Table 5.

Table 5. Performance metrics.

Metric	Description	Significance
MSE	Mean Squared Error	Evaluates prediction accuracy including outliers
mAP	Mean Average Precision	Measures the ability to detect highlights that match the ground truth
Coverage Ratio	The proportion of predicted highlight segments that contain the actual highlights (ground truth).	Evaluation of the ability to correctly match the start and end positions of highlights.

Table 5. *Cont.*

Metric	Description	Significance
F1-Score	$\frac{2 \cdot \text{Precision} \cdot \text{Recall}}{\text{Precision} + \text{Recall}}$	Evaluates both the accuracy of the highlights detected by the model and its ability to avoid missing relevant highlights.

The results of the experiments using the performance indicators in Table 5 are shown in Table 6.

Table 6. Comparison of average performance by complexity group.

Model	Params (M)	MACs (G)	Complexity	MSE	mAP	Coverage	F1-Score
SPOT	~94.5	~825	Low	0.065	0.504	0.78	0.85
			Medium	0.070	0.662	0.80	0.87
			High	0.080	0.562	0.85	0.92
TimeSformer	~89.1	~409.1	Low	0.060	0.452	0.78	0.85
			Medium	0.071	0.561	0.79	0.86
			High	0.090	0.503	0.78	0.85
3D-CNNN	~33	~60	Low	0.087	0.434	0.834	0.44
			Medium	0.084	0.482	0.745	0.36
			High	0.056	0.502	0.603	0.33
MH-DETR	~37	~95	Low	0.078	0.52	0.45	0.60
			Medium	0.073	0.55	0.48	0.80
			High	0.068	0.54	0.46	0.80

Experimental results demonstrated that the proposed SPOT model outperformed the baseline TimeSformer model in terms of mAP and F1-Score, thereby validating its improved highlight detection capability. For MSE, TimeSformer showed a slight advantage in the low-complexity group, while both models exhibited similar performance in the medium-complexity group. In contrast, in the high-complexity group, SPOT achieved an MSE of 0.080, representing a clear improvement over TimeSformer's 0.090. This indicates that SPOT can perform more precise and stable highlight predictions in scenarios with high visual complexity.

In terms of computational cost, SPOT requires more parameters (~94.5M vs. ~89.1M) and higher FLOPs (~825G vs. ~409G MACs) than TimeSformer under the same tokenization setting, due to the additional CNN branch and the increased token sequence length. Nevertheless, these results indicate that the extra cost is justified, as SPOT provides consistently better accuracy across key metrics, particularly in high-complexity scenarios.

Furthermore, when compared to a model trained solely with a 3D CNN on the same dataset, SPOT achieved superior performance across all evaluation metrics (MSE, mAP, Coverage, and F1-Score). This supports the effectiveness of the hybrid architecture that combines local feature extraction via CNN with global relationship modeling using a Transformer, compared to a single 3D CNN-based approach. While a pure 3D CNN captures spatial-temporal features within limited receptive fields, it struggles to model long-range dependencies and contextual relationships. By contrast, SPOT leverages the CNN to encode fine-grained local patterns and the Transformer to capture global temporal dynamics, leading to more accurate highlight detection across diverse video types.

In addition, a performance comparison with the state-of-the-art model MH-DETR on our dataset showed that, while SPOT achieved overall performance comparable to MH-DETR, it outperformed MH-DETR in most cases within the high-complexity group. It should be noted, however, that MH-DETR processes refined individual frames as input, whereas SPOT takes the raw video itself as input—a difference that is likely to have influenced the results to some extent. These findings suggest that SPOT is particularly well-suited for analyzing videos with frequent scene transitions and significant changes in key objects or actions.

Figure 5 illustrates the trend that the performance of the SPOT model improves as the number of parameters in the CNN backbone increases.

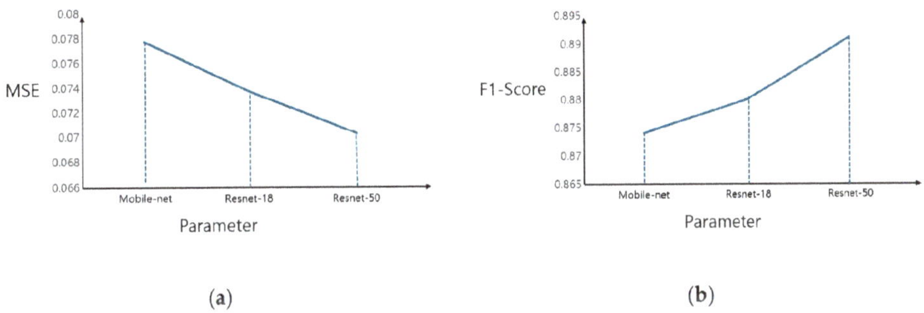

Figure 5. SPOT performance changes as the CNN encoder changes: (**a**) MSE versus parameters; (**b**) F1-score versus parameters.

The graph in the upper-left corner illustrates the relationship between the number of backbone parameters and model performance, showing a gradual improvement as the parameter count increases in the order of MobileNetV3-Small, ResNet18, and ResNet50. These results experimentally demonstrate that the parallel integration of CNNs and Transformer effectively overcomes the limitations of Transformer-only architectures in learning local visual information, thereby functioning as a highlight inference model robust to variations in video complexity.

4.3. Ablation Study

In this study, to analyze the performance contribution of each module in the SPOT model to highlight extraction, a series of ablation experiments were conducted, as shown in Table 7, in which specific modules were removed or replaced with alternative designs.

Table 7. Ablation study: "√" indicates that the corresponding module/component is included in the model.

Test Name	Module				MSE	mAP	Coverage	F1-Score
	CFAGL Block	CNN Encoder	Spatial Encoder	Temporal Encoder				
SPOT	√	√	√	√	0.065	0.576	0.810	0.880
Ablation 1 (sum)		√	√	√	0.072	0.094	0.264	0.223

Table 7. *Cont.*

Test Name	Module				MSE	mAP	Coverage	F1-Score
	CFAGL Block	CNN Encoder	Spatial Encoder	Temporal Encoder				
Ablation 1 (avg)		√	√	√	0.071	0.096	0.268	0.226
Ablation 1 (mul)		√	√	√	0.080	0.084	0.242	0.198
Ablation 2			√	√	0.0737	0.505	0.783	0.853
Ablation 3		√		√	0.073	0.141	0.315	0.278
Ablation 4	√	√	√		0.071	0.174	0.174	0.227

The dataset used in these experiments was not divided based on complexity. The reason is that, while the primary experiments in this paper focused on performance differences according to complexity levels (low, medium, high)—as emphasized throughout the study—the purpose of the ablation experiments is to examine how the presence or structural variation in each block affects performance. Therefore, dividing the dataset by complexity was not necessary in this context.

First, to assess the contribution of the Cross-Attention Fusion of Global and Local features (CAFGL) module, the module was removed, and experiments were conducted using only a simple fusion of the local and global features, as described in Equations (21)–(23). This is because the limitations of such simple fusion methods are evident.

$$F_{sum} = Localfeature + Globalfeature \tag{21}$$

$$F_{avg} = \frac{1}{2}(Localfeature + Globalfeature) \tag{22}$$

$$F_{mul} = Localfeature \odot Globalfeature \tag{23}$$

First, as shown in Equation (21), the addition method assigns equal weights to features with different semantic properties, which can lead to conflicts in importance or the cancelation of information. The study Attentional Feature Fusion [46] pointed out that such simple summation can cause an information bottleneck when merging features with semantic discrepancies, thereby failing to ensure sufficient representational capacity. This effect is also reflected in our experiments, as evidenced by the results of Ablation 1 (sum) in Table 7.

Similarly, Equation (22) computes a simple average, which suffers from problems analogous to those in Equation (21). Averaging treats the information from the two domains equally without reflecting the independent significance of each feature, ultimately weakening the representational power of the fused information. A recent study proposing an Adaptive Feature Fusion technique [47] mentioned that traditional averaging-based fusion could degrade a model's generalization performance and dilute critical information depending on the context. This effect is also reflected in our experiments, as evidenced by the results of Ablation 1 (avg) in Table 7.

Finally, Equation (23) fuses features through multiplication. This approach only activates when both input features are strongly expressed; if one feature is weak, the overall fusion result may collapse to an insignificant value. The study Attentional Feature Fusion [45] reported that multiplication-based fusion can cause information loss when there is an imbalance in the importance of the features, directly affecting visual recognition performance. This effect is also reflected in our experiments, as evidenced by the results of Ablation 1 (mul) in Table 7.

Considering these limitations of non-CAFGL fusion methods, the CAFGL used in the SPOT model enables sophisticated information integration by reflecting the relative importance of each feature while also accounting for their mutual context. This capability significantly contributes to improving highlight prediction performance in SPOT, where the fusion of local and global features is essential.

Next, to evaluate the impact of the CNN Encoder, we compared the performance using the original TimeSformer architecture. The results revealed an overall decrease in performance, with a particularly pronounced drop in prediction accuracy for high-complexity videos.

To assess the influence of the Spatial Encoder, we removed this module and performed predictions using only spatial features at the single-frame level. This resulted in a noticeable degradation in overall performance, as the model failed to sufficiently capture important objects or events. In particular, ignoring spatial-level relationships and the distribution of subjects often led to missing frames that should have been identified as highlights. This demonstrates that the SPOT model relies not only on simple visual features but also on its ability to capture the spatial composition and interactions within a scene.

Finally, to verify the role of the Temporal Encoder, we removed this module and replaced it with a structure that simply averages frame-level features before prediction. This modification led to a significant drop in performance across all datasets, with particularly severe degradation in videos where the temporal progression of events was critical. This result underscores the decisive importance of learning and preserving temporal contextual information for highlight prediction performance.

Overall, these findings confirm that the superior performance of the SPOT model is achieved through the CAFGL module, which integrates CNN and Transformer branches, and the Temporal Encoder, which captures temporal dependencies. Notably, SPOT demonstrates more stable and robust performance in high-complexity video environments compared to pure Transformer-based models such as TimeSformer.

5. Conclusions and Future Studies

In this study, we proposed the SPOT model, which combines CNN and TimeSformer to improve the precision of video highlight prediction in response to the growing demand for short-form and highlight videos. This hybrid architecture was designed to learn both local and global features simultaneously. In particular, by scaling the CNN backbone from MobileNetV3-Small to ResNet18 and ResNet50, the number of parameters increased, enabling the extraction of richer local features, which, when fused with the Transformer, led to overall performance improvements. As a result, SPOT achieved superior highlight prediction performance in complex scenes (with up to a 0.01 reduction in MSE), allowing for the automatic extraction of short-form content from large-scale video collections—a format that aligns with the rapidly growing viewing trend. Moreover, SPOT outperformed the SOTA benchmark MH-DETR in complex scenes.

The proposed SPOT model was designed to enhance the global spatio-temporal representation learning capability of TimeSformer by incorporating a CNN-based encoder that effectively captures local visual patterns. This hybrid structure contributed to overall performance gains, particularly in improving highlight prediction precision in complex scenes. However, the addition of the CNN module increased the number of parameters and computational cost, resulting in higher resource consumption during both training and inference. SPOT tended to have longer training times compared to TimeSformer, which could pose a significant limitation for large-scale dataset processing or real-time applications such as mobile environments; therefore, future work will focus on improving computational efficiency through model compression (e.g., pruning, quantization) and optimization techniques.

The video dataset used in this study is a typical multimodal dataset composed of temporal information, visual information (frames, thumbnails, etc.), and audio information. However, the highlight extraction of SPOT relies solely on temporal and visual frame information, which limits its ability to capture semantic cues from the audio track. We sincerely appreciate the reviewer's suggestion in this regard, as audio signals can indeed provide important cues that effectively reveal highlight moments. For example, audio features can be extracted using MFCC (Mel-Frequency Cepstral Coefficients) [48] and then fed into a CNN-based encoder for learning. Such an approach would allow the integration of complementary semantic information with the visual context of video scenes. In future work, we plan to extend our system by incorporating not only audio but also other multimodal sources such as subtitles and visual metadata (e.g., thumbnails), thereby leveraging richer contextual information for video highlight extraction. These advancements are expected to contribute to a wide range of real-world video platform applications, including automatic editing and summarization.

Author Contributions: Conceptualization, S.K.; methodology, S.K.; formal analysis, S.K.; software, S.K.; validation, S.K.; investigation, J.L. and S.P.; resources, S.K.; supervision, J.L. and S.P.; project administration, S.K.; writing—original draft preparation, S.K.; writing—review and editing, S.K., J.L. and S.P. All authors have read and agreed to the published version of the manuscript.

Funding: This research was supported by the MSIT (Ministry of Science, ICT), Korea, under the Global Research Support Program in the Digital Field program (RS-2024-00428758) supervised by the IITP (Institute for Information and Communications Technology Planning and Evaluation).

Institutional Review Board Statement: Not applicable.

Informed Consent Statement: Not applicable.

Data Availability Statement: The data presented in this study are available on YouTube-8M at https://research.google.com/youtube8m/ (accessed on 8 September 2025).

Acknowledgments: During the preparation of this manuscript, Korean text was translated into English. The authors have reviewed and edited the output and take full responsibility for the content of this publication.

Conflicts of Interest: The authors declare no conflicts of interest.

References

1. Lin, D.C.-E.; Caba Heilbron, F.; Lee, J.-Y.; Wang, O.; Martelaro, N. Videogenic: Identifying Highlight Moments in Videos with Professional Photographs as a Prior. In Proceedings of the 16th Conference on Creativity & Cognition, Chicago, IL, USA, 23–26 June 2024; pp. 328–346.
2. Vora, D.; Kadam, P.; Mohite, D.D.; Kumar, N.; Kumar, N.; Radhakrishnan, P.; Bhagwat, S. AI-driven video summarization for optimizing content retrieval and management through deep learning techniques. *Sci. Rep.* **2025**, *15*, 4058. [CrossRef] [PubMed]
3. Xiong, B.; Kalantidis, Y.; Ghadiyaram, D.; Grauman, K. Less is More: Learning Highlight Detection from Video Duration. In Proceedings of the IEEE/CVF Conference on Computer Vision and Pattern Recognition, Long Beach, CA, USA, 15–20 June 2019; pp. 1258–1267.
4. Zeng, C. Unveiling the impact of short videos: Consumption behavior and decision-making in the digital age. *Highlights Bus. Econ. Manag.* **2023**, *21*, 469–474. [CrossRef]
5. Arslan, S.; Tanberk, S. Key frame extraction with attention based deep neural networks. *arXiv* **2023**, arXiv:2306.13176. [CrossRef]
6. Violot, C.; Elmas, T.; Bilogrevic, I.; Humbert, M. Shorts vs. Regular Videos on YouTube: A Comparative Analysis of User Engagement and Content Creation Trends. In Proceedings of the 16th ACM Web Science Conference, New York, NY, USA, 21–24 May 2024; pp. 213–223.

7. Zannettou, S.; Nemes-Nemeth, O.; Ayalon, O.; Goetzen, A.; Gummadi, K.P.; Redmiles, E.M.; Roesner, F. Analyzing User Engagement with TikTok's Short Format Video Recommendations Using Data Donations. In Proceedings of the 2024 CHI Conference on Human Factors in Computing Systems, Honolulu, HI, USA, 11–16 May 2024; pp. 1–16.
8. Chen, Z.; Liu, P.; Piao, J.; Xu, F.; Li, Y. Shorter is different: Characterizing the dynamics of short-form video platforms. *arXiv* **2024**, arXiv:2410.16058. [CrossRef]
9. Van Daele, T.; Iyer, A.; Zhang, Y.; Derry, J.C.; Huh, M.; Pavel, A. Making Short-Form Videos Accessible with Hierarchical Video Summaries. In Proceedings of the 2024 CHI Conference on Human Factors in Computing Systems, Honolulu, HI, USA, 11–16 May 2024; pp. 1–17.
10. Peronikolis, M.; Panagiotakis, C. Personalized Video Summarization: A comprehensive survey of methods and datasets. *Appl. Sci.* **2024**, *14*, 4400. [CrossRef]
11. Manic, M. Short-form video content and consumer engagement in digital landscapes. *Bull. Transilv. Univ. Brasov. Ser. V Econ. Sci.* **2024**, *17*, 45–52. [CrossRef]
12. Islam, Z.; Paul, S.; Rochan, M. Unsupervised Video Highlight Detection by Learning from Audio and Visual Recurrence. In Proceedings of the 2025 IEEE/CVF Winter Conference on Applications of Computer Vision (WACV), Tucson, AZ, USA, 28 February–4 March 2025; pp. 8702–8711.
13. Xu, Y.; Sun, Y.; Zhai, B.; Jia, Y.; Du, S. MH-DETR: Video Moment and Highlight Detection with Cross-Modal Transformer. In Proceedings of the 2024 International Joint Conference on Neural Networks (IJCNN), Yokohama, Japan, 30 June–5 July 2024; pp. 1–8.
14. Zhao, P.; He, Z.; Zhang, F.; Lin, S.; Zhou, F. Ld-detr: Loop decoder detection transformer for video moment retrieval and highlight detection. *arXiv* **2025**, arXiv:2501.10787.
15. Zhang, T.; Cui, W.; Liu, S.; Jiang, F. SC-HVPPNet: Spatial and Channel Hybrid-Attention Video Post-Processing Network with CNN and Transformer. In Proceedings of the 2024 IEEE International Conference on Multimedia and Expo (ICME), Niagara Falls, ON, Canada, 15–19 July 2024; pp. 1–6.
16. Xiong, T.; Wei, W.; Xu, K.; Chen, D. SA-DETR: Span Aware Detection Transformer for Moment Retrieval. In Proceedings of the 31st International Conference on Computational Linguistics, Abu Dhabi, United Arab Emirates, 19–24 January 2025; pp. 7634–7647.
17. Sun, H.; Zhou, M.; Chen, W.; Xie, W. Tr-DETR: Task-Reciprocal Transformer for Joint Moment Retrieval and Highlight Detection. In Proceedings of the AAAI Conference on Artificial Intelligence, Philadelphia, PA, USA, 25 February–4 March 2024; pp. 4998–5007.
18. Arnab, A.; Sun, C.; Schmid, C. Unified Graph Structured Models for Video Understanding. In Proceedings of the IEEE/CVF International Conference on Computer Vision, Montreal, QC, Canada, 10–17 October 2021; pp. 8117–8126.
19. Tang, Y.; Bi, J.; Xu, S.; Song, L.; Liang, S.; Wang, T.; Zhang, D.; An, J.; Lin, J.; Zhu, R. Video understanding with large language models: A survey. *arXiv* **2023**, arXiv:2312.17432. [CrossRef]
20. Zeng, Z.; McDuff, D.; Song, Y. Contrastive learning of global and local video representations. *Adv. Neural Inf. Process. Syst.* **2021**, *34*, 7025–7040.
21. Sun, G.; Liu, Y.; Ding, H.; Wu, M.; Van Gool, L. Learning local and global temporal contexts for video semantic segmentation. *IEEE Trans. Pattern Anal. Mach. Intell.* **2024**, *46*, 6919–6934. [CrossRef]
22. Wei, F.; Wang, B.; Ge, T.; Jiang, Y.; Li, W.; Duan, L. Learning Pixel-Level Distinctions for Video Highlight Detection. In Proceedings of the IEEE/CVF Conference on Computer Vision and Pattern Recognition, New Orleans, LA, USA, 18–24 June 2022; pp. 3073–3082.
23. Badamdorj, T.; Rochan, M.; Wang, Y.; Cheng, L. Contrastive Learning for Unsupervised Video Highlight Detection. In Proceedings of the IEEE/CVF Conference on Computer Vision and Pattern Recognition, New Orleans, LA, USA, 18–24 June 2022; pp. 14042–14052.
24. Xu, J.; Liu, S.; Chen, G.; Liu, Q. Highlight Detection and Removal Method Based on Bifurcated-CNN. In Proceedings of the International Conference on Intelligent Robotics and Applications, Harbin, China, 1–3 August 2022; pp. 307–318.
25. Al-Saad, M.; Ramaswamy, L.; Bhandarkar, S. F4D: Factorized 4D Convolutional Neural Network for Efficient Video-level Representation Learning. *arXiv* **2023**, arXiv:2401.08609.
26. Paul, D.; Parvez, M.R.; Mohammed, N.; Rahman, S. VideoLights: A Cross-Modal Cross-Task Transformer Model for Joint Video Highlight Detection and Moment Retrieval. *arXiv* **2024**, arXiv:2412.01558.
27. Azad, R.; Kazerouni, A.; Azad, B.; Khodapanah Aghdam, E.; Velichko, Y.; Bagci, U.; Merhof, D. Laplacian-Former: Overcoming the Limitations of Vision Transformers in Local Texture Detection. In Proceedings of the International Conference on Medical Image Computing and Computer-Assisted Intervention, Vancouver, BC, Canada, 8–12 October 2023; pp. 736–746.
28. Pereira, G.A.; Hussain, M. A review of transformer-based models for computer vision tasks: Capturing global context and spatial relationships. *arXiv* **2024**, arXiv:2408.15178. [CrossRef]

29. Li, K.; Wang, Y.; Zhang, J.; Gao, P.; Song, G.; Liu, Y.; Li, H.; Qiao, Y. Uniformer: Unifying convolution and self-attention for visual recognition. *IEEE Trans. Pattern Anal. Mach. Intell.* **2023**, *45*, 12581–12600. [CrossRef] [PubMed]
30. Peng, Z.; Huang, W.; Gu, S.; Xie, L.; Wang, Y.; Jiao, J.; Ye, Q. Conformer: Local Features Coupling Global Representations for Visual Recognition. In Proceedings of the IEEE/CVF international conference on computer vision, Montreal, QC, Canada, 10–17 October 2021; pp. 367–376.
31. Bertasius, G.; Wang, H.; Torresani, L. Is Space-Time Attention all You Need for Video Understanding? In Proceedings of the International Conference on Machine Learning, Online, 18–24 July 2021; p. 4.
32. Menon, V.V.; Feldmann, C.; Amirpour, H.; Ghanbari, M.; Timmerer, C. VCA: Video Complexity Analyzer. In Proceedings of the 13th ACM Multimedia Systems Conference, Athlone, Ireland, 14–17 June 2022; pp. 259–264.
33. Alaa, T.; Mongy, A.; Bakr, A.; Diab, M.; Gomaa, W. Video Summarization Techniques: A Comprehensive Review. *arXiv* **2024**, arXiv:2410.04449. [CrossRef]
34. Li, T.; Sun, Z.; Xiao, X. Unsupervised modality-transferable video highlight detection with representation activation sequence learning. *IEEE Trans. Image Process.* **2024**, *33*, 1911–1922. [CrossRef]
35. Lee, M.J.; Gong, D.; Cho, M. Video Summarization with Large Language Models. In Proceedings of the Computer Vision and Pattern Recognition Conference, Nashville, TN, USA, 11–15 June 2025; pp. 18981–18991.
36. Tang, K.-S.; So, H.-J.; Rappa, N. Examining the Multimodal Design of Explainer Videos: A multimodal Content Analysis of Khan Academy Online Resources. *SSRN Electron. J.* 2023. [CrossRef]
37. Aminbeidokhti, M.; Pedersoli, M.; Cardinal, P.; Granger, E. Emotion Recognition with Spatial Attention and Temporal Softmax Pooling. In Proceedings of the International Conference on Image Analysis and Recognition, Waterloo, ON, Canada, 27–29 August 2019; pp. 323–331.
38. Tran, D.; Bourdev, L.; Fergus, R.; Torresani, L.; Paluri, M. Learning Spatiotemporal Features with 3d Convolutional Networks. In Proceedings of the IEEE International Conference on Computer Vision, Santiago, Chile, 7–13 December 2015; pp. 4489–4497.
39. Hassan, E. Learning video actions in two stream recurrent neural network. *Pattern Recognit. Lett.* **2021**, *151*, 200–208. [CrossRef]
40. Arnab, A.; Dehghani, M.; Heigold, G.; Sun, C.; Lučić, M.; Schmid, C. Vivit: A Video Vision Transformer. In Proceedings of the IEEE/CVF International Conference on Computer Vision, Montreal, BC, Canada, 11–17 October 2021; pp. 6836–6846.
41. Chen, X.; Shi, S.; Ma, T.; Zhou, J.; See, S.; Cheung, K.C.; Li, H. M3Net: Multimodal Multi-task Learning for 3D Detection, Segmentation, and Occupancy Prediction in Autonomous Driving. *arXiv* **2025**, arXiv:2503.18100. [CrossRef]
42. Chen, J.; Ho, C.M. Mm-vit: Multi-Modal Video Transformer for Compressed Video Action Recognition. In Proceedings of the IEEE/CVF Winter Conference on Applications of Computer Vision, Waikoloa, HI, USA, 3–8 January 2022; pp. 1910–1921.
43. Wu, C.; Yin, S.; Qi, W.; Wang, X.; Tang, Z.; Duan, N. Visual chatgpt: Talking, drawing and editing with visual foundation models. *arXiv* **2023**, arXiv:2303.04671. [CrossRef]
44. Xiao, B.; Yin, X.; Kang, S.-C. Vision-based method of automatically detecting construction video highlights by integrating machine tracking and CNN feature extraction. *Autom. Constr.* **2021**, *129*, 103817. [CrossRef]
45. Sul, J.; Han, J.; Lee, J. Hisum: A large-scale dataset for video highlight detection and summarization. *Adv. Neural Inf. Process. Syst.* **2023**, *36*, 40542–40555.
46. Dai, Y.; Gieseke, F.; Oehmcke, S.; Wu, Y.; Barnard, K. Attentional Feature Fusion. In Proceedings of the IEEE/CVF Winter Conference on Applications of Computer Vision, Waikoloa, HI, USA, 3–8 January 2021; pp. 3560–3569.
47. Mungoli, N. Adaptive feature fusion: Enhancing generalization in deep learning models. *arXiv* **2023**, arXiv:2304.03290. [CrossRef]
48. Kim, D.-H.; Son, W.-H.; Kwak, S.-S.; Yun, T.-H.; Park, J.-H.; Lee, J.-D. A hybrid deep learning emotion classification system using multimodal data. *Sensors* **2023**, *23*, 9333. [CrossRef] [PubMed]

electronics

MDPI

Article

Ensemble-Based Knowledge Distillation for Identification of Childhood Pneumonia

Grega Vrbančič * and Vili Podgorelec

Intelligent Systems Laboratory, Faculty of Electrical Engineering and Computer Science, University of Maribor, 2000 Maribor, Slovenia; vili.podgorelec@um.si
* Correspondence: grega.vrbancic@um.si

Abstract

Childhood pneumonia remains a key cause of global morbidity and mortality, highlighting the need for accurate and efficient diagnostic tools. Ensemble methods have proven to be among the most successful approaches for identifying childhood pneumonia from chest X-ray images. However, deploying large, complex convolutional neural network models in resource-constrained environments presents challenges due to their high computational demands. Therefore, we propose a novel ensemble-based knowledge distillation method for identifying childhood pneumonia from X-ray images, which utilizes an ensemble of classification models to distill the knowledge to a more efficient student model. Experiments conducted on a chest X-ray dataset show that the distilled student model achieves comparable (statistically not significantly different) predictive performance to that of the Stochastic Gradient with Warm Restarts ensemble method (F1-score on average 0.95 vs. 0.96, respectively), while significantly reducing inference time and decreasing FLOPs by a factor of 6.5. Based on the obtained results, the proposed method highlights the potential of knowledge distillation to enhance the efficiency of complex methods, making them more suitable for utilization in environments with limited computational resources.

Keywords: knowledge distillation; convolutional neural networks; childhood pneumonia

1. Introduction

Childhood pneumonia remains a significant global health challenge, responsible for over 700,000 deaths annually among children under five and accounting for approximately 14% of all deaths in this age group [1]. The burden is particularly high in developing regions such as South Asia, and West and Central Africa, where incidence rates reach up to 2500 and 1620 cases per 100,000 children, respectively, well above the global average of 1400 cases per 100,000 children [2]. Therefore, accurate and timely diagnosis is essential for effective treatment. However, in many low-resource settings, access to expert radiologic interpretation of chest X-ray images is limited, hindering prompt diagnosis and therapy [3].

Recent advancements in deep learning, especially with the utilization of convolutional neural networks (CNNs), have demonstrated high predictive performance in detecting various pathologies from medical images [4,5], including pneumonia [6,7], tubercolosis [8], and COVID-19 [9,10]. Such state-of-the-art models tend to be complex and computationally demanding, presenting challenges for their deployment in real-world, resource-constrained environments such as rural clinics or mobile health platforms [11]. Moreover, their computational complexity also increases vulnerability to adversarial attacks, posing serious risks in clinical practice [12]. Recent approaches, such as style contrastive learning [13], aim to mitigate these issues by learning representations prone to noise in data or imaging artifacts. While promising, these methods often rely on large-scale models and contrastive frameworks that remain computationally intensive, limiting their immediate applicability in real-world deployment scenarios. This concern further reinforces the motivation for developing models that are both computationally efficient and robust in real-world applications. Such approaches, in general, require substantial computational resources during the training phase, but on the other hand, often yield distilled neural network models with significantly lower inference time. This trade-off has led to an active line of research focused on developing lightweight and resilient architectures, particularly for the purpose of deployment in resource-constrained settings. From the perspective of efficient and sustainable neural network model deployment, such approaches align with the principles of Green AI [14].

To address these challenges, various strategies and methods were developed, including model pruning [15], quantization [16], and low-rank factorization [17]. While effective in reducing model size and inference latency, these methods often require post hoc tuning and may result in degraded predictive performance. Among these, knowledge distillation (KD) has emerged as an auspicious approach [18]. In the process of KD, a smaller, "student" model learns to replicate the behavior of a larger, computationally complex "teacher" model without significant loss in predictive performance [18]. Knowledge distillation techniques have been applied to reduce the complexity of neural networks for detecting diseases in various medical image analysis tasks [19], such as COVID-19, pneumonia, and tuberculosis from chest X-rays [20], facilitating their use in automated medical applications [21].

A common limitation across previous efforts is their reliance on a single teacher model, which can restrict the diversity of knowledge transferred to the student and may limit generalizability in complex diagnostic tasks. To address this, the use of multiple teacher models has gained attention [22,23]. The problem of utilizing a multiple teachers approach in the process of knowledge distillation is the significant amount of computational complexity needed to obtain a diverse group of models, since it is required in order to train multiple, usually deep, neural network architectures, which limit their practical applicability. However, in the past, ensemble methods [7,24–26] have demonstrated great predictive performance and are capable of creating a diverse group of ensemble models, often without significantly increasing computational complexity in the training phase. Therefore, we propose an ensemble knowledge distillation method (EKD) which uses a selection of top-performing ensemble models as teachers in the process of distilling their knowledge into a single student model, with the goal of maintaining predictive performance and ability to generalize, while significantly reducing computational complexity in the inference time. The predictive and inference performance of the proposed EDK method is evaluated for the task of identifying childhood pneumonia from chest X-ray images. The main contribution of our research is as follows:

- We propose an ensemble knowledge distillation method for image classification, utilizing multiple teacher models obtained from the SGDRE method. This approach reduces the distilled student model's complexity and computational demands.

  This main contribution is further supported by the following:

- A comprehensive empirical evaluation of the presented EKD method is conducted, addressing the task of identifying childhood pneumonia from chest X-ray images.
- An in-depth analysis and comparison are performed to assess the predictive performance and computational complexity of the distilled student model relative to both the SGDRE method and a conventionally trained student model.

The remainder of this paper is structured as follows. Section 2 presents the methods and materials used. Section 3 describes the experimental setup, including evaluation methods and metrics. Section 4 presents the experimental results in detail, followed by a discussion in Section 5. Finally, Section 6 concludes the study by summarizing the presented work and highlighting potential future work.

2. Related Work

In recent years, numerous studies have explored KD for improving the computational efficiency of deep neural networks, particularly in medical imaging applications. In the context of chest X-rays, KD has proven effective for compressing complex networks while preserving performance [20,21]. For example, KD has been employed to distill knowledge from large networks trained on expert-labeled datasets to smaller models designed for edge deployment in disease classification and segmentation tasks [19].

Several recent studies have further refined the KD process. Prototype-based knowledge distillation methods have been proposed to tackle challenges in medical segmentation, particularly when only single-modal data is available [27]. Such approaches aim to transfer semantic structures through compact class representations. For instance, Wang et al. [27] proposed a prototype knowledge distillation approach that transfers intra-class and inter-class feature variations from a multi-modal teacher to a single-modal student, enhancing segmentation performance even when only single-modal data is available. In a recent study [28], Asham et al. propose a lightweight deep learning model leveraging optimizing KD process by training multiple candidate teacher models and finding the most suitable one. Galih et al. [29] proposed an approach which employs the Vision Transformer (ViT) architecture as the teacher model and MobileNet as the student model in order to reduce computational complexity of student model. To achieve the same goal, Ghosh in their study [30] proposed a KD approach where models pretrained on the ImageNet dataset serve as teacher models. Additionally, Bi et al. [31] developed a Multi-Prototype Embedding Refinement method for semi-supervised medical image segmentation, capturing intra-class variations by clustering voxel embeddings along multiple prototypes per class. Such methods demonstrate the potential of using representative and interpretable feature structures to enhance model learning efficiency and generalization.

However, a common limitation across these efforts is the reliance on a single teacher model. This can restrict the diversity of knowledge transferred to the student and may limit generalizability in complex diagnostic tasks. To address this, the use of multiple teachers has gained attention [22,23,32]. This approach allows the student model to learn from a more diverse ensemble of teacher models, potentially capturing complementary information. For example, Li et al. [32] proposed a dual online knowledge distillation strategy to connect heterogenous networks with the developed multi-scale feature refinement module and thus transfer the knowledge from different sources. Cheng et al. [23] proposed an approach that integrates both localized and globalized frequency attention techniques, aiming to substantially enhance the distillation process. Additionally, Fukuda et al. [22] employed a KD approach using multiple models, including very deep networks and Long Short-Term Memory (LSTM) models, to train a standard CNN model, demonstrating the versatility of the KD process.

However, a common problem of utilizing a multiple teachers approach in the process of knowledge distillation is the significant computational complexity needed to obtain a diverse group of models, since it is required in order to train multiple, usually deep, neural network architectures, which limits their practical applicability. In contrast to aforementioned approaches, our proposed EKD method utilizes the SGDRE method for the purpose of obtaining multiple teacher models in the single training process and thus reducing computational complexity.

3. Materials and Methods

3.1. Knowledge Distillation

Knowledge distillation (KD) is the process of transferring knowledge from a large, computationally complex model, usually a deep neural network, to a smaller, more efficient model that retains comparable predictive performance while being computationally feasible for deployment in more resource-constrained environments. The inspiration behind the idea was drawn from natural processes, particularly biological metamorphosis, in which many insects, such as butterflies, undergo two distinct life stages optimized for different functions. Larval stage is optimized for consuming resources and growing, which is an analogy for training large complex models, and adult stage is optimized for efficiency, mobility, and reproduction, like the predictive models should be when feasible for deployment.

The principle behind knowledge distillation is based on utilizing soft labels—the teacher model's output actions (logits)—as opposed to utilizing definite class labels only, to train the student models. These soft labels convey additional information regarding the inter-class relationships that are not present in the one-hot encoded ground truth labels. Formally, given an input x, a teacher model with parameters θ_T produces output signal $z_T = f_{\theta_T}(x)$. Similarly, a student model with parameters θ_S produces output signal $z_S = f_{\theta_S}(x)$.

The knowledge transfer is achieved by introducing a temperature parameter T in the softmax function to generate soft probability distributions:

$$p_i^T(x) = \frac{\exp(z_{T,i}/T)}{\sum_j \exp(z_{T,j}/T)}$$

$$p_i^S(x) = \frac{\exp(z_{S,i}/T)}{\sum_j \exp(z_{S,j}/T)}$$

where $p_i^T(x)$ and $p_i^S(x)$ can be interpreted as probabilities of class i for input x from the teacher and student models, respectively. The temperature parameter T controls the softness of the probability distribution. When $T = 1$, we obtain the standard softmax outputs. As T increases, the probability distribution becomes more uniform, placing more weight on the relative relations between classes.

The student model is then trained to optimize a combined loss function:

$$\mathcal{L}(\theta_S) = \alpha \mathcal{L}_{CE}(y, \sigma(z_S)) + (1 - \alpha)\mathcal{L}_{KD}(p^T, p^S)$$

where $\mathcal{L}_{CE}$ is the standard cross-entropy loss between the one-hot encoded ground truth labels y and the student's predictions with a standard softmax $\sigma(\cdot)$. $\mathcal{L}_{KD}$ is the knowledge distillation loss, typically implemented as the Kullback–Leibler (KL) divergence between the teacher's and student's soft probability distributions.

Advancements in knowledge distillation have expanded beyond the original formulation, one of which is transferring not only the outputs but also the intermediate representation [33]. Additionally, distilling knowledge from an ensemble of teacher models into a single student model [34,35] is also gaining attention in recent years.

3.2. SGDRE Method

Stochastic gradient descent (SGD) with warm restarts (SGDRE) [7] is an ensemble method that periodically resets the learning rate of the SGD optimized to encourage convergence to the local minima. Building upon this idea, the SGDRE method constructs an ensemble of models from a single training run by capturing multiple model snapshots at different restart points using the warm restarts mechanism. These snapshots, representing models converged to different local optima, are then used collectively as teacher models to transfer diverse knowledge to the student model during the knowledge distillation process. The conceptual design of the method is depicted in Figure 1. The SGDRE method results in enhanced performance for image classification tasks, particularly in the context of medical image analysis.

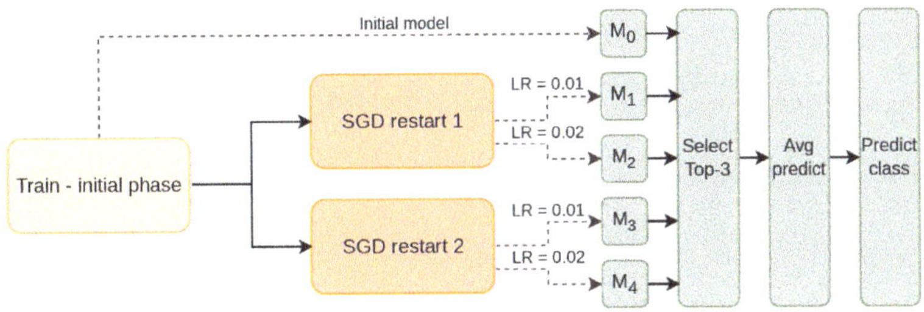

Figure 1. Conceptual diagram of SGDRE method.

The key improvement introduced in this study lies in the modification of the training process, where, in contrast to conventional practice, in which the learning rate is gradually decreased through the training process, here the learning rate is periodically increased with the utilization of SGD with warm restarts. The SGD with warm restarts mechanism was initially presented in [36]. The main goal of this mechanism was to address the main SGD issue, which is that it is likely to converge prematurely, which can result in inferior solutions, especially in the case of deep neural network architectures. The SGDRE method uses the aforementioned mechanism with three different learning rate annealing strategies presented in Figure 2, to obtain a diverse set of candidate ensemble models through one training process.

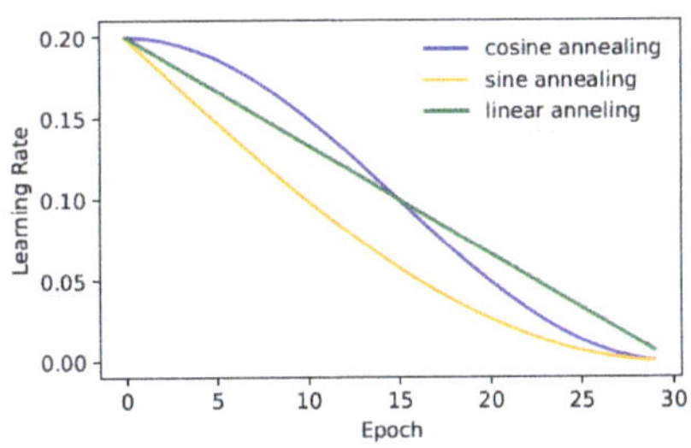

Figure 2. Presentation of three different learning rate annealing strategies employed in the process of SGDRE training.

As can be observed in Figure 1, the method consists of three training phases. The whole training process is designed to efficiently work under the limited training budget—limited number of epochs. In the initial training phase, the SGDRE is trained with the SGD optimizer, linearly reducing the initial learning rate for 50 epochs. After the initial training phase, the SGD learning rate is increased to 0.01 and 0.02, employing the sine decrease of the learning rate and early stopping mechanism, monitoring the area under the ROC curve (AUC) metric, which is calculated after each training epoch. The process of increasing the learning rate is then repeated with the only difference being the utilization of a cosine learning rate decay; however, the starting point of this process remains the same, after the initial training phase. Each warm restart is budgeted with an equal number of epochs, which is calculated based on the initial training budget subtracted by the epochs consumed in the initial training phase. Such a process of employing warm restarts with different initial learning rates and annealing strategies encourages a broader exploration of the loss surface, to uncover potentially more diverse and higher-quality solutions, and can also help improve generalization performance. The models obtained in this process are then evaluated. The top three individually best-performing models based on AUC scores are selected for the purpose of the ensemble method. The predictions of selected models are combined using the averaging approach, and the computed average finally serves as a final ensemble prediction.

In the original SGDRE study [7], the CNN architecture proposed by Stephen et al. [37] was utilized, which has already been demonstrated to be successful at solving the classification task to identify pneumonia based on the X-ray images. The architecture is composed of four convolutional layers (with 32, 64, and two with 128 filters) paired with max-pooling layers, followed by a flatten layer, a dropout layer (dropout rate 0.5), and two fully connected layers (with 512 and 1 neurons). All convolutional layers use 3×3 kernels with ReLU activation. The proposed CNN architecture results in 6,795,394 trainable parameters.

3.3. Ensemble Knowledge Distillation

Based on the presented SGDRE method, we propose an ensemble-based knowledge distillation method, EKD, for the task of identifying childhood pneumonia from chest X-ray images. The method leverages multiple teacher models to distill the knowledge into a more compact student model. The process involves training an SGDRE method from which we obtain ensemble models that achieved acceptable performance and distilling their knowledge into a single student model. The conceptual diagram of the method is presented in Figure 3.

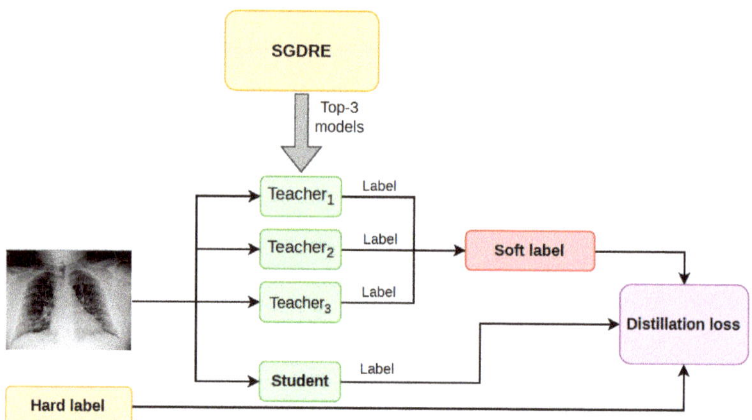

Figure 3. Conceptual diagram of ensemble knowledge distillation method EKD.

From the SGDRE method, we obtain the top three best-performing models, which are selected based on the AUC metric. Although the models output class probabilities via the softmax layer, we calculate AUC in a one-vs-rest manner by treating the softmax score for each class as a continuous-valued prediction. After the selection, the three teacher models are in the process of training, utilized for the purpose of distilling the knowledge through the computed soft label. Soft label combines the predicted labels of each teacher model into one unified label. Given an input sample x, the probability distribution predicted by each of the teacher models is calculated as:

$$p_k(y|x) = \sigma(z_k/T) \tag{1}$$

where z_k denotes the logits produced by the k-th teacher model and σ denotes the softmax function. The teachers' combined soft label p_{soft} is then calculated as the average of all teachers' predictions:

$$p_{soft}(y|x) = \frac{1}{K}\sum_{k=1}^{K} p_k(y|x) \tag{2}$$

In such a manner, the calculated soft labels reflect the diversity of multiple teacher models, capturing richer information than hard labels. The calculated soft label, together with the predicted label from the student model, and the ground-truth hard label, are afterward combined into the distillation loss value. The composite distillation loss value balances the true label loss and the soft label loss, and can be formally expressed as:

$$\mathcal{L}_{KD} = \alpha \cdot \mathcal{L}_{CE}(y, \text{softmax}(\hat{z})) + (1-\alpha) \cdot T^2 \cdot \mathcal{L}_{CE}(p_{\text{soft}}, \sigma(\hat{z}/T)) \tag{3}$$

where $\mathcal{L}_{CE}$ is the categorical cross-entropy loss, y denotes the ground truth labels, $\hat{z}$ represents the student model's logits, T is the temperature parameter which controls the probability distribution during the loss computation, and α is a weighting factor balancing both p_{soft} loss and true label loss. The factor T^2 is included to preserve the relative contributions of the soft targets during training. The distillation loss value calculated in such a manner is further used in the process of training the student model, serving as the loss metric.

3.4. Dataset

The Chest X-ray images dataset is a publicly available dataset [38], originally collected and presented by Kermany et al. [39]. Chest X-ray images were collected from retrospective cohorts of pediatric patients aged 1 to 5 years from Guangzhou Women and Children's Medical Center, Guangzhou, China. After the process of collecting the images, each image went through a rigorous process of quality control, removing all low-quality or unreliable scans. Finally, two expert physicians were utilized in grading the diagnoses of chest X-ray images prior to them being approved for use in the process of training the CNN [38].

In the preprocessing phase, we have resized the original X-ray images, which have different sizes, to a uniform size of 200 × 200 pixels. The total number of samples in the data set is 5858, which is unevenly distributed between the two classes. The "normal" class includes the X-ray images that do not show signs of pneumonia, and the "pneumonia" class contains the X-ray images that are diagnosed with pneumonia. The distribution between the classes can be observed in Figure 4. We can see class imbalance where the pneumonia-diagnosed images represent 72.96% of all the image samples, and the remaining 27.04% X-ray images of normal lungs.

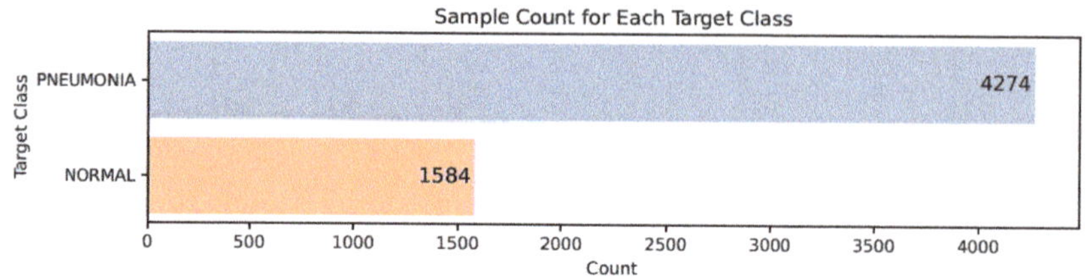

Figure 4. Class distribution of the dataset.

Two sample chest X-ray images used for training and evaluation of the compared methods can be observed in Figure 5, where the sample a represents the X-ray image of a healthy lung, while the sample b represents the X-ray image of lungs indicating pneumonia.

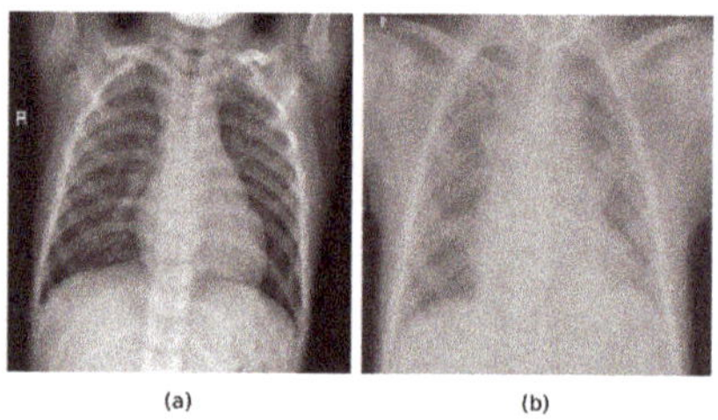

Figure 5. Samples representing each of the categories of X-ray images in the dataset: (**a**) represents an X-ray image of healthy lungs, (**b**) represents X-ray image of lungs indicating pneumonia.

4. Experimental Framework

The proposed method for knowledge distillation from ensemble models to a single student model was evaluated on the task of childhood pneumonia identification based on the X-ray images. To objectively evaluate the performance of the proposed ensemble knowledge distillation method, EKD, we compared its performance with that of the ensemble method. Additionally, we conducted an experiment where we conventionally trained the student CNN architecture using randomly initialized weights in order to determine whether the utilization of the proposed method is justified. Therefore, in total, we conducted four experiments:

- Trained student CNN architecture in a conventional manner. The method is denoted as Student.
- Trained the SGDRE method, denoted as a SGDRE.
- Trained the proposed ensemble knowledge distillation method, utilizing the teacher models obtained by the SGDRE method, denoted as EKD.
- Trained the student model using knowledge distillation utilizing only one teacher from SGDRE method, denoted as KD.

All experiments were conducted on a computer with an octa-core Intel i7-6700 processor, 16 GB of RAM, and an Nvidia GeForce GTX 1660 Ti with 6 GB of memory, running on the Linux Mint 6 Debian edition operating system.

The following subsections present the evaluation method and metrics, the utilized student CNN architecture, and parameter settings for each of the conducted experiments.

4.1. Evaluation Methods and Metrics

We adopted a well-established 10-fold cross-validation approach as suggested by Demšar et al. [40], to assess the predictive performance of the predictive models produced by the proposed ensemble knowledge distillation method for identification of childhood pneumonia. This approach involves partitioning the dataset into ten equal subsets. In each iteration, nine subsets are used for training of the method, while the remaining subset serves as the test set. In such a manner, the process is repeated ten times, with each subset once serving as the test set. With 10-fold cross-validation, we mitigate variance by averaging over multiple data partitions and ensure that the model's performance is not overly dependent on a particular data partition. The predictive performances of the compared methods are evaluated through common classification metrics such as accuracy, F1 score, AUC, and Cohen's kappa score. Additionally, we captured the training time, the number of epochs consumed, and the inference time to inspect and analyze the performance from a computational complexity standpoint.

The accuracy metric is one the most commonly used metrics for evaluating the performance of classification algorithms [40]. It represents the proportion of correct predictions out of the total number of predictions. Formally, we can express the accuracy metric as:

$$Accuracy = \frac{TP + TN}{TP + TN + FP + FN} \tag{4}$$

where TP are correctly classified positive instances, TN are correctly classified negative instances, FP are negative instances incorrectly classified as positive, and FN are positive instances incorrectly classified as negative.

Since the accuracy metric can be misleading, especially when dealing with unbalanced datasets, it is common to use the F1-score [41] metric, which is often used in such scenarios. It represents the harmonic mean of the precision and recall, balancing the trade-offs between those two metrics. We can formally express the F1-score metric as:

$$F1\text{-}score = 2 \times \frac{P \times R}{P + R} \tag{5}$$

where P denotes the precision metric, which can be expressed as

$$P = \frac{TP}{TP + FP} \tag{6}$$

and R denotes the recall metric formally expressed as

$$R = \frac{TP}{TP + FN}. \tag{7}$$

The area under the curve (AUC) metric is also widely used to evaluate the discriminatory ability of classifiers [42]. It measures the area under the receiver operating characteristic (ROC) curve, while ROC is defined as the true positive rate (TPR), against the false positive rate (FPR) across various values of a classification threshold. The AUC represents the probability that the classifier will assign a higher score to a randomly chosen positive instance than to a randomly chosen negative one. The classifier's performance is then summarized across all possible threshold values, thus forming a family of classifiers parameterized by the decision threshold. In this context, the parameter is the classification threshold, which is used to convert the model's continuous output scores into binary predictions. By varying this threshold, a family of thresholded classifiers is created, each with different TP rate and FP rate values. The AUC metric can be formally expressed as:

$$\int_0^1 TPR(\theta) dFPR(\theta) \tag{8}$$

where m denotes the model and θ denotes the classification threshold.

Cohen's kappa [43] is a statistical measure developed initially to quantify inter-rater agreement, but it is also widely used to evaluate the level of agreement between a classifier's predicted class and the ground truth class. It compares an observed accuracy to an expected accuracy (chance), while taking into account random chance, which generally makes it less misleading than simply using accuracy as a metric. Formally, the Cohen's kappa metric can be expressed as:

$$\kappa = \frac{p_o - p_e}{1 - p_e} \tag{9}$$

where p_o is the relative observed agreement among raters, and p_e is the hypothetical probability of chance agreement. The interpretation of the metric values depends on several definitions, one being proposed by Landis and Koch [44] in which they described the values <0 as no agreement, 0–0.20 as slight, 0.21–0.40 as fair, 0.41–0.60 as moderate, 0.61–0.80 as substantial, and 0.81–1 as almost perfect agreement.

4.2. Student CNN Architecture

The architecture of the student CNN, graphically presented in Figure 6, is based on the architecture presented by Stephen et al. [37]. However, we modified it to facilitate effective feature extraction and classification with a minimalistic structure. The architecture comprises a serial combination of convolutional layers, normalization layers, pooling layers, and fully connected layers. The input to the network is a 200 × 200 × 1 grayscale X-ray image. The first convolutional layer applies 32 filters of size 3 × 3 with ReLU [45] activation function and Glorot uniform [46] weight initialization, and follows it with a batch normalization layer to stabilize training. For the purpose of dimension reduction, a maximization pooling layer of size 2 × 2 and a stride of 2 downsamples is utilized. The second convolutional layer is defined with 64 kernels with the same kernel size, activation function, and initialization, with batch normalization and a further max-pooling operation as in the previous combination. Following the second convolutional block is a flatten layer to transform the feature maps to a one-dimensional vector. Next is a fully connected layer comprising 32 neurons, ReLU activation, and L2 regularization ($\lambda = 0.01$)—where the normalization of the weights is added as a penalty term to the loss function to help prevent overfitting. Next, a dropout layer with a dropout rate of 0.5 is applied. Finally, the output layer consists of two neurons that use a softmax activation function, giving class probabilities for binary classification.

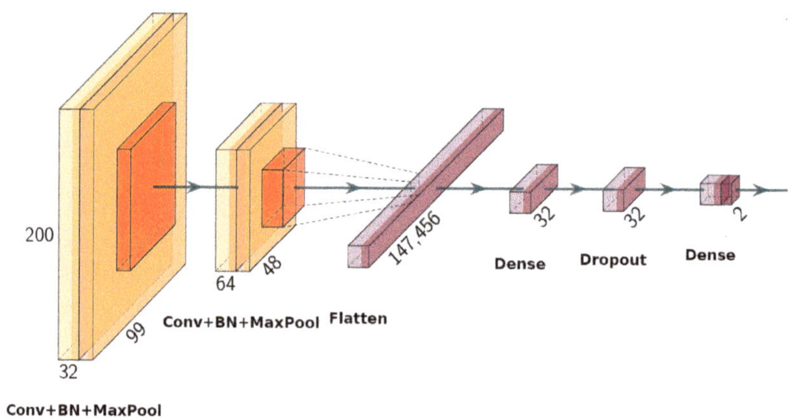

Figure 6. Graphical representation of the utilized student CNN architecture.

The total number of trainable parameters in the presented student CNN architecture is 4,737,698, which is significantly smaller compared to the teacher model architecture presented in Section 3.2, with 6,795,394 trainable parameters. This reduction in model complexity highlights the effectiveness of the distillation approach. Additionally, through reduced total parameters, the student model potentially minimizes the surface area for adversarial attacks, aligning with recent findings that overparameterized models may be more vulnerable to such threats [12].

4.3. Parameter Settings

All the experiments were conducted utilizing a 10-fold cross-validation approach with the parameter settings presented in Table 1. For all methods, the total number of epochs available for training was set to 100. The training was conducted utilizing a mini-batch strategy for all experiments, with the batch size set to 32, which is a common choice in medical imaging to balance between stability and computational efficiency. The Student, KD, and EKD models were trained using the Adam optimizer function since it provides better convergence in settings involving soft targets and KD. On the other hand, the SGDRE method was trained using the SGD optimizer, consistent with the approach proposed in the original SGDR method [36], which benefits from a high initial learning rate and different annealing strategies leading to different local minima. Regarding the initial learning rate, for Student it was set to 2×10^{-3}, for SGDRE to 1×10^{-1} based on SGDR recommendations, and for KD/EKD to 1×10^{-4}, following common practices in knowledge distillation tasks where lower learning rates help in stabilizing the learning from soft targets [18]. For both methods, the early stopping mechanism was employed in order to prevent potential overfitting, with patience set to 10. The SGDRE is not utilizing the early stopping mechanism, since it consumes all the given budget of epochs in order to obtain multiple models. All methods except the knowledge distillation-based (KD and EKD) methods utilize the categorical cross-entropy, while the KD and EKD utilize a custom distillation loss presented in the previous section. Since the distillation loss is computed using values α and temperature T, we set those values to 0.5 and 3.0, respectively. The selection of those parameter values was guided by recent studies [47,48], where such parameter values yielded stable results.

Table 1. Parameter settings of the conducted experiments.

Parameter	Student	SGDRE	KD/EKD
No. of epochs	100	100	100
Batch size	32	32	32
Optimizer	Adam	SGD	Adam
Initial learning rate	1×10^{-3}	1×10^{-1}	1×10^{-4}
Loss function	categorical cross-entropy	categorical cross-entropy	distillation loss
Early stopping [1]	10	10	10
Alpha (α)	-	-	0.5
Initial temperature T	-	-	3.0

[1] Values represent the patience when the early stopping mechanism is being employed.

5. Results

Throughout the study, we focused on pursuing the following research questions:

- RQ1: Can the proposed EKD method reduce the computational complexity of the SGDRE method without compromising predictive performance?
  - RQ1.1 Does the proposed EKD method achieve comparable predictive performance while reducing computational complexity?

- RQ1.2 Does the distilled model achieve faster inference time than the ensemble method?
- RQ2: Does the proposed EKD method outperform the same student CNN architecture trained with a conventional approach?

The results obtained from the conducted experiments, in line with the defined research questions, are comprehensively presented in Table 2, where each metric value is reported as the average over 10 folds for each method, along with the corresponding standard deviation. The emphasized values in the table highlight the best-performing classifier among those compared.

Table 2. Comparison of averaged metrics obtained over 10-fold cross-validation. Displayed are accuracy, AUC, F1 score, Cohen's kappa coefficient, consumed numbers of epochs (Epochs), train time (in seconds), and inference time (in seconds) with associated standard deviations.

Metrics	Student	SGDRE	KD	EKD
Accuracy	0.87 ± 0.05	**0.96 ± 0.01**	0.86 ± 0.09	0.95 ± 0.01
AUC	0.85 ± 0.05	**0.95 ± 0.01**	0.79 ± 0.19	0.94 ± 0.01
F1	0.87 ± 0.05	**0.96 ± 0.01**	0.83 ± 0.14	0.95 ± 0.01
Kappa	0.69 ± 0.10	**0.89 ± 0.01**	0.57 ± 0.37	0.87 ± 0.02
Epochs	**18.20** ± 6.65	97.90 ± 0.30	20.70 ± 8.67	23.30 ± 6.54
Train time	**114.00 ± 39.66**	634.70 ± 53.98	373.20 ± 148.58	528.10 ± 140.03
Inference time	**1.29** ± 0.08	6.67 ± 1.00	1.40 ± 0.13	1.32 ± 0.09

Bold values represent the best achieved score for each metric.

As can be observed from the table, the highest predictive performance is achieved by the SGDRE method, closely followed by the proposed EKD method, which lags by 0.01 in terms of accuracy, AUC, and F1 metric, and by 0.02 in the kappa statistic. In contrast, the KD model yields the worst results, closely followed by the Student model. However, in terms of training and inference time, we can observe that in this case, the best performing is Student model, followed by the KD and EKD methods. Focusing on the training time, the best performing is Student model with an average of 114.00 s, while the EKD and SGDRE methods consumed more time to train on average, 634.70 s and 528.10 s, respectively. Regarding inference time, we can see that the lowest inference time was also achieved by the Student model, followed closely by the EKD and KD methods. On the other side, the worst inference time was achieved by the SGDRE method. Additionally, we can observe that the other methods achieved comparable results from the inference standpoint, far lower than the more computationally complex SGDRE method. Thus, it can be inferred that the EKD method is capable of achieving comparable predictive performance to that of the SGDRE method with lower computational complexity.

5.1. Predictive Performance Comparison

In Figure 7, the achieved accuracy values of the compared methods are presented in the form of violin plots. The violin plot is a combination of a box plot and a density plot, providing a deeper understanding of the distribution of metric values across 10 folds. The width of the violin plot represents the density of values in a range, meaning the wider the plot, the more values are presented in that range. The horizontal lines in each of the violin plots from top to bottom represent the maximum, median, and minimum values, while the white circle denotes the mean value.

Looking at the accuracy comparison, the EKD method achieves a high value of 0.95 with a standard deviation of 0.01, almost on par with the SGDRE method, which achieved 0.96. The difference between those two is only 0.01 on average. However, both of the mentioned methods outperformed the KD model by a large amount, 0.09 and 0.10, respectively, as well as the Student model. Looking at the standard deviations, we can also observe that SGDRE and EKD methods have drastically smaller standard deviations in comparison to the KD and Student models.

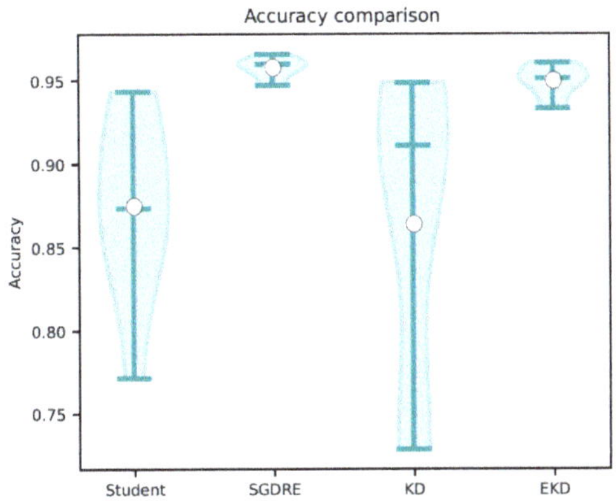

Figure 7. Violin plot comparing the accuracy metric over 10 folds.

As is the case with the accuracy, we can also observe a similar pattern when comparing the AUC values presented in Figure 8. The delta between the best and second-best performing methods, namely SGDRE and EKD method, is at 0.01, while the delta between SGDRE and the worst-performing KD model is 0.16. Similar to the accuracy values distribution, we can also observe that the density of AUC values for the SGDRE and EKD methods is not as scattered as it can be observed with the KD and Student. Additionally, the KD model achieved by far the lowest AUC value, while the maximum value is similar to the worst performing fold of EKD model.

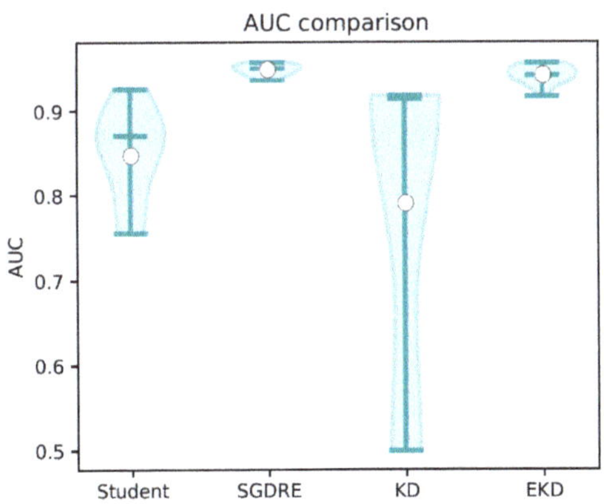

Figure 8. Violin plot comparing the AUC metric over 10 folds.

Focusing on the F1 values presented in Figure 9, we can see that the distribution of values across all methods is practically the same as was in the case of the AUC metric. The only difference is in the delta between the worst performing KD model and the best performing SDGRE model, which is in the case of the F1 metric set at 0.13.

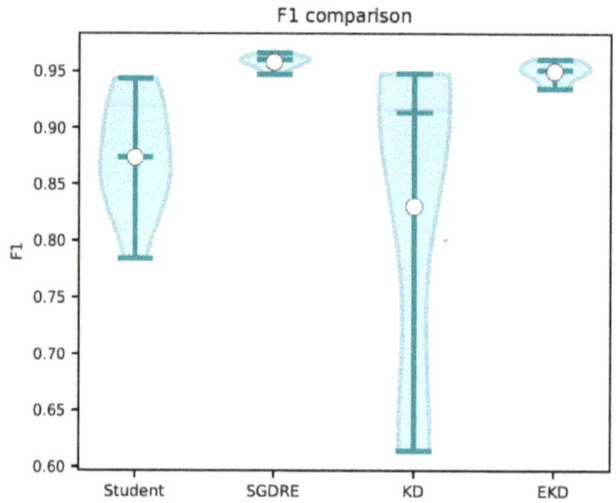

Figure 9. Violin plot comparing the F1 metric over 10 folds.

Figure 10 depicts the violin plots of kappa statistic values over 10 folds. In terms of achieved average kappa values, the best performing method is again the SGDRE method, achieving 0.89, followed closely by EKD method with 0.87, while the Student and KD models achieved 0.69 and 0.57, respectively. Looking at the delta values when comparing the SGDRE and EKD methods, we can observe a difference of 0.02. On the other hand, when comparing the SGDRE method against the KD model, the difference is 0.32. Interpreting the kappa statistic, based on the definition proposed by Landis and Koch [44], the SGDRE and EKD methods on average achieved almost perfect agreement, the Student model achieved substantial agreement, while the KD model achieved moderate agreement.

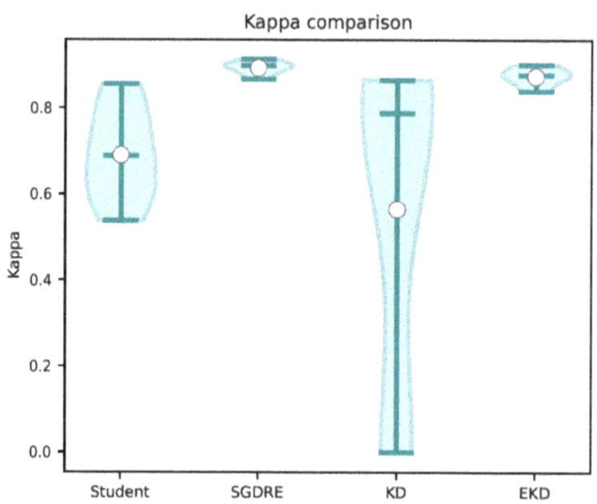

Figure 10. Violin plot comparing the Kappa metric over 10 folds.

5.2. Computational Complexity Comparison

Figure 11 depicts the distribution of achieved inference times of the compared methods over 10 folds. These times are indicative of the computational complexity of each method during the inference. It must be noted that the inference time of a fixed architecture is inherently constant under deterministic conditions; any observed fluctuations are due to measurement noise introduced by interpreter-level overhead (e.g., from Python 3.11.3) or background operating system processes. Therefore, the observed minor differences in inference time between EKD, KD, and Student models are practically insignificant. As observed in the figure, the SGDRE method is by far the worst performing, trailing behind the second best EKD method by 5.36 s. It would be expected that the SGDRE method would take three times more inference time than the EKD, Student, or KD methods. However, in the case of the SGDRE method, we must also take into consideration the fact that there is some overhead when combining the predictions of each ensemble model. The distribution of the inference times of the SGDRE method is much more scattered than in the case of the compared methods. Such long inference times can be attributed to the fact that the SGDRE method needs to perform three predictions for each given test sample in order to compute the final prediction. When comparing the two best-performing methods, we can observe that the inference times are practically the same, with an average difference of 0.2 s.

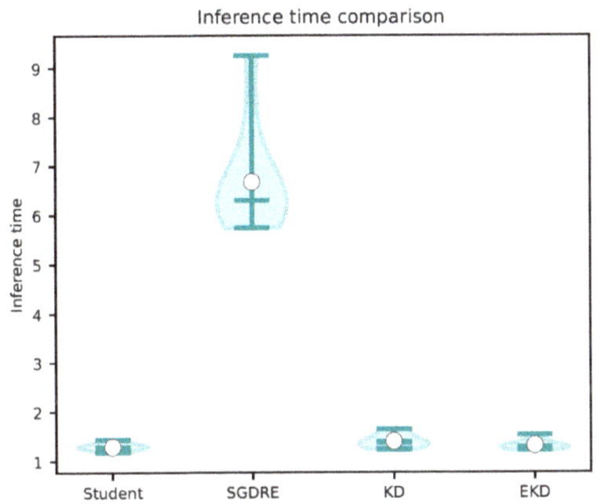

Figure 11. Violin plot comparing the inference time metric over 10 folds.

In addition to the measured inference time, we also conducted a comparison between the SGDRE and the proposed EKD method. In Table 3, the number of trainable parameters of the compared methods are presented together with the required FLOPs. As we can observe, the EKD method has a clear advantage also in that aspect due to the reduced size of the student CNN architecture. In terms of the reduction ratio, the number of trainable parameters was reduced by 4.31 times, while the FLOPs were reduced by 6.5 times.

Table 3. Comparison of SGDRE method and Student/EKD model trainable parameters and FLOPs.

Metric	SGDRE	Student/EKD [1]	Reduction Ratio
Parameters	20,386,182	4,737,698	4.31×
FLOPs	2,486,904,420	382,573,292	6.5×

[1] Student and EKD method have the same CNN architecture.

5.3. Statistical Analysis

In order to assess the statistical significance of the obtained results, we followed the procedure suggested by Demšar [40]. First, we conducted a Shapiro–Wilk test to determine whether the values of each metric are normally distributed. Since the hypothesis was rejected, meaning the values are not normally distributed, we employed the Friedman test as suggested by calculating the asymptotic significance for all compared methods on all 10 folds. The results of the conducted test are presented in Table 4 together with the rank averages for each method and metric.

Table 4. Statistical results of Friedman test.

	Friedman Test	Rank Averages [1]			
Metric	**All Three**	**Student**	**SGDRE**	**KD**	**EKD**
Accuracy	**<0.001**	3.60	**1.15**	3.3	1.95
AUC	**<0.001**	3.70	**1.40**	3.3	1.60
F1	**<0.001**	3.60	**1.20**	3.30	1.90
Kappa	**<0.001**	3.70	**1.20**	3.20	1.90
Time	**<0.001**	**1.00**	3.60	2.30	3.10
Epochs	**<0.001**	**1.60**	4.00	2.00	2.40

[1] Lowest average rank at the specific metric represents the better performing method. Bold values represent the best achieved score.

Observing the results of the conducted Friedman test, we can see that there are statistically significant ($p < 0.001$) differences between methods regardless of the metric. Therefore, we continue with the post hoc statistical analysis, conducting the Wilcoxon signed-rank test, which can be used to compare the statistical equality of two methods over the same sample. Since there were multiple comparisons between the methods, we applied the Holm–Bonferroni correction, which is used to control the family-wise error rate when conducting multiple hypothesis tests. The results of the conducted signed-rank test are presented in Table 5. The table presents the pairwise comparison of models' predictive performance methods for each metric. The emphasized values in the table represent the statistically significant differences, with a significance level of 95%. Focusing on the comparison between the Student and SGDRE, we can observe that there is a statistically significant difference between the compared methods for all metrics. Combining the results with the achieved rank averages presented in Table 4, we can observe that for the metrics accuracy, AUC, F1, and kappa, the SGDRE achieved a lower average rank, so it is considered better performing. However, for the metrics, time, epochs, and inference time, it is the other way around. Comparing the Student model with the EKD method, we can observe that there is a statistically significant difference for metrics accuracy, AUC, F1, Kappa, and training time. Looking at the average ranks, we can see that the proposed EKD method achieved statistically significantly better results for all the predictive metrics, and the Student model achieved statistically significantly lower training time. Those findings support the decision to utilize the proposed EKD method instead of training the Student network in a conventional manner (i.e., without knowledge distillation). If the EKD method does not yield a statistically significant performance improvement, the Student architecture would be a more reasonable choice in terms of training time.

Table 5. Results of Wilcoxon test with Holm–Bonferroni correction applied.

Metric	Student vs. SGDRE	Student vs. EKD	KD vs. EKD	SGDRE vs. EKD
Accuracy	**0.047**	**0.047**	**0.047**	0.297
AUC	**0.047**	**0.047**	**0.047**	0.422
F1	**0.047**	**0.047**	**0.047**	0.297
Kappa	**0.047**	**0.047**	**0.047**	0.297
Time	**0.047**	**0.047**	0.420	0.422
Epochs	**0.047**	0.422	0.422	**0.047**

Bold values represent the best achieved score.

When comparing the two knowledge distillation approaches, KD and EKD, we observe a statistically significant difference in the metrics of accuracy, AUC, F1, and Kappa. Inspecting the average ranks, we can see that the proposed EKD method achieves statistically significantly better results across all predictive metrics. In contrast, differences in training and inference times are statistically insignificant, as expected, since both approaches use the same student architecture.

Finally, comparing the best performing SGDRE method with the proposed EKD method, we can see that the statistically significant differences are only present for the metrics epochs and inference time. The predictive performance metrics and training time are not statistically significantly different; therefore, we can confirm that the predicting performance of the proposed EKD method is comparable to the more computationally complex SGDRE method. Focusing on the metrics epochs and inference time, looking at the average ranks achieved, we can see that the EKD method achieved, on average, lower ranks than the SGDRE method. Thus, the proposed method is statistically significantly better performing in terms of epochs needed to train and, more importantly, achieves faster inference time, due to reduced computational complexity.

5.4. Comparison with Some Existing Methods

Several studies have used the same chest X-ray dataset to detect childhood pneumonia. However, it is important to note that not every study employed the same evaluation methodology (using k-fold cross-validation versus using simple train test split approach). As a result the comparison may not be entirely objective, but it can still provide a general sense of the predictive performance landscape across different approaches.

Kermany et al. [39] presented a method which utilizes the transfer learning approach using the Inception V3 CNN architecture. The authors reported an accuracy of 92.8%, which lags behind the proposed EKD method by 3.2%.

A study conducted by Stephen et al. [37] proposed a specific custom CNN architecture that achieved an accuracy of 93.7%. In comparison, the proposed EKD method outperforms this by a margin of 2.3%.

In [28], Asham et al. presented a lightweight deep learning model with KD, which achieved an accuracy of 97.92%, exceeding that of the EKD method by 1.92%. However, the experiments conducted by Asham et al. employed a simple train/validation/test split methodology, which could have contributed to the reported predictive performance difference.

Kundu et al. [49] reported that their proposed ensemble method achieved an average accuracy of 98.81% and an average F1 score of 98.97, surpassing the EKD method by 2.81 and 3.79, respectively. While it is not uncommon for ensemble methods to outperform single-model methods on specific tasks, they pose challenges for deployment in resource-constrained environments due to increased computational complexity during inference.

Singh et al. [19] proposed an efficient detection method based on Vision Transformers. The authors conducted extensive performance evaluation relative to other architectures utilizing the same dataset. Their proposed Vision Transformer method achieved an accuracy of 97.61% and an F1 score of 0.95. Compared to the EKD method, this represents a 1.61% higher accuracy, while on average achieving the same F1 score. Additionally, from the computational complexity standpoint, we can also observe that proposed EKD method has around 17 times fewer trainable parameters than the Vision Transformers method, which translates to significantly shorter training and inference time.

6. Discussion

Following an in-depth analysis of the experimental results, we confirm that the model trained using our proposed EKD method achieved predictive performance comparable to that of the more computationally complex SGDRE method when applied to the task of identifying childhood pneumonia from X-ray images. The predictive metrics were statistically insignificantly different from the SGDRE method, while the inference time was significantly different. Observing the average ranks proved that the proposed EKD achieved on average a lower rank; therefore, it is better performing in terms of inference time. Additionally, the computational complexity of the proposed EKD method in comparison to the SGDRE method was reduced by a factor of 6.5× in terms of FLOPs standpoint and 4.31× in terms of the number of trainable parameters.

When comparing the predictive performance of the EKD model with that of the Student and KD methods, we observed that the EKD model significantly outperformed both in all classification metrics by a great margin. These findings support the utilization of the proposed EKD method instead of utilizing the Student CNN architecture and training it in a conventional manner. However, the training time of the Student method was significantly better than that achieved by the EKD method. We can attribute this to the fact that in the process of knowledge distillation, for each iteration of training, it is needed to obtain the prediction of teacher models in order to compute the soft labels. Therefore, the training time is increased in comparison to the conventional training of CNN.

Based on the obtained empirical results, we can confirm that the proposed EKD method can match the predictive performance of the more complex SGDRE method in the task of childhood pneumonia identification, while simultaneously reducing both computational complexity and inference time.

Although the reported performance remains strong, a limitation of the current study is the absence of explicit strategies to address class imbalance in the training data. Future work will explore the use of data augmentation, re-sampling, and class weighting techniques to further enhance model fairness and ensure more robust detection of underrepresented classes.

7. Conclusions

In this study, we proposed an ensemble-based knowledge distillation method for classification problems and applied it to the task of identifying childhood pneumonia from X-ray images. The method utilizes the SGDRE approach for the purpose of obtaining a homogeneous group of specialized CNN models, which are utilized as a group of teacher models. From the obtained group of models, the top three most suitable models are selected as the teacher models in the process of distilling the knowledge to a smaller, more efficient student CNN model.

The model trained using the proposed method was empirically evaluated on the task of childhood pneumonia identification and compared with both the SGDRE ensemble method and the Student CNN architecture trained using a conventional approach. Statistical analysis of the obtained results demonstrated that the proposed EKD method significantly outperformed the conventionally trained Student model and achieved comparable performance to the more computationally complex SGDRE method, while providing statistically significantly faster inference times.

In future work, we would like to expand our work to explore the possibility of implementing fully automatic, adaptive computation of the distillation loss throughout the knowledge distillation process, with the goal of further improving the predictive performance of the proposed method.

Author Contributions: Conceptualization, G.V. and V.P.; methodology, G.V.; software, G.V.; validation, G.V.; formal analysis, G.V.; investigation, G.V.; resources, G.V.; data curation, G.V.; writing—original draft preparation, G.V.; writing—review and editing, V.P.; visualization, G.V.; supervision, V.P.; project administration, V.P.; funding acquisition, V.P. All authors have read and agreed to the published version of the manuscript.

Funding: This research was funded by the Slovenian Research and Innovation Agency, Research Core Funding No. P2-0057.

Institutional Review Board Statement: Not applicable.

Informed Consent Statement: Not applicable.

Data Availability Statement: The data used in our study are publicly accessible through the Mendeley Data platform https://data.mendeley.com/datasets/rscbjbr9sj/2 (accessed on 14 January 2025).

Conflicts of Interest: The authors declare no conflicts of interest.

Abbreviations

The following abbreviations are used in this manuscript:

CNN	Convolutional Neural Network
AI	Artificial Intelligence
KD	Knowledge Distillation
LSTM	Long Short-Term Memory
EKD	Ensemble Knowledge Distillation
SGD	Stochastic Gradient Descent
SGDRE	Stochastic Gradient Descent with warm Restarts Ensemble
AUC	Area Under the Curve
ROC	Receiver operating characteristic
FLOPs	Floating Point Operations per Second

References

1. World Health Organization. Pneumonia in Children. 2022. Available online: https://www.who.int/news-room/fact-sheets/detail/pneumonia (accessed on 10 March 2025).
2. UNICEF. Pneumonia in Children Statistics—UNICEF DATA. 2024. Available online: https://data.unicef.org/topic/child-health/pneumonia/ (accessed on 10 March 2025).
3. Fawole, O.A.; Kelly, M.S.; Steenhoff, A.P.; Feemster, K.A.; Crotty, E.J.; Rattan, M.S.; David, T.; Mazhani, T.; Shah, S.S.; Andronikou, S.; et al. Interpretation of pediatric chest radiographs by non-radiologist clinicians in Botswana using World Health Organization criteria for endpoint pneumonia. *Pediatr. Radiol.* **2020**, *50*, 913–922. [CrossRef]
4. Kim, H.E.; Cosa-Linan, A.; Santhanam, N.; Jannesari, M.; Maros, M.E.; Ganslandt, T. Transfer learning for medical image classification: A literature review. *BMC Med. Imaging* **2022**, *22*, 69. [CrossRef] [PubMed]
5. Cai, L.; Gao, J.; Zhao, D. A review of the application of deep learning in medical image classification and segmentation. *Ann. Transl. Med.* **2020**, *8*, 713. [CrossRef]
6. Rahman, T.; Chowdhury, M.E.; Khandakar, A.; Islam, K.R.; Islam, K.F.; Mahbub, Z.B.; Kadir, M.A.; Kashem, S. Transfer learning with deep convolutional neural network (CNN) for pneumonia detection using chest X-ray. *Appl. Sci.* **2020**, *10*, 3233. [CrossRef]
7. Vrbančič, G.; Podgorelec, V. Efficient ensemble for image-based identification of Pneumonia utilizing deep CNN and SGD with warm restarts. *Expert Syst. Appl.* **2022**, *187*, 115834. [CrossRef]
8. Iqbal, A.; Usman, M.; Ahmed, Z. Tuberculosis chest X-ray detection using CNN-based hybrid segmentation and classification approach. *Biomed. Signal Process. Control* **2023**, *84*, 104667. [CrossRef]
9. Vrbačič, G.; Pečnik, Š.; Podgorelec, V. Hyper-parameter optimization of convolutional neural networks for classifying COVID-19 X-ray images. *Comput. Sci. Inf. Syst.* **2022**, *19*, 327–352. [CrossRef]
10. Sejuti, Z.A.; Islam, M.S. A hybrid CNN–KNN approach for identification of COVID-19 with 5-fold cross validation. *Sens. Int.* **2023**, *4*, 100229. [CrossRef]
11. Luo, X.; Liu, D.; Kong, H.; Huai, S.; Chen, H.; Xiong, G.; Liu, W. Efficient Deep Learning Infrastructures for Embedded Computing Systems: A Comprehensive Survey and Future Envision. *ACM Trans. Embed. Comput. Syst.* **2024**, *24*, 1–100. [CrossRef]
12. Muoka, G.W.; Yi, D.; Ukwuoma, C.C.; Mutale, A.; Ejiyi, C.J.; Mzee, A.K.; Gyarteng, E.S.; Alqahtani, A.; Al-antari, M.A. A comprehensive review and analysis of deep learning-based medical image adversarial attack and defense. *Mathematics* **2023**, *11*, 4272. [CrossRef]
13. Wang, Z.; Tao, H.; Zhou, H.; Deng, Y.; Zhou, P. A content-style control network with style contrastive learning for underwater image enhancement. *Multimed. Syst.* **2025**, *31*, 60. [CrossRef]
14. Schwartz, R.; Dodge, J.; Smith, N.A.; Etzioni, O. Green ai. *Commun. ACM* **2020**, *63*, 54–63. [CrossRef]
15. He, Y.; Xiao, L. Structured pruning for deep convolutional neural networks: A survey. *IEEE Trans. Pattern Anal. Mach. Intell.* **2023**, *46*, 2900–2919. [CrossRef] [PubMed]

16. Rokh, B.; Azarpeyvand, A.; Khanteymoori, A. A comprehensive survey on model quantization for deep neural networks in image classification. *ACM Trans. Intell. Syst. Technol.* **2023**, *14*, 1–50. [CrossRef]
17. Lin, S.; Ji, R.; Chen, C.; Tao, D.; Luo, J. Holistic cnn compression via low-rank decomposition with knowledge transfer. *IEEE Trans. Pattern Anal. Mach. Intell.* **2018**, *41*, 2889–2905. [CrossRef] [PubMed]
18. Hinton, G.; Vinyals, O.; Dean, J. Distilling the knowledge in a neural network. *arXiv* **2015**. [CrossRef]
19. Singh, S.; Kumar, M.; Kumar, A.; Verma, B.K.; Abhishek, K.; Selvarajan, S. Efficient pneumonia detection using Vision Transformers on chest X-rays. *Sci. Rep.* **2024**, *14*, 2487. [CrossRef]
20. Kabir, M.M.; Mridha, M.; Rahman, A.; Hamid, M.A.; Monowar, M.M. Detection of COVID-19, pneumonia, and tuberculosis from radiographs using AI-driven knowledge distillation. *Heliyon* **2024**, *10*, e26801. [CrossRef]
21. Khan, I.U.; Aslam, N. A deep-learning-based framework for automated diagnosis of COVID-19 using X-ray images. *Information* **2020**, *11*, 419. [CrossRef]
22. Fukuda, T.; Suzuki, M.; Kurata, G.; Thomas, S.; Cui, J.; Ramabhadran, B. Efficient Knowledge Distillation from an Ensemble of Teachers. In Proceedings of the Interspeech, Stockholm, Sweden, 20–24 August 2017; pp. 3697–3701. [CrossRef]
23. Cheng, X.; Zhou, J. LGFA-MTKD: Enhancing Multi-Teacher Knowledge Distillation with Local and Global Frequency Attention. *Information* **2024**, *15*, 735. [CrossRef]
24. Müller, D.; Soto-Rey, I.; Kramer, F. An analysis on ensemble learning optimized medical image classification with deep convolutional neural networks. *IEEE Access* **2022**, *10*, 66467–66480. [CrossRef]
25. Khan, F.; Siva Prasad, B.V.V.; Syed, S.A.; Ashraf, I.; Ramasamy, L.K. An efficient, ensemble-based classification framework for big medical data. *Big Data* **2022**, *10*, 151–160. [CrossRef]
26. Namamula, L.R.; Chaytor, D. Effective ensemble learning approach for large-scale medical data analytics. *Int. J. Syst. Assur. Eng. Manag.* **2024**, *15*, 13–20. [CrossRef]
27. Wang, S.; Yan, Z.; Zhang, D.; Wei, H.; Li, Z.; Li, R. Prototype knowledge distillation for medical segmentation with missing modality. In Proceedings of the ICASSP 2023—2023 IEEE International Conference on Acoustics, Speech and Signal Processing (ICASSP), Rhodes Island, Greece, 4–10 June 2023; pp. 1–5. [CrossRef]
28. Asham, M.A.; Al-Shargabi, A.A.; Al-Sabri, R.; Meftah, I. A lightweight deep learning model with knowledge distillation for pulmonary diseases detection in chest X-rays. *Multimed. Tools Appl.* **2024**, *84*, 14885–14913. [CrossRef]
29. Galih, B.S.N.; Novamizanti, L.; Akhyar, F. Identification of Lung Disease via X-Ray Images Using Knowledge Distillation and Vision Transformer. In Proceedings of the 2024 International Conference on Intelligent Cybernetics Technology & Applications (ICICyTA), Bali, Indonesia, 17–19 December 2024; pp. 1234–1238. [CrossRef]
30. Ghosh, R. Determining top fully connected layer's hidden neuron count for transfer learning, using knowledge distillation: A case study on chest X-ray classification of pneumonia and COVID-19. *J. Digit. Imaging* **2021**, *34*, 1349–1358. [CrossRef]
31. Bi, Y.; Che, E.; Chen, Y.; He, Y.; Qu, J. Multi-Prototype Embedding Refinement for Semi-Supervised Medical Image Segmentation. *arXiv* **2025**. [CrossRef]
32. Li, G.; Huang, C.; Zhou, X.; Hu, L.; Wu, J.; Zhang, H. DOKD-MFR: Integrating Dual Online Knowledge Distillation with Multi-scale Feature Refinement for pneumonia image recognition. *Biomed. Signal Process. Control* **2025**, *110*, 108047. [CrossRef]
33. Romero, A.; Ballas, N.; Kahou, S.E.; Chassang, A.; Gatta, C.; Bengio, Y. Fitnets: Hints for thin deep nets. *arXiv* **2014**. [CrossRef]
34. You, S.; Xu, C.; Xu, C.; Tao, D. Learning from multiple teacher networks. In Proceedings of the 23rd ACM SIGKDD International Conference on Knowledge Discovery and Data Mining, Halifax, NS, Canada, 13–17 August 2017; pp. 1285–1294. [CrossRef]
35. Gou, J.; Yu, B.; Maybank, S.J.; Tao, D. Knowledge distillation: A survey. *Int. J. Comput. Vis.* **2021**, *129*, 1789–1819. [CrossRef]
36. Loshchilov, I.; Hutter, F. Sgdr: Stochastic gradient descent with warm restarts. *arXiv* **2016**. [CrossRef]
37. Stephen, O.; Sain, M.; Maduh, U.J.; Jeong, D.U. An efficient deep learning approach to pneumonia classification in healthcare. *J. Healthc. Eng.* **2019**, *2019*, 4180949. [CrossRef]
38. Kermany, D. Labeled optical coherence tomography (oct) and chest x-ray images for classification. *Mendeley Data* **2018**. [CrossRef]
39. Kermany, D.S.; Goldbaum, M.; Cai, W.; Valentim, C.C.; Liang, H.; Baxter, S.L.; McKeown, A.; Yang, G.; Wu, X.; Yan, F.; et al. Identifying medical diagnoses and treatable diseases by image-based deep learning. *Cell* **2018**, *172*, 1122–1131. [CrossRef]
40. Demšar, J. Statistical comparisons of classifiers over multiple data sets. *J. Mach. Learn. Res.* **2006**, *7*, 1–30.
41. Van Rijsbergen, C.J. *Information Retrieval*, 2nd ed.; Butterworth-Heinemann: Newton, MA, USA, 1979.
42. Ballabio, D.; Grisoni, F.; Todeschini, R. Multivariate comparison of classification performance measures. *Chemom. Intell. Lab. Syst.* **2018**, *174*, 33–44. [CrossRef]
43. Cohen, J. A coefficient of agreement for nominal scales. *Educ. Psychol. Meas.* **1960**, *20*, 37–46. [CrossRef]
44. Landis, J.R.; Koch, G.G. The measurement of observer agreement for categorical data. *Biometrics* **1977**, *33*, 159–174. [CrossRef]
45. Fukushima, K. Visual feature extraction by a multilayered network of analog threshold elements. *IEEE Trans. Syst. Sci. Cybern.* **1969**, *5*, 322–333. [CrossRef]

46. Glorot, X.; Bengio, Y. Understanding the difficulty of training deep feedforward neural networks. In Proceedings of the Thirteenth International Conference on Artificial Intelligence and Statistics. JMLR Workshop and Conference Proceedings, Sardinia, Italy, 13–15 May 2010; pp. 249–256.
47. Li, Z.; Li, X.; Yang, L.; Zhao, B.; Song, R.; Luo, L.; Li, J.; Yang, J. Curriculum temperature for knowledge distillation. In Proceedings of the AAAI Conference on Artificial Intelligence, Washington, DC, USA, 7–14 February 2023; Volume 37, pp. 1504–1512. [CrossRef]
48. Chi, Z.; Zheng, T.; Li, H.; Yang, Z.; Wu, B.; Lin, B.; Cai, D. Normkd: Normalized logits for knowledge distillation. *arXiv* **2023**. [CrossRef]
49. Kundu, R.; Das, R.; Geem, Z.W.; Han, G.T.; Sarkar, R. Pneumonia detection in chest X-ray images using an ensemble of deep learning models. *PLoS ONE* **2021**, *16*, e0256630. [CrossRef]

electronics

MDPI

Article

Video Compression Using Hybrid Neural Representation with High-Frequency Spectrum Analysis

Jian Hua Zhao *, Xue Jun Li * and Peter Han Joo Chong

Department of Electrical and Electronic Engineering, Auckland University of Technology, Auckland 1010, New Zealand; peter.chong@aut.ac.nz

* Correspondence: jianhua.zhao@autuni.ac.nz (J.H.Z.); xuejun.li@aut.ac.nz (X.J.L.); Tel.: +64-9-921-9999 (X.J.L.)

Abstract

Recent advancements in implicit neural representations have shown substantial promise in various domains, particularly in video compression and reconstruction, due to their rapid decoding speed and high adaptability. Building upon the state-of-the-art Neural Representations for Videos, the Expedite Neural Representation for Videos and Hybrid Neural Representation for Videos primarily enhance performance by optimizing and expanding the embedded input of the Neural Representations for Videos network. However, the core module in Neural Representations for Videos network, responsible for video reconstruction, has garnered comparatively less attention. This paper introduces a novel High-frequency Spectrum Hybrid Network, which leverages high-frequency information from the frequency domain to generate detailed image reconstructions. The central component of this approach is the High-frequency Spectrum Hybrid Network block, an innovative extension of the module in Neural Representations for Videos network, which integrates the High-frequency Spectrum Convolution Module into the original framework. The high-frequency spectrum convolution module emphasizes the extraction of high-frequency features through a frequency domain attention mechanism, significantly enhancing both performance and the recovery of local details in video images. As an enhanced module in the Neural Representations for Videos network, it demonstrates exceptional adaptability and versatility, enabling seamless integration into a wide range of existing Neural Representations for Videos network architectures without requiring substantial modifications to achieve improved results. In addition, this work introduces the High-frequency Spectrum loss function and the Multi-scale Feature Reuse Path to further mitigate the issue of blurriness caused by the loss of high-frequency details during image generation. Experimental evaluations confirm that the proposed High-frequency Spectrum Hybrid Network surpasses the performance of the Neural Representations for Videos, the Expedite Neural Representation for Videos, and the Hybrid Neural Representation for Videos, achieving improvements of +5.75 dB, +4.53 dB, and +1.05 dB in peak signal-to-noise ratio, respectively.

Keywords: video compression; artificial intelligence; implicit neural representation; high-frequency spectrum

1. Introduction

Global internet traffic has been experiencing a steady growth rate of approximately 22% annually, currently surpassing 33 exabytes per day [1]. This rapid increase is largely driven by the rising demand for high-definition video across various applications, such as

https://doi.org/10.3390/electronics14132574

video conferencing, security surveillance, medical care, agriculture, forestry, and online video streaming platforms like YouTube and Netflix. Despite advancements in hardware storage and network transmission technologies, the sheer size of uncompressed raw video files continues to pose significant challenges in terms of storage capacity and bandwidth requirements. As a result, video compression has emerged as a critical area of research, focused on developing methods that reduce the volume of video data while preserving as much visual quality as possible after reconstruction.

Traditionally, video encoding has relied on techniques such as the discrete cosine transform (DCT) [2] and predictive coding across spatial and temporal domains. However, deep learning-based video compression algorithms offer considerable advantages, particularly in terms of end-to-end optimization, improved quality retention, and enhanced compression ratios. Prominent works in this domain include learning-based modules for adapting conventional codecs [3–8] and end-to-end video compression models [9–16]. Moreover, Neural Representations for Video (NeRV), models [17–20], which are based on implicit neural representations, have garnered widespread attention due to their simplicity, high adaptability, and exceptionally fast decoding speeds. Notable recent advancements include the Expedite Neural Representation for Videos (E-NeRV) [18] and Hybrid Neural Representation for Videos (HNeRV) [19], which offer significant improvements in the efficient reconstruction of video frames with superior quality compared to the original NeRV model [17].

Although E-NeRV [18] and HNeRV [19] have achieved promising results, research on NeRV still faces several limitations and challenges.

Firstly, while both E-NeRV [18] and HNeRV [19] achieve marginal improvements by adjusting the number of channels in NeRV blocks, their superior performance primarily arises from the optimization of the input embeddings in the NeRV network. In [17], Chen et al. used frame indices, which are simple scalar values, as temporal input embeddings. E-NeRV [18] further enhanced this approach by incorporating spatial coordinates as spatial embeddings. HNeRV [19] enriches the spatial embeddings by extracting feature maps from the ground-truth video images, employing ConvNeXt [21] (a regular Convolutional Neural Network (CNN)) as an encoder. While improving the quality of input embeddings is a highly effective strategy for enhancing model performance, increasing the efficiency of the NeRV block itself remains a critical concern.

Secondly, the current best-performing model, HNeRV [19], exhibits limitations in generating visually coherent images, leading to the loss of texture and edges. Figure 1 provides an illustrative example. HNeRV [19] fails to capture the edge details of the nose and mouth when reconstructing a character's face, and introduces noise points that affect color uniformity across the face. We hypothesize that the narrow receptive field and absence of high-frequency information are the primary causes of this phenomenon. First, small convolutional kernels are limited in the range of features they can capture, which can lead to incorrect pixel values being generated by the network. Although increasing kernel size effectively expands the receptive field and improves performance, it also results in a significant increase in network parameters, which grows quadratically. Second, convolution is a weighted summation operation that tends to produce smooth, low-frequency information over broad regions rather than high-frequency signals with sharp local variations. This limitation hinders the network's ability to accurately reconstruct object edges and texture details. Although high-frequency details may be prioritized under a constrained compression ratio, the human visual system remains highly sensitive to such details, such as textures and edges. Loss of these elements causes videos to appear blurred, which is especially noticeable in scenes requiring fine detail, such as satellite imagery, medical videos, and game streaming.

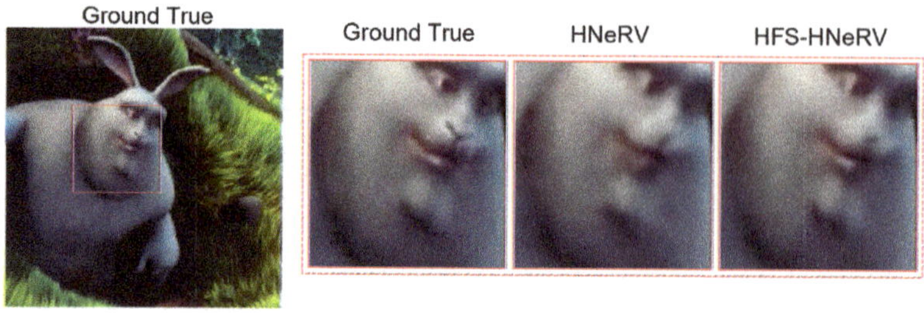

Figure 1. An example of missing texture and edges.

In light of these challenges, our research is motivated by the following considerations:

- Existing NeRV-type methods primarily focus on incorporating multimodal or enhanced input data to improve video reconstruction, rather than enhancing the intrinsic performance of the network modules themselves. Although modifying the input data is less likely to introduce fluctuations in model parameters to affect the compression rate, it remains essential to design a new core module to enhance the intrinsic performance of the network.
- Although current NeRV-type approaches can learn implicit representations of video frames, they lack dedicated modeling of high-frequency information, resulting in insufficient detail reconstruction. Therefore, a novel fundamental module capable of reconstructing high-frequency content is required.

Based on the aforementioned motivations, we propose an innovative approach called High-frequency Spectrum Hybrid Neural Representation for Video (HFS-HNeRV). Figure 2 illustrates the primary architecture and workflow of HFS-HNeRV. To address the first challenge, we introduce the HFS-HNeRV block, which enhances the basic NeRV module by incorporating a high-frequency spectrum convolution module (HFSCM). HFSCM includes a high-spectral attention mechanism based on the channel–spatial attention structure of CBAM [22] and GAM [23], along with an additional convolutional layer. Channel attention reweights each channel in the feature map by integrating the information of all channels for each pixel, encouraging the model to focus on channels that are most critical to overall semantics. Spatial attention allows the model to highlight regions that are vital to global semantics along the spatial dimension. Moreover, since the channel dimension can be greatly reduced in spatial attention, a larger receptive field (such as a large convolution kernel) can be applied without substantially increasing the number of parameters. This design allows the model to integrate a wider range of local contextual information with only a minimal increase in parameter count, thereby considering more global semantic information when redistributing weights. After the attention module accentuates the important feature information, the subsequent convolutional layers not only expand the receptive field but also further fuse these attention-weighted features to generate richer and higher-quality feature representations. This modification significantly improves video frame reconstruction while maintaining a stable parameter count. The HFS-HNeRV block also exhibits excellent compatibility and generalizability, making it easily integrable into a wide range of NeRV networks without necessitating significant changes to the original architecture.

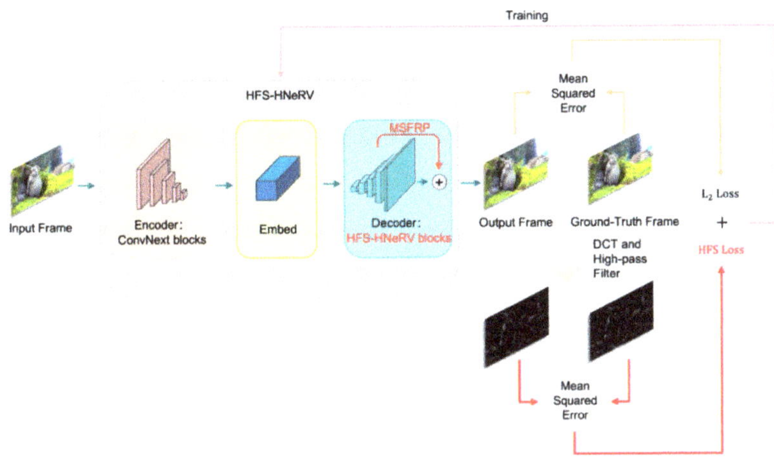

Figure 2. Our proposed HFS-HNeRV enables the model to focus on the details of edges and textures in the image by introducing the HFS attention mechanism, HFS loss, and multi-scale feature reuse.

To address the second challenge, the proposed HFSCM includes a novel high-frequency enhancement attention mechanism, which leverages the Haar wavelet transform to strengthen high-frequency components. This technique effectively captures the high-frequency features within the feature map, facilitating the restoration of edge details and textures, thereby enhancing the overall image quality. Additionally, the attention mechanism enables the module to better extract and fuse global information, partially mitigating the issue of insufficient receptive fields. Furthermore, HFSCM incorporates a dual convolutional layer structure, which further refines the features enhanced by the high-frequency spectrum attention mechanism (HFSAM), resulting in richer feature representations.

We also propose a high-frequency spectrum loss function to aid in the training of the model. This loss function extracts high-frequency signals from both the predicted and ground-truth images via Fourier transform and high-pass filters and then computes the mean square error (MSE) between them. The high-frequency spectrum (HFS) loss is integrated into the overall loss function alongside the MSE loss, with a hyperparameter introduced to adjust its weight relative to the total error. This adjustment allows the model to reduce the disproportionate influence of low-frequency components, thereby encouraging greater focus on generating finer image details, such as edges and textures.

Finally, inspired by classical image and video super-resolution networks, we introduce several modifications to the decoder's structure. Specifically, we incorporate a multi-scale feature reuse path (MSFRP), which enriches the final output feature representations by fusing feature maps from different scale layers.

In summary, our work makes the following contributions:

- We propose a novel NeRV module, HFS-HNeRV block, which can be easily integrated into various NeRV networks without substantial modifications to the network architecture.
- We introduce a new loss function specifically designed for high-frequency information generation, enhancing the model's capacity to reconstruct image details.
- We optimize the NeRV network design by incorporating MSFRP into the current NeRV framework.

2. Related Works

2.1. Implicit Neural Representations

Implicit neural representations [24], often applied in image [25,26] or scene reconstruction [27,28], are techniques that utilize neural networks to represent geometric shapes or environments. For example, Neural Radiance Fields (NeRFs) [28] can reconstruct a 3D scene using provided 3D coordinates. In NeRV [17], the entire video or image sequence is implicitly represented by a neural network instead of being stored in the traditional form of frame data. The network learns the mapping from input (such as timestamps or spatial coordinates) to output (image frames) so that it can quickly decode the video frames based on frame indices. Unlike explicit representations, implicit representations store most of the information in the network's parameters, which significantly reduces storage requirements. However, implicit representations come with several drawbacks. They demand substantial resources during the training process—such as extensive training time, large datasets, and significant computational power—which makes their application in real-time scenarios challenging. Additionally, the complexity of these models can lead to instability during training.

2.2. Video Compression

Video compression seeks to reduce the size of video data while preserving as much quality as possible. Conventional video compression standards, such as H.264 [29] and H.265 [30], have been widely used across many fields. In the past decade, deep learning has introduced new possibilities for advancements in video compression techniques. Traditional methods typically involve four core technologies: predictive coding, transform coding, entropy coding, and motion compensation. Learning-based video compression approaches primarily focus on replacing or enhancing these key components [3–8]. Additionally, Refs. [9–13] have explored end-to-end video compression models. However, a novel approach called Neural Representations for Videos (NeRV) [17] has been introduced, which uses neural networks to implicitly represent video by overfitting the network to memorize video frames. By compressing the neural network, NeRV achieves the goal of video compression.

2.3. Video Super-Resolution

Video super-resolution is a technique widely applied in fields such as remote sensing and telemedicine to enhance both the resolution and visual clarity of video frames. At its core, it primarily involves upsampling methods, including interpolation, pixel shuffle, and deconvolution. The deep learning-based approaches to video super-resolution can be broadly classified into single-frame [31–35] and multi-frame methods [36–41]. Given that video is essentially a sequence of consecutive images forming a dynamic visual record, single-frame super-resolution networks are largely extensions of image super-resolution techniques. Prominent examples include the Super-Resolution Convolutional Neural Network (SRCNN) [31], Very Deep Super-Resolution (VDSR) [32], and the Super-Resolution Generative Adversarial Network (SRGAN) [35]. In contrast, multi-frame super-resolution networks exploit the inter-frame information present in videos, and these methods can be further subdivided into those that align video frames and unaligned methods. Approaches based on optical flow estimation [38,39] and deformable convolution [40,41] are key examples of the former, whereas those employing 3D convolution [42,43] and recurrent convolutional neural networks [44,45] exemplify the latter. The primary objective of video super-resolution is to upsample low-resolution videos into high-resolution counterparts. This procedure bears similarities to how NeRV [17] incrementally upsamples an embedding into a complete video image, thus creating some overlap in the methodologies used in these two areas. Low-quality videos can be considered compressed versions of their high-resolution counterparts. NeRV-like approaches may draw inspiration from video super-resolution techniques, such as more sophisticated network designs (encoder–decoder model and Generative Adversarial Network (GAN) [46]) and enhanced upsampling mechanisms (such as bilinear interpolation and Sub-pixel Convolution). Nevertheless, since the parameter count in NeRV models directly influences the compression ratio, any method that substantially increases model complexity should be applied judiciously. For more detailed comparisons of video super-resolution models, please refer to [47–49].

2.4. Frequency Domain Image Analysis

Although images have traditionally been processed in the spatial domain for computer vision tasks, recent studies [50,51] have demonstrated that frequency domain analysis offers distinct advantages, particularly in image compression. The HFSAM proposed in this study differs from these prior works in several key aspects.

The core concept of LC-FDNet [50] is adaptive frequency decomposition (AFD), which extracts low-frequency (LF) and high-frequency (HF) latents from input images, followed by separate compression. Specifically, the high frequency compressor retains the residual information between the original image and the high-frequency prediction generated by the network, leveraging entropy coding for compression. The principal objective of this approach is to extract and compress the low- and high-frequency components separately, thereby mitigating information loss during the compression process.

DBPN [51] separates the low- and high-frequency latents by using average pooling. These latents are subsequently processed through a dual-layer attention mechanism to generate an attention map. In the process of obtaining the final output latent, they recall the low frequency and high frequency latents to emphasize these fine-grained features again. In our approach, we integrate the Haar wavelet transform into the spatial attention component to extract high-frequency information, further weighting the LH, HL, and HH components using hyperparameters. This weighting strategy ensures that these high-frequency details receive emphasis in the generated attention map.

Similarly, the Frequency-Aware Transformer [52] introduces the frequency-decomposed window attention (FDWA) mechanism to achieve frequency decomposition, grounded in the theoretical foundation that small local window attention can effectively capture high-frequency information, as discussed by [53]. This effect closely resembles that of the Haar wavelet transform, which also produces the LL, LH, HL and HH maps. Fundamentally, both methods serve to decompose images into their low- and high-frequency components. Structurally, FDWA integrates self-attention with window attention, making it particularly well suited for transformer architectures. In contrast, Convolutional Neural Networks (CNNs) can achieve a similar effect more efficiently by directly applying the Haar wavelet transform for frequency decomposition and integrating spatial and channel attention mechanisms to enhance the representation of edges and texture details.

3. Proposed Method

Figure 3a,b show the overall structure of the HFS-HNeRV network. In Section 3.1, we will explain the structure and function of the key parts in the HFS-HNeRV block. Section 3.2 is an introduction to MSFRP. Finally, the HFS loss function is described in Section 3.3.

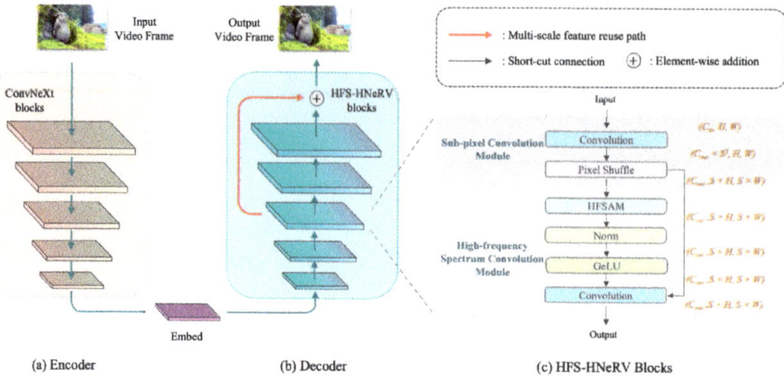

Figure 3. The structure of HFS-HNeRV. (**a**) Encoder: we employ ConvNeXt as the encoder to downsample the input video frames into smaller embeddings. (**b**) Decoder: we employ the HFS-HNeRV blocks to build the decoder for upsampled images and add MSFRP to reuse the feature maps of the third layer. (**c**) HFS-HNeRV blocks: In the HFS-HNeRV blocks, we introduce a residual structure that, through dual convolutional layers, further enriches the generated features by leveraging the attention maps produced by HFSAM.

3.1. HFS-HNeRV Block

As can be seen in Figure 3c, HFS-HNeRV block is composed of a sub-pixel convolution module and HFSCM.

3.1.1. Sub-Pixel Convolution Module

For the first half of the HFS-HNeRV block, we retain the sub-pixel convolution (SPC) module. It has been employed as a basic module in previous NeRV-type works. Detailed information can be found in [33]. Here, we only give a brief introduction.

The SPC module integrates a convolutional layer with a pixel shuffle layer. In the convolutional process, as shown in Figure 3c, the input feature map adheres to the dimensions $X \in \mathbb{R}^{H\times W\times C}$, while the output feature map is represented as $Y \in \mathbb{R}^{H\times W\times S^2C}$. This dimensionality enhancement can be interpreted as the network layer extracting features, which subsequently serve as references for generating more contextually relevant features. A reduction in the number of input or output channels will significantly degrade the performance of this network layer. Although increasing the size of the convolutional kernel can improve network efficiency, it also results in a considerable increase in the number of model parameters. Therefore, to ensure parameter stability, the original kernel size and channel configuration have been maintained.

3.1.2. High-Frequency Spectrum Convolution Module

HFSCM is primarily composed of two components: a high-frequency spectrum attention mechanism and an additional convolutional layer. As depicted in Figure 3c, the entire module adopts a residual block structure.

The high-frequency spectrum attention mechanism (HFSAM) consists of two key parts: the channel attention layer and the frequency domain spatial attention layer. The channel attention layer employs a dual multi-layer perceptron structure to produce a channel attention map by extracting global information from the feature vectors at each $H \times W$ position within the feature map $\mathbf{F}_1$, as demonstrated in Figure 4a. This process can be expressed by the following formula:

$$\mathbf{C}_{Atten} = \sigma(MLP(GeLU(MLP(\mathbf{F}_1)))) \quad (1)$$

$$\mathbf{F}_2 = (\mathbf{F}_1 \otimes \mathbf{C}_{Atten}) + \mathbf{F}_1 \tag{2}$$

where σ denotes the sigmoid function. $GeLU$ represents the GeLU activation function. $\otimes$ represents the element-wise multiplication. MLP represents the multi-layer perceptron. $Conv$ represents a convolutional layer.

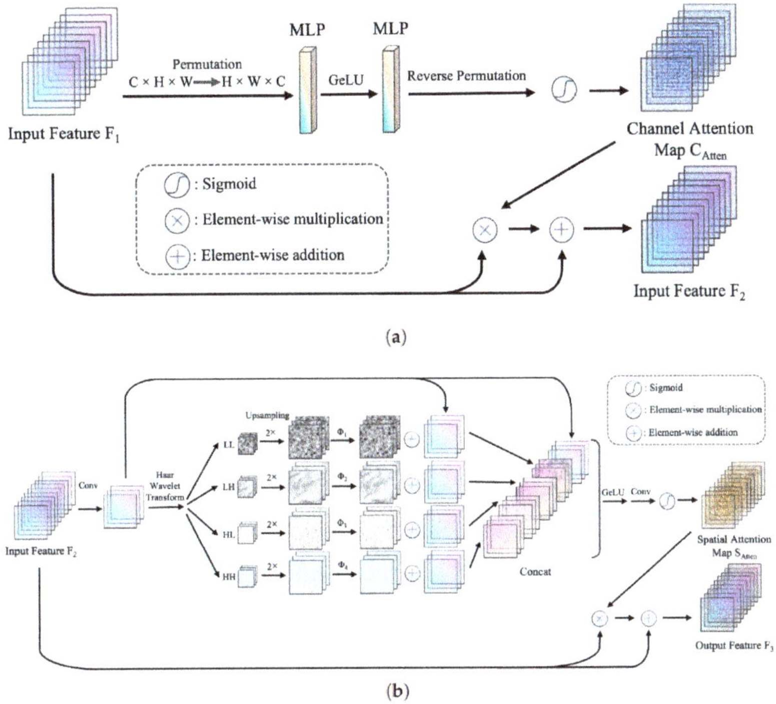

Figure 4. (**a**) Channel Attention: This part employs dual multi-layer perceptron to integrate the intra-channel contextual information of the input features, computing the output feature map through a residual structure. (**b**) Spatial Attention: We enhance high-frequency information by incorporating Haar wavelet transform into the spatial attention mechanism. Note that 2× symbolizes the two-fold upsampling operation.

Before introducing the frequency domain spatial attention layer, we briefly describe the processing of the Haar wavelet transform on the feature map. The Haar wavelet basis functions are defined by the scaling function $\phi(t)$ and the wavelet function $\psi(t)$:

$$\phi(t) = \begin{cases} 1, & 0 \le t < 1 \\ 0, & \text{otherwise} \end{cases} \tag{3}$$

$$\psi(t) = \begin{cases} 1, & 0 \le t < \frac{1}{2} \\ -1, & \frac{1}{2} \le t < 1 \\ 0, & \text{otherwise} \end{cases} \tag{4}$$

For a one-dimensional signal x of length N, the corresponding low- and high-frequency operators are denoted A_k and D_k, respectively:

$$A_k = \frac{x_{2k} + x_{2k+1}}{\sqrt{2}} \tag{5}$$

$$D_k = \frac{x_{2k} - x_{2k+1}}{\sqrt{2}} \tag{6}$$

where $k \in \{0, 1, \dots, \frac{N}{2} - 1\}$.

Since the Haar wavelet transform is applied to the feature map on a channel-by-channel basis, only a two-dimensional Haar wavelet transform is required. First, the operator transforms each row of the feature map to obtain a new matrix $\mathbf{F}'$:

$$\mathbf{F}' = \begin{bmatrix} A_{0,0} & A_{0,1} & \dots & A_{0,W/2} & D_{0,0} & D_{0,1} & \dots & D_{0,W/2} \\ A_{1,0} & A_{1,1} & \dots & A_{1,W/2} & D_{1,0} & D_{1,1} & \dots & D_{1,W/2} \\ \vdots & \vdots & \ddots & \vdots & \vdots & \vdots & \ddots & \vdots \\ A_{H,0} & A_{H,1} & \dots & A_{H,W/2} & D_{H,0} & D_{H,1} & \dots & D_{H,W/2} \end{bmatrix} \tag{7}$$

Next, the columns of $\mathbf{F}'$ are transformed to yield the matrix $\mathbf{F}_{Haar}$:

$$\mathbf{F}_{Haar} = \begin{bmatrix} LL_{0,0} & LL_{0,1} & \dots & LL_{0,W/2} & LH_{0,0} & LH_{0,1} & \dots & LH_{0,W/2} \\ LL_{1,0} & LL_{1,1} & \dots & LL_{1,W/2} & LH_{1,0} & LH_{1,1} & \dots & LH_{1,W/2} \\ \vdots & \vdots & \ddots & \vdots & \vdots & \vdots & \ddots & \vdots \\ LL_{H/2,0} & LL_{H/2,1} & \dots & LL_{H/2,W/2} & LH_{H/2,0} & LH_{H/2,1} & \dots & LH_{H/2,W/2} \\ HL_{0,0} & HL_{0,1} & \dots & HL_{0,W/2} & HH_{0,0} & HH_{0,1} & \dots & HH_{0,W/2} \\ HL_{1,0} & HL_{1,1} & \dots & HL_{1,W/2} & HH_{1,0} & HH_{1,1} & \dots & HH_{1,W/2} \\ \vdots & \vdots & \ddots & \vdots & \vdots & \vdots & \ddots & \vdots \\ HL_{H/2,0} & HL_{H/2,1} & \dots & HL_{H/2,W/2} & HH_{H/2,0} & HH_{H/2,1} & \dots & HH_{H/2,W/2} \end{bmatrix} \tag{8}$$

Finally, the matrix $\mathbf{F}_{Haar}$ is partitioned into four sub-regions:

$$\mathbf{F}_{Haar} = \begin{bmatrix} LL & LH \\ HL & HH \end{bmatrix} \tag{9}$$

where LL denotes the low–low subband, representing the approximation coefficients after applying low-pass filtering in both horizontal and vertical directions. LH represents the low–high subband, containing vertical detail coefficients obtained by low-pass filtering horizontally and high-pass filtering vertically. HL represents the high–low subband, containing horizontal detail coefficients obtained by high-pass filtering horizontally and low-pass filtering vertically. HH denotes the high–high subband, capturing diagonal detail coefficients after applying high-pass filtering in both horizontal and vertical directions. More detailed information about the Haar wavelet transform can be found in [54].

In the frequency domain spatial attention layer, as depicted in Figure 4b, the initial convolutional layer is designed to reduce the number of channels in the input feature map $\mathbf{F}_2$. This reduction primarily aims to minimize the number of parameters in the attention layer, ensuring computational efficiency. Following this, the feature map undergoes decomposition into various frequency component sub-maps through the Haar wavelet transform, producing the low frequency–low frequency (LL) map, low frequency–high frequency (LH) map, high frequency–low frequency (HL) map, and high frequency–high frequency (HH) map. After decomposition, the sub-maps are upsampled to match the original feature map's dimensions. Each of these four sub-maps is then multiplied by a set of distinct enhancement weights, followed by element-wise addition with the original input feature map. These four enhanced sub-maps are concatenated with the input feature map, forming an enriched feature representation. The concatenated feature map is subsequently processed through a sequence of layers, including normalization, activation, convolution, and sigmoid functions, resulting in the generation of the spatial attention map $\mathbf{S}_{Atten}$. The incorporation of the Haar wavelet transform enables the analysis of frequency domain information, allowing the HFSCM to capture high-frequency features more effectively. This leads to the restoration of edge details and textures within the image, thereby improving the overall quality of image generation. Additionally, the use of the attention mechanism strengthens the module's ability to extract and integrate global information, partially alleviating the issue of insufficient receptive field. The calculation process for spatial attention is described as follows:

$$\mathbf{F}_{LL}, \mathbf{F}_{HL}, \mathbf{F}_{LH}, \mathbf{F}_{HH} = Up(DWT_{Haar}(Conv(\mathbf{F}_2))) \tag{10}$$

$$\mathbf{F}_{LL2} = \Phi_1 \mathbf{F}_{LL} + \mathbf{F}_2 \tag{11}$$

$$\mathbf{F}_{HL2} = \Phi_2 \mathbf{F}_{HL} + \mathbf{F}_2 \tag{12}$$

$$\mathbf{F}_{LH2} = \Phi_3 \mathbf{F}_{LH} + \mathbf{F}_2 \tag{13}$$

$$\mathbf{F}_{HH2} = \Phi_4 \mathbf{F}_{HH} + \mathbf{F}_2 \tag{14}$$

$$\mathbf{S}_{Atten} = \sigma(Conv(GeLU(Concat(\mathbf{F}_2, \mathbf{F}_{LL2}, \mathbf{F}_{HL2}, \mathbf{F}_{LH2}, \mathbf{F}_{HH2})))) \tag{15}$$

$$\mathbf{F}_3 = (\mathbf{F}_2 \otimes \mathbf{S}_{Atten}) + \mathbf{F}_2 \tag{16}$$

where Up denotes the bilinear interpolation operation, and DWT_{Haar} represents the Haar wavelet transform. Φ represents the enhancement factor of the frequency maps. $\mathbf{F}_{LL}$, $\mathbf{F}_{HL}$, $\mathbf{F}_{LH}$, and $\mathbf{F}_{HH}$ represent the feature maps for the LL, HL, LH and HH sub-bands, respectively. $Concat$ represents the concatenation operation that merges multiple tensors.

In addition, we introduced extra convolutional layers following the HFSAM (as shown in Figure 3c) to allow the network to better focus on and exploit the high-frequency features enhanced by the HFSAM. The additional convolutional layers expand the receptive field, thereby enhancing the model's ability to represent intricate high-frequency details. The shortcut connection contributes to the overall stability of the module during training to avoid the problem of gradient disappearance. The following formula can be used to express how the feature map is calculated:

$$\mathbf{F}_{out} = Conv(GeLU(HFS_{Atten}(\mathbf{F}_1))) \oplus \mathbf{F}_1 \tag{17}$$

where $\oplus$ denotes the element-wise addition.

3.2. Multi-Scale Feature Reuse Path

MSFRP, whose structure is shown in Figure 5, enables the model to capture more information at different scales and further enhances the model's expressiveness. In the NeRV-based network, avoiding growth of the number of parameters is an essential prerequisite. Therefore, we decide to upsample the feature map produced by the model's third-to-last layer via the bilinear interpolation method to the same size as the final output feature map of the model. Specifically, the feature maps from $L3$ layers (160×320) are first reduced to the channels at 3 through a 1×1 convolutional layer. Then, they are resized to a common spatial resolution (640×1280) via bilinear interpolation. Finally, the aligned feature maps are fused by element-wise addition. Bilinear interpolation is a technique that involves two linear interpolations in a two-dimensional plane grid cell. Assuming that the coordinates of the four corners of the grid cell are $f(0,0)$, $f(1,0)$, $f(0,1)$ and $f(1,1)$, the bilinear interpolation polynomial formula can be expressed as

$$f(x,y) = \sum_{i=0}^{1}\sum_{j=0}^{1} a_{ij}x^i y^j = a_{00} + a_{10}x + a_{01}y + a_{11}xy \tag{18}$$

$$
\begin{aligned}
a_{00} &= f(0,0), \\
a_{10} &= f(1,0) - f(0,0), \\
a_{01} &= f(0,1) - f(0,0) \\
a_{11} &= f(1,1) + f(0,0) - (f(1,0) + f(0,1))
\end{aligned}
\tag{19}
$$

Detailed information on bilinear interpolation can be found in [55].

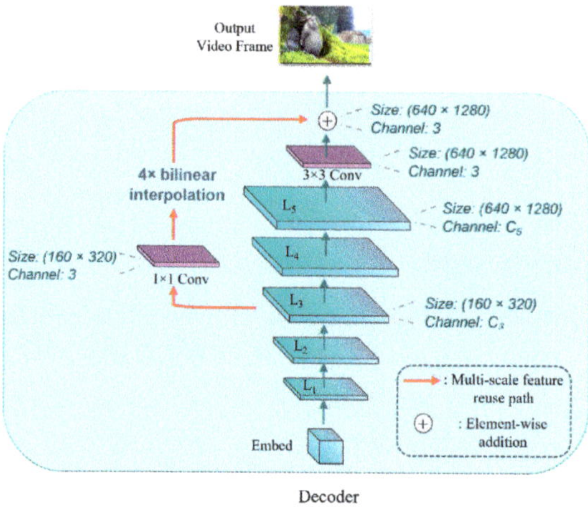

Figure 5. The structure of MSFRP.

3.3. High-Frequency Spectrum Loss

The MSE loss function is widely used in various downstream tasks within computer vision. To further direct the model's focus towards high-frequency features in images, we introduce the HFS loss, which is based on the Fourier transform and high-pass filters, and incorporate it into the total loss function.

Specifically, we first transform both the predicted and ground-truth images into the frequency domain by employing the 2D discrete Fourier transform (DFT), implemented via PyTorch's torch.fft.fft2. The zero-frequency component is shifted to the center of the spectrum to facilitate the application of a high-pass filter.

The high-pass filter is constructed as a binary circular mask that suppresses low-frequency components. Specifically, for a frequency spectrum of size $H \times W$, we set a square region of size $(2m)^2$, centered at $(H/2, W/2)$, to zero. Here, m is a tunable cutoff parameter controlling the frequency threshold. The mask is broadcasted across batch and channel dimensions to match the shape of the input tensors.

After masking, we apply an amplification factor g to the remaining high-frequency components to emphasize fine-grained details such as edges and textures. Then, the filtered and enhanced frequency spectra are transformed back to the spatial domain by using the inverse 2D DFT. The HFS loss is defined as the mean square error between the spatial domain reconstructions derived from the high-frequency components of the predicted and ground-truth images.

The DFT and inverse DFT of a two-dimensional image can be represented as follows:

$$
F(u,v) = \frac{1}{HW} \sum_{x=0}^{H-1} \sum_{y=0}^{W-1} f(x,y) e^{-j2\pi\left(\frac{ux}{H} + \frac{vy}{W}\right)} \tag{20}
$$

$$
f(x,y) = \sum_{u=0}^{H-1} \sum_{v=0}^{W-1} F(u,v) e^{j2\pi\left(\frac{ux}{H} + \frac{vy}{W}\right)} \tag{21}
$$

where H and W represent the height and width of the image, respectively. x and y denote the spatial coordinates within the image, and u and v represent frequency coordinates within the spectrum.

Given a video sequence $V = \{v_t\}_{t=1}^{T} \in \mathbb{R}^{T\times H\times W\times 3}$ and a frame index t, we have a predicted image $\mathbf{I}_t^{\text{pred}}$ and a ground-truth image $\mathbf{I}_t^{\text{gt}}$. The formulae for MSE loss and HFS Loss are expressed as

$$\mathcal{L}_{\text{MSE}} = \frac{1}{H\times W\times C}\sum_{i=1}^{H}\sum_{j=1}^{W}\sum_{c=1}^{C}\left(\mathbf{I}_{i,j,c}^{\text{pred}} - \mathbf{I}_{i,j,c}^{\text{gt}}\right)^2 \tag{22}$$

$$\mathcal{L}_{\text{HFS}} = \frac{1}{H\times W\times C}\sum_{i=1}^{H}\sum_{j=1}^{W}\sum_{c=1}^{C}\left(iFFT(g\cdot M\cdot FFT(\mathbf{I}_{i,j,c}^{\text{pred}})) - iFFT(g\cdot M\cdot FFT(\mathbf{I}_{i,j,c}^{\text{gt}}))\right)^2 \tag{23}$$

where H and W represent the height and width of the image, respectively. C represents the number of channels of the image. $\mathbf{I}_{i,j,c}^{\text{pred}}$ and $\mathbf{I}_{i,j,c}^{\text{gt}}$ represent the predicted image and ground-truth image, respectively. FFT, $iFFT$, M and g denote discrete Fourier transform, inverse discrete Fourier transform, binary high-pass filter mask, and high-frequency amplification factor, respectively.

The total loss function can be expressed as

$$\mathcal{L}_{\text{total}} = \mathcal{L}_{\text{MSE}}(\mathbf{I}_t^{\text{pred}}, \mathbf{I}_t^{\text{gt}}) + \beta\mathcal{L}_{\text{HFS}}(\mathbf{I}_t^{\text{pred}}, \mathbf{I}_t^{\text{gt}}) \tag{24}$$

where β is the weight that controls the influence of HFS loss. It is set to 0.12 in the experiments.

4. Experiments

In this section, we will conduct ablation experiments on HFSCM, HFS loss, and MSFRP, and discuss their effectiveness in detail. We will initially go over the experimental setting and dataset that were employed in this study. Following Section 4.1, we will demonstrate the effectiveness of HFSCM, HFS loss, and MSFRP through ablation experiments in Section 4.2. Finally, Section 4.3 will show the performance of HFS-HNeRV in video compression tasks, including performance indicators and comparison of generated images.

4.1. Dataset and Implementation Details

In this paper, we utilize the hybrid representation network architecture of HNeRV. Therefore, most of the experimental settings are consistent with HNeRV. For the dataset, we adopt the Big Buck Bunny (the Big Buck Bunny dataset is available at https://github.com/haochen-rye/HNeRV (accessed on 25 June 2024)), a widely used open-source animated video, which includes 132 frames with resolution of 720 × 1280, cropped to the center with a resolution of 640 × 1280. The selected segments depict an animal coming out of a tree hole and stretching as it stands upright, covering a range of scenes with different levels of motion (from static to moving objects) and texture complexity (such as smooth backgrounds and detailed foliage or grass). To evaluate the model's performance on a publicly available benchmark, we applied center cropping to the UVG dataset (the UVG dataset is available at https://ultravideo.fi/dataset.html (accessed on 28 December 2024)) (7 videos in full HD resolution (1920 × 1080) with a frame rate of 120 frames per second (fps)), resulting in a resolution of 480 × 960. They include fast motion (such as a speedboat, bee wings, and running horse), high-frequency textures (such as long hair, petals and waves), and rich structural information, making it suitable for evaluating the generalization and robustness of video reconstruction models. For performance metrics, we retained the same settings as those in HNeRV [19], specifically the peak-signal-to-noise ratio (PSNR) and multi-scale structural similarity index measure (MS-SSIM). Moreover, we selected multiple regions within the images to conduct a human visual quality comparison. During training, we used the Adam optimizer with $\beta = (0.9, 0.999)$ and a weight decay of 0. Furthermore, we set the learning rate to 0.001 with cosine learning rate decay. Unless otherwise stated, all experimental models are baselined with model size of 1.5 M, training epochs of 300, and bit per pixel (bpp) of 0.109. All experiments were conducted on one laptop-based RTX 3060 GPU. the reported performance results were also measured on this GPU to reflect parallel execution, excluding data loading and preprocessing overhead.

4.2. Ablation Study

In this section, we will present and discuss the relevant ablation experiments of HFSCM, HFS loss, and MSFRP, and explain their related parameter settings.

4.2.1. HFSCM

As shown in Table 1, inserting the attention module after the upsampling layer can significantly enhance model's performance. Furthermore, HFSCM only introduces few parameters since the number of channels is kept low after the upsampling layer. The convolution layer after the attention mechanism can further combine local and global information to enhance the expressive capability of the model. Also, the residual structure not only prevents the gradient vanishing problem but also contributes positively to the performance of the model. The attention mechanism involves the convolution kernel size k in spatial attention. As mentioned earlier, a larger convolution kernel size will have a positive impact on model performance (as shown in Table 2). However, increasing the number of convolution kernels directly results in a growth in model parameters. Therefore, we conducted ablation experiments under conditions where the number of parameters and bit rate were kept at comparable levels (as shown in Table 3), and we then selected $k = 7$ as a trade-off between model complexity and performance. Table 4 shows that the additional convolutional layers indeed have a significant positive impact on the performance of the model.

Table 1. Comparison of module ablation experimental results.

Component	SPC	HFSCM	MSFRP	HFS Loss	PSNR	MS-SSIM
HNeRV	✓	×	×	×	35.57	0.9773
Variant 1	✓	✓	×	×	36.36	0.9806
Variant 2	✓	✓	✓	×	36.38	0.9808
HFS-HNeRV (Ours)	✓	✓	✓	✓	36.62	0.9814

Table 2. Ablation of kernel size k under unconstrained settings (with $r = 5$).

k	PSNR	MS-SSIM	bpp (≈M)	Params (≈)
3	36.33	0.9801	0.103	1.39
5	36.49	0.9809	0.106	1.43
7	36.62	0.9814	0.110	1.49
9	36.69	0.9819	0.115	1.58

Table 3. Ablation of kernel size k under parameter and bitrate constraints (with $r = 5$).

k	PSNR	MS-SSIM	bpp (≈M)	Params (≈)
3	36.57	0.9812	0.110	1.49
5	36.60	0.9813	0.110	1.50
7	36.62	0.9814	0.109	1.49
9	36.47	0.9808	0.109	1.49

Table 4. Ablation of additional convolutional layer in HFSCM.

Module	PSNR	MS-SSIM
HFSCM (sigle convolutional layer)	35.95	0.9785
HFSCM (dual convolutional layer)	36.62	0.9814

4.2.2. MSFRP

As can be seen in Table 1, the performance of variant 2 proves the effectiveness of reusing features of different scales. Considering that deconvolution or pixel shuffle will bring additional parameter burden, we apply the bilinear interpolation method rather than sub-pixel convolution or deconvolution. We consider that the output features of the third-to-last layer not only retain rich original feature information but also have a moderate level of feature abstraction. Upon comparison, it is clear that reusing the features of the third-to-last output layer has the best effect (Table 5). Since reusing the first layer necessitates upsampling by a factor of up to 64×, and the fifth layer serves as the network's final output, the results from these two layers are excluded from Table 5.

Table 5. Ablation of reusing different feature layers.

Layer (Resolution)	Scale	PSNR	MS-SSIM
Layer2 (40 × 80)	16×	36.54	0.9814
Layer3 (160 × 320)	4×	36.62	0.9814
Layer4 (320 × 640)	2×	36.56	0.9813

4.2.3. HFS Loss

HFS loss extracts the high-frequency features of generated images and ground-truth images through Fourier transform and high-pass filters before calculating the error between them. Table 1 demonstrates that the application of HFS loss can significantly boost the performance of the model. Table 6 shows the performance parameters of the model at different training cycles and the convergence of HFS loss. We set the threshold m and enhancement factor g of the high-pass filter to $m \in \{10, 15, 20, 25\}$ and $g \in \{1.0, 2.0, 3.0, 4.0\}$, respectively. The PSNR results are shown in Tables 7 and 8. The optimal hyperparameter settings are found to be $m = 17$ and $g = 3.0$.

Table 6. HFS loss ablation at different epochs.

Epoch	HFS Loss	PSNR
30	9.17×10^{-3}	27.83
120	3.20×10^{-3}	32.08
210	1.95×10^{-3}	35.68
300	1.59×10^{-3}	36.62

Table 7. Threshold m ablation (with $g = 3.0$).

m	PSNR	MS-SSIM
10	36.56	0.9813
15	36.61	0.9814
20	36.62	0.9814
25	36.62	0.9814

Table 8. Enhancement factor g ablation (with $m = 17$).

g	PSNR	MS-SSIM
1.0	36.45	0.9810
2.0	36.55	0.9813
3.0	36.62	0.9814
4.0	36.62	0.9814

4.3. Main Results

4.3.1. Video Regression

In comparison to existing methods, our approach demonstrates improvements in both model performance metrics and human visual perception. All experiments were conducted using the Big Buck Bunny dataset. As shown in Table 9, with a model size of 1.5 M, HFS-HNeRV outperforms NeRV, E-NeRV, and HNeRV across various training epochs. Furthermore, when the training epochs are set to 300, HFS-HNeRV continues to deliver superior performance with 1.5 M parameters (Table 10). Table 11 shows that HFS-HNeRV can still maintain its performance advantage over HNeRV on the UVG dataset. Significantly, NeRV-based methods perform well on HoneyBee but show relatively poor performance on Ready and Yacht. This phenomenon can be analyzed from two main aspects: content complexity and motion intensity. First, regarding content complexity, the main subject in HoneyBee is a bee, which occupies only a small region in the entire frame. The background primarily consists of flowers and grass with simple structures and similar color distributions. This implies that the model needs to learn fewer and less complex visual features. In contrast, Yacht and Ready contain abundant high-frequency details (such as water ripples, human contours, and hair), which place higher demands on the model's representational capacity. Although our method achieves notable improvements over HNeRV on these videos, the overall performance remains inferior compared to its results on other video sequences. Second, in terms of motion intensity, the primary objects in Yacht and Ready have significant movements. While NeRV-based methods do not rely on motion estimation, large inter-frame differences mean that the model must learn more temporal features to complete the reconstruction.

Regarding visual quality, the experimental benchmark was established with 300 training epochs and a model size of 1.5 M. As illustrated in Figure 6, the textures around the edges of smaller objects in the image appear noticeably sharper and more complete. Additionally, the images generated by HFS-HNeRV exhibit significantly fewer abrupt color shifts, contributing to a more cohesive and natural overall visual appearance.

Table 9. PSNR(dB) results on Bunny with different model sizes.

Size	0.75 M	1.5 M	3.0 M
NeRV	28.46	30.87	33.21
E-NeRV	30.95	32.09	36.72
HNeRV	32.81	35.57	37.43
HFS-HNeRV (Ours)	34.17	36.62	38.82

Table 10. PSNR(dB) results on Bunny with different trainning epochs.

Epoch	300	600	1200
NeRV	30.87	31.68	32.13
E-NeRV	32.09	33.2	34.15
HNeRV	35.57	36.19	36.93
HFS-HNeRV (Ours)	36.62	37.37	37.89

Table 11. PSNR(dB) results at resolution 480 × 960, on UVG dataset.

Video	Beauty	Bosph	Honey	Jockey	Ready	Shake	Yacht	avg.
HNeRV	35.08	36.86	39.42	34.05	28.05	35.53	31.87	34.41
HFS-HNeRV (Ours)	35.04	37.66	39.53	34.88	29.04	35.75	32.36	34.89

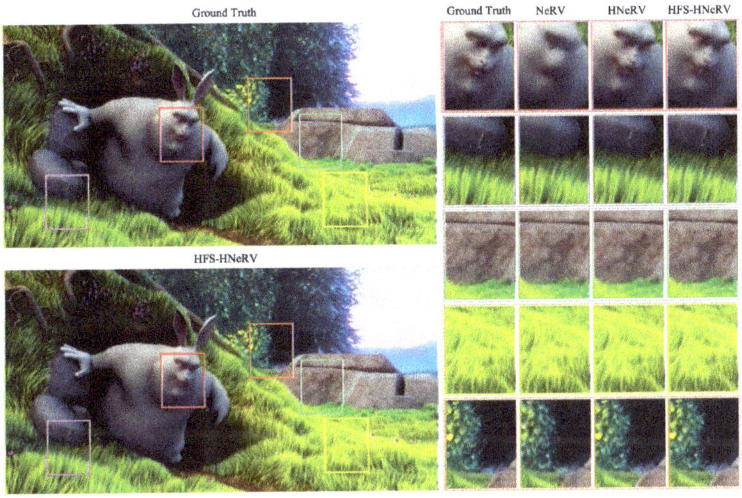

Figure 6. Visual quality comparison of videos at 0.109 bpp. On the left, we compare one overall video frame generated by HFS-HNeRV with the ground truth. On the right, we compare NeRV, HNeRV, and HFS-HNeRV by extracting and analyzing five patches from the images. It can be observed that HFS-HNeRV consistently outperforms in various aspects, including facial details, small objects (such as the contour of a blade of grass), local region details (such as the texture of rocks and grass), and low-contrast objects (such as a leaf in darkness).

4.3.2. Video Compression

For the video compression task, we employed embedded quantization (8 bits), model quantization (8 bits), and model entropy coding. Figure 7a,b show the rate-distortion performance of HNeRV, HFS-HNeRV, and traditional compression methods (H.264 and H.265), respectively. Although a performance gap remains between NeRV-type methods and conventional compression technologies, HFS-HNeRV outperforms HNeRV, clearly demonstrating that the three proposed components collectively contribute to advancing the performance of NeRV-type architectures.

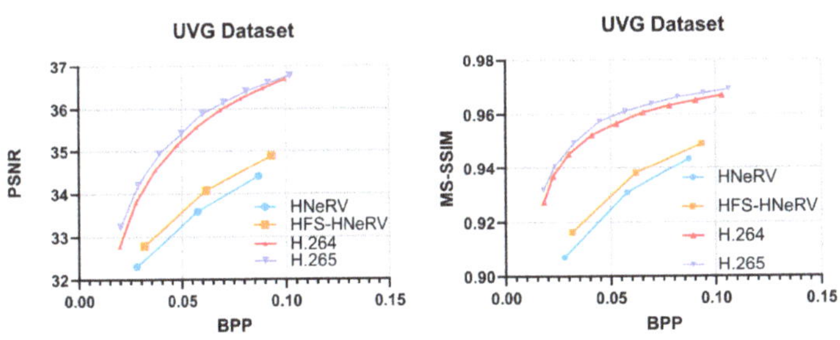

Figure 7. (**a**) PSNR(dB) results on UVG dataset. (**b**) MS-SSIM results on UVG dataset.

4.3.3. Model Complexity

We mainly discuss the model complexity from the perspectives of model parameter count and decoding speed.

For the traditional methods, we directly cite the FPS values of H.264 and H.265 reported in previous work. Since these methods were evaluated using four CPU threads on Intel Xeon 4216 processors, the setup is closer to real-world application scenarios. For the NeRV method, due to the significant performance gap caused by the mobile version of the RTX 3060 GPU, we benchmarked HNeRV and HFS-HNeRV by using the RTX A6000 GPU, whose performance is more comparable to that of a four-core Xeon CPU.

In terms of model complexity, we have made careful efforts to avoid or control the increase in the number of parameters. For instance, the HFS loss does not introduce any additional parameters, and the MSFRP is implemented with bilinear interpolation to minimize parameter overhead. While the introduction of the attention mechanism inevitably adds some parameters, we counteract this by reducing the number of channels across all network layers. This ensures that the total number of model parameters remains consistent across all comparison experiments. The experimental results demonstrate that this trade-off is worthwhile. Our model achieves superior performance under the same parameter budget.

As for decoding speed, compared with traditional compression methods and other NeRV-based approaches, our method shows significantly lower decoding speed (as illustrated in Figure 8). This is primarily due to the additional operations frequently performed within the network—such as wavelet transforms and frequency domain calculations—which introduce higher computational complexity and memory overhead. As a result, the current inference speed of our method is limited.

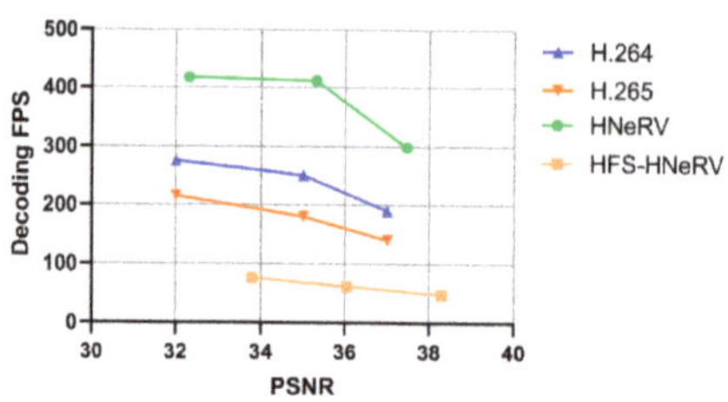

Figure 8. Decoding FPS comparison.

5. Conclusions

In this paper, we present HFS-HNeRV, a NeRV network optimized for learning high-frequency features within the frequency domain. To support its training, we introduce a specialized loss function designed to target high-frequency features, thereby improving the model's performance to reproduce fine details such as edges and textures. Specifically, we propose the HFSCM and the HFS loss, which enable the model to more effectively focus on and learn high-frequency information in the frequency domain.

Quantitative results reveal that HFS-HNeRV significantly outperforms other NeRV-based networks, including NeRV, E-NeRV, and HNeRV, achieving improvements in PSNR of +5.75 dB, +4.53 dB, and +1.05 dB, respectively. In terms of visual reconstruction quality, HFS-HNeRV demonstrates superior performance in restoring edge textures and produces images with more cohesive and natural color distributions. Importantly, both HFSCM and HFS loss exhibit a high degree of flexibility, allowing them to be easily integrated into a variety of NeRV architectures, thus offering substantial benefits for tasks related to video compression and reconstruction.

6. Future Work

For future work, we plan to explore the following three aspects:

- The decoding speed of the model needs to be enhanced. The current method still lags behind traditional compression techniques in terms of decoding efficiency, which is a critical factor in practical applications (particularly in scenarios with real-time requirements). To address this limitation, we aim to investigate more efficient frequency domain transformation methods and network simplification strategies to enhance inference speed.
- The model's adaptability to diverse types of video content needs to be strengthened. As observed from its performance on the UVG dataset, the proposed method remains sensitive to video characteristics, which means that videos featuring rapid motion or complex backgrounds often result in performance degradation. To improve robustness, we will consider incorporating motion estimation mechanisms and enhancing the compression and reconstruction capabilities for high-frequency information.
- We should carefully balance parameter configurations and performance metrics. Given the method's strict constraints on model size, any newly introduced components or parameter adjustments that significantly increase the number of parameters should be thoroughly evaluated. Therefore, we plan to conduct more comprehensive ablation studies to identify the optimal configuration strategies.

Author Contributions: Conceptualization, J.H.Z. and X.J.L.; methodology, J.H.Z. and X.J.L.; software, J.H.Z.; validation, J.H.Z.; formal analysis, J.H.Z.; investigation, J.H.Z.; resources, J.H.Z. and X.J.L.; data curation, J.H.Z. and X.J.L.; writing—original draft preparation, J.H.Z., X.J.L. and P.H.J.C.; writing—review and editing, J.H.Z., X.J.L. and P.H.J.C.; visualization, J.H.Z. and X.J.L.; supervision, X.J.L. and P.H.J.C.; project administration, X.J.L. and P.H.J.C. All authors have read and agreed to the published version of the manuscript.

Funding: This work was funded by the Vice-Chancellor's Doctoral Scholarship at Auckland University of Technology, New Zealand.

Data Availability Statement: Data are contained within the article.

Acknowledgments: This article is a revised and expanded version of a paper entitled "HFS-HNeRV: High-Frequency Spectrum Hybrid Neural Representation for Videos", which was presented at the 6th ACM International Conference on Multimedia in Asia (MMASIA '24), held in Auckland, New Zealand, on 28 December 2024.

Conflicts of Interest: The authors declare no conflicts of interest.

References

1. Tirana, K.; Elmazi, D. 5G Impact on the Flow of Wireless Internet Traffic. In Proceedings of the 2024 International Conference on Computing, Networking, Telecommunications & Engineering Sciences Applications (CoNTESA), Tirana, Albania, 18–19 December 2024; pp. 1–4.
2. Pratt, W.K.; Kane, J.; Andrews, H.C. Hadamard transform image coding. *Proc. IEEE* **1969**, *57*, 58–68. [CrossRef]
3. Zhang, Z.T.; Yeh, C.H.; Kang, L.W.; Lin, M.H. Efficient CTU-based intra frame coding for HEVC based on deep learning. In Proceedings of the 2017 Asia-Pacific Signal and Information Processing Association Annual Summit and Conference (APSIPA ASC), Kuala Lumpur, Malaysia, 12–15 December 2017; pp. 661–664.
4. Wang, Y.; Fan, X.; Liu, S.; Zhao, D.; Gao, W. Multi-scale convolutional neural network-based intra prediction for video coding. *IEEE Trans. Circuits Syst. Video Technol.* **2019**, *30*, 1803–1815. [CrossRef]
5. Schneider, J.; Sauer, J.; Wien, M. Dictionary learning based high frequency inter-layer prediction for scalable HEVC. In Proceedings of the 2017 IEEE Visual Communications and Image Processing (VCIP), St. Petersburg, FL, USA, 10–13 December 2017; pp. 1–4.
6. Wang, Z.; Ma, C.; Liao, R.L.; Ye, Y. Multi-density convolutional neural network for in-loop filter in video coding. In Proceedings of the 2021 Data Compression Conference (DCC), Snowbird, UT, USA, 23–26 March 2021, pp. 23–32.

7. Huang, Z.; Guo, X.; Shang, M.; Gao, J.; Sun, J. An efficient qp variable convolutional neural network based in-loop filter for intra coding. In Proceedings of the 2021 Data Compression Conference (DCC), Snowbird, UT, USA, 23–26 March 2021; pp. 33–42.
8. Ho, M.M.; Zhou, J.; He, G.; Li, M.; Li, L. SR-CL-DMC: P-frame coding with super-resolution, color learning, and deep motion compensation. In Proceedings of the IEEE/CVF Conference on Computer Vision and Pattern Recognition Workshops, Seattle, WA, USA, 14–19 June 2020; pp. 124–125.
9. Lu, G.; Zhang, X.; Ouyang, W.; Chen, L.; Gao, Z.; Xu, D. An end-to-end learning framework for video compression. *IEEE Trans. Pattern Anal. Mach. Intell.* **2020**, *43*, 3292–3308. [CrossRef] [PubMed]
10. Hu, Z.; Xu, D.; Lu, G.; Jiang, W.; Wang, W.; Liu, S. Fvc: An end-to-end framework towards deep video compression in feature space. *IEEE Trans. Pattern Anal. Mach. Intell.* **2022**, *45*, 4569–4585. [CrossRef] [PubMed]
11. Agustsson, E.; Minnen, D.; Johnston, N.; Balle, J.; Hwang, S.J.; Toderici, G. Scale-space flow for end-to-end optimized video compression. In Proceedings of the IEEE/CVF Conference on Computer Vision and Pattern Recognition, Seattle, WA, USA, 14–19 June 2020; pp. 8503–8512.
12. Fu, L.; Wang, P.; Wang, X. An Improved Neural Network Approach to End-to-end Video Compression. In Proceedings of the 5th International Conference on Computer Information and Big Data Applications, Wuhan China, 26–28 April 2024; pp. 57–61.
13. Liu, B.; Chen, Y.; Machineni, R.C.; Liu, S.; Kim, H.S. Mmvc: Learned multi-mode video compression with block-based prediction mode selection and density-adaptive entropy coding. In Proceedings of the IEEE/CVF Conference on Computer Vision and Pattern Recognition, Vancouver, BC, Canada, 17–24 June 2023; pp. 18487–18496.
14. Zou, N.; Zhang, H.; Cricri, F.; Tavakoli, H.R.; Lainema, J.; Aksu, E.; Hannuksela, M.; Rahtu, E. End-to-End Learning for Video Frame Compression with Self-Attention. In Proceedings of the IEEE/CVF Conference on Computer Vision and Pattern Recognition (CVPR) Workshops, Seattle, WA, USA, 13–19 June 2020.
15. Rippel, O.; Nair, S.; Lew, C.; Branson, S.; Anderson, A.G.; Bourdev, L. Learned Video Compression. In Proceedings of the IEEE/CVF International Conference on Computer Vision (ICCV), Seoul, Republic of Korea, 27 October–2 November 2019.
16. Wang, S.; Zhao, Y.; Gao, H.; Ye, M.; Li, S. End-to-end video compression for surveillance and conference videos. *Multimed. Tools Appl.* **2022**, *81*, 42713–42730. [CrossRef]
17. Chen, H.; He, B.; Wang, H.; Ren, Y.; Lim, S.N.; Shrivastava, A. Nerv: Neural representations for videos. *Adv. Neural Inf. Process. Syst.* **2021**, *34*, 21557–21568.
18. Li, Z.; Wang, M.; Pi, H.; Xu, K.; Mei, J.; Liu, Y. E-nerv: Expedite neural video representation with disentangled spatial-temporal context. In *Computer Vision—ECCV 2022, Proceedings of the 17th European Conference, Tel Aviv, Israel, 23–27 October 2022*; Springer: Cham, Switzerland, 2022; pp. 267–284.
19. Chen, H.; Gwilliam, M.; Lim, S.N.; Shrivastava, A. Hnerv: A hybrid neural representation for videos. In Proceedings of the IEEE/CVF Conference on Computer Vision and Pattern Recognition, Vancouver, BC, Canada, 17–24 June 2023; pp. 10270–10279.
20. Zhao, J.; Li, X.J.; Chong, P.H.J. HFS-HNeRV: High-Frequency Spectrum Hybrid Neural Representation for Videos. In Proceedings of the 6th ACM International Conference on Multimedia in Asia, Auckland, New Zealand, 3–6 December 2024; pp. 1–7.
21. Liu, Z.; Mao, H.; Wu, C.Y.; Feichtenhofer, C.; Darrell, T.; Xie, S. A convnet for the 2020s. In Proceedings of the IEEE/CVF Conference on Computer Vision and Pattern Recognition, New Orleans, LA, USA, 18–24 June 2022; pp. 11976–11986.
22. Woo, S.; Park, J.; Lee, J.Y.; Kweon, I.S. Cbam: Convolutional block attention module. In Proceedings of the European Conference on Computer Vision (ECCV), Munich, Germany, 8–14 September 2018; pp. 3–19.
23. Liu, Y.; Shao, Z.; Hoffmann, N. Global attention mechanism: Retain information to enhance channel-spatial interactions. *arXiv* **2021**, arXiv:2112.05561.
24. Mehta, I.; Gharbi, M.; Barnes, C.; Shechtman, E.; Ramamoorthi, R.; Chandraker, M. Modulated periodic activations for generalizable local functional representations. In Proceedings of the IEEE/CVF International Conference on Computer Vision, Montreal, BC, Canada, 11–17 October 2021; pp. 14214–14223.
25. Strümpler, Y.; Postels, J.; Yang, R.; Gool, L.V.; Tombari, F. Implicit neural representations for image compression. In *Computer Vision—ECCV 2022, Proceedings of the 17th European Conference, Tel Aviv, Israel, 23–27 October 2022*; Springer: Cham, Switzerland, 2022; pp. 74–91.
26. Chen, Y.; Liu, S.; Wang, X. Learning continuous image representation with local implicit image function. In Proceedings of the IEEE/CVF Conference on Computer Vision and Pattern Recognition, Nashville, TN, USA, 20–25 June 2021; pp. 8628–8638.
27. Jiang, C.; Sud, A.; Makadia, A.; Huang, J.; Nießner, M.; Funkhouser, T. Local implicit grid representations for 3d scenes. In Proceedings of the IEEE/CVF Conference on Computer Vision and Pattern Recognition, Seattle, WA, USA, 14–19 June 2020; pp. 6001–6010.
28. Mildenhall, B.; Srinivasan, P.P.; Tancik, M.; Barron, J.T.; Ramamoorthi, R.; Ng, R. Nerf: Representing scenes as neural radiance fields for view synthesis. *Commun. ACM* **2021**, *65*, 99–106. [CrossRef]
29. Wiegand, T.; Sullivan, G.J.; Bjontegaard, G.; Luthra, A. Overview of the H. 264/AVC video coding standard. *IEEE Trans. Circuits Syst. Video Technol.* **2003**, *13*, 560–576. [CrossRef]

30. Sullivan, G.J.; Ohm, J.R.; Han, W.J.; Wiegand, T. Overview of the high efficiency video coding (HEVC) standard. *IEEE Trans. Circuits Syst. Video Technol.* **2012**, *22*, 1649–1668. [CrossRef]
31. Dong, C.; Loy, C.C.; He, K.; Tang, X. Learning a deep convolutional network for image super-resolution. In *Computer Vision–ECCV 2014, Proceedings of the 13th European Conference, Zurich, Switzerland, 6–12 September 2014*; Part IV; Springer: Cham, Switzerland, 2014; pp. 184–199.
32. Kim, J.; Lee, J.K.; Lee, K.M. Accurate image super-resolution using very deep convolutional networks. In Proceedings of the IEEE Conference on Computer Vision and Pattern Recognition, Las Vegas, NV, USA, 27–30 June 2016; pp. 1646–1654.
33. Shi, W.; Caballero, J.; Huszár, F.; Totz, J.; Aitken, A.P.; Bishop, R.; Rueckert, D.; Wang, Z. Real-time single image and video super-resolution using an efficient sub-pixel convolutional neural network. In Proceedings of the IEEE Conference on Computer Vision and Pattern Recognition, Las Vegas, NV, USA, 27–30 June 2016; pp. 1874–1883.
34. Shocher, A.; Cohen, N.; Irani, M. "zero-shot" super-resolution using deep internal learning. In Proceedings of the IEEE Conference on Computer Vision and Pattern Recognition, Salt Lake City, UT, USA, 18–23 June 2018; pp. 3118–3126.
35. Ledig, C.; Theis, L.; Huszar, F.; Caballero, J.; Cunningham, A.; Acosta, A.; Aitken, A.; Tejani, A.; Totz, J.; Wang, Z.; et al. Photo-realistic single image super-resolution using a generative adversarial network. In Proceedings of the IEEE Conference on Computer Vision and Pattern Recognition, Honolulu, HI, USA, 21–26 July 2017; Volume 2017, pp. 4681–4690.
36. Chan, K.C.; Wang, X.; Yu, K.; Dong, C.; Loy, C.C. Basicvsr: The search for essential components in video super-resolution and beyond. In Proceedings of the IEEE/CVF Conference on Computer Vision and Pattern Recognition, Nashville, TN, USA, 20–25 June 2021; pp. 4947–4956.
37. Sajjadi, M.S.; Vemulapalli, R.; Brown, M. Frame-recurrent video super-resolution. In Proceedings of the IEEE Conference on Computer Vision and Pattern Recognition, Salt Lake City, UT, USA, 18–23 June 2018; pp. 6626–6634.
38. Xue, T.; Chen, B.; Wu, J.; Wei, D.; Freeman, W.T. Video enhancement with task-oriented flow. *Int. J. Comput. Vis.* **2019**, *127*, 1106–1125. [CrossRef]
39. Kim, T.H.; Sajjadi, M.S.; Hirsch, M.; Scholkopf, B. Spatio-temporal transformer network for video restoration. In Proceedings of the European Conference on Computer Vision (ECCV), Munich, Germany, 8–14 September 2018; pp. 106–122.
40. Tian, Y.; Zhang, Y.; Fu, Y.; Xu, C. Tdan: Temporally-deformable alignment network for video super-resolution. In Proceedings of the IEEE/CVF Conference on Computer Vision and Pattern Recognition, Seattle, WA, USA, 14–19 June 2020; pp. 3360–3369.
41. Ying, X.; Wang, L.; Wang, Y.; Sheng, W.; An, W.; Guo, Y. Deformable 3d convolution for video super-resolution. *IEEE Signal Process. Lett.* **2020**, *27*, 1500–1504. [CrossRef]
42. Kim, S.Y.; Lim, J.; Na, T.; Kim, M. Video super-resolution based on 3D-CNNS with consideration of scene change. In Proceedings of the 2019 IEEE International Conference on Image Processing (ICIP), Taipei, Taiwan, 22–25 September 2019; pp. 2831–2835.
43. Liu, H.; Zhao, P.; Ruan, Z.; Shang, F.; Liu, Y. Large motion video super-resolution with dual subnet and multi-stage communicated upsampling. *Proc. AAAI Conf. Artif. Intell.* **2021**, *35*, 2127–2135. [CrossRef]
44. Zhu, X.; Li, Z.; Zhang, X.Y.; Li, C.; Liu, Y.; Xue, Z. Residual invertible spatio-temporal network for video super-resolution. *Proc. AAAI Conf. Artif. Intell.* **2019**, *33*, 5981–5988. [CrossRef]
45. Isobe, T.; Jia, X.; Gu, S.; Li, S.; Wang, S.; Tian, Q. Video super-resolution with recurrent structure-detail network. In *Computer Vision—ECCV 2020, Proceedings of the 16th European Conference, Glasgow, UK, 23–28 August 2020*; Part XII; Springer: Cham, Switzerland, 2020; pp. 645–660.
46. Goodfellow, I.J.; Pouget-Abadie, J.; Mirza, M.; Xu, B.; Warde-Farley, D.; Ozair, S.; Courville, A.; Bengio, Y. Generative adversarial nets. In Proceedings of the 27th International Conference on Neural Information Processing Systems, Lake Tahoe, NV, USA, 5–10 December 2013; pp. 2672–2680.
47. Liu, H.; Ruan, Z.; Zhao, P.; Dong, C.; Shang, F.; Liu, Y.; Yang, L.; Timofte, R. Video super-resolution based on deep learning: A comprehensive survey. *Artif. Intell. Rev.* **2022**, *55*, 5981–6035. [CrossRef]
48. Baniya, A.A.; Lee, T.K.; Eklund, P.W.; Aryal, S. A survey of deep learning video super-resolution. *IEEE Trans. Emerg. Top. Comput. Intell.* **2024**, *8*, 2655–2676. [CrossRef]
49. Wang, Z.; Chen, J.; Hoi, S.C. Deep learning for image super-resolution: A survey. *IEEE Trans. Pattern Anal. Mach. Intell.* **2020**, *43*, 3365–3387. [CrossRef] [PubMed]
50. Rhee, H.; Jang, Y.I.; Kim, S.; Cho, N.I. LC-FDNet: Learned lossless image compression with frequency decomposition network. In Proceedings of the IEEE/CVF Conference on Computer Vision and Pattern Recognition, New Orleans, LA, USA, 18–24 June 2022; pp. 6033–6042.
51. Gao, G.; You, P.; Pan, R.; Han, S.; Zhang, Y.; Dai, Y.; Lee, H. Neural image compression via attentional multi-scale back projection and frequency decomposition. In Proceedings of the IEEE/CVF International Conference on Computer Vision, Montreal, BC, Canada, 11–17 October 2021; pp. 14677–14686.
52. Li, H.; Li, S.; Dai, W.; Li, C.; Zou, J.; Xiong, H. Frequency-aware transformer for learned image compression. *arXiv* **2023**, arXiv:2310.16387.
53. Pan, Z.; Cai, J.; Zhuang, B. Fast vision transformers with hilo attention. *Adv. Neural Inf. Process. Syst.* **2022**, *35*, 14541–14554.

54. Porwik, P.; Lisowska, A. The Haar-wavelet transform in digital image processing: Its status and achievements. *Mach. Graph. Vis.* **2004**, *13*, 79–98.
55. Kidner, D.; Dorey, M.; Smith, D. What's the point? Interpolation and extrapolation with a regular grid DEM. In Proceedings of the Fourth International Conference on GeoComputation, Fredericksburg, VA, USA, 25–28 July 1999.

electronics

MDPI

Article

Attentive Multi-Scale Features with Adaptive Context PoseResNet for Resource-Efficient Human Pose Estimation

Ali Zakir [1], Sartaj Ahmed Salman [1], Gibran Benitez-Garcia [1,*] and Hiroki Takahashi [1,2]

1 Graduate School of Informatics and Engineering, The University of Electro-Communications, Chofugaoka 1-5-1, Chofu 182-8585, Japan; a2240012@edu.cc.uec.ac.jp (A.Z.); s2140019@edu.cc.uec.ac.jp (S.A.S.); rocky@inf.uec.ac.jp (H.T.)

2 AI Exploration/Meta-Networking Research Center, The University of Electro-Communications, Chofugaoka 1-5-1, Chofu 182-8585, Japan

* Correspondence: gibran@ieee.org

Abstract: Human Pose Estimation (HPE) remains challenging due to scale variation, occlusion, and high computational costs. Standard methods often struggle to capture detailed spatial information when keypoints are obscured, and they typically rely on computationally expensive deconvolution layers for upsampling, making them inefficient for real-time or resource-constrained scenarios. We propose AMFACPose (Attentive Multi-scale Features with Adaptive Context PoseResNet) to address these limitations. Specifically, our architecture incorporates Coordinate Convolution 2D (CoordConv2d) to retain explicit spatial context, alleviating the loss of coordinate information in conventional convolutions. To reduce computational overhead while maintaining accuracy, we utilize Depthwise Separable Convolutions (DSCs), separating spatial and pointwise operations. At the core of our approach is an Adaptive Feature Pyramid Network (AFPN), which replaces costly deconvolution-based upsampling by efficiently aggregating multi-scale features to handle diverse human poses and body sizes. We further introduce Dual-Gate Context Blocks (DGCBs) that refine global context to manage partial occlusions and cluttered backgrounds. The model integrates Squeeze-and-Excitation (SE) blocks and the Spatial–Channel Refinement Module (SCRM) to emphasize the most informative feature channels and spatial regions, which is particularly beneficial for occluded or overlapping keypoints. For precise keypoint localization, we replace dense heatmap predictions with coordinate classification using Multi-Layer Perceptron (MLP) heads. Experiments on the COCO and CrowdPose datasets demonstrate that AMFACPose surpasses the existing 2D HPE methods in both accuracy and computational efficiency. Moreover, our implementation on edge devices achieves real-time performance while preserving high accuracy, confirming the suitability of AMFACPose for resource-constrained pose estimation in both benchmark and real-world environments.

Keywords: human pose estimation; multi-scale features; edge computing; dual-gate context blocks; adaptive feature pyramid network

1. Introduction

Human Pose Estimation (HPE) is a critical subfield of Computer Vision (CV) focused on locating and connecting human body joints, i.e., keypoints, in images or video sequences. Accurate pose estimation enables machines to analyze human posture and motion, facilitating a wide range of applications, including video surveillance, human–computer interaction, medical rehabilitation, and autonomous driving [1]. Despite significant advancements in deep learning (DL) and convolutional neural networks (CNNs) [2], HPE continues to face several core challenges. These include scale variation, where subjects can appear at vastly different resolutions, the occlusion of keypoints by objects or other individuals, and stringent computational requirements that frequently hinder real-time deployment [3,4].

Early approaches relied on hand-crafted features combined with probabilistic models, offering interpretability but limited accuracy in complex scenarios, such as occlusions, varied lighting conditions, and cluttered backgrounds [5]. The emergence of CNNs significantly improved feature extraction capabilities. For instance, the pioneering work of DeepPose directly regressed keypoint coordinates but struggled with stability in multi-modal distributions [4]. Subsequently, heatmap-based methods emerged, transforming coordinate regression into spatial heatmap prediction, notably improving robustness and accuracy. Approaches such as Stacked Hourglass Networks [6] and SimpleBaseline [7] refined heatmap-based architectures, although at the expense of increased computational overhead due to complex upsampling procedures.

To reduce these computational demands while maintaining accuracy, High-Resolution Networks (HRNets) preserve spatial resolution throughout the network, significantly improving precision, albeit with substantial computational complexity [8]. Recognizing this trade-off, transformer-based models such as HRFormer [9], TokenPose [10], and ViTPose [11] leveraged global self-attention mechanisms, enabling more accurate keypoint estimation by modeling global contextual relationships. However, these approaches often introduced even greater computational complexity and parameter demands, making practical deployment challenging.

To address these efficiency challenges, coordinate classification approaches have recently emerged, such as SimCC [12], reformulating keypoint localization as a discrete classification task, significantly reducing the quantization errors inherent in heatmap-based methods. Building on this paradigm, AECA-PRNetCC further enhanced performance by incorporating adaptive channel attention mechanisms, thereby achieving a balance between accuracy and computational efficiency [13].

Despite these improvements, two major issues persist. Firstly, most advanced methods face a fundamental accuracy–computation trade-off, as higher accuracy typically demands greater computational complexity, complicating real-world deployment. Secondly, existing approaches still suffer from precision limitations in localizing keypoints under occlusion or scale variations, partly due to ineffective local feature refinement and global contextual reasoning capabilities.

In response, we propose AMFACPose (Attentive Multi-scale Features with Adaptive Context PoseResNet), a novel framework designed to address these challenges in 2D HPE. Our model begins with a ResNet structure [14], which we modified by replacing the standard convolution layers with Coordinate Convolution 2D (CoordConv2d) [15] to preserve explicit spatial coordinates, as well as by removing the average pooling and fully connected layers. This design retains the model's feature-extraction capabilities while reducing computational overhead. We also replace the standard 7×7 convolution in the initial layer with a series of 3×3 CoordConv2d layers, each followed by Batch Normalization (BN) and Mish activation, thereby improving the model's ability to capture fine-grained features. Furthermore, throughout the four stages of ResBlocks, we employ Depthwise Separable Convolutions (DSCs) [16] to further reduce computational costs without compromising accuracy, separating spatial and pointwise operations into distinct phases.

A key component of our design is the Adaptive Feature Pyramid Network (AFPN), which replaces computationally expensive deconvolution-based upsampling with an efficient multi-scale feature fusion strategy. By aggregating feature maps at different resolutions, AFPN ensures the robust handling of diverse poses and body sizes without incurring the high overhead of traditional upsampling layers. Building on the AFPN, we introduce Dual-Gate Context Blocks (DGCBs) to refine global contextual information, which is essential for managing occlusions and cluttered backgrounds. To further enhance feature representation, our approach incorporates Squeeze-and-Excitation (SE) blocks and a Spatial–Channel Refinement Module (SCRM). SE adaptively recalibrates channel-wise feature responses, while SCRM simultaneously optimizes spatial and channel dimensions, amplifying critical cues. This collaboration of multi-scale aggregation, global context gating, and attention-based refinement significantly improves the visibility of obscured or overlapping joints, ultimately producing more accurate and efficient pose estimation. We adopt a coordinate classification approach instead of generating dense heatmaps. Specifically, each joint's feature representation is passed through Multi-Layer Perceptron (MLP) heads that output discrete horizontal and vertical coordinate estimates, alleviating the quantization errors typical of heatmap-based pipelines and removing the memory and computational overhead required for large-scale heatmap generation and post-processing. This design preserves localization precision while reducing both model size and inference latency. Unlike previous coordinate classification approaches such as SimCC and AECA-PRNetCC, our AMFACPose model uniquely combines explicit spatial awareness through CoordConv2d, multi-scale feature fusion via AFPN, and dual-path attention mechanisms, delivering superior accuracy while maintaining low computational cost, making it highly suitable for real-time deployment in resource-constrained environments.

The following three fundamental contributions emerge from this work:

1. We propose a modified ResNet backbone that replaces the standard convolutions with CoordConv2d and DSC, reducing computational overhead while preserving strong feature extraction capabilities. To further elevate feature quality, the backbone incorporates SE blocks and an SCRM, adaptively enhancing critical regions and channels, which is particularly valuable for partially visible or overlapping keypoints.
2. To eliminate costly deconvolution-based upsampling, we introduce an AFPN that efficiently aggregates multi-scale feature maps. Building on the AFPN, DGCBs refine global context, ensuring the robust handling of scale variations, cluttered backgrounds, and complex human poses across varying resolutions.
3. We validate our AMFACPose model on the COCO and CrowdPose datasets, achieving notable improvements in both accuracy and efficiency over the existing methods. Moreover, our model performance on edge devices demonstrates the practicality of these design choices for deployment in diverse, resource-constrained settings.

The remainder of this paper is organized as follows: Section 2 reviews the key developments in HPE, situating our work within the existing literature. Section 3 introduces the proposed AMFACPose framework, detailing each of its core components, including the modified ResNet backbone and the AFPN with DGCBs. Section 4 explains the experimental setup, datasets, and implementation specifics. Section 5 presents our empirical findings, comparing them against SOTA methods on benchmarks such as COCO and CrowdPose. We also discuss the performance of our model on edge devices in Section 6 and provide ablation studies in Section 7 to isolate the contributions of each architectural component. Finally, Section 8 concludes the paper by summarizing our primary insights and suggesting directions for future research in resource-efficient and high-accuracy 2D HPE.

2. Related Work

DL has substantially transformed 2D HPE by automating feature extraction, leading to improvements in both accuracy and computational efficiency. Early research explored regression-based methods for direct keypoint coordinate prediction. Although these approaches initially faced consistency challenges, the Residual Log-likelihood Estimation (RLE) [17] achieved good performance comparable to leading heatmap-based techniques. However, these methods continue to face challenges in handling scale variations and occlusions.

A significant development in 2D HPE occurred with the adoption of two-dimensional Gaussian heatmaps for joint localization. Initially transforming the coordinate prediction task into heatmap generation [18], these methods achieved greater stability. Further progress came from architectures like the Stacked Hourglass Network [6], which utilized symmetric encoder–decoder structures with repeated pooling and upsampling to capture multi-scale features. However, heatmap-based methods can suffer high computational costs due to the requirement for dense heatmaps, large upsampling layers, and post-processing operations such as non-maximum suppression. To alleviate these burdens, FasterPose [19] introduced a more streamlined design, while Dense layer and Identity block Parallel Network (IDPNet) [20] implemented lightweight architectural choices targeted toward resource-constrained deployments.

Despite the accuracy benefits of heatmap-based approaches, quantization errors remain a persistent issue. These errors arise from discretizing joint locations onto the heatmap's pixel grid, which can reduce precision as resolution declines. Various minimization techniques have been proposed, including Taylor expansion [21] to refine predictions around the heatmap peak response, and one-dimensional heatmaps [22], which compress spatial dimensionality without sacrificing localization quality. Furthermore, recent work highlights the role of unbiased data processing in reducing systematic bias [23]. Attention mechanisms, whether spatial and channel-based, also help address occlusions and cluttered scenes. Examples include spatially oriented channel attention for better joint discernment [24] and adaptive efficient channel attention for refined feature recalibration [13].

Given the rising demand for real-time and mobile HPE applications, a critical line of research focuses on designing computationally efficient, accurate architectures. While high-resolution representation learning [8] preserves spatial detail throughout the network, it often leads to significant memory overhead. For instance, SimCC [12] reframed HPE to be compatible with both CNN and Transformer architectures, eliminating the need for dense heatmap predictions. Building on this, A. Zakir et al. [25] proposed an efficient bridge attention integration mechanism that enhances feature representation while maintaining computational efficiency.

An important and emerging direction in HPE focuses on confidence score calibration and keypoint visibility estimation for robust occlusion handling. Jiang et al. [26] introduced HPCVNet, which jointly calibrates confidence scores and explicitly classifies keypoint visibility, achieving a mAP of 77.6 on COCO. In contrast, our method adopts an implicit occlusion-handling strategy using attention-driven modules such as AFPN and DGCB. Without requiring auxiliary visibility branches, AMFACPose achieves 76.6 mAP on COCO and demonstrates strong performance on occlusion-heavy benchmarks such as CrowdPose. These strategies reflect a distinct approach to handling partial visibility and overlapping joints in 2D pose estimation.

Building on these developments, we propose AMFACPose, a unified and lightweight pose estimation framework. Unlike heatmap-based pipelines, AMFACPose employs a coordinate classification strategy, avoiding deconvolution layers, dense heatmaps, and post-processing stages. This design achieves a practical balance between high localization accuracy and computational efficiency, making it well suited for real-world applications constrained by latency, memory, and power.

3. AMFACPose

In 2D HPE, the task is to determine the spatial configuration of human body joints, i.e., keypoints, within an RGB image or video frame [27]. Let the pose **P** be represented by N keypoints, each defined by a 2D coordinate (x_n, y_n). For instance, $N = 17$ in the COCO dataset [27]. Formally, for each individual in the input, the goal is to estimate:

$$\mathbf{P} = \{(x_n, y_n)\}_{n=1}^{N}. \quad (1)$$

To address the challenges of occlusion, scale variation, and excessive computational overhead, we propose AMFACPose as illustrated in Figure 1. Our approach uses a ResNet34 backbone [14] that we modified by integrating CoordConv2d [15] and DSC [16], producing an efficient feature extractor that maintains strong spatial representation. Within this backbone, we incorporate attention modules—SE blocks [28] and an SCRM—to highlight keypoints, relevant channels, and local features, ensuring robust performance under partial occlusions or complex scenes. Next, AFPN fuses multi-scale features extracted from the backbone, retaining both global context and fine-grained details. We then refine these fused features using DGCBs, which selectively enhance relevant contextual information while suppressing background noise. Finally, instead of the commonly used heatmap-based and regression-based approachs, AMFACPose utilizes coordinate classification, thereby avoiding the computationally intensive generation of dense heatmaps and simplifying the inference pipeline. The subsequent sections provide an in-depth exploration of each component, illustrating how AMFACPose successfully balances efficiency with accurate and robust keypoint localization.

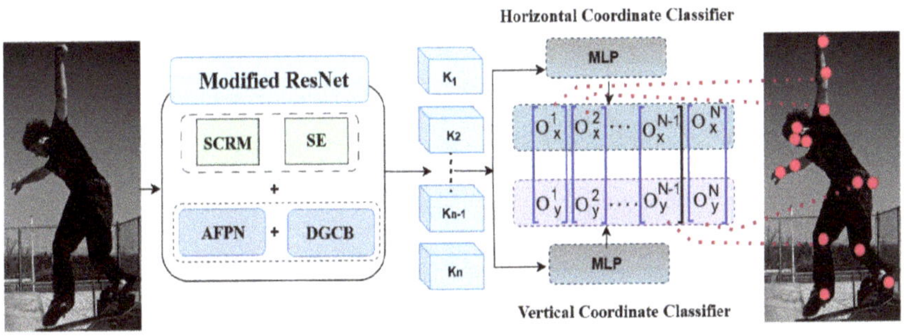

Figure 1. Comprehensive architectural design of AMFACPose for 2D HPE using coordinate classification.

3.1. Modified ResNet Backbone

Recent pose estimation frameworks, such as HRNet [8], Simple Baseline [7], and Stacked Hourglass Networks [6], preserve high-resolution feature representations to achieve precise body–joint localization. Although these high-capacity models attain competitive accuracy, they typically demand substantial computational resources, limiting real-time deployment on edge devices. Vision Transformers [29] likewise exhibit strong performance but often face latency challenges due to expensive self-attention operations.

To balance representational power and computational efficiency, we adopt ResNet34 as our backbone. Compared with deeper variants like ResNet50 or ResNet101, ResNet34 retains the skip connections essential for stable gradient flow [30] yet lowers parameter counts and FLoating-point OPerations (FLOPs). This design offers fine-grained feature extraction necessary for accurate joint detection without incurring prohibitive overhead.

Figure 2 presents an overview of our modified ResNet34 architecture. We remove the final average pooling and fully connected layers, preserving spatial detail in deeper stages and allowing subtle body part cues to remain accessible. Furthermore, the standard 7×7 input convolution is replaced by a sequence of 3×3 convolutions interleaved with CoordConv2d. Each basic block of the ResNet34 is also enhanced with DSC to reduce computational complexity while maintaining expressive capacity. This modified backbone thus strikes a favorable balance between accuracy and real-time feasibility, serving as the foundation for AMFACPose.

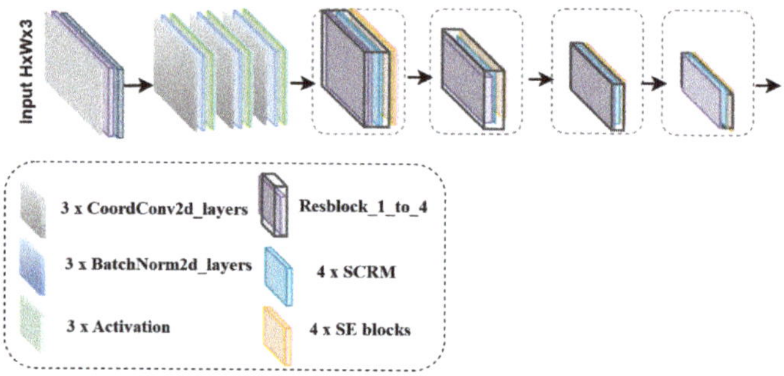

Figure 2. Architecture overview of modified ResNet as feature extractor.

3.1.1. Integration of CoordConv2d for Enhanced Spatial Awareness

The network's initial stem, as shown in Figure 2, incorporates CoordConv2d to embed explicit spatial features at the earliest stage. Let $\mathbf{X} \in \mathbb{R}^{B \times C \times H \times W}$ denote the input tensor, where B is the batch size, C is the channel count, and H, W are spatial dimensions. We first construct normalized coordinate grids $\mathbf{X}_{\text{coord}}, \mathbf{Y}_{\text{coord}} \in [-1,1]^{H \times W}$, providing a consistent reference frame for each pixel location. Four learnable parameters $\alpha_x, \beta_x, \alpha_y, \beta_y$ then adaptively scale and shift these coordinates, as follows:

$$\mathbf{X}' = \left(\mathbf{X} \mid \alpha_x \mathbf{X}_{\text{coord}} + \beta_x \mid \alpha_y \mathbf{Y}_{\text{coord}} + \beta_y \right) \in \mathbb{R}^{B \times (C+2) \times H \times W}. \quad (2)$$

After concatenation, a standard 3×3 convolution processes both the original feature maps and these position-aware channels in tandem.

Algorithm 1 summarizes the key steps of CoordConv2d. By retaining explicit spatial information, the stem ensures improved joint localization even under occlusions or viewpoint shifts. The learnable parameters α and β enable flexible adjustment to variations in scale and perspective.

Algorithm 1 Coordinate-enhanced convolution layer

Input: Feature tensor $\mathbf{X} \in \mathbb{R}^{B \times C \times H \times W}$
Output: Enhanced feature maps $\widetilde{\mathbf{X}}$
Step 1: Coordinate Grid Initialization
Initialize normalized grids $\mathbf{X}_{\text{coord}}, \mathbf{Y}_{\text{coord}} \in [-1,1]^{H \times W}$.
Step 2: Learnable Parameters
$\alpha_x, \beta_x, \alpha_y, \beta_y$ are updated by backpropagation.
Step 3: Coordinate Transformation
$\mathbf{X}'_{\text{coord}} \leftarrow \alpha_x \mathbf{X}_{\text{coord}} + \beta_x$, $\mathbf{Y}'_{\text{coord}} \leftarrow \alpha_y \mathbf{Y}_{\text{coord}} + \beta_y$.
Step 4: Feature Concatenation
$\mathbf{X}' \leftarrow [\mathbf{X} \mid \mathbf{X}'_{\text{coord}} \mid \mathbf{Y}'_{\text{coord}}] \in \mathbb{R}^{B \times (C+2) \times H \times W}$.
Step 5: Convolution
$\widetilde{\mathbf{X}} \leftarrow \text{Conv2D}(\mathbf{X}')$.
Step 6: Output
return $\widetilde{\mathbf{X}}$.

3.1.2. Depthwise Separable Convolutions for Efficiency

Maintaining spatial detail is crucial for pose estimation, yet computational efficiency is equally important for real-time systems. To address this, each Residual block in ResNet34 replaces the standard 2D convolutions with DSC. In the following equation, a depthwise step applies a unique spatial filter to each input channel:

$$\mathbf{X}_{\text{depthwise}} = \text{Conv2D}_{\text{depthwise}}(\mathbf{X}), \tag{3}$$

where the total parameter count and FLOPs are significantly reduced. A subsequent 1×1 pointwise convolution integrates cross-channel information, as follows:

$$\widetilde{\mathbf{X}} = \text{Conv2D}_{1\times 1}(\mathbf{X}_{\text{depthwise}}). \tag{4}$$

Within our Residual blocks, skip connections [14] preserve gradient flow across these separable layers, retaining the ability to learn rich features. When downsampling is needed, e.g., for stride 2, a lightweight residual path aligns the input and output dimensions without adding substantial overhead. Integrating CoordConv2d-based positional encoding and DSC provides a streamlined expressive backbone, striking a strong balance between accuracy and speed. This backbone then serves as the basis for the subsequent modules in AMFACPose.

3.2. *Adaptive Feature Pyramid Network (AFPN)*

Multi-scale feature fusion is central to effective pose estimation, since body parts can appear at various scales and contextual features may span multiple receptive fields. Traditional approaches, including feature pyramid networks with top–down pathways [31], often rely on deconvolution layers or complex lateral connections, which can amplify computational costs. To address this, we introduce an AFPN that unifies multi-scale representations while preserving critical spatial details, as illustrated in Figure 3.

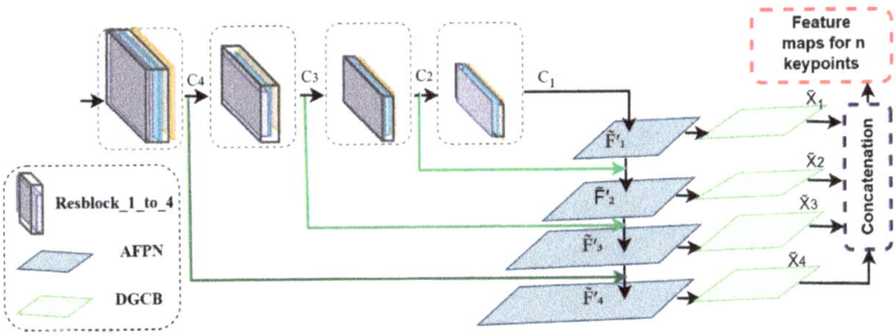

Figure 3. Overview of AFPN architecture. Diagram illustrates four ResNet blocks producing multi-scale feature maps (C_1, C_2, C_3, C_4) that are processed through AFPN and DGCB before concatenation for keypoint feature map generation.

Let $\{C_1, C_2, C_3, C_4\}$ be the feature maps produced by the modified ResNet34 backbone at consecutive stages, as shown in Figure 3, each with a distinct resolution. A 1×1 convolution is applied to each C_i to standardize the channel dimension, as expressed in the following:

$$\mathbf{F_i} = \text{Conv}_{1\times 1}(C_i) \quad \text{for } i \in \{1,2,3,4\}. \tag{5}$$

For each feature map $\mathbf{F}_i$, we apply a DGCB (detailed in Section 3.3) to generate a refined feature representation using two learnable masks—a context mask and a gating mask. Both masks are generated by small convolutional networks with trainable parameters. Formally, the DGCB's refinement is represented as follows:

$$\mathbf{A}_i = \mathrm{DGCB}(\mathbf{F}_i), \tag{6}$$

where the DGCB internally performs an element-wise multiplication between the input feature map and the context and gating masks, as further explained in Section 3.3, Equation (11).

Both $\mathbf{F}_i$ and $\mathbf{A}_i$ are subsequently upsampled to match the spatial resolution of $\mathbf{F}_4$, where the arrow operator $\uparrow(\cdot,\cdot)$ indicates bilinear interpolation, and $\mathrm{size}(F_4)$ represents the height and width of F_4, as shown in the following:

$$\tilde{\mathbf{F}}_i = \uparrow(F_i, \mathrm{size}(F_4)), \quad \tilde{\mathbf{A}}_i = \uparrow(A_i, \mathrm{size}(F_4)). \tag{7}$$

Each feature map $\tilde{F}_i$ is then modulated by its corresponding refined representation $\tilde{A}_i$, as follows:

$$\tilde{\mathbf{F}}_i' = \tilde{F}_i \odot \tilde{A}_i, \tag{8}$$

where $\odot$ denotes the element-wise product. The refined outputs from all scales, $\{\tilde{F}_1', \tilde{F}_2', \tilde{F}_3', \tilde{F}_4'\}$, are concatenated and passed through a 1×1 convolution, as follows:

$$\mathbf{X} = \mathrm{Concat}(\tilde{F}_1', \tilde{F}_2', \tilde{F}_3', \tilde{F}_4'), \quad \mathbf{F}_{\mathrm{out}} = \mathrm{Conv}_{1\times 1}(X). \tag{9}$$

The bilinear upsampling in $\uparrow(\cdot,\cdot)$ ensures all features share the same spatial dimensions, enabling their direct combination.

This operation fuses high-level semantics from deeper layers with localized details from shallower ones, producing a consolidated multi-scale feature tensor F_{out} that captures both global context and fine-grained cues.

The AFPN utilizes bilinear interpolation rather than deconvolution to reduce complexity, and it employs our parameterized DGCB to selectively highlight informative features. This design yields a compact architecture well suited for real-time or resource-limited applications. The resulting multi-scale representation serves as a foundation for subsequent pose estimation modules, enabling more accurate keypoint localization under a broad range of poses and imaging conditions.

The use of bilinear interpolation for upsampling in the AFPN is guided by both theoretical rationale and empirical effectiveness. Bilinear interpolation provides a computationally efficient, parameter-free method for resizing feature maps, making it particularly attractive for real-time or resource-constrained scenarios. In contrast to deconvolution, which increases model complexity and may introduce checkerboard artifacts, bilinear interpolation performs deterministic, smooth upsampling without additional learnable weights.

In our design, the potential limitations of bilinear interpolation, such as information loss or aliasing, are addressed through two mechanisms. First, a 1×1 convolution (Equation (5)) is applied before upsampling, which helps to suppress high-frequency noise and standardize channel dimensions. Second, the upsampled features are modulated by context-aware masks generated from DGCBs (Equation (8)), which selectively enhance salient regions and suppress irrelevant or noisy activation. This combination preserves critical spatial cues while maintaining efficiency.

Unlike traditional Feature Pyramid Networks that rely on fixed top–down pathways for multi-scale feature fusion, the AFPN introduces several architectural enhancements for more effective scale handling beyond the computational advantages of bilinear interpolation. Conventional FPNs typically apply direct addition or fixed-weight fusion, which may overlook the relative importance of scale-specific features. In contrast, the

AFPN integrates Dual-Gate Context Blocks that generate adaptive, context-aware masks to selectively emphasize the most informative features at each scale. Additionally, while traditional FPNs often fuse features sequentially, risking the dilution of fine-grained details from lower levels, the AFPN employs parallel aggregation followed by concatenation and fusion, preserving resolution-specific information. These distinctions collectively enable the AFPN to maintain strong keypoint localization performance across a range of object sizes and challenging visual conditions, while remaining efficient enough for deployment in resource-constrained environments.

3.3. Dual-Gate Context Blocks (DGCBs)

HPE frequently encounters ambiguities stemming from partial occlusions, multiple overlapping individuals, and cluttered scenes. Although previous strategies introduce GCBs or similar modules to incorporate scene-level features [32,33], most rely on a single attention mechanism that may not sufficiently separate background noise from body–joint features. In contrast, our proposed DGCB module learns two distinct masks, a context mask and a gating mask, that work together to refine feature representations and enhance joint localization.

Let $\mathbf{X} \in \mathbb{R}^{B\times C\times H\times W}$ be the feature map at a particular scale. A Global Average Pooling (GAP) operation condenses this tensor to $\mathrm{GAP}(\mathbf{X}) \in \mathbb{R}^{B\times C\times 1\times 1}$. Two parallel sets of 1×1 convolutions with ReLU and sigmoid activations process this pooled descriptor, as follows:

$$\mathbf{M}^c(\mathbf{X}) = \sigma\big(\mathbf{W}_2^c\delta(\mathbf{W}_1^c\mathrm{GAP}(\mathbf{X}))\big), \quad \mathbf{M}^g(\mathbf{X}) = \sigma\big(\mathbf{W}_2^g\delta(\mathbf{W}_1^g\mathrm{GAP}(\mathbf{X}))\big), \tag{10}$$

where $\delta(\cdot)$ and $\sigma(\cdot)$ denote ReLU and sigmoid activations, and $\mathbf{W}_1^c, \mathbf{W}_2^c, \mathbf{W}_1^g, \mathbf{W}_2^g$ are separate trainable weights, where c and g represent the contextual and gated information.

Although both branches appear structurally similar, they learn to serve distinct functional purposes through several mechanisms. First, the weight parameters are initialized independently and updated separately during training, allowing them to evolve toward different feature spaces. Second, the multiplicative interaction in the final output creates complementary specialization between branches; the network benefits when each mask focuses on different aspects of the input features rather than learning redundant information. Through this design, the context branch captures high-level global semantics features, while the gating branch selectively filters these contextual features based on local activation relevance.

Both masks are broadcast to the shape $\mathbb{R}^{B\times C\times H\times W}$ and applied element-wise to the input, as expressed in the following equation:

$$\widetilde{\mathbf{X}} = \mathbf{X} \odot M^c(\mathbf{X}) \odot M^g(\mathbf{X}), \tag{11}$$

where $\odot$ denotes element-wise multiplication.

Each scale in the AFPN incorporates a DGCB to refine features prior to the final fusion step. Although DGCBs add only two small 1×1 convolutions per scale, they minimally increase computational overhead while substantially boosting keypoint visibility under occlusions or complex backgrounds. Their design segregates global scene information from localized gating cues, fostering more resilient pose estimation in cluttered or overlapping scenarios. A schematic of the DGCB's internal architecture, illustrating the context mask and gating mask flow, is provided in Figure 4.

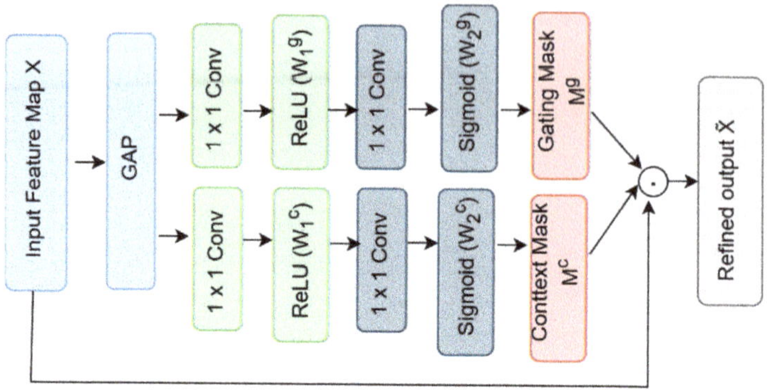

Figure 4. Architecture of DGCB. Two parallel sets of 1×1 convolution paths produce a context mask and a gating mask, each conditioned on the GAP features. These masks are broadcast and multiplied element-wise with the original input, enhancing relevant body–joint features while suppressing background interference.

3.4. Attention Mechanisms: Squeeze-and-Excitation and Spatial–Channel Refinement

Channel- and spatial-level attention can enhance the discriminative power of convolutional backbones for HPE. The proposed architecture incorporates the following two supportive modules: the classical SE block [28], which recalibrates feature channels globally, and a novel SCRM, which jointly emphasizes both channel and spatial dimensions. Although both modules utilize channel-wise weighting, their mechanisms differ fundamentally. SE blocks use a fully-connected bottleneck structure to capture global inter-channel dependencies, while the SCRM integrates a lightweight convolutional transformation for channel attention directly fused with spatial attention. These differences result in collaborative behavior during learning and inference.

3.4.1. Squeeze-and-Excitation (SE) Blocks

Each SE block adaptively re-weights channels based on a global context vector [28], effectively amplifying body part features and suppressing less relevant activations. Formally, let $\mathbf{X} \in \mathbb{R}^{B \times C \times H \times W}$ be the incoming feature map. GAP yields $\mathbf{z} = \mathrm{pool}(\mathbf{X}) \in \mathbb{R}^{B \times C \times 1 \times 1}$. A small fully connected (FC) network equivalent to 1×1 convolutions, equipped with ReLU and sigmoid activations, has parameters $\mathbf{W}_1, \mathbf{W}_2$, as expressed in the following:

$$\mathbf{s} = \sigma(\mathbf{W}_2 \delta(\mathbf{W}_1 \mathbf{z})), \tag{12}$$

where $\delta(\cdot)$ and $\sigma(\cdot)$ denote the ReLU and sigmoid functions, respectively. The resulting channel attention vector $\mathbf{s} \in \mathbb{R}^{B \times C \times 1 \times 1}$ is broadcast and multiplied element-wise with $\mathbf{X}$, as follows:

$$\widetilde{\mathbf{X}} = \mathbf{X} \odot \mathbf{s}. \tag{13}$$

Integrating an SE block after each of the ResNet34 backbone's four residual blocks ensures that channel refinements benefit from multi-scale global context. Figure 5 visually summarizes the main steps of the SE module.

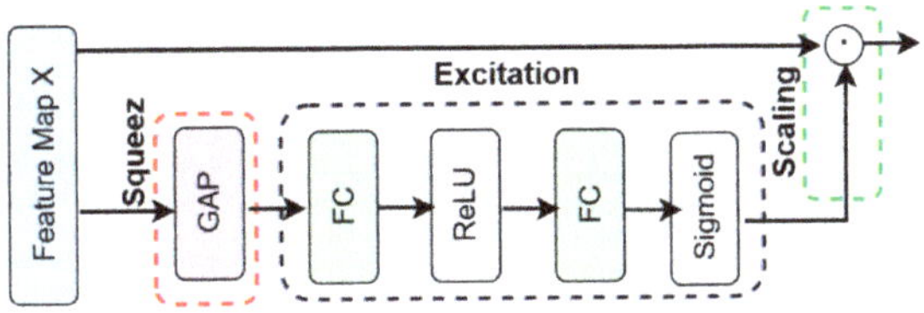

Figure 5. Architecture of SE Module. SE block applies GAP to each channel, producing a single descriptor vector. Two FC layers with ReLU and sigmoid activations re-weight channels based on their global importance, allowing network to emphasize key body part features.

3.4.2. Spatial–Channel Refinement Module (SCRM)

While SE blocks excel at global-channel-level recalibration, local spatial dependencies are crucial for accurately locating body joints, especially under occlusions. Addressing this need, our novel SCRM provides a simultaneous refinement of both the spatial and channel dimensions through a dual-attention mechanism. Let $\mathbf{X} \in \mathbb{R}^{B \times C \times H \times W}$ be the input feature map. An Adaptive Average Pooling (AAP) operation condenses $\mathbf{X}$ to $\mathrm{AAP}(\mathbf{X}) \in \mathbb{R}^{B \times C \times 1 \times 1}$, which is then transformed into a channel attention vector by a 1D convolution, as shown in the following:

$$\mathbf{X_c} = \sigma(\mathrm{BN}(\mathrm{Conv1D}(\mathrm{pool}(\mathbf{X})))), \tag{14}$$

where $\sigma(\cdot)$ and $\mathrm{BN}(\cdot)$ represent the sigmoid and BN functions, respectively. In parallel, a depthwise 3×3 convolution with BN and sigmoid activation extracts a spatial attention mask, as follows:

$$\mathbf{X_s} = \sigma(\mathrm{BN}(\mathrm{Conv2D_{depthwise}}(\mathbf{X}))). \tag{15}$$

Broadcasting both $\mathbf{X_c}$ and $\mathbf{X_s}$ to $\mathbb{R}^{B \times C \times H \times W}$ and multiplying them element-wise with $\mathbf{X}$ yields the following:

$$\widetilde{\mathbf{X}} = \mathbf{X} \odot \mathbf{X_c} \odot \mathbf{X_s}. \tag{16}$$

Although channel attention in SCRM is similar to SE, several critical distinctions differentiate their functionalities and effects. First, the channel attention generation differs architecturally. SE uses a bottleneck FC structure, compressing channel dimensions and modeling global inter-channel dependencies in a non-linear transformation, thereby capturing abstract relationships among the channels. In contrast, SCRM maintains the original channel dimensionality via 1D convolution, preserving channel-specific information without dimensionality reduction, thereby modeling simpler yet spatially aware channel relationships.

Second, the most significant distinction lies in the SCRM's simultaneous integration of spatial attention, which SE blocks lack entirely. By coupling channel emphasis ($\mathbf{X_c}$) with spatial filtering ($\mathbf{X_s}$), the SCRM enables the network to focus on which feature channels matter and where within the spatial field they should be emphasized. This dual optimization is particularly beneficial for the accurate localization of joints under challenging conditions such as partial occlusions or complex human poses. Unlike sequential attention methods such as CBAM [33], which apply spatial and channel attention independently in sequence, the SCRM fuses them in a single step for improved efficiency. Thus, the global channel recalibration of SE blocks and the combined spatial–channel refinement of the SCRM provide attention functionalities and collectively improve the robustness and accuracy of the model. Figure 6 outlines the SCRM's structure and highlights its combined spatial–channel approach.

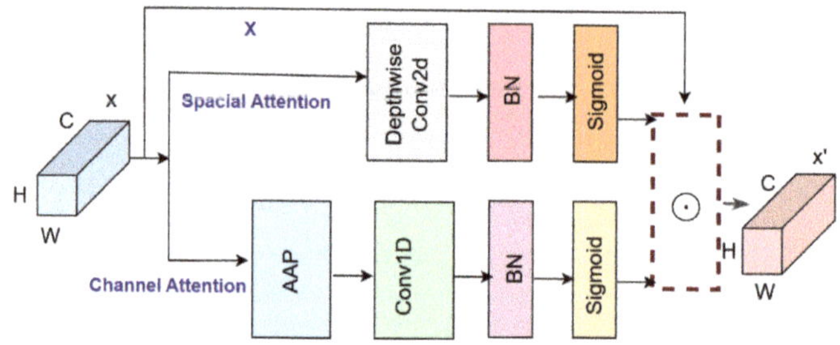

Figure 6. Overview of SCRM structure. A 1D convolutional layer generates channel attention from globally pooled features, while a depthwise 3×3 convolution extracts spatial attention. Multiplying both attention maps into the original feature refines local body part features and strengthens channel emphasis, helping to resolve occlusions or overlapping subjects.

3.5. AMFACPose Head and Coordinate Classification

Most HPE frameworks generate heatmaps for each joint and use peak-finding or regression to extract (x, y) coordinates, which can inflate memory usage and computational complexity [7,8,24]. In AMFACPose, we replace heatmaps with a coordinate classification approach that directly predicts discrete (x, y) indices for each joint. This methodology reduces the overhead of creating high-resolution heatmaps, enabling efficient inference without compromising accuracy.

3.5.1. Final Feature Reorganization

After passing through the modified ResNet34 backbone, AFPN, and attention modules, i.e., DGCBs, SE, and SCRM, the network outputs a fused feature map $\mathbf{F} \in \mathbb{R}^{B \times C \times H' \times W'}$, where B is the batch size, C is the number of channels, and (H', W') denotes the reduced spatial dimensions. To enable per-joint classification, the channel dimension C is reshaped into $(\mathrm{N} \times d)$, where d represents an embedding size for each joint, as expressed in the following:

$$\mathbf{F}' = \text{reshape}\Big(\mathbf{F}, B, \mathrm{N}, d, (H' \times W')\Big). \tag{17}$$

This transformation allocates a dedicated d-dimensional embedding for every joint at each spatial location, ensuring that subsequent classifiers can learn rich features specific to each keypoint.

3.5.2. Discrete Coordinate Classification

We discretize the continuous input space (W, H) into N_x and N_y bins along the horizontal and vertical axes, respectively, as follows:

$$N_x = W \times k, \quad N_y = H \times k, \tag{18}$$

where $k \geq 1$ is a scaling factor that controls the granularity of coordinate discretization. Each ground-truth joint coordinate (x_i, y_i) is mapped to a discrete location in $\{1, \ldots, N_x\} \times \{1, \ldots, N_y\}$.

In our implementation, we adopt $k = 2$, following the design choice proposed by Li et al. [12]. This value achieves a strong balance between prediction granularity and computational efficiency. Larger values of k lead to finer bins, which increase memory and computation requirements with limited benefit, while smaller values reduce model cost but introduce quantization artifacts that degrade localization precision.

For each joint i, the reorganized feature $\mathbf{F}_i' \in \mathbb{R}^{B \times d \times (H' \times W')}$ is fed into two MLPs equipped with Mish activation functions, as follows:

$$\mathbf{p}_x^i = \mathrm{MLP}_x(\mathbf{F}_i') \in \mathbb{R}^{N_x}, \quad \mathbf{p}_y^i = \mathrm{MLP}_y(\mathbf{F}_i') \in \mathbb{R}^{N_y}. \tag{19}$$

where $\mathbf{p}_x^i$ and $\mathbf{p}_y^i$ represent discrete probability distributions over the set of possible x- and y-bins. Algorithm 2 outlines this procedure.

Algorithm 2 AMFACPose: keypoint estimation process

Require: RGB image I of size $H \times W \times 3$
Ensure: Predicted keypoint coordinates $\{o_x^1, o_y^1, \ldots, o_x^N, o_y^N\}$ for N keypoints
Feature Extraction:
  Process I through the modified ResNet backbone to obtain fused feature map $\mathbf{F}$ of size (B, C, H', W')
Feature Reorganization:
  Reshape $\mathbf{F}$ to $\mathbf{F}'$ of size $(B, \mathrm{N}, d,\ H' \times W')$
Discretization Setup:
  Let $k \geq 1$ be the scaling factor
  Set $N_x = W \times k$ and $N_y = H \times k$
for $i = 1, \ldots, \mathrm{N}$ **do**
    Horizontal Classification:
      $\mathbf{p}_x^i \leftarrow \mathrm{MLP}_x(\mathbf{F}_i')$
    Vertical Classification:
      $\mathbf{p}_x^i \leftarrow \mathrm{MLP}_y(\mathbf{F}_i')$
end for
return Keypoint coordinates $\{o_x^1, o_y^1, \ldots, o_x^N, o_y^N\}$

By framing joint location prediction as a classification problem, AMFACPose streamlines the output space, bypasses large heatmaps, and simplifies post-processing. The MLP-based classifiers with Mish activations can learn complex spatial dependencies, ultimately leading to improved localization precision. This framework also reduce memory usage, making the model more suitable for real-time and resource-constrained scenarios.

3.6. AMFACPose Loss Function: KLDDiscretLoss

Conventional HPE often adopts Mean Squared Error (MSE) [7] or L1-based losses, which assume continuous error distributions [34]. However, in our coordinate classification framework, joint positions are discretized into bins along the x- and y-axes, rendering such regression-focused objectives less optimal. To address this discrepancy, we propose KLDDiscretLoss, a divergence-based criterion grounded in Kullback–Leibler Divergence (KLD) [35]. By treating pose estimation as a classification problem, KLDDiscretLoss directly compares predicted probability distributions with discrete ground-truth distributions, thereby capturing the inherent uncertainties of joint positions.

A key advantage of KLDDiscretLoss is that it models probability distributions rather than point estimates. This perspective is particularly beneficial when joint locations are ambiguous due to scale variations, occlusions, or overlapping body parts. In order to refine the network's confidence calibration, we incorporate two additional mechanisms—label smoothing [36] and temperature scaling [37]. Label smoothing allocates a small fraction of the ground-truth probability mass uniformly across all coordinate bins, preventing overfitting and minimizing cases where the network becomes overconfident in a single discrete location.

Temperature scaling, controlled by a parameter T, modifies the softmax logits by $\frac{1}{T}$. When $T > 1$, the resulting distributions become softer, reflecting higher uncertainty in the model's predictions; when $T < 1$, the distributions sharpen, forcing the network to commit more strongly to specific bins. The temperature value plays an important role in situations involving occlusion or pose ambiguity. A moderately sharpened output distribution encourages the model to focus on likely joint locations, improving spatial localization while still expressing uncertainty. In our experiments, we set $T = 0.8$, which we found to provide a favorable trade-off between sharpness and calibration. This choice was guided by early empirical validation and is consistent with insights from a previous study on model calibration [37]. It allows the network to remain confident in its predictions without becoming overly rigid or under-responsive in uncertain contexts, such as occluded joints.

Concretely, let o_x^i and o_y^i denote the predicted logits for x- and y-coordinates of the i-th joint, and let $\text{gt}(o_x^i)$ and $\text{gt}(o_y^i)$ be the corresponding ground-truth distributions. A joint-specific weight W_i is assigned to emphasize harder-to-detect keypoints, such as hands or feet. The KLDDiscretLoss for the i-th joint is given by the following:

$$\text{Loss}_\text{i} = W_i \times \left[\text{KLD}\left(\log\left[\text{Softmax}\left(\frac{o_x^i}{T}\right)\right], \text{gt}(o_x^i)\right) + \text{KLD}\left(\log\left[\text{Softmax}\left(\frac{o_x^i}{T}\right)\right], \text{gt}(o_x^i)\right)\right], \tag{20}$$

where $\text{Softmax}(\frac{o_x^i}{T})$ and $\text{Softmax}(\frac{o_y^i}{T})$ convert the scaled logits into probability distributions. The total KLDiscretLoss is then computed as the mean across all N joints, as follows:

$$\text{KLDDiscretLoss} = \frac{1}{N}\sum_{i=1}^{N} \text{Loss}_i. \tag{21}$$

Compared to regression-based losses such as SmoothL1 or MSE, KLDDiscretLoss offers a principled advantage under occlusion. Regression losses penalize deviations from ground-truth coordinates without accounting for uncertainty, which can result in overconfident and unreliable predictions for occluded or ambiguous joints. In contrast, KLDDiscretLoss allows the network to express uncertainty by distributing probability mass across plausible locations. This soft probabilistic output creates natural error bounds. If a joint is fully occluded, the prediction can approach a uniform distribution, with the error exceeding the expected value by up to half the discretization range. Empirically, this advantage is reflected in our CrowdPose performance, where AMFACPose achieves 65.9 AP in the hard subset, demonstrating robustness in severe occlusion scenarios. Thus, KLDDiscretLoss provides a more reliable and uncertainty-aware mechanism for keypoint localization than point-based regression losses.

Our PyTorch-based implementation [38] processes the (x, y) distributions for each joint independently, facilitating the straightforward integration of label smoothing and temperature scaling in the preprocessing steps. This structure also enables fine-grained control over which joints receive higher weighting, enabling the model to spend more capacity on challenging joints or underrepresented body parts. By guiding the network to produce calibrated probability distributions rather than single-point predictions, KLDiscretLoss enhances robustness against partial visibility, background clutter, and pose variability.

4. Experimental Setup

4.1. Datasets

We conducted comprehensive evaluations of AMFACPose using two established benchmarks in HPE—the MS COCO [27] and CrowdPose datasets [39]. These datasets were selected for their complementary characteristics, enabling a thorough assessment of our model across diverse scenarios.

The MS COCO 2017 dataset serves as a primary benchmark for HPE evaluation, containing over 200,000 images with approximately 250,000 annotated person instances.

Each instance is labeled with 17 keypoints, encompassing facial features i.e., eyes, ears, nose, and body joints such as shoulders, elbows, wrists, hips, knees, ankles. The dataset is partitioned into 118,000 training images, 5000 validation images, and a separate test set. MS COCO's strength lies in its diversity, featuring varied poses, scales, and occlusions in natural contexts, thereby providing a robust evaluation framework for model generalization.

On the other hand, the CrowdPose dataset [39] specifically addresses the challenges of pose estimation in crowded scenarios. Comprising 20,000 images with approximately 80,000 person instances, CrowdPose annotates 14 keypoints per person, focusing on body joints i.e., shoulders, elbows, wrists, hips, knees, ankles, while excluding facial landmarks. The dataset is divided into 10,000 training, 2000 validation, and 8000 testing sets. CrowdPose's distinctive feature is its emphasis on person-to-person occlusions and high-density scenarios, presenting more challenging conditions than the typical pose estimation datasets. This characteristic makes it particularly valuable for evaluating our model's performance in real-world crowded environments, where accurate pose estimation is crucial yet technically challenging.

4.2. Evaluation Metrics

Our model's performance evaluation utilizes the Object Keypoint Similarity (OKS) metric, which provides a rigorous assessment of keypoint localization accuracy. The OKS metric quantifies the similarity between predicted and ground-truth keypoint positions through the following formulation:

$$\text{OKS} = \frac{\sum_i \delta(v_i > 0) \exp\left(-\frac{d_i^2}{2s^2k_i^2}\right)}{\sum_i \delta(v_i > 0)} \tag{22}$$

where d_i represents the Euclidean distance between the predicted and ground-truth positions for the i-th keypoint, s denotes the person instance scale, k_i is a keypoint-specific normalization constant, and v_i indicates keypoint visibility. The indicator function $\delta(v_i > 0)$ ensures evaluation focuses exclusively on visible keypoints. We used average precision (AP) as our primary performance metric, calculated across ten OKS thresholds ranging from 0.50 to 0.95 in 0.05 increments. This comprehensive range allows for a detailed performance assessment at various precision levels. We specifically report AP_{50} and AP_{75} corresponding to OKS thresholds of 0.50 and 0.75, providing insights into the model's performance at different precision requirements. Scale-specific metrics AP_M and AP_L evaluate performance on medium- and large-sized instances, respectively. Additionally, we compute average recall (AR) following similar protocols to AP, offering complementary insights into the model's detection capabilities.

For the CrowdPose dataset evaluation, we maintain consistency with MS COCO by utilizing the same fundamental OKS metric while incorporating additional crowd-specific measures. These include AP metrics stratified by scene complexity, AP_{easy} , AP_{medium}, and AP_{hard}. Scene complexity classification is determined by the crowding level, computed as the average Intersection over Union of the ground-truth bounding boxes within each image. This stratified evaluation framework enables a detailed assessment of our model's performance across varying levels of scene complexity and person-to-person occlusion. Through this comprehensive evaluation framework, combining standard OKS-based metrics with crowd-specific measures, we ensure a thorough assessment of our model's keypoint localization capabilities across diverse scenarios. This approach validates the model's reliability in both general and crowded environments, providing a complete understanding of its real-world applicability.

4.3. Implementation Details

Our implementation strategy emphasizes training stability, efficient resource utilization, and strong generalization for real-world pose estimation. We implemented comprehensive data augmentation techniques including random horizontal flips, rotational variations from $-30°$ to $+30°$, and scale adjustments from 0.7 to 1.3 [40]. These augmentations were implemented using the PyTorch 1.12.1 framework, ensuring efficient and reliable model training.

Training proceeds for 140 epochs, with a batch size of 32 to maintain a balance between gradient stability and computational throughput. Six parallel data-processing workers further accelerate input pipelines. The initial learning rate is set to 1×10^{-5}, enabling gradual convergence while preventing overshooting of local minima. We used the Mish activation function [41] in the ResNet, a smooth and non-monotonic alternative to ReLU that has demonstrated effectiveness in minimizing vanishing gradients [42] and improving feature extraction in deeper models.

To refine parameter updates and manage regularization, we adopt the AdamW optimizer [43], which decouples weight decay from the main optimization steps. This separation grants more precise control over the magnitude of regularization and often produces better generalization performance [44]. Empirical studies [45] show that AdamW outperforms classical optimizers in complex tasks by maintaining stable gradients and resisting overfitting, making it particularly suitable for the challenges posed by dense keypoint localization.

The full AMFACPose model—which includes the AFPN, DGCBs, and other attention modules—requires approximately 78 h to converge, while the baseline ResNet34 model converges in approximately 42 h under the same training schedule. Despite the modest increase in training time, the additional modules yield significant accuracy gains, justifying their computational cost.

5. Results and Discussion

This section presents a comprehensive quantitative and qualitative evaluation of the proposed AMFACPose framework. We first detail its performance on the MS COCO dataset, highlighting both accuracy and scalability. Subsequently, we examine resource–efficiency trade-offs and analyze the model's behavior under congested scenarios using the CrowdPose dataset. Finally, we provide qualitative examples of the model predictions, illustrating AMFACPose's versatility across diverse real-world conditions.

5.1. Performance on COCO Dataset

Table 1 compares AMFACPose with several SOTA 2D HPE models on the MS COCO dataset, including multiple recent approaches. Utilizing a ResNet34 backbone with an input resolution of 384 × 288, AMFACPose achieves an AP of 76.6, surpassing coordinate-based methods such as AECA-PRNetCC, with an AP of 76.0, and SimCC, with an AP of 73.4. Additionally, AMFACPose marginally outperforms the strong heatmap-based baseline HRNet-W48, which achieves an AP of 76.3. The method also demonstrates superior performance compared to recently introduced techniques, such as BR-Pose with an AP of 75.3, various PCDPose models exhibiting AP scores ranging from 73.5 to 74.3, SDPose variants achieving AP scores between 73.5 and 73.7, and the CSDNet-m/12 model with an AP of 75.0. Many of these methods rely on the robust HRNet backbone, emphasizing the competitive advantage of AMFACPose's coordinate classification pipeline, which achieves comparable or superior accuracy without incurring significant computational overhead from heatmap generation and post-processing.

Table 1. Quantitative comparison on MS COCO; accuracy metrics across different model architectures and input configurations.

Model	Backbone	Input	AP	AP_{50}	AP_{75}	AP_M	AP_L	AR
Heatmap-based								
SimpleBaseline [7]	ResNet-50	384 × 288	72.2	89.3	78.9	68.1	79.7	77.6
	ResNet-101	384 × 288	73.6	89.6	80.3	69.9	81.1	79.1
HRNet [8]	HRNet-W32	384 × 288	75.8	90.6	82.7	71.9	82.8	81.0
	HRNet-W48	384 × 288	76.3	90.8	82.9	72.3	**83.4**	**81.2**
TokenPose-L/D24 [10]	CNN	256 × 192	75.8	90.3	82.5	72.3	82.7	80.6
TokenPose-L/D6 [10]	CNN	256 × 192	75.4	90.0	81.8	71.8	82.4	80.4
BR-Pose [46]	HRNet-W32	256 × 192	75.3	90.6	82.5	71.7	81.9	80.4
PCDPose-B [47]	HRNet-W32	256 × 192	74.3	89.7	81.4	70.8	81.0	79.5
PCDPose-S-V2 [47]	HRNet-W32	256 × 192	74.1	89.5	81.1	70.7	81.0	79.3
PCDPose-S-V1 [47]	HRNet-W32	256 × 192	73.5	89.6	80.9	69.8	80.9	78.9
SDPose-B [48]	CNN	256 × 192	73.7	89.6	80.4	70.3	80.5	79.1
SDPose-S-V2 [48]	CNN	256 × 192	73.5	89.5	80.4	70.1	80.3	78.7
CSDNet-m/12 [49]	HRNet-W32	256 × 192	75.0	89.9	81.7	71.4	81.9	80.1
Regression-based								
PRTR [50]	ResNet-50	384 × 288	68.2	88.2	75.2	63.2	76.2	76.0
	ResNet-101	384 × 288	70.1	88.8	77.6	65.7	77.4	77.5
	HRNet-W32	384 × 288	73.1	89.4	79.8	68.8	80.4	79.8
Coordinate-based								
SimCC [12]	ResNet-50	384 × 288	73.4	89.2	80.0	69.7	80.6	78.8
AECA-PRNetCC [13]	ResNet34	384 × 288	76.0	92.5	82.4	73.3	80.7	79.0
AMFACPose	**ResNet34**	**384 × 288**	**76.6**	**92.6**	**83.7**	**73.9**	81.2	79.3
	ResNet34	256 × 256	75.6	**92.6**	81.8	72.5	80.2	78.2
	ResNet18	384 × 288	73.1	91.6	79.5	70.3	78.0	76.0
	ResNet18	256 × 256	72.1	91.5	79.4	69.1	76.7	75.0

A detailed analysis of the threshold-specific metrics reveals strong performances at both moderate and stricter accuracy levels. Specifically, AMFACPose achieves an AP_{50} of 92.6 and an AP_{75} of 83.7. Additionally, the method demonstrates balanced effectiveness across different object scales, achieving an AP_M of 73.9 and an AP_L of 81.2. These results show the effectiveness of the Adaptive Feature Pyramid Network and the attention modules in managing subjects of varying sizes and enhancing global and local contextual understanding, even under challenging conditions such as partial occlusions or diverse poses. To further investigate the trade-offs between resource efficiency and accuracy, evaluations with smaller input resolutions, such as 256 × 256, and lighter backbones, such as ResNet18, were conducted. These configurations consistently maintain AP scores above 72.0, demonstrating AMFACPose's adaptability to varying computational constraints. Notably, the most compact configuration with ResNet18 at a resolution of 256 × 256 still achieves an AP of 72.1, competitively close to several recent, larger-architecture methods. This adaptability highlight the practical applicability of AMFACPose, particularly for deployment in real-world scenarios involving edge devices with limited computational resources.

5.2. Model Complexity and Resource Efficiency

Table 2 presents a comparative summary of AMFACPose alongside recent 2D HPE models, emphasizing accuracy and computational efficiency. With a ResNet34 backbone at 384 × 288 input, AMFACPose achieves an AP of 76.6 using only 3.8 M parameters and 5.2 GFLOPs. This reflects a substantial improvement over HRNet-W48, which reports a slightly lower AP of 76.3 but requires 63.6 M parameters and 32.9 GFLOPs. Compared to

AECA-PRNetCC, which achieves an AP of 76.0 with 29.0 M parameters and 8.3 GFLOPs, AMFACPose delivers similar accuracy at a fraction of the computational cost.

Table 2. Model complexity on MS COCO: AP, parameters (M), and FLOPs (G) for leading 2D HPE methods.

Model	Backbone	Input	AP	Params (M)	FLOPs (G)
Heatmap-based					
SimpleBaseline [7]	ResNet-50	384 × 288	72.2	34.0	18.6
	ResNet-101	384 × 288	73.6	53.0	26.7
HRNet [8]	HRNet-W32	384 × 288	75.8	28.5	16.0
	HRNet-W48	384 × 288	76.3	63.6	32.9
TokenPose-L/D24 [10]	CNN	256 × 192	75.8	27.5	11.0
TokenPose-L/D6 [10]	CNN	256 × 192	75.4	20.8	9.1
BR-Pose [46]	HRNet-W32	256 × 192	75.3	31.3	9.0
PCDPose-B [47]	HRNet-W32	256 × 192	74.3	13.8	5.2
PCDPose-S-V2 [47]	HRNet-W32	256 × 192	74.1	7.7	6.7
PCDPose-S-V1 [47]	HRNet-W32	256 × 192	73.5	8.0	4.5
SDPose-B [48]	CNN	256 × 192	73.7	13.2	5.2
SDPose-S-V2 [48]	CNN	256 × 192	73.5	6.2	4.7
CSDNet-m/12 [49]	HRNet-W32	256 × 192	75.0	17.4	6.9
Regression-based					
PRTR [50]	ResNet-50	384 × 288	68.2	41.5	11.0
	ResNet-101	384 × 288	70.1	60.4	19.1
	HRNet-W32	384 × 288	73.1	57.2	21.6
Coordinate-based					
SimCC [12]	ResNet-50	384 × 288	73.4	36.8	20.2
AECA-PRNetCC [13]	ResNet34	384 × 288	76.0	29.0	8.3
AMFACPose	ResNet34	384 × 288	76.6	3.8	5.2
	ResNet34	256 × 256	75.6	3.6	3.1
	ResNet18	384 × 288	73.1	2.5	3.2
	ResNet18	256 × 256	72.1	2.4	1.9

Recent models further highlight AMFACPose's efficiency. BR-Pose reaches 75.3 AP with 31.3 M parameters and 9.0 GFLOPs. PCDPose variants yield AP scores from 73.5 to 74.3, with 7.7–13.8 M parameters and 4.5–6.7 GFLOPs. SDPose methods achieve 73.5–73.7 AP with 6.2–13.2 M parameters and 4.7–5.2 GFLOPs, while CSDNet-m/12 reaches 75.0 AP with 17.4 M parameters and 6.9 GFLOPs. In all cases, AMFACPose offers better accuracy with significantly lower resource requirements, supporting its deployment in constrained environments.

Further reductions are achieved using ResNet18. At 256 × 256 input, AMFACPose maintains 72.1 AP with only 2.4 M parameters and 1.9 GFLOPs, showing its adaptability to low-power applications without severe performance loss.

We also visualize these trade-offs in Figure 7, which plots the AP on the vertical axis versus model parameters on the horizontal axis. The size and color of each bubble correspond to FLOPs, and the outline color denotes the underlying methodology, which are heatmap-based, regression-based, and coordinate-based. As shown, AMFACPose configurations appear near the lower-parameter, lower-FLOP regions while achieving competitive accuracy. In contrast, HRNet-W48 occupies a higher-parameter area with significantly higher computational cost for a similar AP score. These findings point to the efficacy of AMFACPose's coordinate classification pipeline and lightweight design components, making it well suited for resource-constrained scenarios.

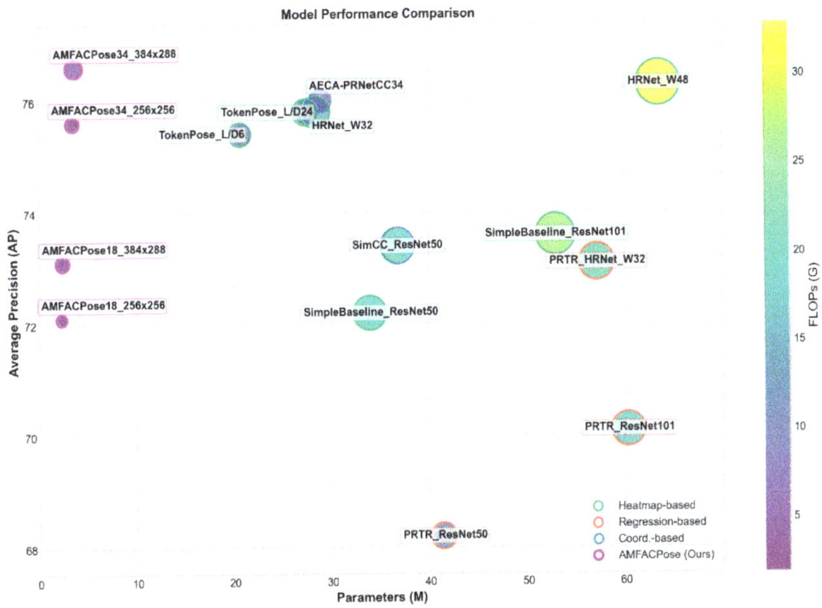

Figure 7. Comparative visualization of model efficiency. Bubbles represent both size and color of FLOPs, while x-axis shows parameter count, and y-axis depicts AP. AMFACPose with purple outline maintains high AP with fewer parameters and FLOPs compared to various SOTA models.

While demonstrating significant improvements in computational efficiency, AMFACPose also introduces several practical trade-offs. The use of DSC and the AFPN substantially reduces computation to 5.2 GFLOPs, compared to 32.9 GFLOPs in HRNet-W48, while maintaining competitive AP scores. This design enables real-time performance even on edge devices such as Jetson platforms, as discussed in Section 6. However, the coordinate classification strategy, while efficient, involves discretizing the coordinate space, which may introduce localization limitations for small joints (e.g., wrists or ankles) when high precision is required. In such cases, high-resolution heatmap regression may provide better granularity. Moreover, while our approach handles moderate occlusions effectively using attention modules such as DGCBs and the SCRM, it does not incorporate explicit visibility classification. Competing works such as HPCVNet [26], which achieves 77.6 mAP on COCO, model keypoint visibility directly, offering added robustness in scenarios with extreme occlusion or dense overlapping subjects. These trade-offs reflect the broader goal of balancing accuracy, interpretability, and deployment feasibility in real-world pose estimation systems.

5.3. Performance on CrowdPose Dataset

We further evaluated AMFACPose on the CrowdPose dataset [39], known for emphasizing challenging scenarios involving person-to-person occlusions and complex group interactions. As detailed in Table 3, AMFACPose utilizing a ResNet34 backbone achieves a leading AP score of 75.3, along with AP_{50} and AP_{75} values of 93.4 and 81.0, respectively. This performance surpasses established frameworks such as PRTR with an AP of 71.6, HRFormer with 72.6, and ED-Pose with Swin-L, which achieves 73.1. Furthermore, AMFACPose demonstrates higher accuracy than recent methods, including GroupPose with an AP of 74.1, MAQT with 74.3, and CCAM-Person with 74.4.

Across varying levels of difficulty, AMFACPose maintains strong performance, reporting an AP_{easy} of 82.1 and AP_{medium} of 76.4. This highlights its capability to accurately estimate poses under moderate occlusions. Although the model yields a slightly lower AP_{hard} of 65.9 compared to CCAM-Person at 66.9 and MAQT at 66.7, it remains highly competitive. These results emphasize the contribution of adaptive multi-scale feature fusion and dual-gate context blocks in resolving complex occlusions and effectively separating overlapping human joints.

Our strong performance on CrowdPose's challenging occlusion scenarios validates AMFACPose's approach to occlusion handling through feature enhancement rather than explicit visibility classification as in HPCVNet [26]. While HPCVNet achieves slightly higher mAP on COCO (77.6 vs. 76.6), its performance on occlusion-heavy datasets like CrowdPose has not been established. The combination of multi-scale feature fusion via the AFPN and contextual refinement through DGCBs in our approach proves particularly effective for distinguishing overlapping subjects in real-world scenarios.

Altogether, AMFACPose combines high accuracy with low parameter complexity and reliable performance in crowded visual scenes. The integration of attention-guided multi-scale processing and a coordinate classification framework makes it particularly well suited for real-time applications and deployment in embedded environments, where both precision and efficiency are essential.

Table 3. Performance evaluation of SOTA 2D HPE models on CrowdPose; AP scores across easy, medium, and hard tiers.

Model	Backbone	AP	AP_{50}	AP_{75}	AP_{easy}	AP_{medium}	AP_{hard}
Sim.Baseline [7]	ResNet-50	60.8	81.4	65.7	71.4	61.2	51.2
HRNet [8]	HigherHRNet-W48	67.6	87.4	72.6	75.8	68.1	58.9
DEKR [51]	DEKR-W48	68.0	85.5	73.4	76.6	68.8	58.4
ED-Pose [52]	ResNet-50	69.9	88.6	75.8	77.7	70.6	60.9
PRTR [50]	Swin-L	71.6	90.4	78.3	77.3	72.0	65.8
HRFormer [9]	HRFormer-B	72.6	89.6	77.2	76.6	73.5	59.5
ED-Pose [52]	Swin-L	73.1	90.5	79.8	80.5	73.8	63.8
HDA-Pose [53]	YOLOv8	73.7	92.3	77.5	79.8	75.0	66.1
GroupPose [54]	Swin-L	74.1	91.3	80.4	80.8	74.7	66.4
MAQT [55]	HRNet-S	74.3	91.5	80.5	80.9	74.8	66.7
CCAM-Person [56]	YOLOv8	74.4	92.7	78.4	80.4	75.7	66.9
AMFACPose	**ResNet34**	**75.3**	**93.4**	**81.0**	**82.1**	**76.4**	65.9

Bold values indicate the proposed method and the best performance in each evaluation metric.

5.4. Qualitative Analysis

Figure 8 depicts representative AMFACPose outputs on the COCO dataset, demonstrating the framework's adaptability to diverse poses, occlusions, and environmental conditions. In high-action sports scenarios such as tennis, the model accurately tracks rapid limb movements without sacrificing fine-grained joint precision. Outdoor settings, ranging from skateboarding parks to beach environments, highlight the system's resilience to shifting backgrounds, lighting variations, and dynamic body configurations. Even in multi-person scenes where individuals overlap, AMFACPose reliably distinguishes each subject's joints, showing the effectiveness of its multi-scale fusion and gating modules. These qualitative observations align with the quantitative metrics reported earlier, suggesting AMFACPose's potential for real-world deployment in applications demanding both accuracy and computational efficiency.

Figure 8. Qualitative examples of AMFACPose's predictions on COCO images under diverse scenarios, including fast sports movements, overlapping subjects, and challenging lighting conditions. Results illustrate model's robustness to occlusions, pose variations, and multi-person interactions.

To further investigate the effectiveness of our proposed DGCB module in handling occlusion, we visualize attention maps with and without the DGCB enabled. As shown in Figure 9, we evaluate a sample image where a subject's hands and shoulders are partially occluded by flowers. The attention maps indicate that when the DGCB is active, the model maintains more focused attention on the occluded joints. The difference map (rightmost panel) highlights the regions where attention increases (red) or decreases (blue), showing that the DGCB effectively enhances attention near occluded keypoints.

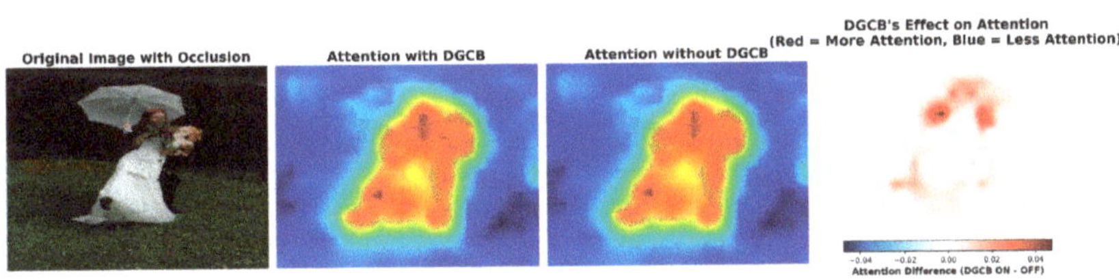

Figure 9. Visualization of DGCB's effectiveness in handling occlusion. (**Left**): Original occluded image. (**Center**): Attention maps with and without DGCB. (**Right**): Difference map (DGCB ON–OFF), showing improved focus in red and decreased attention in blue.

Figure 10 provides a detailed view of the occluded region. Zoomed attention maps clearly show that the DGCB helps maintain activation on partially hidden body parts. The additional focus around occluded limbs demonstrates how the DGCB leverages global context to refine local attention, improving keypoint localization under challenging visibility conditions.

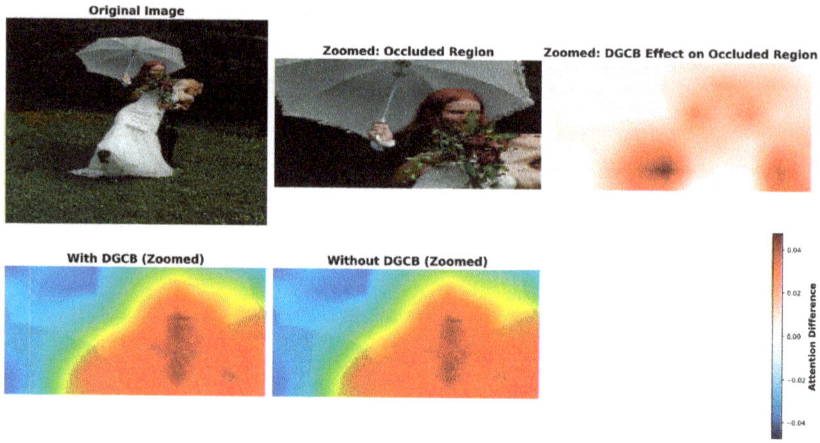

Figure 10. Zoomed qualitative analysis of DGCB's effect on occluded body parts. Top row: Original image and zoomed region. Bottom row: Attention with and without DGCB, showing stronger activation on occluded subject's upper body when DGCB is used.

These qualitative results reinforce our quantitative findings on the CrowdPose benchmark and provide visual evidence that DGCBs significantly enhance occlusion robustness in AMFACPose.

6. Performance and Efficiency Analysis

Figure 11 offers a visual overview of the speed–accuracy trade-offs for 2D HPE models, highlighting how AP correlates with inference speed on an RTX 3060 GPU. Each marker's size denotes the model's overall performance, while the green-shaded area represents the "sweet spot", where a favorable balance of high AP and real-time throughput emerges. AMFACPose, with a ResNet34 backbone, resides within this region, emphasizing its ability to maintain robust accuracy while achieving competitive frame rates. In comparison, alternative approaches often sacrifice accuracy for speed, or vice versa, reinforcing AMFACPose's balanced design.

Table 4 summarizes AMFACPose's performance across multiple hardware platforms, including the Jetson Orin Nano-8 at 15 W, Orin NX-8 at 20 W, Orin NX-16 at 25 W, and two desktop GPUs, which are RTX 4090 and RTX 3060. Using a ResNet34 backbone with a 384 × 288 input on the Orin Nano-8, this configuration processes each frame in 67.82 ms, corresponding to 14.74 fps. The more powerful Orin NX-16 reduces inference time to 45.97 ms and yields 21.75 fps. High-end GPUs offer even higher throughput, where the same setup runs at 6.74 ms per frame, i.e., 148.45 fps, on the RTX 4090 and 9.90 ms, i.e., 101.04 fps, on the RTX 3060. Reducing the input resolution to 256 × 256 substantially increases speed, especially on lower-wattage devices. For instance, the ResNet34 variant at 256 × 256 runs at 23.59 fps on the Orin Nano-8, scaling to over 30 fps on the Orin NX-8 and exceeding 100 fps on the RTX 3060.

Switching to a ResNet18 backbone trades off some precision for even greater efficiency. At a 384 × 288 input, this lighter configuration processes frames in 43.15 ms with 23.18 fps on the Orin Nano-8. This improves to 29.64 ms with 33.74 fps on the Orin NX-16, and further reduces to under 5 ms per frame with 201.10 fps on the RTX 4090. The 256 × 256 variant pushes the fps further across all devices; it reaches 36.02 fps on the Orin Nano-8 and scales to 50.45 fps on the Orin NX-16, while desktop GPUs offer well over 150 fps with modest sacrifices in accuracy relative to the ResNet34 backbone. These observations confirm that AMFACPose can flexibly adapt to various computational budgets, ranging from highly constrained edge platforms to powerful desktop workstations, while retaining a competitive balance between speed and precision.

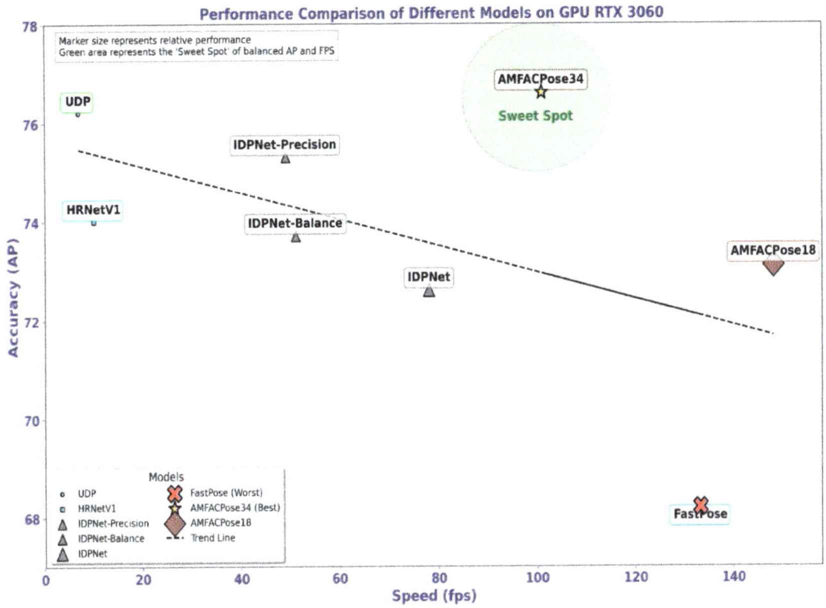

Figure 11. Speed–accuracy trade-offs for various models on RTX 3060 GPU. Each marker's size indicates relative performance, and green zone denotes "sweet spot" balancing high AP with fps. AMFACPose achieves notable accuracy in this region without incurring heavy computational costs.

Table 4. Performance analysis of AMFACPose model across different hardware platforms.

Model	Backbone	Input	AP	Orin Nano-8 (15 W) ms/fps	Orin NX-8 (20 W) ms/fps	Orin NX-16 (25 W) ms/fps	RTX 4090 ms/fps	RTX 3060 ms/fps
AMFACPose	ResNet34	384 × 288	76.6	67.82/14.74	52.90/18.90	45.97/21.75	6.74/148.45	9.90/101.04
		256 × 256	75.6	42.46/23.59	33.18/30.23	29.28/34.16	6.46/154.80	8.75/114.31
	ResNet18	384 × 288	73.1	43.15/23.18	33.05/29.89	29.64/33.74	4.97/201.10	6.75/148.19
		256 × 256	72.1	27.76/36.02	22.21/45.03	19.82/50.45	4.85/206.39	6.15/162.53

Table 5 places AMFACPose alongside prominent 2D HPE methods on an RTX 3060. Even with the ResNet34 backbone, the model obtains 101.0 fps, surpassing the speed of most competing solutions and matching or outperforming many in accuracy. The ResNet18 setup, although slightly lower in AP at 73.1, pushes throughput to 148.1 fps. Models like UDP with ResNet152 reach comparable precision but operate at only 6.9 fps, highlighting AMFACPose's efficiency advantages. The results of Table 5 are visualized in Figure 11. Across diverse settings and hardware, these results demonstrate that our architecture consistently maintains a favorable trade-off between accuracy and real-time usability, making it a versatile choice for applications that demand both precision and scalability.

Table 5. Comparison of AMFACPose with other methods on RTX_3060.

Model	Backbone	AP	GPU–RTX-3060 (fps)
UDP [28]	ResNet152	76.2	6.9
HRNetV1 [8]	HRNetV1-w32	74.0	10.0
IDPNet-Precision [20]	IDPNet-1286	75.3	49.0
IDPNet-Balance [20]	IDPNet-1143	73.7	51.0
IDPNet [20]	DPNet-1132	72.6	78.0
FastPose [19]	LPN-50	68.2	133.0
AMFACPose	ResNet34	76.6	101.0
	ResNet18	73.1	148.1

7. Ablation Study

A systematic ablation study was conducted to evaluate the contribution of each core component in AMFACPose. Table 6 reports the results on the MS COCO dataset using a ResNet34 backbone with an input resolution of 384 × 288. Starting from the baseline, we incrementally added the AFPN, DGCBs, SCRM, SE blocks, and CoordConv2d layers, enabling a detailed assessment of both the accuracy and computational cost associated with each module.

Table 6. Ablation study analysis of performance and computational cost of AMFACPose components on COCO dataset.

Model Variant	AP	AP_{50}	AP_{75}	AP_M	AP_L	AR	Params (M)	FLOPs (G)
Baseline (ResNet34)	72.4	91.3	78.3	69.3	77.3	75.3	3.3	4.7
+AFPN	73.2	91.5	79.3	69.9	78.5	76.3	3.5	5.0
+DGCBs	73.4	91.5	79.9	70.1	78.8	76.9	3.6	5.0
+SCRM	75.4	92.5	82.0	72.6	80.2	78.8	3.6	5.2
+SE	76.3	92.6	82.8	73.0	81.2	79.0	3.8	5.2
+CoordConv2d **(Full AMFACPose)**	**76.6**	**92.6**	**83.7**	**73.9**	**81.2**	**79.3**	**3.8**	**5.2**

The bold is used to highlight our complete proposed method (Full AMFACPose).

The baseline configuration achieves an AP of 72.4 with 3.3 M parameters and 4.70 GFLOPs, serving as the initial reference. Adding the AFPN increases AP to 73.2 while slightly increasing the model size to 3.5 M parameters and 5.0 GFLOPs, demonstrating the benefit of efficient multi-scale feature aggregation. Introducing DGCBs further improves AP to 73.4, with parameters at 3.6 M and FLOPs at 5.0, highlighting better contextual encoding with minimal cost.

A more substantial performance gain comes from integrating the SCRM module, which increases AP to 75.4 while maintaining 3.6 M parameters and 5.2 GFLOPs. This shows the effectiveness of joint spatial and channel refinement. The inclusion of SE blocks lifts AP to 76.3, with a modest increase to 3.8 M parameters and no additional GFLOP cost, due to lightweight global re-weighting.

Finally, adding CoordConv2d brings the model to its full configuration, achieving an AP of 76.6, along with 92.6 AP_{50}, 83.7 AP_{75}, 73.9 AP_M, and 81.2 AP_L. The model remains compact with 3.8 M parameters and 5.2 GFLOPs.

Importantly, this analysis directly addresses concerns about the integration of multiple attention mechanisms. Across the entire architecture, AMFACPose improves AP by 4.2 while increasing parameter count by just 0.5 M and computation by 0.5 GFLOPs. These results confirm that the proposed modules—the AFPN, DGCBs, SCRM, and SE blocks—work collaboratively and efficiently, making the full model highly suitable for real-time and resource-constrained environments.

8. Conclusions and Future Work

This paper presents AMFACPose, an efficient architecture for 2D HPE that addresses key challenges in scale variation and occlusion while maintaining minimal computational requirements. Through the integration of specialized components—the AFPN, DGCBs, SE blocks, and SCRM—our coordinate-based classification approach achieves high localization accuracy without the computational overhead typical of heatmap-based methods. Extensive evaluations on the COCO and CrowdPose datasets demonstrate AMFACPose's effectiveness, outperforming state-of-the-art approaches while maintaining significantly lower parameter counts and faster inference speeds across various hardware platforms. The architecture's adaptability is particularly evident in its consistent performance across resource-constrained edge devices and high-performance GPUs.

Despite its advantages, AMFACPose—like most vision models—may experience performance degradation under extreme conditions such as low-light environments or severe motion blur. Addressing these limitations requires future extensions that integrate spatiotemporal information or leverage cross-modality learning. We also acknowledge the ethical implications of pose estimation technologies, particularly in surveillance contexts, where privacy concerns are critical. Responsible deployment must be guided by transparent governance, informed consent, and equitable data representation to avoid bias and ensure fairness across demographic groups.

Future research directions include extending AMFACPose to 3D pose estimation and multi-view configurations, integrating temporal information for dynamic motion analysis, and developing domain adaptation techniques for limited-data scenarios. Additional focus will be placed on power-optimization strategies for embedded and mobile deployments, further enhancing the model's practical utility in resource-constrained environments.

Author Contributions: Conceptualization, A.Z., S.A.S. and H.T.; Methodology, A.Z.; Software, A.Z. and S.A.S.; Validation, S.A.S. and G.B.-G.; Formal analysis, G.B.-G.; Investigation, A.Z.; Writing—review & editing, G.B.-G. and H.T.; Supervision, H.T.; Project administration, H.T. All authors have read and agreed to the published version of the manuscript.

Funding: This research received no external funding.

Data Availability Statement: The data presented in this study are available in this article.

Conflicts of Interest: The authors declare no conflicts of interest.

Abbreviations

HPE	Human Pose Estimation
DL	Deep Learning
DSC	Depthwise Separable Convolutions
MLPs	Multi-Layer Perceptron
GAP	Global Average Pooling
AFPN	Adaptive Feature Pyramid Network
DGCB	Dual-Gate Context Block
SE	Squeeze-and-Excitation
SCRM	Spatial–Channel Refinement Module
CoordConv2d	Coordinate Convolution 2D
KLDiscretLoss	Kullback–Leibler Divergence-based Discrete Loss
MSE	Mean Squared Error
OKS	Object Keypoint Similarity
AP	Average Precision
AR	Average Recall
IoU	Intersection over Union

CNN	Convolutional Neural Network
GPU	Graphics Processing Unit
GFLOPs	Giga FLoating-point Operation
fps	Frames Per Second
BN	Batch Normalization
ReLU	Rectified Linear Unit
COCO	Common Objects in Context
FPN	Feature Pyramid Network
SOTA	State-Of-The-Art

References

1. Bertasius, G.; Feichtenhofer, C.; Tran, D.; Shi, J.; Torresani, L. Learning Temporal Pose Estimation from Sparsely-Labeled Videos. In Proceedings of the Advances in Neural Information Processing Systems (NeurIPS), Vancouver, BC, Canada, 8–14 December 2019; pp. 3003–3014.
2. Krizhevsky, A.; Sutskever, I.; Hinton, G.E. ImageNet Classification with Deep Convolutional Neural Networks. *Adv. Neural Inf. Process. Syst.* **2012**, *25*, 1097–1105. Available online: https://proceedings.neurips.cc/paper_files/paper/2012/file/c399862d3b9d6b76c8436e924a68c45b-Paper.pdf (accessed on 15 April 2025). [CrossRef]
3. Cao, Z.; Simon, T.; Wei, S.E.; Sheikh, Y. Realtime Multi-Person 2D Pose Estimation Using Part Affinity Fields. In Proceedings of the IEEE Conference on Computer Vision and Pattern Recognition (CVPR), Honolulu, HI, USA, 21–26 July 2017; pp. 7291–7299. [CrossRef]
4. Toshev, A.; Szegedy, C. DeepPose: Human Pose Estimation via Deep Neural Networks. In Proceedings of the IEEE Conference on Computer Vision and Pattern Recognition (CVPR), Columbus, OH, USA, 23–28 June 2014; pp. 1653–1660. [CrossRef]
5. Yang, Y.; Ramanan, D. Articulated Human Detection with Flexible Mixtures of Parts. *IEEE Trans. Pattern Anal. Mach. Intell.* **2013**, *35*, 2878–2890. [CrossRef] [PubMed]
6. Newell, A.; Yang, K.; Deng, J. Stacked Hourglass Networks for Human Pose Estimation. In *Computer Vision—ECCV 2016*; Leibe, B., Matas, J., Sebe, N., Welling, M., Eds.; Springer: Amsterdam, The Netherlands, 2016; pp. 483–499. [CrossRef]
7. Xiao, B.; Wu, H.; Wei, Y. Simple Baselines for Human Pose Estimation and Tracking. In Proceedings of the European Conference on Computer Vision (ECCV), Munich, Germany, 8–14 September 2018; pp. 466–481. [CrossRef]
8. Sun, K.; Xiao, B.; Liu, D.; Wang, J. Deep High-Resolution Representation Learning for Human Pose Estimation. In Proceedings of the IEEE/CVF Conference on Computer Vision and Pattern Recognition (CVPR), Long Beach, CA, USA, 16–20 June 2019; pp. 5693–5703. [CrossRef]
9. Yuan, Y.; Fu, R.; Huang, L.; Lin, W.; Zhang, C.; Chen, X.; Wang, J. HRFormer: High-Resolution Transformer for Dense Prediction. *arXiv* **2021**, arXiv:2110.09408. [CrossRef]
10. Li, Y.; Zhang, S.; Wang, Z.; Yang, S.; Yang, W.; Xia, S.-T.; Zhou, E. TokenPose: Learning Keypoint Tokens for Human Pose Estimation. In Proceedings of the IEEE/CVF International Conference on Computer Vision (ICCV), Montreal, QC, Canada, 11–17 October 2021; pp. 11313–11322. [CrossRef]
11. Xu, Y.; Zhang, J.; Zhang, Q.; Tao, D. ViTPose: Simple Vision Transformer Baselines for Human Pose Estimation. *Adv. Neural Inf. Process. Syst.* **2022**, *35*, 38571–38584. Available online: https://proceedings.neurips.cc/paper_files/paper/2022/file/fbb10d319d44f8c3b4720873e4177c65-Paper-Conference.pdf (accessed on 10 April 2025).
12. Li, Y.; Yang, S.; Liu, P.; Zhang, S.; Wang, Y.; Wang, Z.; Yang, W.; Xia, S.T. SimCC: A Simple Coordinate Classification Perspective for Human Pose Estimation. In Proceedings of the European Conference on Computer Vision (ECCV), Tel Aviv, Israel, 23–27 October 2022; pp. 89–106. [CrossRef]
13. Zakir, A.; Salman, S.A.; Benitez-Garcia, G.; Takahashi, H. AECA-PRNetCC: Adaptive Efficient Channel Attention-Based PoseResNet for Coordinate Classification in 2D Human Pose. In Proceedings of the 38th International Conference on Image and Vision Computing New Zealand (IVCNZ), Auckland, New Zealand, 29 November–1 December 2023; pp. 1–6. [CrossRef]
14. He, K.; Zhang, X.; Ren, S.; Sun, J. Deep Residual Learning for Image Recognition. In Proceedings of the IEEE Conference on Computer Vision and Pattern Recognition (CVPR), Las Vegas, NV, USA, 27–30 June 2016; pp. 770–778. [CrossRef]
15. Liu, R.; Lehman, J.; Molino, P.; Such, F.P.; Frank, E.; Sergeev, A.; Yosinski, J. An Intriguing Failing of Convolutional Neural Networks and the CoordConv Solution. In Proceedings of the Advances in Neural Information Processing Systems (NeurIPS), Montréal, QC, Canada, 3–8 December 2018; pp. 9605–9616. [CrossRef]
16. Chollet, F. Xception: Deep Learning with Depthwise Separable Convolutions. In Proceedings of the IEEE Conference on Computer Vision and Pattern Recognition (CVPR), Honolulu, HI, USA, 21–26 July 2017; pp. 1251–1258. [CrossRef]

17. Li, J.; Bian, S.; Zeng, A.; Wang, C.; Pang, B.; Liu, W.; Lu, C. Human Pose Regression with Residual Log-Likelihood Estimation. In Proceedings of the IEEE/CVF International Conference on Computer Vision (ICCV), Online, 11–17 October 2021; pp. 11025–11034. [CrossRef]
18. Tompson, J.J.; Jain, A.; LeCun, Y.; Bregler, C. Joint Training of a Convolutional Network and a Graphical Model for Human Pose Estimation. *Adv. Neural Inf. Process. Syst.* **2014**, *27*, 1799–1807. [CrossRef]
19. Dai, H.; Shi, H.; Liu, W.; Wang, L.; Liu, Y.; Mei, T. FasterPose: A Faster Simple Baseline for Human Pose Estimation. *ACM Trans. Multimed. Comput. Commun. Appl.* **2022**, *18*, 1–16. [CrossRef]
20. Liu, H.; Wu, J.; He, R. IDPNet: A Light-Weight Network and Its Variants for Human Pose Estimation. *J. Supercomput.* **2024**, *80*, 6169–6191. [CrossRef]
21. Zhang, F.; Zhu, X.; Dai, H.; Ye, M.; Zhu, C. Distribution-Aware Coordinate Representation for Human Pose Estimation. In Proceedings of the IEEE/CVF Conference on Computer Vision and Pattern Recognition (CVPR), Online, 14–19 June 2020; pp. 7093–7102. [CrossRef]
22. Yin, S.; Wang, S.; Chen, X.; Chen, E.; Liang, C. Attentive One-Dimensional Heatmap Regression for Facial Landmark Detection and Tracking. In Proceedings of the 28th ACM International Conference on Multimedia (ACM MM), Seattle, WA, USA, 12–16 October 2020; pp. 538–546. [CrossRef]
23. Huang, J.; Zhu, Z.; Guo, F.; Huang, G. The Devil Is in the Details: Delving into Unbiased Data Processing for Human Pose Estimation. In Proceedings of the IEEE/CVF Conference on Computer Vision and Pattern Recognition (CVPR), Online, 14–19 June 2020; pp. 5700–5709. [CrossRef]
24. Zakir, A.; Salman, S.A.; Takahashi, H. SOCA-PRNet: Spatially Oriented Attention-Infused Structured-Feature-Enabled PoseResNet for 2D Human Pose Estimation. *Sensors* **2023**, *23*, 110. [CrossRef] [PubMed]
25. Zakir, A.; Salman, S.A.; Benitez-Garcia, G.; Takahashi, H. EBA-PRNetCC: An Efficient Bridge Attention-Integration PoseResNet for Coordinate Classification in 2D Human Pose Estimation. In Proceedings of the 19th International Joint Conference on Computer Vision, Imaging and Computer Graphics Theory and Applications (VISIGRAPP), Rome, Italy, 27–29 February 2024; pp. 133–144. [CrossRef].
26. Jiang, Z.; Ji, H.; Yang, C.-Y.; Hwang, J.-N. 2D Human Pose Estimation Calibration and Keypoint Visibility Classification. In Proceedings of the IEEE International Conference on Acoustics, Speech and Signal Processing (ICASSP), Seoul, Republic of Korea, 14–19 April 2024; pp. 6095–6099. [CrossRef]
27. Lin, T.-Y.; Maire, M.; Belongie, S.; Hays, J.; Perona, P.; Ramanan, D.; Dollár, P.; Zitnick, C.L. Microsoft COCO: Common Objects in Context. In Proceedings of the European Conference on Computer Vision (ECCV), Zurich, Switzerland, 6–12 September 2014; pp. 740–755. [CrossRef]
28. Hu, J.; Shen, L.; Sun, G. Squeeze-and-Excitation Networks. In Proceedings of the IEEE Conference on Computer Vision and Pattern Recognition (CVPR), Salt Lake City, UT, USA, 18–23 June 2018; pp. 7132–7141. [CrossRef]
29. Dosovitskiy, A.; Beyer, L.; Kolesnikov, A.; Weissenborn, D.; Zhai, X.; Unterthiner, T.; Dehghani, M.; Minderer, M.; Heigold, G.; Gelly, S.; et al. An Image is Worth 16 × 16 Words: Transformers for Image Recognition at Scale. *arXiv* **2020**, arXiv:2010.11929. [CrossRef]
30. Zagoruyko, S.; Komodakis, N. Wide Residual Networks. In Proceedings of the British Machine Vision Conference (BMVC), York, UK, 19–22 September 2016; pp. 87.1–87.12. [CrossRef]
31. Lin, T.-Y.; Dollár, P.; Girshick, R.; He, K.; Hariharan, B.; Belongie, S. Feature Pyramid Networks for Object Detection. In Proceedings of the IEEE Conference on Computer Vision and Pattern Recognition (CVPR), Honolulu, HI, USA, 21–26 July 2017; pp. 2117–2125. [CrossRef]
32. Cao, Y.; Xu, J.; Lin, S.; Wei, F.; Hu, H. GCNet: Non-local Networks Meet Squeeze-Excitation Networks and Beyond. In Proceedings of the IEEE/CVF International Conference on Computer Vision (ICCV) Workshops, Seoul, Republic of Korea, 27–28 October 2019; pp. 1971–1980. [CrossRef]
33. Woo, S.; Park, J.; Lee, J.-Y.; Kweon, I.S. CBAM: Convolutional Block Attention Module. In Proceedings of the European Conference on Computer Vision (ECCV), Munich, Germany, 8–14 September 2018; pp. 3–19. [CrossRef]
34. Carreira, J.; Agrawal, P.; Fragkiadaki, K.; Malik, J. Human Pose Estimation with Iterative Error Feedback. In Proceedings of the IEEE Conference on Computer Vision and Pattern Recognition (CVPR), Las Vegas, NV, USA, 27–30 June 2016; pp. 4733–4742. [CrossRef]
35. Kullback, S.; Leibler, R.A. On Information and Sufficiency. *Ann. Math. Stat.* **1951**, *22*, 79–86. [CrossRef]
36. Szegedy, C.; Vanhoucke, V.; Ioffe, S.; Shlens, J.; Wojna, Z. Rethinking the Inception Architecture for Computer Vision. In Proceedings of the IEEE Conference on Computer Vision and Pattern Recognition (CVPR), Las Vegas, NV, USA, 27–30 June 2016; pp. 2818–2826. [CrossRef]
37. Guo, C.; Pleiss, G.; Sun, Y.; Weinberger, K.Q. On Calibration of Modern Neural Networks. In Proceedings of the 34th International Conference on Machine Learning (ICML), Sydney, Australia, 6–11 August 2017; pp. 1321–1330. [CrossRef]

38. PyTorch Documentation. *torch.nn.KLDivLoss*. Available online: https://pytorch.org/docs/stable/generated/torch.nn.KLDivLoss.html (accessed on 1 February 2025).
39. Li, J.; Wang, C.; Zhu, H.; Mao, Y.; Fang, H.-S.; Lu, C. CrowdPose: Efficient Crowded Scenes Pose Estimation and a New Benchmark. In Proceedings of the IEEE/CVF Conference on Computer Vision and Pattern Recognition (CVPR), Long Beach, CA, USA, 15–20 June 2019; pp. 10863–10872. [CrossRef]
40. Shorten, C.; Khoshgoftaar, T.M. A Survey on Image Data Augmentation for Deep Learning. *J. Big Data* **2019**, *6*, 60. [CrossRef]
41. Misra, D. Mish: A Self Regularized Non-Monotonic Activation Function. *arXiv* **2019**, arXiv:1908.08681. [CrossRef]
42. Ramachandran, P.; Zoph, B.; Le, Q.V. Searching for Activation Functions. *arXiv* **2017**, arXiv:1710.05941. [CrossRef]
43. Loshchilov, I.; Hutter, F. Decoupled Weight Decay Regularization. In Proceedings of the International Conference on Learning Representations (ICLR), Vancouver, BC, Canada, 30 April–3 May 2017. [CrossRef]
44. Zhang, M.; Lucas, J.; Ba, J.; Hinton, G.E. Lookahead Optimizer: k Steps Forward, 1 Step Back. In Proceedings of the Advances in Neural Information Processing Systems (NeurIPS), Vancouver, BC, Canada, 8–14 December 2019; Volume 32, pp. 9597–9608. [CrossRef]
45. Bello, I.; Zoph, B.; Vasudevan, V.; Le, Q.V. Neural Optimizer Search with Reinforcement Learning. In Proceedings of the International Conference on Machine Learning (ICML), Sydney, Australia, 6–11 August 2017; pp. 459–468. [CrossRef]
46. Liu, Z.; Liu, L.; Hao, S. BR-Pose: Enhancing Human Pose Estimation Through Bi-level Routing Attention and Multi-level Weight Fusion. *Vis. Comput.* **2025**, 1–12. [CrossRef]
47. Tian, Z.; Fu, W.; Woźniak, M.; Liu, S. PCDPose: Enhancing the Lightweight 2D Human Pose Estimation Model with Pose-enhancing Attention and Context Broadcasting. *Pattern Anal. Appl.* **2025**, *28*, 59. [CrossRef]
48. Chen, S.; Zhang, Y.; Huang, S.; Yi, R.; Fan, K.; Zhang, R.; Chen, P.; Wang, J.; Ding, S.; Ma, L. SDPose: Tokenized Pose Estimation via Circulation-Guide Self-Distillation. In Proceedings of the IEEE/CVF Conference on Computer Vision and Pattern Recognition (CVPR), Seattle, WA, USA, 16–22 June 2024; pp. 1082–1090. [CrossRef]
49. Zhang, F.; Shi, Q.; Ma, Y. Combining Self-attention and Depth-wise Convolution for Human Pose Estimation. *SIViP* **2024**, *18*, 5647–5661. [CrossRef]
50. Li, K.; Wang, S.; Zhang, X.; Xu, Y.; Xu, W.; Tu, Z. Pose Recognition with Cascade Transformers. In Proceedings of the IEEE/CVF Conference on Computer Vision and Pattern Recognition (CVPR), Nashville, TN, USA, 20–25 June 2021; pp. 1944–1953. [CrossRef]
51. Geng, Z.; Sun, K.; Xiao, B.; Zhang, Z.; Wang, J. Bottom-Up Human Pose Estimation via Disentangled Keypoint Regression. In Proceedings of the IEEE/CVF Conference on Computer Vision and Pattern Recognition (CVPR), Nashville, TN, USA, 20–25 June 2021; pp. 14676–14686. [CrossRef]
52. Yang, J.; Zeng, A.; Liu, S.; Li, F.; Zhang, R.; Zhang, L. Explicit Box Detection Unifies End-to-End Multi-Person Pose Estimation. *arXiv* **2023**, arXiv:2302.01593. [CrossRef]
53. Dong, C.; Tang, Y.; Zhang, L. HDA-Pose: A Real-Time 2D Human Pose Estimation Method Based on Modified YOLOv8. *Signal Image Video Process.* **2024**, *18*, 5823–5839. [CrossRef]
54. Liu, H.; Chen, Q.; Tan, Z.; Liu, J.-J.; Wang, J.; Su, X.; Li, X.; Yao, K.; Han, J.; Ding, E.; et al. GroupPose: A Simple Baseline for End-to-End Multi-Person Pose Estimation. In Proceedings of the IEEE/CVF International Conference on Computer Vision (ICCV), Paris, France, 2–6 October 2023; pp. 15029–15038. [CrossRef]
55. Liang, H.; Wang, C.; Shao, M.; Zhang, Q. MAQT: Multi-scale attention and query-optimized transformer for end-to-end pose estimation. *J. Supercomput.* **2025**, *81*, 429. [CrossRef]
56. Dong, C.; Du, G. An enhanced real-time human pose estimation method based on modified YOLOv8 framework. *Sci. Rep.* **2024**, *14*, 8012. [CrossRef] [PubMed]

electronics

MDPI

Article

Multi-Head Hierarchical Attention Framework with Multi-Level Learning Optimization Strategy for Legal Text Recognition

Ke Zhang [1], Yufei Tu [2], Jun Lu [1,3], Zhongliang Ai [4,*], Zhonglin Liu [5], Licai Wang [1] and Xuelin Liu [6]

1 Big Data Research and Development Center, North China Institute of Computing Technology, Beijing 100083, China; zhangke_ucas@163.com (K.Z.)
2 School of Computer Science, Beijing University of Posts and Telecommunications, Beijing 100876, China; tuyufei@bupt.edu.cn
3 China Academy of Electronics and Information Technology, Beijing 100041, China
4 Strategic Planning Research Institute of CETC, Beijing 100041, China
5 China Justice Big Data Institute Co., Ltd., Beijing 100041, China; liuzhonglin@cjbdi.com
6 China Satellite Network Group Co., Ltd., Beijing 100020, China
* Correspondence: aizl067@sina.com

Abstract: Owing to the rapid increase in the amount of legal text data and the increasing demand for intelligent processing, multi-label legal text recognition is becoming increasingly important in practical applications such as legal information retrieval and case classification. However, traditional methods have limitations in handling the complex semantics and multi-label characteristics of legal texts, making it difficult to accurately extract feature and effective category information. Therefore, this study proposes a novel multi-head hierarchical attention framework suitable for multi-label legal text recognition tasks. This framework comprises a feature extraction module and a hierarchical module. The former extracts multi-level semantic representations of text, while the latter obtains multi-label category information. In addition, this study proposes a novel hierarchical learning optimization strategy that balances the learning needs of multi-level semantic representation and multi-label category information through data preprocessing, loss calculation, and weight updating, effectively accelerating the convergence speed of framework training. We conducted comparative experiments on the legal domain dataset CAIL2021 and the general multi-label recognition datasets AAPD and Web of Science (WOS). The results indicate that the method proposed in this study is significantly superior to mainstream methods in legal and general scenarios, demonstrating excellent performance. The study findings are expected to be widely applied in the field of intelligent processing of legal information, improving the accuracy of intelligent classification of judicial cases and further promoting the digitalization and intelligence process of the legal industry.

Keywords: multi-head hierarchical attention; multi-level learning optimization strategy; legal text; multi-label recognition

1. Introduction

Legal text classification falls under the category of text hierarchical multi-label classification tasks. As a subtask within the natural language processing (NLP) field, general text hierarchical multi-label classification aims to assign labels to texts based on a given label hierarchy, where each input text can correspond to multiple different labels structured hierarchically. Multi-label hierarchical text classification plays a significant role in various domains, such as news categorization, legal applications, and document management, owing to its alignment with real-world application requirements [1,2]. Unlike traditional

https://doi.org/10.3390/electronics14101946

flat classification methods, hierarchical multi-label classification tasks require capturing the associations between texts and categories, as well as taking into account the hierarchical relationships and correlations between categories. However, increasing the number of categories and hierarchical levels introduces challenges such as an imbalanced sample distribution and semantic similarity between hierarchical labels [3,4], further complicating the task.

Legal text classification tasks exhibit distinct characteristics compared with traditional multi-label text classification, including stronger semantic reasoning logic embedded in labels and limited labeled samples. Identifying these labels requires contextual semantic analysis combined with factual content and underlying legal logic, further increasing task complexity. An example of a legal text classification task is shown in Figure 1. For a factual description of a loan relationship case, the deep-level labels (level-3) include "joint liability guarantee, scope of guarantee, other costs for realizing creditor's rights, guarantee period, attorney fee". The intermediate-level labels (level-2) are "guarantee, scope of guarantee, other costs, period of duty guarantee, other costs", while the shallow-level labels (level-1) comprise "guarantee, guarantee, calculation of private lending principal, 'statute of limitations, period of duty guarantee, exclusion period', calculation of private lending principal". Here, the level-3 labels "joint liability guarantee" and "scope of guarantee" both fall under the level-1 category "guarantee", whereas the level-3 label "guarantee period" belongs to the level-1 category "statute of limitations, period of duty guarantee, exclusion period". Although "joint liability guarantee", "scope of guarantee", and "guarantee period" all appear to relate to "guarantee" on the surface, legally, they belong to two distinct categories. Accurate classification requires literal interpretation and precise legal semantic analysis.

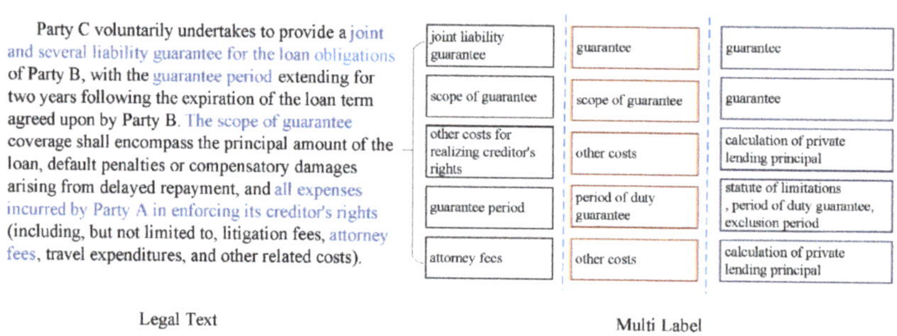

Figure 1. The task of multi-label recognition of legal text.

Scholars have dedicated efforts to exploring efficient and accurate hierarchical text classification methods to address the aforementioned challenges. Several studies have proposed model design strategies incorporating hierarchical structures to tackle issues such as class imbalance and hierarchical relationship modeling. Zhou et al. [5] employed directed graphs to represent hierarchical labels and used a hierarchy-sensitive structural encoder to model labels, effectively integrating hierarchical label information into text and label semantics. Chen et al. [6]'s hierarchy-aware semantics matching network (Hi-Match) performs representation learning on texts and hierarchical labels, using separate text and label encoders to extract semantic features. The model then calculates correlations between text and label embeddings within a joint semantic embedding space to identify multi-label types, defining distinct optimization objectives based on the two representation vectors to enhance hierarchical multi-label text classification performance. However, these methods suffer from insufficient semantic representation of label hierarchies and the inability to resolve imbalanced sample distribution. An increasing number of researchers have recently adopted contrastive learning approaches to optimize hierarchical label semantic representation and address sample distribution imbalance. Zhang et al. [7] introduced a hierarchy-aware and label balanced model (HALB), which utilizes multi-label negative supervision to push text representations of samples with different labels further apart. In addition, to mitigate label imbalance in hierarchical text classification, asymmetric loss is applied to compute classification loss, enabling the model to focus on learning from difficult samples and balance the contribution of positive and negative labels to the loss function.

Furthermore, scholars have improved classification performance by optimizing multi-label semantic representations [4], augmenting negative samples [8], or incorporating external knowledge [3,9] to further enhance the accuracy of multi-label recognition. Chen et al. [3] proposed a few-shot hierarchical multi-label classification framework based on ICL and LLM, leveraging contrastive learning to accurately retrieve text keywords from a retrieval database and improve hierarchical label recognition accuracy. However, these approaches primarily address either imbalanced sample distribution or hierarchical semantic representation issues individually, failing to resolve both challenges synchronously. Zhang et al. [4] combined multi-label contrastive learning with K-nearest neighbors (MLCL-KNN), enabling text representations of sample pairs with more shared labels to be closer while separating pairs without common labels. Zhou et al. [5] designed a hierarchical sequence ranking (HiSR) method to generate diverse negative samples that maximize contrastive learning effectiveness, enhancing the ability of the model to distinguish fine-grained labels by emphasizing differences between true labels and generated negatives. Feng et al. [9] categorized external knowledge into micro-knowledge (basic concepts associated with individual class labels) and macro-knowledge (correlations between class labels), using them to improve discriminative power in text and semantic label representations.

This study addresses these limitations and capitalizes on the advantages of prototype networks in handling imbalanced sample distributions by proposing a multi-label recognition method for legal texts based on hierarchical prototypical networks. In particular, we employ the Sentence-BERT model [10] to obtain a unified long-text embedding vector representation. A hierarchical prototype network architecture is designed for multi-level label recognition, in which a hierarchical prototype structure is constructed according to the data label levels and relationships. In addition, a hierarchical prototype network loss function is proposed. By integrating inter-layer correlation information between labels and prototypes at different levels, the method achieves unified optimization of cross-level prototype parameters within the prototype network, thereby enhancing the accuracy of multi-level label recognition under conditions of uneven sample distribution.

The main contributions of this article are as follows:

(1) We propose a new multi-head hierarchical attention framework suitable for multi-label legal text recognition tasks, which mainly comprises a feature extraction module and a hierarchical module. The feature extraction module is mainly used to extract multi-level semantic representations of the text, while the hierarchical module is used to obtain multi-label category information.
(2) We propose a novel hierarchical learning optimization strategy that considers multi-level semantic representation and multi-label classification information learning requirements through data preprocessing, loss calculation, and weight updating, effectively improving the convergence speed of framework training.
(3) We conduct comparative experiments on the legal domain dataset CAIL2021 and the general multi-label recognition datasets AAPD and Web of Science (WOS). The experimental results show that the proposed method is significantly superior to mainstream methods in legal and general scenarios.

2. Related Work

2.1. Multi-Label Representation

The prototype neural network [11] utilizes neural networks to project inputs into a latent embedding space, where multiple reference points (class prototypes) are defined. The model improves classification accuracy by optimizing the mapping function and prototype representations. During inference, the Euclidean distance between the input embedding and each class prototype is computed to assign labels.

Prototype neural networks have demonstrated robust performance in few-shot classification tasks, particularly in image classification [11] and open-domain problems [12]. Their applications in NLP include entity recognition [13], text classification [14], and relation extraction [15,16]. In multi-intent recognition, Luo et al. [17] introduced an intent fusion feature extraction mechanism and an intent separation mechanism to eliminate irrelevant noise, thereby improving multi-label classification. Xian et al. [18] employed a single-layer recurrent neural network to generate text vector representations, further refining classification performance via a mean-value prototype neural network.

While current hierarchical multi-label recognition methods effectively capture label dependencies, they remain less effective in handling long-tail distributions. Conversely, prototype learning methods exhibit strong robustness in few-shot multi-label classification but lack adequate modeling of hierarchical labels. We attempt to bridge this gap by proposing a hierarchical prototype neural network that integrates hierarchical multi-label learning and prototype-based classification, enhancing accuracy in hierarchical multi-label recognition.

2.2. Multi-Label Text Recognition

Multi-label recognition of legal texts represents a specialized subdomain within multi-label classification, necessitating the precise identification of domain-specific terminologies and hierarchical structures from lengthy legal documents. Compared with general multi-label recognition tasks, legal text classification is distinguished by its strict sentence structures, systematic semantic tagging, specialized domain-specific terminology requiring expert interpretation, and long-tailed data distributions. These characteristics render legal text classification more challenging and complex than general tasks. Current research in this domain can be categorized into three primary approaches based on hierarchical traversal methods: flat methods, local methods, and global methods.

The flat method simplifies the hierarchical multi-label classification problem into a standard multi-label classification task. This approach assumes mutual independence between labels at different hierarchical levels, flattening them into a single-layer label prediction or focusing solely on terminal-level label prediction. For instance, Peng et al. [19] integrated TextCNN, RNN, and attention-based capsule networks to optimize classification networks for multi-label tasks. Liu et al. [20] proposed XML-CNN, which incorporates bottleneck layers and dynamic max-pooling to enhance hierarchical label recognition. However, this assumption disregards the inherent hierarchical structure of legal labels. In addition, the resulting label predictions fail to capture inter-label hierarchical dependencies, yielding suboptimal practical classification accuracy.

The local method utilizes independent classifiers for different hierarchical levels, progressively predicting labels from lower to higher levels. For instance, Cai et al. [21] developed a hierarchical support vector machine (HSVM) that constructs separate SVM classifiers for each level and integrates discriminant functions to maintain hierarchical consistency. Cerri et al. [22] utilized multiple neural networks independently trained through transfer learning to enhance hierarchical classification. Wehrmann et al. [23] introduced a hierarchical multi-label classification network (HMCN) that jointly models local classification dependencies and global hierarchical information, optimizing classification at local and global levels. However, this method propagates classification errors from lower levels upward, increasing uncertainty in higher-level predictions. In addition, it amplifies erroneous predictions at intermediate levels, leading to a gradual decline in prediction accuracy as the hierarchy ascends, an undesirable phenomenon in which classification performance deteriorates progressively across hierarchical tiers.

Global methods typically involve a single classifier that fully integrates hierarchical category information into the classification process, designing optimization strategies to capture hierarchical label relationships and enabling direct prediction of hierarchical labels [24]. Zhou et al. [5] proposed the hierarchy-aware global model (HiAGM) for hierarchical label prediction, which combines a bidirectional tree long short-term memory network (Bi-TreeLSTM) with a graph convolutional network (GCN) to model label hierarchical relationships. Chen et al. [6] developed a Hi-Match network that models text and hierarchical multi-label semantics. They transformed label recognition into a semantic matching problem, incorporating hierarchical information by calculating the semantic similarity between texts and hierarchical labels. As such, they achieved hierarchical label identification. Deng et al. [25] addressed the long-tail distribution challenge of last-level labels by proposing the HTCinfoMax model, which introduces text-label mutual information maximization and prior label matching to filter irrelevant information. Zhang et al. [4] developed MLCL-KNN to further optimize semantic representations across different hierarchy levels, designing a label contrastive learning method that pulls text representations of sample pairs with more shared labels closer while pushing pairs without common labels apart. During inference, KNN retrieves nearest neighbor samples to enhance multi-label recognition accuracy. Furthermore, Zhang et al. [7] and Zhou et al. [8] improved semantic label discriminability using negative sample augmentation and sibling label contrastive learning, respectively, to boost hierarchical label recognition performance. Nooten et al. [26] explored the effects of label-aware loss and contrastive loss in Euclidean and hyperbolic spaces on hierarchical label semantic representations.

3. Methods

3.1. Problem Description

Legal text multi-label recognition falls under hierarchical multi-label classification, where the objective is to identify hierarchically structured legal labels from a given factual description. The set of all multi-labels forms a hierarchical structure, defined as $C = (C^1, C^2, \cdots, C^H)$, where H represents the depth of the hierarchical label structure. The classification set of the i-th layer is denoted as $C^i = \{c_1, c_2, \cdots\} \in \{0,1\}^{|C^i|}$, and $|C^i|$ is the total number of labels at that level. The hierarchical structure T resembles a forest in data structures, where the depth of the label hierarchy corresponds to the depth of trees in the forest, each parent node may correspond to multiple child nodes, and a child node belongs to only one parent node.

The formal definition of the legal text multi-label recognition problem is as follows: Let D denote the dataset containing N data samples

$$D = \{(X_1, Y_1), (X_2, Y_2), \cdots, (X_N, Y_N)\} \tag{1}$$

where X_i represents the input legal text comprising L words:

$$X_i = \{w_1, w_2, \cdots, w_L\} \tag{2}$$

Y_i denotes the corresponding hierarchical multi-label set, where

$$Y_i = \{y_1, y_2, \cdots, y_H\},\ y_i \subset C^i\ and\ Y_i \subset T \quad (3)$$

Let the multi-label recognition model be Ω, then the legal text multi-label recognition task can be represented as a classification model Ω learned using the sample set D and hierarchical structure T that can predict the multi-label set for legal text Y_i corresponding to the input text.

$$\Omega(X_i, \theta) \rightarrow Y_i, Y_i \subset T \quad (4)$$

where θ is a parameter of model Ω.

3.2. Multi-Head Hierarchical Attention Framework

The overall framework of the legal text multi-label recognition model based on the hierarchical prototype neural network proposed in this study is shown in Figure 2. This framework comprises two parts, the feature extraction module on the left and the hierarchical module on the right. The feature extraction module mainly comprises a vector encoder and a multi-head attention layer. The text sentence vector encoder is responsible for encoding the input text to generate an initial sentence vector, which serves as the semantic representation of the text while preserving contextual dependencies and key semantic features. Subsequently, multiple multi-head attention layers are used to hierarchically represent sentence vectors, enabling the extraction of semantic representations at each level. The hierarchical module calculates the semantic distance between different levels and their corresponding prototype representations for multi-level label recognition. Figure 2 shows a scenario with three label levels, corresponding to the legal dataset (CAIL2021). The subsequent description of the method is based on this three-layer label structure. The model can be extended to accommodate different depths of hierarchical labels (e.g., 2 layers, 4 layers). Depending on the label hierarchy of the target task, the depth of the feature extraction layer and prototype network in the model can be adjusted accordingly. Model parameters are optimized by calculating the loss function.

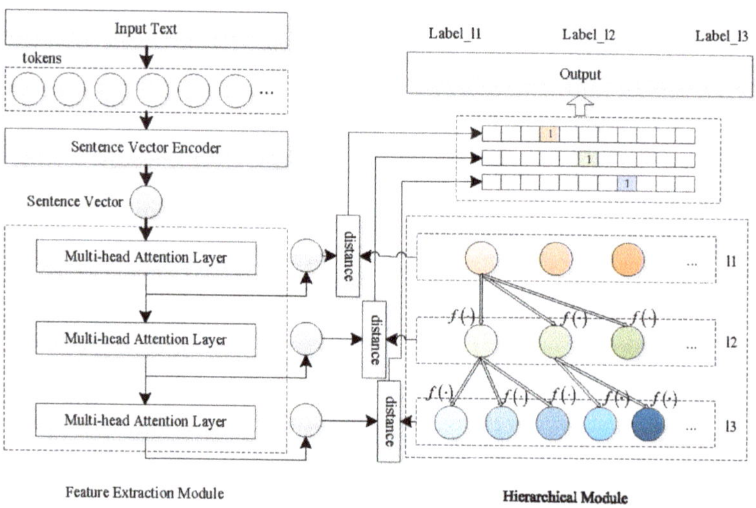

Figure 2. Overall Framework.

3.3. Feature Extraction Module

This study effectively extracts the multi-level semantic representation from the input legal text by utilizing the Sentence-BERT model [10] to obtain the initial sentence vector E from the input text $\{w_1, w_2, \cdots, w_N\}$. Sentence-BERT is a supervised sentence embedding model that extends the BERT architecture by incorporating a mean pooling layer, enabling the extraction of fixed-length sentence embeddings. By leveraging a Siamese network architecture, it compares semantic embeddings of input text with manually annotated reference samples, optimizing model parameters using a contrastive learning strategy. This process enhances the semantic representation capacity of sentence vectors.

Multi-head attention mechanisms are utilized to extract hierarchical semantic information at different levels to align with the multi-level label structure [27]. Each multi-head attention layer captures semantic features at increasing depths, thereby enabling progressive abstraction of textual representations. Given a three-level hierarchical label structure, the multi-level sentence vector representation is computed as follows:

$$\begin{cases} H_1 = Multihead(E) \\ H_2 = Multihead(H_1) \\ H_3 = Multihead(H_2) \end{cases} \tag{5}$$

where H_1, H_2, and H_3 denote sentence vector representations at three different hierarchical depths while $Multihead(\cdot)$ represents the transformation function applied at each level, implemented using multi-head attention mechanisms.

3.4. Hierarchical Module

Conventional prototype neural networks typically employ a single-layer structure, which fails to capture hierarchical relationships between label classes, leading to suboptimal recognition accuracy. This study overcomes this limitation by proposing a hierarchical prototype neural network model that incorporates a transition matrix to define prototype transitions between adjacent hierarchical levels. The model simultaneously optimizes prototype parameters across all hierarchical levels, ensuring global optimization of multi-label classification.

The hierarchical prototype representations are formally defined as follows:

$$\begin{aligned} P &= \{P_1, P_2, P_3\} \\ &= \left\{\left\{m_{1k}^{l1}, m_{2k}^{l1}, \cdots, m_{xk}^{l1}\right\}, \left\{m_{1k}^{l2}, m_{2k}^{l2}, \cdots, m_{yk}^{l2}\right\}, \left\{m_{1k}^{l3}, m_{2k}^{l3}, \cdots, m_{zk}^{l3}\right\}\right\} \end{aligned} \tag{6}$$

where $l1$, $l2$, and $l3$ correspond to the prototype parameters at three different hierarchical depths, x, y, and z represent the number of prototype labels at each respective level, and k denotes the number of prototypes under each prototype label.

Let $\mathbf{A}$ denote the connection matrix between the prototype parameters of the first and second levels, with a dimensionality of $y \times x$. A_{ij} represents the connection between the i-th prototype parameter in the first level and the j-th prototype parameter in the second level. If the j-th prototype parameter in the second level corresponds to the i-th prototype parameter in the first level, the value is 1; otherwise, it is 0. $\mathbf{B}$ denotes the connection matrix between the prototype parameters of the second and third levels, with a dimensionality of $z \times y$. The equations for calculating the prototypes at different levels are given as follows:

$$P_2 = \mathbf{A} \cdot f(P_1) \tag{7}$$

$$P_3 = \mathbf{B} \cdot f(P_2) \tag{8}$$

$f(\cdot)$ represents the transformation operation between prototypes at different levels. The calculation of prototype parameters is implemented using an attention mechanism layer, and a mean pooling layer is applied to process the parameter calculation results. This stabilizes the distribution of prototype parameters and enables the model to converge quickly.

3.5. Hierarchical Label Classification

Traditional prototype neural networks are primarily designed for single-label classification tasks, where they compute the distance between the feature representation and multiple prototypes and assign the class of the nearest prototype to the input data. The classification process is defined as follows:

$$x \in class \quad \arg\max_{i=1}^{C} g_i(x) \tag{9}$$

g_i is the discriminant function corresponding to the i-th class:

$$g_i(x) = -\min_{j=1}^{K} \|\Omega(X_i;\theta) - m_{ij}\|_2^2 \tag{10}$$

In addition, g_i can also represent the matching value of sample x to the i-th class.

However, multi-label recognition tasks require assigning zero or more labels to a single sample, making the minimum-distance approach unsuitable as it is inherently limited to single-label classification. Yang et al. [12] sought to address this by proposing a distance-based prototype neural network for hierarchical multi-label classification. Their method computes distances between hierarchical multi-labels and prototypes, introducing a threshold-based decision mechanism; no label is assigned if the minimum prototype distance of a sample exceeds a pre-defined threshold. However, the sample is assigned all corresponding labels if the distance to at least one prototype falls below the threshold. For a sample x, which does not correspond to any label,

$$\max_{i=1}^{C} g_i(x) < threshold \tag{11}$$

For a sample x corresponding to one or more labels, the label set is defined as follows:

$$\{i; \min_{j=1}^{K} \|\Omega(X_i;\theta) - m_{ij}\|_2^2 > -threshold, i \in (1,2,3,\ldots,C)\} \tag{12}$$

Parent–child constraints are applied to ensure hierarchical consistency, enforcing structural dependencies by considering only prototype distances within the same hierarchical parent–child relationships.

3.6. Loss Function

Traditional single-label classification employs loss functions such as DCE [12] and OVA [28], which optimize the distance between text embeddings and prototype representations. However, these methods are incompatible with multi-label classification, as they do not account for multi-label assignments. This study introduces a hierarchical cross-entropy loss function that optimizes text embedding representations and prototype parameters to address this limitation, ensuring compliance with the multi-label constraints in Equation (12).

For an input x_i, the multi-level text vector representation is computed, followed by confidence-level estimation for each prototype class, as follows:

$$\hat{y}^{l1} = \max_{k}\left(\sigma\left(\lambda d\left(\Omega^{l1}(x_i;\theta), m_{ik}^{l1}\right)\right)\right) \tag{13}$$

where σ represents the sigmoid function, and d is the distance function (using cosine similarity). During the calculation, the maximum distance between the text vector representation and the model distance within the same class is taken as its confidence level value with respect to the current class. The loss function for the model output at the current level and its corresponding prototype is defined as follows:

$$loss^{l1} = -\left(y^{l1} \log\left(\hat{y}^{l1}\right)\right) - \left(1 - y^{l1}\right) \log\left(1 - \hat{y}^{l1}\right) \tag{14}$$

The losses of the model are obtained by summing the three levels of losses as follows:

$$Loss = loss^{l1} + loss^{l2} + loss^{l3} \tag{15}$$

3.7. Implementation Details

All experiments were conducted on a high-performance computing server running CentOS 7.6. The system specifications include two RTX-TITAN 24 GB GPUs and eight 32 GB memory modules. The experimental environment was set up under the PyTorch 1.7.1 framework, utilizing the transformers model library [29], with Python version 3.7.6.

For the CAIL2021 dataset, the model employs the three-layer hierarchical structure described above. For the AAPD and WOS datasets, which have label depths of two layers, we modify the feature extraction and hierarchical modules to align with this label hierarchy. In particular, the multi-layer sentence representation is restricted to H_1 and H_2, the hierarchical prototype representation is defined as $P = \{P_1, P_2\}$, and the loss function is optimized as $Loss = loss^{l1} + loss^{l2}$.

During the training process, the data in the training samples were first preprocessed. Legal text data typically exhibits strong structural characteristics and considerable length. In our actual training procedure, we processed the data from the training samples of the CAIL12021 dataset as follows: (1) Based on the characteristics of legal data and label types, we segmented the lengthy document data, retaining only key sections such as the trial process, the appellant's claim, the respondent's defense, and the court's findings. In addition, excessively long sentences within the training samples were truncated to improve processing efficiency. (2) Sentences and labels in the factual description section were extracted separately and treated as independent data entries. Finally, we constructed a corresponding label set for the samples according to the number of model labels, thereby obtaining all the required training sample data.

This study employs the AdamW optimizer with weight_decay set to 0.001, a mini-batch size of 8, and an initial learning rate of 1e-8. In addition, a warmup strategy was adopted to adjust the learning rate.

4. Experimental Results

4.1. Datasets and Evaluation Criteria

We utilized the CAIL2021 case label prediction dataset [30] as the primary experimental resource to validate the effectiveness of the proposed hierarchical prototype neural network. The labels in the CAIL2021 case label prediction task dataset are curated by legal experts and represent factual labels for private lending cases. These labels are applied to publicly available judgment documents, constructing a case label prediction dataset. The CAIL2021 dataset comprises 2496 legal text samples, with labels categorized into three hierarchical levels, classified as evidence, private lending relationships, contract parties, and contract performance. The number of label types at each level is 11, 75, and 234. The dataset is split into training, validation, and test sets in an 8:1:1 ratio, respectively, with an average of 7.6 labels per sentence.

Considering the limited sample size in the CAIL2021 dataset and the current unavailability of other legal multi-label recognition datasets, we also selected the WOS [31] and AAPD [32] datasets to supplement our validation of the effectiveness of the proposed model for general-level multi-label classification tasks. Despite the relatively shallow depth of the label hierarchy in these two datasets (comprising only two levels), the abundance of labels and samples within them provides an effective supplementary means to assess the capabilities of the model in multi-label classification tasks, particularly under conditions characterized by a high number of labels and uneven sample distribution. The detailed distribution of the three benchmark datasets is presented in Table 1, while the distribution of sample counts across different labels is illustrated in Figure 3. The sample distributions in these datasets vary significantly, enabling an effective evaluation of the performance of the model under conditions of uneven sample distribution.

Table 1. Dataset statistics.

Datasets	Label Total Quantity	Label Depth	Label Quantity	Training/Validation/Test
CAIL2021	320	3	11/75/234	1996/250/250
WOS	141	2	7/134	30,070/7518/9397
AAPD	61	2	9/52	5380/1000/1000

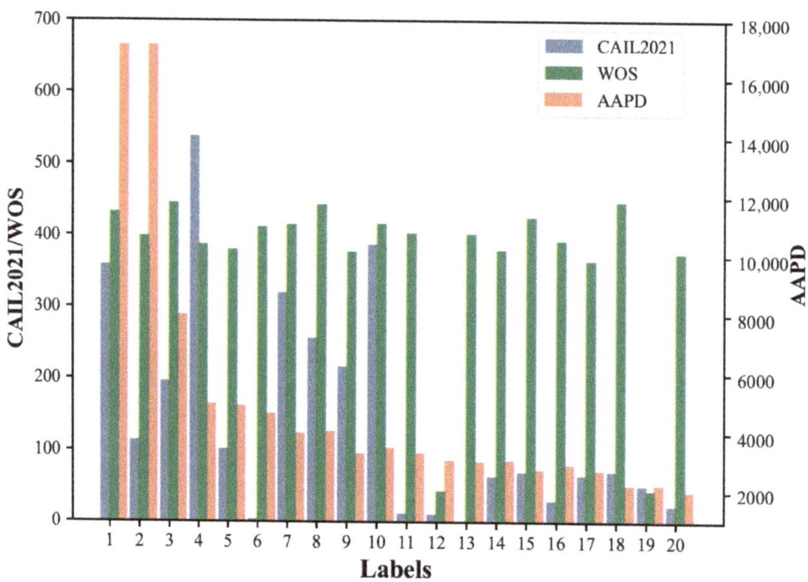

Figure 3. Distribution of samples with different labels in the dataset.

The study assessed model performance using micro-F1 and macro-F1, which are widely used in multi-label classification tasks [33]. Micro-F1 is a micro-averaging algorithm that focuses more on the overall classification performance, while macro-F1 is a macro-averaging method that emphasizes the classification performance of each individual class.

4.2. Experimental Results

We evaluated the performance of the proposed hierarchical prototype neural network by comparing it with general deep learning models, including TextRCNN [5], BERT [6], and SGM [32], as well as the top-performing model from the CAIL 2021 competition

Phase-1. Since Micro-F1 was the primary evaluation metric used in the competition, the experimental results for the CAIL2021 dataset are summarized in Table 2.

Table 2. Experimental results of CAIL2021 dataset.

Model	Accuracy	Recall Rate	Micro-F1
TextRCNN	73.32	37.18	49.34
BERT	72.72	42.62	53.74
SGM	63.29	48.22	54.74
CAIL 2021-Top1	57.40	53.00	55.10
Method in this study	67.57	56.06	61.28

To demonstrate the effectiveness of the proposed method, we conducted a rigorous evaluation of the statistical significance of the performance improvement. Specifically, the CAIL2021 dataset was randomly partitioned into training, validation, and test sets in an 8:1:1 ratio. Subsequently, five independent random experiments were carried out, and the results are summarized in Table 3. A paired samples *t*-test was employed to perform significance analysis. Using the experimental data, we evaluated the significance of differences between the proposed method and the micro-f1 means of TextRNN, BERT, and SGM. The detailed significance analysis is presented in Table 4. As shown in Table 4, the performance improvement of the proposed method is statistically significant ($p < 0.05$) compared to other attention-based models. These evaluation results indicate that our method exhibits substantial advantages over alternative approaches.

Table 3. Results of Models on CAIL2021 datasets.

Models	Micro-F1				
TextRCNN	49.34	49.28	49.31	48.93	49.19
BERT	53.74	52.88	53.66	53.23	52.59
SGM	54.74	53.95	54.02	54.61	53.71
Ours	61.28	61.27	61.13	61.07	60.53

Table 4. Significance analysis of the performance improvement of the proposed model compared to other models.

Models	TextRCNN	Ours	BERT	Ours	SGM	Ours
$\mu(\%)$	49.21	61.06	53.22	61.06	54.21	61.06
σ	0.028	0.095	0.244	0.095	0.199	0.095
n	5		5		5	
ρ	0.284		0.671		0.579	
Δ	0		0		0	
df	4		4		4	
$tStat$	−86.78		−47.72		−41.78	
$P(T < t)$	5.29×10^{-8}		5.77×10^{-7}		9.81×10^{-7}	
t	2.132		2.132		2.132	

The experimental results demonstrate that the proposed method significantly enhances multi-label recognition performance. Compared with the top-performing model in the CAIL 2021 competition, our approach achieves a 6.18% improvement in the micro-F1 score, substantially outperforming commonly used deep learning models for this task. This suggests that our method effectively captures core semantic information within hierarchical levels while better integrating cross-layer semantic relationships, ultimately yielding superior results. A rigorous comparative evaluation was performed between the conventional binary cross-entropy (BCE) loss function and our novel optimization strategy under identical experimental configurations. Figure 4 systematically illustrates the loss trajectories throughout the training process, revealing a distinct convergence pattern: The proposed methodology achieves stable convergence at approximately 40,000 iterations, demonstrating a two-fold acceleration in convergence rate compared to the BCE baseline requiring 80,000 iterations.

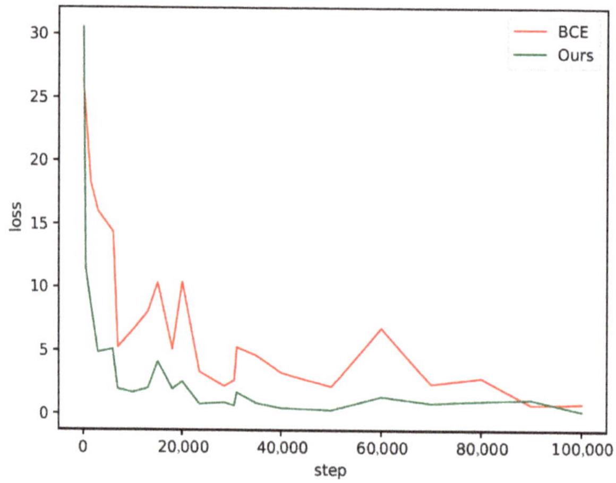

Figure 4. Convergence Dynamics of Training Loss.

The generalizability of the proposed method is further validated by conducting experiments on WOS and AAPD, two widely used multi-label text classification datasets. Comparisons were made against Retrieval [3], TextRCNN [5], Hi-Match [6], Hi-AGM [5], HGCLR [34], MLCL-KNN [4], HiSR [8], HALB [7], DPT [35] and MLCL [26], with the results presented in Table 5.

The experimental results show that the proposed method consistently outperforms state-of-the-art approaches across multiple datasets. The model achieved the highest micro-F1 score (88.24%) and a competitive macro-F1 score (80.24%) on the WOS dataset, as well as the leading micro-F1 score (81.21%) and a substantial macro-F1 score (57.65%) on the AAPD dataset. These results demonstrate its efficacy in general multi-label text classification tasks. The success of this method can be attributed primarily to its ability to effectively capture label semantics at multiple levels and address the challenge of imbalanced sample distribution. This further confirms that the semantic analysis of latent embedding space and the effective integration of cross-layer label semantic relationships represent a viable approach applicable to multi-label text classification tasks, including legal-specific domains. The proposed model exhibits superior domain-specific effectiveness and remarkable task generalization capability.

Table 5. Experimental results of multi-label recognition dataset.

Model	Dataset	Micro-F1	Macro-F1
Retrieval	WOS	81.38	73.82
	AAPD	-	-
HARNN	WOS	81.50	69.69
	AAPD	79.58	48.83
HiMatch	WOS	86.20	80.53
	AAPD	80.74	57.16
HiAGM	WOS	85.82	80.28
	AAPD	80.33	56.72
HGCLR	WOS	87.11	81.20
	AAPD	-	-
MLCL-KNN	WOS	87.37	81.88
	AAPD	-	-
HiSR	WOS	87.52	82.04
	AAPD	-	-
HALB	WOS	87.45	82.04
	AAPD	-	-
DPT	WOS	87.25	81.51
	AAPD	-	-
MLCL	WOS	87.35	77.82
	AAPD	81.75	58.75
Ours	WOS	88.24	80.24
	AAPD	81.21	57.65

Compared with the relatively lower accuracy in the legal text multi-label recognition task, the model achieved high accuracy on the WOS and AAPD datasets. Following the analysis, the differences in the accuracy of the model are mainly reflected in (1) the different languages of the datasets, (2) the differences in the number of labels, and (3) the differences in the sample size. The observed discrepancies in the experimental results further validate the viewpoint hypothesized in this study that "legal multi-label classification represents a complex scenario characterized by abundant label types, demanding semantic correlations and strong hierarchical dependencies between labels". Traditional multi-label recognition approaches often struggle to deliver satisfactory performance when handling such intricate tasks involving legal texts, particularly owing to their limitations in addressing the sophisticated hierarchical interdependencies and semantic associations inherent in legal label systems.

4.3. Ablation Experiment

An ablation study was conducted on the multi-label legal text recognition dataset (CAIL2021) to examine the contribution of different model components. The independent effects of key components were evaluated by removing the multi-layer loss function (Layer), which converts multi-level labels into a single-layer structure, and the batch normalization (BN) layer [36], which ensures stable distribution of prototype parameters. The results are presented in Table 6.

Table 6. Experimental results of the CAIL2021 dataset.

Method	Accuracy	Recall Rate	Micro-F1
Ours -layer-BN	70.23	53.63	60.82
Ours -layer	71.68	52.48	60.60
Ours -BN	68.70	54.83	60.99
Ours	67.57	56.06	61.28

As outlined in Table 6, the proposed method achieves the best performance. When removing the "Layer" component, the recall rate and F1-score of the model decreased, indicating that this mechanism effectively captures the hierarchical structural relationships between labels. The layer-wise approach leverages inter-label dependencies to partially rectify erroneous predictions, thereby significantly enhancing recall capability and improving the adaptability of the model to the complexity of multi-label tasks. Similarly, ablation of the BN layer resulted in notable performance degradation, suggesting that BN enhances model stability and optimizes the balance between recall and the F1-score by normalizing parameter distributions and mitigating training fluctuation. The complete model achieved optimal F1-score performance, which collectively verifies the rationality of our architectural design and the effectiveness of the proposed technical solutions.

5. Conclusions

This study focuses on the task of multi-label legal text recognition, innovatively constructing a multi-head hierarchical attention framework and supporting a new hierarchical learning optimization strategy. In terms of method construction, the framework achieves precise extraction of multi-level semantic representations of text and effective acquisition of multi-label category information through the collaborative operation of the feature extraction and hierarchical modules. Concurrently, the hierarchical learning optimization strategy successfully breaks the shackles of traditional methods in balancing multi-level semantic and multi-label category information learning, accelerates the convergence speed of framework training, and lays a solid foundation for efficient and accurate multi-label legal text recognition. In the experimental verification phase, the proposed method showed significant advantages compared with mainstream methods on the CAIL2021 legal field dataset and the general multi-label recognition datasets AAPD and WOS. The model can complete tasks more accurately and efficiently, whether it is multi-label recognition of complex legal text in legal scenarios or facing diverse text types in general scenarios. This highlights the strong generalization ability and adaptability of this method. However, the model can be further optimized in terms of cross-level label modeling, such as employing a learnable soft-linked hierarchical label association approach to enhance the robustness and generalizability of the model to real-world legal data. This approach improves the adaptability of the model to challenges such as category interference, label variations, and semantic ambiguity between different labels.

The study findings are expected to be widely applied to the intelligent processing of legal information, such as assisting legal practitioners in quickly searching and classifying massive legal literature, improving the accuracy of intelligent classification of judicial cases, and further promoting the digitalization and intelligence process of the legal industry. Concurrently, this method provides new ideas for related NLP tasks. Future research can explore and expand its potential value to text processing in other professional fields.

Author Contributions: Conceptualization, K.Z.; methodology, K.Z., Y.T., J.L., Z.A. and Z.L.; software, K.Z. and L.W.; validation, L.W. and Z.A.; formal analysis, L.W. and K.Z.; investigation, K.Z., Z.L. and Z.A.; resources, L.W., J.L. and Z.A.; data curation, K.Z. and L.W.; writing—original draft preparation,

K.Z., Y.T. and Z.L.; writing—review and editing, K.Z., Y.T., J.L., X.L. and Z.A.; visualization, J.L., L.W., X.L. and Z.A.; supervision, L.W.; funding acquisition, L.W. and K.Z. All authors have read and agreed to the published version of the manuscript.

Funding: The work in this paper was supported by the National Natural Science Foundation of China under Grant No. U23B2056, and the National Key Research and Development Program of China under Grant No. 2022YFC3340900.

Institutional Review Board Statement: Not applicable.

Informed Consent Statement: Not applicable.

Data Availability Statement: All the datasets used in this research are publicly accessible.

Conflicts of Interest: Author Zhonglin Liu was employed by the company China Justice Big Data Institute Co., Ltd. Author Xuelin Liu was employed by the company China Satellite Network Group Co., Ltd. The remaining authors declare that the research was conducted in the absence of any commercial or financial relationships that could be construed as a potential conflict of interest .

Abbreviations

The following abbreviations are used in this study:

CAIL	Challenge of AI in Law
HSVM	Hierarchical support vector machine
HMCN	Hierarchical multi-label classification network
Hi-Match	Hierarchy-aware semantics matching network
Bi-TreeLSTM	Bidirectional tree long short-term memory
GCN	Graph convolutional networks
HiAGM	Hierarchy-aware global model

References

1. Zangari, A.; Marcuzzo, M.; Rizzo, M.; Giudice, L.; Albarelli, A.; Gasparetto, A. Hierarchical text classification and its foundations: A review of current research. *Electronics* **2024**, *13*, 1199. [CrossRef]
2. Caled, D.; Won, M.; Martins, B.; Silva, M.J. A hierarchical label network for multi-label eurovoc classification of legislative contents. In Proceedings of the Digital Libraries for Open Knowledge: 23rd International Conference on Theory and Practice of Digital Libraries, TPDL 2019, Oslo, Norway, 9–12 September 2019; Springer International Publishing: Berlin/Heidelberg, Germany, 2019; pp. 238–252.
3. Chen, H.; Zhao, Y.; Chen, Z.; Wang, M.; Li, L.; Zhang, M.; Zhang, M. Retrieval-style in-context learning for few-shot hierarchical text classification. *Trans. Assoc. Comput. Linguist.* **2024**, *12*, 1214–1231. [CrossRef]
4. Zhang, J.; Li, Y.; Shen, F.; He, Y.; Tan, H.; He, Y. Hierarchical text classification with multi-label contrastive learning and KNN. *Neurocomputing* **2024**, *577*, 127323. [CrossRef]
5. Zhou, J.; Ma, C.P.; Long, D.K.; Xu, G.W.; Ding, N.; Zhang, H.Y.; Xie, P.J.; Liu, G.S. Hierarchy-aware global model for hierarchical text classification. In Proceedings of the 58th Annual Meeting of the Association for Computational Linguistics (ACL), Online, 5–10 July 2020; pp. 1106–1117.
6. Chen, H.B.; Ma, Q.L.; Lin, Z.X.; Yan, J.Y. Hierarchy-aware label semantics matching network for hierarchical text classification. In Proceedings of the 59th Annual Meeting of the Association for Computational Linguistics and the 11th International Joint Conference on Natural Language Processing (ACL), Online, 1–6 August 2021; pp. 4370–4379.
7. Zhang, J.; Li, Y.; Shen, F.; Xia, C.; Tan, H.; He, Y. Hierarchy-aware and label balanced model for hierarchical text classification. *Knowl.-Based Syst.* **2024**, *300*, 112153. [CrossRef]
8. Zhou, J.; Zhang, L.; He, Y.; Fan, R.; Zhang, L.; Wan, J. A Novel Negative Sample Generation Method for Contrastive Learning in Hierarchical Text Classification. In Proceedings of the 31st International Conference on Computational Linguistics, Abu Dhabi, UAE, 19–24 January 2025; pp. 5645–5655.
9. Feng, Z.; Mao, K.; Zhou, H. Adaptive micro-and macro-knowledge incorporation for hierarchical text classification. *Expert Syst. Appl.* **2024**, *248*, 123374. [CrossRef]
10. Reimers, N.; Iryna, G. Sentence-BERT: Sentence Embeddings using Siamese BERT-Networks. In Proceedings of the 2019 Conference on Empirical Methods in Natural Language Processing and the 9th International Joint Conference on Natural Language Processing (EMNLP-IJCNLP), Hong Kong, China, 3–7 November 2019; pp. 3982–3992.

11. Snell, J.; Swersky, K.; Zemel, R. Prototypical networks for few-shot learning. In Proceedings of the 31st International Conference on Neural Information Processing Systems (NeurIPS), Long Beach, CA, USA, 3–9 December 2017; pp. 4080–4090.
12. Yang, H.M.; Zhang, X.Y.; Yin, F.; Yang, Q.; Liu, C.L. Convolutional prototype network for open set recognition. *IEEE Trans. Pattern Anal. Mach. Intell.* **2020**, *44*, 2358–2370. [CrossRef]
13. Ren, Q. Fine-Grained Entity Typing with Prototypical Networks. *J. Chin. Inf. Process.* **2020**, *34*, 65–72.
14. Yang, Y.Y.; Xie, M.X.; Cao, J.X.; Wang, X.B.; Liu, T.W.; Du, Y.H. Adversarial Sample Generation for Chinese Classification Model. *Comput. Eng.* **2023**, *49*, 54–62.
15. Gao, T.Y.; Han, X.; Liu, Z.Y.; Sun, M.S. Hybrid attention-based prototypical networks for noisy few-shot relation classification. In Proceedings of the 32th AAAI Conference on Artificial Intelligence (AAAI), Honolulu, HI, USA, 27 January–1 February 2019; pp. 6407–6414.
16. Liu, H.X.; Dong, C.; Gou, Z.N.; Gao, K. Few-Shot Relation Extraction Method Fusing with Hybrid Representation. *Comput. Eng.* **2023**, *49*, 63–68.
17. Luo, S.Y.; He, J. Few-shot Multi-intent Recognition with Intent Information. *J. Chin. Inf. Process.* **2023**, *37*, 61–70.
18. Xian, Y.T.; Xiang, Y.; Yu, Z.T.; Wen, Y.H.; Wang, H.B.; Zhang, Y.F. Mean Prototypical Network for Text Classification. *J. Chin. Inf. Process.* **2020**, *34*, 73–80.
19. Peng, H.; Li, J.X.; Wang, S.Z.; Wang, L.H.; Gong, Q.R.; Yang, R.Y.; Li, B.; Philip, S.Y.; He, L.F. Hierarchical taxonomy-aware and attentional graph capsule RCNNs for large-scale multi-label text classification. *IEEE Trans. Knowl. Data Eng.* **2019**, *33*, 2505–2519. [CrossRef]
20. Liu, J.Z.; Chang, W.C.; Wu, Y.X.; Yang, Y.M. Deep learning for extreme multi-label text classification. In Proceedings of the 40th International ACM SIGIR Conference on Research and Development in Information Retrieval (SIGIR), Shinjuku, Tokyo, Japan, 7–11 August 2017; pp. 115–124.
21. Cai, L.J.; Hofmann, T. Hierarchical document categorization with support vector machines. In Proceedings of the 13th ACM International Conference on Information and Knowledge Management (CIKM), Washington, DC, USA, 8–13 November 2004; pp. 78–87.
22. Cerri, R.; Barros, R.C.; de Carvalho, A.C.P.L.F.; Jin, Y.C. Reduction strategies for hierarchical multi-label classification in protein function prediction. *BMC Bioinform.* **2016**, *17*, 373. [CrossRef] [PubMed]
23. Wehrmann, J.; Cerri, R.; Barros, R. Hierarchical multi-label classification networks. In Proceedings of the 35th International Conference on Machine Learning (ICML), Stockholm, Sweden, 10–15 July 2018; pp. 5075–5084.
24. Cao, Y.K.; Wei, Z.Y.; Tang, Y.J.; Jin, C.K.; Li, Y.F. Hierarchical Label Text Classification Method with Deep Label Assisted Classification Task. *Comput. Eng. Appl.* **2024**, *60*, 105–112.
25. Deng, Z.F.; Peng, H.; He, D.X.; Li, J.X.; Yu, P.S. HTCInfoMax: A global model for hierarchical text classification via information maximization. *arXiv* **2021**, arXiv:2104.05220.
26. Van Nooten, J.; Daelemans, W. Jump To Hyperspace: Comparing Euclidean and Hyperbolic Loss Functions for Hierarchical Multi-Label Text Classification. In Proceedings of the 31st International Conference on Computational Linguistics, Abu Dhabi, UAE, 19–24 January 2025; pp. 4260–4273.
27. Vaswani, A.; Shazeer, N.; Parmar, N.; Uszkoreit, J.; Jones,L.; Gomez, A.N.; Kaiser, L.; Polosukhin, I. Attention is All you Need. In Proceedings of the 31st International Conference on Neural Information Processing Systems (NeurIPS), Long Beach, CA, USA, 3–9 December 2017; pp. 6000–6010.
28. Liu, C.L. One-vs-all training of prototype classifier for pattern classification and retrieval. In Proceedings of the 20th IAPR International Conference on Pattern Recognition (ICPR), Istanbul, Turkey, 23–26 August 2010; pp. 3328–3331.
29. Wolf, T.; Debut, L.; Sanh, V.; Chaumond, J.; Delangue, C.; Moi, A.; Cistac, P.; Rault, T.; Louf, R.; Funtowicz, M.; et al. Transformers: State-of-the-art natural language processing. In Proceedings of the 2020 Conference on Empirical Methods in Natural Language Processing (EMNLP), Online, 16–20 November 2020; pp. 38–45
30. Challenge of AI in Law(CAIL). Available online: http://cail.cipsc.org.cn/task_summit.html?raceID=6&cail_tag=2021 (accessed on 24 February 2025).
31. Kowsari, K.; Brown, D.E.; Heidarysafa, M.; Meimandi, K.J.; Gerber, M.S; Barnes, L.E. Hdltex: Hierarchical deep learning for text classification. In Proceedings of the 2017 16th IEEE International Conference on Machine Learning and Applications (ICMLA), Cancun, Mexico, 18–21 December 2017; pp. 364–371.
32. Yang, P.C.; Sun, X.; Li, W.; Ma, S.M.; Wu, W.; Wang, H.F. SGM: Sequence generation model for multi-label classification. *arXiv* **2018**, arXiv:1806.04822.
33. Gopal, S.; Yang, Y.M. Recursive regularization for large-scale classification with hierarchical and graphical dependencies. In Proceedings of the 19th ACM SIGKDD International Conference on Knowledge Discovery and Data Mining (KDD), Chicago, IL, USA, 11–14 August 2013; pp. 257–265.

34. Wang, Z.H.; Wang, P.Y.; Huang, L.Z.; Sun, X.; Wang, H.F. Incorporating Hierarchy into Text Encoder: A Contrastive Learning Approach for Hierarchical Text Classification. In Proceedings of the 60th Annual Meeting of the Association for Computational Linguistics (ACL), Dublin, Ireland, 22–27 May 2022; pp. 7109–7119.
35. Xiong, S.; Zhao, Y.; Zhang, J.; Mengxiang, L.; He, Z.; Li, X.; Song, S. Dual prompt tuning based contrastive learning for hierarchical text classification. In Proceedings of the Findings of the Association for Computational Linguistics ACL 2024, Bangkok, Thailand, 11–16 August 2024; pp. 12146–12158.
36. Ioffe, S.; Szegedy, C. Batch normalization: Accelerating deep network training by reducing internal covariate shift. In Proceedings of the 2020 International Conference on Machine Learning (ICML), Online, 16–22 November 2020; pp. 448–456

electronics

MDPI

Article

Detection of Exoplanets in Transit Light Curves with Conditional Flow Matching and XGBoost

Stefano Fiscale [1,2,*], Alessio Ferone [3], Angelo Ciaramella [3], Laura Inno [1,2,3], Massimiliano Giordano Orsini [1], Giovanni Covone [2,4,5] and Alessandra Rotundi [1,3]

1 UNESCO Chair "Environment, Resources and Sustainable Development", Department of Science and Technology, Parthenope University of Naples, 80133 Naples, Italy; laura.inno@uniparthenope.it (L.I.); massimiliano.giordanoorsini001@studenti.uniparthenope.it (M.G.O.); alessandra.rotundi@uniparthenope.it (A.R.)

2 Istituto Nazionale di Astrofisica, Osservatorio Astronomico di Capodimonte, Salita Moiariello, 16, 80131 Naples, Italy

3 Department of Science and Technology, Centro Direzionale di Napoli, Parthenope University of Naples, 80143 Naples, Italy; alessio.ferone@uniparthenope.it (A.F.); angelo.ciaramella@uniparthenope.it (A.C.)

4 Department of Physics "Ettore Pancini", University of Naples Federico II, 80138 Naples, Italy; giovanni.covone@unina.it

5 INFN Section of Naples, Via Cinthia 6, 80126 Naples, Italy

* Correspondence: stefano.fiscale001@studenti.uniparthenope.it

Abstract: NASA's space-based telescopes Kepler and Transiting Exoplanet Survey Satellite (TESS) have detected billions of potential planetary signatures, typically classified with Convolutional Neural Networks (CNNs). In this study, we introduce a hybrid model that combines deep learning, dimensionality reduction, decision trees, and diffusion models to distinguish planetary transits from astrophysical false positives and instrumental artifacts. Our model consists of three main components: (i) feature extraction using the CNN VGG19, (ii) dimensionality reduction through t-Distributed Stochastic Neighbor Embedding (t-SNE), and (iii) classification using Conditional Flow Matching (CFM) and XGBoost. We evaluated the model on two Kepler and one TESS datasets, achieving F1-scores of 98% and 100%, respectively. Our results demonstrate the effectiveness of VGG19 in extracting discriminative patterns from data, t-SNE in projecting features in a lower dimensional space where they can be most effectively classified, and CFM with XGBoost in enabling robust classification with minimal computational cost. This study highlights that a hybrid approach leveraging deep learning and dimensionality reduction allows one to achieve state-of-the-art performance in exoplanet detection while maintaining a low computational cost. Future work will explore the use of adaptive dimensionality reduction methods and the application to data from upcoming missions like the ESA's PLATO mission.

Keywords: exoplanet detection; deep learning; dimensionality reduction; diffusion models; decision trees

1. Introduction

Since the discovery of 51 Pegasi b [1], the identification of exoplanets—planets orbiting stars other than the Sun—has become one of the most rapidly evolving research fields combining a wide range of expertise from astrophysics to data science [2]. Over the past two decades, space-based telescopes such as NASA's Kepler [3] and the Transiting Exoplanet Survey Satellite (TESS) [4] have revolutionized this field by collecting photometric measurements from hundreds of thousands of stars. By using the transit method [5], these telescopes have identified a large number of periodic signals due to real planets, astrophysical events (e.g., eclipsing binaries and stellar variability), and other phenomena (e.g., instrumental systematics). The human-based analysis is the most reliable approach to classify these signals as expert astronomers can handle a wide range of possible scenarios based on their expertise [6,7]. However, the manual examination of these signals presents two major drawbacks. First, human judgment is not objective, and some astronomers might disagree on labels assigned to some signals. Second, this process is highly time-consuming considering that astronomers need to be trained on this task [8] and that labeling a single signal might require from a few hours up to several days as the visual examination of Data Validation reports provided for the signal of interest [9] is required at least.

To address these issues, Convolutional Neural Networks (CNNs) [10] became the standard in classifying these signals [11–15], from their first implementation by Shallue C. and Vanderburg A. [16] (hereinafter SV18) with Astronet. These CNNs detect the most relevant patterns in transit signals through a feature extraction block—which is typically based on the architecture of the CNN VGG19 [17]—thus performing classification leveraging the universal approximation property of a Multi-Layer Perceptron (MLP) [18–20]. Over time, the architecture of these networks has been optimized, leading to significant performance gains up to 99% of classification accuracy on real exoplanet signals [21,22].

However, such CNNs are designed assuming that features useful for humans in their analysis are equally relevant to the model in solving the task at hand. Processing linearly dependent input features unnecessarily increase the complexity of the network [23], both in terms of data collection and preparation, and model's parameter optimization. Moreover, the higher the number of model's parameters requiring optimization, the larger the volume of training data needs to be in order for the optimization algorithm to converge to a stable local minimum; in this field, the ratio of the dataset size to the number of model parameters is still heavily skewed toward the latter. CNNs face two major limitations: their classifier is highly complex, consisting of hundreds of thousands to millions of parameters, and they lack interpretability, which is crucial here to understand the reasoning behind model predictions.

Decision trees such as Random Forests (RFs) [24] and Gradient Boosted Trees (GBTs) [25,26], including XGBoost, have demonstrated their effectiveness in approximating complex distributions with lower computational costs than MLPs. These models are universal approximators like MLPs [27] but obtain particularly better classification performance on tabular data [28]. Previous efforts demonstrated the effectiveness of RF classifiers in classifying planetary candidates across ground- and space-based surveys [29–32].

Another promising approach to preserve classification accuracy while reducing model complexity is dimensionality reduction (DR). Methods like t-Distributed Stochastic Neighbor Embedding (t-SNE) [33] can effectively project high-dimensional data into lower-dimensional embedding while preserving data structures, making them highly suitable for data processing before classification. Integrating the potential of these models can facilitate the development of a more efficient classifier. In this context, Armstrong D. et al. [30] and Schanche N. et al. [32] introduced innovative approaches, respectively, employing the combination of RFs and a Self-Organizing Map (SOM) for classifying transit signals in the Next-Generation Transit Survey (NGTS) [34] data and RFs coupled with a CNN for processing data from the Wide Angle Search for Planets (WASP) [35] survey.

In this paper, we propose an innovative approach to perform a multi-class classification of the signals detected in Kepler and TESS data, in planet candidate (PC), astrophysical false positive (AFP), and non-transiting phenomenon (NTP). Our approach is based on a model consisting of three main components:

1. Feature extraction, performed using the widely adopted CNN VGG19, which transforms input signals into high-dimensional feature vectors;
2. Dimensionality reduction, performed by the t-SNE method, which maps the high-dimensional features to a lower dimensional space, where they can be most effectively classified;
3. Classification, implemented by Conditional Flow Matching (CFM) and XGBoost [36].

Our model achieves competitive performance compared to the state of the art, with an F1-score of 99% on Kepler data and 100% on a TESS dataset, operating on very small inputs in size terms compared to other approaches in the literature.

Our results reveal that the application of t-SNE on the feature vectors produced by VGG19 enhances classification capabilities of the model than classical VGG-based CNNs classifying feature vectors with a MLP.

With this model, we continue to build on the most relevant architectures in the context of exoplanets detection (i.e., CNNs and decision trees), with the innovation of merging them in a single data processing pipeline. This work highlights the advantages of combining deep learning with dimensionality reduction and decision tree classifiers, offering an effective and efficient solution for exoplanet detection.

The rest of the paper is organized as follows: Related works are presented in Section 2, where we also define the contribution and novelty of our approach. The Kepler and TESS data used in this work are described in Section 3.1, while a theoretical background on the three main components of our model is provided in Section 3.2. We explain our model's architectural details in Section 4, showing the results in Section 5. A discussion is reported in Section 6, including a comparison with related works, and conclusions are drawn in Section 7.

2. Related Works

This section provides an overview of the evolution of ML models for the classification of TCEs. Since numerous contributions have been made in this field, we summarize in Table 1 the specifics about the most relevant model architectures in order to highlight the key differences between prior studies and our approach.

The first ML models developed for the binary classification of TCEs were based on RFs, namely, Autovetter [29] and Robovetter [37]. These models were employed to classify thousands of Kepler TCEs and played a key role in generating two of the largest labeled datasets available for this survey: Kepler Q1–Q17 Data Release 24 and 25. Both approaches were designed to process a broad set of inputs, including scalar planetary features, centroid motion and difference image analysis, odd–even transit differences, secondary view, and phase-folded light curves (all these features are described in the caption of Table 1).

Subsequent efforts demonstrated that integrating different ML techniques lead to better classification performance. SOMs were applied to Kepler and K2 [38] data [39], while RF and SOM (RFC + SOM) combinations were tested on NGTS [30,34] data, and a model based on RF and CNN was applied on WASP data [32,35]. These hybrid approaches leveraged the strengths of different methods to improve robustness in TCE classification. These models used a limited set of input features, with SOM processing phase-folded light curves representing the transit shapes, while RFC + SOM integrates planetary parameters without centroid or secondary eclipse information. Although centroid information could help in identifying some false-positive scenarios such as background eclipsing binaries, in their work, Armstrong D. et al. [30] decided to not use this feature due to the risk to discard blended transiting planets, which instead remain candidates worthy of further analysis.

The introduction of deep learning revolutionized TCE classification, with CNN-based models becoming the standard. Astronet [16] was one of the first CNNs specifically designed for Kepler TCEs classification, processing a global view and its zoomed-in representation (the local view). Since then, CNN-based models have been used on various surveys, including K2 [11] and TESS [13,40]. Some models further increased input dimensionality by incorporating stellar and transit parameters alongside multiple light curves representations [14,41]. The evolution of CNNs culminated in two of the best models: Exominer [21] for Kepler and Astronet-Triage-v2 [22] for TESS. As shown in Table 1, both models process a combination of light curve representations (e.g., global and local views and secondary eclipse) and stellar and transit parameters to classify TCEs. Given that the input information processed by these models corresponds almost entirely to that used by astronomers during manual vetting, efforts to enhance their interpretability have become increasingly relevant. In this context, a notable contribution was proposed by Salinas H. et al. [42]. The authors of this study presented a Transformer-based approach for the binary classification of TESS TCEs, processing global and local views, centroid information, and stellar and planetary features.

Table 1. Comparison of different model architectures. For each model, we report the network architecture and the classification task (binary: 2c, or multi-class: >2c) and, if the model uses stellar features (St.f), planetary features (Pl.f, including transit period, transit duration, transit depth difference, etc.), centroid information (C, pixel-level information about the location of the variation in brightness for the detected transit), phase-folded flux (Pff, consisting of light curves with different data binning such as global and local views), odd–even (two consecutive transits), secondary view (Sv, consisting of the dip in star brightness when the detected object passes behind its star), difference image (Diff.img, used to evaluate whether the transit occurs out of the central pixel where the target star is supposed to be). The ✓ symbol indicates that the corresponding feature is used as an input parameter in the model; conversely, the symbol × indicates that the feature is not employed by the model.

Model [Ref.]	Architecture	Task	St.f.	Pl.f.	C	Pff	Odd–Even	Sv	Diff.img.
Robovetter	Decision Tree	3c	×	✓	✓	✓	✓	✓	✓
Autovetter	Decision Tree	3c	✓	✓	✓	✓	✓	✓	✓
Armstrong D. et al. [39]	SOM	2c	×	×	×	✓	×	×	×
Armstrong D. et al. [30]	RFC + SOM	2c	×	✓	×	×	×	×	×
Astronet	CNN	2c	×	×	×	✓	×	×	×
Astronet-K2 [11]	CNN	2c	✓	✓	×	✓	×	×	×
Exonet [41]	CNN	2c	✓	×	✓	✓	×	×	×
Genesis [43]	CNN	2c	✓	×	✓	✓	×	×	×
Astronet-Triage [13]	CNN	2c	×	×	×	✓	×	×	×
Astronet-Vetting [13]	CNN	2c	×	✓	×	✓	×	✓	×
Astronet-Triage-v2	CNN	5c	✓	✓	×	✓	×	✓	×
Exominer	CNN	2c	✓	✓	✓	✓	✓	✓	✓
Salinas H. et al. [42]	Transformer	2c	✓	✓	✓	✓	×	×	×
This work	CNN + DR + CFM + XGBoost	3c	×	×	×	✓	×	×	×

Our approach integrates the key strengths of previous models into a unified framework. We adopt CNN architecture based on VGG19 as feature extractor, a choice consistent with previous works such as Astronet, Astronet-Triage, and Astronet-Triage-v2. However, instead of relying on the CNN for end-to-end classification as previous works already tested, we show that classification performance improves when features are projected into lower-dimensional spaces by t-SNE and that decision trees are used to exploit their capabilities in discriminating tabular data. We simplified the input to only the global view, deciding not to process as input the other light curves that differ from the global view in binning size (e.g., local view). Furthermore, the dimensionality reduction using t-SNE enhances computational efficiency and enables interpretability through the visualization of data in a two-dimensional space, providing insight into model predictions. A performance comparison with state-of-the-art models is provided in Section 6.4.

3. Background

Since our aim is developing a model to classify signals detected in transit light curves, this section is intended to provide all the necessary background information about the data used in this work (Section 3.1) and the operation of the methods that make up our model (Section 3.2).

3.1. Data

We work with light curves in which periodic transits of potential planetary nature, called Threshold-Crossing-Events (TCEs), were detected. Section 3.1.1 briefly explains how light curves are produced by the Kepler and TESS telescopes and how TCEs are detected. For a more detailed overview on this, we refer the reader to Jenkins J. et al. [44] and Jenkins J. et al. [45]. Section 3.1.2 provides details about the composition of TCEs datasets used. The process of input data preparation is described in Section 3.1.3.

3.1.1. From Light Curves to Threshold Crossing Events

The Kepler and TESS space telescopes were designed to gather photometric observations for a set of target stars from which light curves are extracted with a technique called aperture photometry. This technique consists of extracting the flux values of a target star from each photometric observation by summing the pixel values within a predefined aperture, optimized to maximize the signal-to-noise ratio (SNR). The resulting one-dimensional signal represents the variation in stellar brightness as a function of time, forming a light curve. An example of Kepler light curve is depicted in the top panel of Figure 1.

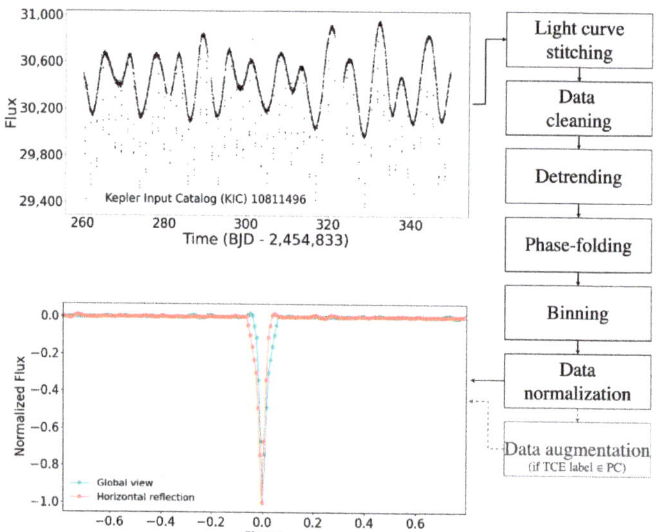

Figure 1. Our data preparation pipeline processes each TCE through several steps. First, we retrieve the corresponding light curve files from the MAST archive (for sake of simplicity, we show a single Kepler quarter for Kepler Input Catalog (KIC) star 10811496). These light curves are merged into a single signal (light curve stitching step), from which not-a-numbers and outliers have been filtered out (data cleaning step). During the detrending step, we eliminate any non-transit flux variation. The cleaned signal is phase-folded according to the TCE's period (phase-folding). Finally, we bin and normalize the data to create a 1×201-length global view, where the median flux is set to 0 and the maximum transit depth to -1 (binning and data normalization steps). The resulting signal is horizontally reflected if it belongs to the PC class (data augmentation step).

During its nine year service until 2018, Kepler monitored approximately 156,000 stars in a fixed region of the sky up to 4000 light years from the Earth, in the constellations of Lyra and Cygnus. The stellar flux measurements were sampled at 29.4 min cadence. Observations for each target star were divided into quarters of ∼90 days, after which the spacecraft rotated 90 degrees to maintain its solar panels pointed toward the Sun.

The observation strategy has changed with TESS, with the telescope scanning the entire sky in a 200-light-year range, dividing the sky into 26 sectors each observed for 27 days. TESS is designed to observe ∼200,000 target stars at a 2 min cadence (short cadence data) and to collect Full-Frame Images of each sector at 10 and 30 min cadences (long cadence data).

Both missions employ similar pipelines for data reduction and TCEs detection: the Kepler Science Operations Center (KSOC) [44] and the Science Processing Operations Center (SPOC) [45] for Kepler and TESS, respectively. These pipelines perform bias and flat field calibration, aperture photometry, and systematic corrections before identifying TCEs via the Transiting Planet Search module [46]. While SPOC is responsible for processing TESS short cadence data, long cadence data are processed by the MIT Quick Look Pipeline (QLP) [47].

3.1.2. Catalogs of Threshold Crossing Events Used in This Work

When TPS detects periodic dimming, i.e., TCEs, in the pre-processed stellar light curves, each TCE is examined by astronomers through automated tools [48] whose outputs are visually analyzed so that a label can be assigned to it [6,7]. This process, intent on determining the nature of each TCE, is called vetting.

In this study, we use three catalogs of labeled TCEs from which we produce the input representations we fed to our model. These catalogs provide for each TCE a set of physical (both planetary and stellar) and statistical parameters used for its classification and characterization. The parameters of these catalogs we used are those related to transit properties, i.e., transit period, duration, and the time of the first detected transit (defined as epoch), along with the column defining the label of the TCE. We employ these transit parameters during the pre-processing method, as described in Section 3.1.3.

- Kepler Q1–Q17 Data Release 24 ($\mathcal{D}_{K24}$). This catalog comprises 20,367 TCEs identified by the KSOC pipeline in Kepler light curves. These TCEs were automatically classified by Autovetter [29,49] into planet candidates (PCs), astrophysical false positives (AFPs), non-transiting phenomena (NTP), and unknown (UNK). To minimize the uncertainty of our dataset labels, we adopted the approach employed for the first time by SV18 by discarding all TCEs labeled as UNK. This filtering resulted in a final dataset of 3600 PCs, 9596 AFPs, and 2541 NTPs.
- Kepler Q1–Q17 Data Release 25 ($\mathcal{D}_{K25}$). This set is the final version of TCEs detected by the Kepler mission [50], comprising 34,032 TCEs automatically dispositioned by the Robovetter algorithm [37], that is an ensemble of decision trees trained on a dataset of labeled transits.
  The primary distinction between this catalog and $\mathcal{D}_{K24}$ lies in a higher number of long-period TCEs (approximately 372 days), resulting in $\mathcal{D}_{K25}$ being a TCE dataset characterized by a lower SNR. With longer orbital periods, the number of observed transits decreases, limiting the increase in SNR during our data preparation pipeline. Before generating model inputs from this catalog, we performed the following filtering operation. We removed all TCEs with the rogue flag set to 1, which correspond to cases with fewer than three detected transits, erroneously included in this catalog due to a bug in the Kepler pipeline. For our PC class, we selected the 2726 confirmed and 1382 candidate planets from the Cumulative KOI catalog (The Cumulative KOI catalog

contains the most precise information on all the Kepler TCEs labeled as confirmed and candidate planet, as well as false positive. Further information about Kepler tables of TCEs can be found at the following link: https://exoplanetarchive.ipac.caltech.edu/docs/Kepler_KOI_docs.html, accessed on 9 August 2024). Our AFP class includes the 3946 TCEs labeled as false positive in the Cumulative KOI table, while the NTP class contains the 21,098 TCEs from the Kepler Data Release (DR) 25 catalog that do not appear in the Cumulative KOI table.

- TESS TEY23 ($\mathcal{D}_{TEY23}$). This catalog contains a subset of 24,952 TCEs detected by QLP in TESS long cadence data for which Tey E. et al. [22] (hereafter TEY23) provided dispositions across a three-year vetting process. The authors used five labels to classify these TCEs: "periodic eclipsing signal", "single transit", "contact eclipsing binaries", "junk", and "not-sure" (see Section 2.4 of their paper for further details on the labeling process). To improve the reliability of our dataset, we filtered out (i) 5340 TCEs for which the authors did not provide a consensus label and (ii) all the TCEs labeled as "single transit" and "not-sure", thus obtaining 2613 periodic eclipsing signals (we will identify as E), which include both planet candidates and non-contact eclipsing binaries, 738 contact eclipsing binaries (B) and 15,791 junk (J).

We divided each dataset in 80% training and 20% test splits. In dividing the dataset into the training test, we created splits by preserving the same percentage for each class as in the complete set. By doing so, we avoided getting unbalanced splits toward one of the classes. Table 2 summarizes the composition of these datasets.

Table 2. Composition of the three datasets used in this study. For each class *, we report the total number of TCEs and their distribution in training (80%) and test (20%) sets. * Classes. PC: Planet Candidate, AFP: Astrophysical False Positive, NTP: Non-Transiting Phenomenon, E: Periodic Eclipsing Signal, B: Contact Eclipsing Binary, and J: Junk. [a] The number of samples for the PC classes was doubled as described in Section 3.1.3.

Dataset [Ref.]	Class	Total	Training	Test
Kepler Q1–Q17 DR24 [49]	PC	[a] 7200	5760	1440
	AFP	9596	7676	1920
	NTP	2541	2033	508
	Total	19,337	15,469	3868
Kepler Q1–Q17 DR25 [50]	PC	[a] 8216	6573	1643
	AFP	3946	3162	784
	NTP	21,098	16,950	4148
	Total	33,260	26,685	6575
TESS TEY23 [22]	E	2613	1647	966
	B	738	598	140
	J	15,791	13,327	2464
	Total	19,142	15,572	3570

3.1.3. Data Preparation

The TCEs detected by the KSOC, SPOC, and QLP pipelines still remain signals dominated by the brightness of their host star, in our case, representing noise. To prevent our model from learning the noise, we generate a standard one-dimensional representation for each TCE: a binned and phase-folded light curve devoid of any variability except that of the transit of interest. The methodology we adopted to generate such representations has been widely used in this context of exoplanets detection with Machine Learning (ML) since it was proposed by SV18, and it is described below.

This data preparation pipeline consists of two main blocks: data cleaning—where inconsistent data such as not-a-number and outliers are removed—and data smoothing—where any variability in light curve brightness except that caused by TCE is flattened.

First, we download from the Mikulski Archive for Space Telescopes (MAST) (https://archive.stsci.edu/, accessed on 19 June 2020 for $\mathcal{D}_{K24}$, 20 May 2023 for $\mathcal{D}_{TEY23}$ and 9 August 2024 for $\mathcal{D}_{K25}$) the light curves of the stars around which the TCEs of the catalogs $\mathcal{D}_{K24}$, $\mathcal{D}_{K25}$, and $\mathcal{D}_{TEY23}$ orbit. For each TCE, we apply the following operations:

- Stitching the light curves. A TCE can be associated with multiple segments (Kepler quarters or TESS sectors) of the light curve of its host star. This depends mainly on the observing strategy of the telescope. We generate a single light curve by sequentially appending segments, which we then normalize by the median value calculated over the entire signal;
- Data cleaning. From the resulting light curve, we discard all not-a-numbers and outliers beyond $\pm 3\sigma$ of the stellar flux;
- Detrending. In order to remove any non-TCE-related variability, we divide the cleaned flux data by an interpolating polynomial of degree 3 computed using the Savitzky–Golay method with filter window set to 11. During detrending, we preserve flux measurements related to TCE transit by applying a mask calculated based on TCE transit period and duration;
- Phase-folding and binning. This detrended signal is folded on the relative TCE period and binned with a time bin size of 30 min (When developing this data pre-processing pipeline, we tested time bin sizes of 2, 10, and 30 min, which correspond to the data sampling rates of the Kepler and TESS telescopes. The best results in terms of the shape of the resulting transit were obtained using the 30 min value).
  Following the same methodology used by SV18 and Yu L. et al. [13], we linearly interpolate any empty bin so as to generate an input signal of length 201;
- Normalizing the binned signal. The binned signal is then normalized to 0-median and maximum transit depth to -1. We define the binned and normalized transit as *global view*, consisting of the one-dimensional input we fed to our model;
- Data augmentation on the PC class. Since our main goal is to train a model able to minimize the number of misclassified planets, we double the number of samples belonging to this class in the $\mathcal{D}_{K24}$ and $\mathcal{D}_{K25}$ datasets. More precisely, we apply a horizontal reflection to the global views of the PC TCEs. We decided to not adopt the same procedure to the eclipsing signals (E class) of $\mathcal{D}_{TEY23}$ since Tey E. et al. [22] declared that this set of planets also contains a fraction of non-contact eclipsing binaries, and we want to minimize the risk of increasing the number of eclipsing binaries contaminating the E class because of our purpose of identifying exoplanets.

The schema of this data preparation pipeline is depicted in Figure 1.

This pipeline is highly time-consuming because of (i) the large number of light curves to be processed ($\sim$64,000); (ii) the multiple scans to be performed on each of them; (iii) the high number of data points for each light curves, up to 70,000. To speed up this process, we parallelized this pipeline by distributing the workload over multiple nodes as described in Fiscale S. et al. [51] as the operations on different light curves are independent.

3.2. Components of Our Model

Our model combines neural networks and other methods for feature extraction, dimensionality reduction, and the classification of global views. Below, we provide a theoretical background of each component of our model.

3.2.1. Convolutional Neural Network and VGG19

A Convolutional Neural Network [10,52] is a deep learning model consisting of two main blocks: (i) feature extraction—where the input is subjected to a series of operations such as application of convolutional filters, non-linear activation functions such as Rectified Linear Unit (ReLU), and spatial dimensionality reduction, i.e., pooling. The aim is to extract increasingly complex features from the data and identifying possible patterns, undetectable by manual examination, useful in solving the task at hand; (ii) classification—where the features extracted from the previous block are processed through a classifier, which is typically a MLP.

In this work, we exploited the feature extraction block of VGG19 to extract from our input data, the global views, and their most relevant features. The details of this process are described in Step 1 of Section 4.

3.2.2. Dimensionality Reduction and t-SNE

Dimensionality reduction methods aim to project high-dimensional data in a lower-dimensional space while preserving as much of the significant structure of the data as possible. Among the several dimensionality reduction algorithms (e.g., Isomap [53], Locally Linear Embedding [54], and Laplacian Eigenmaps [55]), we used t-SNE. It is a non-linear method that improves the Stochastic Neighbor Embedding algorithm [56] in terms of cost function optimization and solving the crowding problem (A comprehensive technical description of the t-SNE algorithm, including a quantitative analysis of how it preserves the local and global structure of high-dimensional data, can be found in the original paper by Van der Maaten L. and Hinton G. [33]. In particular, Sections 3.2 and 3.3 and Figures 1 and 2 of the aforementioned paper illustrate how the algorithm addresses the crowding problem and enhances cluster separation in the embedded space). t-SNE generates a two- or three-dimensional representation of input data as follows.

Let $\mathcal{X} = \{\vec{x}_i\}_{i=1}^{m} \in \mathbb{R}^N$ the set of input data belonging to the N-dimensional space and $\mathcal{Y} = \{\vec{y}_i\}_{i=1}^{m} \in \mathbb{R}^d$ the counterpart set of projections into the output lower-dimensional space, where $d \in \{2,3\} : d \leq N$. In the input space, the pairwise similarities are modeled as conditional probabilities $p_{j|i}$, with

$$p_{j|i} = \frac{\exp(-||\vec{x}_i - \vec{x}_j||^2/2\sigma_i^2)}{\sum_{k\neq i}\exp(-||\vec{x}_i - \vec{x}_k||^2/2\sigma_i^2))} \tag{1}$$

where σ_i is the variance of the gaussian distribution centered in the i-th sample. These conditional probabilities are symmetric since $p_{ij} = (p_{j|i} + p_{i|j})/2m$.

In the output space, similarities are modeled by using the t-Student distribution with one degree of freedom:

$$q_{ij} = \frac{(1 + ||\vec{y}_i - \vec{y}_j)||^2)^{-1}}{\sum_{k\neq l}(1 + ||\vec{y}_k - \vec{y}_l)||^2)^{-1}} \tag{2}$$

The aim is to determine the points $\vec{y}_i$ so that the Kullback–Leibler (KL) divergence [57] between the two conditional probabilities distributions is minimized:

$$\mathrm{KL}(P||Q) = \sum_{i\neq j} p_{ij} \log \frac{p_{ij}}{q_{ij}} \tag{3}$$

The minimization of the quantity KL$(P||Q)$ is computed with the gradient descent algorithm with momentum and adaptive learning rate (see Equation (5) in Van der Maaten L. and Hinton G. [33]). The momentum term increases during the gradient descent iterations, while the learning rate is updated according the method provided by Jacobs R.A. [58]. A full derivation of the t-SNE gradient can be found in Appendix A of the original paper. As the authors described in their Section 3.4, the optimization process is improved by the use of the "early exaggeration" trick, which forces the method to model large distances among the low dimensional representation of the samples based on their membership cluster. In other words, the distance between two samples of different clusters is maximized, as we found in our experiments and show in Figure 2.

We relied on t-SNE to reduce the dimensionality of feature vectors obtained from VGG19. Step 2 of Section 4 reports the details of this operation. We demonstrate in Section 5 that this dimensionality reduction places the data in a space where the classifier is able to define better separation surfaces that are highly discriminative than those learned from state-of-the-art CNNs, which work in higher dimensionality embeddings. The limitations of this technique are discussed in Section 6.5.

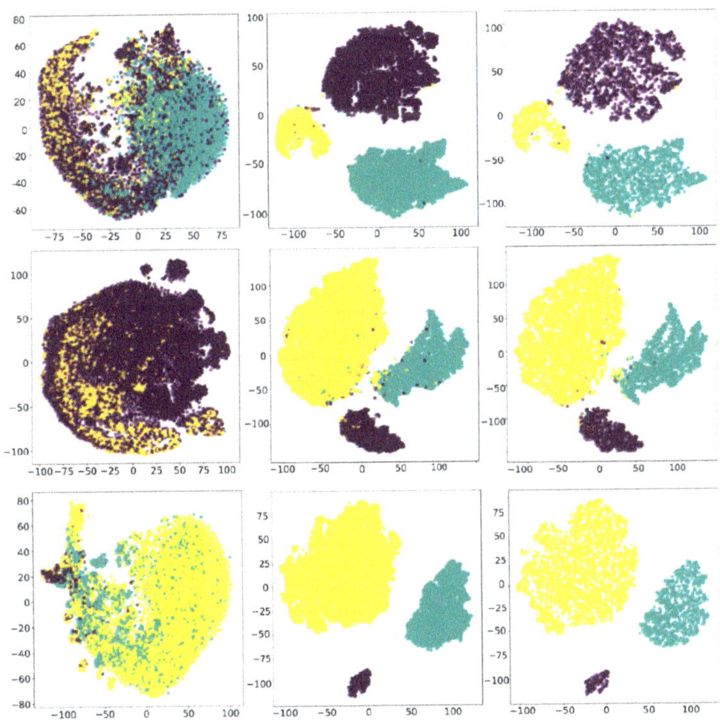

Figure 2. For each dataset, we show the representations of the global views ($\mathcal{D}$, left column), $\mathcal{D}_{2-train}$ (middle column), and $\mathcal{D}_{2-test}$ (right column) in the two-dimensional space defined by t-SNE. (First row) Kepler Q1–Q17 Data Release 24; (second row) Kepler Q1–Q17 Data Release 25; (third row) TESS TEY23. The application of VGG19 for extracting features from the global views ensures a highly effective separation among the three clusters of TCEs on each dataset. Purple points indicate samples belonging to the AFP class (or class B), green points represent samples from the PC class (or class E), and yellow points correspond to the NTP class (or class J).

3.2.3. Gradient-Boosted Trees and XGBoost

Gradient-boosted trees (GBTs) consist of a set of sequentially trained decision trees highly robust in the classification of tabular data [59–62]. Each new tree is constructed with the aim of correcting errors made by previous trees. In a classification context, the final prediction on a given sample is obtained by the majority vote from the predictions of all the trees. In this study, we used eXtreme Gradient Boosting (XGBoost) [63], which differs from GBTs as the trees are constructed in parallel, rather than sequentially. In addition, XGBoost extends traditional gradient boosting by including regularization elements in the objective function, thus improving generalization and preventing overfitting issues, which is very important in exoplanet detection as the majority of datasets are highly imbalanced toward the not-PC classes.

3.2.4. Diffusion Models and Conditional Flow Matching

Diffusion models are the new frontier of generative models, long characterized by the domain of Generative Adversarial Networks [64]. Diffusion models iteratively transform input samples with the injection of noise and then learn to reverse this process, reconstructing the original samples distribution, by solving a Stochastic Differential Equation.

Conditional Flow Matching [36] is a diffusion model used in both generative and classification tasks [65]. CFM transforms an input sample through a learned vector field varying in time $t \in [0,1]$, mapping its original distribution to a Gaussian distribution over n_t steps. This mapping is achieved by applying a series of invertible transformations (e.g., affine and planar transformations) on the sample, constrained by the labels of input data in supervised learning scenarios. At step n_t, the sample follows the reverse process by solving an Ordinary Differential Equation (ODE) so that the original data distribution can be reconstructed.

XGBoost plays a dual role in this framework. During the forward process, a new XGBoost model is trained at each step to estimate the vector field, providing a more efficient alternative than using a classical neural network [36,66]. Additionally, a final XGBoost is applied on the reconstructed sample at the end of the reverse process to perform classification.

We implemented CFM and XGBoost within our model by exploiting the approach provided by Jolicoeur-Martineau A. et al. [36].

4. Method

This section details the pipeline that we designed for the classification of global views, starting with feature extraction through a CNN, followed by dimensionality reduction via t-SNE, and concluding with classification using Conditional Flow Matching and XGBoost. We leverage the strengths of each component in our pipeline to achieve robust generalization performance in lower-dimensional spaces.

Let

$$\mathcal{D} = \{(\vec{x}_1, y_1), (\vec{x}_2, y_2), \ldots, (\vec{x}_n, y_n)\}$$

be the input dataset composed by n samples. Each sample $\{\vec{x}_i\}_{i=1}^{n} \in \mathbb{R}^N$ consists of a global view of size $N = 201$, with

$$\{y_i\}_{i=1}^{n} \in \mathcal{Y} = \{\mathrm{AFP}, \mathrm{PC}, \mathrm{NTP}, \mathrm{E}, \mathrm{B}, \mathrm{J}\}$$

indicating its label. The datasets $\mathcal{D}_{K24}$, $\mathcal{D}_{K25}$, and $\mathcal{D}_{TEY23}$ are separately processed through the following steps.

1. Feature extraction. We extract the features from the global views with the feature extraction block of VGG19. This model is independently trained on each dataset until

overfitting on the global views. Since VGG19 is exclusively used as feature extractor, its training can be extended until overfitting the dataset in order to guarantee the most representative features are extracted. For each of the n global views, the VGG19's feature extraction branch produces a one-dimensional feature map of size 2560, once flattened. We trained VGG19 for 300 epochs on each dataset, with a learning rate of 1×10^{-3}, batch size of 128, and pooling size and stride fixed to 3 and 2, respectively, by using Adam [67] as the optimization algorithm. As highlighted from the number of TCEs for each class in Table 2, all our datasets are imbalanced toward one of the three classes. Typically, such an imbalance is toward the class of non-astrophysical transits (classes NTP and J). To address class imbalance, we used class weighting when training VGG19. The weights for each class were computed using the Inverse Class Frequency technique [68].
The n 2560-length feature vectors, we denote as $\mathcal{D}_1^{n\times 2560}$, are saved at the end of the last training epoch.

2. Dimensionality reduction. The resulting feature vectors are projected into a two-dimensional embedding defined by t-SNE. By processing $\mathcal{D}_1$, t-SNE produces (In our experiments, we also evaluated the classification performance of our model by processing three-dimensional data produced by t-SNE, rather than exclusively two-dimensional data. However, the best performance was obtained by processing data in two dimensions) a representation $\mathcal{D}_2^{n\times 2}$.
As shown in Step 2 of Figure 3, the input $\mathcal{D}_1$ of t-SNE is divided in two subsets (We discuss the application of this strategy in Section 6.5):

   - $\mathcal{D}_{1-train}$ (80% of data), used to generate $\mathcal{D}_{2-train}$, which will be used as training set for the Conditional Flow Matching;
   - The entire dataset $\mathcal{D}_1$, from which $\mathcal{D}_2$ is obtained. We extract from this representation the set $\mathcal{D}_{2-test}$, containing the data that will be used when assessing the Conditional Flow Matching performance.

   Our experiments revealed that running t-SNE for 3000 iterations, with a perplexity of 50, best maximized the separation of TCEs classes in the two-dimensional space.
   The two-dimensional projections obtained by t-SNE for training and test data are shown in middle and right panels of Figure 2, respectively.
   We emphasize that a quantitative assessment of how well t-SNE preserves the clustering structure of the data—particularly in terms of local and global neighborhood relationships—is thoroughly discussed in the original work by Van der Maaten L. and Hinton G. [33]. In our study, we focus on the practical impact this dimensionality reduction has in the context of TCE classification, showing the related evidence in Figures 2 and 4 and Table 3.

3. Classification with CFM and XGBoost. Following the methodology described in Jolicoeur-Martineau A. et al. [36] and Li A. et al. [65], we performed TCE classification by processing $\mathcal{D}_2$ with CFM and XGBoost (Step 3). Each sample of $\mathcal{D}_2$ is mapped into the vector field of the CFM from $t = 0$ to $t = 1$ in $n_t = 50$ steps. At each step, an XGBoost is trained to estimate the vector field. The sample at time $t = 1$ is processed with an ODE, returning the output sample that is fed to an additional XGBoost, responsible for the TCE classification [65].
   Due to the low dimensionality of the input and the good separability between classes of TCEs provided by t-SNE, a very accurate classification performance is obtained as early as n_t = 50 noise levels. Each of the n_t XGBoosts has 100 decision trees of maximum depth of 2 and has been trained for 30 epochs with 63 steps per epoch. An extended discussion on finding the sub-optimal hyperparameters configuration is provided in Section 6.

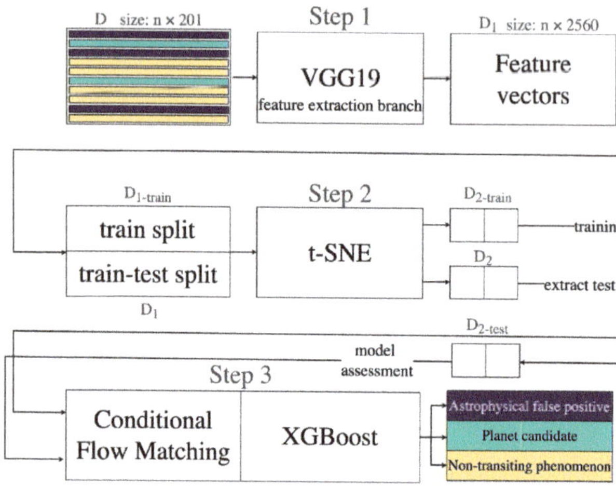

Figure 3. Architecture of our model. *STEP 1*: The input dataset $\mathcal{D}$, containing n global views labeled as AFP (or B, purple rectangles), PC (or E, green rectangles), NTP (or J, yellow rectangles), is processed by VGG19. For each global view, VGG19 produces a feature vector of size 2560. We define the entire set $\mathcal{D}_1$. *STEP 2*: We generate two splits of data from $\mathcal{D}_1$: $\mathcal{D}_{1-train}$, containing the 80% of feature vectors to be used for training in STEP 3, and $\mathcal{D}_1$, which corresponds to the entire dataset obtained in STEP 1. We use t-SNE to project the two splits separately into a two-dimensional space, obtaining $\mathcal{D}_{2-train}$ and $\mathcal{D}_2$. *STEP 3*: We train the CFM with XGBoost on $\mathcal{D}_{2-train}$ and evaluate its performance on $\mathcal{D}_{2-test}$, the subset of $\mathcal{D}_2$ containing only the test data. XGBoost performs multi-class classification of TCEs into AFP (or B), PC (or E), and NTP (or J).

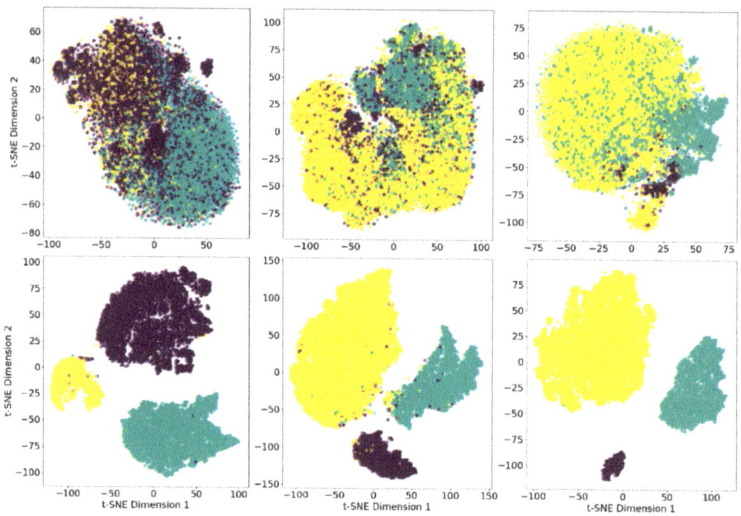

Figure 4. Visual comparison between the features extracted by DART-Vetter (**top row**) and VGG19 (**bottom row**) in the two-dimensional embedding defined by t-SNE. The features extracted from the global views of $\mathcal{D}_{K24}$, $\mathcal{D}_{K25}$, and $\mathcal{D}_{TEY23}$ are depicted in the left, middle, and right panels, respectively. Purple points indicate samples belonging to the AFP class (or class B), green points represent samples from the PC class (or class E), and yellow points correspond to the NTP class (or class J).

Table 3. Performance of different vetting models. Our precision, recall, and F1-scores for Kepler data are computed by averaging the scores of Table 4 obtained on each class. Other model scores are taken from the reference manuscripts. The best results on Kepler and TESS datasets are highlighted in boldface.

Model [Ref.]	Survey	Precision	Recall	F1-Score
SOM [39]	Kepler	0.864	0.865	0.864
SOM [39]	K2	0.945	0.972	0.958
RFC + SOM [30]	NGTS	0.901	0.914	0.907
Exominer [21]	Kepler	0.968	0.974	0.971
Exominer-Basic [21]	TESS	0.88	0.73	0.79
Astronet-Triage-v2 [22]	TESS	0.84	0.99	0.909
Transformer [42]	TESS	0.809	0.8	0.805
This work	Kepler	**0.974**	**0.987**	**0.980**
This work	TESS	**1.0**	**1.0**	**1.0**

Table 4. Classification performance of the model across three datasets: Kepler Q1–Q17 Data Release (DR) 24, Data Release 25, and TESS TEY23. The metrics, computed on test samples, show the ability of our model in distinguishing between TCEs of different natures, including Astrophysical False Positives (AFP), Planet Candidates (PC), and Non-Transiting Phenomena (NTP) in the Kepler datasets. For the TESS dataset, the classification involves TCEs whose nature could be non-contact eclipsing binaries (B), eclipsing signals (E), and Junk (J). For Kepler DR24, individual class misclassification rates are provided, showing particularly strong performance in identifying planet candidates (0.42% misclassification rate). On Kepler DR25, our model exhibits a global misclassification rate of 2.1% across all classes, while on TESS TEY23, it achieves robust predictions performance, with a 0% misclassification rate.

Dataset	Class	Precision	Recall	F1-Score	Misclass. Rate (%)
Kepler Q1–Q17 DR24	AFP	0.9943	0.9932	0.9937	1.25
	PC	0.9972	0.9986	0.9979	0.42
	NTP	0.9803	0.9803	0.9803	3.93
Kepler Q1–Q17 DR25	AFP	0.910	0.985	0.946	2.1
	PC	0.971	0.996	0.983	
	NTP	0.997	0.972	0.984	
TESS TEY23	B	1.000	1.000	1.000	0.0
	E	1.000	1.000	1.000	
	J	1.000	1.000	1.000	

5. Results

The results obtained from the model on the three datasets under this study are presented in this section. On each dataset, we evaluated the classification performance in terms of precision, recall, F1-score, and misclassification rate for each class [69]. Table 4 reports these results. In general, the discriminatory capabilities of the model on each dataset are competitive with those obtained from state-of-the-art models [21,22].

5.1. Application on Kepler Q1–Q17 Data Release 24

The model achieves high predictive accuracy across all three classes of $\mathcal{D}_{K24}$, with noteworthy results in the identification of planets. The results are reported in the first block of Table 4 and discussed below.

On the PC class, we obtain a precision of 0.9972, a recall of 0.9986, and an F1-score of 0.9979, with a misclassification rate of 0.042, indicating a very robust distinction between planetary signals and false positives or non-transiting phenomena. On the AFP class, the precision is 0.9943, recall 0.9932, and F1-score is 0.9937, resulting in a misclassification rate of 0.0125. The NTP class, while more challenging due to its variability in the nature of transits (including any transit not consistent with astrophysical ones), maintains optimal classification metrics, with a precision, recall, and F1-score of 0.9803 and a misclassification rate of 0.0393.

Analyzing the confusion matrix in left panel of Figure 5, we observe 25 TCE misclassified. The majority of these misclassifications occur between the AFP and NTP classes, counting 19 samples. These samples correspond to the purple and yellow points in the top right panel of Figure 2, which are located in regions of the two-dimensional space close to the center of a cluster to which they do not belong. For the PC class, our model misclassifies only two planets, labeling them as AFP. Meanwhile, there are only three false positives: two AFPs and one NTP, which are the purple and yellow points in the green cluster of the top right panel in Figure 2.

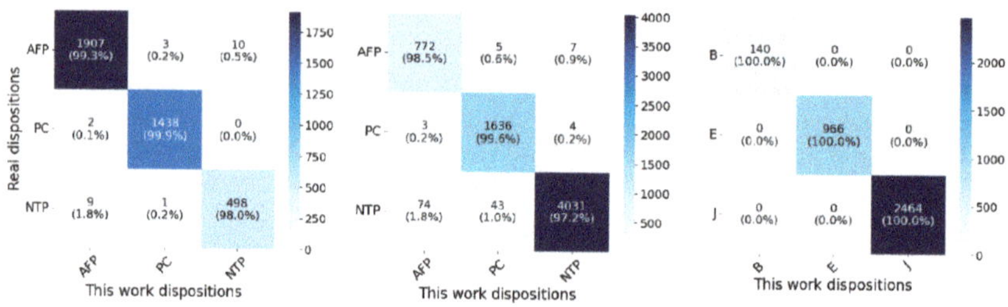

Figure 5. Confusion matrices computed on the test sets of $\mathcal{D}_{K24}$ (**left panel**), $\mathcal{D}_{K25}$ (**middle panel**), and $\mathcal{D}_{TEY23}$ (**right panel**). The high classification performance of Conditional Flow Matching with XGBoost is evident from the diagonal elements of each matrix, with a percentage of correctly classified samples for each class ranging from 97% to 100%. On both Kepler and TESS data, our model retrieves at least 99.6% of planets during classification.

These results demonstrate the effectiveness of our model in distinguishing the TCEs of the three classes, particularly in the identification of planet candidates.

5.2. *Application on Kepler Q1–Q17 Data Release 25*

Compared to the DR24 dataset, the higher number of long-period TCEs with a lower SNR in $\mathcal{D}_{K25}$ slightly affects the classification accuracy of our model. Nevertheless, discrete classification performance is achieved on this dataset as well. The second block of Table 4 displays the results we present below.

For the AFP class, the model achieves a precision of 0.910, a recall of 0.985, and an F1-score of 0.946. For the PC class, very high scores are obtained: precision is 0.971, recall is 0.996, and F1-score is 0.983. For the NTP class, the model exhibits the highest precision of 0.997, along with a recall of 0.972 and an F1-score of 0.984.

The middle panel confusion matrix in Figure 5 shows that the number of misclassified planets is very low. The model successfully identifies 1636 planets out of 1643 total samples, with only seven misclassifications. Three are associated with the AFP class and four to the NTP class. Regarding these four TCEs, we focus the reader's attention on the middle right panel of Figure 2. Among the five planets (green points) projected by t-SNE near regions dominated by NTPs, only four are classified as NTP. Our model is able to retrieve one of them during classification, despite the fact that its position in the two-dimensional space seemed to compromise its classification. The number of false positives is relatively high (48, including 43 NTPs and 5 AFPs). These samples are visible in middle right panel of Figure 2. The presence of a small cluster of yellow points and five purple points falling into the green cluster of the PCs can be observed. For these points, the model is unable to provide the correct label.

Overall, the misclassification rate of 0.021 further confirms the robust discrimination capabilities of the model on all three classes of TCEs, despite their imperfect separation in the two-dimensional space.

The results obtained on the two Kepler datasets show that the greatest uncertainty in the model lies in the discrimination between AFP and NTP class samples. However, the percentage of misclassifications between these two classes is extremely low ($\sim$2%) and involves samples located at the edges of the clusters (as shown in the rightmost panels of Figure 2), suggesting that further analysis on these cases would not make significant contributions to the overall evaluation of the model. We recall that the main goal is to minimize the fraction of misclassified PCs as they represent the signals of greatest scientific interest. In this regard, our model performs very well: the maximum percentage of misclassified planets is 0.4% in $\mathcal{D}_{K25}$, a value that is very small. As mentioned in Section 3.1.2, $\mathcal{D}_{K25}$ is known to contain a higher fraction of long-period planets than $\mathcal{D}_{K24}$, resulting in fewer available transits and, consequently, a lower SNR of TCEs. This aspect may justify a slight increase in the misclassifications from $\mathcal{D}_{K24}$ (0.1%) to $\mathcal{D}_{K25}$ (0.4%). In Section 6.6, we discuss instead the problem of label noise, whereby a TCE of a given class (e.g., AFP) may change its disposition over time or be labeled differently by different teams of astronomers.

5.3. Application on TESS TEY23

As highlighted in third block of Table 4, our model shows impressive performance in classifying non-contact eclipsing binaries, eclipsing signals, and junk. The model correctly classifies all samples with no misclassified TCEs. As a result, precision, recall, and F1-score all reach their maximum value of 1, with a misclassification rate of 0%. The confusion matrix on this dataset is shown in right panel of Figure 5. The correct classification of all samples is mainly due to their perfect separation in two-dimensional space, as visible in the bottom right panel of Figure 2.

The results on the TESS dataset demonstrate that the prediction of our model is consistent with the labels assigned by experts, which we considered as ground truth. For the two Kepler datasets, our predictions align with the automated labels produced by Autovetter and Robovetter. These findings suggest that the proposed method exhibits strong robustness when applied to real data.

6. Discussion

6.1. The Contribution of VGG19 and t-SNE in TCEs Classification

The use of VGG19 for extracting features from the global views proved to be crucial in ensuring a highly discriminative representation of TCEs.

Initially, we evaluated the use of the CNN provided by Fiscale S. et al. [15] as a feature extractor that we will call DART-Vetter. This model, developed to classify Kepler and TESS TCEs, processes the global view through five convolutional blocks. Each block consists of a one-dimensional convolutional layer followed by ReLU activation, spatial dropout, max pooling, and batch normalization. The number of filters in the convolutional layers increases exponentially from 16 to 256. The extracted features are then flattened and classified through a single fully connected layer. Feature extraction from the global views of the three datasets was performed following the same procedure described in Section 4 (Steps 1 and 2). DART-Vetter was trained until overfitting on each dataset, and the extracted features were stored at the final training epoch.

However, the classification performance on feature vectors produced by DART-Vetter was poor. For this reason, we evaluated the use of VGG19. This network has already been widely used in the context of exoplanet identification, demonstrating its effectiveness since the introduction of Astronet, whose network architecture is clearly based on that of VGG19, as shown in Figure 7 of their paper [16].

Figure 4 presents a visual comparison of the features obtained from DART-Vetter (top panel) and VGG19 (bottom panel) for the $\mathcal{D}_{K24}$ (left panel), $\mathcal{D}_{K25}$ (middle panel), and $\mathcal{D}_{TEY23}$ (right panel) datasets. The results indicate that VGG19 provides a significantly more effective class separation, with minimal overlap between different classes, unlike the features extracted by DART-Vetter, where class overlap is more noticeable.

The left column of Figure 2 shows, for each dataset, the two-dimensional representations of global views before features are extracted from them using VGG19. Middle and right columns depict the two-dimensional representation—defined by t-SNE—of the features extracted from this network on the training and test data, respectively. The clear class separation achieved after feature extraction and dimensionality reduction confirms that VGG19 captures robust discriminative features, while t-SNE further enhances their separability, as highlighted by the results of Table 3. This near perfect separability facilitated the training of Conditional Flow Matching and XGBoost, enabling them to learn well-defined decision surfaces resulting in a very low misclassification rate.

Thus, the high classification accuracy of our model is mainly due to the key role of combining feature extraction and dimensionality reduction for the identification of most relevant patterns within the global views.

6.2. Reducing the High Computational Complexity and Memory Demand When Training the Conditional Flow Matching with XGBoost

In this section, we discuss a key factor we had to handle during the design of the model and which directed us toward the use of dimensionality reduction methods.

Training our CFM with XGBoost on the feature vectors extracted from VGG19 would have required an extremely high computational cost, making the whole process shown in Figure 3 impractical. We trained CFM and XGBoost with the methodology provided by Jolicoeur-Martineau A. et al. [36], which requires training n_t models, where the levels of noise n_t should take values in [50, 100]. In addition, each model needs to be trained on a duplication of the input dataset. For example, on Kepler Q1–Q17 Data Release 25, it would have been necessary to replicate the dataset at least 50 times, bringing the overall size to more than 1.6 million samples, each with 2560 features. This would have required significantly more memory resources than were available on our machine and training times on the order of several days, also hampering the hyperparameters fine-tuning. An even more critical issue concerned the scalability of the model: even if we had obtained good results, such an onerous process would have made it difficult for other users to exploit the model on their own laptops. The application of t-SNE proved its effectiveness also in addressing this issue by compressing the input vectors from 2560 to only 2 features.

This compression allowed us to preserve the discriminative patterns learned from VGG19 on the global views while ensuring efficient training of CFM with XGBoost and easily reproducible model configuration on common hardware.

To further assess the ability of t-SNE in mapping the feature vectors into a two-dimensional space, we made a comparison with Principal Component Analysis (PCA). As illustrated in Figure 6, t-SNE outperforms PCA in preserving class separability within the lower dimensional embedding. Left and central panels of Figure 6 (top row) demonstrate that when features from the $\mathcal{D}_{K24}$ and $\mathcal{D}_{K25}$ datasets are projected using PCA, they are partially overlapped and spread across significantly larger regions, resulting in poor cluster definition. For each dataset, the standard deviations (σ_1, σ_2) of the first two principal components are $\mathcal{D}_{K24}$: (2903.8, 1551.8); $\mathcal{D}_{K25}$: (407.0, 224.2); $\mathcal{D}_{TEY23}$: (18.0, 5.8).

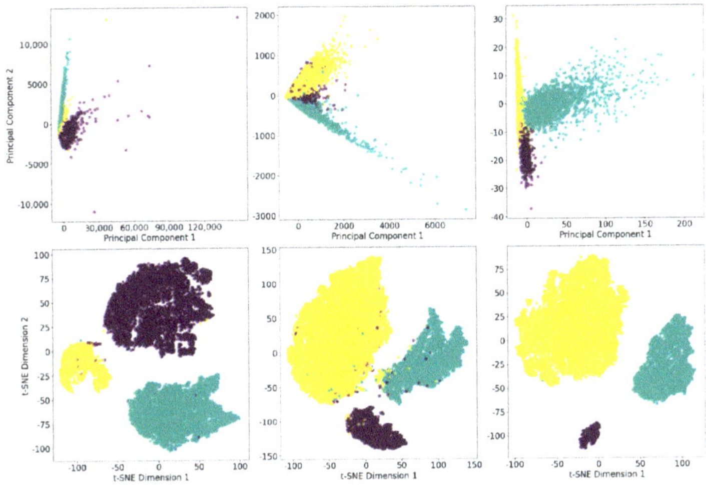

Figure 6. Comparison between t-SNE (**bottom row**) and Principal Component Analysis (PCA (**top row**)) in dimensionality reduction. Two-dimensional features for $\mathcal{D}_{K24}$, $\mathcal{D}_{K25}$, and $\mathcal{D}_{TEY23}$ are shown in the left, middle, and right panels, respectively. Purple points indicate samples belonging to the AFP class (or class B), green points represent samples from the PC class (or class E), and yellow points correspond to the NTP class (or class J).

This wider spreading occurs because data with PCA are linearly mapped to the directions with largest variance, causing high variance classes to distribute across larger regions.

On the other hand, t-SNE maps the same features into more compact embedding while effectively preserving the separation between the three TCE classes. The better ability of t-SNE to project TCEs features into well-defined regions corresponding to their respective classes justifies our choice to adopt this method for dimensionality reduction in our pipeline.

6.3. Finding the Hyperparameter Configuration Optimizing Classification Accuracy

During the experiments, we conducted a systematic analysis of classification performance by varying the Conditional Flow Matching and XGBoost hyperparameters. As suggested in Jolicoeur-Martineau A. et al. [36], we tested noise levels in the range [50, 100], with discrete increments of 10 units. The optimal number of decision trees was evaluated by considering sets in [100, 500], each time increasing by 100 units. Given the two-dimensional inputs of our Step 3, an extensive exploration of the maximum depth of the trees was not necessary, limiting the analysis to architectures with depths of no more than four levels. The number of training epochs of decision trees was estimated in [10, 100], with increments of 10. The batch size for each epoch was chosen by preferring powers of 2 in order to optimize computational efficiency and maximize the use of available hardware resources. The value of 63 steps for each epoch allowed us to process batch sizes of similar size to 256. The experiments conducted revealed that the performance does not improve as model complexity increases. This result finds a natural interpretation in Occam's razor heuristic, according to which, given equal performance, simpler models are preferable to their more complex counterparts.

6.4. Comparison with State-of-the-Art Vetting Models

In this section, we compare the predictive performance of our model with those achieved by state-of-the-art vetting models. Table 5 reports the technical details regarding the models we compare with, while Table 3 summarizes the performance of these comparison models. Direct comparisons should be made with caution as these models are trained and tested on datasets from different surveys, varying in training and test set size and pre-processing methods. Additionally, each model applies a specific classification threshold, which is typically optimized on recall to minimize the fraction of misclassified planets.

Table 5. Technical details regarding the deep learning models we compare for classification performance in Table 3. For each model, we provide information about the architecture and training hyperparameters. Input branches indicate the number of input channels through which the model processes data. The column Figure Ref. refers to the figure in the original article where the network architecture is shown. We derived the information displayed in this table from reference articles (and from related source codes when available). We were not able to retrieve the related information for the element denoted with the "-" symbol.

Hyperparameters	**Models**		
	Exominer	Astronet-Triage-v2	Salinas H. et al. [42]
Architecture	CNN	CNN	Transformer
Figure Ref.	Figure 9	Figure 8	Figure 2
Input branches	8	7	3
Activation	ReLU	ReLU	Attention Mechanism *
Regularization	Dropout	Dropout	Dropout
Fully-connected	4×128	4×512	Linear ($X \rightarrow 2$) *
Output	Sigmoid	Sigmoid	Softmax *
Optimizer	Adam	Adam	Adam
Training	-	20,000 steps	60 epochs
Learning rate	6.73×10^{-5}	1×10^{-3}	1×10^{-3}
Batch size	-	64	100
Model selection	10-fold CV	10-fold CV	10-fold CV
	Armstrong D. et al. [39] Kepler	Armstrong D. et al. [39] K2	Armstrong D. et al. [30]
Architecture	SOM	SOM	RFC + SOM
Grid dimension	20×20	8×8	20×20
Radius	20	<20	20
Training epochs	500	500	300
Learning rate	0.1	0.1	0.1

* Softmax in the final layer, Attention Mechanism within the Transformer blocks. X represents the concatenated output dimension of the encoders.

Exominer achieves a precision of 0.96 and recall of 0.97, while Astronet-Triage-v2 attains 0.84 and 0.99, respectively. Despite their ability to minimize the fraction of false negatives, these models were designed to process human-relevant input features, some of which are linearly dependent. For example, the local view is essentially a global view with a different bin size. Including such redundant features increases model complexity without significantly improving generalization capabilities [23,43,70]. In addition, high-dimensional inputs increase the risk that the network will need substantial architectural changes to be applied to data from different surveys. This limitation is evident in the degraded performance of Exominer when applied to TESS data (Exominer-Basic), where its precision and recall drop to 0.88 and 0.73, respectively. While reducing input redundancy is crucial for optimizing model effectiveness, astronomers often prioritize interpretability to understand the reasoning behind model predictions. Salinas H. et al. [42] introduced a Transformer-based approach designed to enhance interpretability. However, its performance remains below that of Exominer and Astronet-Triage-v2, achieving a precision of 0.809 and recall of 0.8.

The SOM-based model proposed by Armstrong D. et al. [39] proves its robustness on K2 data, with an F1-score = 0.958, but the performance deterioratea on the Kepler dataset, where the F1-score is 0.864.

Compared to all previous approaches, our model achieves the highest scores on both Kepler and TESS datasets, with an F1-score of 0.980 and 1.0, respectively. Notably, this performance is achieved without increasing input dimensionality, consequently making our model easily transferable across surveys. Our implementation choices supported by promising results suggest that projecting the learned features into lower dimensional spaces and then classifying them by exploiting the capabilities of decision trees as universal approximators may be sufficient to outperform more complex models.

6.5. Current Limitations of Our Model

The current limitation of our approach is the use of t-SNE for dimensionality reduction. Unlike deep learning models, t-SNE lacks optimizable parameters and, therefore, cannot learn dynamic mappings from high- to low-dimensional space through a training phase. Consequently, to guarantee that the two-dimensional projection of training data is not influenced by test data during dimensionality reduction (as described in Step 2 of Section 4), we had to split $\mathcal{D}_1$ into distinct subsets.

Additionally, t-SNE is computationally expensive on large datasets as it requires computing pairwise distances. Although this method presents these drawbacks, it proved to be effective in preserving class separability in the lower-dimensional embeddings of both our TCE datasets and benchmark datasets of images and handwritten digits [71].

To address these limitations, we plan to replace t-SNE with methods that can learn dynamic mapping, such as Variational Autoencoder (VAE).

6.6. The Noise Affecting TCE Labels and Lack of Benchmark Dataset

In this section, we discuss what we consider to be a central challenge in the field of exoplanet detection: the presence of label noise affecting the classification of TCEs. It is well known by the exoplanet community that TCE labels are subject to uncertainty as they may evolve over time with the availability of new observations and through manual vetting by experts. Consequently, a certain degree of ambiguity is to be expected. For example, this issue is mentioned in Exominer and found in Astronet-Triage-v2, where Table A1 in Tey E. et al. [22] highlights certain disagreements among astronomers regarding TCE dispositions, with some cases lacking a Consensus Label. Further discrepancies in the TCE label can be found in Cacciapuoti L. et al. [6] and Magliano C. et al. [7], who independently examined and relabeled subsets of TCEs from the ExoFOP catalog, sometimes diverging from the labels provided by the TESS Follow-up Program Observing Group (TFOPWG; [72]). Labels change over time, observable in the "View all TFOPWG Disposition" field of ExoFOP, further confirming this underlying ambiguity.

Supervised models for exoplanet detection are evaluated on these datasets, labeled by different research teams, and a universally accepted "ground-truth" dataset for model assessment does not yet exist. This constitutes a significant limitation that makes direct comparisons across studies inherently difficult. This remains an open issue in the field and warrants further attention from the exoplanet community.

7. Conclusions

We presented a model to distinguish planetary signals from false positives in Kepler and TESS transit light curves. Our approach combines deep learning, dimensionality reduction, diffusion models, and decision trees. More precisely, we used VGG19 for feature extraction, t-SNE for dimensionality reduction, and Conditional Flow Matching with XGBoost for classification. The proposed model was evaluated on three datasets achieving F1-scores of 98% on Kepler data and 100% on the TESS dataset TEY23, which represents a performance improvement over the best-performing models on Kepler (1% better than Exominer) and on TESS (10% better than Astronet-Triage-v2). The architecture we designed guarantees low computational complexity in data collection, preparation, and processing. Our Python code (version 3.10.15), implemented using the PyTorch library (version 1.9.5) [73], is freely available at the following link: https://github.com/stefanofisc/dartvetter_cfm.

We relied on the effectiveness of VGG19 as a feature extractor, as illustrated in Figure 4, and the results reported in Table 3 proved that t-SNE significantly enhances class separability. While VGG19 extracts highly discriminative patterns, these features lie in a high-dimensional space, which can affect the ability of the classifier to define optimal decision boundaries. By contrast, projecting these features into a two-dimensional space via t-SNE facilitates the learning of well-defined separation surfaces. This enables CFM and XGBoost to achieve high classification accuracy with substantially lower computational and memory demands. We carefully considered the potential risk of overfitting while designing our pipeline. Consequently, we employed several strategies to reduce this risk, particularly in preventing the model from being biased toward the majority class, as detailed in Section 4. Furthermore, without dimensionality reduction, training CFM on high-dimensional feature vectors, with the method developed by Jolicoeur-Martineau A. et al. [36], would have been infeasible due to the need for dataset duplication for each noise level.

Future work will explore alternative dimensionality reduction techniques, such as Variational Autoencoder, to further optimize the feature representation.

Another important aspect to be addressed in future developments is the exploration of more data augmentation methods, such as statistically based undersampling and oversampling [74]. In the present work, our aim was to extend the PC class in order to construct the largest and most reliable dataset representation for evaluating our model. To this end, we employed a simple yet effective oversampling technique, consisting of horizontally flipping the global views of the PC class. This approach preserves the statistical properties of the original signals as it does not leverage on synthetic signal injections or noise distortions. On the other hand, undersampling could be considered in scenarios where training and evaluation are performed exclusively on real data. In this context, one could randomly select a representative subset from the majority classes (i.e., NTP, J, and AFP). However, while this approach may help balance the class distribution, it carries the risk of discarding informative examples crucial for capturing the diversity of non-planetary signals. This may, in turn, introduce bias and negatively affect the generalization capabilities of our model. Among the various augmentation techniques, we believe statistically based oversampling appears to be the most promising avenue for future exploration. Architectures such as VAEs and diffusion models offer the possibility to sample new data from a learned latent space, enabling the generation of realistic variations of planetary signals. These synthetic samples tend to preserve the underlying statistical distribution of the original data, potentially enhancing the robustness of our model without compromising data representation.

Additionally, we plan to extend the application of our model to upcoming transit surveys, including ESA's PLAnetary Transits and Oscillations of stars (PLATO) [75], to assess its generalization capabilities on new data.

Author Contributions: Conceptualization, S.F. and A.F.; methodology, S.F., A.F. and A.C.; software, S.F.; validation, S.F., A.F. and A.C.; formal analysis, S.F., A.F. and A.C.; investigation, S.F. and A.F.; resources, S.F., A.F. and A.C.; data curation, S.F., A.F. and A.C.; writing—original draft preparation, S.F.; writing—review and editing, S.F., A.F., A.C., L.I., G.C., M.G.O. and A.R.; visualization, S.F., A.F., A.C., L.I., M.G.O., G.C. and A.R.; supervision, A.F., A.C., L.I. and A.R.; project administration, A.F. All authors have read and agreed to the published version of the manuscript.

Funding: This research received no external funding.

Data Availability Statement: The data presented in this study are available in Mikulski Archive for Space Telescopes at http://archive.stsci.edu/missions/kepler/lightcurves/tarfiles/DOI_LINKS/Q0-17_LC+SC/ (Kepler data, accessed on 19 June 2020 for Kepler Q1–Q17 Data Release 24 and on 9 August 2024 for Kepler Q1–Q17 Data Release 25) and https://archive.stsci.edu/tess/bulk_downloads/bulk_downloads_ffi-tp-lc-dv.html#lc (TESS data, accessed on 20 May 2023), reference number [T98304] (Kepler) and reference number [t9-nmc8-f686] (TESS).

Acknowledgments: This research has made use of the NASA Exoplanet Archive, which is operated by the California Institute of Technology, under contract with the National Aeronautics and Space Administration under the Exoplanet Exploration Program. This paper includes data collected by the Kepler mission and obtained from the MAST data archive at the Space Telescope Science Institute (STScI). Funding for the Kepler mission is provided by the NASA Science Mission Directorate. STScI is operated by the Association of Universities for Research in Astronomy, Inc., under NASA contract NAS 5–26555. This paper includes data collected with the TESS mission, obtained from the MAST data archive at the Space Telescope Science Institute (STScI). Funding for the TESS mission is provided by the NASA Explorer Program. STScI is operated by the Association of Universities for Research in Astronomy, Inc., under NASA contract NAS 5–26555.

Conflicts of Interest: The authors declare no conflicts of interest.

References

1. Mayor, M.; Queloz, D. A Jupiter-mass companion to a solar-type star. *Nature* **1995**, *378*, 355–359. [CrossRef]
2. Giordano Orsini, M.; Ferone, A.; Inno, L.; Giacobbe, P.; Maratea, A.; Ciaramella, A.; Bonomo, A.S.; Rotundi, A. A data-driven approach for extracting exoplanetary atmospheric features. *Astron. Comput.* **2025**, *52*, 100964. [CrossRef]
3. Koch, D.G.; Borucki, W.J.; Basri, G.; Batalha, N.M.; Brown, T.M.; Caldwell, D.; Christensen-Dalsgaard, J.; Cochran, W.D.; DeVore, E.; Dunham, E.W.; et al. Kepler mission design, realized photometric performance, and early science. *Astrophys. J. Lett.* **2010**, *713*, L79. [CrossRef]
4. Ricker, G.R.; Winn, J.N.; Vanderspek, R.; Latham, D.W.; Bakos, G.Á.; Bean, J.L.; Berta-Thompson, Z.K.; Brown, T.M.; Buchhave, L.; Butler, N.R.; et al. Transiting exoplanet survey satellite. *J. Astron. Telesc. Instrum. Syst.* **2015**, *1*, 014003. [CrossRef]
5. Deeg, H.J.; Alonso, R. Transit photometry as an exoplanet discovery method. *arXiv* **2018**, arXiv:1803.07867.
6. Cacciapuoti, L.; Kostov, V.B.; Kuchner, M.; Quintana, E.V.; Colón, K.D.; Brande, J.; Mullally, S.E.; Chance, Q.; Christiansen, J.L.; Ahlers, J.P.; et al. The TESS Triple-9 Catalog: 999 uniformly vetted exoplanet candidates. *Mon. Not. R. Astron. Soc.* **2022**, *513*, 102–116. [CrossRef]
7. Magliano, C.; Kostov, V.; Cacciapuoti, L.; Covone, G.; Inno, L.; Fiscale, S.; Kuchner, M.; Quintana, E.V.; Salik, R.; Saggese, V.; et al. The TESS Triple-9 Catalog II: A new set of 999 uniformly vetted exoplanet candidates. *Mon. Not. R. Astron. Soc.* **2023**, *521*, 3749–3764. [CrossRef]
8. Kostov, V.B.; Kuchner, M.J.; Cacciapuoti, L.; Acharya, S.; Ahlers, J.P.; Andres-Carcasona, M.; Brande, J.; de Lima, L.T.; Di Fraia, M.Z.; Fornear, A.U.; et al. Planet Patrol: Vetting Transiting Exoplanet Candidates with Citizen Science. *Publ. Astron. Soc. Pac.* **2022**, *134*, 044401. [CrossRef]
9. Tenenbaum, P.; Jenkins, J.M. *TESS Science Data Products Description Document: EXP-TESS-ARC-ICD-0014 Rev D*; No. ARC-E-DAA-TN61810; NASA: Washington, DC, USA, 2018.
10. LeCun, Y.; Boser, B.; Denker, J.S.; Henderson, D.; Howard, R.E.; Hubbard, W.; Jackel, L.D. Backpropagation applied to handwritten zip code recognition. *Neural Comput.* **1989**, *1*, 541–551. [CrossRef]
11. Dattilo, A.; Vanderburg, A.; Shallue, C.J.; Mayo, A.W.; Berlind, P.; Bieryla, A.; Calkins, M.L.; Esquerdo, G.A.; Everett, M.E.; Howell, S.B.; et al. Identifying exoplanets with deep learning. II. Two new super-Earths uncovered by a neural network in K2 data. *Astron. J.* **2019**, *157*, 169. [CrossRef]
12. Chaushev, A.; Raynard, L.; Goad, M.R.; Eigmüller, P.; Armstrong, D.J.; Briegal, J.T.; Burleigh, M.R.; Casewell, S.L.; Gill, S.; Jenkins, J.S.; et al. Classifying exoplanet candidates with convolutional neural networks: Application to the Next Generation Transit Survey. *Mon. Not. R. Astron. Soc.* **2019**, *488*, 5232–5250. [CrossRef]
13. Yu, L.; Vanderburg, A.; Huang, C.; Shallue, C.J.; Crossfield, I.J.; Gaudi, B.S.; Daylan, T.; Dattilo, A.; Armstrong, D.J.; Ricker, G.R.; et al. Identifying exoplanets with deep learning. III. Automated triage and vetting of TESS candidates. *Astron. J.* **2019**, *158*, 25. [CrossRef]
14. Osborn, H.P.; Ansdell, M.; Ioannou, Y.; Sasdelli, M.; Angerhausen, D.; Caldwell, D.; Jenkins, J.M.; Räissi, C.; Smith, J.C. Rapid classification of TESS planet candidates with convolutional neural networks. *Astron. Astrophys.* **2020**, *633*, A53. [CrossRef]

15. Fiscale, S.; Inno, L.; Ciaramella, A.; Ferone, A.; Rotundi, A.; De Luca, P.; Galletti, A.; Marcellino, L.; Covone, G. Identifying Exoplanets in TESS Data by Deep Learning. In *Applications of Artificial Intelligence and Neural Systems to Data Science*; Springer Nature: Singapore, 2023; pp. 127–135.
16. Shallue, C.J.; Vanderburg, A. Identifying exoplanets with deep learning: A five-planet resonant chain around Kepler-80 and an eighth planet around Kepler-90. *Astron. J.* **2018**, *155*, 94. [CrossRef]
17. Simonyan, K.; Zisserman, A. Very deep convolutional networks for large-scale image recognition. *arXiv* **2014**, arXiv:1409.1556.
18. Cybenko, G. Approximation by superpositions of a sigmoidal function. *Math. Control Signals Syst.* **1989**, *2*, 303–314. [CrossRef]
19. Bishop, C.M. *Neural Networks for Pattern Recognition*; Oxford University Press: Oxford, UK, 1995.
20. Hornik, K.; Stinchcombe, M.; White, H. Multilayer feedforward networks are universal approximators. *Neural Netw.* **1989**, *2*, 359–366. [CrossRef]
21. Valizadegan, H.; Martinho, M.J.; Wilkens, L.S.; Jenkins, J.M.; Smith, J.C.; Caldwell, D.A.; Twicken, J.D.; Gerum, P.C.; Walia, N.; Hausknecht, K.; et al. ExoMiner: A highly accurate and explainable deep learning classifier that validates 301 new exoplanets. *Astrophys. J.* **2022**, *926*, 120. [CrossRef]
22. Tey, E.; Moldovan, D.; Kunimoto, M.; Huang, C.X.; Shporer, A.; Daylan, T.; Muthukrishna, D.; Vanderburg, A.; Dattilo, A.; Ricker, G.R.; et al. Identifying exoplanets with deep learning. V. Improved light-curve classification for TESS full-frame image observations. *Astrophys. J.* **2023**, *165*, 95. [CrossRef]
23. Guyon, I.; Elisseeff, A. An introduction to variable and feature selection. *J. Mach. Learn. Res.* **2003**, *3*, 1157–1182.
24. Breiman, L. Random forests. *Mach. Learn.* **2001**, *45*, 5–32. [CrossRef]
25. Friedman, J.; Hastie, T.; Tibshirani, R. Additive logistic regression: A statistical view of boosting (with discussion and a rejoinder by the authors). *Ann. Stat.* **2000**, *28*, 337–407. [CrossRef]
26. Friedman, J.H. Greedy function approximation: A gradient boosting machine. *Ann. Stat.* **2001**, *29*, 1189–1232. [CrossRef]
27. Royden, H.L.; Fitzpatrick, P. *Real Analysis*; Macmillan: New York, NY, USA, 1968; Volume 2.
28. Shwartz-Ziv, R.; Armon, A. Tabular data: Deep learning is not all you need. *Inf. Fusion* **2022**, *81*, 84–90. [CrossRef]
29. McCauliff, S.D.; Jenkins, J.M.; Catanzarite, J.; Burke, C.J.; Coughlin, J.L.; Twicken, J.D.; Tenenbaum, P.; Seader, S.; Li, J.; Cote, M. Automatic classification of Kepler planetary transit candidates. *Astrophys. J.* **2015**, *806*, 6. [CrossRef]
30. Armstrong, D.J.; Günther, M.N.; McCormac, J.; Smith, A.M.; Bayliss, D.; Bouchy, F.; Burleigh, M.R.; Casewell, S.; Eigmüller, P.; Gillen, E.; et al. Automatic vetting of planet candidates from ground-based surveys: Machine learning with NGTS. *Mon. Not. R. Astron. Soc.* **2018**, *478*, 4225–4237. [CrossRef]
31. Caceres, G.A.; Feigelson, E.D.; Babu, G.J.; Bahamonde, N.; Christen, A.; Bertin, K.; Meza, C.; Curé, M. Autoregressive planet search: Application to the Kepler mission. *Astrophys. J.* **2019**, *158*, 58. [CrossRef]
32. Schanche, N.; Cameron, A.C.; Hébrard, G.; Nielsen, L.; Triaud, A.H.; Almenara, J.M.; Alsubai, K.A.; Anderson, D.R.; Armstrong, D.J.; Barros, S.C.; et al. Machine-learning approaches to exoplanet transit detection and candidate validation in wide-field ground-based surveys. *Mon. Not. R. Astron. Soc.* **2019**, *483*, 5534–5547. [CrossRef]
33. Van der Maaten, L.; Hinton, G. Visualizing data using t-SNE. *J. Mach. Learn. Res.* **2008**, *9*, 2579–2605.
34. Wheatley, P.J.; West, R.G.; Goad, M.R.; Jenkins, J.S.; Pollacco, D.L.; Queloz, D.; Rauer, H.; Udry, S.; Watson, C.A.; Chazelas, B.; et al. The next generation transit survey (NGTS). *Mon. Not. R. Astron. Soc.* **2018**, *475*, 4476–4493. [CrossRef]
35. Pollacco, D.L.; Skillen, I.; Cameron, A.C.; Christian, D.J.; Hellier, C.; Irwin, J.; Lister, T.A.; Street, R.A.; West, R.G.; Anderson, D.; et al. The WASP project and the SuperWASP cameras. *Publ. Astron. Soc. Pac.* **2006**, *118*, 1407. [CrossRef]
36. Jolicoeur-Martineau, A.; Fatras, K.; Kachman, T. Generating and imputing tabular data via diffusion and flow-based gradient-boosted trees. In *International Conference on Artificial Intelligence and Statistics*; PMLR: Birmingham, UK, 2024; pp. 1288–1296.
37. Coughlin, J.L.; Mullally, F.; Thompson, S.E.; Rowe, J.F.; Burke, C.J.; Latham, D.W.; Batalha, N.M.; Ofir, A.; Quarles, B.L.; Henze, C.E.; et al. Planetary candidates observed by Kepler. VII. The first fully uniform catalog based on the entire 48-month data set (Q1–Q17 DR24). *Astrophys. J. Suppl. Ser.* **2016**, *224*, 12. [CrossRef]
38. Howell, S.B.; Sobeck, C.; Haas, M.; Still, M.; Barclay, T.; Mullally, F.; Troeltzsch, J.; Aigrain, S.; Bryson, S.T.; Caldwell, D.; et al. The K2 mission: Characterization and early results. *Publ. Astron. Soc. Pac.* **2014**, *126*, 398. [CrossRef]
39. Armstrong, D.J.; Pollacco, D.; Santerne, A. Transit shapes and self organising maps as a tool for ranking planetary candidates: Application to kepler and k2. *Mon. Not. R. Astron. Soc.* **2016**, *461*, 2461–2473.
40. Poleo, V.T.; Eisner, N.; Hogg, D.W. NotPlaNET: Removing False Positives from Planet Hunters TESS with Machine Learning. *Astron. J.* **2024**, *168*, 100. [CrossRef]
41. Ansdell, M.; Ioannou, Y.; Osborn, H.P.; Sasdelli, M.; Smith, J.C.; Caldwell, D.; Jenkins, J.M.; Räissi, C.; Angerhausen, D. Scientific domain knowledge improves exoplanet transit classification with deep learning. *Astrophys. J. Lett.* **2018**, *869*, L7. [CrossRef]
42. Salinas, H.; Pichara, K.; Brahm, R.; Pérez-Galarce, F.; Mery, D. Distinguishing a planetary transit from false positives: A Transformer-based classification for planetary transit signals. *Mon. Not. R. Astron. Soc.* **2023**, *522*, 3201–3216. [CrossRef]
43. Visser, K.; Bosma, B.; Postma, E. Exoplanet detection with Genesis. *J. Astron. Instrum.* **2022**, *11*, 2250011. [CrossRef]

44. Jenkins, J.M.; Caldwell, D.A.; Chandrasekaran, H.; Twicken, J.D.; Bryson, S.T.; Quintana, E.V.; Clarke, B.D.; Li, J.; Allen, C.; Tenenbaum, P.; et al. Overview of the Kepler science processing pipeline. *Astrophys. J. Lett.* **2010**, *713*, L87. [CrossRef]
45. Jenkins, J.M.; Twicken, J.D.; McCauliff, S.; Campbell, J.; Sanderfer, D.; Lung, D.; Mansouri-Samani, M.; Girouard, F.; Tenenbaum, P.; Klaus, T.; et al. The TESS science processing operations center. In *Software and Cyberinfrastructure for Astronomy IV*; SPIE: Bellingham, WA, USA, 2016; Volume 9913, pp. 1232–1251.
46. Jenkins, J.M.; Tenenbaum, P.; Seader, S.; Burke, C.J.; McCauliff, S.D.; Smith, J.C.; Twicken, J.D.; Chandrasekaran, H. *Kepler Data Processing Handbook: Transiting Planet Search*; Kepler Science Document KSCI-19081-002; NASA Ames Research Center: Mountain View, CA, USA, 2017; p. 9.
47. Kunimoto, M.; Huang, C.; Tey, E.; Fong, W.; Hesse, K.; Shporer, A.; Guerrero, N.; Fausnaugh, M.; Vanderspek, R.; Ricker, G. Quick-look pipeline lightcurves for 9.1 million stars observed over the first year of the TESS Extended Mission. *RNAAS* **2021**, *5*, 234. [CrossRef]
48. Kostov, V.B.; Mullally, S.E.; Quintana, E.V.; Coughlin, J.L.; Mullally, F.; Barclay, T.; Colón, K.D.; Schlieder, J.E.; Barentsen, G.; Burke, C.J. Discovery and Vetting of Exoplanets. I. Benchmarking K2 Vetting Tools. *Astron. J.* **2019**, *157*, 124. [CrossRef]
49. Catanzarite, J.H. *Autovetter Planet Candidate Catalog for Q1–Q17 Data Release 24*; NASA Ames Research Center: Mountain View, CA, USA, 2015.
50. Thompson, S.E.; Coughlin, J.L.; Hoffman, K.; Mullally, F.; Christiansen, J.L.; Burke, C.J.; Bryson, S.; Batalha, N.; Haas, M.R.; Catanzarite, J.; et al. Planetary candidates observed by Kepler. VIII. A fully automated catalog with measured completeness and reliability based on data release 25. *Astrophys. J. Suppl. Ser.* **2018**, *235*, 38. [CrossRef] [PubMed]
51. Fiscale, S.; De Luca, P.; Inno, L.; Marcellino, L.; Galletti, A.; Rotundi, A.; Ciaramella, A.; Covone, G.; Quintana, E. A GPU algorithm for outliers detection in TESS light curves. In *International Conference on Computational Science*; Springer: Cham, Switzerland, 2021; pp. 420–432.
52. LeCun, Y.; Bengio, Y.; Hinton, G. Deep learning. *Nature* **2015**, *521*, 436–444. [CrossRef]
53. Tenenbaum, J.B.; Silva, V.D.; Langford, J.C. A global geometric framework for nonlinear dimensionality reduction. *Science* **2000**, *290*, 2319–2323. [CrossRef] [PubMed]
54. Roweis, S.T.; Saul, L.K. Nonlinear dimensionality reduction by locally linear embedding. *Science* **2000**, *290*, 2323–2326. [CrossRef]
55. Belkin, M.; Niyogi, P. Using manifold stucture for partially labeled classification. *Adv. Neural Inf. Process. Syst.* **2002**, *15*, 1505–1512.
56. Hinton, G. Stochastic neighbor embedding. *Adv. Neural Inf. Process. Syst.* **2003**, *15*, 857–864.
57. Csiszár, I. I-divergence geometry of probability distributions and minimization problems. *Ann. Probab.* **1975**, *3*, 146–158. [CrossRef]
58. Jacobs, R.A. Increased rates of convergence through learning rate adaptation. *Neural Netw.* **1988**, *1*, 295–307. [CrossRef]
59. Zhang, C.; Liu, C.; Zhang, X.; Almpanidis, G. An up-to-date comparison of state-of-the-art classification algorithms. *Expert Syst. Appl.* **2017**, *82*, 128–150. [CrossRef]
60. Touzani, S.; Granderson, J.; Fernandes, S. Gradient boosting machine for modeling the energy consumption of commercial buildings. *Energy Build.* **2018**, *158*, 1533–1543. [CrossRef]
61. Machado, M.R.; Karray, S.; De Sousa, I.T. LightGBM: An effective decision tree gradient boosting method to predict customer loyalty in the finance industry. In Proceedings of the 2019 14th International Conference on Computer Science & Education (ICCSE), Toronto, ON, Canada, 19–21 August 2019; pp. 1111–1116.
62. Ma, B.; Meng, F.; Yan, G.; Yan, H.; Chai, B.; Song, F. Diagnostic classification of cancers using extreme gradient boosting algorithm and multi-omics data. *Comput. Biol. Med.* **2020**, *121*, 103761. [CrossRef] [PubMed]
63. Chen, T.; He, T.; Benesty, M.; Khotilovich, V.; Tang, Y.; Cho, H.; Chen, K.; Mitchell, R.; Cano, I.; Zhou, T. Xgboost: Extreme gradient boosting. In *R Package Version 0.4-2*; The R Project for Statistical Computing: Vienna, Austria, 2015; Volume 1, pp. 1–4.
64. Goodfellow, I.; Pouget-Abadie, J.; Mirza, M.; Xu, B.; Warde-Farley, D.; Ozair, S.; Courville, A.; Bengio, Y. Generative adversarial nets. *Adv. Neural Inf. Process. Syst.* **2014**, *27*, 2672–2680.
65. Li, A.C.; Prabhudesai, M.; Duggal, S.; Brown, E.; Pathak, D. Your diffusion model is secretly a zero-shot classifier. In Proceedings of the IEEE/CVF International Conference on Computer Vision, Paris, France, 1–6 October 2023; pp. 2206–2217.
66. Chen, R.T.; Rubanova, Y.; Bettencourt, J.; Duvenaud, D.K. Neural ordinary differential equations. *Adv. Neural Inf. Process. Syst.* **2018**, *31*, 6572–6583.
67. Kingma, D.P.; Ba, J. Adam: A method for stochastic optimization. *arXiv* **2014**, arXiv:1412.6980.
68. Lertnattee, V.; Theeramunkong, T. Analysis of inverse class frequency in centroid-based text classification. In Proceedings of the IEEE International Symposium on Communications and Information Technology, 2004. ISCIT 2004, Sapporo, Japan, 26–29 October 2004; Volume 2, pp. 1171–1176.
69. Goodfellow, I.; Bengio, Y.; Courville, A.; Bengio, Y. *Deep Learning*; MIT Press: Cambridge, UK, 2016; Volume 1, No. 2.
70. Visser, K.; Bosma, B.; Postma, E. Size does matter: Exoplanet detection with a sparse convolutional neural network. *Astron. Comput.* **2022**, *41*, 100654. [CrossRef]

71. Gisbrecht, A.; Schulz, A.; Hammer, B. Parametric nonlinear dimensionality reduction using kernel t-SNE. *Neurocomputing* **2015**, *147*, 71–82. [CrossRef]
72. Guerrero, N.M.; Seager, S.; Huang, C.X.; Vanderburg, A.; Soto, A.G.; Mireles, I.; Hesse, K.; Fong, W.; Glidden, A.; Shporer, A.; et al. The TESS objects of interest catalog from the TESS prime mission. *Astrophys. J. Suppl. Ser.* **2021**, *254*, 39. [CrossRef]
73. Imambi, S.; Prakash, K.B.; Kanagachidambaresan, G.R. PyTorch. In *Programming with TensorFlow: Solution for Edge Computing Applications*; Springer Nature: Cham, Switzerland, 2021; pp. 87–104.
74. Braga, F.C.; Roman, N.T.; Falceta-Gonçalves, D. The Effects of Under and Over Sampling in Exoplanet Transit Identification with Low Signal-to-Noise Ratio Data. In *Brazilian Conference on Intelligent Systems*; Springer International Publishing: Cham, Switzerland, 2022; pp. 107–121.
75. Rauer, H.; Catala, C.; Aerts, C.; Appourchaux, T.; Benz, W.; Brandeker, A.; Christensen-Dalsgaard, J.; Deleuil, M.; Gizon, L.; Goupil, M.J.; et al. The PLATO 2.0 mission. *Exp. Astron.* **2014**, *38*, 249–330. [CrossRef]

MDPI AG
Grosspeteranlage 5
4052 Basel
Switzerland
Tel.: +41 61 683 77 34

Electronics Editorial Office
E-mail: electronics@mdpi.com
www.mdpi.com/journal/electronics

www.ingramcontent.com/pod-product-compliance
Lightning Source LLC
Chambersburg PA
CBHW061812210926
51850CB00006B/680
9783725879755